CONTEMPORARY CREATIVE NONFICTION

I & EYE

B. Minh Nguyen
Purdue University

Porter Shreve
Purdue University

PEARSON
Longman

New York   San Francisco   Boston
London   Toronto   Sydney   Tokyo   Singapore   Madrid
Mexico City   Munich   Paris   Cape Town   Hong Kong   Montreal

Vice President and Editor-in-Chief: Joseph Terry
Executive Managing Editor: Erika Berg
Executive Marketing Manager: Ann Stypuloski
Production Manager: Denise Phillip
Project Coordination, Text Design, and Electronic Page Makeup:
    WestWords, Inc.
Cover Designer/Manager: Wendy Ann Fredericks
Cover Art: Marsha Burns, *My Bathroom Window,* 1999. Courtesy
    of the artist and Charles Cowles Gallery, NY.
Manufacturing Buyer: Lucy Hebard
Printer and Binder: Hamilton Printing Company
Cover Printer: Coral Graphic Services

For permission to use copyrighted material, grateful acknowledgement is made to the copyright holders on pp. 383–384, which are hereby made part of this copyright page.

Library of Congress Cataloging-in-Publication Data

Contemporary creative nonfiction : I & eye / [compiled by] B. Minh Nguyen,
    Porter Shreve.
        p. cm.
    Includes bibliographical references and index.
    ISBN 0-321-19817-4 (pbk.)
1. College readers. 2. Creative writing (Higher education)—Problems, exercises,
etc. 3. English language—Rhetoric—Problems, exercises, etc. 4. Autobiography—
Authorship—Problems, exercises, etc. 5. Journalism—Authorship—Problems,
exercises, etc. 6. Essay—Authorship—Problems, exercises, etc. 7. Report
writing—Problems, exercises, etc. I. Nguyen, B. Minh. II. Shreve, Porter.
PE1417.C65223 2004
808'.0427—dc22

                                                                2004005539

Please visit our website at http://www.ablongman.com

ISBN 0-321-19817-4

        6 7 8 9 10   12 11 10 09 08

Contents

Alternate Contents by Creative Nonfiction Forms

Memoir

Meditation

Personal Essay

Process Analysis

Segmented Writing

LITERARY JOURNALISM

Preface

As creative nonfiction instructors, we have searched for the ideal contemporary anthology in this emerging field; our colleagues at various colleges and universities agree that there is a need for a collection that is comprehensive yet diverse, updated, and fresh. This anthology meets that need, offering memoirs, essays, and literary journalism that teach craft and provide a wide range of voices and forms.

The pieces in this anthology were all published after the mid-1960s in North America, around the time that Tom Wolfe, Joan Didion, and others were introducing a form of narrative reporting that came to be known as "New Journalism." At the same time, novelists, essayists, short story writers, and poets were continuing to write imaginative essays, criticism, and memoirs of great formal variety. In *Contemporary Creative Nonfiction: I & Eye* we aim to bridge the divide between personal essays and memoirs and literary journalism, providing works and commentaries that cover the autobiographical and biographical, the subjective and objective, within the same collection.

Our focus, mainly due to limits on length, is on North American prose. We have chosen 45 essays and 15 craft commentaries that bring together a full range of forms, modes, and voices in contemporary creative nonfiction. We have blended "contemporary classics" by writers such as John McPhee, John Edgar Wideman, Edward Hoagland, Annie Dillard, and Maxine Hong Kingston with the work of many new voices, among them Edwidge Danticat, Sarah Vowell, Richard McCann, Meghan Daum, and Lê Thi Diem Thúy. The result is not only a composite picture of North American life since the mid-1960s but a measure of the scope and depth of creative nonfiction as an art form.

Besides its range and diversity, *Contemporary Creative Nonfiction: I & Eye* is a flexible text:

- It is well suited for all levels of creative nonfiction, from introductory to advanced, offering excellent models of memoir, essay, and literary nonfiction technique. The general introduction and the introductions that precede each section provide context as well as information on the various craft strategies that the authors use in the pieces.

- Our inclusion of both personal and journalistic creative nonfiction makes *Contemporary Creative Nonfiction: I & Eye* a comprehensive text. Because most courses emphasize personal essay and memoir, we selected 30 personal pieces, 15 literary journalistic pieces, and 15 craft pieces. As we note in the introductions, several works here bridge the divide between the "I" and the "Eye." Our categories are meant not to restrict but to expand, generating debate over the implicit question, "What makes a work personal or journalistic, subjective or objective?"

We have also included a range of apparati to enrich the teaching and reading of the pieces.

- The two tables of contents offer organization and flexibility, arranging the pieces both by subject and by form. Each section in the main Table of Contents—Portraits, Place, Creativity and the Arts, Nature and Science, and Culture and Society—is subdivided into the personal "I" and the journalistic "Eye", with a separate section for Craft Essays. The Alternate Table of Contents is divided by form: Memoir, Meditation, Personal Essay, Process Analysis, Segmented Writing, and Literary Journalism. This organization is geared toward helping instructors plan their lessons and helping students approach the wide-ranging field of creative nonfiction. The categories are suggestions, rather than absolutes, and are meant to be tools for navigation and structure.

- The main Introduction provides useful information on the definition, history, and development of creative nonfiction, and is divided into four categories: the "I" (personal essay and memoir), the "Eye" (literary journalism), the idea of truth, and the use of literary elements. The additional section introductions provide background context on personal and journalistic creative nonfiction within each subject, emphasizing craft considerations such as style and form.

- The 15 craft essays, by such major contributors to the field as Joan Didion, Phillip Lopate, and Tracy Kidder, discuss the writing and shaping of creative nonfiction. Subjects include the personal point of veiw, the art of note taking, the role of emotion in critical writing, and how to access memory through the senses.

- Appendix I offers 20 substantial and adaptable writing prompts, arranged in sections that match the organization of the book. Inspired by and drawing upon many of the essays, these prompts serve as springboards for student writing.

- Appendix II includes suggestions for further reading in the field of contemporary creative nonfiction. Along with the Author Biographies at the end of the book, Appendix II points students to memoirs, essay collections, and works of literary journalism, arranged in sections that correspond with the organization of the book.

In closing, we would like to thank the instructors who reviewed our preliminary materials and offered invaluable recommendations and advice: Marilyn

Abildskov, University of Iowa; Susan Atefat-Peckham, Georgia College & State University; Jocelyn Bartkevicius, University of Central Florida; Joseph Bathanti, Appalachian State University; Bob Cowser, St. Lawrence University; Candice Favilla, Southwestern Oregon Community College; Melissa A. Goldthwaite, Ohio State University; Connie Griffin, Boston College; Colleen McElroy, University of Washington; Dianne McPherson, Ithaca College; Kathy O'Shaughnessey, Portland Community College; Marie C. Paretti, Virginia Tech; Sydney Plum, University of Connecticut; Mike Raymond, Stetson University; Dennis Read, Denison University; Carlo Rotella, Boston College; Alison Russell, Xavier University; David Seal, Pacific Lutheran University; Heather Sellers, Hope College; Sheryl St. Germain, Iowa State University; Steve Tollefson, University of California, Berkeley; Bronwyn Williams, University of Louisville. Thanks to Gerry Canavan, Tom Christopher, Brian Crocker, Fay Dacey, Ruth Dickey, Chad Holley, Jeremy Isaac, Jay Parr, Ezra Plemons, Eileen Pollack, Lori Reese, Davy Rothbart, Jillian Weise, and Lee Zacharias. Thanks also to the English Department and M.F.A. Program in Creative Writing at the University of Michigan, the English Department and M.F.A. Program in Creative Writing at the University of North Carolina at Greensboro, and the English Department and M.F.A. program in Creative Writing at Purdue University. Special thanks to Michele Cronin, Beth Keister, Jami Darby, Teresa Ward, Rebecca Gilpin, and our editor Erika Berg at Longman.

B. Minh Nguyen
Porter Shreve

Introduction

The field of creative nonfiction—which has also been called "the fourth genre," "the literature of fact," "the art of truth," and "literary nonfiction"—is often defined by what it is not: not poetry, not fiction, not drama. It draws on these genres, incorporating elements such as lyricism, story arc, and dialogue, yet it demands one crucial aspect that the other genres do not: truth. As Annie Dillard has said, "The essay can do everything a poem can do, and everything a short story can do—everything but fake it."

In secondary school most of us were taught to write standard five-paragraph essays of exposition and argumentation, in which information occupied the core and personal perspective was usually forbidden outright. Such requirements—thesis statements, the objective voice, or the absolute absence of the "I"—happily are no longer required of us. Having abandoned such restrictions, creative nonfiction often seems hard to define because it is continually pushing boundaries.

Today, creative nonfiction is an umbrella term encompassing personal essays, memoirs, and literary journalism. Or, comprehensively, the "I" and the "Eye." The "I" includes personal essays—reflections that emerge from personal concerns or experiences—and memoirs, in which writers remember and explore significant moments from their past. The "Eye," influenced by traditional journalism, focuses more on observing subjects beyond personal experience. In this anthology we present a variety of forms—meditations on art, personal political writing, essays on place and landscape, profiles, critical analyses, and experiential journalism—and put the personal and the literary journalistic side by side.

The "I"

The categories of "I" & "Eye" are not meant to be mutually exclusive. A work of personal nonfiction, after all, must engage in ideas both about and beyond the self; as Phillip Lopate says, it "is not self-absorbed navel-gazing." As readers and writers we should be able to see a connection between our own and another person's story. The role of the "I," whether intense and emotional as in John Edgar Wideman's selection from *Brothers and Keepers* or critical and humorous as in Meghan Daum's "Music Is My Bag," is that of someone inviting us into his or her world, vision, and experiences. In its varying modes, a work of personal nonfiction may be a remembrance of childhood; it may be an essay that contemplates the connection between personal and social history; it may be a study in self-discovery and identity.

In a traditional essay we may find rational argument, reasoning, opinion, or contemplation. The roots of such essays go back to the French writer Michel de Montaigne (1533–1592), who focused on observations and minutiae of daily life and human processes, and further back to Seneca (A.D. 3–65), who incorporated in some of his works a rhetorical, almost conversational style with the reader/listener. As the essay evolved it began incorporating techniques such as dialogue and scenes, which had been previously seen only in fiction and drama. In the mid–nineteenth century in the United States, Ralph Waldo Emerson and Henry David Thoreau helped establish a new direction for nonfiction. Their essays on nature, particularly Thoreau's, included intense observation, description, and immersion into landscape, and influenced essayists such as John Muir and Rachel Carson, and contemporary writers such as Annie Dillard, Barry Lopez, and Gretel Ehrlich, who often return to subjects of the natural world. The sense of the personal here is key—going beyond information to rumination. Today, many personal essays draw on experiences emerging from personal spaces, be they spaces of nature, history, childhood, family, or culture. Here, we find what Lopate has called "the hallmark of the personal essay"—"intimacy."

A prominent form of personal creative nonfiction is the memoir, because it mines the material of personal history. Often this material is rooted in childhood and all of its concomitant factors of growing awareness and understanding. Jamaica Kincaid, Tony Earley, and Stuart Dybek are some of the writers here who draw on childhood memories. More than just anecdotes and remembrances, these are ways for writers to reflect on the people and events that influenced their lives. While a memoir involves self-exploration, it also transcends the boundaries of individual experience. While these parameters are subject to argument and matters of perception, we think that the pieces included here represent the strongest possible examples of what the memoir can do, showing us another person's view of the world, drawing us into that life.

Many of the personal essays in this anthology incorporate elements of memoir, along with meditation, discursiveness, and observation. This mixing of modes pushes the field of creative nonfiction even further: represented here are lyrical narratives (Naomi Shihab Nye's "Thank You in Arabic"), essays that connect distinct points of memory and experience (Chang-rae Lee's "Coming Home Again"), experimental works involving shards of memory and anecdote (Wayne Koestenbaum's "Celebrity Dreaming"), essays that focus on the personal interpretation of a subject (Gerald Early's "Life with Daughters: Watching the Miss America Pageant"). The voices and styles range from contemplative to sardonic, wistful to passionate, comedic to elegiac. The common thread shared by all the personal essays is the inward "I," the self-exploration and search for understanding that, in turn, invites us to do the same.

The "Eye"

The category of what we call literary journalism emerges from traditional essays and reportage, which focus on information and accuracy. While components of journalistic observation and witness remain crucial to literary journalism, it has expanded to include the author's presence and perspective. This radical shift occurred in the 1960s, when writers such as Joan Didion, Tom Wolfe, and Gay Talese challenged the traditional structure of journalism by incorporating distinct voices—a technique usually seen in fiction—as well as dialogue and dramatic action. Rather than simply reporting an account of something that happened, these writers of what came to be called New Journalism reconstructed scenes, used extensive research, and immersed themselves in their subjects, understanding them thoroughly in order to write authentically. While Wolfe and Talese kept the "I" in the shadows of the narrative, Didion often incorporates it, connecting her personal life to the ideas and places she investigated. A classic mode of journalistic creative nonfiction is the profile piece, such as Tom Wolfe's "Yeager" from *The Right Stuff* in which the author focuses on observing the life and behavior of one particular person or group. Here the observant "Eye" witnesses and studies different worlds, people, and contexts. Contemporary literary journalism has inherited these elements of New Journalism and continues to forge ahead, at times obscuring the boundaries between outward and inward views.

It might generally be said that personal creative nonfiction explores personal identity through subjects such as place, politics, and nature, and journalistic creative nonfiction explores those subjects from an observer's vantage point. Yet these distinctions may often be more helpful for purposes of organization and discussion than for definition. We do not wish to pigeonhole all of the essays into one absolute category. A work such as Beverly Lowry's "Secret Ceremonies of Love and Death," for instance, is a kind of "bridge" piece blurring the line between personal and journalistic. Other essays also float in between, drawing on aspects of both camps; in another example, Lawrence Otis Graham's "Invisible Man" draws on personal experiential research in order to examine the insidiousness of racism.

Some of the essays here, such as Susan Orlean's "Meet the Shaggs," are more clearly influenced by traditional journalism while others, such as Atul Gawande's "Final Cut," follow the mode of traditional essay-writing. Though the personal "I" does not appear in traditional journalism, it often appears in this category of literary journalistic creative nonfiction. The first-person narrative voice may be used liberally, as in James Alan McPherson's "Saturday Night, and Sunday Morning"; minimally, as in Diane Ackerman's "The Psychopharmacology of Chocolate"; or not at all, as in Tom Wolfe's "Yeager." While journalistic creative nonfiction may acknowledge the role of the author as witness and observer, ultimately it stays focused on the world of observation outside the self.

The Idea of Truth

One element that sets creative nonfiction apart from other literary genres is the use of truth. Traditional journalism and reportage, of course, require facts, objectivity, and a kind of voicelessness—the disappearance of the author. New Journalism incorporated a greater emphasis on perception; the stance was still a form of witness, but offered a more descriptive, less strictly objective point of view. Literary journalism can go even further in its emphasis on perception, and personal creative nonfiction further still: feelings, perception, and memory all combine to create, rather than simply tell, what is true.

It makes sense that, when it comes to the idea of truth, journalistic creative nonfiction would have tighter restrictions than personal creative nonfiction. Though it need not focus on providing all the facts, as reportage pieces do, literary journalism is based in observation and actuality. At the same time, how the world is perceived and described is filtered through the writing and perception of each author. Here again lies the difference between a report and a work of literary journalism: the former is concerned with the transmission of facts; the latter is based in fact, but allows viewpoint and voice to inform the facts, making truth both root and creation.

A friend recently talked about a memory she'd shared with her parents. Remember, she said to them, when I was 10 and we were on vacation in California, and we ate at that restaurant that served crêpes suzette? I thought that was the most romantic thing a person could eat. But her parents said, Wait—that wasn't a restaurant. That was your aunt's house, and your aunt made the crêpes.

What the parents remembered—perhaps correctly, perhaps not—may be different from what our friend remembered, but the emotional truth remains the same: the feeling of romance and newness, becoming aware of the world through the glamorous idea of crêpes suzette.

And this example we just told: notice that we paraphrased our friend. We may not have remembered the exact words she used, but the essence of the story is true. Likewise, at its core, personal creative nonfiction is concerned with the truth of feeling. Otherwise, we might as well be transcribing everything. Creative nonfiction *is* creative; it is not as reliant on facts and accuracy in the way a newspaper article must be. Rather, creative nonfiction writers acknowledge the uses and limits of perception and memory. This is particularly so for personal essays and memoirs, which draw upon layers of the past.

You've probably heard the cliché that there are three sides to every story: your side, their side, and the truth. Creative nonfiction is testament to the idea that there may *only* be your side and their side, that especially when it comes to personal essays and memoirs the nature of "truth" is bound so inescapably by personal viewpoints that it can never be charted and pinpointed. In a bad breakup each person has his or her own idea of what went wrong and whom to blame—rarely do they agree, and rarely is there a "correct" answer. Facts are often replaced by opinion, belief, and emotion.

When it comes to memory and perception, then, the idea of truth is murky—there is no one truth, no one viewpoint, no one way to describe how something felt or occurred. What constitutes "truth" can be a wide definition, filtered through interpretation, experience, and language. A personal piece such as Tony Earley's "Somehow Form a Family," for instance, shows us through narrative and language the writer's truth about how he grew up.

A work of personal creative nonfiction cannot guarantee accuracy—nor does it need to—but it must still, at its core, be emotionally true. Writing creative nonfiction requires not just truth but also honesty to ourselves, else why write it at all? Honesty—as much as it is possible—shows through in the creative process as we figure out why we are writing and what we are trying to say. The act of writing may be an exploration of that truth and honesty, or a discovery of it; it may lead to realizations we hadn't yet fully processed about ourselves. Personal creative nonfiction is, in a sense, raw—there is no cloaking of the author behind the narrator, no way to disguise the truth that must inform the personal work. As Bret Lott says in his essay "Toward a Definition of Creative Nonfiction":

> The self, however at the center of what you are writing or however tangential, must inform the heart of the tale you are telling. It is indeed *self* that is the *creative* element of creative non-fiction. Without you and who you are, a piece of writing that tells what happened is simply nonfiction: a police report. But when I begin to incorporate the sad and glorious fact that the way I see it shapes and forms what it is to be seen, I end up with creative nonfiction.

The Use of Literary Elements

Creative nonfiction brings together two elements from the genres of fiction and poetry that may seem at first to contradict each other: narrative and freedom from narrative. Some form of narrative license, or the act of storytelling, is one of the most frequently used elements in creative nonfiction. A narrative can provide a scenic anchor to an essay, immediately catching the reader's attention, and it can provide a jumping-off point for the ideas that emerge. The element of narrative creates greater freedom for the creative nonfiction writer, and some works of personal creative nonfiction read almost like short stories. Here, the ideas in the essay may not just unfold with the narrative but may also be the narrative itself, as we see in Dorothy Allison's selection from *Two or Three Things I Know for Sure*.

Gerald Early's "Life with Daughters: Watching the Miss America Pageant," on the other hand, centers itself in a narrative about watching the pageant. From there, Early weaves in discussions of history, race, and beauty culture. As in stories, creative nonfiction narratives may also revolve around the characterization of a main figure. A more journalistic profile piece such as Susan Orlean's "Meet the Shaggs" is one example, and a personal profile piece such as Bernard Cooper's "Picking Plums" is another. And yet, an essay may eschew narrative altogether, as in Lê Thi Diem Thúy's collagelike "The Gangster We Are All Looking For." Or, like a poem, it may focus on the development of imagery, as Margaret Atwood does in "The Female Body."

Many of the works here, including Susan Allen Toth's "Cinematypes: Going to the Movies" and John McPhee's "The Search for Marvin Gardens," involve segmentation: essays divided into sections, often a collection of images, memories, observations. This structure, which may seem like a disparate gathering of moments, asks the reader to make connections and conclusions as the various segments accumulate and play off of each other. Section breaks can suggest the fragmentation of memory and underscore leaps in time and narration. A segmented essay is also useful for generating a particular tone or voice. It may create a distancing effect, for instance, that suggests the author's state of mind, as in Toth's essay. That same sense of distance, however, can also be used to generate a greater emotional response, as in Michael Herr's "Illumination Rounds," which feels taut, as if there is no room for anything but tense, necessary description.

Voice is another major element that creative nonfiction borrows from the other genres. By *voice* we mean the distinctive way in which the author tells a story—his or her particular way of rendering language, events, and perspective. Narrative voice is connected to point of view: is the author in the background, observing events in an intense, lively way, as in Tom Wolfe's "Yeager"? Or perhaps the author's point of view is up front and center, speaking directly to the reader as in Lucy Grealy's "Mirrorings." In this memoir, voice not only steers the experience of the nonfiction work but also carries the heart of its truth.

These elements—narrative, voice, structure—are just a few of the literary techniques used in creative nonfiction to establish intimacy or distance, memoir or pure observation. While the creative nonfiction essays here deal, in some form, with the exploration of ideas, lives, and beliefs, they do so in radically different ways. Some of the essays contain implicit forms of argument, whether perspectives on personal experience (Bharati Mukherjee's "Two Ways to Belong in America") or perspectives on social issues (Susan Sontag's selection from *AIDS and Its Metaphors*). These are not "thesis"-driven essays, however, but complex considerations of various points of view. Other essays here layer narrative moments and ideas into segments that ask the reader to draw connections between the literal and the figurative, the past and the present. Through such various structures, styles, and subjects, each author's particular voice shines through.

The authority of truth is at the center of creative nonfiction, and so is the role of the author. In fiction and poetry the "I" is a speaker or a character, not necessarily the author and, indeed, not assumed to be the author. In nonfiction we trust that the "I"—whether the personal "I," the "I" in the shadows, or the unnamed observer—is the author. We can trust that the author is speaking to us, giving us observations, experiences, and memories that ring true to him or herself—and to us.

Because the field of creative nonfiction is ever-expanding and resistant to clear definition, we created our categories as an organizational guide. In essence, we think the field may be most readily approachable first by subject (see "Table of Contents"), then by form (see "Alternate Table of Contents"). We have found that in seeking to define creative nonfiction we circle back to questions like "What is this essay *about*?" "What is an author trying to say?" and "Where does one begin writing?" We suggest that subject is a good place to begin.

At first we tried to list the works alphabetically and by year of publication, but this approach seemed chaotic, even overwhelming. The categories we've chosen are meant as tools for organization, whether for understanding all the things an essay can do, or understanding all the different ways one might approach the writing of an essay. After all, in writing and revising we need to have a central subject.

Certainly a work listed under one subject may cross over into another, just as a work of journalistic nonfiction may cross over into the personal. Stephen Jay Gould's "A Biological Homage to Mickey Mouse," for instance, is a scientific study of Mickey Mouse yet at the same time draws on ideas of the cartoon figure as a particular embodiment of cultural ideals. Chang-rae Lee's "Coming Home Again" focuses on his relationship with his mother within the contexts of place—his mother's house and his boarding school. Both of these essays could arguably be included in other sections as well—Culture and Society, or Portraits. But we find that these essays, while drawing on various themes and elements from other categories, maintain a greater focus on scientific inquiry in Gould's case and on the sense of place as connected to identity and familial relationships in Lee's case.

In its best form an essay is complex and composed of layers of meaning. Our subject categories are not meant to be rigid divisions, but rather suggestions for approach. The craft essays in each section are also organized by subject but not limited by them. Patricia Hampl's "Reviewing Anne Frank," for instance, is in the category of Creativity and the Arts because it deals with the formidable task of assessing a literary classic; the essay is also about the process of writing.

Our goal here is to offer a wide range of voices, forms, and styles. With an understanding that most readers and writers in creative nonfiction classes lean more toward the personal, we included 30 personal works and 15 literary journalistic works. In Portraits, the viewpoints look both inward—at the self, as in Jamaica Kincaid's "Biography of a Dress"—and outward, at others, as in Susan Orlean's "Meet the Shaggs." The writings on Place touch on the subject literally and metaphorically, from the examination of a city in James Alan McPherson's "Saturday Night, and Sunday Morning" to the idea of home in Naomi Shihab Nye's "Thank You in Arabic."

The section on Creativity and the Arts examines the role of the arts on the self and in a community, from David Sedaris's "The Drama Bug" to Dagoberto Gilb's "Steinbeck." The forces of biology, nature, and the senses are represented in Nature and Science, from Terry Tempest Williams's "The Clan of One-Breasted Women" to Atul Gawande's "Final Cut." In the section on Culture and Society, writers focus on the connections between politics and the self, from deeply personal narratives such as Dorothy Allison's selection from *Two or Three Things I Know for Sure* to social investigations such as Susan Sontag's selection from *AIDS and Its Metaphors*. In addition, 15 craft essays explore topics of observation, revision, and the role of the "I"; many of them, including Annie Dillard's contemporary classic "Seeing," also function as models of creative nonfiction essay writing.

As Cynthia Ozick says, "No one is freer than the essayist—free to leap out in any direction, to hop from thought to thought. . . . The marvel is that out of this apparent causelessness, out of this scattering of idiosyncratic seeing and telling, a coherent world is made." So the writers of contemporary creative nonfiction in this collection create coherent, marvelous worlds through radically varied approaches. In this anthology you will find that every subject, from self-identity to the world of nature, is closely examined. As with the very question "What is creative nonfiction?" there are no absolute answers or tidy definitions. In terms of form, range, and craft possibilities, the works here give a comprehensive view of all that creative nonfiction has to offer.

Works Cited

Annie Dillard, "Introduction." *The Best American Essays 1988*. Houghton Mifflin, 1988.
Phillip Lopate, "On the Necessity of Turning Oneself Into a Character."
Phillip Lopate, "Introduction." *The Art of the Personal Essay*. Doubleday, 1994.
Bret Lott, "Toward a Definition of Creative Nonfiction."

PART

I

— Portraits —

When it comes to finding material, the most readily available source is the self: personal identity, history, family, who we are, and what has shaped us. The essays and memoirs included in this section are all based in these ideas: some go by way of childhood recollections, others focus on portraying other people. These works, then, are portraits not only of the writers themselves but also of different lives, the "I" & "Eye" sometimes separate, sometimes yoked together.

The danger in writing memoir is solipsism, a self-absorption that fails to illuminate or discover ideas beyond pure personal experience. The works that incorporate memoir in this section show us how how to avoid such a pitfall. Lucy Grealy's "Mirrorings," for instance, though confessional in voice, expands into ideas about beauty and self-image. Lê Thi Diem Thúy's lyrical "The Gangster We Are All Looking For" is composed of the author's memories, but at the same time contemplates metaphors of immigration and arrival. Both writers begin and return to personal experience, using them as guideposts for narrative and idea, but they don't simply stay there. Other memoir-driven works here— "Picking Plums," Bernard Cooper's often elegiac inquiry into his father's life; Jamaica Kincaid's "Biography of a Dress" and Tony Earley's "Somehow Form a Family," two different portraits of childhood; and John Edgar Wideman's emotionally raw selection from *Brothers and Keepers*—center around an author's relationship to family members. They also ponder ideas that emerge from defining objects—food, clothing, television, prison—that function as major metaphors in the works. These are explorations not just of selfhood, but of the development of identity within familial and cultural contexts. Perhaps so many writers of memoirs and personal essays return to childhood because it is a locus of endless reimagining; as we look back upon how we grew up, we can begin to understand the forces and people who shaped us, and how we in turn shaped them.

In the "Eye" subcategory of literary journalistic pieces, Tom Wolfe's "Yeager" from *The Right Stuff* is a classic of New Journalism. Here, the "I" is a background observer, not seen on the page but felt in the perspective and voice of the piece. Using vivid description and narration, the author seems to be experiencing everything right alongside Yeager. The author is invisible, yet he breathes through his subject. Beverly Lowry's "Secret Ceremonies of Life and Death," on the other hand, can be seen as a link between the personal and the journalistic; the essay is about death-row inmate Karla Faye Tucker, yet it is also about the unlikely friendship between these two women. We placed this essay in the journalistic section because, though it does involve aspects of the personal, the primary focus is on the "Eye" looking outward. While Wolfe is a pure observer, and Lowry is very much involved in her subject, Susan Orlean in "Meet the Shaggs," a group portrait of an obscure rock group, takes the role of interviewer, a reporter seeking answers.

A central impetus behind these profiles is the understanding that every life and every person are rich with stories, conflicts, and ideas that can be seen through social, cultural, and historical frameworks. Using elements such as narrative and dialogue, creative nonfiction portraits shape their subjects into characters whose experiences are in some way resonant. The Shaggs, after all, are not just a music group but also a view into a family, and an emblem of a particular time and place in late 1960s America.

Questions of veracity can loom large in writing literary journalism, particularly when focusing on another person as the subject. Writers must struggle to capture the essence of a character without being overly swayed by personal bias (or being unable to recognize such bias). The three craft essays in this section offer guidance on such matters. In "Making the Truth Believable," Tracy Kidder uses his own experiences to navigate issues such as honesty and the true observer's point of view. In their respective pieces "On the Necessity of Turning Oneself into a Character" and "The Singular First Person," Phillip Lopate and Scott Russell Sanders discuss the often tricky role of the "I" in personal essays. Lopate offers advice to the writer on how to portray the self on the page, and Sanders stresses the necessity of discovering a unique voice. As he writes, "It is the *singularity* of the first person—its warts and crotchets and turn of voice—that lures many of us into reading essays, and that lingers with us after we finish."

The "I"

Bernard Cooper

Picking Plums

It has been nearly a year since my father fell while picking plums. The bruises on his leg have healed, and except for a vague absence of pigmentation where the calf had blistered, his recovery is complete. Back in the habit of evening constitutionals, he navigates the neighborhood with his usual stride—"Brisk," he says, "for a man of eighty-five"—dressed in a powder blue jogging suit that bears the telltale stains of jelly doughnuts and Lipton tea, foods which my father, despite doctor's orders, hasn't the will to forsake.

He broke his glasses and his hearing aid in the fall, and when I first stepped into the hospital room for a visit, I was struck by the way my father—head cocked to hear, squinting to see— looked so much older and more remote, a prisoner of his failing senses. "Boychik?" he asked, straining his face in my general direction. He fell back into a stack of pillows, sighed a deep sigh, and without my asking described what had happened:

"There they are, all over the lawn. Purple plums, dozens of them. They look delicious. So what am I supposed to do? Let the birds eat them? Not on your life. It's my tree, right? First I fill a bucket with the ones from the ground. Then I get the ladder out of the garage. I've climbed the thing a hundred times before. I make it to the top, reach out my hand, and . . . who knows what happens. Suddenly I'm an astronaut. Up is down and vice versa. It happened so fast I didn't have time to piss in my pants. I'm flat on my back, not a breath in me. Couldn't have called for help if I tried. And the pain in my leg—you don't want to know."

"Who found you?"

"What?"

I move closer, speak louder.

"Nobody found me," he says, exasperated. "Had to wait till I could get up on my own. It seemed like hours. I'm telling you, I thought it was all over. But eventually I could breathe normal again and—don't ask me how; God only knows—I got in the car and drove here myself." My father shifted his weight and grimaced. The sheet slid off his injured leg, the calf swollen, purple as a plum, what the doctor called "an insult to the tissue."

Throughout my boyhood my father possessed a surplus of energy, or it possessed him. On weekdays he worked hard at the office, and on weekends he gardened in our yard. He was also a man given to unpredictable episodes of anger. These rages were never precipitated by a crisis—in the face of illness or accident my father remained steady, methodical, even optimistic; when the chips were down he was an incorrigible joker, an inveterate backslapper, a sentry at the bedside—but something as simple as a drinking glass left out on the table could send him into a frenzy of invective. Spittle shot from his lips. Blood ruddied his face. He'd hurl the glass against the wall.

His temper rarely intimidated my mother. She'd light a Tareyton, stand aside, and watch my father flail and shout until he was purged of the last sharp word. Winded and limp, he'd flee into the living room, where he would draw the shades, sit in his wing chair, and brood for hours.

Even as a boy, I understood how my father's profession had sullied his view of the world, had made him a wary man, prone to explosions. He spent hours taking depositions from jilted wives and cuckolded husbands. He conferred with a miserable clientele: spouses who wept, who spat accusations, who pounded his desk in want of revenge. At the time, California law required that grounds for divorce be proven in court, and toward this end my father carried in his briefcase not only the usual legal tablets and manila files but bills for motel rooms, matchbooks from bars, boxer shorts blooming with lipstick stains.

After one particularly long and vindictive divorce trial, he agreed to a weekend out of town. Mother suggested Palm Springs, rhapsodized about the balmy air, the cacti lit by colored lights, the street named after Bob Hope. When it finally came time to leave, however, my mother kept thinking of things she forgot to pack. No sooner would my father begin to back the car out of the driveway than my mother would shout for him to stop, dash into the house, and retrieve what she needed. A carton of Tareytons. An aerosol can of Solarcaine. A paperback novel to read by the pool. I sat in the backseat, motionless and mute; with each of her excursions back inside, I felt my father's frustration mount. When my mother insisted she get a package of Saltine crackers in case we got hungry along the way, my father glared at her, bolted from the car, wrenched every piece of luggage from the trunk, and slammed it shut with such a vengeance the car rocked on its springs.

Through the rear window, my mother and I could see him fling two suitcases, a carryall, and a makeup case yards above his balding head. The sky was a huge and cloudless blue; gray chunks of luggage sailed through it, twisting and spinning and falling to earth like the burned-out stages of a booster rocket. When a piece of luggage crashed back to the asphalt, he'd pick it up and hurl it again. With every effort, an involuntary, animal grunt issued from the depths of his chest.

Finally, the largest suitcase came unlatched in mid-flight. Even my father was astonished when articles of his wife's wardrobe began their descent from the summer sky. A yellow scarf dazzled the air like a tangible strand of sunlight. Fuzzy slippers tumbled down. One diaphanous white slip drifted over the driveway and, as if guided by an invisible hand, draped itself across a hedge. With that, my father barreled by us, veins protruding on his temple and neck, and stomped into the house. "I'm getting tired of this," my mother grumbled. Before she stooped to pick up the mess—a vast and random geography of clothes—she flicked her cigarette onto the asphalt and ground the ember out.

One evening, long after I'd moved away from home, I received a phone call from my father telling me that my mother had died the night before. "But I didn't know it happened," he said.

He'd awakened as usual that morning, ruminating over a case while he showered and shaved. My mother appeared to be sound asleep, one arm draped across her face, eyes sheltered beneath the crook of her elbow. When he sat on the bed to pull up his socks, he'd tried not to jar the mattress and wake her. At least he *thought* he'd tried not to wake her, but he couldn't remember, he couldn't be sure. Things looked normal, he kept protesting—the pillow, the blanket, the way she lay there. He decided to grab a doughnut downtown and left in a hurry. But that night my father returned to a house suspiciously unlived-in. The silence caused him to clench his fists, and he called for his wife—"Lillian, Lillian"—as he drifted through quiet, unlit rooms, walking slowly up the stairs.

I once saw a photograph of a woman who had jumped off the Empire State Building and landed on the roof of a parked car. What is amazing is that she appears merely to have leapt into satin sheets, to be deep in a languid and absolute sleep. Her eyes are closed, lips slightly parted, hair fanned out on a metal pillow. Nowhere is there a trace of blood, her body caught softly in its own impression.

As my father spoke into the telephone, his voice about to break—"I should have realized. I should have known"—that's the state in which I pictured my mother: a long fall of sixty years, an uncanny landing, a miraculous repose.

My father and I had one thing in common after my mother's heart attack: we each maintained a secret life. Secret, at least, from each other.

I'd fallen for a man named Travis Mask. Travis had recently arrived in Los Angeles from Kentucky, and everything I was accustomed to—the billboards lining the Sunset strip, the 7-Elevens open all night—stirred in him a strong allegiance; "I love this town," he'd say every day. Travis's job was to collect change from food vending machines throughout the city. During dinner he would tell me about the office lobbies and college cafeterias he had visited, the trick to opening different machines, the noisy cascade of nickles and dimes. Travis Mask was enthusiastic. Travis Mask was easy to please. In bed I called him by his full name because I found the sound of it exciting.

My father, on the other hand, had fallen for a woman whose identity he meant to keep secret. I knew of her existence only because of a dramatic change in his behavior: he would grow mysterious as quickly and inexplicably as he had once grown angry. Though I resented being barred from this central fact of my father's life, I had no intention of telling him I was gay. It had taken me thirty years to achieve even a modicum of intimacy with the man, and I didn't want to risk a setback. It wasn't as if I was keeping my sexual orientation a secret; I'd told relatives, co-workers, friends. But my father was a man who whistled at waitresses, flirted with bank tellers, his head swiveling like a radar dish toward the nearest pair of breasts and hips. Ever since I was a child my father reminded me of the wolf in cartoons whose ears shoot steam, whose eyes pop out on springs, whose tongue unfurls like a party favor whenever he sees a curvaceous dame. As far as my father was concerned, desire for women fueled the world, compelled every man without exception—his occupation testified to that—was a force as essential as gravity. I didn't want to disappoint him.

Eventually, Travis Mask was transferred to Long Beach. In his absence my nights grew long and ponderous, and I tried to spend more time with my father in the belief that sooner or later an opportunity for disclosure would present itself. We met for dinner once a month in a restaurant whose interior was dim and crimson, our interaction friendly but formal, both of us cautiously skirting the topic of our private lives; we'd become expert at the ambiguous answer, the changed subject, the half-truth. Should my father ask if I was dating, I'd tell him yes, I had been seeing someone. I'd liked them very much, I said, but they were transferred to another city. Them. They. My attempt to neuter the pronouns made it sound as if I were courting people en masse. Just when I thought this subterfuge was becoming obvious, my father began to respond in kind: "Too bad I didn't get a chance to meet them. Where did you say they went?"

Avoidance also worked in reverse: "And how about you, Dad? Are you seeing anybody?"

"Seeing? I don't know if you'd call it *seeing*. What did you order, chicken or fish?"

During one dinner we discovered that we shared a fondness for nature programs on television, and from that night on, when we'd exhausted our comments about the meal or the weather, we'd ask if the other had seen the show about the blind albino fish that live in underwater caves, or the one about the North American moose whose antlers, coated with green moss, provide camouflage in the underbrush. My father and I had adapted like those creatures to the strictures of our shared world.

And then I met her.

I looked up from a rack of stationery at the local Thrifty one afternoon and there stood my father with a willowy black woman in her early forties. As she waited for a prescription to be filled, he drew a finger through her hair, nuzzled the nape of her neck, the refracted light of his lenses causing his cheeks to glow. I felt like a child who was witness to something forbidden: his father's helpless, unguarded ardor for an unfamiliar woman. I didn't know whether to run or stay. Had he always been attracted to young black women? Had I ever known him well? Somehow I managed to move myself toward them and mumble hello. They turned around in unison. My father's eyes widened. He reached out and cupped my shoulder, struggled to say my name. Before he could think to introduce us, I shook the woman's hand, startled by its softness. "So you're the son. Where've you been hiding?" She was kind and cordial, though too preoccupied to engage in much conversation, her handsome features furrowed by a hint of melancholy, a sadness which I sensed had little to do with my surprise appearance. Anna excused herself when the pharmacist called her name.

Hours after our encounter I could still feel the softness of Anna's hand, the softness that stirred my father's yearning. He was seventy-five years old, myopic and hard of hearing, his skin loose and liver-spotted, but one glimpse of his impulsive public affection led me to the conclusion that my father possessed, despite his age, a restless sexual energy. The meeting left me elated, expectant. My father and I had something new in common: the pursuit of our unorthodox passions. We were, perhaps, more alike than I'd realized. After years of relative estrangement, I'd been given grounds for a fresh start, a chance to establish a stronger connection.

But none of my expectations mattered. Later that week they left the country.

The prescription, it turned out, was for a psychotropic drug. Anna had battled bouts of depression since childhood. Her propensity for unhappiness gave my father a vital mission: to make her laugh, to wrest her from despair. Anna worked as an elementary-school substitute teacher and managed a few rental properties in South-Central Los Angeles, but after weeks of functioning normally, she would take to my father's bed for days on end, blank and immobile beneath the quilt she had bought to brighten up the room, unaffected by his jokes, his kisses and cajoling. These spells of depression came without warning and ended just as unexpectedly. Though they both did their best to enjoy each other during the periods of relative calm, they lived, my father later lamented, like people in a thunderstorm, never knowing when lightning would strike. Thinking that a drastic change might help Anna shed a recent depression, they pooled their money and flew to Europe.

They returned with snapshots showing the two of them against innumerable backdrops: the Tower of London, the Vatican, Versailles; monuments, obelisks, statuary. In every pose their faces were unchanged, the faces of people who want to be happy, who try to be happy, and somehow can't.

As if in defiance of all the photographic evidence against them, they were married the following month at the Church of the Holy Trinity. I was one of only two guests at the wedding. The other was an uncle of Anna's. Before the ceremony began he shot me a glance which attested, I was certain, to an incredulity as great as mine. The vaulted chapel rang with prerecorded organ music, an eerie and pious overture. Light filtered through stained-glass windows, chunks of sweet color that reminded me of Jell-O. My old Jewish father and his Episcopalian lover appeared at opposite ends of the dais, walking step by measured step toward a union in the center. The priest, swimming in white vestments, was somber and almost inaudible. Cryptic gestures, odd props; I watched with a powerful, wordless amazement. Afterward, as if the actual wedding hadn't been surreal enough, my father and Anna formed a kind of receiving line (if two people can constitute a line) in the church parking lot, where the four of us, bathed by hazy sunlight, exchanged pleasantries before the newlyweds returned home for a nap; their honeymoon in Europe, my father joked, had put the cart before the horse.

During the months after the wedding, when I called my father, he answered as though the ringing of the phone had been an affront. When I asked him what the matter was he'd bark, "What makes you think there's something the matter?" I began to suspect that my father's frustration had given rise to those ancient rages. But my father had grown too old and frail to sustain his anger for long. When we saw each other—Anna was always visiting relatives or too busy or tired to join us—he looked worn, embattled, and the pride I had in him for attempting an interracial marriage, for risking condemnation in the eyes of the world, was overwhelmed now by concern. He lost weight. His hands began to shake. I would sit across from him in the dim, red restaurant and marvel that this bewildered man had once hurled glasses against a wall and launched Samsonite into the sky.

Between courses I'd try to distract my father from his problems by pressing him to unearth tidbits of his past, as many as memory would allow. He'd often talk about Atlantic City, where his parents had owned a small grocery. Sometimes my mother turned up in the midst of his sketchy regressions. He would smooth wrinkles from the tablecloth and tell me no one could take her place. He eulogized her loyalty and patience, and I wondered whether he could see her clearly— her auburn hair and freckled hands—wondered whether he wished she were here to sweep up after his current mess. "Remember," he once asked me, without a hint of irony or regret, "what fun we had in Palm Springs?" Then he snapped back into the present and asked what was taking so long with our steaks.

The final rift between my father and Anna must have happened suddenly; she left behind several of her possessions, including the picture of Jesus that sat on the sideboard in the dining room next to my father's brass menorah. And along with Anna's possessions were stacks of leather-bound books, *Law of Torts, California Jurisprudence,* and *Forms of Pleading and Practice,* embossed along their spines. Too weak and distracted to practice law, my father had retired, and the house became a repository for the contents of his former office. I worried about him being alone, wandering through rooms freighted with history, crowded with the evidence of two marriages, fatherhood, and a long and harrowing career; he had nothing to do but pace and sigh and stir up dust. I encouraged him to find a therapist, but as far as my father was concerned, psychiatrists were all conniving witch doctors who fed off the misery of people like Anna.

Brian, the psychotherapist I'd been living with for three years (and live with still), was not at all fazed by my father's aversion to his profession. They'd met only rarely—once we ran into my father at a local supermarket, and twice Brian accompanied us to the restaurant—but when they were together, Brian would draw my father out, compliment him on his plaid pants, ask questions regarding the fine points of law. And when my father spoke, Brian listened intently, embraced him with his cool, blue gaze. My father relished my lover's attention; Brian's cheerfulness and steady disposition must have been refreshing in those troubled, lonely days. "How's that interesting friend of yours?" he sometimes asked. If he was suspicious that Brian and I shared the same house, he never pursued it—until he took his fall from the plum tree.

I drove my father home from the hospital, trying to keep his big unwieldy car, bobbing like a boat, within the lane. I bought him a pair of seersucker shorts because long pants were too painful and constricting. I brought over groceries and my wok, and while I cooked dinner my father sat at the dinette table, leg propped on a vinyl chair, and listened to the hissing oil, happy, abstracted. I helped him up the stairs to his bedroom, where we watched *Wheel of Fortune* and *Jeopardy* on the television and where, for the first time since I was a boy, I sat at his feet and he rubbed my head. It felt so good I'd graze his good leg, contented as a cat. He welcomed my visits with an eagerness bordering on glee and didn't seem to mind being dependent on me for physical assistance; he leaned his bulk on my shoulder wholly, and I felt protective, necessary, inhaling the scents of salve and Old Spice and the base, familiar odor that was all my father's own.

"You know those hostages?" asked my father one evening. He was sitting at the dinette, dressed in the seersucker shorts, his leg propped on the chair. The bruises had faded to lavender, his calf back to its normal size.

I could barely hear him over the broccoli sizzling in the wok. "What about them?" I shouted.

"I heard on the news that some of them are seeing a psychiatrist now that they're back."

"So?"

"Why a psychiatrist?"

I stopped tossing the broccoli. "Dad," I said, "if you'd been held hostage in the Middle East, you might want to see a therapist, too."

The sky dimmed in the kitchen windows. My father's face was a silhouette, his lenses catching the last of the light. "They got their food taken care of, right? And a place to sleep. What's the big deal?"

"You're at gunpoint, for God's sake. A prisoner. I don't think it's like spending a weekend at the Hilton."

"Living alone," he said matter-of-factly, "is like being a prisoner."

I let it stand. I added the pea pods.

"Let me ask you something," said my father. "I get this feeling—I'm not sure how to say it— that something isn't right. That you're keeping something from me. We don't talk much, I grant you that. But maybe now's the time."

My heart was pounding. I'd been thoroughly disarmed by his interpretation of world events, his minefield of non sequiturs, and I wasn't prepared for a serious discussion. I switched off the gas. The red jet sputtered. When I turned around, my father was staring at his outstretched leg. "So?" he said.

"You mean Brian?"

"Whatever you want to tell me, tell me."

"You like him, don't you?"

"What's not to like."

"He's been my lover for a long time. He makes me happy. We have a home." Each declaration was a stone in my throat. "I hope you understand. I hope this doesn't come between us."

"Look," said my father without skipping a beat, "you're lucky to have someone. And he's lucky to have you, too. It's no one's business anyway. What the hell else am I going to say?"

But my father thought of something else before I could speak and express my relief. "You know," he said, "when I was a boy of maybe sixteen, my father asked me to hold a ladder while he trimmed the tree in our backyard. So I did, see, when I suddenly remember I have a date with this bee-yoo-tiful girl, and I'm late, and I run out of the yard. I don't know what got into me. I'm halfway down the street when I remember my father, and I think, 'Oh, boy. I'm in trouble now.' But when I get back I can hear him laughing way up in the tree. I'd never heard him laugh like that. 'You must like her a lot,' he says when I help him down. Funny thing was, I hadn't told him where I was going."

I pictured my father's father teetering above the earth, a man hugging the trunk of a tree and watching his son run down the street in pursuit of sweet, ineffable pleasure. While my father reminisced, night obscured the branches of the plum tree, the driveway where my mother's clothes once floated down like enormous leaves. When my father finished telling the story, he looked at me, then looked away. A moment of silence lodged between us, an old and obstinate silence. I wondered whether nothing or everything would change. I spooned our food onto separate plates. My father carefully pressed his leg to test the healing flesh.

Tony Earley

Somehow Form a Family

In July 1969, I looked a lot like Opie in the second or third season of *The Andy Griffith Show.* I was a small boy with a big head. I wore blue jeans with the cuffs turned up and horizontally striped pullover shirts. I was the brother in a father-mother-brother-sister family. We lived in a four-room house at the edge of the country, at the foot of the mountains, outside a small town in North Carolina, but it could have been anywhere.

On one side of us lived Mr. and Mrs. White. They were old and rich. Their driveway was paved. Mrs. White was the president of the town garden club. When she came to visit Mama she brought her own ashtray. Mr. White was almost deaf. When he watched the news on television, it sounded like thunder in the distance. The Whites had an aluminum travel trailer in which you could see your reflection. One summer they hitched it to their Chrysler and pulled it all the way to Alaska.

On the other side of us lived Mack and Joan. They had just graduated from college. I thought Joan was beautiful, and still do. Mack had a bass boat and a three-tray tackle box in which lurked a bristling school of lures. On the other side of Mack and Joan lived Mrs. Taylor, who was old, and on the other side of Mrs. Taylor lived Mr. and Mrs. Frady, who had a fierce dog. My sister, Shelly, and I called it the Frady dog. The Frady dog lived a long and bitter life. It did not die until well after I had a driver's license.

On the far side of the Whites lived Mr. and Mrs. John Harris; Mr. and Mrs. Burlon Harris lived beyond them. John and Burlon were first cousins. John was a teacher who in the summers fixed lawn mowers, including ours, in a building behind his house. Burlon reminded me of Mr. Greenjeans on *Captain Kangaroo.* He kept horses and let us play in his barn. Shelly once commandeered one of his cats and brought it home to live with us. Burlon did not mind; he asked her if she wanted another one. We rode our bicycles toward Mr. Harris's house as if pulled there by gravity. We did not ride in the other direction; the Frady dog sat in its yard and watched for us.

In July 1969, we did not have much money, but in the hierarchy of southern poor, we were the good kind, the kind you would not mind living on your road. We were clean. Our clothes were clean. My parents worked. We went to church. Easter mornings, Mama stood us in front of the yellowbell bush and took our picture. We had meat at every meal—chicken and cube steak and pork chops and ham—and plenty of milk to drink. We were not trashy. Mrs. White would not sit with her ashtray in the kitchen of trashy people. Trashy people lived in the two houses around the curve past Mr. Harris's. When Daddy drove by those houses we could see that the kids in the yard had dirty faces. They were usually jabbing at something with a stick. Shelly and I were not allowed to ride our bicycles around the curve.

I knew we were poor only because our television was black and white. It was an old Admiral, built in the 1950s, with brass knobs the size of baseballs. Its cabinet was perfectly square, a cube of steel with a painted-on mahogany grain. Hoss on *Bonanza* could not have picked it up by himself. It was a formidable object, but its vertical hold was shot. We gathered around it the night Neil Armstrong walked on the moon, but we could not tell what was happening. The picture flipped up and down. We turned off the lights in the living room so we could see better. We listened to Walter Cronkite. In the distance we could hear Mr. White's color TV rumbling. We changed the channel and listened to Huntley and Brinkley. We could hear the scratchy radio transmissions coming down out of space, but we could not see anything. Daddy got behind the TV with a flashlight. He said, "Is that better? Is that better?" but it never was. Mama said, "Just be thankful you've got a television."

After the Eagle had landed but before the astronauts opened the door and came out, Mack knocked on the door and asked us if we wanted to look at the moon. He was an engineer for a power company and had set up his surveyor's transit in the backyard. Daddy and Shelly and I went with him. We left Mama sitting in the living room in the blue light of the TV. She said she did not want to miss anything. The moon, as I remember it, was full, although I have since learned that it wasn't. I remember that a galaxy of lightning bugs blinked against the black pine trees that grew between our yard and that of the Whites. Mack pointed the transit at the sky. Daddy held me up so I could see. The moon inside the instrument was startlingly bright; the man in the moon was clearly visible, although the men on the moon weren't. "You can't see them or anything," Mack said, which I already knew. I said, "I know that." I wasn't stupid and did not like to be talked to as if I were. Daddy put me down. He and Mack stood for a while and talked. Daddy smoked a ciga-rette. In the bright yard Shelly chased lightning bugs. She did not run, but instead jumped slowly, her feet together. I realized that she was pretending to walk on the moon, pretending that she was weightless. The moon was so bright, it cast a shadow at her feet. I remember these things for sure. I am tempted to say that she was beautiful in the moonlight, and I'm sure she was, but that isn't something I remember noticing that night, only a thing I need to say now.

Eight, maybe nine months later, Shelly and I rode the bus home from school. It was a Thursday, Mama's day off, Easter time. The cherry tree in the garden separating our driveway from that of the Whites was in brilliant, full bloom. We could hear it buzzing from the road. One of us checked the mailbox. We looked up the driveway at our house. Something was wrong with it, but we couldn't tell what. Daddy was adding four rooms on to the house, and we were used to it appearing large and unfinished. We stood in the driveway and stared. Black tar paper was tacked to the outside walls of the new part, but the old part was still covered with white asbestos shingles. In the coming summer, Daddy and a crew of brick masons would finish transforming the house into a split-level ranch style, remarkably similar to the one in which the Bradys would live. I loved the words *split-level ranch-style*. To me they meant "rich."

Shelly and I spotted what was wrong at the same time. A giant television antenna had attached itself to the roof of our house. It was shiny and tall as a young tree. It looked dangerous, as if it would bite, like a praying mantis. The antenna slowly began to turn, as if it had noticed us. Shelly and I looked quickly at each other, our mouths wide open, and then back at the antenna. We sprinted up the driveway.

In the living room, on the spot occupied by the Admiral that morning, sat a magnificent new color TV, a Zenith, with a twenty-one-inch screen. Its cabinet was made of real wood. *Gomer Pyle, U.S.M.C.* was on. I will never forget that. Gomer Pyle and Sergeant Carter were the first two people I ever saw on a color television. The olive green and khaki of their uniforms was dazzling. Above them was the blue sky of California. The sky in California seemed bluer than the sky in North Carolina.

We said, "Is that ours?"

Mama said, "I'm going to kill your daddy." He had charged the TV without telling her. Two men from Sterchi's Furniture had showed up at the house that morning with the TV on a truck. They climbed onto the roof and planted the antenna.

We said, "Can we keep it?"

Mama said, "I don't know," but I noticed she had written the numbers of the stations we could get on the dial of the Channel Master, the small box which controlled the direction the antenna pointed. Mama would never have written on anything she planned on taking back to the store.

The dial of the Channel Master was marked like a compass. Channel 3 in Charlotte lay to the east; Channel 13 in Asheville lay to the west. Channel 7 in Spartanburg and Channel 4 in Greenville rested side by side below them in the south. For years these cities would mark the outside edges of the world as I knew it. Shelly reached out and turned the dial. Mama smacked her on the hand. Gomer grew fuzzy and disappeared. I said, "Mama, she broke it." When the dial stopped turning, Mama carefully turned it back to the south. Gomer reappeared, resurrected. Jim Nabors probably never looked better to anyone, in his whole life, than he did to us right then.

Mama sat us down on the couch and laid down the law. Mama always laid down the law when she was upset. We were not to touch the TV. We could not turn it on, nor could we change the channel. Under no circumstances were we to touch the Channel Master. The Channel Master was very expensive. And if we so much as looked at the knobs that controlled the color, she would whip us. It had taken her all afternoon to get the color just right.

We lived in a split-level ranch-style house, with two maple trees and a rose bush in the front yard, outside a town that could have been named Springfield. We had a color TV. We had a Channel Master antenna that turned slowly on top of our house until it found and pulled from the sky electromagnetic waves for our nuclear family.

We watched *Hee-Haw,* starring Buck Owens and Roy Clark; we watched *All in the Family, The Mary Tyler Moore Show, The Bob Newhart Show, The Carol Burnett Show,* and *Mannix,* starring Mike Connors with Gail Fisher as Peggy; we watched *Gunsmoke* and *Bonanza,* even after Adam left and Hoss died and Little Joe's hair turned gray; we watched *Adam-12* and *Kojak, McCloud, Colombo,* and *Hawaii Five-O;* we watched *Cannon,* a Quinn Martin production and *Barnaby Jones,* a Quinn Martin production, which co-starred Miss America and Uncle Jed from *The Beverly Hillbillies.* Daddy finished the new part of the house and moved out soon thereafter. He rented a trailer in town and took the old Admiral out of the basement with him. We watched *Mutual of Omaha's Wild Kingdom* and *The Wonderful World of Disney.* After school we watched *Gomer Pyle, U.S.M.C., The Beverly Hillbillies, Gilligan's Island,* and *The Andy Griffith Show.* Upstairs, we had rooms of our own. Mama stopped taking us to church.

On Friday nights we watched *The Partridge Family, The Brady Bunch, Room 222, The Odd Couple,* and *Love American Style*. Daddy came to visit on Saturdays. We watched *The Little Rascals* on Channel 3 with Fred Kirby, the singing cowboy, and his sidekick, Uncle Jim. We watched *The Little Rascals* on Channel 4 with Monty Dupuy, the weatherman, and his sidekick, Doohickey. Mornings, before school, we watched *The Three Stooges* with Mr. Bill on Channel 13. Mr. Bill worked alone. The school year Daddy moved out, Mr. Bill showed Bible story cartoons instead of *The Three Stooges*. That year, we went to school angry.

After each of Daddy's visits, Mama said he was getting better. Shelly and I tried to imagine living with the Bradys but realized we would not fit in. They were richer and more popular at school. They did not have Southern accents. One Saturday Daddy brought me a set of golf clubs, which I had asked for but did not expect to get. It was raining that day. I took the clubs out in the yard and very quickly realized that golf was harder than it looked on television. I went back inside and wiped the mud and water off the clubs with Bounty paper towels, the quicker picker upper. Upstairs I heard Mama say, "Do you think he's stupid?" I spread the golf clubs on the floor around me. I tuned in *Shock Theater* on Channel 13 and turned it up loud.

Shelly had a crush on Bobby Brady; I had a crush on Jan. Jan had braces, I had braces. Jan had glasses, I had glasses. Their daddy was an architect. Our daddy lived in a trailer in town with a poster of Wile E. Coyote and the Road Runner on the living room wall. The Coyote held the Road Runner firmly by the neck. The caption on the poster said, "Beep, Beep your ass." I lay in bed at night and imagined being married to Jan Brady but having an affair with Marsha. I wondered how we would tell Jan, what Marsha and I would do then, where we would go. Greg Brady beat me up. I shook his hand and told him I deserved it. Alice refused to speak to me. During this time Mrs. White died. I heard the ambulance in the middle of the night. It sounded like the one on *Emergency*. I opened the door to Mama's room to see if she was OK. She was embarrassed because our dog barked and barked.

Rhoda left *The Mary Tyler Moore Show*. Maude and George Jefferson left *All in the Family*; Florida, Maude's maid, left *Maude*. Daddy moved back in. He watched the news during supper, the TV as loud as Mr. White's. We were not allowed to talk during the news. This was the law. After the news we watched *Rhoda* or *Maude* or *Good Times*. Daddy decided that cutting the grass should be my job. We had a big yard. I decided that I didn't want to do anything he said. Mr. White remarried. The new Mrs. White's daughter died of cancer. The new Mrs. White dug up every flower the old Mrs. White had planted; she cut down every tree and shrub, including the cherry tree in the garden between our driveways. Mama said the new Mrs. White broke her heart. Mr. White mowed and mowed and mowed their grass until it was smooth as a golf course. Mack and Joan paved their driveway.

What I'm trying to say is this: we lived in a split-level ranch-style house; we had a Zenith in the living room and a Channel Master attached to the roof. But Shelly and I fought like Thelma and J.J. on *Good Times*. I wanted to live in Hawaii and work for Steve McGarrett. No bad guy ever got away from McGarrett, except the Chinese master spy Wo Fat. Shelly said McGarrett would never give me a job. In all things Shelly was on Daddy's side; I lined up on Mama's. Friday evenings, when Daddy got home from work, I sneaked outside to snoop around in the glove compartment of his car. I pretended I had a search warrant, that I was Danno on a big case. Shelly reported my snooping to Daddy. I was trying to be a good son.

Every Saturday, before he went to work, Daddy left word that I was to cut the grass before he got home. I stayed in bed until lunch. Shelly came into my room and said, "You better get up." I flipped her the bird. She said, "I'm telling." I got up in time to watch professional wrestling on Channel 3. I hated the bad guys. They did not fight fair. They hid brass knuckles in their trunks and beat the good guys until they bled. They won too often. Mama brought me tomato and onion sandwiches. I could hear Mack on one side and Mr. White on the other mowing their grass. I could hear John Harris and Mr. Frady and Mrs. Taylor's daughter, Lucille, mowing grass. Lucille lived in Charlotte, but came home on weekends just to mow Mrs. Taylor's grass. We had the shaggiest lawn on the road. After wrestling, I watched the *Game of the Week* on Channel 4. Carl Yaztremski of the Boston Red Sox was my favorite baseball player. He had forearms like fenceposts. Nobody messed with him. I listened over the lawn mowers for the sound of Daddy's Volkswagen. Mama came in the living room and said, "Son, maybe you should mow some of the grass before your daddy gets home. You know what's going to happen." I knew what was going to happen. I knew that eventually he would make me mow the grass. I knew that when I was through, Mack would come through the pine trees laughing. He would say, "Charles, I swear that is the laziest boy I have ever seen." Mack had a Snapper Comet riding mower, on which he sat like a king. I never saw him on it that I did not want to bean him with a rock. Daddy would shake his head and say, "Mack, dead lice wouldn't fall off that boy." Every Saturday night we ate out at Scoggin's Seafood and Steak House. *Hee-Haw* came on at seven; *All in the Family* came on at eight.

And then Shelly and I were in high school. We watched *M*A*S*H** and *Lou Grant, Love Boat* and *Fantasy Island.* We watched *Dynasty* and *Dallas.* Opie was Richie Cunningham on *Happy Days.* Ben Cartwright showed up in a black bathrobe on *Battlestar Gallactica.* The Channel Master stopped working, but no one bothered to have it fixed. The antenna was left immobile on the roof in a compromised position: we could almost get most of the channels. One summer Mack built a pool in his backyard. Joan lay in a bikini beside the pool in the sun. The next summer Mack built a fence. This was during the late seventies. Shelly lay in her room with the lights turned off and listened to *Dark Side of the Moon.* On Friday nights she asked me to go out with her and her friends. I always said no. I did not want to miss *The Rockford Files.*

In those days Shelly and I watched *Guiding Light* when we got home from school. It was our soap. I remember that Ed Bauer's beautiful wife Rita left him because he was boring. Shelly said I reminded her of Ed Bauer. She wore her hair like Farrah Fawcett Majors on *Charlie's Angels.* After *Guiding Light* I changed the channel and watched *Star Trek.* I could not stay awake in school. I went to sleep during homeroom. During the day I woke up only long enough to change classes and eat lunch. I watched *Star Trek* when I got home as if it were beamed to our house by God. I did not want to be Captain Kirk, or any of the main characters. I just wanted to go with them. I wanted to wear a red jersey and walk the long, anonymous halls of the Starship Enterprise as it disappeared into space. One day *Star Trek* was preempted by an *ABC After School Special.* I tried to kick the screen out of the TV. I was wearing sneakers, so the glass would not break. Shelly hid in Mama and Daddy's room. I said, "Five-O. Open up." Then I kicked the door off the hinges.

Our family doctor thought I had narcolepsy. He sent me to a neurologist in Charlotte. Mama and Daddy went with me. In Charlotte, an EEG technician attached wires to my head. A small, round amber light glowed high up in the corner of the examination room. I watched the light until I went to sleep. The neurologist said that the EEG looked normal, but that he would talk to us more about the results in a few minutes. He led us to a private waiting room. It was small and bare and paneled with wood. In it were four chairs. Most of one wall was taken up by a darkened glass. I could not see what was on the other side of it. I studied our reflection. Mama and Daddy were trying to pretend that the glass wasn't there. I said, "Pa, when we get back to the Ponderosa, do you want me to round up those steers on the lower forty?"

Daddy said, "What?"
I said, "Damnit, Jim. I'm a doctor."
Daddy said, "What are you talking about?"
Mama said, "Be quiet. They're watching us."

Shelly died on Christmas Eve morning when I was a freshman in college. She had wrecked Mama's car. That night I stayed up late and watched the Pope deliver the Christmas mass from the Vatican. There was nothing else on. Daddy moved out again. My college almost shut down during the week *The Thorn Birds* was broadcast. Professors rescheduled papers and exams. In the basement of my dorm twenty-five nineteen-year-old guys shouted at the TV when the Richard Chamberlain character told the Rachel Ward character he loved God more than he loved her. At age nineteen, it was impossible to love God more than Rachel Ward. My best friend, a guy from Kenya, talked me into switching from *Guiding Light* to *General Hospital*. This was during the glory days of *General Hospital* when Luke and Scorpio roomed together on the Haunted Star. Laura was supposedly dead, but Luke knew in his heart she was still alive; every time he was by himself he heard a Christopher Cross song.

Going home was strange, as if the Mayberry I expected had become Mayberry, R.F.D. Shelly was gone. Daddy was gone. The second Mrs. White died, then Mr. White went away to a nursing home. The Fradys had moved away. John Harris had a heart attack and stopped fixing lawn mowers. Mama mowed our grass by herself with a rider. I stopped going to see Burlon Harris because he teared up every time he tried to talk about Shelly. Mack and Joan had a son named Timmy. Mack and Joan got a divorce. Mack moved to a farm out in the country; Joan moved to town.

Daddy fell in love with Mama my senior year and moved back in. The Zenith began slowly dying. Its picture narrowed into a greenly tinted slit. It stared like a diseased eye into the living room where Mama and Daddy sat. They turned off the lights so they could see better. I became a newspaper reporter. With my first Christmas bonus, I bought myself a television, a nineteen-inch GE. With my second Christmas bonus I bought Mama and Daddy one. They hooked it up to cable. When I visited them on Thursdays we watched *The Cosby Show, Family Ties, Cheers, Night Court,* and *Hill Street Blues*. Daddy gave up on broadcast TV when NBC cancelled *Hill Street Blues* and replaced it with *L.A. Law*. Now he mostly watches the Discovery Channel. Mama calls it the "airplanes and animals channel." They are in the eighteenth year of their new life together. I bear them no grudges. They were very young when I knew them best.

In grad school I switched back to *Guiding Light*. I had known Ed Bauer longer than I had known all but a few of my friends. It pleased me to see him in Springfield every afternoon, trying to do good. I watched *The Andy Griffith Show* twice a day. I could glance at Opie and tell you what year the episode was filmed. I watched the Gulf War from a stool in a bar.

Eventually I married a woman who grew up in a family that watched television only on special occasions—when Billie Jean King played Bobby Riggs, when Diana married Prince Charles. My wife was a student in a seminary. She did not want to meet Ed Bauer, nor could I explain, without sounding pathetic, why Ed Bauer was important to me. The first winter we were married I watched the winter Olympics huddled beneath a blanket in the frigid basement of the house we had rented. This was in a closed-down steel town near Pittsburgh, during the time I contemplated jumping from a bridge into the Ohio River. My wife asked the seminary community to pray for me. Ann B. Davis, who played Alice on *The Brady Bunch* was a member of that community. One day I saw her in the cafeteria at school. She looked much the same as when she played Alice, except that her hair was white, and she wore small, gold glasses. I didn't talk to her. I had heard that she didn't like talking about *The Brady Bunch,* and I could not think of anything to say to her about the world in which we actually lived. I sat in the cafeteria and stared at her as much as I could without anyone noticing. I don't know if she prayed for me or not, but I like to think that she did. I wanted to tell her that I grew up in a split-level ranch-style house outside a small town that could have been named Spring-field, but that something had gone wrong inside it. I wanted to tell her that years ago Alice had been important to me, that my sister and I had looked to Alice for something we could not name, and had at least seen a picture of what love looked like. I wanted to tell her that no one in my family ever raised their voice while the television was on, that late at night even a bad television show could keep me from hearing the silence inside my own heart. I wanted to tell her that Ed Bauer and I were still alive, that both of us had always wanted to do what was right. Ann B. Davis stood, walked over to the trash can, and emptied her tray. She walked out of the cafeteria and into a small, gray town near Pittsburgh. I wanted her to *be* Alice. I wanted her to smile as if she loved me. I wanted her to say, "Buck up, kiddo, everything's going to be all right." And what I'm trying to tell you now is this: I grew up in a split-level ranch-style house outside a town that could have been anywhere. I grew up in front of a television. I would have believed her. </P></BM></READ>

Lucy Grealy

_____

Mirrorings

There was a long period of time, almost a year, during which I never looked in a mirror. It wasn't easy, for I'd never suspected just how omnipresent are our own images. I began by merely avoiding mirrors, but by the end of the year I found myself with an acute knowledge of the reflected image, its numerous tricks and wiles, how it can spring up at any moment: a glass tabletop, a well-polished door handle, a darkened window, a pair of sunglasses, a restaurant's otherwise magnificent brass-plated coffee machine sitting innocently by the cash register.

At the time, I had just moved, alone, to Scotland and was surviving on the dole, as Britain's social security benefits are called. I didn't know anyone and had no idea how I was going to live, yet I went anyway because by happenstance I'd met a plastic surgeon there who said he could help me. I had been living in London, working temp jobs. While in London, I'd received more nasty comments about my face than I had in the previous three years, living in Iowa, New York, and Germany. These comments, all from men and all odiously sexual, hurt and disoriented me. I also had journeyed to Scotland because after more than a dozen operations in the States my insurance had run out, along with my hope that further operations could make any *real* difference. Here, however, was a surgeon who had some new techniques, and here, amazingly enough, was a government willing to foot the bill: I didn't feel I could pass up yet another chance to "fix" my face, which I confusedly thought concurrent with "fixing" my self, my soul, my life.

Twenty years ago, when I was nine and living in America, I came home from school one day with a toothache. Several weeks and misdiagnoses later, surgeons removed most of the right side of my jaw in an attempt to prevent the cancer they found there from spreading. No one properly explained the operation to me, and I awoke in a cocoon of pain that prevented me from moving or speaking. Tubes ran in and out of my body, and because I was temporarily unable to speak after the surgery and could not ask questions, I made up my own explanations for the tubes' existence. I remember the mysterious manner the adults displayed toward me. They asked me to do things: lie still for x-rays, not cry for needles, and so on, tasks that, although not easy, never seemed equal to the praise I received in return. Reinforced to me again and again was how I was "a brave girl" for not crying, "a good girl" for not complaining, and soon I began defining myself this way, equating strength with silence.

Then the chemotherapy began. In the seventies chemo was even cruder than it is now, the basic premise being to poison patients right up to the very brink of their own death. Until this point I almost never cried and almost always received praise in return. Thus I got what I considered the better part of the deal. But now it was like a practical joke that had gotten out of hand. Chemotherapy was a nightmare and I wanted it to stop; I didn't want to be brave anymore. Yet I had grown so used to defining myself as "brave"—i.e., *silent*—that the thought of losing this sense of myself was even more terrifying. I was certain that if I broke down I would be despicable in the eyes of both my parents and the doctors.

The task of taking me into the city for the chemo injections fell mostly on my mother, though sometimes my father made the trip. Overwhelmed by the sight of the vomiting and weeping, my father developed the routine of "going to get the car," meaning that he left the doctor's office before the injection was administered, on the premise that then he could have the car ready and waiting when it was all over. Ashamed of my suffering, I felt relief when he was finally out of the room. When my mother took me, she stayed in the room, yet this only made the distance between us even more tangible. She explained that it was wrong to cry *before* the needle went in; afterward was one thing, but before, that was mere fear, and hadn't I demonstrated my bravery earlier? Every Friday for two and a half years I climbed up onto that big doctor's table and told myself not to cry, and every week I failed. The two large syringes were filled with chemicals so caustic to the vein that each had to be administered very slowly. The whole process took about four minutes; I had to remain utterly still. Dry retching began in the first fifteen seconds, then the throb behind my eyes gave everything a yellow-green aura, and the bone-deep pain of alternating extreme hot and cold flashes made me tremble, yet still I had to sit motionless and not move my arm. No one spoke to me—not the doctor, who was a paradigm of the cold-fish physician; not the nurse, who told my mother I reacted much more violently than many of "the other children"; and not my mother, who, surely overwhelmed by the sight of her child's suffering, thought the best thing to do was remind me to be brave, to try not to cry. All the while I hated myself for having wept before the needle went in, convinced that the nurse and my mother were right, that I was "overdoing it," that the throwing up was psychosomatic, that my mother was angry with me for not being good or brave enough.

Yet each week, two or three days after the injection, there came the first flicker of feeling better, the always forgotten and gratefully rediscovered understanding that to simply be well in my body was the greatest thing I could ask for. I thought other people felt this appreciation and physical joy all the time, and I felt cheated because I was able to feel it only once a week.

Because I'd lost my hair, I wore a hat constantly, but this fooled no one, least of all myself. During this time, my mother worked in a nursing home in a Hasidic community. Hasidic law dictates that married women cover their hair, and most commonly this is done with a wig. My mother's friends were now all willing to donate their discarded wigs, and soon the house seemed filled with them. I never wore one, for they frightened me even when my mother insisted I looked better in one of the few that actually fit. Yet we didn't know how to say no to the women who kept graciously offering their wigs. The cats enjoyed sleeping on them and the dogs playing with them, and we grew used to having to pick a wig up off a chair we wanted to sit in. It never struck us as odd until one day a visitor commented wryly as he cleared a chair for himself, and suddenly a great wave of shame overcame me. I had nightmares about wigs and flushed if I even heard the word, and one night I put myself out of my misery by getting up after everyone was asleep and gathering all the wigs except for one the dogs were fond of and that they had chewed up anyway. I hid all the rest in an old chest.

When you are only ten, which is when the chemotherapy began, two and a half years seem like your whole life, yet it finally did end, for the cancer was gone. I remember the last day of treatment clearly because it was the only day on which I succeeded in not crying, and because later, in private, I cried harder than I had in years; I thought now I would no longer be "special," that without the arena of chemotherapy in which to prove myself no one would ever love me, that I would fade unnoticed into the background. But this idea about *not being different* didn't last very long. Before, I foolishly believed that people stared at me because I was bald. After my hair eventually grew in, it didn't take long before I understood that I looked different for another reason. My face. People stared at me in stores, and other children made fun of me to the point that I came to expect such reactions constantly, wherever I went. School became a battleground.

Halloween, that night of frights, became my favorite holiday because I could put on a mask and walk among the blessed for a few brief, sweet hours. Such freedom I felt, walking down the street, my face hidden! Through the imperfect oval holes I could peer out at other faces, masked or painted or not, and see on those faces nothing but the normal faces of childhood looking back at me, faces I mistakenly thought were the faces everyone else but me saw all the time, faces that were simply curious and ready for fun, not the faces I usually braced myself for, the cruel, lonely, vicious ones I spent every day other than Halloween waiting to see around each corner. As I breathed in the condensed, plastic-scented air under the mask, I somehow thought that I was breathing in normality, that this joy and weightlessness were what the world was composed of, and that it was only my face that kept me from it, my face that was my own mask that kept me from knowing the joy I was sure everyone but me lived with intimately. How could the other children not know it? Not know that to be free of the fear of taunts and the burden of knowing no one would ever love you was all that anyone could ever ask for? I was a pauper walking for a short while in the clothes of the prince, and when the day ended I gave up my disguise with dismay.

I was living in an extreme situation, and because I did not particularly care for the world I was in, I lived in others, and because the world I did live in was dangerous now, I incorporated this danger into my secret life. I imagined myself to be an Indian. Walking down the streets, I stepped through the forest, my body ready for any opportunity to fight or flee one of the big cats that I knew stalked me. Vietnam and Cambodia, in the news then as scenes of catastrophic horror, were other places I walked through daily. I made my way down the school hall, knowing a land mine or a sniper might give themselves away at any moment with the subtle metal click I'd read about. Compared with a land mine, a mere insult about my face seemed a frivolous thing.

In those years, not yet a teenager, I secretly read—knowing it was somehow inappropriate—works by Primo Levi and Elie Wiesel, and every book by a survivor I could find by myself without asking the librarian. Auschwitz, Birkenau: I felt the blows of the capos and somehow knew that because any moment we might be called upon to live for a week on one loaf of bread and some water called soup, the peanut-butter sandwich I found on my plate was nothing less than a miracle, an utter and sheer miracle capable of making me literally weep with joy.

I decided to become a "deep" person. I wasn't exactly sure what this would entail, but I believed that if I could just find the right philosophy, think the right thoughts, my suffering would end. To try to understand the world I was in, I undertook to find out what was "real," and I quickly began seeing reality as existing in the lowest common denominator, that suffering was the one and only dependable thing. But rather than spend all of my time despairing, though certainly I did plenty of that, I developed a form of defensive egomania: I felt I was the only one walking about in the world who understood what was really important. I looked upon people complaining about the most mundane things—nothing on TV, traffic jams, the price of new clothes—and felt joy because I knew how unimportant those things really were and felt unenlightened superiority because other people didn't. Because in my fantasy life I had learned to be thankful for each cold, blanketless night that I survived on the cramped wooden bunks, my pain and despair were a stroll through the country in comparison. I was often miserable, but I knew that to feel warm instead of cold was its own kind of joy, that to eat was a reenactment of the grace of some god whom I could only dimly define, and that to simply be alive was a rare, ephemeral gift.

As I became a teenager, my isolation began. My nonidentical twin sister started going out with boys, and I started—my most tragic mistake of all—to listen to and believe the taunts thrown at me daily by the very boys she and the other girls were interested in. I was a dog, a monster, the ugliest girl they had ever seen. Of all the remarks, the most damaging wasn't even directed at me but was really an insult to "Jerry," a boy I never saw because every day between fourth and fifth periods, when I was cornered by a particular group of kids, I was too ashamed to lift my eyes off the floor. "Hey, look, it's Jerry's girlfriend!" they shrieked when they saw me, and I felt such shame, knowing that this was the deepest insult to Jerry that they could imagine.

When pressed to it, one makes compensations. I came to love winter, when I could wrap up the disfigured lower half of my face in a scarf: I could speak to people and they would have no idea to whom and to what they were really speaking. I developed the bad habit of letting my long hair hang in my face and of always covering my chin and mouth with my hand, hoping it might be mistaken as a thoughtful, accidental gesture. I also became interested in horses and got a job at a rundown local stable. Having those horses to go to each day after school saved my life; I spent all of my time either with them or thinking about them. Completely and utterly repressed by the time I was sixteen, I was convinced that I would never want a boyfriend, not ever, and wasn't it convenient for me, even a blessing, that none would ever want me. I told myself I was free to concentrate on the "true reality" of life, whatever that was. My sister and her friends put on blue eye shadow, blow-dried their hair, and spent interminable hours in the local mall, and I looked down on them for this, knew they were misleading themselves and being overly occupied with the "mere surface" of living. I'd had thoughts like this when I was younger, ten or twelve, but now my philosophy was haunted by desires so frightening I was unable even to admit they existed.

Throughout all of this, I was undergoing reconstructive surgery in an attempt to rebuild my jaw. It started when I was fifteen, two years after chemo ended. I had known for years I would have operations to fix my face, and at night I fantasized about how good my life would finally be then. One day I got a clue that maybe it wouldn't be so easy. An older plastic surgeon explained the process of "pedestals" to me, and told me it would take *ten years* to fix my face. Ten years? Why even bother, I thought; I'll be ancient by then. I went to a medical library and looked up the "pedestals" he talked about. There were gruesome pictures of people with grotesque tubes of their own skin growing out of their bodies, tubes of skin that were harvested like some kind of crop and then rearranged, with results that did not look at all normal or acceptable to my eye. But then I met a younger surgeon, who was working on a new way of grafting that did not involve pedestals, and I became more hopeful and once again began to await the fixing of my face, the day when I would be whole, content, loved.

Long-term plastic surgery is not like in the movies. There is no one single operation that will change everything, and there is certainly no slow unwrapping of the gauze in order to view the final, remarkable result. There is always swelling, sometimes to a grotesque degree, there are often bruises, and always there are scars. After each operation, too frightened to simply go look in the mirror, I developed an oblique method, with several stages. First, I tried to catch my reflection in an overhead lamp: the roundness of the metal distorted my image just enough to obscure details and give no true sense of size or proportion. Then I slowly worked my way up to looking at the reflection in someone's eyeglasses, and from there I went to walking as briskly as possible by a mirror, glancing only quickly. I repeated this as many times as it would take me, passing the mirror slightly more slowly each time until finally I was able to stand still and confront myself.

The theory behind most reconstructive surgery is to take large chunks of muscle, skin, and bone and slap them into the roughly appropriate place, then slowly begin to carve this mess into some sort of shape. It involves long, major operations, countless lesser ones, a lot of pain, and many, many years. And also, it does not always work. With my young surgeon in New York, who with each passing year was becoming not so young, I had two or three soft-tissue grafts, two skin grafts, a bone graft, and some dozen other operations to "revise" my face, yet when I left graduate school at the age of twenty-five I was still more or less in the same position I had started in: a deep hole in the right side of my face and a rapidly shrinking left side and chin, a result of the radiation I'd had as a child and the stress placed upon the bone by the other operations. I was caught in a cycle of having a big operation, one that would force me to look monstrous from the swelling for many months, then having the subsequent revision operations that improved my looks tremendously, and then slowly, over the period of a few months or a year, watching the graft reabsorb back into my body, slowly shrinking down and leaving me with nothing but the scarred donor site the graft had originally come from.

It wasn't until I was in college that I finally allowed that maybe, just maybe, it might be nice to have a boyfriend. I went to a small, liberal, predominantly female school and suddenly, after years of alienation in high school, discovered that there were other people I could enjoy talking to who thought me intelligent and talented. I was, however, still operating on the assumption that no one, not ever, would be physically attracted to me, and in a curious way this shaped my personality. I became forthright and honest in the way that only the truly self-confident are, who do not expect to be rejected, and in the way of those like me, who do not even dare to ask acceptance from others and therefore expect no rejection. I had come to know myself as a person, but I would be in graduate school before I was literally, physically able to use my name and the word "woman" in the same sentence.

Now my friends repeated for me endlessly that most of it was in my mind, that, granted, I did not look like everyone else, but that didn't mean I looked bad. I am sure now that they were right some of the time. But with the constant surgery I was in a perpetual state of transfiguration. I rarely looked the same for more than six months at a time. So ashamed of my face, I was unable even to admit that this constant change affected me; I let everyone who wanted to know that it was only what was inside that mattered, that I had "grown used to" the surgery, that none of it bothered me at all. Just as I had done in childhood, I pretended nothing was wrong, and this was constantly mistaken by others for bravery. I spent a great deal of time looking in the mirror in private, positioning my head to show off my eyes and nose, which were not only normal but quite pretty, as my friends told me often. But I could not bring myself to see them for more than a moment: I looked in the mirror and saw not the normal upper half of my face but only the disfigured lower half.

People still teased me. Not daily, as when I was younger, but in ways that caused me more pain than ever before. Children stared at me, and I learned to cross the street to avoid them; this bothered me, but not as much as the insults I got from men. Their taunts came at me not because I was disfigured but because I was a disfigured *woman.* They came from boys, sometimes men, and almost always from a group of them. I had long, blond hair, and I also had a thin figure. Sometimes, from a distance, men would see a thin blonde and whistle, something I dreaded more than anything else because I knew that as they got closer, their tune, so to speak, would inevitably change; they would stare openly or, worse, turn away quickly in shame or repulsion. I decided to cut my hair to avoid any misconception that anyone, however briefly, might have about my being attractive. Only two or three times have I ever been teased by a single person, and I can think of only one time when I was ever teased by a woman. Had I been a man, would I have had to walk down the street while a group of young women followed and denigrated my sexual worth?

Not surprisingly, then, I viewed sex as my salvation. I was sure that if only I could get someone to sleep with me, it would mean I wasn't ugly, that I was attractive, even lovable. This line of reasoning led me into the beds of several manipulative men who liked themselves even less than they liked me, and I in turn left each short-term affair hating myself, obscenely sure that if only I had been prettier it would have worked—he would have loved me and it would have been like those other love affairs that I was certain "normal" women had all the time. Gradually, I became unable to say "I'm depressed" but could say only "I'm ugly," because the two had become inextricably linked in my mind. Into that universal lie, that sad equation of "if only . . . " that we are all prey to, I was sure that if only I had a normal face, then I would be happy.

The new surgeon in Scotland, Oliver Fenton, recommended that I undergo a procedure involving something called a tissue expander, followed by a bone graft. A tissue expander is a small balloon placed under the skin and then slowly blown up over the course of several months, the object being to stretch out the skin and create room and cover for the new bone. It's a bizarre, nightmarish thing to do to your face, yet I was hopeful about the end results and I was also able to spend the three months that the expansion took in the hospital. I've always felt safe in hospitals: they're the one place I feel free from the need to explain the way I look. For this reason the first tissue expander was bearable— just—and the bone graft that followed it was a success; it did not melt away like the previous ones.

The surgical stress this put upon what remained of my original jaw instigated the deterioration of that bone, however, and it became unhappily apparent that I was going to need the same operation I'd just had on the right side done to the left. I remember my surgeon telling me this at an outpatient clinic. I planned to be traveling down to London that same night on an overnight train, and I barely made it to the station on time, such a fumbling state of despair I was in.

I could not imagine going through it *again,* and just as I had done all my life, I searched and searched through my intellect for a way to make it okay, make it bearable, for a way to *do* it. I lay awake all night on that train, feeling the tracks slip beneath me with an odd eroticism, when I remembered an afternoon from my three months in the hospital. Boredom was a big problem those long afternoons, the days marked by meals and television programs. Waiting for the afternoon tea to come, wondering desperately how I could make time pass, it had suddenly occurred to me that I didn't have to make time pass, that it would do it of its own accord, that I simply had to relax and take no action. Lying on the train, remembering that, I realized I had no obligation to improve my situation, that I didn't have to explain or understand it, that I could just simply let it happen. By the time the train pulled into King's Cross station, I felt able to bear it yet again, not entirely sure what other choice I had.

But there was an element I didn't yet know about. When I returned to Scotland to set up a date to have the tissue expander inserted, I was told quite casually that I'd be in the hospital only three or four days. Wasn't I going to spend the whole expansion time in the hospital? I asked in a whisper. What's the point of that? came the answer. You can just come in every day to the outpatient ward to have it expanded. Horrified by this, I was speechless. I would have to live and move about in the outside world with a giant balloon inside the tissue of my face? I can't remember what I did for the next few days before I went into the hospital, but I vaguely recall that these days involved a great deal of drinking alone in bars and at home.

I had the operation and went home at the end of the week. The only things that gave me any comfort during the months I lived with my tissue expander were my writing and Franz Kafka. I started a novel and completely absorbed myself in it, writing for hours each day. The only way I could walk down the street, could stand the stares I received, was to think to myself, "I'll bet none of them are writing a novel." It was that strange, old, familiar form of egomania, directly related to my dismissive, conceited thoughts of adolescence. As for Kafka, who had always been one of my favorite writers, he helped me in that I felt permission to feel alienated, and to have that alienation be okay, bearable, noble even. In the same way that imagining I lived in Cambodia helped me as a child, I walked the streets of my dark little Scottish city by the sea and knew without doubt that I was living in a story Kafka would have been proud to write.

The one good thing about a tissue expander is that you look so bad with it in that no matter what you look like once it's finally removed, your face has to look better. I had my bone graft and my fifth soft-tissue graft and, yes, even I had to admit I looked better. But I didn't look like me. Something was wrong: was *this* the face I had waited through eighteen years and almost thirty operations for? I somehow just couldn't make what I saw in the mirror correspond to the person I thought I was. It wasn't only that I continued to feel ugly; I simply could not conceive of the image as belonging to me. My own image was the image of a stranger, and rather than try to understand this, I simply stopped looking in the mirror. I perfected the technique of brushing my teeth without a mirror, grew my hair in such a way that it would require only a quick, simple brush, and wore clothes that were simply and easily put on, no complex layers or lines that might require even the most minor of visual adjustments.

On one level I understood that the image of my face was merely that, an image, a surface that was not directly related to any true, deep definition of the self. But I also knew that it is only through appearances that we experience and make decisions about the everyday world, and I was not always able to gather the strength to prefer the deeper world to the shallower one. I looked for ways to find a bridge that would allow me access to both, rather than riding out the constant swings between peace and anguish. The only direction I had to go in to achieve this was to strive for a state of awareness and self-honesty that sometimes, to this day, occasionally rewards me. I have found, I believe, that our whole lives are dominated, though it is not always so clearly translatable, by the question "How do I look?" Take all the many nouns in our lives—car, house, job, family, love, friends—and substitute the personal pronoun "I." It is not that we are all so self-obsessed; it is that all things eventually relate back to ourselves, and it is our own sense of how we appear to the world by which we chart our lives, how we navigate our personalities, which would otherwise be adrift in the ocean of *other* people's obsessions.

One evening toward the end of my year-long separation from the mirror, I was sitting in a café talking to someone—an attractive man, as it happened—and we were having a lovely, engaging conversation. For some reason I suddenly wondered what I looked like to him. What was he *actually* seeing when he saw me? So many times I've asked this of myself, and always the answer is this: a warm, smart woman, yes, but an unattractive one. I sat there in the café and asked myself this old question, and startlingly, for the first time in my life, I had no answer readily prepared. I had not looked in a mirror for so long that I quite simply had no clue as to what I looked like. I studied the man as he spoke; my entire life I had seen my ugliness reflected back to me. But now, as reluctant as I was to admit it, the only indication in my companion's behavior was positive.

And then, that evening in that café, I experienced a moment of the freedom I'd been practicing for behind my Halloween mask all those years ago. But whereas as a child I expected my liberation to come as a result of gaining something, a new face, it came to me now as the result of shedding something, of shedding my image. I once thought that truth was eternal, that when you understood something it was with you forever. I know now that this isn't so, that most truths are inherently unretainable, that we have to work hard all our lives to remember the most basic things. Society is no help; it tells us again and again that we can most be ourselves by looking like someone else, leaving our own faces behind to turn into ghosts that will inevitably resent and haunt us. It is no mistake that in movies and literature the dead sometimes know they are dead only after they can no longer see themselves in the mirror; and as I sat there feeling the warmth of the cup against my palm, this small observation seemed like a great revelation to me. I wanted to tell the man I was with about it, but he was involved in his own topic and I did not want to interrupt him, so instead I looked with curiosity toward the window behind him, its night-darkened glass reflecting the whole café, to see if I could, now, recognize myself.

Jamaica Kincaid

Biography of a Dress

The dress I am wearing in this black-and-white photograph, taken when I was two years old, was a yellow dress made of cotton poplin (a fabric with a slightly unsmooth texture first manufactured in the French town of Avignon and brought to England by the Huguenots, but I could not have known that at the time), and it was made for me by my mother. This shade of yellow, the color of my dress that I am wearing when I was two years old, was the same shade of yellow as boiled corn-meal, a food that my mother was always eager for me to eat in one form (as a porridge) or another (as fongie, the starchy part of my midday meal) because it was cheap and therefore easily available (but I did not know that at the time), and because she thought that foods bearing the colors yellow, green or orange were particularly rich in vitamins and so boiled cornmeal would be particularly good for me. But I was then (not so now) extremely particular about what I would eat, not knowing then (but I do now) of shortages and abundance, having no consciousness of the idea of rich and poor (but I know now that we were poor then), and would eat only boiled beef (which I required my mother to chew for me first and, after she had made it soft, remove it from her mouth and place it in mine), certain kinds of boiled fish (doctor or angel), hard-boiled eggs (from hens, not ducks), poached calf's liver and the milk from cows, and so would not even look at the boiled cornmeal (porridge or fongie). There was not one single thing that I could isolate and say I did not like about the boiled cornmeal (porridge or fongie) because I could not isolate parts of things then (though I can and do now), but whenever I saw this bowl of trembling yellow substance before me I would grow still and silent, I did not cry, that did not make me cry. My mother told me this then (she does not tell me this now, she does not remember this now, she does not remember telling me this now):

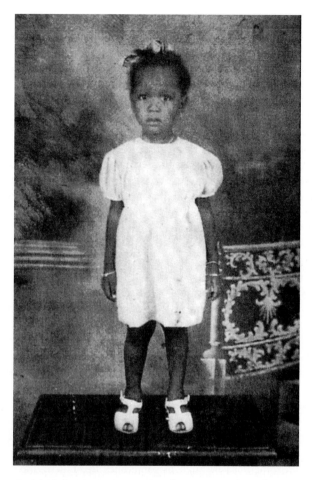

© 1992 by Jamaica Kincaid. Reprinted with permission of The Wylie Agency.

she knew of a man who had eaten boiled cornmeal at least once a day from the time he was my age then, two years old, and he lived for a very long time, finally dying when he was almost one hundred years old, and when he died he had looked rosy and new, with the springy wrinkles of the newborn, not the slack pleats of skin of the aged; as he lay dead his stomach was cut open, and all his insides were a beautiful shade of yellow, the same shade of yellow as boiled cornmeal. I was powerless then (though not so now) to like or dislike this story; it was beyond me then (though not so now) to understand the span of my lifetime then, two years old, and it was beyond me then (though not so now), the span of time called almost one hundred years old; I did not know then (though I do now) that there was such a thing as an inside to anybody, and that this inside would have a color, and that if the insides were the same shade of yellow as the yellow of boiled cornmeal my mother would want me to know about it.

On a day when it was not raining (that would have been unusual, that would have been out of the ordinary, ruining the fixed form of the day), my mother walked to one of the Harneys stores (there were many Harneys who owned stores, and they sold the same things, but I did not know then and I do not know now if they were all of the same people) and bought one-and-a-half yards of this yellow cotton poplin to make a dress for me, a dress I would wear to have my picture taken on the day I turned two years old. Inside, the store was cool and dark, and this was a good thing because outside was hot and overly bright. Someone named Harney did not wait on my mother, but someone named Miss Verna did and she was very nice still, so nice that she tickled my cheek as she spoke to my mother, and I reached forward as if to kiss her, but when her cheek met my lips I opened my mouth and bit her hard with my small child's teeth. Her cry of surprise did not pierce the air, but she looked at me hard, as if she knew me very, very well; and later, much later, when I was about twelve years old or so and she was always in and out of the crazy house, I would pass her on the street and throw stones at her, and she would turn and look at me hard, but she did not know who I was, she did not know who anyone was at all, not at all. Miss Verna showed my mother five flat thick bolts of cloth, white, blue (sea), blue (sky), yellow and pink, and my mother chose the yellow after holding it up against the rich copper color that my hair was then (it is not so now); she paid for it with a one-pound note that had an engraving of the king George Fifth on it (an ugly man with a cruel, sharp, bony nose, not the kind, soft, fleshy noses I was then used to), and she received change that included crowns, shillings, florins and farthings.

My mother, carrying me and the just-bought piece of yellow poplin wrapped in coarse brown paper in her arms, walked out of Mr. Harney's store, up the street a few doors away, and into a store called Murdoch's (because the family who owned it were the Murdochs), and there my mother bought two skeins of yellow thread, the kind used for embroidering and a shade of yellow almost identical to the yellow poplin. My mother not only took me with her everywhere she went, she carried me, sometimes in her arms, sometimes on her back; for this errand she carried me in her arms; she did not complain, she never complained (but later she refused to do it anymore and never gave an explanation, at least not one that I can remember now); as usual, she spoke to me and sang to me in French patois (but I did not understand French patois then and I do not now and so I can never know what exactly she said to me then). She walked back to our house on Dickenson Bay Street, stopping often to hold conversations with people (men and women) she knew, speaking to them sometimes in English, sometimes in French; and if after they said how beautiful I was (for people would often say that about me then but they do not say that about me now), she would laugh and say that I did not liked to be kissed (and I don't know if that was really true then but it is not so now). And that night after we had eaten our supper (boiled fish in a butter-and-lemon-juice sauce) and her husband (who was not my father but I did not know that at the time, I know that now) had gone for a walk (to the jetty), she removed her yellow poplin from its brown wrapper and folded and made creases in it and with scissors made holes (for the arms and neck) and slashes (for an opening in the back and the shoulders); she then placed it along with some ordinary thread (yellow), the thread for embroidering, the scissors and a needle in a basket that she had brought with her from her home in Dominica when she first left it at sixteen years of age.

For days afterward, my mother, after she had finished her usual chores (clothes washing, dish washing, floor scrubbing, bathing me, her only child, feeding me a teaspoon of cod-liver-oil), sat on the sill of the doorway, half in the sun, half out of the sun, and sewed together the various parts that would make up altogether my dress of yellow poplin; she gathered and hemmed and made tucks; she was just in the early stages of teaching herself how to make smocking and so was confined to making straight stitches (up-cable, down-cable, outline, stem, chain); the bodice of the dress appeared simple, plain, and the detail and pattern can only be seen close up and in real life, not from far away and not in a photograph; and much later, when she grew in confidence with this craft, the bodice of my dresses became overburdened with the stitches, chevron, trellis, diamonds, Vandyke, and species of birds she had never seen (swan) and species of flowers she had never seen (tulip) and species of animals she had never seen (bear) in real life, only in a picture in a book.

My skin was not the color of cream in the process of spoiling, my hair was not the texture of silk and the color of flax, my eyes did not gleam like blue jewels in a crown, the afternoons in which I sat watching my mother make me this dress were not cool, and verdant lawns and pastures and hills and dales did not stretch out before me; but it was the picture of such a girl at two years old—a girl whose skin was the color of cream in the process of spoiling, whose hair was the texture of silk and the color of flax, a girl whose eyes gleamed like blue jewels in a crown, a girl whose afternoons (and mornings and nights) were cool, and before whom stretched verdant lawns and pastures and hills and dales—that my mother saw, a picture on an almanac advertising a particularly fine and scented soap (a soap she could not afford to buy then but I can now), and this picture of this girl wearing a yellow dress with smocking on the front bodice perhaps created in my mother the desire to have a daughter who looked like that or perhaps created the desire in my mother to try and make the daughter she already had look like that. I do not know now and I did not know then. And who was that girl really? (I did not ask then because I could not ask then but I ask now.) And who made her dress? And this girl would have had a mother; did the mother then have some friends, other women, did they sit together under a tree (or sit somewhere else) and compare strengths of potions used to throw away a child, or weigh the satisfactions to be had from the chaos of revenge or the smooth order of forgiveness; and this girl with skin of cream on its way to spoiling and hair the color of flax, what did her insides look like, what did she eat? (I did not ask then because I could not ask then and I ask now but no one can answer me, really answer me.)

My second birthday was not a major event in anyone's life, certainly not my own (it was not my first and it was not my last, I am now forty-three years old), but my mother, perhaps because of circumstances (I would not have known then and to know now is not a help), perhaps only because of an established custom (but only in her family, other people didn't do this), to mark the occasion of my turning two years old had my ears pierced. One day, at dusk (I would not have called it that then), I was taken to someone's house (a woman from Dominica, a woman who was as dark as my mother was fair, and yet they were so similar that I am sure now as I was then that they shared the same tongue), and two thorns that had been heated in a fire were pierced through my earlobes. I do not now know (and could not have known then) if the pain I experienced resembled in any way the pain my mother experienced while giving birth to me or even if my mother, in having my ears bored in that way, at that time, meant to express hostility or aggression toward me (but without meaning to and without knowing that it was possible to mean to). For days afterward my earlobes were swollen and covered with a golden crust (which might have glistened in the harsh sunlight, but I can only imagine that now), and the pain of my earlobes must have filled up all that made up my entire being then and the pain of my earlobes must have been unbearable, because it was then that was the first time that I separated myself from myself, and I became two people (two small children then, I was two years old), one having the experience, the other observing the one having the experience. And the observer, perhaps because it was an act of my own will (strong then, but stronger now), my first and only real act of self-invention, is the one of the two I most rely on, the one of the two whose voice I believe to be the true voice; and of course it is the observer who cannot be relied on as the final truth to be believed, for the observer has woven between myself and the person who is having an experience a protective membrane, which allows me to see but only feel as much as I can handle at any given moment. And so . . .

. . . On the day I turned two years old, the twenty-fifth of May 1951, a pair of earrings, small hoops made of gold from British Guiana (it was called that then, it is not called that now), were placed in the bored holes in my earlobes (which by then had healed); a pair of bracelets made of silver from someplace other than British Guiana (and that place too was called one thing then, something else now) was placed one on each wrist; a pair of new shoes bought from Bata's was placed on my feet. That afternoon, I was bathed and powdered, and the dress of yellow poplin, completed, its seams all stitched together with a certainty found only in the natural world (I now realize), was placed over my head, and it is quite possible that this entire act had about it the feeling of being draped in a shroud. My mother, carrying me in her arms (as usual), took me to the studio of a photographer, a man named Mr. Walker, to have my picture taken. As she walked along with me in her arms (not complaining), with the heat of the sun still so overwhelming that it, not gravity, seemed to be the force that kept us pinned to the earth's surface, I placed my lips against one side of her head (the temple) and could feel the rhythm of the blood pulsing through her body; I placed my lips against her throat and could hear her swallow saliva that had collected in her mouth; I placed my face against her neck and inhaled deeply a scent that I could not identify then (how could I, there was nothing to compare it to) and cannot now, because it is not of animal or place or thing, it was (and is) a scent unique to her, and it left a mark of such depth that it eventually became a part of my other senses, and even now (yes, now) that scent is also taste, touch, sight and sound.

And Mr. Walker lived on Church Street in a house that was mysterious to me (then, not now) because it had a veranda (unlike my own house) and it had many rooms (unlike my own house, but really Mr. Walker's house had only four rooms, my own house had one) and the windows were closed (the windows in my house were always open). He spoke to my mother, I did not understand what they said, they did not share the same tongue. I knew Mr. Walker was a man, but how I knew that I cannot say (now, then, sometime to come). It is possible that because he touched his hair often, smoothing down, caressing, the forcibly straightened strands, and because he admired and said that he admired my dress of yellow poplin with its simple smocking (giving to me a false air of delicacy), and because he admired and said that he admired the plaid taffeta ribbon in my hair, I thought that he perhaps wasn't a man at all, I had never seen a man do or say any of those things, I had then only seen a woman do or say those things. He (Mr. Walker) stood next to a black box which had a curtain at its back (this was his camera but I did not know that at the time, I only know it now) and he asked my mother to stand me on a table, a small table, a table that made me taller, because the scene in the background, against which I was to be photographed, was so vast, it overwhelmed my two-year-old frame, making me seem a mere figurine, not a child at all; and when my mother picked me up, holding my by the armpits with her hands, her thumb accidentally (it could have been deliberate, how could someone who loved me inflict so much pain just in passing?) pressed deeply into my shoulder, and I cried out and then (and still now) looked up at her face and couldn't find any reason in it, and could find no malice in it, only that her eyes were full of something, a feeling that I thought then (and am convinced now) had nothing to do with me; and of course it is possible that just at that moment she had realized that she was exhausted, not physically, but just exhausted by this whole process, celebrating my second birthday, commemorating an event, my birth, that she may not have wished to occur in the first place and may have tried repeatedly to prevent, and then, finally, in trying to find some beauty in it, ended up with a yard and a half of yellow poplin being shaped into a dress, teaching herself smocking and purchasing gold hoops from places whose names never remained the same and silver bracelets from places whose names never remained the same. And Mr. Walker, who was not at all interested in my mother's ups and downs and would never have dreamed of taking in the haphazard mess of her life (but there was nothing so unusual about that, every life, I now know, is a haphazard mess), looked on for a moment as my mother, belying the look in her eyes, said kind and loving words to me in a kind and loving voice, and he then walked over to a looking glass that hung on a wall and squeezed with two of his fingers a lump the size of a pinch of sand that was on his cheek; the lump had a shiny white surface and it broke, emitting a tiny plap sound, and from it came a long ribbon of thick, yellow pus that curled on Mr. Walker's cheek imitating, almost, the decoration on the birthday cake that awaited me at home, and my birthday cake was decorated with a series of species of flora and fauna my mother had never seen (and still has not seen to this day, she is seventy-three years old).

After that day I never again wore my yellow poplin dress with the smocking my mother had just taught herself to make. It was carefully put aside, saved for me to wear to another special occasion; but by the time another special occasion came (I could say quite clearly then what the special occasion was and can say quite clearly now what the special occasion was but I do not want to), the dress could no longer fit me, I had grown too big for it.

Lê Thi Diem Thúy

The Gangster We Are All Looking For

Vietnam is a black-and-white photograph of my grandparents sitting in bamboo chairs in their front courtyard. They are sitting tall and proud, surrounded by chickens and roosters. Their feet are separated from the dirt by thin sandals. My grandfather's broad forehead is shining. So too are my grandmother's famed sad eyes. The animals are obliviously pecking at the ground. This looks like a wedding portrait, though it is actually a photograph my grandparents had taken late in life, for their children, especially for my mother. When I think of this portrait of my grandparents in the last years of their life, I always envision a beginning. To what or where, I don't know, but always a beginning.

When my mother, a Catholic schoolgirl from the South, decided to marry my father, a Buddhist gangster from the North, her parents disowned her. This is in the photograph, though it is not visible to the eye. If it were, it would be a deep impression across the soft dirt of my grandparents' courtyard. Her father chased her out of the house, beating her with the same broom she had used every day of her life, from the time she could stand up and sweep to the morning of the very day she was chased away.

The year my mother met my father, there were several young men working at her house, running errands for her father, pickling vegetables with her mother. It was understood by everyone that these men were courting my mother. My mother claims she had no such understanding.

She treated these men as brothers, sometimes as uncles even, later exclaiming in self-defense, "I didn't even know about love then."

Ma says love came to her in a dark movie theater. She doesn't remember what movie it was or why she'd gone to see it, only that she'd gone alone and found herself sitting beside him. In the dark, she couldn't make out his face but noticed he was handsome. She wondered if he knew she was watching him out of the corner of her eye. Watching him without embarrassment or shame. Watching him with a strange curiosity, a feeling that made her want to trace and retrace his silhouette with her fingertips until she'd memorized every feature and could call his face to her in any dark place she passed through. Later, in the shadow of the beached fishing boats on the blackest nights of the year, she would call him to mind, his face a warm companion for her body on the edge of the sea.

In the early days of my parents' courtship, my mother told stories. She confessed elaborate dreams about the end of war: foods she'd eat (a banquet table, mangoes piled high to the ceiling); songs she'd make up and sing, clapping her hands over her head and throwing her hair like a horse's mane; dances she'd do, hopping from one foot to the other. Unlike the responsible favorite daughter or sister she was to her family, with my father, in the forest, my mother became reckless, drunk on her youth and the possibility of love. Ignoring the chores to be done at home, she rolled her pants up to her knees, stuck her bare feet in puddles, and learned to smoke a cigarette.

She tied a vermilion ribbon in her hair. She became moody. She did her chores as though they were favors to her family, forgetting that she ate the same rice and was dependent on the same supply of food. It seemed to her the face that stared back at her from deep inside the family well was the face of a woman she had never seen before. At night she lay in bed and thought of his hands, the way his thumb flicked down on the lighter and brought fire to her cigarette. She began to wonder what the forests were like before the trees were dying. She remembered her father had once described to her the smiling broadness of leaves, jungles thick in the tangle of rich soil.

One evening, she followed my father in circles through the forest, supposedly in search of the clearing that would take them to his aunt's house. They wandered aimlessly into darkness, never finding the clearing or the aunt she knew he never had.

"You're not from here," she said.

"I know."

"So tell me, what's your aunt's name?"

"Xuan."

"Spring?"

"Yes."

She laughed. I can't be here, she thought.

"My father will be looking for me—"

"I'll walk you home. It's not too late."

In the dark, she could feel his hand extending toward her, filling the space between them. They had not touched once the entire evening and now he stood offering his hand to her. She stared at him for a long time. There was a small scar on his chin, curved like her fingernail. It was too dark to see this. She realized she had memorized his face.

My first memory of my father's face is framed by the coiling barbed wire of a prison camp in South Vietnam. My mother's voice crosses through the wire. She is whispering his name and, in this utterance, caressing him. Over and over she calls him to her: "Anh Minh, Anh Minh." His name becomes a tree she presses her body against. The act of calling blows around them like a warm breeze, and when she utters her own name, it is the second half of a verse that began with his. She drops her name like a pebble is dropped into a well. She wants to be engulfed by him. "Anh Minh, em My, Anh Minh. Em, em My."

She is crossing through barbed wire the way some people step through open windows. She arrives warm, the slightest film of sweat on her bare arms. She says, "It's me, it's me." Shy and formal and breathless, my parents are always meeting for the first time. Savoring the sound of a name, marveling at the bone structure.

I trail behind them, the tip of their dragon's tail. I am suspended like a silk banner from the body of a kite. They flick me here and there. I twist and turn in the air, connected to them by this fabric that worms spin.

For a handful of pebbles and my father's sharp profile my mother left home and never returned. Imagine a handful of pebbles. The casual way he tossed them at her as she was walking home from school with her girlfriends. He did this because he liked her and wanted to let her know. Boys are dumb that way, my mother told me. A handful of pebbles, to be thrown in anger, in desperation, in joy. My father threw them in love. Ma says they touched her like warm kisses, these pebbles he had been holding in the sun. Warm kisses on the curve of her back, sliding down the crook of her arm, grazing her ankles and landing around her feet in the hot sand.

What my father told her could have been a story. There was no one in the South to confirm the details of his life. He said he came from a semi-aristocratic Northern family. Unlacing his boot, he pulled out his foot and told her to pay close attention to how his second toe was significantly longer than his other toes. "A sure sign of aristocracy," he claimed. His nose was high, he said, because his mother was French, one of the many mistresses his father kept. He found this out when he was sixteen. That year, he ran away from home and came south.

"There are thieves, gamblers, drunks I've met who remind me of people in my family. It's the way they're dreamers. My family's a garden full of dreamers lying on their backs, staring at the sky, drunk and choking on their dreaming." He said this while leaning against a tree, his arms folded across his bare chest, his eyes staring at the ground, his shoulders golden.

She asked her mother, "What does it mean if your second toe is longer than your other toes?"

"It means . . . your mother will die before your father," her mother said.

"I heard somewhere it's a sign of aristocracy."

"Huh! What do we know about aristocracy?"

My father's toes fascinated my mother. When she looked at his bare feet she saw ten fishing boats, two groups of five. Within each group, the second boat ventured ahead, leading the others. She would climb a tree, stand gripping the branch with her own toes, and stare down at his. She directed him to stand in the mud. There, she imagined what she saw to be ten small boats surrounded by black water, a fleet of junks journeying in the dark.

She would lean back and enjoy this vision, never explaining to him what it was she saw. She left him to wonder about her senses as he stood, cigarette in hand, staring at her trembling ankles, not moving until she told him to.

I was born in the alley behind my grandparents' house. At three in the morning my mother dragged herself out of the bed in the small house she and my father lived in after they married.

He was in prison, so, alone, she began to walk. She cut a crooked line on the beach. Moving in jerky steps, like a ball tossed on the waves, she seemed to be thrown along without direction. She walked to the schoolhouse, sat on the sand, and leaned against the first step. She felt grains of sand pressing against her back. Each grain was a minute pinprick that became increasingly painful to her. She felt as though her back would break out in a wash of blood. She thought, I am going to bleed to death. We are going to die.

In front of the schoolhouse lay a long metal tube. No one knew where it came from. It seemed always to have been there. Children hid in it, crawled through it, spoke to one another at either end of it, marched across it, sat on it, and confided secrets beside it. There had been so little to play with at the school recesses. This long metal tube became everything. A tarp was suspended over it, to shield it from the sun. The tube looked like a blackened log that sat in a room without walls. When the children sat in a line on the tube, their heads bobbing this way and that in conversation, it seemed they were sitting under a canopied raft.

The night I was born, my mother looked at this tube and imagined it to be the badly burnt arm of a dying giant whose body was buried in the sand. She could not decide if he had been buried in the sand and was trying to get out or if he had tried to bury himself in the sand but was unable to pull his arm under in time. In time for what? She had heard a story about a girl in a neighboring town who was killed during a napalm bombing. The bombing happened on an especially hot night when this girl had walked to the beach to cool her feet in the water. They found her floating on the sea. The phosphorus from the napalm made her body glow like a lantern. In her mind, my mother built a canopy for this girl. She started to cry, thinking of the buried giant, the floating girl, these bodies stopped in midstep, on their way somewhere.

She began to walk toward the tube. She had a sudden urge to be inside it. The world felt dangerous to her and she was alone. At the mouth of the tube she bent down; her belly blocked the opening. She tried the other side, the other mouth. Again her belly stopped her. "But I remember," she muttered out loud, "as a girl I sometimes slept in here." This was what she wanted now, to sleep inside the tube.

"Tall noses come from somewhere—"
  "Not from here."
  "Not tall noses."

Eyes insinuate, moving from her nose to mine then back again. Mouths suck air in, form it into the darkest shade of contempt, then spit it at her feet as she walks by. I am riding on her hip. I am the new branch that makes the tree bend, but she walks with her head held high. She knows where she pulled me from. No blue eye.

Ma says war is a bird with a broken wing flying over the countryside, trailing blood and burying crops in sorrow. If something grows in spite of this, it is both a curse and a miracle. When I was born, she cried when I cried, knowing I had breathed war in and she could never shake it out of me. Ma says war makes it dangerous to breathe, though she knows you die if you don't. She says she could have thrown me against the wall, breaking me until I coughed up this war which is killing us all. She could have stomped on it in the dark and danced on it like a madwoman dancing on gravestones. She could have ground it down to powder and spit on it, but didn't I know? War has no beginning and no end. It crosses oceans like a splintered boat filled with people singing a sad song.

Every morning Anh wakes up in the house next to mine, a yellow duplex she and I call a townhouse because we found out from a real estate ad that a townhouse is a house that has an upstairs and a downstairs. My father calls Anh the "chicken-egg girl." Each morning Anh's mother loads a small pushcart with stacks of eggs and Anh walks all over Linda Vista selling eggs. Her back yard is full of chickens and roosters. Sometimes you can see a rooster fly up and balance itself on the back gate, and it will crow and crow, off and on, all day long until dark comes.

We live in the country of California, the province of San Diego, the village of Linda Vista. We live in old Navy Housing, bungalows that were built in the 1940s and '50s. Since the 1980s these bungalows have housed Vietnamese, Cambodian, and Laotian refugees from the Vietnam War. When we moved in, we had to sign a form promising not to push fish bones down the garbage disposal.

We live in a yellow row house on Westinghouse Street. Our house is one story, made of wood and plaster. We are connected to six two-story houses and another one-story house at the other end. Across from our row of houses, separated by a field of brown dirt, sits another row of yellow houses, same as ours and facing us like a sad twin. Linda Vista is full of houses like ours, painted in peeling shades of olive green, baby blue, and sunbaked yellow.

There's new Navy Housing on Linda Vista Road, the long street that takes you out of here. We see the people there watering their lawns, the children riding pink tricycles up and down the cul-de-sacs. We see them in Victory Supermarket, buying groceries with cash. In Kelley Park they have picnics and shoot each other with water guns. At school their kids are Most Popular, Most Beautiful, Most Likely to Succeed. Though there are more Vietnamese, Cambodian, and Laotian kids at the school, we are not Most of anything in the yearbook. They call us Yang because one year a bunch of Laotian kids with the last name Yang came to our school. The Navy Housing kids started calling all the refugee kids Yang.

Yang. Yang. Yang.

Ma says living next to Anh's family reminds her of Vietnam because the blue tarp suspended above Anh's back yard is the bright blue of the South China Sea. Ma says isn't it funny how sky and sea follow you from place to place as if they too were traveling and not just the boat that travels across or between them. Ma says even Anh reminds her of Vietnam, the way she sets out for market each morning.

Ba becomes a gardener. Overnight. He buys a truck full of equipment and a box of business cards from Uncle Twelve, who is moving to Texas to become a fisherman. The business cards read "Tom's Professional Gardening Service" and have a small, green embossed picture of a man pushing a lawn mower. The man's back is to the viewer, so no one who doesn't already know can tell it's not Ba. He says I can be his secretary because I speak the best English. If you call us on the business phone, you will hear me say: "Hello, you have reached Tom's Professional Gardening Service. We are not here right now, but if you leave us a message, we will get back to you as soon as possible. Thank you."

It is hot and dusty where we live. Some people think it's dirty, but they don't know much about us. They haven't seen our gardens full of lemongrass, mint, cilantro, and basil. They've only seen the pigeons pecking at day-old rice and the skinny cats and dogs sitting in the skinny shade of skinny trees as they drive by. Have they seen the berries we pick which turn our lips and fingertips red? How about the small staircase Ba built from our bedroom window to the back yard so I would have a short cut to the clothesline? How about the Great Wall of China which snakes like a river from the top of the steep Crandall Street hill to the slightly curving bottom? Who has seen this?

It was so different at the Green Apartment. We had to close the gate behind us every time we came in. It clanged heavily, and I imagined a host of eyes, upstairs and downstairs, staring at me from behind slightly parted curtains. There were four palm trees planted at the four far corners of the courtyard and a central staircase that was narrow at the top and fanned out at the bottom. The steps were covered in fake grass, like the set of an old Hollywood movie, the kind that stars an aging beauty who wakes up to find something is terribly wrong.

We moved out of the Green Apartment after we turned on the TV one night and heard that our manager and his brother had hacked a woman to pieces and dumped her body into the Pacific Ocean in ten-gallon garbage bags that washed onto the shore. Ma said she didn't want to live in a place haunted by a murdered lady. So we moved to Linda Vista, where she said there were a lot of Vietnamese people like us, people whose only sin was a little bit of gambling and sucking on fish bones and laughing hard and arguing loudly.

Ma shaved all her hair off in Linda Vista because she got mad at Ba for gambling her money away and getting drunk every week watching *Monday Night Football*. Ba gave her a blue baseball cap to wear until her hair grew back, and she wore it backward, like a real bad-ass.

After that, some people in Linda Vista said that Ma was crazy and Ba was crazy for staying with her. But what do some people know?

When the photograph came, Ma and Ba got into a fight. Ba threw the fish tank out the front door and Ma broke all the dishes. They said they never should've been together.

Ma's sister had sent her the photograph from Vietnam. It came in a stiff envelope. There was nothing inside but the photograph, as if anything more would be pointless. Ma started to cry. "Child," she sobbed, over and over again. She wasn't talking about me. She was talking about herself.

Ba said, "Don't cry. Your parents have forgiven you."

Ma kept crying anyway and told him not to touch her with his gangster hands. Ba clenched his hands into tight fists and punched the walls.

"What hands?! What hands?!" he yelled. "Let me see the gangster! Let me see his hands!" I see his hands punch hands punch hands punch blood.

Ma is in the kitchen. She has torn the screen off the window. She is punctuating the pavement with dishes, plates, cups, rice bowls. She sends them out like birds gliding through the sky with nowhere in particular to go. Until they crash. Then she exhales "Huh!" in satisfaction.

I am in the hallway gulping air. I breathe in the breaking and the bleeding. When Ba plunges his hands into the fish tank, I detect the subtle tint of blood in water. When he throws the fish tank out the front door, yelling, "Let me see the gangster!" I am drinking up spilled water and swallowing whole the beautiful colored tropical fish before they hit the ground, caking themselves in brown dirt until just the whites of their eyes remain, blinking at the sun.

All the hands are in my throat, cutting themselves on broken dishes, and the fish swim in circles; they can't see for all the blood.

Ba jumps in his truck and drives away.

When I grow up I am going to be the gangster we are all looking for.

The neighborhood kids are standing outside our house, staring in through the windows and the open door. Even Anh, our chicken-egg seller. I'm sure their gossiping mothers sent them to spy on us. I run out front and dance like a crazy lady, dance like a fish, wiggle my head and throw my body so everything eyes nose tongue comes undone. At first they laugh but then they stop, not knowing what to think. Then I stop and stare each one of them down.

"What're you looking at?" I ask.

"Lookin' at you," one boy says, half giggling.

"Well," I say, with my hand on my hip and my head cocked to one side, "I'm looking at you too," and I give him my evil one-eye look, focusing all my energy into one eye. I stare at him hard like my eye is a bullet and he can be dead.

I turn my back on them and walk into the house.

I find Ma sitting in the windowsill. The curve of her back is inside the bedroom while the rest of her body is outside, on the first step Ba built going from the bedroom to the garden. Without turning to look at me, she says, "Let me lift you into the attic."

"Why?"

"We have to move your grandparents in."

I don't really know what she is talking about, but I say O.K. anyway.

We have never needed the attic for anything. In fact, we have never gone up there. When we moved my grandparents in, Ma simply lifted me up and I pushed the attic door open with one hand, while with the other I slipped in the stiff envelope containing the photograph of my grandparents. I pushed it the length of my arm and down to my fingertips. I pushed it so far it was beyond reach, but Ma said it was enough, they had come to live with us, and sometimes you don't need to see or touch people to know they're there.

Ba came home drunk that night and asked to borrow my blanket. I heard him climbing the tree in the back yard. It took him a long time. He kept missing the wooden blocks that run up and down the tree like a ladder. Ba put them in when he built the steps going from the bedroom window into the garden. If you stand on the very top block, your whole body is hidden by tree branches. Ba put those blocks in for me, so I could win at hide-and-go-seek.

When Ba finally made it onto the roof, he lay down over my room and I could hear him rolling across my ceiling. Rolling and crying. I was scared he would roll off the edge and kill himself, so I went to wake Ma.

She was already awake. She said it would be a good thing if he rolled off. But later I heard someone climb the tree, and all night two bodies rolled across my ceiling. Slowly and firmly they pressed against my sleep, the Catholic schoolgirl and the Buddhist gangster, two dogs chasing each other's tails. They have been running like this for so long, they have become one dog, one tail.

Without any hair and looking like a man, my mother is still my mother, though sometimes I can't see her even when I look and look and look so long all the colors of the world begin to swim and bob around me. Her hands always bring me up, her big peasant hands with the flat, wide nails, wide like her nose and just as expressive. I will know her by her hands and her walk which is at once slow and urgent, the walk of a woman going to the market with her goods securely bound to her side. Even walking empty-handed, my mother suggests invisible bundles whose contents no one but she can unravel. And if I never see her again, I will know my mother by the smell of sea salt and the prints of my own bare feet crossing sand, running to and away from, to and away from, family.

When the eviction notice came, we didn't believe it so we threw it away. It said we had a month to get out. The houses on our block had a new owner who wanted to tear everything down and build better housing for the community. It said we were priority tenants for the new complex, but we couldn't afford to pay the new rent so it didn't matter. The notice also said that if we didn't get out in time, all our possessions would be confiscated in accordance with some section of a law book or manual we were supposed to have known about but had never seen. We couldn't believe the eviction notice so we threw it away.

The fence is tall, silver, and see-through. Chainlink, it rattles when you shake it and wobbles when you lean against it. It circles the block like a bad dream. It is not funny like a line of laundry whose flying shirts and empty pants suggest human birds and vanishing acts. This fence presses sharply against your brain. We three stand still as posts. Looking at it, then at each other—this side and that—out of the corners of our eyes. What are we thinking?

At night we come back with three uncles. Ba cuts a hole in the fence and we step through. Quiet, we break into our own house through the back window. Quiet, we steal back everything that is ours. We fill ten-gallon garbage bags with clothes, pots and pans, flip-flops, the porcelain figure of Mary, and our wooden Buddha. In the arc of four flashlights we find our favorite hairbrushes behind bedposts. When we are done, we are clambering and breathless. We can hear police cars coming to get us, though it's quiet.

We tumble out the window like people tumbling across continents. We are time traveling, weighed down by heavy furniture and bags of precious junk. We find ourselves leaning against Ba's yellow truck. Ma calls his name, her voice reaching like a hand feeling for a tree trunk in darkness.

In the car, Ma starts to cry. "What about the sea?" she asks. "What about the garden?" Ba says we can come back in the morning and dig up the stalks of lemongrass and fold the sea into a blue square. Ma is sobbing. She is beating the dashboard with her fists. "I want to know," she says, "I want to know, I want to know . . . who is doing this to us?" Hiccupping, she says, "I want to know why, why there's always a fence. Why there's always someone on the outside wanting someone . . . something on the inside and between them . . . this . . . sharp fence. Why are we always leaving like this?"

Everyone is quiet when Ma screams.

"Take me back!" she says. "I can't go with you. I've forgotten my mother and father. I can't believe . . . Anh Minh, we've left them to die. Take me back."

Ma wants Ba to stop the car, but Ba doesn't know why. The three uncles, sitting in a line in the back of the truck, think Ma is crazy. They yell in through the window, "My, are you going to walk back to Vietnam?"

"Yeah, are you going to walk home to your parents' house?"

In the silence another laughs.

Ba puts his foot on the gas pedal. Our car jerks forward, then plunges down the Crandall Street hill. Ma says, "I need air, water . . . " I roll the window down. She puts her head in her hands. She keeps crying, "Child." Outside, I see the Great Wall of China. In the glare of the streetlamps, it is just a long strip of cardboard.

In the morning, the world is flat. Westinghouse Street is lying down like a jagged brushstroke of sunburnt yellow. There is a big sign inside the fence that reads

COMING SOON:

CONDOMINIUMS   TOWNHOUSES   FAMILY HOMES

Beside these words is a watercolor drawing of a large, pink complex.

We stand on the edge of the chainlink fence, sniffing the air for the scent of lemongrass, scanning this flat world for our blue sea. A wrecking ball dances madly through our house. Everything has burst wide open and sunk down low. Then I hear her calling them. She is whispering, "Ma/Ba, Ma/Ba." The whole world is two butterfly wings rubbing against my ear.

Listen . . . they are sitting in the attic, sitting like royalty. Shining in the dark, buried by a wrecking ball. Paper fragments floating across the surface of the sea.

Not a trace of blood anywhere except here, in my throat, where I am telling you all this.

John Edgar Wideman
_____

from Brothers and Keepers

When you were a chubby-cheeked baby and I stood you upright, supporting most of your weight with my hands but freeing you just enough to let you feel the spring and bounce of strength in your new, rubbery thighs, when you toddled those first few bowlegged, pigeon-toed steps across the kitchen, did the trouble start then? Twenty-odd years later, when you shuffled through the polished corridor of the Fort Collins, Colorado, courthouse dragging the weight of iron chains and fetters, I wanted to give you my hands again, help you make it across the floor again; I shot out a clenched fist, a black power sign, which caught your eye and made you smile in that citadel of whiteness. You made me realize I was tottering on the edge, leaning on you. You, in your baggy jumpsuit, three days' scraggly growth on your face because they didn't trust you with a razor, manacled hand and foot so you were theatrically displayed as their pawn, absolutely under their domination; you were the one clinging fast, taking the weight, and your dignity held me up. I was reaching for your strength.

Always there. The bad seed, the good seed. Mommy's been saying for as long as I can remember: That Robby . . . he wakes up in the morning looking for the party. She's right, ain't she? Mom's nearly always right in her way, the special way she has of putting words together to take things apart. Every day God sends here Robby thinks is a party. Still up there on the third floor under his covers and he's thinking, Where's it at today? What's it gonna be today? Where's the fun? And that's how he's been since the day the Good Lord put him on this earth. That's your brother, Robert Douglas Wideman.

The Hindu god Venpadigedera returned to earth and sang to the people: Behold, the light shineth in all things. Birds, trees, the eyes of men, all giveth forth the light. Behold and be glad. Gifts wait for any who choose to see. Cover the earth with flowers. Shower flowers to the four corners. Rejoice in the bounty of the light.

The last time we were all together, cousin Kip took a family portrait. Mom and Daddy in a line with their children. The third generation of kids, a nappy-headed row in front. Five of us grown-up brothers and sisters hanging on one another's shoulders. Our first picture together since I don't remember when. We're all standing on Mom's about-to-buckle porch with cousin Kip down in the weeds of the little front yard pointing his camera up at us. I was half-scared those rickety boards would crack and we'd sink, arms still entwined, like some brown *Titanic,* beneath the rippling porch floor.

Before I saw the picture I had guessed how we'd look frozen in shades of black and white. I wasn't too far off. Tish is grinning ear to ear—the proud girl child in the middle who's survived the teasing and protections of her four brothers. Even though he isn't, Gene seems the tallest because of the way he holds that narrow, perfect head of his balanced high and dignified on his long neck. Dave's eyes challenge the camera, meet it halfway and dare it to come any closer, and the camera understands and keeps its distance from the smoldering eyes. No matter what Dave's face seems to be saying—the curl of the lip that could be read as smile or sneer, as warning or invitation—his face also projects another level of ambiguity, the under-ground history of interracial love, sex, and hate, what a light-eyed, brown-skinned man like David embodies when he confronts other people. I'm grinning too (it's obvious Tish is my sister) because our momentary togetherness was a reprieve, a possibility I believed I'd forfeited by my selfishness and hunger for more. Giddy almost, I felt like a rescued prince ringed by his strong, handsome people, my royal brothers and sister who'd paid my ransom. Tickled even by the swell and pitch of the rotting porch boards under my sandals.

You. You are mugging. Your best side dramatically displayed. The profile shot you'd have demanded on your first album, the platinum million seller you'd never cut but knew you could because you had talent and brains and you could sing and mimic anybody and that long body of yours and those huge hands were instruments more flexible and expressive than most people's faces. You knew what you were capable of doing and knew you'd never get a chance to do it, but none of that defeat for the camera, no, only the star's three-quarter profile. Billy Eckstineing your eyes, the Duke of Earl tilting the slim oval of your face forward to emphasize the pout of your full lips, the clean lines of your temples and cheekbones tapering down from the Afro's soft explosion. Your stage would be the poolroom, the Saturday-night basement social, the hangout corner, the next chick's pad you swept into with all the elegance of Smokey Robinson and the Count of Monte Cristo, slowly unbuttoning your cape, inching off your kid gloves, everything pantomimed with gesture and eye flutters till your rap begins and your words sing that much sweeter, purer for the quiet cradling them. You're like that in the picture. Stylized, outrageous under your big country straw hat pushed back off your head. Acting. And Tish, holding up the picture to study it, will say something like, Look at you, boy. You ought to be 'shamed. And your mask will drop and you'll grin cause Tish is like Mom, and ain't no getting round her. So you'll just grin back and you are Robby again at about age seven, cute and everybody's pet, grin at Sis and say, "G'wan, girl."

Daddy's father, our grandfather, Harry Wideman, migrated from Greenwood, South Carolina, to Pittsburgh, Pennsylvania, in 1906. He found a raw, dirty, double-dealing city. He learned its hills and rivers, the strange names of Dagos and Hunkies and Polacks who'd been drawn, as he had, by steel mills and coal mines, by the smoke and heat and dangerous work that meant any strong-backed, stubborn young man, even a black one, could earn pocketfuls of money. Grandpa's personal quest connected him with hordes of other displaced black men seeking a new day in the promised land of the North. Like so many others, he boarded in an overcrowded rooming house, working hard by day, partying hard at night against the keen edge of exhaustion. When his head finally hit the pillow, he didn't care that the sheets were still warm from the body of the man working nights who rented the bed ten hours a day while Harry pulled his shift at the mill.

Harry Wideman was a short, thick, dark man whose mahogany color passed on to Daddy, blended with the light, bright skin of John and Freeda French's daughter Bette to produce the brown we wear. Do you remember anything about him, or were you too young? Have you ever wondered how the city appeared through his eyes, the eyes of a rural black boy far from home, a stranger in a strange land? Have you ever been curious? Grandpa took giant steps forward in time. As a boy not quite old enough to be much help in the fields, his job was looking out for Charley Rackett, his ancient, crippled grandfather, an African, a former slave. Grandpa listened to Charley Rackett's African stories and African words, then lived to see white men on the moon. I think of Grandpa high up on Bruston Hill looking over the broad vista spreading out below him. He's young and alone; he sees things with his loins as much as his eyes. Hills rolling to the horizon, toward the invisible rivers, are breasts and buttocks. Shadowed spaces, nestling between the rounded hills, summon him. Whatever happens to him in this city, whatever he accomplishes will be an answer to the soft, insinuating challenge thrown up at him as he stares over the teeming land. This city will measure his manhood. *Our Father Who Art . . .* I hear prayer words interrupting his dreaming, disturbing the woman shapes his glance fashions from the landscape. The earth turns. He plants his seed. In the blink of an eye he's an old man, close to death. He has watched the children of his children's children born in this city. Some of his children's children dead already. He ponders the wrinkled tar paper on the backs of his hands. Our Father. A challenge still rises from the streets and rooftops the way it once floated up from long-gone, empty fields. And the old man's no nearer now to knowing, to understanding why the call digs so deeply at his heart.

Wagons once upon a time in the streets of Pittsburgh. Delivering ice and milk and coal. Sinking in the mud, trundling over cobblestones, echoing in the sleep of a man who works all day in the mouth of a fiery furnace, who dreams of green fish gliding along the clear, stony bottom of a creek in South Carolina. In the twenty years between 1910 and 1930, the black population of Pittsburgh increased by nearly fifty thousand. Black music, blues and jazz, came to town in places like the Pythian Temple, the Ritz, the Savoy, the Showboat. In the bars on the North Side, Homewood, and the Hill you could get whatever you thought you wanted. Gambling, women, a good pork chop. Hundreds of families took in boarders to earn a little extra change. A cot in a closet in somebody's real home seemed nicer, better than the dormitories with their barracks-style rows of beds, no privacy, one toilet for twenty men. Snores and funk, eternal coming and going because nobody wanted to remain in those kennels one second longer than he had to. Fights, thieves, people dragged in stinking drunk or bloody from the streets, people going straight to work after hanging out all night with some whore and you got to smell him and smell her beside you while you trying to pull your shift in all that heat. Lawd. Lawdy. Got no money in the bank. Joints was rowdy and mean and like I'm telling you if some slickster don't hustle your money in the street or a party-time gal empty your pockets while you sleep and you don't nod off and fall in the fire, then maybe you earn you a few quarters to send home for that wife and them babies waiting down yonder for you if she's still waiting and you still sending. If you ain't got no woman to send for then maybe them few quarters buy you a new shirt and a bottle of whiskey so you can find you some trifling body give all your money to.

The strong survive. The ones who are strong and *lucky.* You can take that back as far as you want to go. Everybody needs one father, two grandfathers, four great-grandfathers, eight great-great-grandfathers, sixteen great-great-great-grandfathers, then thirty-two, then sixty-four, and that's only eight generations backward in time, eight generations linked directly, intimately with what you are. Less than 150 years ago, 128 men made love to 128 women, not all in the same hotel or on the same day but within a relatively short expanse of time, say twenty years, in places as distant as Igboland, New Amsterdam, and South Carolina. Unknown to each other, probably never even coming face to face in their lifetimes, each of these couples was part of the grand conspiracy to produce you. Think of a pyramid balanced on one of its points, a vast cone of light whose sides flare outward, vectors of force like the slanted lines kids draw to show a star's shining. You once were a pinprick of light, a spark whose radiance momentarily upheld the design, stabilized the ever-expanding V that opens to infinity. At some inconceivable distance the light bends, curves back on itself like a ram's horn or conch shell, spiraling toward its greatest compass but simultaneously narrowing to that needle's eye it must enter in order to flow forth bounteously again. You hovered at that nexus, took your turn through that open door.

The old people die. Our grandfathers, Harry Wideman and John French, are both gone now. The greatest space and no space at all separates us from them. I see them staring, dreaming this ravaged city; and we are in the dream, it's our dream, enclosed, enclosing. We could walk down into that valley they saw from atop Bruston Hill and scoop up the houses, dismantle the bridges and tall buildings, pull cars and trucks off the streets, roll up roads and highways and stuff them all like toys into the cotton-picking sacks draped over our shoulders. We are that much larger than the things that happen to us. Accidents like the city poised at the meeting of three rivers, the city strewn like litter over precipitous hills.

Did our grandfathers run away from the South? Black Harry from Greenwood, South Carolina, mulatto white John from Culpepper, Virginia. How would they answer that question? Were they running from something or running to something? What did you figure you were doing when you started running? When did your flight begin? Was escape the reason or was there a destination, a promised land exerting its pull? Is freedom inextricably linked with both, running *from* and running *to*? Is freedom the motive and means and end and everything in between?

I wonder if the irony of a river beside the prison is intentional. The river was brown last time I saw it, mud-brown and sluggish in its broad channel. Nothing pretty about it, a working river, a place to dump things, to empty sewers. The Ohio's thick and filthy, stinking of coal, chemicals, offal, bitter with rust from the flaking hulls of iron-ore barges inching grayly to and from the steel mills. But viewed from barred windows, from tiered cages, the river must call to the prisoners' hearts, a natural symbol of flight and freedom. The river is a path, a gateway to the West, the frontier. Somewhere it meets the sea. Is it somebody's cruel joke, an architect's way of giving the knife a final twist, hanging this sign outside the walls, this river always visible but a million miles away beyond the spiked steel fence guarding its banks?

When I think of the distance between us in terms of miles or the height and thickness of walls or the length of your sentence or the deadly prison regimen, you're closer to me, more accessible than when I'm next to you in the prison visiting room trying to speak and find myself at the edge of a silence vaster than oceans. I turned forty-three in June and you'll be thirty-three in December. Not kids any longer by any stretch of the imagination. You're my little brother and maybe it's generally true that people never allow their little brothers and sisters to grow up, but something more seems at work here, something more damaging than vanity, than wishful thinking that inclines us to keep our pasts frozen, intact, keeps us calling our forty-year-old cronies "the boys" and a grown man "little brother." I think of you as little brother because I have no other handle. At a certain point a wall goes up and easy memories stop.

When I think back, I have plenty of recollections of you as a kid. How you looked. The funny things you said. Till about the time you turned a gangly, stilt-legged, stringbean thirteen, we're still family. Our lives connect in typical, family ways: holidays, picnics, births, deaths, the joking and teasing, the time you were a baby just home from the hospital and Daddy John French died and I was supposed to be watching you while the grown-ups cleaned and cooked, readying the house on Finance Street for visitors, for Daddy John to return and lie in his coffin downstairs. Baby-sitting you in Aunt Geraldine's room while death hovered in there with us and no way I could have stayed in that room alone. Needing you much more than you needed me. You just zzz'ed away in your baby sleep, your baby ignorance. You couldn't have cared less whether death or King Kong or a whole flock of those loose-feathered, giant birds haunting my sleep had gathered round your crib. If the folks downstairs were too quiet, my nerves would get jumpy and I'd snatch you up and walk the floor. Hold you pressed in my arms against my heart like a shield. Or if the night cracks and groans of the house got too loud, I'd poke you awake, worry you so your crying would keep me company.

After you turned thirteen, after you grew a mustache and fuzz on your chin and a voluminous Afro so nobody could call you "Beanhead" anymore, after girls and the move from Shadyside to Marchand Street so you started Westinghouse High instead of Peabody where the rest of us had done our time, you begin to get separate. I have to struggle to recall anything about you till you're real again in prison. It's as if I was asleep for fifteen years and when I awakened you were gone. I was out of the country for three years then lived in places like Iowa City and Philly and Laramie, so at best I couldn't have seen much of you, but the sense of distance I'm trying to describe had more to do with the way I related to you than with the amount of time we spent together. We had chances to talk, opportunities to grow beyond the childhood bonds linking us. The problem was that in order to be the person I thought I wanted to be, I believed I had to seal myself off from you, construct a wall between us.

Your hands, your face became a man's. You accumulated scars, a deeper voice, lovers, but the changes taking place in you might as well have been occurring on a different planet. The scattered images I retain of you from the sixties through the middle seventies form no discernible pattern, are rooted in no vital substance like childhood or family. Your words and gestures belonged to a language I was teaching myself to unlearn. When we spoke, I was conscious of a third party short-circuiting our conversations. What I'd say to you came from the mouth of a translator who always talked down or up or around you, who didn't know you or me but pretended he knew everything.

Was I as much a stranger to you as you seemed to me? Because we were brothers, holidays, family celebrations, and troubles drew us to the same rooms at the same time, but I felt uncomfortable around you. Most of what I felt was guilt. I'd made my choices. I was running away from Pittsburgh, from poverty, from blackness. To get ahead, to make something of myself, college had seemed a logical, necessary step; my exile, my flight from home began with good grades, with good English, with setting myself apart long before I'd earned a scholarship and a train ticket over the mountains to Philadelphia. With that willed alienation behind me, between us, guilt was predictable. One measure of my success was the distance I'd put between us. Coming home was a kind of bragging, like the suntans people bring back from Hawaii in the middle of winter. It's sure fucked up around here, ain't it? But look at me, I got away. I got mine. I didn't want to be caught looking back. I needed home to reassure myself of how far I'd come. If I ever doubted how good I had it away at school in that world of books, exams, pretty, rich white girls, a roommate from Long Island who unpacked more pairs of brand-new jockey shorts and T-shirts than they had in Kaufmann's department store, if I ever had any hesitations or reconsiderations about the path I'd chosen, youall were back home in the ghetto to remind me how lucky I was.

Fear marched along beside guilt. Fear of acknowledging in myself any traces of the poverty, ignorance, and danger I'd find surrounding me when I returned to Pittsburgh. Fear that I was contaminated and would carry the poison wherever I ran. Fear that the evil would be discovered in me and I'd be shunned like a leper.

The "Eye"

Beverly Lowry

Secret Ceremonies of Love and Death

My friend Karla Faye got married last June, changed her last name from Tucker to Brown. This came as no surprise. She'd been calling herself by her new name for a long time already, months before the actual ceremony took place. In the eyes of God, she'd explained, she and Dana Brown had taken their vows, made their commitment already. The only thing left was, as she said, to put it on paper for man's sake. "Love," she ended her letters, "Karla Faye Brown (SMILE!)."

No matter her legal last name, the Texas Department of Correction will continue to call Karla Faye by her inmate identification number, 777, from now until . . . I do what I can to skip over some possibilities. Until whatever happens regarding her case. When the Houston *Chronicle* got wind of the wedding, its page-one story was headlined, "New Bride Can't Leave Death Row." The first sentence of the story began, "Pickax murderer Karla Faye Tucker . . . has married."

I grew up in a time of absolutes. Purity, goodness, evil. Those days, the righteous, honorable, and true soul suited up to do battle against the enemies of God and America (weren't they the same?) and we all knew who they were. The belief in purity makes for sanctimoniousness and—worse—a kind of cynicism that denies people second and third chances. Certainty becomes a razor-toothed trap, which clamps hard down on the heart and spirit. I was raised Christian but not a serious one. Presbyterians went to church, certainly, but church never got in the way of how you lived or what you ate. When I was sixteen, I even went to a religious camp in the Rockies, where I declared myself saved and—standing before a roomful of converts and weeping friends—dedicated my life to Jesus. My conversion also did not seriously change my life. When camp was over, I reverted to former desires: to be a cheerleader and a member of the Sub-Deb Cotillion Club.

Things happen, Compassion softens certainty. Harsh concepts come clean. The curious heart opens, and we begin to understand just how complex good is and how twisted happiness can be. Life does this and that; we end up in situations we once would have thought of as dead-end and hopeless. And yet, once we stop beating our heads against stony facts and come to a point when we can consider the options, we can still manage, not just to convince ourselves, but actually to know and to believe, "This is good. I am content." Considering the issue of hope, Karla Faye quotes Scripture, Romans 4:18, in which Paul, speaking of Abraham, says, "Who, contrary to hope, in hope believed."

Karla Faye didn't personally attend her wedding and, by her request, neither did any of her family or friends. Newspapers didn't get wind of the nuptials until the next day. Karla seriously did not want to get married by proxy; she wanted to stand with Dana Brown hand in hand, so that they could say their vows together. She thought maybe she'd be on bench warrant in Houston for a court date and they could have the service then, or even that a judge might sympathize and give her permission to leave prison for her wedding; but it didn't happen, and in the end proxy was her only choice. But the groom was there, a minister performed the ceremony, and afterwards, Karla Faye's new husband drove to the prison in his car with "Just Married" painted all over it and balloons trailing from the back bumper, so that Karla Faye could see it from the window in her cell as he made the turn to the parking lot by the gates to the visiting room. With the other women on death row, the bride had been having her own ceremony and celebration, with cake and small presents.

The wedding took place on a Saturday, so that Karla Faye and Dana could eat together during their weekly visit, Saturday being the only day TDC allows death-row inmates to have a meal with visitors. But TDC didn't cook that particular night, and so they drank Cokes together and didn't care at all about the food. "The first thing we did," Dana says, "was fall on our knees and pray." He was in his wedding suit, she in prison-issue whites, and the newlyweds had their wedding night visit sitting in hard folding chairs with a shield of Plexiglas between them. They pretended to touch one another through the Plexiglas; they held up their hands in a thumb and forefinger salute, their hand signal for love; they crossed their arms over their chests and rocked back and forth and hugged their own shoulders as a substitute for holding one another; they prayed together for a long, long time. "Mush through the mesh," they call what happens when they are together.

And after their visit, when Dana's two hours were up, Karla went back to her quarters, with the five other women on Texas's death row, where she was locked up in her cell for the night, and after eating dinner with friends, Dana Brown went home to the condominium he has bought, where he and Karla hope, in time, to have a life together. "I am," Karla reported to me in a letter, "definitely the blushing bride, feeling every bit the in-love young married woman."

I met Karla Faye in 1986, two years after the death of my son Peter, who at eighteen had been killed in a hit-and-run occurrence I still refuse to call an accident. Death was on my mind all the time in those years. I felt alone with death, wed to it, in its thrall. I'd done what I could to mend my heart: psychotherapy, psychics, a fortune-teller with candles and cards. Family and friends provided me with soft pillows of love and compassion. And I had, in fact, been able to go on with my life. I seemed better and was, but barely. Crookedly creeping along. Then I saw a newspaper story about Karla Faye, the changes she'd experienced in prison, her newfound religion, the happiness she'd discovered on death row. There was a color picture: Karla Faye with a chipped tooth, chin cupped in one hand, hair curled around her face, those dark soft eyes taking the camera straight on. A pretty young woman in prison whites, she looked sweet and soulful and—I could think of no other word to describe what I saw—*good*. And yet at her trial she had been described by her own lawyer as evil incarnate. I didn't get it. Captivated by what I saw—she was so alive—I wrote and went to see her.

Women don't so much create a friendship as discover it. When I walked into the visiting room and found Karla Faye sitting on her side of the Plexiglas saying "Howdy" and broadly beckoning me over to where she was, I knew I would not easily walk away from whatever this relationship turned out to be. And I sat in the metal folding chair and I asked her questions, and she told me everything. The murders. Her life. Her mother. Sex, drugs. I listened, listened. Then I told her about Peter and how he died, and, to make the point that she *deserved* to be where she was, she asked an amazing question: "Now what if they found the person who hit Peter and they put him on trial and he said, 'But I'm sorry now. I'm different. I've changed.' How would you feel?"

We challenge each other's easy assumptions. When she looked at me—dead-on, not flinching—with the same soft sweetness I saw in the newspaper photo, I had to admit, I didn't know. "See?" she said.

At that time she'd been on death row for two years, in prison for three. I'd lived in Houston when her trial took place. I remembered it well: the double murders, the horrible weapon of death, the reported claims of the defendant—my friend, who was twenty-three at the time—to have felt sexually gratified by what she'd done that horrible night, an erotic peak with every stroke. That braggy statement did Karla in, in the eyes of her jury, and more than likely put her on death row. When I asked her about it, she winced. Of course it wasn't true. She only said it because of who she said it *to,* and how badly she wanted to be one of them—in her druggy sped-up state of mind and tomboy heart wanting to be a tough guy, running with bikers, not wanting to be girly and hesitant, needing instead to be bold, ballsy, a lover of violence and trouble. It was the kind of murder death-penalty advocates use as a test case to prove their point: that there are people who are, oh very unlike the rest of us, people who are born bad. Monstrous, these others, they walk among us, dead to hope and unredeemable, unworthy to enjoy access to the constitutional rights the rest of us hold dear. Or even, to live.

And there she sat, a warm, loving, thinking young woman. She had told about the murders in the penalty phase of her trial, told of her life: the marijuana at eight, heroin at ten. She even testified against the man who gave her lessons in killing, the thirty-five-year-old boyfriend who was with her the night of the murders. I listened to her story and believed. Trusted her. And I thought I could perhaps speak for her, even speak *as* her, and if I did I might understand a little more about the complexities of good and evil and hope and cynicism. And in doing so, I might lift our spirits— hers and mine and even other people's—marginally higher.

Randomness is hard to take. The nighttime chop, where? Here, there? Out of the blue. Having nothing to do with fault, blame or deserving. Fate will do, in a pinch. At the time I met Karla, I was still looking for a narrative that would make my life, my son's death, make sense. Time to time, I still look for it. Peter's death—to state the obvious—changed my life. Hearing Karla's story—hours and hours sitting across from one another in the TDC visiting room, freezing in the ice-cold Texas air-conditioning, doing yoga poses for one another, drinking soft drinks from a machine, separated always by the cloudy Plexiglas—altered that change. There we sat, both of us with death on our minds, swapping stories. I went to see her once a week for about a year. We could not touch—have never—or exchange any items in person. A guard watched over our every move. And so she sent me photographs of herself and her family, wrote long letters describing her childhood, let me in on private information. Some secrets I keep hidden yet. I still go to see her, though not as often now.

People say (but everybody loves Karla now) she is a new person, isn't she? This girl you go to see, she surely is not the Karla Faye who helped commit murder, is she? We long for certainty, the defined personality, the fixed, known thing; childlike, we still believe in it.

The Karla Faye I visit is not new but the Karla who always was, who might have been, the true Karla Faye who walked among us and did wrong but was always herself the warm, thinking, good young woman I know, who only emerged in prison, minus drugs and bikers and the need to be a tough guy. This is who she will be from now on. Karla Faye gave me not only consolation but a broader sense of the scope of human possibility. Once you know how complex action and motivation and a whole long life can be, you adjust your assumptions, reconsider concepts, enlarge whatever notion you once had of the limits of what might be. Cynicism is tried, tested, and hung up like meat on a hook, to be explored, dissected, maybe even discarded.

Hold up the scales. Hope on one end, cynicism on the other. We've heard it all before. "Sure she's a Christian," we say. On death row, wouldn't you be?

Soften. Listen. Give her a chance. I would come home from the prison and lie in bed and at some dark late hour begin to doubt. Was I being gulled? No. Like falling in love, sometimes you simply *know.* Be still. Trust your heart. If she is not truthful and trustworthy—I knew this—nobody ever was.

A couple of months before Karla got married, I met her new husband. Dana Brown is a handsome, easygoing prison minister who travels the world visiting prisons, singing songs with inmates and reading Scripture to them, trying to bring people hope, and to Jesus. I sat in the visiting room with him—us on the free side of the Plexiglas, Karla on the other—and watching them, I thought of all the variations of love I'd known of, all the people who have maintained love through the most god-awful, unimaginable circumstances, and, put in that context, the limitations imposed on the love of these two young people didn't seem that outrageous to me. "People think I'm crazy," Dana shrugged. "That's okay. They don't think I can touch Karla but I do. We touch spirits all the time, visibly, in that room and even when we're not together. I wouldn't change anything." They praised Jesus a lot that day and said how they'd been married in the eyes of the Lord for a long time. They had fasted for a month, prayed hard, waited. Once they declared their love for one another, Dana had to give up the privilege of actually going into the death row unit where Karla lives, to lead the women there in prayer and song. He became an ordinary visitor, like me, permanently stuck on the other side of the Plexiglas.

She is, my friend Karla Faye, the least cynical person I know. As for the death penalty, well—it shames us all. In the end, read enough cases and the truth becomes clear: Who dies by needle or electric current, administered by the state—us—is arbitrary and has more to do with circumstance—economics and race—than the crime committed. Like hit-and-run, it falls on the unlucky ones whose roll of the dice comes up short. No woman has been executed in Texas since 1896, when Chipita Rodriguez was hanged from a hackberry tree for stealing a horse. Now that women run marathons and countries, is it time to punish them equally as well? To bring the statistics up to date with the times? Poke women's arms the same as men's, fill their veins with poison, steal their breath and heartbeat?

One night it either happens. Or it doesn't. The wind turns; there's a new, breeze-born scent in the air, freshly elected governor, the politics of the moment. One night the deal comes down. Somebody says, Go. Stop. Or, Wait.

Sadness, once rooted in the heart, never dies. Appalling, the things that happen, the boy on the highway alone, dying, unattended. Two people murdered in their beds, the young woman sentenced to die. Karla sends me jokes, pretty cards, pictures cut from magazines, a page full of wildly colored women's cowboy boots: Which ones do I like? She describes the house Dana Brown has bought for them and tells me again and again how happy she is. "My spirit," she says, "soars." Sometimes I think about the possibility of her execution, then I don't. I stuff the possibility back in some lost drawer of the mind where we jam the unthinkable.

When I first met Karla, there were four women on death row; now there are six. In letters, she tells me about their legal appeals, their life together. I send her postcards from wherever I go and tell her stories about places, people, my dog. She is not afraid to die, but oh, I don't want her to. Sometimes, working out at the gym, music pounding in black foam buttons in my ears, I hear an upbeat rock song that reminds me of Karla Faye and I imagine that she is with me, and we are laughing and dancing together, twirling in soft skirts to the beat, alive and happy. And I stop working out and stand there and see myself in some big mirror with a dopey smile on my face.

In the end, I can't save Karla Faye, and neither can Dana Brown. The random nighttime chop hits where it will. It's Karla who, *contrary to hope . . .*

More than either of us and whatever happens, *in hope believes.*

Susan Orlean

Meet the Shaggs

Things I Wonder (2:12)

Depending on whom you ask, the Shaggs were either the best band of all time or the worst. Frank Zappa is said to have proclaimed that the Shaggs were "better than the Beatles." More recently, though, a music fan who claimed to be in "the fetal position, writhing in pain," declared on the Internet that the Shaggs were "hauntingly bad," and added, "I would walk across the desert while eating charcoal briquettes soaked in Tabasco for forty days and forty nights *not* to ever have to listen to anything Shagg-related *ever* again." Such a divergence of opinion confuses the mind. Listening to the Shaggs' album *Philosophy of the World* will further confound. The music is winsome but raggedly discordant pop. Something is sort of wrong with the tempo, and the melodies are squashed and bent, nasal, deadpan. Are the Shaggs referencing the heptatonic, angular microtones of Chinese *ya-yueh* court music and the atonal note clusters of Ornette Coleman, or are they just a bunch of kids playing badly on cheap, out-of-tune guitars? And what about their homely, blunt lyrics? Consider the song "Things I Wonder":

> *There are many things I wonder*
> *There are many things I don't*
> *It seems as though the things I wonder most*
> *Are the things I never find out*

Is this the colloquial ease and dislocated syntax of a James Schuyler poem or the awkward innermost thoughts of a speechless teenager?

The Shaggs were three sisters, Helen, Betty, and Dorothy (Dot) Wiggin, from Fremont, New Hampshire. They were managed by their father, Austin Wiggin, Jr., and were sometimes accompanied by another sister, Rachel. They performed almost exclusively at the Fremont town hall and at a local nursing home, beginning in 1968 and ending in 1973. Many people in Fremont thought the band stank. Austin Wiggin did not. He believed his girls were going to be big stars, and in 1969 he took most of his savings and paid to record an album of their music. Nine hundred of the original thousand copies of *Philosophy of the World* vanished right after being pressed, along with the record's shady producer. Even so, the album has endured for thirty years. Music collectors got hold of the remaining copies of *Philosophy of the World* and started a small Shaggs cult. In the mid-seventies, WBCN-FM, in Boston, began playing a few cuts from the record. In 1988, the songs were repackaged and rereleased on compact disc and became celebrated by outsider-music mavens, who were taken with the Shaggs' artless style. Now the Shaggs are entering their third life: *Philosophy of the World* was reissued last spring by RCA Victor and will be released in Germany this winter. The new CD of *Philosophy of the World* has the same cover as the original 1969 album—a photograph of the Wiggin girls posed in front of a dark green curtain. In the picture, Helen is twenty-two, Dot is twenty-one, and Betty is eighteen. They have long blond hair and long blond bangs and stiff, quizzical half-smiles. Helen, sitting behind her drum set, is wearing flowered trousers and a white Nehru shirt; Betty and Dot, clutching their guitars, are wearing matching floral tunics, pleated plaid skirts, and square-heeled white pumps. There is nothing playful about the picture; it is melancholy, foreboding, with black shadows and the queer, depthless quality of an aquarium. Which leaves you with even more things to wonder about the Shaggs.

Shaggs' Own Thing (3:54)

Fremont, New Hampshire, is a town that has missed out on most everything. Route 125, the main highway bisecting New Hampshire, just misses the east side of Fremont; Route 101 just misses the north; the town is neither in the mountains nor on the ocean; it is not quite in the thick of Boston's outskirts, nor is it quite cosseted in the woods. Fremont is a drowsy, trim, unfancy place, rimmed by the Exeter River. Ostentation is expressed only in a few man-size gravestones in the Fremont cemetery; bragging rights are limited to Fremont's being the hometown of the eminent but obscure 1920s meteorologist Herbert Browne and its being the first place a B-52 ever crashed without killing anyone.

In the 1960s, when the Wiggin sisters formed the Shaggs, many people in Fremont raised dairy cows or made handkerchiefs at the Exeter textile mill or built barrels at Spaulding & Frost Cooperage, went to church, tended their families, kept quiet lives. Sometimes the summer light bounces off the black-glass surface of the Exeter River and glazes the big stands of blue pine, and sometimes the pastures are full and lustrous, but ordinary days in southern New Hampshire towns can be mingy and dismal. "Loneliness contributed to severe depression, illness and drunkenness for countless rural families," Matthew Thomas wrote, in his book *History of Fremont, N.H. Olde Poplin: An Independent New England Republic 1764–1997,* which came out last year. "There may have been some nice, pleasant times . . . but for the most part, death, sickness, disease, accidents, bad weather, loneliness, strenuous hard work, insect-infested foods, prowling predatory animals, and countless inconveniences marked day-to-day existence."

When I was in Fremont recently, I asked Matthew Thomas, who is forty-three and the town historian, what it had been like growing up there. He said it was nice but that he had been bored stiff. For entertainment, there were square dances, sledding, an annual carnival with a Beano tent, Vic Marcotte's Barber Shop and Poolroom. (These days, there are weekend grass drags out near Phil Peterson's farm, where the pasture is flat and firm enough to race snowmobiles in the summer.) When the Shaggs were growing up, the Fremont town hall hosted ham-and-bean suppers, boxing matches, dog shows, and spelling bees. The hall is an unadorned box of a building, but its performance theater is actually quite grand. It isn't used anymore, and someone has made off with the red velvet curtain, but it still has a somber dark stage and high-backed chairs, and the gravid air of a place where things might happen. In a quiet community like Fremont, in the dull hours between barn dances, a stage like that might give you big ideas.

Who Are Parents? (2:58)

Where else would Austin Wiggin have got the idea that his daughters should form a rock band? Neither he nor his wife, Annie, was musical; she much preferred television to music, and he, at most, fooled around with a Jew's harp. He wasn't a show-off, dying to be noticed—by all accounts he was an ornery loner who had little to do with other people in town. He was strict and old-fashioned, not a hippie manqué, not a rebel, very disapproving of long hair and short skirts. He was from a poor family and was raising a poor family—seven kids on a mill hand's salary—and music lessons and instruments for the girls were a daunting expense.

And yet the Shaggs were definitely his idea—or, more exactly, his mother's idea. Austin was terribly superstitious. His mother liked to tell fortunes. When he was young, she studied his palm and told him that in the future he would marry a strawberry blonde and would have two sons whom she would not live to see, and that his daughters would play in a band. Her auguries were borne out. Annie was a strawberry blonde, and she and Austin did have two sons after his mother died. It was left to Austin to fulfill the last of his mother's predictions, and when his daughters were old enough he told them they would be taking voice and music lessons and forming a band. There was no debate: His word was law, and his mother's prophecies were gospel. Besides, he chafed at his place in the Fremont social system. It wasn't so much that his girls would make him rich and raise him out of a mill hand's dreary métier; it was that they would prove that the Wiggin kids were not only different from but better than the folks in town.

The girls liked music—particularly Herman's Hermits, Ricky Nelson, and Dino, Desi & Billy— but until Austin foretold their futures they had not planned to become rock stars. They were shy, small-town teenagers who dreamed of growing up and getting married, having children, maybe becoming secretaries someday. Even now, they don't remember ever having dreamed of fame or of making music. But Austin pushed the girls into a new life. He named them the Shaggs, and told them that they were not going to attend the local high school, because he didn't want them traveling by bus and mixing with outsiders, and, more important, he wanted them to practice their music all day. He enrolled them in a Chicago mail-order outfit called American Home School, but he designed their schedule himself: Practice in the morning and afternoon, rehearse songs for him after dinner, and then do calisthenics and jumping jacks and leg lifts or practice for another hour before going to bed. The girls couldn't decide which was worse, the days when he made them do calisthenics or the days when he'd make them practice again before bed. In either case, their days seemed endless. The rehearsals were solemn, and Austin could be cutting. One song in particular, "Philosophy of the World," he claimed they never played right, and he would insist on hearing it again and again.

The Shaggs were not leading rock-and-roll lives. Austin forbade the girls to date before they were eighteen and discouraged most other friendships. They hadn't been popular kids, anyway— they didn't have the looks or the money or the savvy for it—but being in the band, and being home-schooled, set them apart even more. Friday nights, the family went out together to do grocery shopping. Sundays they went to church, and the girls practiced when they got home. Their world was even smaller than the small town of Fremont.

This was 1965. The Beatles had recently debuted on American television. The harmony between generations—at least, the harmony between the popular cultures of those generations— was busting. And yet the sweet, lumpish Wiggin sisters of Fremont, New Hampshire, were playing pop music at their father's insistence, in a band that he directed. Rebellion might have been driving most rock and roll, but in Fremont, Dot Wiggin was writing tributes to her mom and dad, with songs like "Who Are Parents?":

Parents are the ones who really care
Who are parents?
Parents are the ones who are always there
Some kids think their parents are cruel
Just because they want them to obey certain rules . . . .
Parents do understand
Parents do care

Their first public performance was at a talent show in nearby Exeter, in 1968. The girls could barely play their instruments. They didn't think they were ready to appear in public, but Austin thought otherwise. When they opened, with a cover of a loping country song called "Wheels," people in the audience threw soda cans at them and jeered. The girls were mortified; Austin told them they just had to go home and practice more. If they thought about quitting, they thought about it very privately, because Austin would have had no truck with the idea; he was the kind of father who didn't tolerate debate. They practiced more, did their calisthenics, practiced more. Dot wrote the songs and the basic melodies, and she and Betty worked together on the chords and rhythms. Helen made up her drum parts on her own. The songs were misshapen pop tunes, full of shifting time signatures and odd meters and abrupt key changes, with lyrics about Dot's lost cat, Foot Foot, and her yearning for a sports car and how much she liked to listen to the radio.

On Halloween, the Shaggs played at a local nursing home—featuring Dot's song "It's Halloween" in their set—and got a polite response from the residents. Soon afterward, Austin arranged for them to play at the Fremont town hall on Saturday nights. The girls worried about embarrassing themselves, but at the same time they liked the fact that the shows allowed them to escape the house and their bounded world, even if it was just for a night. At that point, the girls had never even been to Boston, which was only fifty miles away.

The whole family took part in the town hall shows. Austin III, the older of the two sons who had been seen in Austin's future, played the maracas; the other son, Robert, played the tambourine and did a drum solo during intermission; Annie sold tickets and ran the refreshment stand. A Pepsi truck would drop off the cases of soda at their green ranch house, on Beede Road, every Friday night. Even though, according to one town hall regular, most people found the Shaggs' music "painful and torturous," sometimes as many as a hundred kids showed up at the dances—practically the whole adolescent population of Fremont. Then again, there really wasn't much else to do in Fremont on a Saturday night. The audience danced and chatted, heckled the band, pelted the girls with junk, ignored them, grudgingly appreciated them, mocked them.

The rumor around town was that Austin forced his daughters to be in the band. There was even talk that he was inappropriately intimate with them. When asked about it years later, Betty said that the talk wasn't true, but Helen said that Austin once was intimate with her. Certainly, the family was folded in on itself; even Austin's father and Annie's mother, after they were both widowed, became romantically involved and lived together in a small house on the Wiggin property. The gossip and criticism only made Austin more determined to continue with the band. It was, after all, his destiny.

I'm So Happy When You're Near (2:12)

"Through the years, this author as town historian has received numerous requests from fans around the country looking for information on 'The Shaggs' and the town they came from," Matthew Thomas wrote in his section about the band. "They definitely have a cult following, and deservedly so, because the Wiggin sisters worked hard and with humble resources to gain respect and acceptance as musicians. To their surprise they succeeded. After all, what other New Hampshire band . . . has a record album worth $300–$500?"

The Beatles' arrival in America piqued Austin. He disliked their moppy hair but was stirred by their success. If they could make it, why couldn't his girls? He wanted to see the Shaggs on television, and on concert tours. Things weren't happening quickly enough for him, though, and this made him unhappy. He started making tapes and home movies of the town hall shows. In March 1969, he took the girls to Fleetwood Studios, outside Boston, to make a record. According to the magazine *Cool and Strange Music!,* the studio engineer listened to the Shaggs rehearse and suggested that they weren't quite ready to record. But Austin insisted on going forward, reportedly telling the engineer, "I want to get them while they're hot." In the album's liner notes, Austin wrote:

> The Shaggs are real, pure, unaffected by outside influences. Their music is different, it is theirs alone. They believe in it, live it. . . . Of all contemporary acts in the world today, perhaps only the Shaggs do what others would like to do, and that is perform only what they believe in, what they feel, not what others think the Shaggs should feel. The Shaggs love you. . . . They will not change their music or style to meet the whims of a frustrated world. You should appreciate this because you know they are pure what more can you ask? . . . They are sisters and members of a large family where mutual respect and love for each other is at an unbelievable high . . . in an atmosphere which has encouraged them to develop their music unaffected by outside influences. They are happy people and love what they are doing. They do it because they love it.

The Wiggins returned to Fleetwood a few years later. By then, the girls were more proficient—they had practiced hundreds of hours since the first recording session—but their playing still inspired the engineer to write, "As the day progressed, I overcame my disappointment and started feeling sorry for this family paying sixty dollars an hour for studio time to record—this?"

I once asked Annie Wiggin if she thought Austin was a dreamer, and after sitting quietly for a few moments she said, "Well, probably. Must have been." If he was, it no doubt got harder to dream as the years went on. In 1973, the Fremont town supervisors decided to end the Saturday night concerts, because—well, no one really remembers why anymore, but there was talk of fights breaking out and drugs circulating in the crowd, and wear and tear on the town hall's wooden floors, although the girls scrubbed the scuff marks off every Sunday. Austin was furious, but the girls were relieved to end the grind of playing every Saturday night. They were getting older and had begun to chafe at his authority. Helen secretly married the first boyfriend she ever had—someone she had met at the dances. She continued living at home for three months after the wedding because she was too terrified to tell Austin what she had done. On the night that she finally screwed up the courage to give him the news, he got out a shotgun and went after her husband. The police joined in and told Helen to choose one man or the other. She left with her husband, and it was months before Austin spoke to her. She was twenty-eight years old.

The Shaggs continued to play at local fairs and at the nursing home. Austin still believed they were going to make it, and the band never broke up. It just shut down in 1975, on the day Austin, who was only forty-seven years old, died in bed of a massive heart attack—the same day, according to Helen, they had finally played a version of "Philosophy of the World" that he praised.

Philosophy of the World (2:56)

Shortly after the newest rerelease of the Shaggs' album, I went to New Hampshire to talk to the Wiggin sisters. A few years after Austin died, Betty and Dot married and moved to their own houses, and eventually Annie sold the house on Beede Road and moved to an apartment nearby. After a while, the house's new owner complained to people in town that Austin's ghost haunted the property. As soon as he could afford it, the new owner built something bigger and nicer farther back on the property, and allowed the Fremont Fire Department to burn the old Wiggin house down for fire-fighting practice.

Dot and Betty live a few miles down the road from Fremont, in the town of Epping, and Helen lives a few miles farther, in Exeter. They don't play music anymore. After Austin died, they sold much of their equipment and let their kids horse around with whatever was left. Dot hung on to her guitar for a while, just in case, but a few years ago she lent it to one of her brothers and hasn't gotten it back. Dot, who is now fifty, cleans houses for a living. Betty, forty-eight, was a school janitor until recently, when she took a better job, in the stockroom of a kitchen goods warehouse. Helen, who suffers from serious depression, lives on disability.

Dot and Betty arranged to meet me at Dunkin' Donuts, in Epping, and I went early so that I could read the local papers. It was a soggy, warm morning in southern New Hampshire; the sky was chalky, and the sun was as gray as gunmetal. Long tractor-trailers idled in the Dunkin' Donuts parking lot and then rumbled to life and lumbered onto the road. A few people were lined up to buy Pick 4 lottery tickets. The clerk behind the doughnut counter was discussing her wedding shower with a girl wearing a fuzzy halter top and platform sneakers. In the meantime, the coffee burned.

That day's Exeter *News-Letter* reported that the recreation commission's kickoff concert would feature Beatle Juice, a Beatles tribute band led by "Brad Delp, former front man of 'Boston,' one of the biggest rock bands New England has ever produced." Southern New Hampshire has regular outbreaks of tribute bands and reunion tours, as if it were in a time zone all its own, one in which the past keeps reappearing, familiar but essentially changed. Some time ago, Dot and her husband and their two sons went to see a revived version of Herman's Hermits. The concert was a huge disappointment for Dot, because her favorite Hermit, Peter (Herman) Noone, is no longer with the band, and because the Hermits' act now includes dirty jokes and crude references.

The Shaggs never made any money from their album until years later, when members of the band NRBQ heard "Philosophy of the World" and were thrilled by its strange innocence. NRBQ's own record label, Red Rooster, released records by such idiosyncratic bands as Jake & the Family Jewels, and they asked the Wiggins if they could compile a selection of songs from the group's two recording sessions. The resulting album, *The Shaggs' Own Thing,* includes the second session at Fleetwood Studios and some live and home recordings. Red Rooster's reissue of *Philosophy of the World* was reviewed in *Rolling Stone* twice in 1980 and was described as "priceless and timeless." The articles introduced the Shaggs to the world.

Three years ago, Irwin Chusid, the author of the forthcoming book *Songs in the Key of Z: The Curious Universe of Outsider Music,* discovered that a company he worked with had bought the rights to the Shaggs' songs, which had been bundled with other obscure music-publishing rights. Chusid wanted to reissue *Philosophy of the World* as it was in 1969, with the original cover and the original song sequence. He suggested the project to Joe Mozian, a vice president of marketing at RCA Victor, who had never heard the band. Mozian was interested in unusual ventures; he had just released some Belgian lounge music from the sixties, which featured such songs as "The Frère Jacques Conga." Mozian says, "The Shaggs were beyond my wildest dreams. I couldn't comprehend that music like that existed. It's so basic and innocent, the way the music business used to be. Their timing, musically, was . . . fascinating. Their lyrics were . . . amazing. It is kind of a bad record — that's so obvious, it's a given. But it absolutely intrigued me, the idea that people would make a record playing the way they do."

The new *Philosophy of the World* was released last March. Even though the record is being played on college radio stations and the reviews have been enthusiastic and outsider art has been in vogue for several years, RCA Victor has sold only a few thousand copies of *Philosophy* so far. Mozian admits that he is disappointed. "I'm not sure why it hasn't sold," he says. "I think people are a little afraid of having the Shaggs in their record collections."

While I was waiting for the Wiggins, I went out to my car to listen to the CD again. I especially love the song "Philosophy of the World," with its wrought-up, clattering guitars and chugging, cockeyed rhythm and the cheerfully pessimistic lyrics about how people are never happy with what they have. I was right in the middle of the verse about how rich people want what poor people have, and how girls with long hair want short hair, when Betty pulled up and opened the door of my car. As soon as she recognized the song, she gasped, "Do you like this?" I said yes, and she said, "God, it's horrible." She shook her head. Her hair no longer rippled down to her waist and no longer had a shelf of shaggy bangs that touched the bridge of her nose; it was short and springy, just to the nape of her neck, the hair of a grown woman without time to bother too much about her appearance.

A few minutes later, Dot drove in. She was wearing a flowered housedress and a Rugrats watch, and had a thin silver band on her thumb. On her middle finger was a chunky ring that spelled "Elvis" in block letters. She and Betty have the same deep blue eyes and thrusting chin and tiny teeth, but Dot's hair is still long and wavy, and even now you can picture her as the girl with a guitar on the cover of the 1969 album. She asked what we were listening to. "What do you think?" Betty said to her. "The *Shaggs*." They both listened for another minute, so rapt that it seemed as if they had never heard the song before. "I never play the record on my own anymore," Dot said. "My son Matt plays it sometimes. He likes it. I don't think I get sentimental when I hear it—I just don't think about playing it."

"I wonder where I put my copies of the album," Betty said. "I know I have one copy of the CD. I think I have some of the albums somewhere."

The Wiggins have received fan letters from Switzerland and Texas, been interviewed for a documentary film, and inspired a dozen Web sites, bulletin boards, and forums on the Internet, but it's hard to see how this could matter much, once their childhood had been scratched out and rewritten as endless days of practicing guitar, and their father, who believed that their success was fated, died before they got any recognition. They are wise enough to realize that some of the long-standing interest in their music is ironic—sheer marvel that anything so unpolished could ever have made it onto a record. "We might have felt special at the time we made the record," Dot said uncertainly. "The really cool part, to me, is that it's thirty years later and we're still talking about it. I never thought we'd really be famous. I never thought we'd even be as famous as we are. I met a girl at the Shop 'n Save the other day who used to come to the dances, and she said she wanted to go out now and buy the CD. And I saw a guy at a fair recently and talked to him for about half an hour about the Shaggs. And people call and ask if they can come up and meet us—that's amazing to me."

Yet when I asked Dot and Betty for the names of people who could describe the town hall shows, they couldn't think of any for days. "We missed out on a lot," Betty said. "I can't say we didn't have fun, but we missed a social life, we missed out on having friends, we missed everything except our music and our exercises. I just didn't think we were good enough to be playing in concerts and making records. At one point, I thought maybe we would make it, but it wasn't really my fantasy." Her fantasy, she said, was to climb into a car with plenty of gas and just drive—not to get anywhere in particular, just to go.

We ordered our coffee and doughnuts and sat at a table near the window. Betty had her two-year-old and eight-month-old granddaughters, Makayla and Kelsey, with her, and Makayla had squirmed away from the table and was playing with a plastic sign that read CAUTION WET FLOOR. Betty often takes care of her grandchildren for her son and her daughter-in-law. Things are tight. The little windfall from their recordings helps, especially since Dot's husband is in poor health and can't work, and Betty's husband was killed in a motorcycle accident six years ago, and Helen is unable to work because of her depression.

For the Wiggins, music was never simple and carefree, and it still isn't. Helen doesn't go out much, so I spoke with her on the phone, and she told me that she hadn't played music since her father died but that country and western echoed in her head all the time, maddeningly so, and so loud that it made it hard for her to talk. When I asked Betty if she still liked music, she thought for a moment and then said that her husband's death had drawn her to country music. Whenever she feels bereft, she sings broken-hearted songs along with the radio. Just then, Makayla began hollering. Betty shushed her and said, "She really does have some kind of voice." A look flickered across her face. "I think, well, maybe she'll take voice lessons someday."

Dot is the only one who is still attached to her father's dream. She played the handbells in her church choir until recently, when she began taking care of one of Helen's children in addition to her own two sons and no longer had the time. She said that she's been writing lyrics for the last two years and hopes to finish them, and to compose the music for them. In the meantime, Terry Adams, of NRBQ, says he has enough material left from the Fleetwood Studio recording sessions for a few more CDs, and he has films of the town hall concerts that he plans to synchronize with sound. The Shaggs, thirty years late, may yet make it big, the way Austin saw it in his dreams. But even that might not have been enough to sate him. The Shaggs must have known this all along. In "Philosophy of the World," the song they never could play to his satisfaction, they sang:

> *It doesn't matter what you do*
> *It doesn't matter what you say*
> *There will always be one who wants things the opposite way*
> *We do our best, we try to please*
> *But we're like the rest we're never at ease*
> *You can never please*
> *Anybody*
> *In this world.*

Tom Wolfe

from The Right Stuff

Yeager

Anyone who travels very much on airlines in the United States soon gets to know the voice of *the airline pilot* . . . coming over the intercom . . . with a particular drawl, a particular folksiness, a particular down-home calmness that is so exaggerated it begins to parody itself (nevertheless!—it's reassuring) . . . the voice that tells you, as the airliner is caught in thunderheads and goes bolting up and down a thousand feet at a single gulp, to check your seat belts because "it might get a little choppy" . . . the voice that tells you (on a flight from Phoenix preparing for its final approach into Kennedy Airport, New York, just after dawn): "Now, folks, uh . . . this is the captain . . . ummmm . . . We've got a little ol' red light up here on the control panel that's tryin' to tell us that the *landin'* gears're not . . . uh . . . *lockin'* into position when we lower 'em . . . Now . . . *I* don't believe that little ol' red light knows what it's *talkin'* about—I believe it's that little ol' red light that iddn' workin' right" . . . faint chuckle, long pause, as if to say, *I'm not even sure all this is really worth going into—still, it may amuse you* . . . "But . . . I guess to play it by the rules, we oughta *humor* that little ol' light . . . so we're gonna take her down to about, oh, two or three hundred feet over the runway at Kennedy, and the folks down there on the ground are gonna see if they caint give us a visual inspection of those ol' landin' gears"—with which he is obviously on intimate ol'-buddy terms, as with every other working part of this mighty ship—"and if I'm right . . . they're gonna tell us everything is cop*acetic* all the way aroun' an' we'll jes take her on in" . . . and, after a couple of low passes over the field, the voice returns: "Well, folks, those folks down there on the ground—it must be too early for 'em or somethin'—I'spect they still got the *sleepers* in their eyes . . . 'cause they say they caint tell if those ol' landin' gears are all the way down or not . . . But, you know, up here in the cockpit we're convinced they're all the way down, so we're jes gonna take her on in . . . And oh" . . . (*I almost forgot*) . . . "while we take a little swing out over the ocean an' empty some of that surplus fuel we're not gonna be needin' anymore—that's what you might be seein' comin' out of the wings—our lovely little ladies . . . if they'll be so kind . . . they're gonna go up and down the aisles and show you how we do what we call 'assumin' the position'" . . . another faint chuckle (*We do this so often, and it's so much fun, we even have a funny little name for it*) . . . and the stewardesses, a bit grimmer, by the looks of them, than *that voice*, start telling the passengers to take their glasses off and take the ballpoint pens and other sharp objects out of their pockets, and they show them *the position*, with the head lowered . . . while down on the field at Kennedy the little yellow emergency trucks start roaring across the field—and even though in your pounding heart and your sweating palms and your broiling brainpan you *know* this is a critical moment in your life, you still can't quite bring yourself to *believe* it, because if it were . . . how could *the captain*, the man who knows the actual situation most intimately . . . how could he keep on drawlin' and chucklin' and driftin' and lollygaggin' in that particular voice of his—

Well!—who doesn't know that voice! And who can forget it!—even after he is proved right and the emergency is over.

That particular voice may sound vaguely Southern or Southwestern, but it is specifically Appalachian in origin. It originated in the mountains of West Virginia, in the coal country, in Lincoln County, so far up in the hollows that, as the saying went, "they had to pipe in daylight." In the late 1940's and early 1950's this up-hollow voice drifted down from on high, from over the high desert of California, down, down, down, from the upper reaches of the Brotherhood into all phases of American aviation. It was amazing. It was *Pygmalion* in reverse. Military pilots and then, soon, airline pilots, pilots from Maine and Massachusetts and the Dakotas and Oregon and everywhere else, began to talk in that poker-hollow West Virginia drawl, or as close to it as they could bend their native accents. It was the drawl of the most righteous of all the possessors of the right stuff: Chuck Yeager.

Yeager had started out as the equivalent, in the Second World War, of the legendary Frank Luke of the 27th Aero Squadron in the First. Which is to say, he was the boon-docker, the boy from the back country, with only a high-school education, no credentials, no cachet or polish of any sort, who took off the feed-store overalls and put on a uniform and climbed into an airplane and lit up the skies over Europe.

Yeager grew up in Hamlin, West Virginia, a town on the Mud River not far from Nitro, Hurricane Whirlwind, Salt Rock, Mud, Sod, Crum, Leet, Dollie, Ruth, and Alum Creek. His father was a gas driller (drilling for natural gas in the coalfields), his older brother was a gas driller, and he would have been a gas driller had he not enlisted in the Army Air Force in 1941 at the age of eighteen. In 1943, at twenty, he became a flight officer, i.e., a non-com who was allowed to fly, and went to England to fly fighter planes over France and Germany. Even in the tumult of the war Yeager was somewhat puzzling to a lot of other pilots. He was a short, wiry, but muscular little guy with dark curly hair and a tough-looking face that seemed (to strangers) to be saying: "You best not be lookin' me in the eye, you peckerwood, or I'll put four more holes in your nose." But that wasn't what was puzzling. What was puzzling was the way Yeager talked. He seemed to talk with some older forms of English elocution, syntax, and conjugation that had been preserved uphollow in the Appalachians. There were people up there who never said they disapproved of anything, they said: "I don't hold with it." In the present tense they were willing to *help* out, like anyone else; but in the past tense they only *holped.* "H'it weren't nothin' I hold with, but I holped him out with it, anyways."

In his first eight missions, at the age of twenty, Yeager shot down two German fighters. On his ninth he was shot down over German-occupied French territory, suffering flak wounds; he bailed out, was picked up by the French underground, which smuggled him across the Pyrenees into Spain disguised as a peasant. In Spain he was jailed briefly, then released, whereupon he made it back to England and returned to combat during the Allied invasion of France. On October 12, 1944, Yeager took on and shot down five German fighter planes in succession. On November 6, flying a propeller-driven P-51 Mustang, he shot down one of the new jet fighters the Germans had developed, the Messerschmit-262, and damaged two more, and on November 20 he shot down four FW-190s. It was a true Frank Luke-style display of warrior fury and personal prowess. By the end of the war he had thirteen and a half kills. He was twenty-two years old.

In 1946 and 1947 Yeager was trained as a test pilot at Wright Field in Dayton. He amazed his instructors with his ability at stunt-team flying, not to mention the unofficial business of hassling. That plus his up-hollow drawl had everybody saying, "He's a natural-born stick 'n' rudder man." Nevertheless, there was something extraordinary about it when a man so young, with so little experience in flight test, was selected to go to Muroc Field in California for the XS-1 project.

Muroc was up in the high elevations of the Mojave Desert. It looked like some fossil landscape that had long since been left behind by the rest of terrestrial evolution. It was full of huge dry lake beds, the biggest being Rogers Lake. Other than sagebrush the only vegetation was Joshua trees, twisted freaks of the plant world that looked like a cross between cactus and Japanese bonsai. They had a dark petrified green color and horribly crippled branches. At dusk the Joshua trees stood out in silhouette on the fossil wasteland like some arthritic nightmare. In the summer the temperature went up to 110 degrees as a matter of course, and the dry lake beds were covered in sand, and there would be windstorms and sandstorms right out of a Foreign Legion movie. At night it would drop to near freezing, and in December it would start raining, and the dry lakes would fill up with a few inches of water, and some sort of putrid prehistoric shrimps would work their way up from out of the ooze, and sea gulls would come flying in a hundred miles or more from the ocean, over the mountains, to gobble up these squirming little throwbacks. A person had to see it to believe it: flocks of sea gulls wheeling around in the air out in the middle of the high desert in the dead of winter and grazing on antediluvian crustaceans in the primordial ooze.

When the wind blew the few inches of water back and forth across the lake beds, they became absolutely smooth and level. And when the water evaporated in the spring, and the sun baked the ground hard, the lake beds became the greatest natural landing fields ever discovered, and also the biggest, with miles of room for error. That was highly desirable, given the nature of the enterprise at Muroc.

Besides the wind, sand, tumbleweed, and Joshua trees, there was nothing at Muroc except for two quonset-style hangars, side by side, a couple of gasoline pumps, a single concrete runway, a few tarpaper shacks, and some tents. The officers stayed in the shacks marked "barracks," and lesser souls stayed in the tents and froze all night and fried all day. Every road into the property had a guardhouse on it manned by soldiers. The enterprise the Army had undertaken in this godforsaken place was the development of supersonic jet and rocket planes.

At the end of the war the Army had discovered that the Germans not only had the world's first jet fighter but also a rocket plane that had gone 596 miles an hour in tests. Just after the war a British jet, the Gloster Meteor, jumped the official world speed record from 469 to 606 in a single day. The next great plateau would be Mach 1, the speed of sound, and the Army Air Force considered it crucial to achieve it first.

The speed of sound, Mach 1, was known (thanks to the work of the physicist Ernst Mach) to vary at different altitudes, temperatures, and wind speeds. On a calm 60-degree day at sea level it was about 760 miles an hour, while at 40,000 feet, where the temperature would be at least sixty below, it was about 660 miles an hour. Evil and baffling things happened in the transonic zone, which began at about .7 Mach. Wind tunnels choked out at such velocities. Pilots who approached the speed of sound in dives reported that the controls would lock or "freeze" or even alter their normal functions. Pilots had crashed and died because they couldn't budge the stick. Just last year Geoffrey de Havilland, son of the famous British aircraft designer and builder, had tried to take one of his father's DH 108s to Mach 1. The ship started buffeting and then disintegrated, and he was killed. This led engineers to speculate that the shock waves became so severe and unpredictable at Mach 1, no aircraft could survive them. They started talking about "the sonic wall" and "the sound barrier."

So this was the task that a handful of pilots, engineers, and mechanics had at Muroc. The place was utterly primitive, nothing but bare bones, bleached tarpaulins, and corrugated tin rippling in the heat with caloric waves; and for an ambitious young pilot it was perfect. Muroc seemed like an outpost on the dome of the world, open only to a righteous few, closed off to the rest of humanity, including even the Army Air Force brass of command control, which was at Wright Field. The commanding officer at Muroc was only a colonel, and his superiors at Wright did not relish junkets to the Muroc rat shacks in the first place. But to pilots this prehistoric throwback of an airfield became . . . shrimp heaven! the ratshack plains of Olympus!

Low Rent Septic Tank Perfection . . . yes; and not excluding those traditional essentials for the blissful hot young pilot: Flying & Drinking and Drinking & Driving.

Just beyond the base, to the southwest, there was a rickety wind-blown 1930's-style establishment called Pancho's Fly Inn, owned, run, and bartended by a woman named Pancho Barnes. Pancho Barnes wore tight white sweaters and tight pants, after the mode of Barbara Stanwyck in *Double Indemnity*. She was only forty-one when Yeager arrived at Muroc, but her face was so weather-beaten, had so many hard miles on it, that she looked older, especially to the young pilots at the base. She also shocked the pants off them with her vulcanized tongue. Everybody she didn't like was an old bastard or a sonofabitch. People she liked were old bastards and sonsabitches, too. "I tol' 'at ol' bastard to get 'is ass on over here and I'd g'im a drink." But Pancho Barnes was anything but Low Rent. She was the granddaughter of the man who designed the old Mount Lowe cable-car system, Thaddeus S. C. Lowe. Her maiden name was Florence Leontine Lowe. She was brought up in San Marino, which adjoined Pasadena and was one of Los Angeles' wealthiest suburbs, and her first husband—she was married four times—was the pastor of the Pasadena Episcopal Church, the Rev. C. Rankin Barnes. Mrs. Barnes seemed to have few of the conventional community interests of a Pasadena matron. In the late 1920's, by boat and plane, she ran guns for Mexican revolutionaries and picked up the nickname Pancho. In 1930 she broke Amelia Earhart's air-speed record for women. Then she barnstormed around the country as the featured performer of "Pancho Barnes's

Mystery Circus of the Air." She always greeted her public in jodhpurs and riding boots, a flight jacket, a white scarf, and a white sweater that showed off her terrific Barbara Stanwyck chest. Pancho's desert Fly Inn had an airstrip, a swimming pool, a dude ranch corral, plenty of acreage for horseback riding, a big old guest house for the lodgers, and a connecting building that was the bar and restaurant. In the barroom the floors, the tables, the chairs, the walls, the beams, the bar were of the sort known as extremely weatherbeaten, and the screen doors kept banging. Nobody putting together such a place for a movie about flying in the old days would ever dare make it as dilapidated and generally go-to-hell as it actually was. Behind the bar were many pictures of airplanes and pilots, lavishly autographed and inscribed, badly framed and crookedly hung. There was an old piano that had been dried out and cracked to the point of hopeless desiccation. On a good night a huddle of drunken aviators could be heard trying to bang, slosh, and navigate their way through old Cole Porter tunes. On average nights the tunes were not that good to start with. When the screen door banged and a man walked through the door into the saloon, every eye in the place checked him out. If he wasn't known as somebody who had something to do with flying at Muroc, he would be eyed like some lame goddamned mouseshit sheepherder from *Shane*.

The plane the Air Force wanted to break the sound barrier with was called the X-I at the outset and later on simply the X-I. The Bell Aircraft Corporation had built it under an Army contract. The core of the ship was a rocket of the type first developed by a young Navy inventor, Robert Truax, during the war. The fuselage was shaped like a 50-caliber bullet—an object that was known to go supersonic smoothly. Military pilots seldom drew major test assignments; they went to highly paid civilians working for the aircraft corporations. The prime pilot for the X-I was a man whom Bell regarded as the best of the breed. This man looked like a movie star. He looked like a pilot from out of *Hell's Angels*. And on top of everything else there was his name: Slick Goodlin.

The idea in testing the X-I was to nurse it carefully into the transonic zone, up to seven-tenths, eight-tenths, nine-tenths the speed of sound (.7 Mach, .8 Mach, .9 Mach) before attempting the speed of sound itself, Mach 1, even though Bell and the Army already knew the X-I had the rocket power to go to Mach 1 and beyond, if there *was* any *beyond*. The consensus of aviators and engineers, after Geoffrey de Havilland's death, was that the speed of sound was an absolute, like the firmness of the earth. The sound barrier was a farm you could buy in the sky. So Slick Goodlin began to probe the transonic zone in the X-I, going up to .8 Mach. Every time he came down he'd have a riveting tale to tell. The buffeting, it was so fierce—and the listeners, their imaginations aflame, could practically see poor Geoffrey de Havilland disintegrating in midair. And the goddamned aerodynamics—and the listeners got a picture of a man in ballroom pumps skidding across a sheet of ice, pursued by bears. A controversy arose over just how much bonus Slick Goodlin should receive for assaulting the dread Mach 1 itself. Bonuses for contract test pilots were not unusual; but the figure of $150,000 was now bruited about. The Army balked, and Yeager got the job. He took it for $283 a month, or $3,396 a year; which is to say, his regular Army captain's pay.

The only trouble they had with Yeager was in holding him back. On his first powered flight in the X-I he immediately executed an unauthorized zero-g roll with a full load of rocket fuel, then stood the ship on its tail and went up to .85 Mach in a vertical climb, also unauthorized. On subsequent flights, at speeds between .85 Mach and .9 Mach, Yeager ran into most known airfoil problems— loss of elevator, aileron, and rudder control, heavy trim pressures, Dutch rolls, pitching and buffeting, the lot—yet was convinced, after edging ever .9 Mach, that this would all get better, not worse, as you reached Mach 1. The attempt to push beyond Mach 1—"breaking the sound barrier"—was set for October 14, 1947. Not being an engineer, Yeager didn't believe the "barrier" existed.

October 14 was a Tuesday. On Sunday evening, October 12, Chuck Yeager dropped in at Pancho's along with his wife. She was a brunette named Glennis, whom he had met in California while he was in training, and she was such a number, so striking, he had the inscription "Glamorous Glennis" written on the nose of his P-51 in Europe and, just a few weeks back, on the X-I itself. Yeager didn't go to Pancho's and knock back a few because two days later the big test was coming up. Nor did he knock back a few because it was the weekend. No, he knocked back a few because night had come and he was a pilot at Muroc. In keeping with the military tradition of Flying & Drinking, that was what you did, for no other reason than that the sun had gone down. You went to Pancho's and knocked back a few and listened to the screen doors banging and to other aviators torturing the piano and the nation's repertoire of Familiar Favorites and to lonesome mouse-turd strangers wandering in through the banging doors and to Pancho classifying the whole bunch of them as old bastards and miserable peckerwoods. That was what you did if you were a pilot at Muroc and the sun went down.

So about eleven Yeager got the idea that it would be a hell of a kick if he and Glennis saddled up a couple of Pancho's dude-ranch horses and went for a romp, a little rat race, in the moonlight. This was in keeping with the military tradition of Flying & Drinking and Drinking & Driving, except that this was prehistoric Muroc and you rode horses. So Yeager and his wife set off on a little proficiency run at full gallop through the desert in the moon-light amid the arthritic silhouettes of the Joshua trees. Then they start racing back to the corral, with Yeager in the lead and heading for the gateway. Given the prevailing conditions, it being nighttime, at Pancho's, and his head being filled with a black sandstorm of many badly bawled songs and vulcanized oaths, he sees too late that the gate has been closed. Like many a hard-driving midnight pilot before him, he does not realize that he is not equally gifted in the control of all forms of locomotion. He and the horse hit the gate, and he goes flying off and lands on his right side. His side hurts like hell.

The next day, Monday, his side still hurts like hell. It hurts every time he moves. It hurts every time he breathes deep. It hurts every time he moves his right arm. He knows that if he goes to a doctor at Muroc or says anything to anybody even remotely connected with his superiors, he will be scrubbed from the flight on Tuesday. They might even go so far as to put some other miserable peckerwood in his place. So he gets on his motorcycle, an old junker that Pancho had given him, and rides over to see a doctor in the town of Rosamond, near where he lives. Every time the goddamned motorcycle hits a pebble in the road, his side hurts like a sonofabitch. The doctor in Rosamond informs him he has two broken ribs and he tapes them up and tells him that if he'll just keep his right arm immobilized for a couple of weeks and avoid any physical exertion or sudden movements, he should be all right.

Yeager gets up before daybreak on Tuesday morning—which is supposed to be the day he tries to break the sound barrier—and his ribs still hurt like a sonofabitch. He gets his wife to drive him over to the field, and he has to keep his right arm pinned down to his side to keep his ribs from hurting so much. At dawn, on the day of a flight, you could hear the X-I screaming long before you got there. The fuel for the X-I was alcohol and liquid oxygen, oxygen converted from a gas to a liquid by lowering its temperature to 297 degrees below zero. And when the lox, as it was called, rolled out of the hoses and into the belly of the X-I, it started boiling off and the X-I started steaming and screaming like a teakettle. There's quite a crowd on hand, by Muroc standards . . . perhaps nine or ten souls. They're still fueling the X-I with the lox, and the beast is wailing.

The X-I looked like a fat orange swallow with white markings. But it was really just a length of pipe with four rocket chambers in it. It had a tiny cockpit and a needle nose, two little straight blades (only three and a half inches thick at the thickest part) for wings, and a tail assembly set up high to avoid the "sonic wash" from the wings. Even though his side was throbbing and his right arm felt practically useless, Yeager figured he could grit his teeth and get through the flight—except for one specific move he had to make. In the rocket launches, the X-1, which held only two and a half minutes' worth of fuel, was carried up to twenty-six thousand feet underneath a B-29. At seven thousand feet, Yeager was to climb down a ladder from the bomb bay of the B-29 to the open doorway of the X-1, hook up to the oxygen system and the radio microphone and earphones, and put his crash helmet on and prepare for the launch, which would come at twenty-five thousand feet. This helmet was a homemade number. There had never been any such thing as a crash helmet before, except in stunt flying. Throughout the war pilots had used the old skin-tight leather helmet-and-goggles. But the X-1 had a way of throwing the pilot around so violently that there was danger of getting knocked out against the walls of the cockpit. So Yeager had bought a big leather football helmet—there were no plastic ones at the time—and he butchered it with a hunting knife until he carved the right kind of holes in it, so that it would fit down over his regular flying helmet and the earphones and the oxygen rig. Anyway, then his flight engineer, Jack Ridley, would climb down the ladder, out in the breeze, and shove into place the cockpit door, which had to be lowered out of the belly of the B-29 on a chain. Then Yeager had to push a handle to lock the door airtight. Since the X-1's cockpit was minute, you had to push the handle with your right hand. It took quite a shove. There was no way you could move into position to get enough leverage with your left hand.

Out in the hangar Yeager makes a few test shoves on the sly, and the pain is so incredible he realizes that there is no way a man with two broken ribs is going to get the door closed. It is time to confide in somebody, and the logical man is Jack Ridley. Ridley is not only the flight engineer but a pilot himself and a good old boy from Oklahoma to boot. He will understand about Flying & Drinking and Drinking & Driving through the goddamned Joshua trees. So Yeager takes Ridley off to the side in the tin hangar and says: Jack, I got me a little ol' problem here. Over at Pancho's the other night I sorta . . . dinged my goddamned ribs. Ridley says, Whattya mean . . . *dinged?* Yeager says, Well, I guess you might say I damned near like to . . . *broke* a coupla the sonsabitches. Whereupon Yeager sketches out the problem he foresees.

Not for nothing is Ridley the engineer on this project. He has an inspiration. He tells a janitor named Sam to cut him about nine inches off a broom handle. When nobody's looking, he slips the broomstick into the cockpit of the X-1 and gives Yeager a little advice and counsel.

So with that added bit of supersonic flight gear Yeager went aloft.

At seven thousand feet he climbed down the ladder into the X-1's cockpit, clipped on his hoses and lines, and managed to pull the pumpkin football helmet over his head. Then Ridley came down the ladder and lowered the door into place. As Ridley had instructed, Yeager now took the nine inches of broomstick and slipped it between the handle and the door. This gave him just enough mechanical advantage to reach over with his left hand and whang the thing shut. So he whanged the door shut with Ridley's broomstick and was ready to fly.

At 26,000 feet the B-29 went into a shallow dive, then pulled up and released Yeager and the X-1 as if it were a bomb. Like a bomb it dropped and shot forward (at the speed of the mother ship) at the same time. Yeager had been launched straight into the sun. It seemed to be no more than six feet in front of him, filling up the sky and blinding him. But he managed to get his bearings and set off the four rocket chambers one after the other. He then experienced something that became known as the ultimate sensation in flying: "booming and zooming." The surge of the rockets was so tremendous, forced him back into his seat so violently, he could hardly move his hands forward the few inches necessary to reach the controls. The X-1 seemed to shoot straight up in an absolutely perpendicular trajectory, as if determined to snap the hold of gravity via the most direct route possible. In fact, he was only climbing at the 45-degree angle called for in the flight plan. At about .87 Mach the buffeting started.

On the ground the engineers could no longer see Yeager. They could only hear . . . that poker-hollow West Virginia drawl.

"Had a mild buffet there . . . jes the usual instability . . . "

Jes the usual instability?

Then the X-I reached the speed of .96 Mach, and that incredible caint-hardlyin' awshuckin' drawl said:

"Say, Ridley . . . make a note here, will ya?" (*if you ain't got nothin' better to do*) " . . . elevator effectiveness *re*-gained."

Just as Yeager had predicted, as the X-I approached Mach 1, the stability improved. Yeager had his eyes pinned on the machometer. The needle reached .96, fluctuated, and went off the scale.

And on the ground they heard . . . that voice:

"Say, Ridley . . . make another note, will ya?" (*if you ain't too bored yet*) " . . . there's somethin' wrong with this ol' machometer . . . " (faint chuckle) " . . . it's gone kinda screwy on me . . . "

And in that moment, on the ground, they heard a boom rock over the desert floor—just as the physicist Theodore von Kármán had predicted many years before.

Then they heard Ridley back in the B-29: "If it is, Chuck, we'll fix it. Personally I think you're seeing things."

Then they heard Yeager's poker-hollow drawl again:

"Well, I guess I am, Jack . . . And I'm still goin' upstairs like a bat."

The X-I had gone through "the sonic wall" without so much as a bump. As the speed topped out at Mach 1.05, Yeager had the sensation of shooting straight through the top of the sky. The sky turned a deep purple and all at once the stars and the moon came out—and the sun shone at the same time. He had reached a layer of the upper atmosphere where the air was too thin to contain reflecting dust particles. He was simply looking out into space. As the X-I nosed over at the top of the climb, Yeager now had seven minutes of . . . Pilot Heaven . . . ahead of him. He was going faster than any man in history, and it was almost silent up here, since he had exhausted his rocket fuel, and he was so high in such a vast space that there was no sensation of motion. He was master of the sky. His was a king's solitude, unique and inviolate, above the dome of the world. It would take him seven minutes to glide back down and land at Muroc. He spent the time doing victory rolls and wing-over-wing aerobatics while Rogers Lake and the High Sierras spun around below.

On the ground they had understood the code as soon as they heard Yeager's little exchange with Ridley. The project was secret, but the radio exchanges could be picked up by anyone within range. The business of the "screwy machometer" was Yeager's deadpan way of announcing that the X-I's instruments indicated Mach 1. As soon as he landed, they checked out the X-I's automatic recording instruments. Without any doubt the ship had gone supersonic. They immediately called the brass at Wright Field to break the tremendous news. Within two hours Wright Field called back and gave some firm orders. A top security lid was being put on the morning's events. That the press was not to be informed went without saying. But neither was anyone else, anyone at all, to be told. Word of the flight was not to go beyond the flight line. And even among the people directly involved—who were there and knew about it, anyway—there was to be no celebrating. Just what was on the minds of the brass at Wright is hard to say. Much of it, no doubt, was a simple holdover from wartime, when every breakthrough of possible strategic importance was kept under wraps. That was what you did—you shut up about them. Another possibility was that the chief at Wright had never quite known what to make of Muroc. There was some sort of weird ribald aerial tarpaper mad-monk squadron up on the roof of the desert out there . . .

In any case, by mid-afternoon Yeager's tremendous feat had become a piece of thunder with no reverberation. A strange and implausible stillness settled over the event. Well . . . there was not supposed to be any celebration, but come nightfall . . . Yeager and Ridley and some of the others ambled over to Pancho's. After all, it was the end of the day, and they were pilots. So they knocked back a few. And they had to let Pancho in on the secret, because Pancho had said she'd serve a free steak dinner to any pilot who could fly supersonic and walk in here to tell about it, and they had to see the look on *her* face. So Pancho served Yeager a big steak dinner and said they were a buncha miserable peckerwoods all the same, and the desert cooled off and the wind came up and the screen doors banged and they drank some more and bawled some songs over the cackling dry piano and the stars and the moon came out and Pancho screamed oaths no one had ever heard before and Yeager and Ridley roared and the old weatherbeaten bar boomed and the autographed pictures of a hundred dead pilots shook and clattered on the frame wires and the faces of the living fell apart in the reflections, and by and by they all left and stumbled and staggered and yelped and bayed for glory before the arthritic silhouettes of the Joshua trees. Shit!—there was no one to tell except for Pancho and the goddamned Joshua trees!

Craft Essays

Tracy Kidder

Making the Truth Believable

When I started writing nonfiction a couple of decades ago there was an idea in the air, which for me had the force of a revelation: that all journalism was inevitably subjective. I was in my 20s then, and although my behavior was somewhat worse than it has been recently, I was quite a moralist. I decided that writers of nonfiction had a moral obligation to write in the first person—really write in the first person, making themselves characters on the page. In this way, I would disclose my biases. I would not hide the truth from the reader. I would proclaim that what I wrote was just my own impression of events. In retrospect it seems clear that this prescription for honesty often served as a license for self-absorption on the page. I was too young and self-absorbed to realize what should have been obvious: that I was less likely to write honestly about myself than about anyone else on earth.

I wrote a book about a murder case in a swashbuckling first person. After it was published and disappeared without a trace, I went back to writing nonfiction articles for the *Atlantic Monthly*, under the tutelage of Richard Todd, then a young editor there. For about 5 years, during which I didn't dare attempt another book, I worked on creating what many writer friends of mine call "voice." I didn't do this consciously. If I had, I probably wouldn't have gotten anywhere. But gradually, I think, I found a writing voice, the voice of a person who was informed, fair-minded, and always temperate—the voice, not of the person I was, but of the person I wanted to be. Then I went back to writing books, and discovered other points of view besides the first person.

Choosing a point of view is a matter of finding the best place to stand, from which to tell a story. The process shouldn't be determined by theory, but driven by immersion in the material itself. The choice of point of view, I've come to think, has nothing to do with morality. It's a choice among tools. On the other hand, the wrong choice can lead to dishonesty. Point of view is primary; it affects everything else, including voice. I've made my choices by instinct sometimes and sometimes by experiment. Most of my memories of time spent writing have merged together in a blur, but I remember vividly my first attempts to find a way to write *Among Schoolchildren,* a book about an inner-city teacher. I had spent a year inside her classroom. I intended, vaguely, to fold into my account of events I'd witnessed there a great deal about the lives of particular children and about the problems of education in America. I tried every point of view that I'd used in previous books, and every page I wrote felt lifeless and remote. Finally, I hit on a restricted third-person narration.

That approach seemed to work. The world of that classroom seemed to come alive when the view of it was restricted mainly to observations of the teacher and to accounts of what the teacher saw and heard and smelled and felt. This choice narrowed my options. I ended up writing something less comprehensive than I'd planned. The book became essentially an account of a year in the emotional life of a schoolteacher.

My choice of the restricted third person also obliged me to write parts of the book as if from within the teacher's mind. I wrote many sentences that contained the phrase "she thought." I felt I could do so because the teacher had told me how she felt and what she thought about almost everything that happened in her classroom. And her descriptions of her thoughts and feeling never seemed self-serving. Believing in them myself, I thought that I could make them believable on the page.

For me, part of the pleasure of reading comes from the awareness that an author stands behind the scenes adroitly pulling the strings. But the pleasure quickly palls at painful reminders of that presence—the times when, for instance, I sense that the author strains to produce yet another clever metaphor. Then I stop believing in what I read, and usually stop reading. Belief is what a reader offers an author, what Coleridge famously called "That willing suspension of disbelief for the moment, which constitutes poetic faith." All writers have to find ways to do their work without disappointing readers into withdrawing belief.

In fiction, believability may have nothing to do with reality or even plausibility. In nonflction, it has everything to do with those things.

I think that the nonfiction writer's fundamental job is to make what is true believable. But for some writers lately the job has clearly become more varied: to make believable what the writer thinks is true (if the writer wants to be scrupulous); to make believable what the writer wishes were true (if the writer isn't interested in scrupulosity); or to make believable what the writer thinks might be true (if the writer couldn't get the story and had to make it up).

I figure that if I call a piece of my own writing nonfiction it ought to be about real people, with their real names attached whenever possible, who say and do in print nothing that they didn't actually say and do. On the cover page of my new book I put a note that reads, "This is a work of nonfiction," and I listed the several names that I was obliged to change in the text. I feared that a longer note would stand between the reader and the spell that I wanted to create, inviting the reader into the world of a nursing home. But the definition of "nonfiction" has become so slippery that I wonder if I shouldn't have written more. So now I'll take this opportunity to explain that I spent a year doing research, that the name of the place I wrote about is its real name, that I didn't change the names of any major characters, and that I didn't invent dialogue or put any thoughts in characters' minds that the characters themselves didn't confess to.

I no longer care what rules other writers set for themselves. If I don't like what someone has written, I can stop reading, which is, after all, the worst punishment a writer can suffer. But the expanded definitions of "nonfiction" have created problems for those writers who define the term narrowly. Many readers now view with suspicion every narrative that claims to be nonfiction. But not all writers make up their stories or the details in them. In fact, scores of very good writers do not—writers such as John McPhee (*Coming into the Country*), Jane Kramer (*The Last Cowboy*), J. Anthony Lukas (*Common Ground*). There are also special cases, which confound categories and all attempts to lay down rules for narrative. I have in mind especially Norman Mailer's *Executioner's Song,* a hybrid of fact and fiction, labeled as such, which I loved reading.

Most writers lack Mailer's powers of invention. Some nonfiction writers do not lack his willingness to invent, but the candor to admit it. Some writers proceed by trying to discover the truth about a situation, and then invent the facts as necessary. Even in these suspicious times, a writer can get away with this. Often no one will know, and the subjects of the story may not care. They may approve. They may not notice. But the writer always knows. I believe in immersion in the events of a story. I take it on faith that the truth lies in the events somewhere, and that immersion in those real events will yield glimpses of that truth. I try to hew to a narrow definition of nonfiction partly in that faith and partly out of fear. I'm afraid that if I started making things up in a story that purported to be about real events and people, I'd stop believing it myself. And I imagine that such a loss of conviction would infect every sentence and make each one unbelievable.

I don't mean to imply that all a person has to do to write good nonfiction is to take accurate notes and reproduce them. The kind of nonfiction I like to read is at bottom storytelling, as gracefully accomplished as good fiction. I don't think any technique should be ruled out to achieve it well. For myself, I rule out only invention. But I don't think that honesty and artifice are contradictory. They work together in good writing of every sort. Artfulness and an author's justified belief in a story can produce the most believable nonfiction.

Phillip Lopate

On the Necessity of Turning Oneself into a Character

In personal essays, nothing is more commonly met than the letter *I.* I think it a perfectly good word, one no writer should be ashamed to use. Especially is first person legitimate for this form, so drawn to the particulars of character and voice. The problem with "I" is not that it is in bad taste, but that fledgling personal essayists may think they've said or conveyed more than they actually have with that one syllable. In their minds, that "I" is swarming with background and a lush, sticky past, and an almost too fatal specificity, whereas the reader, encountering it for the first time in a new piece, sees only a slender telephone pole standing in the sentence, trying to catch a few signals to send on. In truth, even the barest "I" holds a whisper of promised engagement, and can suggest a caress in the midst of more stolid language. What it doesn't do, however, is give us a clear picture of who is speaking.

To do that, the writer needs to build herself into a character. And I use the word *character* much the same way the fiction writer does. E.M. Forster, in *Aspects of the Novel,* drew a famous distinction between "flat" and "round" characters—between those fictional personages seen from the outside who acted with the predicable consistency of caricatures, and those whose complexities or teeming inner lives we came to know. But whether the writer chooses to present characters as flat or round, or a combination, the people on the page—it scarcely matters whether they appear in fiction or nonfiction—will need to become knowable enough in their broad outlines to behave "believably," at the same time as free willed enough to intrigue us with surprises. The art of characterization comes down to establishing a pattern of habits and actions for the person you are writing about and introducing variations into the system. In this respect, building a character is a pedagogic model, because you are teaching the reader what to expect.

So how do you turn *yourself* into a character? First of all, you need to have—or acquire—some distance from yourself. If you are so panicked by any examination of your flaws that all you can do is sputter defensively when you feel yourself attacked, you are not going to get very far in the writing of personal essays. You need to be able to see yourself from the ceiling: to know, for instance, how you are coming across in social situations, and to assess accurately when you are charming, and when you seem pushy, mousy, or ridiculous. From the viewpoint of honest essay writing, it is just as unsatisfactorily distorting to underrate yourself all the time, and think you are far less effective than you actually are, than to give yourself too much credit. The point is to begin to take inventory of yourself so that you can present that self to the reader as a specific, legible character.

A good place to start is your quirks. These are the idiosyncrasies, stubborn tics, antisocial mannerisms, and so on that set you apart from the majority of your fellowmen. There will be more than enough time later to assert your common humanity, or better yet, to let the reader make the mental bridge between your oddities and those of everyone else. But to establish credibility, you would do well to resist coming across at first as absolutely average. Who wants to read about that bland creature, the regular Joe? The mistake many beginning essayists make is to try so hard to be likable and nice, to fit in, that the reader, craving stronger stuff (at the very least, a tone of authority), gets bored. Literature is not a place for conformists, organization men. The skills of the kaffeeklatsch—restraining one's expressiveness, rounding out one's edges, sparing everyone's feelings—will not work as well on the page.

The irony is that most of us suspect—no, we *know*—that underneath it all we *are* common as dirt. But we may still need to maximize that pitiful set of quirks, those small differences that seem to set us apart from others, and project them theatrically, the way actors work with singularities in their physical appearances or vocal textures. In order to turn ourselves into characters, we need to *dramatize* ourselves. I don't mean inventing or adding colorful traits that aren't true; I mean positioning those that are already in us under the most clearly focused, sharply defined light. It's a subtractive process: you need to cut away the inessentials, and highlight just those features in your personality that lead to the most intense contradictions or ambivalence.

An essay needs conflict, just as a short story does. Without conflict, your essay will drift into static mode, repeating your initial observation in a self-satisfied way. What gives an essay dynamism is the need to work out some problem, especially a problem that is not easily resolved. Fortunately, human beings are conflicted animals, so there is no shortage of tensions that won't go away. Good essayists know how to select a topic in advance that will generate enough spark in itself, and how to frame the topic so that it will neither be too ambitious nor too slight—so that its scale will be appropriate for satisfying exploration. If you are serenely unconflicted when you first sit down to write an essay, you may find yourself running out of steam. If you take on a problem that is too philosophically large or historically convoluted, you may choke on the details and give up.

Still, these are technical issues, and I am inclined to think that what stands in the way of most personal essays is not technique but psychology. The emotional preparedness, if you will, to be honest and open to exposure.

The student essayist is torn between two contrasting extremes:

A. "I am so weird that I could never tell on the page what is really, secretly going on in my mind."
B. "I am so boring, nothing ever happens to me out of the ordinary, so who would want to read about me?"

Both extremes are rooted in shame, and both reflect a lack of worldliness. The first response ("I am so weird") exaggerates how isolated one is in one's "wicked" thoughts, instead of recognizing that everyone has strange, surreal, immoral notions. The second response ("My life is so boring and I'm so boring") requires a reeducation so that the student essayists can be brought to acknowledge just those moments in the day, in their loves and friendships, in their family dynamics, in their historical moments, in their interactions with the natural world, that remain genuinely perplexing, vexing, luminous, unresolved. In short, they must be nudged to recognize that life remains a mystery—even one's own so-called boring life. They must also be taught to recognize the charm of the ordinary: that daily life that has nourished some of the most enduring essays.

The use of literary or other models can be a great help in invoking life's mystery. I like to remind myself, as well as my students, of the tonal extremes available to us. It is useful to know we can rant as much as Dostoyevsky's Underground Man or Céline's narrators, that we can speak—as the poet Mayakovski says—"At the Top of My Voice." That we can be passionate as Hazlitt and Baldwin, or even whine, the way Joan Didion sometimes does, albeit with self-aware humor. It is useful to remind students, enamored of David Lynch or Quentin Tarantino movies, that some of that bizarre sensibility can find a place in their essays—that "outlaw" culture does not have to be left outside the schoolhouse. At the same time, it is necessary to introduce them to the sane, thoughtful, considered, responsible essayists like George Orwell or E.B. White. From both sets of models we can then choose how reasonable or hysterical we want to come across at any time: in one piece, seem the soul of reason; in another, a step away from the loony bin.

Mining our quirks is only the beginning of turning ourselves into characters. We are distinguished one from another as much by our pasts, the set of circumstances we are born into, as by the challenges we have encountered along the way, and how we choose to resolve them, given our initial stations in life. It means something very different to have been born the second-oldest boy in an upper-middle-class Korean family that emigrated from Seoul to Los Angeles than to have been born the youngest female in a poor Southern Baptist household of nine.

Ethnicity, gender, religion, class, geography, politics: these are all strong determinants in the development of character. Sometimes they can be made too much of, as in the worst sort of "identity politics," which seeks to explain away all the intangibles of a human being's destiny by this or that social oppression. But we must be bold in working with these categories as starting points: be not afraid to meditate on our membership in this or that community, and the degree to which it has or has not formed us.

When you are writing a memoir, you can set up these categories and assess their importance one by one, and go on from there. When you write personal essays, however, you can never assume that your readers will know a thing about your background, regardless of how many times you have explained it in previous essays. So you must become deft at inserting that information swiftly and casually—"I was born in Brooklyn, New York, of working-class parents"—and not worry about the fact that it may be redundant to your regular readers, if you're lucky enough to have any. In one essay, you may decide to make a big thing of your religious training and very little of your family background; in another, just the opposite; but in each new essay, it would be a good idea to tell the reader both, simply because this sort of information will help to build you into a character.

In this sense, the personal essayist must be like a journalist, who respects the obligation to get in the basic orienting facts—the who, what, where, when, and why—as close to the top of every story as possible.

So now you have sketched yourself to the reader as a person of a certain age, sex, ethnic and religious background, class, and region, possessing a set of quirks, foibles, strengths, and peculiarities. Are you yet a character? Maybe not: not until you have soldered your relationship with the reader, by springing vividly into his mind, so that everything your "I" says and does on the page seems somehow—oddly, piquantly—characteristic. The reader must find you amusing (there, I've said it). Amusing enough to follow you, no matter what essay topic you propose. Whether you are writing this time on world peace or a bar of soap, readers must sense quickly from the first paragraph that you are going to keep them engaged. The trouble is that you cannot amuse the reader unless you are already self-amused. And here we come to one of the main stumbling blocks placed before the writing of personal essays: self-hatred.

It is an observable fact that most people don't like themselves, in spite of being, for the most part, decent enough human beings—certainly not war criminals—and in spite of the many self-help books urging us to befriend and think positively about ourselves. Why this self-dislike should be so prevalent is a matter that would require the best sociological and psychoanalytic minds to elucidate; all I can say, from my vantage point as a teacher and anthologist of the personal essay, is that an odor of self-disgust mars many performances in this genre and keeps many would-be practitioners from developing into full-fledged professionals. They exhibit a form of stuttering, of never being able to get past the initial, superficial self-presentation and diving into the wreck of one's personality with gusto.

The proper alternative to self-dislike is not being pleased with oneself—a smugness equally distasteful to the reader—but being *curious about* oneself. Such self-curiosity (of which Montaigne, the father of the essay, was the greatest exemplar) can only grow out of that detachment or distance from oneself about which I spoke earlier.

I am convinced that self-amusement is a discipline that can be learned; it can be practiced even by people (such as myself) who have at times a strong self-dislike or at least self-mistrust. I may be tired of myself in everyday life, but once I start narrating a situation or set of ideas on the page, I begin to see my "I" in a comic light, and I maneuver him so that he will best amuse the reader. My "I" is not me, entirely, but a character drawn from aspects of myself, in somewhat the same way (less stylized or bold, perhaps) that Chaplin drew the Little Fellow or Jerry Lewis modeled the arrested-development goofball from their experiences. I am willing to let my "I" take his pratfalls; maintaining one's dignity should not be a paramount issue in personal essays. But first must come the urge to entertain the reader. From that impulse everything else follows.

There is also considerable character development in expressing your opinions, prejudices, half-baked ideas, etc., etc., provided you are willing to analyze the flaws in your thinking and to entertain arguments against your hobbyhorses and not be too solemn about it all. The essay thrives on daring, darting flights of thought. You must get in the habit of inviting, not censoring, your most far-fetched, mischievous notions, because even if they prove cockeyed, they may point to an element of truth that would otherwise be inaccessible. When, for instance, I wrote my essay "Against Joie de Vivre," I knew on some level that it was an indefensible position, but I wanted to see how far I could get in taking a curmudgeonly stance against the pursuit of happiness. And indeed, it struck a chord of recognition in many readers, because lots of us are "so glad to be unhappy," at least as much as we "want to be happy." (To quote two old songs.)

Finally, it would do well for personal essayists to follow another rule of fiction writers, who tell you that if you want to reveal someone's character, actions speak louder than words. Give your "I" something to do. It's fine to be privy to all of "I"'s ruminations and cerebral nuances, but consciousness can only take us so far in the illumination of character. Particularly if you are writing a memoir essay, with chronology and narrative, it is often liberating to have the "I" step beyond the observer role and be implicated crucially in the overall action. How many memoir pieces suffer from a self-righteous setup: the writer telling a story in which Mr. or Ms. "I" is the passive recipient of the world's cruelty, the character's first exposure to racism or betrayal, say. There is something off-putting about a nonfiction story in which the "I" character is right and all the others wrong, the "I" infinitely more sinned against than sinning. By showing our complicity in the world's stock of sorrow, we convince the reader of our reality and even gain his sympathy.

How much more complicated and alive is George Orwell's younger self, the "I" in "Such, Such Were the Joys," for having admitted he snitched on his classmates, or James Baldwin's "I" in "Notes of a Native Son," for acknowledging how close he came to the edge with his rages about racism in restaurants. Character is not just a question of sensibility: there are hard choices to be made when a person is put under pressure. And it's in having made the wrong choice, curiously enough, that we are made all the more aware of our freedom and potential for humanity. So it is that remorse is often the starting point for good personal essays, whose working-out brings the necessary self-forgiveness (not to mention self-amusement) to outgrow shame.

I have not touched on some other requirements of the personal essay, such as the need to go beyond the self's quandaries, through research or contextualization, to bring back news of the larger world. Nor have I spoken of the grandeur of the so-called formal essay. Yet even when "I" plays no part in the language of an essay, a firm sense of personality can warm the voice of the impersonal essay narrator. When we read Dr. Johnson and Edmund Wilson and Lionel Trilling, for instance, we feel that we know them as fully developed characters in their own essays, regardless of their not referring personally to themselves.

The need thus exists to make oneself into a character, whether the essay uses a first- or third-person narrative voice. I would further maintain that this process of turning oneself into a character is not self-absorbed navel gazing, but rather a potential release from narcissism. It means you have achieved sufficient distance to begin to see yourself in the round: a necessary precondition to transcending the ego—or at least writing personal essays that can touch other people.

Scott Russell Sanders

The Singular First Person

The first soapbox orator I ever saw was haranguing a crowd beside the Greyhound Station in Providence, Rhode Island, about the evils of fluoridated water. What the man stood on was actually an upturned milk crate, all the genuine soap-boxes presumably having been snapped up by antique dealers. He wore an orange plaid sports coat and matching bow tie and held aloft a bottle filled with mossy green liquid. I don't remember the details of his spiel, except his warning that fluoride was an invention of the Communists designed to weaken our bones and thereby make us pushovers for a Red invasion. What amazed me, as a tongue-tied kid of seventeen newly arrived in the city from the boondocks, was not his message but his courage in delivering it to a mob of strangers. I figured it would have been easier for me to jump straight over the Greyhound Station than to stand there on that milk crate and utter my thoughts.

To this day, when I read or when I compose one of those curious monologues we call the personal essay, I often think of that soapbox orator. Nobody had asked him for his two cents' worth, but there he was declaring it with all the eloquence he could muster. The essay, although enacted in private, is no less arrogant a performance. Unlike novelists and playwrights, who lurk behind the scenes while distracting our attention with the puppet show of imaginary characters, unlike scholars and journalists, who quote the opinions of others and shelter behind the hedges of neutrality, the essayist has nowhere to hide. While the poet can lean back on a several-thousand-year-old legacy of ecstatic speech, the essayist inherits a much briefer and skimpier tradition. The poet is allowed to quit after a few lines, but the essayist must hold our attention over pages and pages. It is a brash and foolhardy form, this one-man or one-woman circus, which relies on the tricks of anecdote, conjecture, memory, and wit to enthrall us.

Addressing a monologue to the world seems all the more brazen or preposterous an act when you consider what a tiny fraction of the human chorus any single voice is. At the Boston Museum of Science an electronic meter records with flashing lights the population of the United States. Figuring in the rate of births, deaths, emigrants leaving the country and immigrants arriving, the meter calculates that we add one fellow citizen every twenty-one seconds. When I looked at it recently, the count stood at 249,958,483. As I wrote that figure in my notebook, the final number jumped from three to four. Another mouth, another set of ears and eyes, another brain. A counter for the earth's population would stand somewhere past five billion at the moment, and would be rising in a blur of digits. Amid this avalanche of selves, it is a wonder that anyone finds the gumption to sit down and write one of those naked, lonely, quixotic letters-to-the-world.

A surprising number do find the gumption. In fact, I have the impression there are more essayists at work in America today, and more gifted ones, than at any time in recent decades. Whom do I have in mind? Here is a sampler: Wendell Berry, Carol Bly, Joan Didion, Annie Dillard, Stephen Jay Gould, Elizabeth Hardwick, Edward Hoagland, Phillip Lopate, Barry Lopez, Peter Matthiessen, John McPhee, Cynthia Ozick, Paul Theroux, Lewis Thomas, Tom Wolfe. No doubt you could make up a list of your own—with a greater ethnic range, perhaps, or fewer nature enthusiasts—a list that would provide equally convincing support for the view that we are blessed right now with an abundance of essayists. We do not have anyone to rival Emerson or Thoreau, but in sheer quantity of first-rate work our time stands comparison with any period since the heyday of the form in the mid-nineteenth century.

Why are so many writers taking up this risky form, and why are so many readers—to judge by the statistics of book and magazine publication—seeking it out? In this era of prepackaged thought, the essay is the closest thing we have, on paper, to a record of the individual mind at work and play. It is an amateur's raid in a world of specialists. Feeling overwhelmed by data, random information, the flotsam and jetsam of mass culture, we relish the spectacle of a single consciousness making sense of a portion of the chaos. We are grateful to Lewis Thomas for shining his light into the dark corners of biology, to John McPhee for laying bare the geology beneath our landscape, to Annie Dillard for showing us the universal fire blazing in the branches of a cedar, to Peter Matthiessen for chasing after snow leopards and mystical insights in the Himalayas. No matter if they are sketchy, these maps of meaning are still welcome. As Joan Didion observes in her own collection of essays, *The White Album,* "We live entirely, especially if we are writers, by the imposition of a narrative line upon disparate images, by the 'ideas' with which we have learned to freeze the shifting phantasmagoria which is our actual experience." Dizzy from a dance that seems to acceler-ate hour by hour, we cling to the narrative line, even though it may be as pure an invention as the shapes drawn by Greeks to identify the constellations.

The essay is a haven for the private, idiosyncratic voice in an era of anonyomous babble. Like the bland-burgers served in their millions along our highways, most language served up in public these days is textureless, tasteless mush. On television, over the phone, in the newspaper, wherever humans bandy words about, we encounter more and more abstractions, more empty formulas. Think of the pablum ladled out by politicians. Think of the fluffy white bread of advertising. Think, lord help us, of committee reports. By contrast, the essay remains stubbornly concrete and particu-lar: it confronts you with an oil-smeared toilet at the Sunoco station, a red vinyl purse shaped like a valentine heart, a bowlegged dentist hunting deer with an elephant gun. As Orwell forcefully argued, and as dictators seem to agree, such a bypassing of abstractions, such an insistence on the concrete, is a politically subversive act. Clinging to this door, that child, this grief, following the zigzag motions of an inquisitive mind, the essay renews language and clears trash from the springs of thought. A century and a half ago, in the rousing manifesto entitled *Nature,* Emerson called on a new generation of writers to cast off the hand-me-down rhetoric of the day, to "pierce this rotten diction and fasten words again to visible things." The essayist aspires to do just that.

As if all these virtues were not enough to account for a renaissance of this protean genre, the essay has also taken over some of the territory abdicated by contemporary fiction. Whittled down to the bare bones of plot, camouflaged with irony, muttering in brief sentences and grade-school vocabulary, peopled with characters who stumble like sleepwalkers through numb lives, today's fashionable fiction avoids disclosing where the author stands on anything. In the essay, you had better speak from a region pretty close to the heart or the reader will detect the wind of phoniness whistling through your hollow phrases. In the essay you may be caught with your pants down, your ignorance and sentimentality showing, while you trot recklessly about on one of your hobby-horses. You cannot stand back from the action, as Joyce instructed us to do, and pare your finger-nails. You cannot palm off your cockamamie notions on some hapless character.

To our list of the essay's contemporary attractions we should add the perennial ones of verbal play, mental adventure, and sheer anarchic high spirits. To see how the capricious mind can be led astray, consider the foregoing paragraph, which drags in metaphors from the realms of toys, clothing, weather, and biology, among others. That is bad enough; but it could have been worse. For example, I began to draft a sentence in that paragraph with the following words: "More than once, in sitting down to beaver away at a narrative, felling trees of memory and hauling brush to build a dam that might slow down the waters of time . . . " I had set out to make some innocent remark, and here I was gnawing down trees and building dams, all because I had let that *beaver* slip in. On this occasion I had the good sense to throw out the unruly word. I don't always, as no doubt you will have noticed. Whatever its more visible subject, an essay is also about the way a mind moves, the links and leaps and jigs of thought. I might as well drag in another metaphor—and another unoffending animal— by saying that each doggy sentence, as it noses forward into the underbrush of thought, scatters a bunch of rabbits that go bounding off in all directions. The essayist can afford to chase more of those rabbits than the fiction writer can, but fewer than the poet. If you refuse to chase any of them, and keep plodding along in a straight line, you and your reader will have a dull outing. If you chase too many, you will soon wind up lost in a thicket of confusion with your tongue hanging out.

The pursuit of mental rabbits was strictly forbidden by the teachers who instructed me in English composition. For that matter, nearly all the qualities of the personal essay, as I have been sketching them, violate the rules that many of us were taught in school. You recall we were supposed to begin with an outline and stick by it faithfully, like a train riding its rails, avoiding sidetracks. Each paragraph was to have a topic sentence pasted near the front, and these orderly paragraphs were to be coupled end-to-end like so many boxcars. Every item in those boxcars was to bear the stamp of some external authority, preferably a footnote referring to a thick book, although appeals to magazines and newspapers would do in a pinch. Our diction was to be formal, dignified, shunning the vernacular. Polysyllabic words derived from Latin were preferable to the blunt lingo of the streets. Metaphors were to be used only in emergencies, and no two of them were to be mixed. And even in emergencies we could not speak in the first person singular.

Already as a schoolboy, I chafed against those rules. Now I break them shamelessly, in particular the taboo against using the lonely capital *I*. Just look at what I'm doing right now. My speculations about the state of the essay arise, needless to say, from my own practice as reader and writer, and they reflect my own tastes, no matter how I may pretend to gaze dispassionately down on the question from a hot-air balloon. As Thoreau declares in his cocky manner on the opening page of *Walden:* "In most books the *I*, or first person, is omitted; in this it will be retained; that, in respect to egotism, is the main difference. We commonly do not remember that it is, after all, always the first person that is speaking. I should not talk so much about myself if there were anybody else whom I knew as well." True for the personal essay, it is doubly true for an essay about the essay: one speaks always and inescapably in the first person singular.

We could sort out essays along a spectrum according to the degree to which the writer's ego is on display—with John McPhee, perhaps, at the extreme of self-effacement, and Norman Mailer at the opposite extreme of self-dramatization. Brassy or shy, center stage or hanging back in the wings, the author's persona commands our attention. For the length of an essay, or a book of essays, we respond to that persona as we would to a friend caught up in a rapturous monologue. When the monologue is finished, we may not be able to say precisely what it was about, any more than we can draw conclusions from a piece of music. "Essays don't usually boil down to a summary, as articles do," notes Edward Hoagland, one of the least summarizable of companions, "and the style of the writer has a 'nap' to it, a combination of personality and originality and energetic loose ends that stand up like the nap of a piece of wool and can't be brushed flat" ("What I Think, What I Am"). We make assumptions about that speaking voice, assumptions we cannot validly make about the narrators in fiction. Only a sophomore is permitted to ask if Huckleberry Finn ever had any children; but even literary sophisticates wonder in print about Thoreau's love life, Montaigne's domestic arrangements, De Quincey's opium habit, Virginia Woolf's depression.

Montaigne, who not only invented the form but nearly perfected it as well, announced from the start that his true subject was himself. In his note "To the Reader" at the beginning of the *Essays,* he slyly proclaimed:

> I want to be seen here in my simple, natural, ordinary fashion, without straining or artifice; for it is myself that I portray. My defects will here be read to the life, and also my natural form, as far as respect for the public has allowed. Had I been placed among those nations which are said to live still in the sweet freedom of nature's first laws, I assure you I should very gladly have portrayed myself here entire and wholly naked.

A few pages after this disarming introduction, we are told of the Emperor Maximilian, who was so prudish about exposing his private parts that he would not let a servant dress him or see him in the bath. The Emperor went so far as to give orders that he be buried in his underdrawers. Having let us in on this intimacy about Maximilian, Montaigne then confessed that he himself, although "bold-mouthed," was equally prudish, and that "except under great stress of necessity or voluptuousness," he never allowed anyone to see him naked. Such modesty, he feared, was unbecoming in a soldier. But such honesty is quite becoming in an essayist. The very confession of his prudery is a far more revealing gesture than any doffing of clothes.

A curious reader will soon find out that the word *essay,* as adapted by Montaigne, means a trial or attempt. The Latin root carries the more vivid sense of a weighing out. In the days when that root was alive and green, merchants discovered the value of goods and alchemists discovered the composition of unknown metals by the use of scales. Just so the essay, as Montaigne was the first to show, is a weighing out, an inquiry into the value, meaning, and true nature of experience; it is a private experiment carried out in public. In each of three successive editions, Montaigne inserted new material into his essays without revising the old material. Often the new statements contradicted the original ones, but Montaigne let them stand, since he believed that the only consistent fact about human beings is their inconsistency. In a celebration called "Why Montaigne Is Not a Bore," Lewis Thomas has remarked of him that "He [was] fond of his mind, and affectionately entertained by everything in his head." Whatever Montaigne wrote about—and he wrote about everything under the sun: fears, smells, growing old, the pleasures of scratching—he weighed on the scales of his own character.

It is the *singularity* of the first person—its warts and crotchets and turn of voice—that lures many of us into reading essays, and that lingers with us after we finish. Consider the lonely, melancholy persona of Loren Eiseley, forever wandering, forever brooding on our dim and bestial past, his lips frosty with the chill of the Ice Age. Consider the volatile, Dionysian persona of D. H. Lawrence, with his incandescent gaze, his habit of turning peasants into gods and trees into flames, his quick hatred and quicker love. Consider that philosophical farmer, Wendell Berry, who speaks with a countryman's knowledge and a deacon's severity. Consider E. B. White, with his cheery affection for brown eggs and dachshunds, his unflappable way of herding geese while the radio warns of an approaching hurricane.

E. B. White, that engaging master of the genre, a champion of idiosyncrasy, introduced his own volume of *Essays* by admitting the danger of narcissism:

> I think some people find the essay the last resort of the egoist, a much too self-conscious and self-serving form for their taste; they feel that it is presumptuous of a writer to assume that his little excursions or his small observations will interest the reader. There is some justice in their complaint. I have always been aware that I am by nature self-absorbed and egoistical; to write of myself to the extent I have done indicates a too great attention to my own life, not enough to the lives of others.

Yet the self-absorbed Mr. White was in fact a delighted observer of the world, and shared that delight with us. Thus, after describing memorably how a circus girl practiced her bareback riding in the leisure moments between shows ("The Ring of Time"), he confessed: "As a writing man, or secretary, I have always felt charged with the safekeeping of all unexpected items of worldly or unworldly enchantment, as though I might be held personally responsible if even a small one were to be lost." That may still be presumptuous, but it is a presumption turned outward on the creation.

This looking outward helps distinguish the essay from pure autobiography, which dwells more complacently on the self. Mass murderers, movie stars, sports heroes, Wall Street crooks, and defrocked politicians may blather on about whatever high jinks or low jinks made them temporarily famous, may chronicle their exploits, their diets, their hobbies, in perfect confidence that the public is eager to gobble up every last gossipy scrap. And the public, according to sales figures, generally is. On the other hand, I assume the public does not give a hoot about my private life. If I write of hiking up a mountain with my one-year-old boy riding like a papoose on my back, and of what he babbled to me while we gazed down from the summit onto the scudding clouds, it is not because I am deluded into believing that my baby, like the offspring of Prince Charles, matters to the great world. It is because I know the great world produces babies of its own and watches them change cloudfast before its doting eyes. To make that climb up the mountain vividly present for readers is harder work than the climb itself. I choose to write about my experience not because it is mine, but because it seems to me a door through which others might pass.

On that cocky first page of *Walden,* Thoreau justified his own seeming self-absorption by saying that he wrote the book for the sake of his fellow citizens, who kept asking him to account for his peculiar experiment by the pond. There is at least a sliver of truth to this, since Thoreau, a town character, had been invited more than once to speak his mind at the public lectern. Most of us, however, cannot honestly say the townspeople have been clamoring for our words. I suspect that all writers of the essay, even Norman Mailer and Gore Vidal, must occasionally wonder if they are ego-maniacs. For the essayist, in other words, the problem of authority is inescapable. By what right does one speak? Why should anyone listen? The traditional sources of authority no longer serve. You cannot justify your words by appealing to the Bible or some other holy text, you cannot merely stitch together a patchwork of quotations from classical authors, you cannot lean on a podium at the Atheneum and deliver your wisdom to a rapt audience.

In searching for your own soapbox, a sturdy platform from which to deliver your opinionated monologues, it helps if you have already distinguished yourself at some other, less fishy form. When Yeats describes his longing for Maud Gonne or muses on Ireland's misty lore, everything he says is charged with the prior strength of his poetry. When Virginia Woolf, in *A Room of One's Own,* reflects on the status of women and the conditions necessary for making art, she speaks as the author of *Mrs. Dalloway* and *To the Lighthouse.* The essayist may also lay claim to our attention by having lived through events or traveled through terrains that already bear a richness of meaning. When James Baldwin writes his *Notes of a Native Son,* he does not have to convince us that racism is a troubling reality. When Barry Lopez takes us on a meditative tour of the far north in *Arctic Dreams,* he can rely on our curiosity about that fabled and forbidding place. When Paul Theroux climbs aboard a train and invites us on a journey to some exotic destination, he can count on the romance of railroads and the allure of remote cities to bear us along.

Most essayists, however, cannot draw on any source of authority from beyond the page to lend force to the page itself. They can only use language to put themselves on display and to gesture at the world. When Annie Dillard tells us in the opening lines of *Pilgrim at Tinker Creek* about the tomcat with bloody paws who jumps through the window onto her chest, why should we listen? Well, because of the voice that goes on to say: "And some mornings I'd wake in daylight to find my body covered with paw prints in blood; I looked as though I'd been painted with roses." Listen to her explaining a few pages later what she is up to in this book, this broody, zestful record of her stay in the Roanoke Valley: "I propose to keep here what Thoreau called 'a meteorological journal of the mind,' telling some tales and describing some of the sights of this rather tamed valley, and exploring, in fear and trembling, some of the unmapped dim reaches and unholy fastnesses to which those tales and sights so dizzyingly lead." The sentence not only describes the method of her literary search, but also exhibits the breathless, often giddy, always eloquent and spiritually hungry soul who will do the searching. If you enjoy her company, you will relish Annie Dillard's essays; if you don't, you won't.

Listen to another voice which readers tend to find either captivating or insufferable:

> That summer I began to see, however dimly, that one of my ambitions, perhaps my governing ambition, was to belong fully to this place, to belong as the thrushes and the herons and the muskrats belonged, to be altogether at home here. That is still my ambition. But now I have come to see that it proposes an enormous labor. It is a spiritual ambition, like goodness. The wild creatures belong to the place by nature, but as a man I can belong to it only by understanding and by virtue. It is an ambition I cannot hope to succeed in wholly, but I have come to believe that it is the most worthy of all.

That is Wendell Berry in "The Long-Legged House" writing about his patch of Kentucky. Once you have heard that stately, moralizing, cherishing voice, laced through with references to the land, you will not mistake it for anyone else's. Berry's themes are profound and arresting ones. But it is his voice, more than anything he speaks about, that either seizes us or drives us away.

Even so distinct a persona as Wendell Berry's or Annie Dillard's is still only a literary fabrication, of course. The first person singular is too narrow a gate for the whole writer to squeeze through. What we meet on the page is not the flesh-and-blood author, but a simulacrum, a character who wears the label *I*. Introducing the lectures that became *A Room of One's Own,* Virginia Woolf reminded her listeners that "'I' is only a convenient term for somebody who has no real being. Lies will flow from my lips, but there may perhaps be some truth mixed up with them; it is for you to seek out this truth and to decide whether any part of it is worth keeping." Here is a part I consider worth keeping: "Women have served all these centuries as looking-glasses possessing the magic and delicious power of reflecting the figure of man at twice its natural size." It is from such elegant, revelatory sentences that we build up our notion of the "I" who speaks to us under the name of Virginia Woolf.

What the essay tells us may not be true in any sense that would satisfy a court of law. As an example, think of Orwell's brief narrative, "A Hanging," which describes an execution in Burma. Anyone who has read it remembers how the condemned man as he walked to the gallows stepped aside to avoid a puddle. That is the sort of haunting detail only an eyewitness should be able to report. Alas, biographers, those zealous debunkers, have recently claimed that Orwell never saw such a hanging, that he reconstructed it from hearsay. What then do we make of his essay? Or has it become the sort of barefaced lie we prefer to call a story?

Frankly, I don't much care what label we put on "A Hanging"—fiction or nonfiction, it is a powerful statement either way—but Orwell might have cared a great deal. I say this because not long ago I was bemused and then vexed to find one of my own essays treated in a scholarly article as a work of fiction. Here was my earnest report about growing up on a military base, my heartfelt rendering of indelible memories, being confused with the airy figments of novelists! To be sure, in writing the piece I had used dialogue, scenes, settings, character descriptions, the whole fictional bag of tricks; sure, I picked and chose among a thousand beckoning details; sure, I downplayed some facts and highlighted others; but I was writing about the actual, not the invented. I shaped the matter, but I did not make it up.

To explain my vexation, I must break another taboo, which is to speak of the author's intent. My teachers warned me strenuously to avoid the intentional fallacy. They told me to regard poems and plays and stories as objects washed up on the page from some unknown and unknowable shores. Now that I am on the other side of the page, so to speak, I think quite recklessly of intention all the time. I believe that if we allow the question of intent in the case of murder, we should allow it in literature. The essay is distinguished from the short story, not by the presence or absence of literary devices, not by tone or theme or subject, but by the writer's stance toward the material.

In composing an essay about what it was like to grow up on that military base, I *meant* something quite different from what I mean when concocting a story. I meant to preserve and record and help give voice to a reality that existed independently of me. I meant to pay my respects to a minor passage of history in an out-of-the-way place. I felt responsible to the truth as known by other people. I wanted to speak directly out of my own life into the lives of others.

You can see I am teetering on the brink of metaphysics. One step farther and I will plunge into the void, wondering as I fall how to prove there is any external truth for the essayist to pay homage to. I draw back from the brink and simply declare that I believe one writes, in essays, with a regard for the actual world, with a respect for the shared substance of history, the autonomy of other lives, the being of nature, the mystery and majesty of a creation we have not made.

When it comes to speculating about the creation, I feel more at ease with physics than with metaphysics. According to certain bold and lyrical cosmologists, there is at the center of black holes a geometrical point, the tiniest conceivable speck, where all the matter of a collapsed star has been concentrated, and where everyday notions of time, space, and force break down. That point is called a singularity. The boldest and most poetic theories suggest that anything sucked into a singularity might be flung back out again, utterly changed, somewhere else in the universe. The lonely first person, the essayist's microcosmic "I," may be thought of as a verbal singularity at the center of the mind's black hole. The raw matter of experience, torn away from the axes of time and space, falls in constantly from all sides, undergoes the mind's inscrutable alchemy, and reemerges in the quirky, unprecedented shape of an essay.

Now it is time for me to step down, before another metaphor seizes hold of me, before you notice that I am standing, not on a soapbox, but on the purest air.

PART

II

— Place —

Place has long been a focal point for essayists and memoirists, from Mark Twain on the Mississippi River and James Baldwin on Paris to Thoreau on Walden Pond and Joan Didion on California. We all have our own attachments to places—homes, communities, or places we've traveled. The very word *home* conjures up associations and emotions for most of us; from close connections to feelings of exile, we cannot help being influenced by where we come from and where we live. Like the subject of Portraits, the concept of Place is rich with possibilities for material: what does our home—our house, our city, our neighborhood—say about us? What places are we drawn to, and why? How is our designation of home emblematic of who we are and what we desire?

The creative nonfiction essays in this section address ideas of landscape, history, and memory. In the personal "I" section, several of the works deal with the immigrant experience, which involves inevitable cultural conflicts and a sense of duality, of floating in between homes and worlds. Chang-rae Lee's memoir piece "Coming Home Again" defines home through his relationship with his mother, while in "Thank You in Arabic" Naomi Shihab Nye writes about her family's experiences living in Jerusalem and America. Both writers grapple with issues of identity, something Judith Ortiz Cofer also does in her segmented essay "Silent Dancing."

The description of one's home—how physical space becomes metaphorical space—can also be seen in Edwidge Danticat's memoir "Westbury Court," which returns to a building where her family once lived. Stuart Dybek's "Field Trips" depicts school as a place of rich and often unintended ironies, while Thomas Lynch's meditative essay "The Undertaking" explores how we deal with the fact of death. Whether relying on the power of flashback and narrative, as in Lee's essay, or incorporating imagination as a structural device as in Cofer's contemporary classic, these works are driven by personal responses to the idea of place.

The literary journalistic essays emphasize cultural and political landscapes of place as seen though the critical "Eye" of a range of observers. Whether a travel narrative or a study of a landmark, the works in this section examine particular places within the context of ideas and ideals these places have come to represent. Sarah Vowell's "What He Said There," for instance, is a commentary on Lincoln and the Gettysburg Address. Structure is significant in James Alan McPherson's "Saturday Night, and Sunday Morning" and John McPhee's "The Search for Marvin Gardens." These essays use narrative and descriptive fragments that deliver, in McPherson's essay, reflections on blues music and Chicago and, in McPhee's essay, a complex portrait of Atlantic City against the backdrop of the Monopoly game.

All of the works in this literary journalistic section use the personal "I" to varying degrees, making hazy that distinction between the personal and the journalistic. These blurring lines, connecting outward with inward observation, hearken back to the very idea behind creative nonfiction and its resistance to set boundaries. The topic of Place can generate immediate and personal reactions, such that the individual experience often becomes commingled with the art of careful observation.

The three craft pieces in this section all address the process of writing about our places in the world. In her excerpt from *The Situation and the Story,* Vivian Gornick suggests that writers "engage with the world, because engagement makes experience, experience makes wisdom, and finally it's wisdom—or rather the movement toward it—that counts." This is a call to action; though we may become, as writers, minute observers of everything that happens, we first have to go out there and interact, participate. To "engage with the world" means more than just thinking and looking out the window. On a similar note, Jonathan Raban's "Notes from the Road" deals with the difficulties of turning notes and observations into cohesive prose. For Raban, "the act of writing itself unlocks the memory-bank, and discovers things that are neither in the notebooks nor to be found in the writer's conscious memory." Finally, André Aciman in "A Literary Pilgrim Progresses to the Past" discusses what it means to write about a place, giving it life and personality, and in turn creating ideas about self-identity.

A house, a pond, a trip, a room, a city, a tourist destination—all can become junctures of memory, association, dislocation, and discovery. The writers in this section offer different ways to approach the shaping of such places into essays that explore and reveal something about ourselves and the world we live in.

THE "I"

Judith Ortiz Cofer

Silent Dancing

We have a home movie of this party. Several times my mother and I have watched it together, and I have asked questions about the silent revelers coming in and out of focus. It is grainy and of short duration, but it's a great visual aid to my memory of life at that time. And it is in color—the only complete scene in color I can recall from those years.

We lived in Puerto Rico until my brother was born in 1954. Soon after, because of economic pressures on our growing family, my father joined the United States Navy. He was assigned to duty on a ship in Brooklyn Yard—a place of cement and steel that was to be his home base in the States until his retirement more than twenty years later. He left the Island first, alone, going to New York City and tracking down his uncle who lived with his family across the Hudson River in Paterson, New Jersey. There my father found a tiny apartment in a huge tenement that had once housed Jewish families but was just being taken over and transformed by Puerto Ricans, overflowing from New York City. In 1955 he sent for us. My mother was only twenty years old, I was not quite three, and my brother was a toddler when we arrived at *El Building,* as the place had been christened by its newest residents.

My memories of life in Paterson during those first few years are all in shades of gray. Maybe I was too young to absorb vivid colors and details, or to discriminate between the slate blue of the winter sky and the darker hues of the snow-bearing clouds, but that single color washes over the whole period. The building we lived in was gray, as were the streets, filled with slush the first few months of my life there. The coat my father had bought for me was similar in color and too big; it sat heavily on my thin frame.

I do remember the way the heater pipes banged and rattled, startling all of us out of sleep until we got so used to the sound that we automatically shut it out or raised our voices above the racket. The hiss from the valve punctuated my sleep (which has always been fitful) like a nonhuman presence in the room—a dragon sleeping at the entrance of my childhood. But the pipes were also a connection to all the other lives being lived around us. Having come from a house designed for a single family back in Puerto Rico— my mother's extended-family home—it was curious to know that strangers lived under our floor and above our heads, and that the heater pipe went through everyone's apartments. (My first spanking in Paterson came as a result of playing tunes on the pipes in my room to see if there would be an answer.) My mother was as new to this concept of beehive life as I was, but she had been given strict orders by my father to keep the doors locked, the noise down, ourselves to ourselves.

It seems that Father had learned some painful lessons about prejudice while searching for an apartment in Paterson. Not until years later did I hear how much resistance he had encountered with landlords who were panicking at the influx of Latinos into a neighbor-hood that had been Jewish for a couple of generations. It made no difference that it was the American phenomenon of ethnic turnover which was changing the urban core of Paterson, and that the human flood could not be held back with an accusing finger.

"You Cuban?" one man had asked my father, pointing at his name tag on the Navy uniform—even though my father had the fair skin and light-brown hair of his north-ern Spanish background, and the name Ortiz is as common in Puerto Rico as Johnson is in the United States.

"No," my father had answered, looking past the finger into his adversary's angry eyes. "I'm Puerto Rican."

"Same shit." And the door closed.

My father could have passed as European, but we couldn't. My brother and I both have our mother's black hair and olive skin, and so we lived in El Building and visited our great-uncle and his fair children on the next block. It was their private joke that they were the German branch of the family. Not many years later that area too would be mainly Puerto Rican. It was as if the heart of the city map were being gradually colored brown— *café con leche*[1] brown. Our color.

The movie opens with a sweep of the living room. It is "typical" immigrant Puerto Rican decor for the time: the sofa and chairs are square and hard-looking, upholstered in bright colors (blue and yellow in this instance), and covered with the transparent plastic that furniture salesmen then were so adept at convincing women to buy. The linoleum on the floor is light blue; if it had been subjected to spike heels (as it was in most places), there were dime-sized indentations all over it that cannot be seen in this movie. The room is full of people dressed up: dark suits for the men, red dresses for the women. When I have asked my mother why most of the women are in red that night, she has shrugged, "I don't remember. Just a coincidence." She doesn't have my obsession for assigning symbolism to everything.

The three women in red sitting on the couch are my mother, my eighteen-year-old cousin, and her brother's girlfriend. The novia is just up from the Island, which is appar-ent in her body language. She sits up formally, her dress pulled over her knees. She is a pretty girl, but her posture makes her look insecure, lost in her full-skirted dress, which she has carefully tucked around her to make room for my gorgeous cousin, her future sister-in-law. My cousin has grown up in Paterson and is in her last year of high school. She doesn't have a trace of what Puerto Ricans call la mancha (literally, the stain: the mark of the new immigrant—something about the posture, the voice, or the humble

---

[1] *café con leche:* Coffee with cream. In Puerto Rico it is sometimes prepared with boiled milk.— Cofer's Note.

demeanor that makes it obvious to everyone the person has just arrived on the main-
land). My cousin is wearing a tight, sequined, cocktail dress. Her brown hair has been
lightened with peroxide around the bangs, and she is holding a cigarette expertly between
her fingers, bringing it up to her mouth in a sensuous arc of her arm as she talks animat-
edly. My mother, who has come up to sit between the two women, both only a few years
younger than herself, is somewhere between the poles they represent in our culture.

It became my father's obsession to get out of the barrio, and thus we were never permitted
to form bonds with the place or with the people who lived there. Yet El Building was a
comfort to my mother, who never got over yearning for *la isla.* She felt surrounded by her
language: The walls were thin, and voices speaking and arguing in Spanish could be heard
all day. *Salsas* blasted out of radios, turned on early in the morning and left on for company. Women seemed to cook rice and beans perpetually—the strong aroma of boiling
red kidney beans permeated the hallways.

Though Father preferred that we do our grocery shopping at the supermarket when he
came home on weekend leaves, my mother insisted that she could cook only with products
whose labels she could read. Consequently, during the week I accompanied her and my little brother to *La Bodega*—a hole-in-the-wall grocery store across the street from El Building. There we squeezed down three narrow aisles jammed with various products. Goya's
and Libby's—those were the trademarks that were trusted by *her mamá,* so my mother
bought many cans of Goya beans, soups, and condiments, as well as little cans of Libby's
fruit juices for us. And she also bought Colgate toothpaste and Palmolive soap. (The final *e*
is pronounced in both these products in Spanish, so for many years I believed that they
were manufactured on the Island. I remember my surprise at first hearing a commercial on
television in which Colgate rhymed with "ate.") We always lingered at La Bodega, for it was
there that Mother breathed best, taking in the familiar aromas of the foods she knew from
Mamá's kitchen. It was also there that she got to speak to the other women of El Building
without violating outright Father's dictates against fraternizing with our neighbors.

Yet Father did his best to make our "assimilation" painless. I can still see him carrying
a real Christmas tree up several flights of stairs to our apartment, leaving a trail of aromatic
pine. He carried it formally, as if it were a flag in a parade. We were the only ones in El
Building that I knew of who got presents on both Christmas day AND *dia de Reyes,* the day
when the Three Kings brought gifts to Christ and to Hispanic children.

Our supreme luxury in El Building was having our own television set. It must have
been a result of Father's guilt feelings over the isolation he had imposed on us, but we
were among the first in the barrio to have one. My brother quickly became an avid
watcher of Captain Kangaroo and Jungle Jim, while I loved all the series showing families.
By the time I started first grade, I could have drawn a map of Middle America as exempli-
fied by the lives of characters in *Father Knows Best, The Donna Reed Show, Leave It to Beaver,*
My Three Sons, and (my favorite) *Bachelor Father,* where John Forsythe treated his adopted
teenage daughter like a princess because he was rich and had a Chinese houseboy to do
everything for him. In truth, compared to our neighbors in El Building, *we* were rich. My
father's Navy check provided us with financial security and a standard of life that the factory workers envied. The only thing his money could not buy us was a place to live away
from the barrio—his greatest wish, Mother's greatest fear.

In the home movie the men are shown next, sitting around a card table set up in one cor-
ner of the living room, playing dominoes. The clack of the ivory pieces was a familiar
sound. I heard it in many houses on the Island and in many apartments in Paterson. In
"Leave It to Beaver," the Cleavers played bridge in every other episode; in my childhood,
the men started every social occasion with a hotly debated round of dominoes. The
women would sit around and watch, but they never participated in the games.

Here and there you can see a small child. Children were always brought to parties
and, whenever they got sleepy, were put to bed in the host's bedroom. Babysitting was a
concept unrecognized by the Puerto Rican women I knew: a responsible mother did not
leave her children with any stranger. And in a culture where children are not considered
intrusive, there was no need to leave the children at home. We went where our mother
went.

Of my preschool years I have only impressions: the sharp bite of the wind in December as
we walked with our parents toward the brightly lit stores downtown; how I felt like a
stuffed doll in my heavy coat, boots, and mittens; how good it was to walk into the five-
and-dime and sit at the counter drinking hot chocolate. On Saturdays our whole family
would walk downtown to shop at the big department stores on Broadway. Mother bought
all our clothes at Penney's and Sears, and she liked to buy her dresses at the women's specialty shops like Lerner's and Diana's. At some point we'd go into Woolworth's and sit at
the soda fountain to eat.

We never ran into other Latinos at these stores or when eating out, and it became
clear to me only years later that the women from El Building shopped mainly in other
places—stores owned by other Puerto Ricans or by Jewish merchants who had philosophically accepted our presence in the city and decided to make us their good customers, if
not real neighbors and friends. These establishments were located not downtown but in
the blocks around our street, and they were referred to generically as *La Tienda, El Bazar,*
La Bodega, La Botánica. Everyone knew what was meant. These were the stores where your
face did not turn a clerk to stone, where your money was as green as anyone else's.

One New Year's Eve we were dressed up like child models in the Sears catalogue: my
brother in a miniature man's suit and bow tie, and I in black patent-leather shoes and a
frilly dress with several layers of crinoline underneath. My mother wore a bright red dress
that night, I remember, and spike heels; her long black hair hung to her waist. Father, who
usually wore his Navy uniform during his short visits home, had put on a dark civilian suit
for the occasion: we had been invited to his uncle's house for a big celebration. Everyone
was excited because my mother's brother Hernan—a bachelor who could indulge himself
with luxuries—had bought a home movie camera, which he would be trying out that
night.

Even the home movie cannot fill in the sensory details such a gathering left imprinted
in a child's brain. The thick sweetness of women's perfumes mixing with the ever-present
smells of food cooking in the kitchen: meat and plantain *pasteles,* as well as the ubiquitous
rice dish made special with pigeon peas—*gandules*—and seasoned with precious *sofrito*[2]
sent up from the Island by somebody's mother or smuggled in by a recent traveler. *Sofrito*
was one of the items that women hoarded, since it was hardly ever in stock at La Bodega.
It was the flavor of Puerto Rico.

The men drank Palo Viejo rum, and some of the younger ones got weepy. The first time I saw a grown man cry was at a New Year's Eve party: he had been reminded of his mother by the smells in the kitchen. But what I remember most were the boiled *pasteles*—plantain or yucca rectangles stuffed with corned beef or other meats, olives, and many other savory ingredients, all wrapped in banana leaves. Everybody had to fish one out with a fork. There was always a "trick" pastel—one without stuffing—and whoever got that one was the "New Year's Fool."

There was also the music. Long-playing albums were treated like precious china in these homes. Mexican recordings were popular, but the songs that brought tears to my mother's eyes were sung by the melancholy Daniel Santos, whose life as a drug addict was the stuff of legend. Felipe Rodríguez was a particular favorite of couples, since he sang about faithless women and brokenhearted men. There is a snatch of one lyric that has stuck in my mind like a needle on a worn groove: *De piedra ha de ser mi cama, de piedra la cabezera . . . la mujer que a mi me quiera . . . ha de quererme de veras. Ay, Ay, Ay, corazón, porque no amas.*[3] . . . I must have heard it a thousand times since the idea of a bed made of stone, and its connection to love, first troubled me with its disturbing images.

The five-minute home movie ends with people dancing in a circle—the creative film-maker must have set it up, so that all of them could file past him. It is both comical and sad to watch silent dancing. Since there is no justification for the absurd movements that music provides for some of us, people appear frantic, their faces embarrassingly intense. It's as if you were watching sex. Yet for years I've had dreams in the form of this home movie. In a recurring scene, familiar faces push themselves forward into my mind's eyes, plastering their features into distorted close-ups. And I'm asking them: "Who is *she*? Who is the old woman I don't recognize? Is she an aunt? Somebody's wife? Tell me who she is."

"See the beauty mark on her cheek as big as a hill on the lunar landscape of her face—well, that runs in the family. The women on your father's side of the family wrinkle early; it's the price they pay for that fair skin. The young girl with the green stain on her wedding dress is *La Novia*—just up from the Island. See, she lowers her eyes when she approaches the camera, as she's supposed to. Decent girls never look at you directly in the face. *Humilde,* humble, a girl should express humility in all her actions. She will make a good wife for your cousin. He should consider himself lucky to have met her only weeks after she arrived here. If he marries her quickly, she will make him a good Puerto Rican–style wife; but if he waits too long, she will be corrupted by the city—just like your cousin there."

"She means me. I do what I want. This is not some primitive island I live on. Do they expect me to wear a black mantilla on my head and go to mass every

---

[2] *sofrito:* A cooked condiment. A sauce composed of a mixture of fatback, ham, tomatoes, and many island spices and herbs. It is added to many typical Puerto Rican dishes for a distinctive flavor.— COFER'S NOTE.

[3] *De piedra ha de ser . . . amas:* Lyrics from a popular romantic ballad (called a *bolero* in Puerto Rico). Freely translated: "My bed will be made of stone, of stone also my headrest (or pillow), the woman who (dares to) loves me, will have to love me for real. *Ay, Ay, Ay,* my heart, why can't you (let me) love. . . . "— COFER'S NOTE.

day? Not me. I'm an American woman, and I will do as I please. I can type faster than anyone in my senior class at Central High, and I'm going to be a secretary to a lawyer when I graduate. I can pass for an American girl anywhere—I've tried it. At least for Italian, anyway—I never speak Spanish in public. I hate these parties, but I wanted the dress. I look better than any of these *humildes* here. My life is going to be different. I have an American boyfriend. He is older and has a car. My parents don't know it, but I sneak out of the house late at night sometimes to be with him. If I marry him, even my name will be American. I hate rice and beans—that's what makes these women fat."

"Your *prima*[4] is pregnant by that man she's been sneaking around with. Would I lie to you? I'm your *Tía Política*,[5] your great-uncle's common-law wife— the one he abandoned on the Island to go marry your cousin's mother. *I* was not invited to this party, of course, but I came anyway. I came to tell you that story about your cousin that you've always wanted to hear. Do you remember the comment your mother made to a neighbor that has always haunted you? The only thing you heard was your cousin's name, and then you saw your mother pick up your doll from the couch and say: 'It was as big as this doll when they flushed it down the toilet.' This image has bothered you for years, hasn't it? You had nightmares about babies being flushed down the toilet, and you wondered why anyone would do such a horrible thing. You didn't dare ask your mother about it. She would only tell you that you had not heard her right, and yell at you for listening to adult conversations. But later, when you were old enough to know about abortions, you suspected.

"I am here to tell you that you were right. Your cousin was growing an *Americanito* in her belly when this movie was made. Soon after she put something long and pointy into her pretty self, thinking maybe she could get rid of the problem before breakfast and still make it to her first class at the high school. Well, *Niña*,[6] her screams could be heard downtown. Your aunt, her mamá, who had been a midwife on the Island, managed to pull the little thing out. Yes, they probably flushed it down the toilet. What else could they do with it—give it a Christian burial in a little white casket with blue bows and ribbons? Nobody wanted that baby—least of all the father, a teacher at her school with a house in West Paterson that he was filling with real children, and a wife who was a natural blonde.

"Girl, the scandal sent your uncle back to the bottle. And guess where your cousin ended up? Irony of ironies. She was sent to a village in Puerto Rico to live with a relative on her mother's side: a place so far away from civilization that you have to ride a mule to reach it. A real change in scenery. She found a man there—women like that cannot live without male company—but believe me, the men in Puerto Rico know how to put a saddle on a woman like her. *La Gringa*,[7] they call her. Ha, ha, ha. *La Gringa* is what she always wanted to be. . . ."

The old woman's mouth becomes a cavernous black hole I fall into. And as I fall, I can feel the reverberations of her laughter. I hear the echoes of her last mocking words: *La Gringa,*

---

[4] *prima:* Female cousin.—COFER'S NOTE.
[5] *Tía Política:* Aunt by marriage.—COFER'S NOTE.
[6] *Niña:* Girl.—COFER'S NOTE.

La Gringa! And the conga line keeps moving silently past me. There is no music in my dream for the dancers.

When Odysseus visits Hades to see the spirit of his mother, he makes an offering of sacrificial blood, but since all the souls crave an audience with the living, he has to listen to many of them before he can ask questions. I, too, have to hear the dead and the forgotten speak in my dream. Those who are still part of my life remain silent, going around and around in their dance. The others keep pressing their faces forward to say things about the past.

My father's uncle is last in line. He is dying of alcoholism, shrunken and shriveled like a monkey, his face a mass of wrinkles and broken arteries. As he comes closer I realize that in his features I can see my whole family. If you were to stretch that rubbery flesh, you could find my father's face, and deep within *that* face—my own. I don't want to look into those eyes ringed in purple. In a few years he will retreat into silence, and take a long, long time to die. *Move back, Tío,* I tell him. *I don't want to hear what you have to say. Give the dancers room to move. Soon it will be midnight. Who is the New Year's Fool this time?*

Edwidge Danticat

Westbury Court

When I was fourteen years old, we lived in a six-story brick building in a cul-de-sac off of Flatbush Avenue, in Brooklyn, called Westbury Court. Beneath the building ran a subway station through which rattled the D, M, and Q trains every fifteen minutes or so. Though there was graffiti on most of the walls of Westbury Court, and hills of trash piled up outside, and though the elevator wasn't always there when we opened the door to step inside and the heat and hot water weren't always on, I never dreamed of leaving Westbury Court until the year of the fire.

I was watching television one afternoon when the fire began. I loved television then, especially the afternoon soap operas, my favorite of which was *General Hospital.* I would bolt out of my last high school class every day, pick up my youngest brother, Karl, from day care, and watch *General Hospital* with him on my lap while doing my homework during the commercials. My other two brothers, André and Kelly, would later join us in the apartment, but they preferred to watch cartoons in the back bedroom.

One afternoon while *General Hospital* and afternoon cartoons were on, a fire started in apartment 6E, across the hall. There in that apartment lived our new neighbors, an African-American mother and her two boys. We didn't know the name of the mother, or the names and ages of her boys, but I venture to guess that they were around five and ten years old.

I didn't know a fire had started until two masked, burly firemen came knocking on our door. My brothers and I rushed out into the hallway filled with smoke and were quickly escorted down to the first floor by some other firemen already on our floor. While

---

[7] *La Gringa:* Derogatory epithet used here to ridicule a Puerto Rican girl who wants to look like a blonde North American.—Cofer's note.

we ran by, the door to apartment 6E had already been knocked over by the fire squad and inside was filled with bright flames and murky smoke.

All of the tenants of the building who were home at that time were crowded on the sidewalk outside. My brothers and I, it seemed, were the last to be evacuated. Clutching my brothers' hands, I wondered if I had remembered to lock our apartment door. Was there anything valuable we could have taken?

An ambulance screeched to a stop in front of the building, and the two firemen who had knocked on our door came out carrying the pliant and lifeless bodies of the two children from across the hall. Their mother jumped out of the crowd and ran toward them, screaming, "My babies—not my babies," as the children were lowered into the back of the ambulance and transferred into the arms of the emergency medical personnel. The fire was started by the two boys, after their mother had stepped out to pick up some groceries at the supermarket down the street. They had been playing with matches.

(Later my mother would tell us, "See, this is what happens to children who play with matches. Sometimes it is too late to say, 'I shouldn't have.'" My brother Kelly, who was fascinated with fire and liked to hold up a match to the middle of his palm until the light fizzled out, gave up this party trick after the fire.)

We were quiet that afternoon when both our parents came home. We were the closest to the fire in the building, and the most religious of our parents' friends saw it as a miracle that we had escaped safe and sound. When my mother asked how come I, the oldest one, hadn't heard the children scream or hadn't smelled the smoke coming from across the hall, I confessed that I had been watching *General Hospital* and was too consumed in the intricate plot.

(After the fire, my mother had us stay with a family on the second floor for a few months, after school. I felt better not having to be wholly responsible for myself and my brothers, in case something like that fire should ever happen again.)

The apartment across the hall stayed empty for a long time, and whenever I walked past it, a piece of its inner skeleton would squeak, and occasionally burnt wood that might have been hanging by a fragile singed thread would crash down and cause a domino effect of further ruptures, unleashed like those children's last cries, which I had not heard because I had been so wrapped up in the made-up drama of a world where, even though the adults' lives were often in turmoil, the children came home to the welcoming arms of waiting mommies and nannies who served them freshly baked cookies on porcelain plates and helped them to remove their mud-soaked boots, if it was raining, lest they soil the lily-white carpets. But should their boots accidentally sully the carpet, or should their bright yellow raincoats inadvertently drip on the sparkling linoleum, there would be a remedy for that as well. And if their house should ever catch fire, a smart dog or a good neighbor would rescue them just in time, and the fire trucks would come right quick because some attentive neighbor would call them.

Through the trail of voices that came up to comfort us, I heard that the children's mother would be prosecuted for negligence and child abandonment. I couldn't help but wonder, would our parents have suffered the same fate had it been my brothers and me who were killed in the fire?

When they began to repair the apartment across the hall, I would occasionally sneak out to watch the workmen. They were shelling the inside of the apartment and replacing everything from the bedroom closets to the kitchen floors. I never saw the mother of the dead boys again and never heard anything of her fate.

A year later, after the apartment was well polished and painted, two blind Haitian brothers and their sister moved in. They were all musicians and were part of a group called les Frères Parent, the Parent Brothers. Once my parents allowed my brothers and me to come home from school to our apartment, I would always listen carefully for our new tenants, so I'd be the first to know if anything went awry.

What I heard coming from the apartment soon after they moved in was music, "engagé" music, which the brothers were composing to protest against the dictatorship in Haiti, from which they had fled. The Parent Brothers and their sister, Lydie, did nothing but rehearse a cappella most days when they were not receiving religious and political leaders from Haiti and from the Haitian community in New York.

The same year after the fire, a cabdriver who lived down the hall in 6J was killed on a night shift in Manhattan; a good friend of my father's, a man who gave great Sunday afternoon parties in 6F, died of cirrhosis of the liver. One day while my brothers and I were at school and my parents were at work, someone came into our apartment through our fire escape and stole my father's expensive camera. That same year a Nigerian immigrant was shot and killed in front of the building across the street. To appease us, my mother said, "Nothing like that ever happens out of the blue. He was in a fight with someone." It was too troublesome for her to acknowledge that people could die randomly, senselessly, at Westbury Court or anywhere else.

Every day on my way back from school, I hurried past the flowers and candles piled in front of the spot where the Nigerian, whose name I didn't know, had been murdered. Still I never thought I was living in a violent place. It was an elevated castle above a clattering train tunnel, a blind alley where children from our building and the building across the street had erected a common basketball court for hot summer afternoon games, an urban yellow brick road where hopscotch squares dotted the sidewalk next to burned-out, abandoned cars. It was home.

My family and I moved out of Westbury Court three years after the fire. Every once in a while, though, the place came up in conversation, linked to either a joyous or a painful memory. One of the girls who had scalded her legs while boiling a pot of water for her bath during one of those no-heat days got married last year. After the burglar had broken into the house and taken my father's camera, my father—an amateur photography buff—never took another picture.

My family and I often reminisce about the Parent Brothers when we see them in Haitian newspapers or on television; we brag that we knew them when, before one of the brothers became a senator in Haiti and the sister, Lydie, became mayor of one of the better-off Haitian suburbs, Pétion-Ville. We never talk about the lost children.

Even now, I question what I remember about the children. Did they really die? Or did their mother simply move away with them after the fire? Maybe they were not even boys at all. Maybe they were two girls. Or one boy and one girl. Or maybe I am struggling to phase them out of my memory altogether. Not just them, but the fear that their destiny could have so easily been mine and my brothers'.

A few months ago, I asked my mother, "Do you remember the children and the fire at Westbury Court?"

Without missing a flutter of my breath, my mother replied, "Oh those children, those poor children, their poor mother. Sometimes it is too late to say, 'I shouldn't have.'"

Stuart Dybek

Field Trips

We took two field trips in grade school. The first was a tour of the Bridewell House of Corrections and the Cook County Jail. The prison complex was on twenty-sixth and California, only blocks away from St. Roman's School, so, herded by nuns into an orderly column with the girls in front and the boys bringing up the rear, our fifth grade class walked there. The nuns must have though it a perfect choice for a field trip as not only was there a suitable cautionary lesson, but it saved on bus fare too.

Filing from school at midmorning felt like a jailbreak. Paired up with pals, we traipsed down California, gaping like tourists at the familiar street coming to life—delivery trucks double-parking before greasy spoons, open doors revealing the dark interiors of bars still exhaling boozy breath from the night before. Some of the kids like Bad Brad Norky—already twice convicted of stealing the class milk money—were hoping to see various relatives who were doing time at County. Others, like my best friend, Rafael Mendoza, were hoping to catch a glimpse of a mob boss, or a mass murderer, or the infamous psychopath Edward Gein, a farmer from the wilds of Illinois who supposedly cannibalized his victims and tanned their skins to make lampshades and clothes. Gein fascinated us. Some years later when I was in high school, I bought a pair of hand-stitched moccasin-top gray suede shoes that when soaked with rain turned a cadaverous shade, and my buddies took to calling them my Gein shoes. That, in turn, developed into a neighborhood expression of appreciation for any article of clothing that looked sharp in an unconventional way: *muy Gein, man,* or *Gein cool!* At the same time, the term could also be used as an insult: "Your mama's a Gein."

Even more than the murderers and celebrity psychos, the main draw at County, at least for the boys, was getting a look at the electric chair. We'd heard it was kept in the basement. Local legend had it that a sudden burst of static on the radio or a blink in TV reception, say, during the *Howdy Doody* show, meant that the power had surged because they'd just fried someone at County. We thought maybe we'd get to shake the hand of the warden or whoever flipped the switch at executions. But, if there was an electric chair there at all, we never got to see it.

Surprisingly, the most memorable part of the trip occurred not at County where the men, penned in what the tour guide informed us were sixty-square-foot cells, mostly ignored us, but rather at Bridewell when they took us through the women's wing. The inmates there, prostitutes mainly, saw the nuns and had some comments about being Brides of Christ that were truly educational:

"Yo, Sisters, what kinda meat do the pope eat on Friday? Nun."

"Hey, Sister Mary Hymen, when I dress up like that I get an extra fifty!"

The nuns didn't respond, but their faces assumed the same impassive, inwardly suffering expressions that the statues of martyrs wore, and they began to hurry us through the rest of the tour.

A hefty female guard rapped the bars with her stick and shouted, "Pipe down, Taffy, there's kids for godssake."

And Taffy laughed, "Shee-it, Bull Moose! When I was their age I was doing my daddy."

And from another cell someone called, "Amen, girl!"

The next year the nuns avoided the jail and instead took us to the stockyards, a trip that required a bus. A rented yellow school bus was already waiting when we got to school that morning, and we filed on, boys sitting on the left side of the aisle, girls on the right. I sat next to a new kid, Joseph Bonnamo. Usually, new kids were quiet and withdrawn, but Bonnamo who'd only been at St. Roman's for a couple weeks was already the most popular boy in the class. Everyone called him Joey B. His father had been a marine lifer and Joey B was used to moving around, he said. He'd moved around so much that he was a grade behind, a year older than everyone else, but he didn't seem ashamed by it. He was a good athlete and the girls all had crushes on him. That included Sylvie Perez, who over the summer had suddenly, to use my mother's word, "developed." Exploded into bloom was closer to the truth. Along with the rest of the boys, I pretended as best I could not to notice—it was too intimidating to those of use who'd been her classmates for years. But not to Joey B.

"Like my old man says, 'Tits that size have a mind of their own,'" he confided to me on the way to the Yards, "and hers are thinking, 'Feel me up, Joey B.'"

"How do you know?"

His hand dropped down and he clutched his crotch. "Telepathy."

"Class," Sister Bull Moose asked, "do you know our tradition when riding a bus on a field trip?"

"A round pound?" Joey whispered to me.

No one raised a hand. We didn't know we had a tradition—as far as we knew we were the first class from St. Roman's ever to take a bus on a field trip.

Sister Bull Moose's real name was Sister Amabilia, but she had a heft to her that meant business, and she wielded the baton she used to conduct choir practice not unlike the guard we'd seen wielding a nightstick at Bridewell a year before, so my friend Rafael had come up with the nickname.

From within her habit, a garment that looked as if it had infinite storage capacity, she produced the pitch pipe also used in choir practice and sustained a note. "Girls start and boys come in on 'Merrily merrily merrily . . .'"

Joey B sang in my ear, "Row row row your boner . . ."

At the Yards there was a regular tour. First stop was the Armour packing plant where the meat was processed into bacon and sausage. I think the entire class was relieved that the smell wasn't as bad as we worried it might be. We knew we had traveled to the source of what in the neighborhood was called "the brown wind" or "the glue pee-ew factory," a stench that settled over the south side of Chicago at least once a week. My father said it was the smell of boiling hooves, hair, and bone rendered down to make soap. I'd once dissected a bar of Ivory on which I'd noticed what appeared to be animal hair to see if there were also fragments of bone and if beneath the soap smell I could detect the reek of the Yards.

We left the processing plant for the slaughterhouse and from a metal catwalk looked upon the scene below where workmen wearing yellow hard hats and white coats smeared with gore heaved sledge hammers down on the skulls of the steers that, urged by electric prods, had filed obediently through wooden chutes.

Every time the hammer connected, my friend Rafael would go, "Ka-Boom!"

The steer would drop, folding at the knees as if his front legs had suddenly been broken.

"That has to smart," Joey B said.

For the finale they took us to where the hogs were slaughtered. A man with hairy, thick, spattered forearms, wearing rubber boots and a black rubber apron shiny with blood, stood holding a butcher knife before a vat of water. An assembly line of huge squealing hogs, suspended by their hind legs, swung past him, and as each hog went by the line would pause long enough for the man to slit the hog's throat. He did it with a practiced, effortless motion and I wondered how long he'd had the job, what it had been like on his first day, and if it was a job I could ever be desperate enough to do. Up to then, my idea of the worst job one could have was bus driver. I didn't think I could drive through rush-hour traffic down the same street over and over while making change as bus drivers had to in those days. But watching the man kill hogs, I began to think that driving a bus might not be so bad.

With each hog there was the same terrified squeal, but louder than a squeal, more like a shriek that became a grunting gurgle of blood. A Niagara of blood splashed to the tile and into a flowing gutter of water where it rushed frothing away. The man would plunge the knife into the vat of water before him and the water clouded pink, then he'd withdraw the shining blade just as the next squealing hog arrived. Meanwhile, the hogs who'd just cranked by, still alive, their mouths, nostrils, and slit throats pumping dark read gouts were swung into a bundle of hanging bodies to bleed. Each new carcass slammed into the others causing a few weak squeals and a fresh gush of blood.

The tour guide apologized that we couldn't see the sheep slaughtered. He said that some people thought the sheep sounded human, like children, and that bothered some people, so they didn't include it on the tour.

It made me wonder who killed the sheep. We'd seen the man with sledgehammers and the man with a knife. How were the sheep slaughtered? Was it a promotion to work with the sheep—some place they sent only the most expert slaughterers—or was it the job that nobody at the Yards wanted?

"Just like the goddamn electric chair," Rafael complained.

"How's that?" Joey B asked.

"They wouldn't let us see the chair when we went to the jail last year."

At the end of the tour on our way out of the processing plant they gave each of us a souvenir hot dog. Not a hot dog Chicago style: poppy seed bun, mustard—never catsup, onion, relish, tomato, pickle, peppers, celery salt. This was a cold hot dog wrapped in a napkin. We hadn't had lunch and everyone was starving. We rode back on the bus eating our hot dogs, while singing, "Frère Jacques."

I was sitting by the window, Joey B beside me, and right across the aisle from him—no accident, probably—was Sylvie Perez. I realized it was a great opportunity, but I could never think of anything to say to girls in a situation like that.

"Sylvie," Joey B said, "you liking that hot dog?"

"It's okay," Sylvie said.

"You look good eating it," he told her.

It sounded like the stupidest thing I'd ever heard, but all she did was blush, smile at him, and take another demure nibble.

I knew it was against the rules, but I cracked open the window of the bus and tried to flick my balled-up hot dog napkin into a passing convertible. Sister Bull Moose saw me do it.

"Why does there always have to be one who's not mature enough to take on trips," she asked rhetorically. For punishment I had to give up my seat and stand in the aisle, which I did to an indifference on the part of Sylvie Perez that was the worst kind of scorn.

"Since you obviously need special attention, Stuart, you can sing us a round," Sister said. Once, during our weekly music hour, looking in my direction, she'd inquired, "Who is singing like an off-key foghorn?" When I'd shut up, still moving my mouth, but only pretending to sing, she'd said, "That's better."

"I don't know the words," I said.

"Oh, I think you do. '*Dor-mez-vous, dor-mez-vous, Bim Bam Boom.*' They're easy."

Joey B patted the now empty seat beside him as if to say to Sylvie, "Now you can sit here."

Sylvie rolled her pretty eyes toward Sister Bull Moose and smiled, and Joey B nodded he understood and smiled back, and they rode like that in silence, communicating telepathically while I sang.

Chang-Rae Lee

Coming Home Again

When my mother began using the electronic pump that fed her liquids and medication, we moved her to the family room. The bedroom she shared with my father was upstairs, and it was impossible to carry the machine up and down all day and night. The pump itself was attached to a metal stand on casters, and she pulled it along wherever she went. From anywhere in the house, you could hear the sound of the wheels clicking out a steady time over the grout lines of the slate-tiled foyer, her main thoroughfare to the bathroom and the kitchen. Sometimes you would hear her halt after only a few steps, to catch her breath or steady her balance, and whatever you were doing was instantly suspended by a pall of silence.

I was usually in the kitchen, preparing lunch or dinner, poised over the butcher block with her favorite chef's knife in my hand and her old yellow apron slung around my neck. I'd be breathless in the sudden quiet, and, having ceased my mincing and chopping, would stare blankly at the brushed sheen of the blade. Eventually, she would clear her throat or call out to say she was fine, then begin to move again, starting her rhythmic *ka-jug;* and only then could I go on with my cooking, the world of our house turning once more, wheeling through the black.

I wasn't cooking for my mother but for the rest of us. When she first moved downstairs she was still eating, though scantily, more just to taste what we were having than from any genuine desire for food. The point was simply to sit together at the kitchen table and array ourselves like a family again. My mother would gently set herself down in her customary chair near the stove. I sat across from her, my father and sister to my left and right, and crammed in the center was all the food I had made—a spicy codfish stew, say, or a casserole of gingery beef, dishes that in my youth she had prepared for us a hundred times.

It had been ten years since we'd all lived together in the house, which at fifteen I had left to attend boarding school in New Hampshire. My mother would sometimes point this out, by speaking of our present time as being "just like before Exeter," which surprised me, given how proud she always was that I was a graduate of the school.

My going to such a place was part of my mother's not so secret plan to change my character, which she worried was becoming too much like hers. I was clever and able enough, but without outside pressure I was readily given to sloth and vanity. The famous school—which none of us knew the first thing about—would prove my mettle. She was right, of course, and while I was there I would falter more than a few times, academically and otherwise. But I never thought that my leaving home then would ever be a problem for her, a private quarrel she would have even as her life waned.

Now her house was full again. My sister had just resigned from her job in New York City, and my father, who typically saw his psychiatric patients until eight or nine in the evening, was appearing in the driveway at four-thirty. I had been living at home for nearly a year and was in the final push of work on what would prove a dismal failure of a novel. When I wasn't struggling over my prose, I kept occupied with the things she usually did—the daily errands, the grocery shopping, the vacuuming and the cleaning, and, of course, all the cooking.

When I was six or seven years old, I used to watch my mother as she prepared our favorite meals. It was one of my daily pleasures. She shooed my away in the beginning, telling me that the kitchen wasn't my place, and adding, in her half-proud, half-deprecating way, that her kind of work would only serve to weaken me. "Go out and play with your friends," she'd snap in Korean, "or better yet, do your reading and homework." She knew that I had already done both, and that as the evening approached there was no place to go save her small and tidy kitchen, from which the clatter of her mixing bowls and pans would ring through the house.

I would enter the kitchen quietly and stand beside her, my chin lodging upon the point of her hip. Peering through the crook of her arm, I beheld the movements of her hands. For *kalbi,* she would take up a butchered short rib in her narrow hand, the flinty bone shaped like a section of an airplane wing and deeply embedded in gristle and flesh, and with the point of her knife cut so that the bone fell away, though not completely, leaving it connected to the meat by the barest opaque layer of tendon. Then she methodically butterflied the flesh, cutting and unfolding, repeating the action until the meat lay out on her board, glistening and ready for seasoning. She scored it diagonally, then sifted sugar into the crevices with her pinched fingers, gently rubbing in the crystals. The sugar would tenderize as well as sweeten the meat. She did this with each rib, and then set them all aside in a large shallow bowl. She minced a half-dozen cloves of garlic, a stub of ginger-root, sliced up a few scallions, and spread it all over the meat. She wiped her hands and took out a bottle of sesame oil, and, after pausing for a moment, streamed the dark oil in two swift circles around the bowl. After adding a few splashes of soy sauce, she thrust her hands in and kneaded the flesh, careful not to dislodge the bones. I asked her why it mattered that they remain connected. "The meat needs the bone nearby," she said, "to borrow its richness." She wiped her hands clean of the marinade, except for her little finger, which she would flick with her tongue from time to time, because she knew that the flavor of a good dish developed not at once but in stages.

Whenever I cook, I find myself working just as she would, readying the ingredients— a mash of garlic, a julienne of red peppers, fantails of shrimp—and piling them in little mounds about the cutting surface. My mother never left me any recipes, but this is how I learned to make her food, each dish coming not from a list or a card but from the aromatic spread of a board.

I've always thought it was particularly cruel that the cancer was in her stomach, and that for a long time at the end she couldn't eat. The last meal I made for her was on New Year's Eve, 1990. My sister suggested that instead of a rib roast or a bird, or the usual overflow of Korean food, we make all sorts of finger dishes that our mother might fancy and pick at.

We set the meal out on the glass coffee table in the family room. I prepared a tray of smoked-salmon canapés, fried some Korean bean cakes, and made a few other dishes I thought she might enjoy. My sister supervised me, arranging the platters, and then with some pomp carried each dish in to our parents. Finally, I brought out a bottle of champagne in a bucket of ice. My mother had moved to the sofa and was sitting up, surveying the low table. "It looks pretty nice," she said. "I think I'm feeling hungry."

This made us all feel good, especially me, for I couldn't remember the last time she had felt any hunger or had eaten something I cooked. We began to eat. My mother picked up a piece of salmon toast and took a tiny corner in her mouth. She rolled it around for a moment and then pushed it out with the tip of her tongue, letting it fall back onto her plate. She swallowed hard, as if to quell a gag, then glanced up to see if we had noticed. Of course we all had. She attempted a bean cake, some cheese, and then a slice of fruit, but nothing was any use.

She nodded at me anyway, and said, "Oh, it's very good." But I was already feeling lost and I put down my plate abruptly, nearly shattering it on the thick glass. There was an ugly pause before my father asked me in a weary, gentle voice if anything was wrong, and I answered that it was nothing, it was the last night of a long year, and we were together, and I was simply relieved. At midnight, I poured out glasses of champagne, even one for my mother, who took a deep sip. Her manner grew playful and light, and I helped her shuffle to her mattress, and she lay down in the place where in a brief week she was dead.

My mother could whip up most anything, but during our first years of living in this country we ate only Korean foods. At my harangue-like behest, my mother set herself to learning how to cook exotic American dishes. Luckily, a kind neighbor, Mrs. Churchill, a tall, florid young woman with flaxen hair, taught my mother her most trusted recipes. Mrs. Churchill's two young sons, palish, weepy boys with identical crew cuts, always accompanied her, and though I liked them well enough, I would slip away from them after a few minutes, for I knew that the real action would be in the kitchen, where their mother was playing guide. Mrs. Churchill hailed from the state of Maine, where the finest Swedish meatballs and tuna casserole and angel food cake in America are made. She readily demonstrated certain techniques—how to layer wet sheets of pasta for a lasagna or whisk up a simple roux, for example. She often brought gift shoeboxes containing curious ingredients like dried oregano, instant yeast, and cream of mushroom soup. The two women, though at ease and jolly with each other, had difficulty communicating, and this was made worse by the often confusing terminology of Western cuisine ("corned beef," "deviled eggs"). Although I was just learning the language myself, I'd gladly play the interlocutor, jumping back and forth between their places at the counter, dipping my fingers into whatever sauce lay about.

I was an insistent child, and, being my mother's firstborn, much too prized. My mother could say no to me, and did often enough, but anyone who knew us—particularly my father and sister—could tell how much the denying pained her. And if I was overconscious of her indulgence even then, and suffered the rushing pangs of guilt that she could inflict upon me with the slightest wounded turn of her lip, I was too happily obtuse and venal to let her cease. She reminded me daily that I was her sole son, her reason for living, and that if she were to lose me, in either body or spirit, she wished that God would mercifully smite her, strike her down like a weak branch.

In the traditional fashion, she was the house accountant, the maid, the launderer, the disciplinarian, the driver, the secretary, and, of course, the cook. She was also my first basketball coach. In South Korea, where girls' high school basketball is a popular spectator sport, she had been a star, the point guard for the national high school team that once won the all-Asia championships. I learned this one Saturday during the summer, when I asked my father if he would go down to the schoolyard and shoot some baskets with me. I had just finished the fifth grade, and wanted desperately to make the middle school team the coming fall. He called for my mother and sister to come along. When we arrived, my sister immediately ran off to the swings, and I recall being annoyed that my mother wasn't following her. I dribbled clumsily around the key, on the verge of losing control of the ball, and flung a flat shot that caromed wildly off the rim. The ball bounced to my father, who took a few not so graceful dribbles and made an easy layup. He dribbled out and then drove to the hoop for a layup on the other side. He rebounded his shot and passed the ball to my mother, who had been watching us from the foul line. She turned from the basket and began heading the other way.

"*Um-mah*," I cried at her, my exasperation already bubbling over, "the basket's over *here!*"

After a few steps she turned around, and from where the professional three-point line must be now, she effortlessly flipped the ball up in a two-handed set shot, its flight truer and higher than I'd witnessed from any boy or man. The ball arced cleanly into the hoop, stiffly popping the chain-link net. All afternoon, she rained in shot after shot, as my father and I scrambled after her.

When we got home from the playground, my mother showed me the photograph album of her team's championship run. For years I kept it in my room, on the same shelf that housed the scrapbooks I made of basketball stars, with magazine clippings of slick players like Bubbles Hawkins and Pistol Pete and George (the Iceman) Gervin.

It puzzled me how much she considered her own history to be immaterial, and if she never patently diminished herself, she was able to finesse a kind of self-removal by speaking of my father whenever she could. She zealously recounted his excellence as a student in medical school and reminded me, each night before I started my homework, of how hard he drove himself in his work to make a life for us. She said that because of his Asian face and imperfect English, he was "working two times the American doctors." I knew that she was building him up, buttressing him with both genuine admiration and her own brand of anxious braggadocio, and that her overarching concern was that I might fail to see him as she wished me to—in the most dawning light, his pose steadfast and solitary.

In the year before I left for Exeter, I became weary of her oft-repeated accounts of my father's success. I was a teenager, and so ever inclined to be dismissive and bitter toward anything that had to do with family and home. Often enough, my mother was the object of my derision. Suddenly, her life seemed so small to me. She was there, and sometimes, I thought, *always* there, as if she were confined to the four walls of our house. I would even complain about her cooking. Mostly, though, I was getting more and more impatient with the difficulty she encountered in doing everyday things. I was afraid for her. One day, we got into a terrible argument when she asked me to call the bank, to question a discrepancy she had discovered in the monthly statement. I asked her why she couldn't call herself. I was stupid and brutal, and I knew exactly how to wound her.

"Whom do I talk to?" she said. She would mostly speak to me in Korean, and I would answer in English.

"The bank manager, who else?"

"What do I say?"

"Whatever you want to say."

"Don't speak to me like that!" she cried.

"It's just that you should be able to do it yourself," I said.

"You know how I feel about this!"

"Well, maybe then you should consider it *practice,*" I answered lightly, using the Korean word to make sure she understood.

Her face blanched, and her neck suddenly became rigid, as if I were throttling her. She nearly struck me right then, but instead she bit her lip and ran upstairs. I followed her, pleading for forgiveness at her door. But it was the one time in our life that I couldn't convince her, melt her resolve with the blandishments of a spoiled son.

When my mother was feeling strong enough, or was in particularly good spirits, she would roll her machine into the kitchen and sit at the table and watch me work. She wore pajamas day and night, mostly old pairs of mine.

She said, "I can't tell, what are you making?"

"*Mahn-doo* filling."

"You didn't salt the cabbage and squash."

"Was I supposed to?"

"Of course. Look, it's too wet. Now the skins will get soggy before you can fry them."

"What should I do?"

"It's too late. Maybe it'll be OK if you work quickly. Why didn't you ask me?"

"You were finally sleeping."

"You should have woken me."

"No way."

She sighed, as deeply as her weary lungs would allow.

"I don't know how you were going to make it without me."

"I don't know, either. I'll remember the salt next time."

"You better. And not too much."

We often talked like this, our tone decidedly matter-of-fact, chin up, just this side of being able to bear it. Once, while inspecting a potato fritter batter I was making, she asked me if she had ever done anything that I wished she hadn't done. I thought for a moment, and told her no. In the next breath, she wondered aloud if it was right of her to have let me go to Exeter, to live away from the house while I was so young. She tested the batter's thickness with her finger and called for more flour. Then she asked if, given a choice, I would go to Exeter again.

I wasn't sure what she was getting at, and I told her that I couldn't be certain, but probably yes, I would. She snorted at this and said it was my leaving home that had once so troubled our relationship. "Remember how I had so much difficulty talking to you? Remember?"

She believed back then that I had found her more and more ignorant each time I came home. She said she never blamed me, for this was the way she knew it would be with my wonderful new education. Nothing I could say seemed to quell the notion. But I knew that the problem wasn't simply the *education;* the first time I saw her again after starting school, barely six weeks later, when she and my father visited me on Parents Day, she had already grown nervous and distant. After the usual campus events, we had gone to the motel where they were staying in a nearby town and sat on the beds in our room. She seemed to sneak looks at me, as though I might discover a horrible new truth if our eyes should meet.

My own secret feeling was that I had missed my parents greatly, my mother especially, and much more than I had anticipated. I couldn't tell them that these first weeks were a mere blur to me, that I felt completely overwhelmed by all the studies and my much brighter friends and the thousand irritating details of living alone, and that I had really learned nothing, save perhaps how to put on a necktie while sprinting to class. I felt as if I had plunged too deep into the world, which, to my great horror, was much larger than I had ever imagined.

I welcomed the lull of the motel room. My father and I had nearly dozed off when my mother jumped up excitedly, murmured how stupid she was, and hurried to the closet by the door. She pulled out our old metal cooler and dragged it between the beds. She lifted the top and began unpacking plastic containers, and I thought she would never stop. One after the other they came out, each with a dish that traveled well—a salted stewed meat, rolls of Korean-style sushi. I opened a container of radish kimchi and suddenly the room bloomed with its odor, and I reveled in the very peculiar sensation (which perhaps only true kimchi lovers know) of simultaneously drooling and gagging as I breathed it all in. For the next few minutes, they watched me eat. I'm not certain that I was even hungry. But after weeks of pork parmigiana and chicken patties and wax beans, I suddenly realized that I had lost all the savor in my life. And it seemed I couldn't get enough of it back. I ate and I ate, so much and so fast that I actually went to the bathroom and vomited. I came out dizzy and sated with the phantom warmth of my binge.

And beneath the face of her worry, I thought, my mother was smiling.

From that day, my mother prepared a certain meal to welcome me home. It was always the same. Even as I rode the school's shuttle bus from Exeter to Logan airport, I could already see the exact arrangement of my mother's table.

I knew that we would eat in the kitchen, the table brimming with plates. There was the *kalbi,* of course, broiled or grilled depending on the season. Leaf lettuce, to wrap the meat with. Bowls of garlicky clam broth with miso and tofu and fresh spinach. Shavings of cod dusted in flour and then dipped in egg wash and fried. Glass noodles with onions and shiitake. Scallion-and-hot-pepper pancakes. Chilled steamed shrimp. Seasoned salads of bean sprouts, spinach, and white radish. Crispy squares of seaweed. Steamed rice with barley and red beans. Homemade kimchi. It was all there—the old flavors I knew, the beautiful salt, the sweet, the excellent taste.

After the meal, my father and I talked about school, but I could never say enough for it to make any sense. My father would often recall his high school principal, who had gone to England to study the methods and traditions of the public schools, and regaled students with stories of the great Eton man. My mother sat with us, paring fruit, not saying a word but taking everything in. When it was time to go to bed, my father said good night first. I usually watched television until the early morning. My mother would sit with me for an hour or two, perhaps until she was accustomed to me again, and only then would she kiss me and head upstairs to sleep.

During the following days, it was always the cooking that started our conversations. She'd hold an inquest over the cold leftovers we ate at lunch, discussing each dish in terms of its balance of flavors or what might have been prepared differently. But mostly I begged her to leave the dishes alone. I wish I had paid more attention. After her death, when my father and I were the only ones left in the house, drifting through the rooms like ghosts, I sometimes tried to make that meal for him. Though it was too much for two, I made each dish anyway, taking as much care as I could. But nothing turned out quite right—not the color, not the smell. At the table, neither of us said much of anything. And we had to eat the food for days.

I remember washing rice in the kitchen one day and my mother's saying in English, from her usual seat, "I made a big mistake."

"About Exeter?"

"Yes. I made a big mistake. You should be with us for that time. I should never let you go there."

"So why did you?" I said.

"Because I didn't know I was going to die."

I let her words pass. For the first time in her life, she was letting herself speak her full mind, so what else could I do?

"But you know what?" she spoke up. "It was better for you. If you stayed home, you would not like me so much now."

I suggested that maybe I would like her even more.

She shook her head. "Impossible."

Sometimes I still think about what she said, about having made a mistake. I would have left home for college, that was never in doubt, but those years I was away at boarding school grew more precious to her as her illness progressed. After many months of exhaustion and pain and the haze of the drugs, I thought that her mind was beginning to fade, for more and more it seemed that she was seeing me again as her fifteen-year-old boy, the one she had dropped off in New Hampshire on a cloudy September afternoon.

I remember the first person I met, another new student, named Zack, who walked to the welcome picnic with me. I had planned to eat with my parents—my mother had brought a coolerful of food even that first day—but I learned of the cookout and told her that I should probably go. I wanted to go, of course. I was excited, and no doubt fearful and nervous, and I must have thought I was only thinking ahead. She agreed wholeheartedly, saying I certainly should. I walked them to the car, and perhaps I hugged them, before saying goodbye. One day, after she died, my father told me what happened on the long drive home to Syracuse.

He was driving the car, looking straight ahead. Traffic was light on the Massachusetts Turnpike, and the sky was nearly dark. They had driven for more than two hours and had not yet spoken a word. He then heard a strange sound from her, a kind of muffled chewing noise, as if something inside her were grinding its way out.

"So, what's the matter?" he said, trying to keep an edge to his voice.

She looked at him with her ashen face and she burst into tears. He began to cry himself, and pulled the car over onto the narrow shoulder of the turnpike, where they stayed for the next half hour or so, the blank-faced cars droning by them in the cold, onrushing night.

Every once in a while, when I think of her, I'm driving alone somewhere on the highway. In the twilight, I see their car off to the side, a blue Olds coupe with a landau top, and as I pass them by I look back in the mirror and I see them again, the two figures huddling together in the front seat. Are they sleeping? Or kissing? Are they all right?

Thomas Lynch
_____

The Undertaking

Every year I bury a couple hundred of my townspeople. Another two or three dozen I take to the crematory to be burned. I sell caskets, burial vaults, and urns for the ashes. I have a sideline in headstones and monuments. I do flowers on commission.

Apart from the tangibles, I sell the use of my building: eleven thousand square feet, furnished and fixtured with an abundance of pastel and chair rail and crown moldings. The whole lash-up is mortgaged and remortgaged well into the next century. My rolling stock includes a hearse, two Fleetwoods, and a minivan with darkened windows our pricelist calls a service vehicle and everyone in town calls the Dead Wagon.

I used to use the *unit pricing method*—the old package deal. It meant that you had only one number to look at. It was a large number. Now everything is itemized. It's the law. So now there is a long list of items and numbers and italicized disclaimers, something like a menu or the Sears Roebuck Wish Book, and sometimes the federally-mandated options begin to look like cruise control or rear-window defrost. I wear black most of the time, to keep folks in mind of the fact we're not talking Buicks here. At the bottom of the list there is still a large number.

In a good year the gross is close to a million, five percent of which we hope to call profit. I am the only undertaker in this town. I have a corner on the market.

The market, such as it is, is figured on what is called *the crude death rate*—the number of deaths every year out of every thousand persons.

Here is how it works.

Imagine a large room into which you coax one thousand people. You slam the doors in January, leaving them plenty of food and drink, color TVs, magazines, and condoms. Your sample should have an age distribution heavy on baby boomers and their children— 1.2 children per boomer. Every seventh adult is an old-timer, who, if he or she wasn't in this big room, would probably be in Florida or Arizona or a nursing home. You get the idea. The group will include fifteen lawyers, one faith healer, three dozen real-estate agents, a video technician, several licensed counselors, and a Tupperware distributor. The rest will be between jobs, middle managers, ne'er-do-wells, or retired.

Now for the magic part—come late December when you throw open the doors, only 991.6, give or take, will shuffle out upright. Two hundred and sixty will now be selling Tupperware. The other 8.4 have become the crude death rate.

Here's another stat.

Of the 8.4 corpses, two-thirds will have been old-timers, five percent will be children, and the rest (slightly less than 2.5 corpses) will be boomers—realtors and attorneys likely—one of whom was, no doubt, elected to public office during the year. What's more, three will have died of cerebral-vascular or coronary difficulties, two of cancer, one each of vehicular mayhem, diabetes, and domestic violence. The spare change will be by act of God or suicide—most likely the faith healer.

The figure most often and most conspicuously missing from the insurance charts and demographics is the one I call The Big One, which refers to the number of people out of every hundred born who will die. Over the long haul, The Big One hovers right around . . . well, dead nuts on one hundred percent. If this were on the charts, they'd call it *death expectancy* and no one would buy futures of any kind. But it is a useful number and has its lessons. Maybe you will want to figure out what to do with your life. Maybe it will make you feel a certain kinship with the rest of us. Maybe it will make you hysterical. Whatever the implications of a one hundred percent death expectancy, you can calculate how big a town this is and why it produces for me a steady if unpredictable labor.

They die around the clock here, without apparent preference for a day of the week, month of the year; there is no clear favorite in the way of season. Nor does the alignment of the stars, fullness of moon, or liturgical calendar have very much to do with it. The where-abouts are neither here nor there. They go off upright or horizontally in Chevrolets and nursing homes, in bathtubs, on the interstates, in ERs, ORs, BMWs. And while it may be that we assign more equipment or more importance to deaths that create themselves in places marked by initials—ICU being somehow better than Greenbriar Convalescent Home—it is also true that the dead don't care. In this way, the dead I bury and burn are like the dead before them, for whom time and space have become mortally unimportant. This loss of interest is, in fact, one of the first sure signs that something serious is about to happen. The next thing is they quit breathing. At this point, to be sure, a *gunshot wound to the chest* or *shock and trauma* will get more ink than a CVA or ASHD, but no cause of death is any less permanent than the other. Any one will do. The dead don't care.

Nor does *who* much matter, either. To say, "I'm OK, you're OK, and by the way, he's dead!" is, for the living, a kind of comfort.

It is why we drag rivers and comb plane wrecks and bomb sites.

It is why MIA is more painful than DOA.

It is why we have open caskets and all read the obits.

Knowing is better than not knowing, and knowing it is you is terrifically better than knowing it is me. Because once I'm the dead guy, whether you're OK or he's OK won't much interest me. You can all go bag your asses, because the dead don't care.

Of course, the living, bound by their adverbs and their actuarials, still do. Now, there is the difference and why I'm in business. The living are careful and oftentimes caring. The dead are careless, or maybe it's care-less. Either way, they don't care. These are unremarkable and verifiable truths.

My former mother-in-law, herself an unremarkable and verifiable truth, was always fond of holding forth with Cagneyesque bravado—to wit: "When I'm dead, just throw me in a box and throw me in a hole." But whenever I would remind her that we did substantially that with everyone, the woman would grow sullen and a little cranky.

Later, over meatloaf and green beans, she would invariably give out with: "When I'm dead just cremate me and scatter the ashes."

My former mother-in-law was trying to make carelessness sound like fearlessness. The kids would stop eating and look at each other. The kids' mother would plead, "Oh Mom, don't talk like that." I'd take out my lighter and begin to play with it.

In the same way, the priest that married me to this woman's daughter—a man who loved golf and gold ciboria and vestments made of Irish linen; a man who drove a great black sedan with a wine-red interior and who always had his eye on the cardinal's job— this same fellow, leaving the cemetery one day, felt called upon to instruct me thus: "No bronze coffin for me. No sir! No orchids or roses or limousines. The plain pine box is the one I want, a quiet Low Mass and the pauper's grave. No pomp and circumstance."

He wanted, he explained, to be an example of simplicity, of prudence, of piety and austerity—all priestly and, apparently, Christian virtues. When I told him that he needn't wait, that he could begin his ministry of good example even today, that he could quit the country club and do his hacking at the public links and trade his brougham for a used Chevette; that free of his Florsheims and cashmeres and prime ribs, free of his bingo nights and building funds, he could become, for Christ's sake, the very incarnation of Francis himself, or Anthony of Padua; when I said, in fact, that I would be willing to assist him in this, that I would gladly distribute his savings and credit cards among the worthy poor of the parish, and that I would, when the sad duty called, bury him for free in the manner he would have, by then, become accustomed to; when I told your man these things, he said nothing at all, but turned his wild eye on me in the way that the cleric must have looked on Sweeney years ago, before he cursed him, irreversibly, into a bird.

What I was trying to tell the fellow was, of course, that being a dead saint is no more worthwhile than being a dead philodendron or a dead angelfish. Living is the rub, and always has been. Living saints still feel the flames and stigmata of this vale of tears, the ache of chastity and the pangs of conscience. Once dead, they let their relics do the leg-work, because, as I was trying to tell this priest, the dead don't care.

Only the living care.

And I am sorry to be repeating myself, but this is the central fact of my business—that there is nothing, once you are dead, that can be done *to you* or *for you* or *with you* or *about you* that will do you any good or any harm; that any damage or decency we do accrues to the living, to whom your death happens, if it really happens to anyone. The living have to live with it. You don't. Theirs is the grief or gladness your death brings. Theirs is the loss or gain of it. Theirs is the pain and the pleasure of memory. Theirs is the invoice for services rendered and theirs is the check in the mail for its payment.

And there is the truth, abundantly self-evident, that seems, now that I think of it, the one most elusive to the old in-laws, the parish priest, and to perfect strangers who are forever accosting me in barber-shops and cocktail parties and parent-teacher conferences, hell-bent or duty-bound to let me in on what it is they want done with them when they are dead.

Give it a rest is the thing I say.

Once you are dead, put your feet up, call it a day, and let the husband or the missus or the kids or a sibling decide whether you are to be buried or burned or blown out of a cannon or left to dry out in a ditch somewhere. It's not your day to watch it, because the dead don't care.

Another reason people are always rehearsing their obsequies with me has to do with the fear of death that anyone in their right mind has. It is healthy. It keeps us from playing in traffic. I say it's a thing we should pass on to the kids.

There is a belief—widespread among the women I've dated, local Rotarians, and friends of my chidren—that I, being the undertaker here, have some irregular fascination with, special interest in, inside information about, even attachment to, *the dead*. They assume, these people, some perhaps for defensible reasons, that I want their bodies.

It is an interesting concept.

But here is the truth.

Being dead is one—the worst, the last—but only one in a series of calamities that afflicts our own and several other species. The list may include, but is not limited to, gingivitis, bowel obstruction, contested divorce, tax audit, spiritual vexation, cash flow problems, political upheaval, and on and on and on some more. There is no shortage of misery. And I am no more attracted to the dead than the dentist is to your bad gums, the doctor to your rotten innards, or the accountant to your sloppy expense records. I have no more stomach for misery that the banker or the lawyer, the pastor or the politico—because misery is careless and is everywhere. Misery is the bad check, the ex-spouse, the mob in the street, and the IRS—who, like the dead, feel nothing and, like the dead, *don't care.*

Which is not to say that the dead do not matter.

They do. They do. Of course they do.

Last Monday morning Milo Hornsby died. Mrs. Hornsby called at 2 A.M. to say that Milo had *expired* and would I take care of it, as if his condition were like any other that could be renewed or somehow improved upon. At 2 A.M., yanked from my REM sleep, I am thinking, put a quarter into Milo and call me in the morning. But Milo is dead. In a moment, in a twinkling, Milo has slipped irretrievably out of our reach, beyond Mrs. Hornsby and the children, beyond the women at the laundromat he owned, beyond his comrades at the Legion Hall, the Grand Master of the Masonic Lodge, his pastor at First Baptist, beyond the mailman, zoning board, town council, and Chamber of Commerce; beyond us all, and any treachery or any kindness we had in mind for him.

Milo is dead.

X's on his eyes, lights out, curtains.

Helpless, harmless.

Milo's dead.

Which is why I do not haul to my senses, coffee and quick shave, Homburg and great coat, warm up the Dead Wagon, and make for the freeway in the early o'clock for Milo's sake. Milo doesn't have any sake anymore. I go for her—for she who has become, in the same moment and the same twinkling, like water to ice, the Widow Hornsby. I go for her—because she still can cry and care and pray and pay my bill.

The hospital that Milo died in is state-of-the-art. There are signs on every door declaring a part or a process or bodily function. I like to think that, taken together, the words would add up to The Human Condition, but they never do. What's left of Milo, the remains, are in the basement, between SHIPPING & RECEIVING and LAUNDRY ROOM. Milo would like that if he were still liking things. Milo's room is called PATHOLOGY.

The medical-technical parlance of death emphasizes disorder.

We are forever dying of failures, of anomalies, of insufficiencies, of dysfunctions, arrests, accidents. These are either chronic or acute. The language of death certificates—Milo's says "Cardiopulmonary Failure"—is like the language of weakness. Likewise, Mrs. Hornsby, in her grief, will be said to be breaking down or falling apart or going to pieces, as if there were something structurally awry with her. It is as if death and grief were not part of The Order of Things, as if Milo's failure and his widow's weeping were, or ought to be, sources of embarrassment. "Doing well" for Mrs. Hornsby would mean that she is bearing up, weathering the storm, or being strong for the children. We have willing pharmacists to help her with this. Of course, for Milo, doing well would mean he was back upstairs, holding his own, keeping the meters and monitors bleeping.

But Milo is downstairs, between SHIPPING & RECEIVING and LAUNDRY ROOM, in a stainless-steel drawer, wrapped in white plastic top to toe, and—because of his small head, wide shoulders, ponderous belly, and skinny legs, and the trailing white binding cord from his ankles and toe tag—he looks, for all the world, like a larger than life-size sperm.

I sign for him and get him out of there. At some level, I am still thinking Milo gives a shit, which by now, of course, we all know he doesn't—because the dead don't care.

Back at the funeral home, upstairs in the embalming room, behind a door marked PRIVATE, Milo Hornsby is floating on a porcelain table under florescent lights. Unwrapped, outstretched, Milo is beginning to look a little more like himself—eyes wide open, mouth agape, returning to our gravity. I shave him, close his eyes, his mouth. We call this *setting the features*. These are the features—eyes and mouth—that will never look the way they would have looked in life when they were always opening, closing, focusing, signaling, telling us something. In death, what they tell us is that they will not be doing anything anymore. The last detail to be managed is Milo's hands—one folded over the other, over the umbilicus, in an attitude of ease, of repose, of retirement.

They will not be doing anything anymore, either.

I wash his hands before positioning them.

When my wife moved out some years ago, the children stayed here, as did the dirty laundry. It was big news in a small town. There was the gossip and the goodwill that places like this are famous for. And while there was plenty of talk, no one knew exactly what to say to me. They felt helpless, I suppose. So they brought casseroles and beef stews, took the kids out to the movies or canoeing, brought their younger sisters around to visit me. What Milo did was send his laundry van around twice a week for two months, until I found a housekeeper. Milo would pick up five loads in the morning and return them by lunchtime, fresh and folded. I never asked him to do this. I hardly knew him. I had never been in his home or his laundromat. His wife had never known my wife. His children were too old to play with my children.

After my housekeeper was installed, I went to thank Milo and pay the bill. The invoices detailed the number of loads, the washers and the dryers, detergent, bleaches, fabric softeners. I think the total came to sixty dollars. When I asked Milo what the charges were for pick-up and delivery, for stacking and folding and sorting by size, for saving my life and the lives of my children, for keeping us in clean clothes and towels and bed linen, "Never mind that" is what Milo said. "One hand washes the other."

I place Milo's right hand over his left hand, then try the other way. Then back again. Then I decide that it doesn't matter. One hand washes the other either way.

The embalming takes me about two hours.

It is daylight by the time I am done.

Every Monday morning, Ernest Fuller comes to my office. He was damaged in some profound way in Korea. The details of his damage are unknown to the locals. Ernest Fuller has no limp or anything missing so everyone thinks it was something he saw in Korea that left him a little simple, occasionally perplexed, the type to draw rein abruptly in his day-long walks, to consider the meaning of litter, pausing over bottle caps and gum wrappers. Ernest Fuller has a nervous smile and a dead-fish handshake. He wears a baseball cap and thick eyeglasses. Every Sunday night Ernest goes to the supermarket and buys up the tabloids at the checkout stands with headlines that usually involve Siamese twins or movie stars or UFOs. Ernest is a speed reader and a math whiz but because of his damage, he has never held a job and never applied for one. Every Monday morning, Ernest brings me clippings of stories under headlines like: 601 LB MAN FALLS THRU COFFIN—A GRAVE SITUATION or EMBALMER FOR THE STARS SAYS ELVIS IS FOREVER. The Monday morning Milo Hornsby died, Ernest's clipping had to do with an urn full of ashes, somewhere in East Anglia, that made grunting and groaning noises, that whistled sometimes, and that was expected to begin talking. Certain scientists in England could make no sense of it. They had run several tests. The ashes' widow, how-ever, left with nine children and no estate, is convinced that her dearly beloved and greatly reduced husband is trying to give her winning numbers for the lottery. "Jacky would never leave us without good prospects," she says. "He loved his family more than anything." There is a picture of the two of them, the widow and the urn, the living and the dead, flesh and bronze, the Victrola and the Victrola's dog. She has her ear cocked, waiting.

We are always waiting. Waiting for some good word or the winning numbers. Waiting for a sign or wonder, some signal from our dear dead that the dead still care. We are gladdened when they do outstanding things, when they arise from their graves or fall through their caskets or speak to us in our waking dreams. It pleases us no end, as if the dead still cared, had agendas, were yet alive.

But the sad and well-known fact of the matter is that most of us will stay in our caskets and be dead a long time, and that our urns and graves will never make a sound. Our reason and requiems, our headstones or High Masses, will neither get us in nor keep us out of heaven. The meaning of our lives, and the memories of them, belong to the living, just as our funerals do. Whatever being the dead have now, they have by the living's faith alone.

We heat graves here for winter burials, as a kind of foreplay before digging in, to loosen the frost's hold on the ground before the sexton and his backhoe do the opening. We buried Milo in the ground on Wednesday. The mercy is that what we buried there, in an oak casket, just under the frost line, had ceased to be Milo. Milo had become the idea of himself, a permanent fixture of the third person and past tense, his widow's loss of appetite and trouble sleeping, the absence in places where we look for him, our habits of him breaking, our phantom limb, our one hand washing the other.

Naomi Shihab Nye

Thank You in Arabic

Shortly after my mother discovered my brother had been pitching his Vitamin C tablets behind the stove for years, we left the country. Her sharp alert, "Now the truth be known!" startled us at the breakfast table as she poked into the dim crevice with the nozzle of her vacuum. We could hear the pills go click, click, up the long tube.

My brother, an obedient child, a bright-eyed, dark-skinned charmer who scored high on all his tests and trilled a boy's sweet soprano, stared down at his oatmeal. Four years younger than I, he was also the youngest and smallest in his class. Somehow he maintained an intelligence and dignity more notable than that of his older, larger companions, and the pills episode, really, was a pleasant surprise to me.

Companions in mischief are not to be underestimated, especially when everything else in your life is about to change.

We sold everything we had and left the country. The move had been brewing for months. We took a few suitcases each. My mother cried when the piano went. I wished we could have saved it. My brother and I had sung so many classics over its keyboard—"Look for the Silver Lining" and "Angels We Have Heard on High"—that it would have been nice to return to a year later, when we came straggling back. I sold my life-size doll and my toy sewing machine. I begged my mother to save her red stove for me, so I could have it when I grew up—no one else we knew had a red stove. So my mother asked some friends to save it for me in their barn.

Our parents had closed their imported-gifts stores, and our father had dropped out of ministerial school. He had attended the Unity School of Christianity for a few years, but decided not to become a minister after all. We were relieved, having felt like impostors the whole time he was enrolled. He wasn't even a Christian, to begin with, but a gently non-practicing Muslim. He didn't do anything like fasting or getting down on his knees five times a day. Our mother had given up the stern glare of her Lutheran ancestors, raising my brother and me in the Vedanta Society of St. Louis. When anyone asked what we were, I said, "Hindu." We had a Swami, and sandalwood incense. It was over our heads, but we liked it and didn't feel very attracted to the idea of churches and collection baskets and chatty parish good-will.

Now and then, just to keep things balanced, we attended the Unity Sunday School. My teacher said I was lucky my father came from the same place Jesus came from. It was a passport to notoriety. She invited me to bring artifacts for Show and Tell. I wrapped a red and white *keffiyah* around my friend Jimmy's curly blond head while the girls in lacy socks giggled behind their hands. I told about my father coming to America from Palestine on the boat and throwing his old country clothes overboard before docking at Ellis Island. I felt relieved he'd kept a few things, like the *keffiyah* and its black braided band. Secretly it made me mad to have lost the blue pants from Jericho with the wide cuffs he told us about.

I enjoyed standing in front of the group talking about my father's homeland. Stories felt like elastic bands that could stretch and stretch. Big fans purred inside their metal shells. I held up a string of olive wood camels. I didn't tell our teacher about the Vedanta Society. We were growing up ecumenical, though I wouldn't know that word till a long time later in college. One night I heard my father say to my mother in the next room, "Do you think they'll be confused when they grow up?" and knew he was talking about us. My mother, bless her, knew we wouldn't be. She said, "At least we're giving them a choice." I didn't know then that more clearly than all the stories of Jesus, I'd remember the way our Hindu swami said a single word three times, "Shanti, shanti, shanti"—peace, peace, peace.

Our father was an excellent speaker—he stood behind pulpits and podiums easily, delivering gracious lectures on "The Holy Land" and "The Palestinian Question." He was much in demand during the Christmas season. I think that's how he had fallen into the ministerial swoon. While he spoke, my brother and I hovered toward the backs of the auditoriums, eyeing the tables of canapés and tiny tarts, slipping a few into our mouths or pockets.

What next? Our lives were entering a new chapter, but I didn't know its title yet.

We had never met our Palestinian grandmother, Sitti Khadra, or seen Jerusalem, where our father had grown up, or followed the rocky, narrow alleyways of the Via Dolorosa, or eaten an olive in its own neighborhood. Our mother hadn't either. The Arabic customs we knew had been filtered through the fine net of folktales. We did not speak Arabic, though the lilt of the language was familiar to us—our father's endearments, his musical blessings before meals—but that language had never lived in our mouths.

And that's where we were going, to Jerusalem. We shipped our car, a wide golden Impala the exact color of a cigarette filter, over on a boat. We would meet up with it later.

The first plane flight of my whole life was the night flight out of New York City across the ocean. I was fourteen years old. Every glittering light in every skyscraper looked like a period at the end of the sentence. Good-bye, our lives.

We stopped in Portugal for a few weeks. We were making a gradual transition. We stopped in Spain and Italy and Egypt, where the pyramids shocked me by sitting right on the edge of the giant city of Cairo, not way out in the desert as I had imagined them. While we waited for our baggage to clear customs, I stared at six tall African men in brilliantly patterned dashikis negotiating with an Egyptian customs agent and realized I did not even know how to say "Thank you" in Arabic. How was this possible? The most elemental and important of human phrases in my father's own tongue had evaded me till now. I tugged on his sleeve, but he was busy with visas and passports. "Daddy," I said. "Daddy, I have to know. Daddy, tell me. Daddy, why didn't we ever *learn?*" An African man adjusted his turban. Always thereafter, the word *shookrun,* so simple, with a little roll in the middle, would conjure up the vast African baggage, the brown boxes looped and looped in African twine.

We stayed one or two nights at the old Shepherd's Hotel downtown, but couldn't sleep because of the heat and honking traffic beneath our windows. So our father moved us to the famous Mena House Hotel next to the pyramids. We rode camels for the first time, and our mother received a dozen blood-red roses at her hotel room from a rug vendor who apparently liked her pale brown ponytail. The belly dancer at the hotel restaurant twined a gauzy pink scarf around my brother's astonished ten-year-old head as he tapped his knee in time to her music. She bobbled her giant cleavage under his nose, huge bosoms prickled by sequins and sweat.

Back in our rooms, we laughed until we fell asleep. Later that night, my brother and I both awakened burning with fever and deeply nauseated, though nobody ever threw up. We were so sick that a doctor hung a Quarantine sign in Arabic and English on our hotel room door the next day. Did he know something we didn't know? I kept waiting to hear that we had malaria or typhoid, but no dramatic disease was ever mentioned. We lay in bed for a week. The aged doctor tripped over my suitcase every time he entered to take our temperatures. We smothered our laughter. "Shookrun," I would say. But as soon as he left, to my brother, "I feel bad. How do you feel?"

"I feel really, really bad."

"I think I'm dying."

"I think I'm already dead."

At night we heard the sound and lights show from the pyramids drifting across the desert air to our windows. We felt our lives stretching out across thousands of miles. The Pharaohs stomped noisily through my head and churning belly. We had eaten spaghetti in the restaurant. I would not be able to eat spaghetti again for years.

Finally, finally, we appeared in the restaurant again, thin and weakly smiling, and ordered the famous Mena House *shorraba,* lentil soup, as my brother nervously scanned the room for the belly dancer. Maybe she wouldn't recognize him now.

In those days Jerusalem, which was then a divided city, had an operating airport on the Jordanian side. My brother and I remember flying in upside down, or in a plane dramatically tipped, but it may have been the effect of our medicine. The land reminded us of a dropped canvas, graceful brown hillocks and green patches. Small and provincial, the airport had just two runways, and the first thing I observed as we climbed down slowly from the stuffy plane was all my underwear strewn across one of them. There were my flowered cotton briefs and my pink panties and my slightly embarrassing raggedy ones and my extra training bra, alive and visible in the breeze. Somehow my suitcase had popped open in the hold and dropped its contents the minute the men pried open the cargo door. So the first thing I did on the home soil of my father was recollect my under-wear, down on my knees, the posture of prayer over that ancient holy land.

Our relatives came to see us at a hotel. Our grandmother was very short. She wore a long, thickly embroidered Palestinian dress, had a musical, high-pitched voice and a low, gut-tural laugh. She kept touching our heads and faces as if she couldn't believe we were there. I had not yet fallen in love with her. Sometimes you don't fall in love with people immedi-ately, even if they're your own grandmother. Everyone seemed to think we were all too thin.

We moved into a second-story flat in a stone house eight miles north of the city, among fields and white stones and wandering sheep. My brother was enrolled in the Friends Girls School and I was enrolled in the Friends Boys School in the town of Ramal-lah a few miles farther north—it seemed a little confused. But the Girls School offered grades one through eight in English and high school continued at the Boys School. Most local girls went to Arabic-speaking schools after eighth grade.

I was a freshman, one of seven girl students among two hundred boys, which would cause me problems later. I was called in from the schoolyard at lunchtime, to the office of our counselor who wore shoes so pointed and tight her feet bulged out pinkly on top.

"You will not be talking to them anymore," she said. She rapped on the desk with a pencil for emphasis.

"To whom?"

"All the boy students at this institution. It is inappropriate behavior. From now on, you will only speak with the girls."

"But there are only six other girls! And I only like one of them!" My friend was Anna, from Italy, whose father ran a small factory that made matches. I'd visited it once with her. It felt risky to walk the aisles among a million filled matchboxes. Later we visited the fac-tory that made olive oil soaps and stacked them in giant pyramids to dry.

"No, thank you," I said. "It's ridiculous to say that girls should only talk to girls. Did I say anything bad to a boy? Did anyone say anything bad to me? They're my friends. They're like my brothers. I won't do it, that's all."

The counselor conferred with the headmaster and they called a taxi. I was sent home with a note requesting that I transfer to a different school. The charge: insolence. My mother, startled to see me home early and on my own, stared out the window when I told her.

My brother came home from his school as usual, full of whistling and notebooks. "Did anyone tell you not to talk to girls?" I asked him. He looked at me as if I'd gone goofy. He was too young to know the troubles of the world. He couldn't even imagine them.

"You know what I've been thinking about?" he said. "A piece of cake. That puffy white layered cake with icing like they have at birthday parties in the United States. Wouldn't that taste good right now?" Our mother said she was thinking about mayonnaise. You couldn't get it in Jerusalem. She'd tried to make it and it didn't work. I felt too gloomy to talk about food.

My brother said, "Let's go let Abu Miriam's chickens out." That's what we always did when we felt sad. We let our fussy landlord's red and white chickens loose to flap around the yard happily, puffing their wings. Even when Abu Miriam shouted and waggled his cane and his wife waved a dishtowel, we knew the chickens were thanking us.

My father went with me to the St. Tarkmanchatz Armenian School, a solemnly ancient stone school tucked deep into the Armenian Quarter of the Old City of Jerusalem. It was another world in there. He had already called them on the telephone and tried to enroll me, though they didn't want to. Their school was for Armenian students only, kindergarten through twelfth grade. Classes were taught in three languages, Armenian, Arabic and English, which was why I needed to go there. Although most Arab students at other schools were learning English, I needed a school where classes were actually taught in English—otherwise I would have been staring out the windows triple the usual amount.

The head priest wore a long robe and a tall cone-shaped hat. He said, "Excuse me, please, but your daughter, she is not an Armenian, even a small amount?"

"Not at all," said my father. "But in case you didn't know, there is a stipulation in the educational code books of this city that says no student may be rejected solely on the basis of ethnic background, and if you don't accept her, we will alert the proper authorities."

They took me. But the principal wasn't happy about it. The students, however, seemed glad to have a new face to look at. Everyone's name ended in *-ian,* the beautiful, musical Armenian ending—Boghossian, Minassian, Kevorkian, Rostomian. My new classmates started calling me Shihabian. We wore uniforms, navy blue pleated skirts for the girls, white shirts, and navy sweaters. I waited during the lessons for the English to come around, as if it were a channel on television. While my friends were on the other channels, I scribbled poems in the margins of my pages, read library books, and wrote a lot of letters filled with exclamation points. All the other students knew three languages with three entirely different alphabets. How could they carry so much in their heads? I felt humbled by my ignorance. Again and again and again. One day I felt so frustrated in our physics class—still another language—that I pitched my book out the open window. The professor made me go collect it. All the pages had let loose at the seams and were flapping into the gutters along with the white wrappers of sandwiches.

Every week the girls had a hands-and-fingernails check. We had to keep our nails clean and trim, and couldn't wear any rings. Some of my new friends would invite me home for lunch with them, since we had an hour-and-a-half break and I lived too far to go to my own house.

Their houses were a thousand years old, clustered beehive fashion behind ancient walls, stacked and curled and tilting and dark, filled with pictures of unsmiling relatives and small white cloths dangling crocheted edges. We ate spinach pies and white cheese. We dipped our bread in olive oil, as the Arabs did. We ate small sesame cakes, our mouths full of crumbles. They taught me to say, "I love you" in Armenian, which sounded like *yes-kay-see-goo-see-rem*. I felt I had left my old life entirely.

Every afternoon I went down to the basement of the school where the kindergarten class was having an Arabic lesson. Their desks were pint-sized, their full white smocks tied around their necks. I stuffed my fourteen-year-old self in beside them. They had rosy cheeks and shy smiles. They must have thought I was a very slow learner.

More than any of the lessons, I remember the way the teacher rapped the backs of their hands with his ruler when they made a mistake. Their little faces puffed up with quiet tears. This pained me so terribly I forgot all my words. When it was my turn to go to the blackboard and write in Arabic, my hand shook. The kindergarten students whispered hints to me from the front row, but I couldn't understand them. We learned horribly useless phrases: "Please hand me the bellows for my fire." I wanted words simple as tools, simple as *food* and *yesterday* and *dreams*. The teacher never rapped my hand, especially after I wrote a letter to the city newspaper, which my father edited, protesting such harsh treatment of young learners. I wished I had known how to talk to those little ones, but they were just beginning their English studies and didn't speak much yet. They were at the same place in their English that I was in my Arabic.

From the high windows of St. Tarkmanchatz, we could look out over the Old City, the roofs and flapping laundry and television antennas, the pilgrims and churches and mosques, the olive-wood prayer beads and fragrant *falafel* lunch stands, the intricate interweaving of cultures and prayers and songs and holidays. We saw the barbed wire separating Jordan from Israel then, the bleak, uninhabited strip of no-man's land reminding me how little education saved us after all. People who had differing ideas still came to blows, imagining fighting could solve things. Staring out over the quiet roofs of afternoon, it seemed so foolish to me. I asked my friends what they thought about it and they shrugged.

"It doesn't matter what we think about it. It just keeps happening. It happened in Armenia too, you know. Really, really bad in Armenia. And who talks about it in the world news now? It happens everywhere. It happens in *your* country one by one, yes? Murders and guns. What can we do?"

Sometimes after school, my brother and I walked up the road that led past the crowded refugee camp of Palestinians who owned even less than our modest relatives did in the village. The kids were stacking stones in empty tin cans and shaking them. We waved our hands and they covered their mouths and laughed. We wore our beat-up American tennis shoes and our old sweatshirts and talked about everything we wanted to do and everywhere else we wished we could go.

"I want to go back to Egypt," my brother said. "I sort of feel like I missed it. Spending all that time in bed instead of exploring—what a waste."

"I want to go to Greece," I said. "I want to play a violin in a symphony orchestra in Austria." We made up things. I wanted to go back to the United States most of all. Suddenly I felt like a patriotic citizen. One of my friends, Sylvie Markarian, had just been shipped off to Damascus, Syria, to marry a man who was fifty years old, a widower. Sylvie was exactly my age—we had turned fifteen two days apart. She had never met her future husband before. "Tell your parents no thank you," I urged her. I thought this was the most revolting thing I had ever heard of. "Tell them you *refuse*."

Sylvie's eyes were liquid, swirling brown. I could not see clear to the bottom of them.

"You don't understand," she told me. "In United States you say no. We don't say no. We have to follow someone's wishes. This is the wish of my father. Me, I am scared. I never slept away from my mother before. But I have no choice. I am going because they tell me to go." She was sobbing, sobbing on my shoulder. And I was stroking her long, soft hair. After that, I carried two fists inside, one for Sylvie and one for me.

Most weekends my family went to the village to sit with the relatives. We sat and sat and sat. We sat in big rooms and little rooms, in circles, on chairs or on woven mats or brightly-covered mattresses piled on the floor. People came in and out to greet my family. Sometimes even donkeys and chickens came in and out. We were like movie stars or dignitaries. They never seemed to get tired of us.

My father translated the more interesting tidbits of conversation, the funny stories my grandmother told. She talked about angels and food and money and people and politics and gossip and old memories from my father's childhood, before he emigrated away from her. She wanted to make sure we were going to stick around forever, which made me feel very nervous. We ate from mountains of rice and eggplant on large silver trays—they gave us plates of our own since it was not our custom to eat from the same plate as other people. We ripped the giant wheels of bread into triangles. Shepherds passed through town with their flocks of sheep and goats, their long canes and cloaks, straight out of the Bible. My brother and I trailed them to the edge of the village, past the lentil fields to the green meadows studded with stones, while the shepherds pretended we weren't there. I think they liked to be alone, unnoticed. The sheep had differently colored dyed bottoms, so shepherds could tell their flocks apart.

During these long, slow, smoke-stained weekends—the men still smoked cigarettes a lot in those days, and the old *taboon,* my family's mounded bread-oven, puffed billowy clouds outside the door—my crying jags began. I cried without any warning, even in the middle of a meal. My crying was usually noiseless but dramatically wet—streams of tears pouring down my cheeks, onto my collar or the back of my hand.

Everything grew quiet.

Someone always asked in Arabic, "What is wrong? Are you sick? Do you wish to lie down?"

My father made valiant excuses in the beginning. "She's overtired," he said. "She has a headache. She is missing her friend who moved to Syria. She is feeling homesick."

My brother stared at me as if I had just landed from Planet X.

Worst was our drive to school every morning, when our car came over the rise in the highway and all Jerusalem lay sprawled before us in its golden, stony splendor pockmarked with olive trees and automobiles. Even the air above the city had a thick, religious texture, as if it were a shining brocade filled with broody incense. I cried hardest then. All those hours tied up in school lay just ahead. My father pulled over and talked to me. He sighed. He kept his hands on the steering wheel even when the car was stopped and said, "Someday, I promise you, you will look back on this period in your life and have no idea what made you so unhappy here."

"I want to go home." It became my anthem. "This place depresses me. It weighs too much. I hate all these old stones that everybody keeps kissing. I'm sick of pilgrims. They act so pious and pure. And I hate the way people stare at me here." Already I'd been involved in two street skirmishes with boys who stared too hard and long, clucking with their tongues. I'd socked one in the jaw and he socked me back. I hit the other one straight in the face with my purse.

"You could be happy here if you tried harder," my father said. "Don't compare it to the United States all the time. Don't pretend the United States is perfect. And look at your brother—he's not having any problems!"

"My brother is eleven years old."

I had crossed the boundary from uncomplicated childhood where happiness was a good ball and a horde of candy-coated Jordan almonds.

One problem was that I had fallen in love with four different boys who all played in the same band. Two of them were even twins. I never quite described it to my parents, but I wrote reams and reams of notes about it on loose-leaf paper that I kept under my sweaters in my closet.

Such new energy made me feel reckless. I gave things away. I gave away my necklace and a whole box of shortbread cookies that my mother had been saving. I gave my extra shoes away to the gypsies. One night when the gypsies camped in a field down the road from our house, I thought about their mounds of white goat cheese lined up on skins in front of their tents, and the wild *oud* music they played deep into the black belly of the night, and I wanted to go sit around their fire. Maybe they could use some shoes.

I packed a sack of old loafers that I rarely wore and walked with my family down the road. The gypsy mothers stared into my shoes curiously. They took them into their tents. Maybe they would use them as vases or drawers. We sat with small glasses of hot, sweet tea until a girl bellowed from deep in her throat, threw back her head, and began dancing. A long bow thrummed across the strings. The girl circled the fire, tapping and clicking, trilling a long musical wail from deep in her throat. My brother looked nervous. He was remembering the belly dancer in Egypt, and her scarf. I felt invisible. I was pretending to be a gypsy. My father stared at me. Didn't I recognize the exquisite oddity of my own life when I sat right in the middle of it? Didn't I feel lucky to be here? Well, yes I did. But sometimes it was hard to be lucky.

When we left Jerusalem, we left quickly. Left our beds in our rooms and our car in the drive-way. Left in a plane, not sure where we were going. The rumbles of fighting with Israel had been growing louder and louder. In the barbed-wire no-man's land visible from the windows of our house, guns cracked loudly in the middle of the night. We lived right near the edge. My father heard disturbing rumors at the newspaper that would soon grow into the infamous Six-Day War of 1967. We were in England by then, drinking tea from thin china cups and scanning the newspapers. Bombs were blowing up in Jerusalem. We worried about the village. We worried about my grandmother's dreams, which had been getting worse and worse, she'd told us. We worried about the house we'd left, and the chickens, and the children at the refugee camp. But there was nothing we could do except keep talking about it all.

My parents didn't want to go back to Missouri because they'd already said good-bye to everyone there. They thought we might try a different part of the country. They weighed the virtues of various states. Texas was big and warm. After a chilly year crowded around the small gas heaters we used in Jerusalem, a warm place sounded appealing. In roomy Texas, my parents bought the first house they looked at. My father walked into the city newspaper and said, "Any jobs open around here?"

I burst out crying when I entered a grocery store—so many different kinds of bread.

A letter on thin blue airmail paper reached me months later, written by my classmate, the bass player in my favorite Jerusalem band. "Since you left," he said, "your empty desk reminds me of a snake ready to strike. I am afraid to look at it. I hope you are having a better time than we are."

Of course I was, and I wasn't. *Home* had grown different forever. *Home* had doubled. Back *home* again in my own country, it seemed impossible to forget the place we had just left: the piercing call of the *muezzin* from the mosque at prayer time, the dusky green tint of the olive groves, the sharp, cold air that smelled as deep and old as my grandmother's white sheets flapping from the line on her roof. What story hadn't she finished?

Our father used to tell us that when he was little, the sky over Jerusalem crackled with meteors and shooting stars almost every night. They streaked and flashed, igniting the dark. Some had long golden tails. For a few seconds, you could see their whole swooping trails lit up. Our father and his brothers slept on the roof to watch the sky. "There were so many of them, we didn't even call out every time we saw one."

During our year in Jerusalem, my brother and I kept our eyes cast upwards whenever we were outside at night, but the stars were different since our father was a boy. Now the sky seemed too orderly, stuck in place. The stars had learned where they belonged. Only people on the ground kept changing.

The "Eye"

John McPhee

The Search for Marvin Gardens

Go. I roll the dice—a six and a two. Through the air I move my token, the flatiron, to Vermont Avenue, where dog packs range.

The dogs are moving (some are limping) through ruins, rubble, fire damage, open garbage. Doorways are gone. Lath is visible in the crumbling walls of the buildings. The street sparkles with shattered glass. I have never seen, anywhere, so many broken windows. A sign—"Slow, Children at Play"—has been bent backward by an automobile. At the lighthouse, the dogs turn up Pacific and disappear. George Meade, Army engineer, built the lighthouse—brick upon brick, six hundred thousand bricks, to reach up high enough to throw a beam twenty miles over the sea. Meade, seven years later, saved the Union at Gettysburg.

I buy Vermont Avenue for $100. My opponent is a tall, shadowy figure, across from me, but I know him well, and I know his game like a favorite tune. If he can, he will always go for the quick kill. And when it is foolish to go for the quick kill he will be foolish. On the whole, though, he is a master assessor of percentages. It is a mistake to underestimate him. His eleven carries his top hat to St. Charles Place, which he buys for $140.

The sidewalks of St. Charles Place have been cracked to shards by through-growing weeds. There are no buildings. Mansions, hotels once stood here. A few street lamps now drop cones of light on broken glass and vacant space behind a chain-link fence that some great machine has in places bent to the ground. Five plane trees—in full summer leaf, flecking the light—are all that live on St. Charles Place.

Block upon block, gradually, we are cancelling each other out—in the blues, the lavenders, the oranges, the greens. My opponent follows a plan of his own devising. I use the Hornblower & Weeks opening and the Zuricher defense. The first game draws tight, will soon finish. In 1971, a group of people in Racine, Wisconsin, played for seven hundred and sixty-eight hours. A game begun a month later in Danville, California, lasted eight hundred and twenty hours. These are official records, and they stun us. We have been playing for eight minutes. It amazes us that Monopoly is thought of as a long game. It is possible to play to a complete, absolute, and final conclusion in less than fifteen minutes, all within the rules as written. My opponent and I have done so thousands of times. No wonder we are sitting across from each other now in this best-of-seven series for the international singles championship of the world.

On Illinois Avenue, three men lean out from second-story windows. A girl is coming down the street. She wears dungarees and a bright-red shirt, has ample breasts and a Hadendoan Afro, a black halo, two feet in diameter. Ice rattles in the glasses in the hands of the men.

"Hey, sister!"

"Come on up!"

She looks up, looks from one to another to the other, looks them flat in the eye.

"What for?" she says, and she walks on.

I buy Illinois for $240. It solidifies my chances, for I already own Kentucky and Indiana. My opponent pales. If he had landed first on Illinois, the game would have been over then and there, for he has houses built on Boardwalk and Park Place, we share the railroads equally, and we have cancelled each other everywhere else. We never trade.

In 1852, R. B. Osborne, an immigrant Englishman, civil engineer, surveyed the route of a railroad line that would run from Camden to Absecon Island, in New Jersey, traversing the state from the Delaware River to the barrier beaches of the sea. He then sketched in the plan of a "bathing village" that would surround the eastern terminus of the line. His pen flew glibly, framing and naming spacious avenues parallel to the shore—Mediterranean, Baltic, Oriental, Ventnor—and narrower transsecting avenues: North Carolina, Pennsylvania, Vermont, Connecticut, States, Virginia, Tennessee, New York, Kentucky, Indiana, Illinois. The place as a whole had no name, so when he had completed the plan Osborne wrote in large letters over the ocean, "Atlantic City." No one ever challenged the name, or the names of Osborne's streets. Monopoly was invented in the early nineteen-thirties by Charles B. Darrow, but Darrow was only transliterating what Osborne had created. The railroads, crucial to any player, were the making of Atlantic City. After the rails were down, houses and hotels burgeoned from Mediterranean and Baltic to New York and Kentucky. Properties—building lots—sold for as little as six dollars apiece and as much as a thousand dollars. The original investors in the railroads and the real estate called themselves the Camden & Atlantic Land Company. Reverently, I repeat their names: Dwight Bell, William Coffin, John DaCosta, Daniel Deal, William Fleming, Andrew Hay, Joseph Porter, Jonathan Pitney, Samuel Richards—founders, fathers, forerunners, archetypical masters of the quick kill.

My opponent and I are now in a deep situation of classical Monopoly. The torsion is almost perfect—Boardwalk and Park Place versus the brilliant reds. His cash position is weak, though, and if I escape him now he may fade. I land on Luxury Tax, contiguous to but in sanctuary from his power. I have four houses on Indiana. He lands there. He concedes.

Indiana Avenue was the address of the Brighton Hotel, gone now. The Brighton was exclusive—a word that no longer has retail value in the city. If you arrived by automobile and tried to register at the Brighton, you were sent away. Brighton-class people came in private railroad cars. Brighton-class people had other private railroad cars for their horses—dawn rides on the firm sand at water's edge, skirts flying. Colonel Anthony J. Drexel Biddle—the sort of name that would constrict throats in Philadelphia—lived, much of the year, in the Brighton.

Colonel Sanders' fried chicken is on Kentucky Avenue. So is Clifton's Club Harlem, with the Sepia Revue and the Sepia Follies, featuring the Honey Bees, the Fashions, and the Lords.

My opponent and I, many years ago, played 2,428 games of Monopoly in a single season. He was then a recent graduate of the Harvard Law School, and he was working for a downtown firm, looking up law. Two people we knew—one from Chase Manhattan, the other from Morgan, Stanley—tried to get into the game, but after a few rounds we found that they were not in the conversation and we sent them home. Monopoly should always be *mano a mano* anyway. My opponent won 1,199 games, and so did I. Thirty were ties. He was called into the Army, and we stopped just there. Now, in Game 2 of the series, I go immediately to jail, and again to jail while my opponent seines property. He is dumb-foundingly lucky. He wins in twelve minutes.

Visiting hours are daily, eleven to two; Sunday, eleven to one; evenings, six to nine. "NO MINORS, NO FOOD, Immediate Family Only Allowed in Jail." All this above a blue steel door in a blue cement wall in the windowless interior of the basement of the city hall. The desk sergeant sits opposite the door to the jail. In a cigar box in front of him are pills in every color, a banquet of fruit salad an inch and a half deep—leapers, co-pilots, footballs, truck drivers, peanuts, blue angels, yellow jackets, redbirds, rainbows. Near the desk are two soldiers, waiting to go through the blue door. They are about eighteen years old. One of them is trying hard to light a cigarette. His wrists are in steel cuffs. A military policeman waits, too. He is a year or so older than the soldiers, taller, studious in appearance, gentle, fat. On a bench against a wall sits a good-looking girl in slacks. The blue door rattles, swings heavily open. A turnkey stands in the doorway. "Don't you guys kill yourselves back there now," says the sergeant to the soldiers.
    "One kid, he overdosed himself about ten and a half hours ago," says the M.P.
    The M.P., the soldiers, the turnkey, and the girl on the bench are white. The sergeant is black. "If you take off the handcuffs, take off the belts," says the sergeant to the M.P. "I don't want them hanging themselves back there." The door shuts and its tumblers move. When it opens again, five minutes later, a young white man in sandals and dungarees and a blue polo shirt emerges. His hair is in a ponytail. He has no beard. He grins at the good-looking girl. She rises, joins him. The sergeant hands him a manila envelope. From it he removes his belt and a small notebook. He borrows a pencil, makes an entry in the notebook. He is out of jail, free. What did he do? He offended Atlantic City in some way. He spent a night in the jail. In the nineteen-thirties, men visiting Atlantic City went to jail, directly to jail, did not pass Go, for appearing in topless bathing suits on the beach. A city statute requiring all men to wear full-length bathing suits was not seriously challenged until 1937, and the first year in which a man could legally go bare-chested on the beach was 1940.

Game 3. After seventeen minutes, I am ready to begin construction on overpriced and sluggish Pacific, North Carolina, and Pennsylvania. Nothing else being open, opponent concedes.

The physical profile of streets perpendicular to the shore is something like a playground slide. It begins in the high skyline of Boardwalk hotels, plummets into warrens of "side-avenue" motels, crosses Pacific, slopes through church missions, convalescent homes, burlesque houses, rooming houses, and liquor stores, crosses Atlantic, and runs level through the bombed-out ghetto as far—Baltic, Mediterranean—as the eye can see. North Carolina Avenue, for example, is flanked at its beach end by the Chalfonte and the Haddon Hall (908 rooms, air-conditioned), where, according to one biographer, John Philip Sousa (1854–1932) first played when he was twenty-two, insisting, even then, that everyone call him by his entire name. Behind these big hotels, motels—Barbizon, Catalina—crouch. Between Pacific and Atlantic is an occasional house from 1910—wooden porch, wooden mullions, old yellow paint—and two churches, a package store, a strip show, a dealer in fruits and vegetables. Then, beyond Atlantic Avenue, North Carolina moves on into the vast ghetto, the bulk of the city, and it looks like Metz in 1919, Cologne in 1944. Nothing has actually exploded. It is not bomb damage. It is deep and complex decay. Roofs are off. Bricks are scattered in the street. People sit on porches, six deep, at nine on a Monday morning. When they go off to wait in unemployment lines, they wait sometimes two hours. Between Mediterranean and Baltic runs a chainlink fence, enclosing rubble. A patrol car sits idling by the curb. In the back seat is a German shepherd. A sign on the fence says, "Beware of Bad Dogs."

Mediterranean and Baltic are the principal avenues of the ghetto. Dogs are everywhere. A pack of seven passes me. Block after block, there are three-story brick row houses. Whole segments of them are abandoned, a thousand broken windows. Some parts are intact, occupied. A mattress lies in the street, soaking in a pool of water. Wet stuffing is coming out of the mattress. A postman is having a rye and a beer in the Plantation Bar at nine-fifteen in the morning. I ask him idly if he knows where Marvin Gardens is. He does not. "HOOKED AND NEED HELP? CONTACT N.A.R.C.O." "REVIVAL NOW GOING ON, CONDUCTED BY REVEREND H. HENDERSON OF TEXAS." These are signboards on Mediterranean and Baltic. The second one is upside down and leans against a boarded-up window of the Faith Temple Church of God in Christ. There is an old peeling poster on a warehouse wall showing a figure in an electric chair. "The Black Panther Manifesto" is the title of the poster, and its message is, or was, that "the fascists have already decided in advance to murder Chairman Bobby Seale in the electric chair." I pass an old woman who carries a bucket. She wears blue sneakers, worn through. Her feet spill out. She wears red socks, rolled at the knees. A white handkerchief, spread over her head, is knotted at the corners. Does she know where Marvin Gardens is? "I sure don't know," she says, setting down the bucket. "I sure don't know. I've heard of it somewhere, but I just can't say where." I walk on, through a block of shattered glass. The glass crunches underfoot like coarse sand. I remember when I first came here—a long train ride from Trenton, long ago, games of poker in the train—to play basketball against Atlantic City. We were half black, they were all black. We scored forty points, they scored eighty, or something like it. What I remember most is that they had glass backboards—glittering, pendent, expensive glass backboards, a rarity then in high schools, even in colleges, the only ones we played on all year.

I turn on Pennsylvania, and start back toward the sea. The windows of the Hotel Astoria, on Pennsylvania near Baltic, are boarded up. A sheet of unpainted plywood is the door, and in it is a triangular peep-hole that now frames an eye. The plywood door opens. A man answers my question. Rooms there are six, seven, and ten dollars a week. I thank him for the information and move on, emerging from the ghetto at the Catholic Daughters of America Women's Guest House, between Atlantic and Pacific. Between Pacific and the Boardwalk are the blinking vacancy signs of the Aristocrat and Colton Manor motels. Pennsylvania terminates at the Sheraton-Seaside—thirty-two dollars a day, ocean corner. I take a walk on the Boardwalk and into the Holiday Inn (twenty-three stories). A guest is registering. "You reserved for Wednesday, and this is Monday," the clerk tells him. "But that's all right. We have *plenty* of rooms." The clerk is very young, female, and has soft brown hair that hangs below her waist. Her superior kicks her.

He is a middle-aged man with red spiderwebs in his face. He is jacketed and tied. He takes her aside. "Don't say 'plenty,'" he says. "Say 'You are fortunate, sir. We have rooms available.'"

The face of the young woman turns sour. "We have all the rooms you need," she says to the customer, and, to her superior, "How's that?"

Game 4. My opponent's luck has become abrasive. He has Boardwalk and Park Place, and has sealed the board.

Darrow was a plumber. He was, specifically, a radiator repairman who lived in Germantown, Pennsylvania. His first Monopoly board was a sheet of linoleum. On it he placed houses and hotels that he had carved from blocks of wood. The game he thus invented was brilliantly conceived, for it was an uncannily exact reflection of the business milieu at large. In its depth, range, and subtlety, in its luck-skill ratio, in its sense of infrastructure and socioeconomic parameters, in its philosophical characteristics, it reached to the profundity of the financial community. It was as scientific as the stock market. It suggested the manner and means through which an underdeveloped world had been developed. It was chess at Wall Street level. "Advance token to the nearest Railroad and pay owner twice the rental to which he is otherwise entitled. If Railroad is unowned, you may buy it from the Bank. Get out of Jail, free. Advance token to nearest Utility. If unowned, you may buy it from Bank. If owned, throw dice and pay owner a total ten times the amount thrown. You are assessed for street repairs: $40 per house, $115 per hotel. Pay poor tax of $15. Go to Jail. Go directly to Jail. Do not pass Go. Do not collect $200."

The turnkey opens the blue door. The turnkey is known to the inmates as Sidney K. Above his desk are ten closed-circuit-TV screens—assorted viewpoints of the jail. There are three cellblocks—men, women, juvenile boys. Six days is the average stay. Showers twice a week. The steel doors and the equipment that operates them were made in San Antonio. The prisoners sleep on bunks of butcher block. There are no mattresses. There are three prisoners to a cell. In winter, it is cold in here. Prisoners burn newspapers to keep warm. Cell corners are black with smudge. The jail is three years old. The men's block echoes with chatter. The man in the cell nearest Sidney K. is pacing. His shirt is covered with broad stains of blood. The block for juvenile boys is, by contrast, utterly silent—empty corridor, empty cells. There is only one prisoner. He is small and black and appears to be thirteen. He says he is sixteen and that he has been alone in here for three days.

"Why are you here? What did you do?"

"I hit a jitney driver."

The series stands at three all. We have split the fifth and sixth games. We are scrambling for property. Around the board we fairly fly. We move so fast because we do our own banking and search our own deeds. My opponent grows tense.

Ventnor Avenue, a street of delicatessens and doctors' offices, is leafy with plane trees and hydrangeas, the city flower. Water Works is on the mainland. The water comes over in submarine pipes. Electric Company gets power from across the state, on the Delaware River, in Deepwater. States Avenue, now a wasteland like St. Charles, once had gardens running down the middle of the street, a horse-drawn trolley, private homes. States Avenue was as exclusive as the Brighton. Only an apartment house, a small motel, and the All Wars Memorial Building—monadnocks spaced widely apart—stand along States Avenue now. Pawnshops, convalescent homes, and the Paradise Soul Saving Station are on Virginia Avenue. The soul-saving station is pink, orange, and yellow. In the windows flanking the door of the Virginia Money Loan Office are Nikons, Polaroids, Yashicas, Sony TVs, Underwood typewriters, Singer sewing machines, and pictures of Christ. On the far side of town, beside a single track and locked up most of the time, is the new railroad station, a small hut made of glazed firebrick, all that is left of the lines that built the city. An authentic phrenologist works on New York Avenue close to Frank's Extra Dry Bar and a church where the sermon today is "Death in the Pot." The church is of pink brick, has blue and amber windows and two red doors. St. James Place, narrow and twisting, is lined with boarding houses that have wooden porches on each of three stories, suggesting a New Orleans made of salt-bleached pine. In a vacant lot on Tennessee is a white Ford station wagon stripped to the chassis. The windows are smashed. A plastic Clorox bottle sits on the driver's seat. The wind has pressed newspaper against the chain-link fence around the lot. Atlantic Avenue, the city's principal thoroughfare, could be seventeen American Main Streets placed end to end—discount vitamins and Vienna Corset shops, movie theatres, shoe stores, and funeral homes. The Boardwalk is made of yellow pine and Douglas fir, soaked in pentachlorophenol. Downbeach, it reaches far beyond the city. Signs everywhere—on windows, lampposts, trash baskets—proclaim "Bienvenue Canadiens!" The salt air is full of Canadian French. In the Claridge Hotel, on Park Place, I ask a clerk if she knows where Marvin Gardens is. She says, "Is it a floral shop?" I ask a cabdriver, parked outside. He says, "Never heard of it." Park Place is one block long, Pacific to Boardwalk. On the roof of the Claridge is the Solarium, the highest point in town—panoramic view of the ocean, the bay, the salt-water ghetto. I look down at the rooftops of the side-avenue motels and into swimming pools. There are hundreds of people around the rooftop pools, sunbathing, reading—many more people than are on the beach. Walls, windows, and a block of sky are all that is visible from these pools—no sand, no sea. The pools are craters, and with the people around them they are countersunk into the motels.

The seventh, and final, game is ten minutes old and I have hotels on Oriental, Vermont, and Connecticut. I have Tennessee and St. James. I have North Carolina and Pacific. I have Boardwalk, Atlantic, Ventnor, Illinois, Indiana. My fingers are forming a "V." I have mortgaged most of these properties in order to pay for others, and I have mortgaged the others to pay for the hotels. I have seven dollars. I will pay off the mortgages and build my reserves with income from the three hotels. My cash position may be low, but I feel like a rocket in an underground silo. Meanwhile, if I could just go to jail for a time I could pause there, wait there, until my opponent, in his inescapable rounds, pays the rates of my hotels. Jail, at times, is the strategic place to be. I roll boxcars from the Reading and move the flatiron to Community Chest. "Go to Jail. Go directly to Jail."

The prisoners, of course, have no pens and no pencils. They take paper napkins, roll them tight as crayons, char the ends with matches, and write on the walls. The things they write are not entirely idiomatic; for example, "In God We Trust." All is in carbon. Time is required in the writing. "Only humanity could know of such pain." "God So Loved the World." "There is no greater pain than life itself." In the women's block now, there are six blacks, giggling, and a white asleep in red shoes. She is drunk. The others are pushers, prostitutes, an auto thief, a burglar caught with pistol in purse. A sixteen-year-old accused of murder was in here last week. These words are written on the wall of a now empty cell: "Laying here I see two bunks about six inches thick, not counting the one I'm laying on, which is hard as brick. No cushion for my back. No pillow for my head. Just a couple scratchy blankets which is best to use it's said. I wake up in the morning so shivery and cold, waiting and waiting till I am told the food is coming. It's on its way. It's not worth waiting for, but I eat it anyway. I know one thing when they set me free I'm gonna be good if it kills me."

How many years must a game be played to produce an Anthony J. Drexel Biddle and chestnut geldings on the beach? About half a century was the original answer, from the first railroad to Biddle at his peak. Biddle, at his peak, hit an Atlantic City streetcar conductor with his fist, laid him out with one punch. This increased Biddle's legend. He did not go to jail. While John Philip Sousa led his band along the Boardwalk playing "The Stars and Stripes Forever" and Jack Dempsey ran up and down in training for his fight with Gene Tunney, the city crossed the high curve of its parabola. Al Capone held conventions here—upstairs with his sleeves rolled, apportioning among his lieutenant governors the states of the Eastern seaboard. The natural history of an American resort proceeds from Indians to French Canadians via Biddles and Capones. French Canadians, whatever they may be at home, are Visigoths here. Bienvenue Visigoths!

My opponent plods along incredibly well. He has got his fourth railroad, and patiently, unbelievably, he has picked up my potential winners until he has blocked me everywhere but Marvin Gardens. He has avoided, in the fifty-dollar zoning, my increasingly petty hotels. His cash flow swells. His railroads are costing me two hundred dollars a minute. He is building hotels on States, Virginia, and St. Charles. He has temporarily reversed the current. With the yellow monopolies and my blue monopolies, I could probably defeat his lavenders and his railroads. I have Atlantic and Ventnor. I need Marvin Gardens. My only hope is Marvin Gardens.

There is a plaque at Boardwalk and Park Place, and on it in relief is the leonine profile of a man who looks like an officer in a metropolitan bank—"Charles B. Darrow, 1889–1967, inventor of the game of Monopoly." "Darrow," I address him, aloud. "Where is Marvin Gardens?" There is, of course, no answer. Bronze, impassive, Darrow looks south down the Boardwalk. "Mr. Darrow, please, where is Marvin Gardens?" Nothing. Not a sign. He just looks south down the Boardwalk.

My opponent accepts the trophy with his natural ease, and I make, from notes, remarks that are even less graceful than his.

Marvin Gardens is the one color-block Monopoly property that is not in Atlantic City. It is a suburb within a suburb, secluded. It is a planned compound of seventy-two handsome houses set on curvilinear private streets under yews and cedars, poplars and willows. The compound was built around 1920, in Margate, New Jersey, and consists of solid buildings of stucco, brick, and wood, with slate roofs, tile roofs, multi-mullioned porches, Giraldic towers, and Spanish grilles. Marvin Gardens, the ultimate outwash of Monopoly, is a citadel and sanctuary of the middle class. "We're heavily patrolled by police here. We don't take no chances. Me? I'm living here nine years. I paid seventeen thousand dollars and I've been offered thirty. Number one, I don't want to move. Number two, I don't need the money. I have four bedrooms, two and a half baths, front den, back den. No basement. The Atlantic is down there. Six feet down and you float. A lot of people have a hard time finding this place. People that lived in Atlantic City all their life don't know how to find it. They don't know where the hell they're going. They just know it's south, down the Boardwalk."

James Alan McPherson

Saturday Night, and Sunday Morning

"One of these days I'm go'n show you how nice a man can be
One of these days I'm go'n show you how nice a man can be
I'ma buy you a brand new Cadillac.
After, always speak some good words about me."
                                                                —*Muddy Waters*

People say it is always cold in Chicago.

Once in the dining room of the Hyde Park Hilton, I saw a father and son arguing over Sunday dinner. The father wore a dark blue gabardine suit with shoulder pads, a colored shirt, and a striped tie. The son's three-piece suit linked him with the commercial life of the city. The father's tentative manner, in that upscale hotel, defined him as self-consciously lower class. The son's manner was smooth, manicured, consciously geared to the decor of the dining room. The father did not "belong" in the dining room of the Hyde Park Hilton. The son did. The son kept saying, "But Dad, can't you see?" The father could not see. The father kept insisting on what the Bible says. The son kept making exceptions. They were discussing the son's responsibility toward a woman who was bearing his child. Each seemed determined to pull the other into an alien world.

The winter of 1985 is bitterly cold. It is the coldest day on record, and people have been warned to stay indoors. It is Saturday. At the entrance to the El station, at State and Randolph, two frostbitten boys try to sell at half-price the Sunday edition of the *Tribune*. Down on the platform, the man selling newspapers behind the concession stand is Asian. Along the platform a young black man, in a formal black suit and white shirt and black bow tie and black gloves and black sunshades, is tap-dancing. People waiting for the El, mostly white, applaud and toss coins into his top hat, upturned on the cement platform. Still another black man, handcuffed, is being led away by two Chicago policemen. One policeman also leads a lean German shepherd on a leash. The second officer, escorting an enraged white female, follows behind. The polished handcuffs on the young man's wrists catch the cold yellow light. He seems to be crying without sound.

People pretend they do not see.

During the 1980s, as traditionally, *money* best defined what Chicago runs on. People come to this city because they want to do well. Its traditions are rooted in fur trading, riverboats, railroads, stockyards, banks, commodity futures, and in buildings so tall they almost swagger in the wind off Lake Michigan. This city is unabashed in its commitment to material values, ruggedly honest about its areas of corruption. But it is also a city of great contradictions. Its downtown skyline competes with New York, Atlanta, Houston, San Francisco; its neighborhoods are rigidly ethnic and provincial. It is a city always in the process of reforming; it never seems able to get away from the same old gang. Its overt allegiances are to material values; its covert allegiances, the texture of its soul, are extremely complicated. There are probably more active places of worship in Chicago—Protestant, Catholic, and Jewish—than in any other city in the country. Chicago has contributed more to the arts than any other city; it is still self-conscious in comparing itself to New York. It is one of the most racially polarized of American cities; it is a city still capable of profound human gestures.

Perhaps Chicago is all that can be expected of America.

During the 1930s, the young Richard Wright, in search of values to replace those he thought he had left behind in Mississippi, expressed personal contempt for the public values of Chicago. "Perhaps it would be possible for the Negro to become reconciled to his plight," he wrote in *American Hunger,* "if he could be made to believe that his sufferings were for some remote, high, sacrificial end; but sharing the culture that condemns him, and seeing that a lust for trash is what blinds the nation to his claims, is what set storms to rolling in his soul."

> "Precious Lord, take my hand, lead me on, let me stand,
> I am tired, I am weak, I am worn . . . "
> —*Thomas Dorsey*

During the same time Wright lived there, Mahalia Jackson, Thomas Dorsey, and Muddy Waters came to Chicago. Like many thousands of other Mississippians, they brought with them an idiom, a technique for transcending personal storms, that Wright had somehow bypassed. They used aspects of this idiom to confront, and then to transcend, the hard facts of life. From within their roles as entertainers, from behind the various masks that provided safety, they provided Chicago's material culture with a spiritual optimism. It was Studs Terkel who, back in the 1940s, recognized the value of Mahalia Jackson's music and helped it reach a wider audience. And it was a white Chicago promoter who brought Muddy Waters from the small clubs of the South Side of Chicago to the folk festival at Newport, Rhode Island, in 1960.

Several decades later, these two giants still define the blues idiom.

Saturday Night

During his last set that evening at the Checkerboard, Buddy Guy said to his audience, "I would like your support in helping to make it possible for part of Forty-second Street to be named for Muddy Waters. He did the most to make this street famous, and I think the city should honor him." Buddy Guy was a young blues artist with a rising reputation. Small clubs like the Checkerboard, and Theresa's further down Forty-second Street, supported him. Only those who value authenticity of feeling, the "real" blues, come to these clubs. They are mostly black people, middle-aged or older, whose roots are close to the rural South. For them, the music is not entertainment. It is an organic part of a settled way of life. Groups of white students from the University of Chicago come here, especially on the weekends, but they are not really in the idiom, the felt experience. Still, they brave the cold, and the warnings of black cab drivers ("Don't flash any money. They'll knock you in the head!"), to get a feel for the authentic blues. The armed black policemen, or guards, at the doors of the clubs are there to ensure the safety of the white patrons. But still the mostly black audience sets the musical standard. Next to the front door, beside the armed black guard, a sad-faced, middle-aged black woman sits alone, playing her nightly game of solitaire. Next to the bandstand, an old black man, probably a laborer, does a slow grind to the music. Two women, one toothless and wrinkled and the other young, wearing a red headrag, embrace closely as they dance together. They seem to be supporting each other's souls. Behind my table a man is singing to himself. Suddenly he gets up, walks around the room, and says, "I got the blues! I got the blues!" He stops at my table and makes a statement: "My daughter died last week from heroin. Went out to Michael Reece Hospital, she was layin' up in bed, needle holes swole up in her neck big as a basketball. She was the baddest one of my kids. Monday, I'm takin' her ass down to Clarksdale, Mississippi, and put her six feet under. I'm go'n bury her right. I ain't go'n bury her wrong."

He asks for a contribution for the funeral and I give it to him. Then he goes up onto the small stage and sings.

I try to hear his feelings for his daughter *beneath* the words of his song. But the electrified guitars, in their mocking commentary, seem much too loud and playful. The singer seems to be crying from within his song. I find myself remembering another blues artist, a much older man named John Jackson—a gravedigger by profession and a musician by necessity—of Rappahannock, Virginia. I remember the night he was told, during a gig, that his second son was dying, this one of cancer. To outpourings of sympathy from friends, John Jackson said, "Yes, ma'am. Yes suh. I thank y'all." Then he continued with his music, making very joyful sounds on his blues banjo. John Jackson confirmed for me my suspicion that inside the best musicians is a very delicate mechanism, one guarded at all costs, trained by hard experience to transform deep pain into a kind of beauty. This mechanism, or perhaps it might be called a style, is completely integrated into the fabric of the musician's personal life. The best of them would be incapable of crying. The best of audiences would not allow it.

The blues singer steps down from the platform while the audience applauds politely. He is introduced, to all newcomers, as Muddy Waters, Jr. He passes my table as he moves back to his own. "My *main* man," he whispers to me. "My daughter has some children and I'm tryin' to do the best I can for them."

I give him more money.

While leaving the Checkerboard I observe to the guard how well Muddy is holding up under his tragic loss.

"What loss?" the guard asks.

I detail the circumstances of his daughter's death.

The guard laughs. "Man," he says, "Muddy ain't got no daughter. You give him money? He told that same shit about his mama last week, right in this club, and she was alive and well up in her own house."

It came to me that I was only a tourist from Iowa, someone who lives apart from the current uses of the blues idiom. It also came to me that the idiom had gone desperately commercial. The narrative statement had become detached from its ritual base, and survives now as a form of folklore. There was now *crying* in it.

Sunday Morning

Chicago is an urban center that is receptive to black folk art in all its forms. The many blues and jazz clubs, and the hundreds of churches, are expressions of a rural cultural tradition. How peasant traditions have been able to survive within a highly technological and commercial culture is a profound mystery. Perhaps it has to do with the midwestern lack of pretension, or with a predisposition toward democratic values, or even with Chicago's unofficial policy of ethnic segregation. Whatever has sustained its vitality, it was the cohesive power of this core culture that was the basis of Harold Washington's election as mayor. His sagging campaign finally came together on the coattails of one song, "Move On Up a Little Higher," sung at a rally by Curtis Mayfield.

The core culture is part of the city and at the same time is apart from it. To see the complex simplicity of the connection, one only has to sit on the rear seat in the last car on the El, the one going south, and watch the downtown skyscrapers become toylike and small. One can actually feel the hold of hierarchy diminishing. And, briefly, it becomes clear that Chicago is still a prairie town, one whose various outlying sections have a loose relationship with the controlling powers in the skyscrapers. This arrangement encourages a closeness with one's own ethnic roots.

> "I can't say one thing and then do another,
> Be a saint by day and a devil under cover,
> I got to live the life I sing about in my song. . ."
>
> *—Mahalia Jackson*

The purest expression of the blues idiom was once found in the black Baptist churches. Hundreds of them thrive on the south and west sides of the city: First Baptist, Christian Tabernacle, Greater Salem Baptist. It was at Greater Salem that Mahalia Jackson reached a national and international audience. She was the greatest of gospel singers, and her aristocratic presence still dominates this expression of the idiom. Each January 28, the anniversary of her death in 1972, Studs Terkel plays a retrospective in her honor. He had great love for her. Now, several decades later, in the hums and phrasings of individual singers, one can hear the style she imposed on a folk form. Inside the churches, on Sunday mornings, one can *feel* that her definition of gospel music ("Having faith with a little *bounce* added") still holds true.

Inside Shiloh Baptist, on Forty-ninth Street, one feels a sense of redemption and renewal. For almost half an hour, a slender young girl leads a two-hundred-voice choir in urging a full congregation to "Don't Give Up." Although the organ is electrified, and although the choir is being "conducted" as if it were a symphony, the spirit *is* there, among the people. The call and response between the girl and the choir is hypnotic. Time stops, and she is a priestess performing an ancient ritual function. People shout, dance, wave hands, shake tambourines, are "possessed," transcend private selves and are redeemed into a common spiritual body. They become a collective soul, all essentially equal, before God. The minister comes, now that the preparatory work is over, and begins what soon becomes a jazzlike riff on one line in the Book of Matthew. The message is unimportant. His sole function is to keep the spirit active among his people. Trained nurses in white uniforms rush back and forth, reviving those whose souls have been released from tremendous burdens. For a while, it seems absolutely evident that "Jesus Is on the Main Line," and that one only has to tell Him what one wants. Feeling the collective faith and spirit of the people, it becomes clearer why Christianity is the most radical of religions, why the bedrock and basic values of American society cannot erode. The resilience, the optimistic dream of a foundation in the future, are rooted in churches such as these. It is no accident that gospel music is an essential idiom in evangelical Christianity. It speaks directly to the soul.

"When you get a song in your heart," Mahalia Jackson said, "and you just sing it, it makes you forget about everything. It's good when we can be on one accord. It's good to be on one accord. . . ." The serenity and eloquent economy, the personal dignity, that characterized Mahalia's rendition of gospel can still be heard in the voices of some singers. But like the blues, the basic form has become somewhat standardized. In many of the churches, the idiom has shifted back toward its roots in dance music, threatening to deprive the individual singer of her ritual significance. It is difficult to appreciate the vocabulary of a moan when it is heard against a background of electrified music. The orchestration of the choir, the incorporation of electrified organs and guitars, the almost predictable up-tempo—these are concessions to trends that have become a part of *most* American music. One consequence is that the same arrangements of sounds flow out of a variety of different churches in Chicago each Sunday morning. It is almost as if the technological bias in the outside culture has begun to impose its own highest value, the interchangeability of all parts, on the spiritual values basic to the transcendent ambitions of the idiom. One has the sense, after listening to the music for a while, of human souls encased in metal cages struggling to rise above them. One misses the feel of a *single* human soul speaking out of its own inner calm to the collective soul. One misses the *silence* of the spirit as it descends, or is made manifest, among the congregants. As one misses the simple lyrical compassion that a single human voice and a piano once had for each other. Perhaps I miss only certain people—Mahalia Jackson, Thomas Dorsey—whose personal sounds said that they had gone through the fires and had come out *redeemed.* The purifying work of the fire was in their voices.

In Chicago, the sacred and the secular are inextricably linked. It is a sophisticated commercial city, but it respects artistic integrity. It is ethnically segregated, but it allows each group to preserve its own culture. It is a cold city, but it preserves many islands of human warmth. It has provided a home for the blues idiom, and it has nurtured a few giants. Their influence and the standards they set still dominate the popular culture of the city. The names of developing musicians in the idiom suggest a continuing stance of apprenticeship: Muddy Waters, Jr., Buddy Guy, Sons of Blues. They perform at the Checkerboard and at Theresa's, against the old standard. But they also perform on the

North Side, before ethnically mixed, middle-class audiences, at the Kingston Mines, the Blues, the Wise Fool. They seem to know that their roots go back to the South Side, and from there to the rural towns of Mississippi and Alabama, to the tough experiences of *life* that went into the making of the idiom. Many of the current singers seem to have not yet settled the philosophical distinction between the requirements of folk art and the requirements of entertainment. Some of them guide their audiences from one set into another with a certain promise. "We go'n play some Muddy Waters for you. We go'n be right back and play some Muddy Waters for you. . . ."

One expects that in time, and through the hard lessons of the *life* behind the expressions of the idiom, some of them eventually will.

On that trip nine years ago, I went into Chicago looking for something much better than what I saw. Perhaps I expected to see areas of "purity" in my own ethnic community, some kind of muscular resolve, derived from the traditions of the blues idiom, to forego participation in the general cannibalizing of basic values which characterized that bleak time. Instead I saw what was there: human beings trying to make it as best they could.

It has become an easy cliché by now to say that corruption, public as well as personal, became normative during those years. The stance I took, while trying to explore the cultural life of the city, was bemused disbelief. I did not want to believe that those people who were hit the hardest by Reagan's policies would actually participate in the corruption of the very aesthetic forms created by their ancestors to fortify their souls against oppression. I suppose I nursed a romantic expectation that the mere fact of physical segregation would insulate black people, and our values, from the basic corruption of that time. But the cities, as everyone knew except me, had been written off. Poverty and homelessness had been placed on the back burners of national consciousness.

The word "decadence" is now gaining currency as a way of defining, in 1994, the state of the American soul. I would sharpen it to mean a debilitated, spiritless level of existence, such as what I saw in Chicago, and was defined by Ortega y Gassett in *The Dehumanization of Art:*

> The acute dissociation between past and present is the sign of our times, a generic factor of the epoch, and with it arises a suspicion, more or less vague, which engenders the restlessness peculiar to life in our times. Present day man feels alone on the face of the earth, and suspects that the dead did not die "in jest but in earnest," not ritually but factually, and can no longer help us. The remnants of the traditional spirit have evaporated. Norms, models, standards are of no further use. We must resolve our problems without the active collaboration of the past, totally confined to the present—whether our problems be in art, science, or politics. Modern man finds himself alone, without any living shadow at his side . . . That is what always happens at high noon. . . .

I saw in Chicago nine years ago a period just before "high noon." It is now some time past that hour and little has changed to help renew the vitality of the blues idiom or the Chicago landscape against which it once thrived. The cities have been abandoned as a total loss. Yet there are some hopeful signs. The jazz musician Wynton Marsalis, in his ongoing attempt to renew the blues idiom, has taken it back to its ritual beginnings in the African American church. His recent "In This House on This Morning" is the most "pure" and ritually based sound that I have heard in the idiom since Pharoah Sander's "Journey to the One" just at the beginning of the madness that was the 1980s. Perhaps the black American community will reclaim through its musicians, after all, its old enclaves of artistic purity.

Sarah Vowell

What He Said There

There are children playing soccer on a field at Gettysburg where the Union Army lost the first day's fight. Playing soccer, like a bunch of Belgians—and in the middle of football season no less. Outside of town, there's a billboard for a shopping mall said to be "*The* Gettysburg Address For Shopping." Standing on the train platform where Abraham Lincoln disembarked from Washington on November 18, 1863, there's a Confederate soldier, a reenactor. "Which direction is south?" I ask him, trying to re-create the presidential moment. When the fake Johnny Reb replies that he doesn't know, I scold him, "Dude, you're from there!" Around the corner, the citizens of Gettysburg stand in line at the Majestic Theater for the 2:10 showing of *Meet the Parents*. Bennett, the friend I'm with, makes a dumb joke about Lincoln meeting his in-laws, the Todds. "Things did not go well," he says.

It is November 19, 2000, the 137th anniversary of the cemetery dedication ceremony at which Lincoln delivered a certain speech. "Four score and seven years ago," Lincoln said, referring to the Declaration of Independence in 1776, "our fathers brought forth on this continent a new nation, conceived in Liberty, and dedicated to the proposition that all men are created equal." Always start with the good news.

I could say that I've come to Gettysburg as a rubbernecking tourist, that I've shown up to force myself to mull over the consequences of a war I never think about. Because that would make a better story—a gum-chewing, youngish person who says "like" too much, comes face to face with the horrors of war and Learns Something. But, like, this story isn't like that. Fact is, I think about the Civil War all the time, every day. I can't even use a cotton ball to remove my eye makeup without spacing out about slavery's favorite cash crop and that line from Lincoln's Second Inaugural Address that "it may seem strange that any men should dare to ask a just God's assistance in wringing their bread from the sweat of other men's faces." Well, that, and why does black eyeliner smudge way more than brown?

I guess Gettysburg is a pilgrimage. And, like all pilgrims, I'm a mess. You don't cross state lines to attend the 137th anniversary of anything unless something's missing in your life.

The fighting at Gettysburg took place between July 1 and July 3, 1863. The Union, under the command of General George Meade, won. But not at first, and not with ease. In the biggest, bloodiest battle ever fought on U.S. soil, 51,000 men were killed, wounded, or missing. I am interested enough in that whopping statistic to spend most of the day being driven around the immense battlefield. Interested enough to walk down a spur on Little Round Top to see the monument to the 20th Maine, where a bookish but brave college professor named Joshua Lawrence Chamberlain ran out of ammo and ordered the bayonets that held the Union's ground. Interested enough to stop at the Copse of Trees—where the Confederate General George Pickett aimed his thousands of soldiers who were mowed down at the climax—and sit on a rock and wonder how many Southern skulls were cracked open on it.

I care enough about the 51,000 to visit the graves, semicircular rows of stones with the otherwise forgotten names of Jeremiah Davis and Jesse Wills and Wesley Raikes laid right next to Hiram Hughes. And the little marble cubes engraved with numbers assigned the unknown. Who was 811? Or 775? The markers for the unknowns are so minimal and so beautiful I catch myself thinking of these men as sculptures. Here, they are called "bodies." There are slabs chiseled MASSACHUSETTS 159 BODIES and CONNECTICUT 22 BODIES and WISCONSIN 73 BODIES.

So I pay my respects to the bodies, but I'll admit that I am more concerned with the 272 words President Lincoln said about them. The best the slaughtered can usually hope for is a cameo in some kind of art. Mostly, we living need a *Guernica* to remind us of Guernica. In the Gettysburg Address, Lincoln said of the men who shed their blood, "The world will little note, nor long remember, what we say here, but it can never forget what they did here." Who did he think he was kidding? We only think of them because of him. Robert E. Lee hightailed it out of Gettysburg on the Fourth of July, the same day the Confederates surrendered Vicksburg to U. S. Grant—a big deal at the time because it gave the Feds control of the Mississippi. And yet who these days dwells on Vicksburg, except for the park rangers who work there and a handful of sore losers who whine when they're asked to take the stars and bars off their godforsaken state flags?

The Gettysburg Address is more than a eulogy. It's a soybean, a versatile little problem solver that can be processed into seemingly infinite, ingenious products. In this speech, besides cleaning up the founding fathers' slavery mess by calling for a "new birth of freedom," Lincoln comforted grieving mothers who would never bounce grandchildren on their knees and ran for reelection at the same time. Lest we forget, he came to Washington from Illinois. Even though we think of him as the American Jesus, he had a little Mayor Daley in him too. Lincoln the politician needed the win at Gettysburg and, on the cusp of an election year, he wanted to remind the people explicitly that they could win the war if they just held on, while implicitly reminding them to use their next presidential ballot to write their commander in chief a thank-you note.

Privately, Lincoln has mixed feelings about Gettysburg because he's certain the war could have ended right here if only General Meade had not let General Lee get away. According to a letter written right after the battle, Lincoln is "deeply mortified" that "Meade and his noble army had expended all the skill, and toil, and blood, up to the ripe harvest, and then let the crop go to waste." Because Lincoln is a good man, he does not say this in front of the families who came to the cemetery to hear that their loved ones "shall not have died in vain." Because he is a good politician, he looks on the bright side. Though I personally suspect that in Lincoln's first draft, the line about how "it is for us the living, rather, to be dedicated here to the unfinished work which they who fought here have thus far so nobly advanced" was simply "Goddamn fucking Meade."

Abraham Lincoln is one of my favorite writers. "The mystic chords of memory." "Better angels of our nature." "The father of waters flows unvexed to the sea." All those brilliant phrases I'd admired for so long, and yet I never truly thought of him as a writer until I visited the David Wills house in Gettysburg's town square.

In 1863, Wills was charged by Pennsylvania's governor to oversee the battlefield's cleanup and the construction of the cemetery. His house, now a museum, is where Lincoln stayed the night before delivering the address. I walk into the room where Lincoln slept, with its flowerdy carpet and flowerdy walls, with its canopy bed and its water pitcher and towels, and for several minutes the only possible thought is that he was here. There's the window he leaned out of the night of the 18th, teasing the crowd outside that he had nothing to say. And, this being a sweet old-fashioned tourist trap, there's a gangly Lincoln mannequin in white shirtsleeves, hunched over a small table, his long legs poking out the side. He's polishing the speech. The myth is that he wrote it on the back of an envelope on the train, but probably he's been slaving over it for days and days. Still, he doesn't finish it until he's in this room, the morning of the 19th, the morning he's to deliver it.

To say that Abraham Lincoln was a writer is to say that he was a procrastinator. How many deadlines have I nearly blown over the years, slumped like Lincoln, fretting over words that didn't come out until almost too late? Of course, the stakes are lower when one is under pressure to think up insightful things to say about the new Brad Pitt movie instead of, say, saving the Union. On the other hand, I've whipped out Aerosmith record reviews that are longer than the Gettysburg Address, so where's *my* mannequin?

Looking at Lincoln rushing to stave off failure, I felt so close to him. Or let's say I felt closer. My grandest hope for my own hastily written sentences is that they would keep a stranger company on an airplane. Abraham Lincoln could turn a pretty phrase such as "I invoke the considerate judgment of mankind" and put it in the proclamation that *freed the slaves*. Even Mailer wouldn't claim to top that.

At the Gettysburg National Cemetery, there's a ceremony every November 19 to celebrate the anniversary of Lincoln's speech. I sit down on a folding chair among the shivering townspeople. A brass band from Gettysburg High School plays the national anthem. The eminent Yale historian James McPherson delivers a speech he may have written a long time ago to make college students feel bad. Because when he accuses the audience of taking our democracy for granted, there's a rustling in the crowd. While people who commemorate the anniversary of the Gettysburg Address surely have a lot of problems, taking democracy for granted isn't one of them. New Jersey's governor, Christine Todd Whitman, then takes the podium, proclaiming, "Our government doesn't have all the answers, and it never will." That is code for "Sorry about that icky photo that shows me laughing as I frisk an innocent black man on a State Police ride-along."

I sit through all of this, impatient. I didn't come here for the opening acts. Like a Van Halen concertgoer who doesn't high-five his friend until he hears the first bar of "Jump," all I've been waiting for is for the Lincoln impersonator James Getty to stand up and read the Gettysburg Address already. This is what Garry Wills says happened after Lincoln stopped talking in 1863: "The crowd departed with a new thing in its ideological luggage, that new constitution Lincoln had substituted for the one they brought there with them. They walked off, from those curving graves on the hillside, under a changed sky, into a different America." This is what happened after the Lincoln impersonator stopped talking in the year 2000: The eight-year-old boy sitting next to me pointed at Getty and asked his mom, "Isn't that guy too short?"

I glance at the kid with envy. He's at that first, great, artsy-craftsy age when Americans learn about Abraham Lincoln. How many of us drew his beard in crayon? We built models of his boyhood cabin with Elmer's glue and toothpicks. We memorized the Gettysburg Address, reciting its ten sentences in stovepipe hats stapled out of black construction paper. The teachers taught us to like Washington and to respect Jefferson. But Lincoln—him they taught us to love.

Craft Essays

André Aciman

A Literary Pilgrim Progresses to the Past

What my dentist cried out one day after finally removing an unsuspected fourth nerve from one of my molars comes to mind each time I try to understand myself as a writer. Do I, as a writer, have what he called a "hidden nerve"?

Don't all writers have a hidden nerve, call it a secret chamber, something irreducibly theirs, which stirs their prose and makes it tick and turn this way or that, and identifies them, like a signature, though it lurks far deeper than their style, or their voice or other telltale antics?

A hidden nerve is what every writer is ultimately about. It's what all writers wish to uncover when writing about themselves in this age of the personal memoir. And yet it's also the first thing every writer learns to sidestep, to disguise, as though this nerve were a deep and shameful secret that needs to be swathed in many sheaths. Some don't even know they've screened this nerve from their own gaze, let alone another's. Some crudely mistake confession for introspection. Others, more cunning perhaps, open tempting shortcuts and roundabout passageways, the better to mislead everyone. Some can't tell whether they're writing to strip or hide that secret nerve.

I have no idea to which category I belong.

As for a sheath, however, I'd spot mine in a second. It is place. I begin my inward journey by writing about place. Some do so by writing about love, war, suffering, cruelty, power, God or country. I write about place, or the memory of place. I write about a city called Alexandria, which I'm supposed to have loved, and about other cities that remind me of a vanished world to which I allegedly wish to return. I write about exile, remembrance and the passage of time. I write—so it would seem—to recapture, to preserve and return to the past, though I might just as easily be writing to forget and put that past behind me.

And yet my hidden nerve lies quite elsewhere. To work my way closer to it, I'd have to write about loss and feeling unhinged in provisional places where everyone else seems to have a home and a place, and where everyone knows what he wants, who he is and who he's likely to become.

My Alexandrians, however, have an unsteady foothold wherever they stand; they shift time zones, life passions, loyalties and accents with the unwieldly sense that the real world swims before them, that they are strangers in it, that they're never quite entitled to it. Yet peel this second sheath, and you'll find another.

I may write about place and displacement, but what I'm really writing about is dispersion, evasion, ambivalence: not so much a subject as a move in everything I write. I may write about little parks in New York that remind me of Rome and about tiny squares in Paris that remind me of New York, and about so many spots in the world that will ultimately take me back to Alexandria. But this crisscrossed trajectory is simply my way of showing how scattered and divided I am about everything else in life.

I may never mention dispersion or evasion by name. But I write around them. I write away from them. I write from them, the way some people write around loneliness, guilt, shame, failure, disloyalty, the better to avoid staring at them.

Ambivalence and dispersion run so deep that I don't know whether I like the place I've chosen to call my home, any more than I know whether I like the writer or even the person I am when no one's looking. And yet the very act of writing has become my way of finding a space and of building a home for myself, my way of taking a shapeless, marshy world and firming it up with paper, the way the Venetians firm up eroded land by driving wooden piles into it.

I write to give my life a form, a narrative, a chronology; and, for good measure, I seal loose ends with cadenced prose and add glitter where I know things were quite lusterless. I write to reach out to the real world, though I know that I write to stay away from a world that is still too real and never as provisional or ambivalent as I'd like it to be. In the end it's no longer, and perhaps never was, the world that I like, but writing about it. I write to find out who I am; I write to give myself the slip. I write because I am always at one remove from the world but have grown to like saying so.

Thus I turn to Alexandria, the mythical home of paradox. But Alexandria is merely an alibi, a mold, a construct. Writing about Alexandria helps me give a geographical frame to a psychological mess. Alexandria is the nickname I give this mess. Ask me to be intimate, and I'll automatically start writing about Alexandria.

I'll write about diaspora and dispossession, but these big words hold my inner tale together, the way lies help keep the truth afloat. I use the word *exile,* not because I think it is the right term, but because it approximates something far more intimate, more painful, more awkward: exile from myself, in the sense that I could so easily have had another life, lived elsewhere, loved others, been someone else.

If I keep writing about places, it is because some of them are coded ways of writing about myself: like me, they are always somewhat dated, isolated, uncertain, thrust precariously in the middle of larger cities, places that have become not just stand-ins for Alexandria, but stand-ins for me. I walk past them and think of me.

Let me turn the clock back thirty years.

It is October 1968, and I've just arrived in New York City. Mornings are nippy. It's my second week here. I have found a job in the mailroom at Lincoln Center. During my rounds at 10:30 every morning the plaza is totally empty and its fountain silent. Here every day I am always reminded of my very early childhood, when my mother would take me for long walks along a quiet plantation road far beyond our home.

There is something serene and peaceful in this memory. I go out every morning knowing that as soon as I get a whiff of a nippy Manhattan breeze, I'll encounter the memory of those plantation mornings and the hand that held mine along these long walks.

Fast-forward more than two decades. It is 1992. On certain warm summer days at noon I go to pick up my mother on Sixtieth Street, where she still works as an office clerk. We buy fruit and sandwiches on Broadway and walk awhile until we find a shady stone bench at Lincoln Center's Damrosch Park. At times I bring my two-year-old son, who'll scamper about, eating a spoonful, then run back to hide in between raised flowers beds.

Afterward he and I walk my mother back to her office; we say good-bye, then head toward Broadway to catch the bus across from a tiny park where Dante's statue stands. I tell him of Paolo and Francesca, and of cruel Gianciotto, and of Farinata the exile and Count Ugolino who starved with his children.

Dante's statue still reminds me of the tales I told my son then; it reminds me of this park and of other small parks I've since written about, and of how I felt guilty as a son, letting my mother hold so menial a job in her seventies, taking her out for a walk when it was clearly too warm for her, and how, to write a memoir about our life in Egypt, I had hired a full-time baby-sitter who was only too glad to have the time off whenever I'd take my son to lunches that I resented sometimes because they'd steal me from my desk. I think back to that summer and to my explosive snubs whenever my mother complained I'd arrived too late again.

One day, after losing my temper and making her cry at lunch, I went home and wrote about how she would sit in our balcony in Alexandria smoking a cigarette, and of how the wind had fanned her hair on the day she came to pick me up at school after someone had called home saying I had been suspended that day. Together we rode the tram downtown, naming the stations one by one.

Now, whenever I look back to those hot afternoons at Lincoln Center, I see two boys, me and my son, and I see my mother both as she was during those summer lunches in the early '90s and as I remembered her on our walks along the plantation road two and a half decades earlier. But the one mother most clearly limned on those stone benches at Damrosch Park is the one riding the tram with me: serene, ebullient, carefree, catching the light of the sun on her face as she recited the names of the stations to me.

I did not lie about the names of the tram stations, but I did make up the scene about her coming to school that day. It doesn't matter. For this scene's hidden nerve lay somewhere else: in my wanting to stay home and write, in not knowing which mother I was writing about, in wishing she could be young once more, or that I might be her young boy again, or that both of us might still be in Egypt, or that we should be grateful we weren't.

Perhaps it had something to do with my failure to rescue her from work that day, which I'd inverted into her rescuing me from school; or perhaps with my reluctance to believe that an entirely invented scene could have so cathartic an effect, and that lies do purge the mind of mnemonic dead weight.

I don't know. Perhaps writing opens up a parallel universe into which, one by one, we'll move all of our dearest memories and rearrange them as we please.

Perhaps this is why all memoirists lie. We alter the truth on paper so as to alter it in fact; we lie about our past and invent surrogate memories the better to make sense of our lives and live the life we know was truly ours. We write about our life, not to see it as it was, but to see it as we wish others might see it, so we may borrow their gaze and begin to see our life through their eyes, not ours.

Only then, perhaps, would we begin to understand our life story, or to tolerate it and ultimately, perhaps, to find it beautiful; not that any life is ever beautiful, but the measure of a beautiful life is perhaps one that sees its blemishes, knows they can't be forgiven and, for all that, learns each day to look the other way.

Vivian Gornick

from The Situation and the Story

I began my own working life in the 1970s as a writer of what was then called personal journalism, a hybrid term meaning part personal essay, part social criticism. On the barricades for radical feminism, it had seemed natural to me from the minute I sat down at the typewriter to use myself—that is, to use my own response to a circumstance or an event—as a means of making some larger sense of things. At the time, of course, that was a shared instinct. Many other writers felt similarly compelled. The personal had become political, and the headlines metaphoric. We all felt implicated. We all felt that immediate experience signified. Wherever a writer looked, there was a narrative line to be drawn from the political tale being told on a march, at a party, during a chance encounter. Three who did it brilliantly during those years were Joan Didion, Tom Wolfe, and Norman Mailer.

From the beginning I saw the dangers of this kind of writing, saw what remarkable focus it would take to maintain the right balance between me and the story. Personal journalism had already thrown up many examples of people rushing into print with no clear idea of the relation between narrator and subject; writers were repeatedly falling into the pit of confessionalism or therapy on the page or naked self-absorption.

I don't know how well or how consistently I practiced what I had begun to preach to myself, but invariably I took it as my task to keep the narrating self subordinated to the idea in hand. I knew that I was never to tell an anecdote, fashion a description, indulge in a speculation whose point turned on me. I was to use myself only to clarify the argument, develop the analysis, push the story forward. I thought my grasp of the situation accurate and my self-consciousness sufficient. The reliable reporter in me would guarantee the trustworthy narrator.

One day a book editor approached me with an idea that struck a note of response. I had confided in her the tale of an intimate friendship I'd made with an Egyptian whose childhood in Cairo had strongly resembled my own in the Bronx. The resemblance had induced an ardent curiosity about "them"; and now I was being invited to go to Egypt, to write about middle-class Cairenes.

I said yes with easy pleasure, assuming that I would do in Cairo what I had been doing in New York. That is, I'd put myself down in the middle of the city, meet the people, turn them into encounters, use my own fears and prejudices to let them become themselves, and then I'd *make* something of it.

But Cairo was not New York, and personal journalism turned out not exactly the right job description.

The city was a bombardment of stimuli—dusty, crowded, noisy, alive and in pain—and the people—dark, nervous, intelligent; ignorant, volatile, needy; familiar, somehow very familiar—after all, how far from the idiom of excitable ghetto Jews was that of urban Muslims. The familiarity was my downfall. It excited and confused me. I fell in love with it and I romanticized it, made a mystery of the atmosphere and of myself in it. Who was I? Who were *they? Where* was I, and what was it all about? The problem was I didn't really want the answers to these questions. I found the "unknowingness" of things alluring. I thought it fine to lose myself in it. But when one makes a romance out of not knowing, the reliable reporter is in danger of becoming the untrustworthy narrator. And to a large degree she did.

I spent six hardworking months in Cairo. Morning, noon, and night I was out with Egyptians: doctors, housewives, journalists; students, lawyers, guides; friends, neighbors, lovers. It seemed to me that there was no more interesting thing in the world to do than to hang out with these people who smoked passionately, spoke with intensity, were easily agitated, and seemed consumed with a nervous tenderness applied to themselves and to one another. I thought their condition profound, and I identified with it. Instead of analyzing my subject, I merged with my subject. The Egyptians loved their own anxiety, thought it made them poetic. I got right into it, loving and dramatizing it as much as they did. Anecdote after anecdote collected in my notes, each one easily suffused with the fever of daily life in Cairo. Merely to reproduce it, I thought, would be to tell a story.

Such identification in writing has its uses and its difficulties, and in my book on Egypt the narration reflects both. On the one hand, the prose is an amazement of energy, crowded with description and response. On the other, the sentences are often rhetorical, the tone ejaculatory, the syntax overloaded. Where one adjective will do, three are sure to appear. Where quiet would be useful, agitation fills the page. Egypt was a country of indiscriminate expressiveness overflowing its own margins. My book does this curious thing: it mimics Egypt itself. That is its strength and its limitation.

It seemed to me for a long time that the problem had been detachment: I hadn't had any, hadn't even known it was a thing to be prized; that, in fact, without detachment there can be no story; description and response, yes, but no story. Even so, the confusion went deeper. When I had been a working journalist, politics had provided me with a situation, and polemics had given me my story. Now, in Egypt, I was in free fall, confused by a kind of writing whose requirements I did not understand but whose power I felt jerked around by. It wasn't personal journalism I was trying to write; it was personal narrative. It would be years before I sat down at the desk with sufficient command of the distinction to control the material. That is, to serve the situation and tell the kind of story I now wanted to tell.

Every work of literature has both a situation and a story. The situation is the context or circumstance, sometimes the plot; the story is the emotional experience that preoccupies the writer: the insight, the wisdom, the thing one has come to say. In *An American Tragedy* the situation is Dreiser's America; the story is the pathological nature of hunger for the world.

In Edmund Gosse's memoir *Father and Son* the situation is fundamentalist England in the time of Darwin; the story is the betrayal of intimacy necessary to the act of becoming oneself. In a poem called "In the Waiting Room" Elizabeth Bishop describes herself at the age of seven, during the First World War, sitting in a dentist's office, turning the pages of *National Geographic,* listening to the muted cries of pain her timid aunt utters from within. That's the situation. The story is a child's first experience of isolation: her own, her aunt's, and that of the world.

Augustine's *Confessions* remains something of a model for the memoirist. In it, Augustine tells the tale of his conversion to Christianity. That's the situation. In this tale, he moves from an inchoate sense of being to a coherent sense of being, from an idling existence to a purposeful one, from a state of ignorance to one of truth. That's the story. Inevitably, it's a story of self-discovery and self-definition.

The subject of autobiography is always self-definition, but it cannot be self-definition in the void. The memoirist, like the poet and the novelist, must engage with the world, because engagement makes experience, experience makes wisdom, and finally it's the wisdom—or rather the movement toward it—that counts. "Good writing has two characteristics," a gifted teacher of writing once said. "It's alive on the page and the reader is persuaded that the writer is on a voyage of discovery." The poet, the novelist, the memoirist—all must convince the reader they have some wisdom, and are writing as honestly as possible to arrive at what they know. To the bargain, the writer of personal narrative must also persuade the reader that the narrator is reliable. In fiction a narrator may be—and often famously is—unreliable (as in *The Good Soldier, The Great Gatsby,* Philip Roth's Zuckerman novels). In nonfiction, never. In nonfiction the reader must believe that the narrator is speaking truth. Invariably, of nonfiction it is asked, "Is this narrator trustworthy? Can I believe what he or she is telling me?"

How do nonfiction narrators make themselves trustworthy? A question perhaps best answered by example.

"In Moulmein, in Lower Burma," George Orwell writes in "Shooting an Elephant," "I was hated by large numbers of people—the only time in my life that I have been important enough for this to happen to me. I was sub-divisional police officer of the town, and in an aimless, petty kind of way anti-European feeling was very bitter. No one had the guts to raise a riot, but if a European woman went through the bazaars alone somebody would probably spit betel juice over her dress. As a police officer I was an obvious target and was baited whenever it seemed safe to do so. When a nimble Burman tripped me up on the football field and the referee (another Burman) looked the other way, the crowd yelled with hideous laughter. This happened more than once. In the end the sneering yellow faces of young men that met me everywhere, the insults hooted after me when I was at a safe distance, got badly on my nerves. The young Buddhist priests were the worst of all. There were several thousands of them in the town and none of them seemed to have anything to do except stand on street corners and jeer at Europeans.

"All this was perplexing and upsetting. For at that time I had already made up my mind that imperialism was an evil thing and the sooner I chucked up my job and got out of it the better. Theoretically—and secretly, of course—I was all for the Burmese and all against their oppressors, the British. As f r the job I was doing, I hated it more bitterly than I can perhaps make clear. In a job like that you see the dirty work of Empire at close quarters. The wretched prisoners huddling in the stinking cages of the lock-ups, the grey, cowed faces of the long-term convicts, the scarred buttocks of the men who had been flogged with bamboos—all these oppressed me with an intolerable sense of guilt. But I could get nothing into perspective. I was young and ill-educated and I had had to think out my problems in the utter silence that is imposed on every Englishman in the East. I did not even know that the British Empire is dying, still less did I know that it is a great deal better than the younger empires that are going to supplant it. All I knew was that I was stuck between my hatred of the empire I served and my rage against the evil-spirited little beasts who tried to make my job impossible. With one part of my mind I thought of the British Raj as an unbreakable tyranny, as something clamped down, in *saecula saeculorum,* upon the will of prostrate peoples; with another part I thought that the greatest joy in the world would be to drive a bayonet into a Buddhist priest's guts. Feelings like these are the normal by-products of imperialism; ask any Anglo-Indian official, if you can catch him off duty."

The man who speaks those sentences *is* the story being told: a civilized man made murderous by the situation he finds himself in. We believe this about him because the writing makes us believe it. Paragraph upon paragraph—composed in almost equal part of narration, commentary, and analysis—attests to a reflective nature now regarding its own angry passions with a visceral but contained distaste. The narrator records his rage, yet the writing is not enraged; the narrator hates Empire, yet his hate is not out of control; the narrator shrinks from the natives, yet his repulsion is tinged with compassion. At all times he is possessed of a sense of history, proportion, and paradox. In short, a highly respectable intelligence confesses to having been *reduced* in a situation that would uncivilize anyone, including you the reader.

This man became the Orwell persona in countless books and essays: the involuntary truth speaker, the one who implicates himself not because he wants to but because he has no choice. He is the narrator created to demonstrate the dehumanizing effect of Empire on all within its reach, the one whose presence alone—"I am the man, I was there"—is an indictment.

It was politics that Orwell was after: the politics of his time. That was the situation into which he interjected this persona: the one who alone could tell the story he wanted told. Orwell himself—in unaesthetic actuality—was a man often at the mercy of his own mean insecurities. In life he could act and sound ugly: revisionist biographies now have him not only a sexist and an obsessed anti-communist but possibly an informer as well. Yet the persona he created in his nonfiction—an essence of democratic decency—was something genuine that he pulled from himself, and then shaped to his writer's purpose. *This* George Orwell is a wholly successful fusion of experience, perspective, and personality that is fully present on the page. Because he *is* so present, we feel that we know who is speaking. The ability to make us believe that we know who is speaking is the trustworthy narrator achieved.

From journalism to the essay to the memoir: the trip being taken by a nonfiction persona deepens, and turns ever more inward.

Jonathan Raban

Notes from the Road

When I travel I keep a notebook—actually a Grumbacher sketchbook, ring-bound, 8 1/2 by 11 inches, with a hundred sheets of heavyweight drawing paper. Blotched and swollen, its pages parting company with their binding-wire, the notebook is my main solace when I dine alone at some cheerless eatery where the only remedy for the microwaved chicken is in the ketchup bottle. Writing in it gives me occupation and identity when I might otherwise recognize myself as an aging, unkempt drifter without visible means of support. So it's scribble, scribble, scribble all through dinner. Into the notebook go long descriptions of landscape and character; some fuzzy intellection; scraps of conversation; diagrammatic drawings; paras from the local paper; weather notes; shopping lists; inventories of interiors (the sad cafe gets grimly itemized); skeletal anecdotes; names of birds, trees and plants, culled from the wonderfully useful Peterson guides; phone numbers of people whom I'll never call; the daily target-practice of a dozen or so experimental similes.

"Looks like you're a rider," says the career-waitress with fried hair, whom I gratefully overtip for not saying "Looks like you're a bum."

From my last piece of serious traveling, a solo round-trip by boat from Seattle to Juneau, Alaska, I came back with 3 notebooks stuffed with such writing—the raw material (supposedly) for the book I am now trying to begin. Home, at this desk, seated at this typewriter, I find myself wading through the notebooks with familiar irritation. If the man who wrote them had been hired by me as my researcher, I'd sack him for gross neglect of duty.

My dim-bulb alter ego. The notebooks expose him as short-sighted and long-winded by turns. Bogged down in the quotidian details of his adventure, he can't see the wood for the trees. He travels, but can't remember why he's traveling. He's short of wit, and rarely passes up an opportunity to whine. He asks all the wrong questions (when he remembers to ask any questions at all). He's at his worst when trying hardest to "write": I have to skip page after page of phony lyricism, in search of one memorable fact. The chipped flint of the waves? Give me a break. The mauve ring on the page, left by a glass of British Columbian plonk (than which no plonk in the world is plonkier), is more articulate than my man's laborious notebook-writing. It reminds me that—as he sat at that bar in Prince Rupert, the nib of his Papermate racing across the page—a scene was going on beside his shoulder . . . two angry women; one pregnant, one in fishnet tights . . . They'll find a place in the book; his blessed seascape won't. Why didn't he write about them? Why didn't he listen to the row more closely? Because, in our ill-matched duo, he's the traveler and I'm the writer, and the two are chalk and cheese. He can be a character in my story—a useful stooge—but he can never be its author, for all his tiresome literary pretensions.

Traveling (and one might as well say living) turns us into creatures of hap and contingency. We are forever navigating in fog, where the sensations of the moment are intense, and both our point of departure and our intended destination are lost to view in our concentration on the overwhelming here-and-now. Things are constantly happening, but we're in no position to judge their meaning and significance. The rumble of a ship's engine in the murk may turn out to be the sightless bulk carrier that will run us down and send us to a watery grave. Or it may not. As the case may be. The fogbound navigator, all ears for sounds of distant danger, fails to keep his eyes on the depth-sounder, and runs himself aground on the silent reef. So it is with the poor mutt who keeps my notebooks for me, because the narrative of the journey is kept hidden from him until the journey's over. Blundering through the world in zero visibility, he leaves a record only of his misapprehensions—the scary ship that faded into nothing, the impending storm that never blew, the promising channel that led nowhere. Only by the merest accident (for contingency cuts both ways) does he happen to light, occasionally, on something that will still seem to him important when the voyage is done.

Writing—real writing, in the iron discipline of a book—is the mirror-opposite of traveling. A book is a strictly subordinated world. Its logic, of symbol and metaphor, is at once tantalizingly suggestive and ruthlessly exclusive. From the moment that a narrative begins to develop its own momentum, it insists on what it needs and what it has no time for. It's at his peril that the writer loses sight of where the book began and where it's destined to find an ending. (Endings almost invariably change as the book develops, but the sense of an ending is crucial, even if it turns out to be nothing like the ending.) Writing is—in the terms of Philosophy 101—all cause, cause, cause, where traveling is a long cascade of one damn contingency after another. Good writing demands the long view, under a sky of unbroken blue; good traveling requires one to submit to the fogginess of things, the short-term, minute-by-minute experiencing of the world. It's no wonder that my alter ego and I are on such chronic bad terms.

So—tossing the notebooks into the dunce's corner of my workroom, and feeding a clean sheet of paper into the IBM Quietwriter—I'm at last about to find out what really happened to my mobile, purblind self on his travels; what it all meant, and how his voyage fits into the larger story that the book must eventually unfold. Now—touch wood—comes the interesting bit, where the act of writing itself unlocks the memory-bank, and discovers things that are neither in the notebooks nor to be found in the writer's conscious memory.

You try a phrase out: It rings false. That's not it—it wasn't like that. . . . You have to mail a stack of rejection slips to yourself before you hit on the phrase that rings true, or nearly true. Successive errors narrow the field to an increasingly fine band, then—Snap! When you do find a match between the provisional words in your head and that shadowy, half-buried recollection of events, there's no mistaking it; it's as plain as a pair of jacks on the table. Sentence by slow sentence, you begin to discover the world as it truly was— which is nearly always at variance, and sometimes wildly so, with how it was seen at the time by the dumb cluck with the Papermate.

He has his uses. He can be relied on (generally) for names, dates, the odd line of dialogue, the exact wording of a public notice—the basic facts and figures in the story. But on anything of larger importance, he's a tainted witness, too caught up in the proceedings to give a reliable account of them. For the truth of the matter, go not to him but to the language—testing words against the cloudy stuff of past experience, until you get the decisive fit that signals yes, that's how it was; that's what really happened.

Novelists will understand this process well enough—it's more or less how things come to happen in a work of realist fiction. But journalists—wedded to the notepad, the tape recorder, the "verified quote," the querulous gnome in the fact-checking department—may curl their lips in scorn at my habit of trusting the contents of my head more than I trust the documentary evidence of the notebooks. To them I'd offer this remark, made by the Barbizon school painter Jean Francois Millet: "One man may paint a picture from a careful drawing made on the spot, and another may paint the same scene from memory, from a brief but strong impression; and the last may succeed better in giving the character, the physiognomy of the place, though all the details may be inexact."

Just so. For the next 12 months or so, I mean to leave the notebooks in the corner of the room, to the spiders and the rising damp, and go fishing, instead, in the deep and haunted lake of memory.

Tight lines!

PART

III

— Creativity and the Arts —

Whether high art or popular culture, the creative world offers a way for writers to examine individual and cultural identity in terms of taste, aesthetics, and expression. The books we read, the music we love, the movies we remember—all can say a great deal about who we are.

The creative world is fertile ground for essayists, as it involves the act and idea of interpretation. Since good writers are also good readers, it is no surprise that writers such as Charles Simic in "The Necessity of Poetry," Dagoberto Gilb in "Steinbeck," and Leslie Marmon Silko in "Language and Literature from a Pueblo Indian Perspective" are interested in literary process. While each uses a different structure and focal point, they all explore what it means to write, read, and define literature. Other arts examined in this section include the movies (Susan Allen Toth's "Cinematypes: Going to the Movies"), the dramatic arts (David Sedaris's "The Drama Bug"), music (Meghan Daum's "Music Is My Bag"), and visual art (Saul Bellow's "Graven Images" and John Updike's "Fast Art"). Finally, Wayne Koestenbaum in "Celebrity Dreaming" takes on the pop culture subject of celebrities. This essay, like many of the works here, draws connections between imagination, identity, and desire.

The variety of voices, styles, and structures in the "I" section includes the postmodern (Simic and Koestenbaum), elements of satire (Daum), the use of narrative fragments (Toth), and voice-driven critical analysis (Gilb). A personal essay on creativity and the arts involves an immediate link between self-exploration and arts-exploration: the movies Toth watches, for instance, become metaphors for her relationships with men; and the novels of John Steinbeck become for Gilb a call for more literature about social injustice.

In the "Eye" section, we find inheritors of a long tradition of literary and artistic criticism. These works consider cultural ideas through styles of singular voice and perspective. While the first-person narrator is often invoked, as in Bellow's "Graven Images," the primary focus is on analysis. Silko's piece, which draws on oral tradition, and Updike's summation of the career of Andy Warhol, are very different in theme and form, yet both seek to understand the effect, meaning, and development of arts within social contexts.

The three essays on craft in this section all ruminate on the tension and discovery inherent in essay writing. Patricia Hampl's "Reviewing Anne Frank" discusses the process of writing about a profound literary and historical subject. Cynthia Ozick's "She: Portrait of the Essay as a Warm Body" is an insightful exploration of all that the essay—"a thing of the imagination"—can do. Bret Lott's "Toward a Definition of Creative Nonfiction" is not only a valuable craft piece but also a personal essay about the act of writing and the "responsibility" we have "as human beings to answer for and to our lives." This sentiment is true of the personal essay as well as of the best works of criticism. The art of writing, like the other arts represented in this section, is a constant and necessary source for inquiry.

The "I"

Meghan Daum

Music Is My Bag

Picture a fifteen-year-old boy with the early traces of a mustache who hangs out in the band room after school playing the opening bars of a Billy Joel song on the piano, and who, in an unsuccessful attempt at a personal style, wears a fedora hat and a scarf decorated with a black-and-white design of a piano keyboard. He is the boy who, in addition to having taught himself some tunes from the *Songs in the Attic* sheet music he bought at the local Sam Ash, probably plays the trombone in the marching band, and also no doubt experienced a seminal moment one afternoon as he vaguely flirted with a not-yet-kissed clarinet-playing girl, a girl who is none too popular but whose propensity for leaning on the piano as he plays the opening chords of "Captain Jack" clued him in to the hitherto unimagined social possibilities of the marching band.

If the clarinet-playing girl is an average student musician, she carries her plastic Selmer in the standard-issue black plastic case. If she has demonstrated any kind of proficiency, she carries her Selmer in a tote bag that reads MUSIC IS MY BAG. The boy in the piano-key scarf definitely has music as his bag. He may not yet have the tote bag, but the hat, the Billy Joel, and the euphoria brought on by a sexual awakening centered entirely around band is all he needs to be delivered into the unmistakable world of Music Is My Bag.

I grew up in that world. The walls of my parents' house were covered with framed art posters from musical events: the San Francisco Symphony's 1982 production of *St. Matthew Passion,* the Metropolitan Opera's 1976 production of *Aida,* the original Broadway production of *Sweeney Todd.* Ninety percent of the books on the shelves were about music, if not actual musical scores. Childhood ceramics projects made by my brother and me were painted with eighth notes and treble clef signs. We owned a deck of cards with portraits of the great composers on the back. A baby grand piano overtook the room that would have been the dining room if my parents hadn't forgone a table and renamed it "the music room." This room also contained an imposing hi-fi system and a $300 wooden music stand. Music played at all times: Brahms, Mendelssohn, cast recordings of Sondheim musicals, a cappella Christmas albums. When my father sat down with a book he read musical scores, humming quietly and tapping his foot. When I was ten my mother decided we needed to implement a before-dinner ritual akin to saying grace, so she composed a short song, asking us all to contribute a lyric, and we held hands and sang it before eating. My lyric was, "There's a smile on our face and it seems to say all the wonderful things we've all done today." My mother insisted on harmonizing at the end. She also did this when singing "Happy Birthday."

Harmonizing on songs like "Happy Birthday" is a clear indication of the Music Is My Bag personality. If one does not have an actual bag that reads MUSIC IS MY BAG—as did the violist in the chamber music trio my mother set up with some women from the Unitarian Church—a $300 music stand will more than suffice. To avoid confusion, let me also say that there are many different Bags in life. Some friends of my parents have a $300 dictionary stand, a collection of silver bookmarks, and once threw a dinner party wherein the guests had to dress up as members of the Bloomsbury group. These people are Literature Is My Bag. I also know people who belong to Movies Are My Bag; they are easily detectable by key chains shaped like projectors, outdated copies of *Halliwell's Film Guide,* and one too many T-shirts from obscure venues like the San Jose Film Festival. Cats Are My Bag people are too well-known to require explanation, and the gaudiness of their paraphernalia—the figurines, coffee-table books, and refrigerator magnets—tends to give the category dominance over the slightly more subtle Dogs Are My Bag. Perhaps the most annoying Bag is Where I Went to College Is My Bag: Yale running shorts, plastic Yale tumblers, Yale Platinum Visa cards, and, yes, even Yale screen savers—all in someone pushing forty, the perennial contributor to the class notes.

Having a Bag connotes the state of being overly interested in something yet, in a certain way, not interested enough. It has a hobbyish quality to it, a sense that the enthusiasm developed at a time when the person was lacking in some significant area of social or intellectual life. Music Is My Bag is the mother of all Bags, not just because in the early 1980s some consumer force of the public-radio-fund-drive variety distributed a line of tote bags displaying that slogan but because its adherents—or "music lovers," as they tend to call themselves—give off an aura that distinguishes them from the rest of the population. It's an aura that has to do with a sort of benign cluelessness, a condition that even in middle age smacks of that phase between prepubescence and real adolescence.

Music Is My Bag people have a sexlessness to them, a pastiness. They can never seem to find a good pair of jeans. You can easily spot them on the street: the female French horn player in concert dress hailing a cab to Lincoln Center at around seven in the evening, her earrings too big, her hairstyle unchanged since 1986. The fifty-something recording engineer with the running shoes and the shoulder bag. The Indiana marching band kids in town for the Macy's Thanksgiving Day Parade, snapping photos of one another in front of the Hard Rock Cafe, having sung their parts from the band arrangement of *Hello, Dolly!* the whole way on the bus, thinking, *knowing,* that it won't get any better than this. Like all Music Is My Bag people, they are too much in love with trappings and memorabilia, saving the certificates of participation from regional festivals, the composer-a-month calendars, the Mostly Mozart posters. Their sincerity trumps all attempts at snideness. The boys' sarcasm falls short of irony; the girls will never be great seducers. They will all grow up to look like high school band directors no matter what profession they choose, with pets named Wolfgang and Gershwin and hemlines that are never quite right.

I played the oboe, which is not an instrument to be taken lightly. The oboist runs a high risk of veering deeply into Music Is My Bag, mostly because getting beyond the entry level requires an absorption with technique that can render a person vulnerable to certain vagaries of the wind ensemble subculture, which inevitably concerns itself with the sociopolitical superstructure of the woodwind section. Within this subtype, the oboist faces the twin temptations of narcissism, in contemplating the disproportionate number of solo passages written for the oboe, and pride, because it is she who sounds the A that tunes the orchestra.

The oboe is a difficult instrument, beautiful when played well, horrible when played poorly. Yet even when it produces a lovely sound, it is not an instrument for the vain. The embouchure puckers the face into an unnatural grimace, an expression well documented in the countless photographs from my childhood that suggest some sort of facial deformity: the lipless girl. Then there is the question of moisture. Oboe playing revolves almost entirely around saliva. Spit gets caught in the keys and the joints and must be blown out using cigarette rolling paper as a blotter (a scandalous drugstore purchase for a twelve-year-old girl). Spit accumulates on the floor if you play for too long. Spit must be constantly sucked out from both sides of the reed. Fragile and temperamental, the reed is the oboe player's chronic medical condition. It must be tended to constantly. It must be wet but never too wet, hard enough to emit a decent sound but soft enough to blow air through. The oboist must never stray far from liquid; the reed is forever in her mouth or in a paper cup of water that teeters on the music stand or being doused at a drinking fountain in Parsippany High School at the North Jersey Regional Band and Orchestra audition. After a certain age, the student oboist must learn to make her own reeds, building them from bamboo using knives and shavers—a seemingly eighteenth-century exercise that ought to require an apprenticeship. But oboists, occupying a firm, albeit wet, patch of ground under the tattered umbrella of Music Is My Bag, never quite live in the same era as everyone else.

Although I did, at one point, hold the title of second-best high school player in the state of New Jersey, I was a mediocre oboist. My discipline was lacking, my enthusiasm virtually nil, and my comprehension of rhythm (in keeping with a lifelong math phobia) held me back considerably. But being without an aptitude for music was, in my family, tantamount to being a Kennedy who knows nothing of politics. Aptitude was something, perhaps even the only thing, I possessed. As indifferent to the oboe as I was—and I once began an orchestra rehearsal without noticing that I had neglected to screw the bell, the entire bottom portion, onto the rest of my instrument—I managed to be good enough to play in the New Jersey All-State High School Orchestra as well as in a local adult symphony. I even gained acceptance to a music conservatory. These aren't staggering accomplishments unless you consider the fact that I rarely practiced. If I had practiced with any regularity and determination I could have been, as my parents would have liked me to be, one of those kids who was schlepped to Juilliard on Saturdays. If I had practiced slightly more than that I could have gone to Juilliard for college. If I had practiced a lot I could have ended up in the New York Philharmonic.

And yet I didn't practice. I haven't picked up the oboe since my junior year in college, where, incidentally, I sat first chair in the orchestra even though I did not practice once the entire time.

I never practiced and yet I always practiced. My memory is of always being unprepared, yet I was forced to sit in the chair for so many hours that I suspect something else must have been at work, a lack of consciousness, a failure of concentration, an inability to practice on my own. "Practice" was among the top five words spoken in our family, the other four being Meghan, Mom, Dad, and Evan. Today, almost ten years since I last practiced, the word has finally lost the resonance of our usage. I now think of practice in terms of law or medicine. There is a television show called *The Practice,* and it seems odd to me that I never associate the word sprawled across the screen with the word that was woven relentlessly through our family discourse. For my entire childhood and adolescence, practicing was both a given and a punishment. When we were bad, we practiced. When we were idle, we practiced. Before dinner and TV and friends coming over and bedtime and a thousand other things that beckoned with possibility, we practiced. "You have practicing and homework," my mother said every day. In that order. My father said the same thing without the part about homework.

Much of the reason I could never quite get with the oboe-playing program was that I developed, at a very young age, a deep contempt for the Music Is My Bag world. Instead of religion, my family had music, and it was the church against which I rebelled. I had clergy for parents: my father was a professional composer and arranger, a keyboard player and trombonist, who scored the Gulf War for ABC; my mother was a pianist and music educator of the high-school-production-of-*Carousel* genre. My own brother was a reluctant Christ figure. A typically restless second child in youth (he quit piano lessons but later discovered he could play entirely by ear), my brother recently completed the final mix of a demo CD of songs he wrote and performed in the style of mid-eighties pop, late Doobie Brothers groove. His Los Angeles house is littered with Billy Joel and Bruce Hornsby sheet music, back issues of *Stereo Review,* the liner notes to the digital remastering of John Williams's score for *Star Wars.* Music is the bag.

I compose songs in my sleep. I can't do it awake. I'll dream of songwriters singing onstage. I'll hear them perform new songs, songs I've never heard, songs I therefore must have written. In childhood I never put one thought toward composing a song. It would have been like composing air, creating more of something of which there was already quite enough. Wind players such as flutists and saxophonists need as much air as they can get. Oboists are always trying to get rid of air. They calibrate what they need to get the reed to vibrate, end up using even less, and dispense with the rest out of the corners of their mouths. It's all about exhaling. On an eighth rest, they're as likely to blow air out as they are to steal a breath. There's always too much of everything for oboists: too much air, too many bars when they're not playing and too many bars when there's hardly anyone playing but them, too many percussion players dropping triangles on the floor, too many violinists playing "Eleanor Rigby" before the rehearsal starts.

Most orchestras have only two oboists, first chair and second chair, pilot and copilot. The second oboist is the perpetual back-up system, the one on call, the one who jumps in and saves the other when his reed dries up in the middle of a solo, when he misses his cue, when he freezes in panic before trying to hit a high D. I've been first oboist and I've been second oboist, and first is better, though not by much. It's still the oboe. Unlike the gregarious violinist or the congenial cellist, the oboist is a lone wolf. To play the oboe in an orchestra is to complete an obstacle course of solos and duets with the first flutist, who if she is hardcore Music Is My Bag will refer to herself as a "flautist." Oboe solos dot the great symphonies like land mines, the pizzicati that precede them are drum rolls, the conductor's pointing finger is an arrow for the whole audience to see: here comes the oboe, two bars until the oboe, now, *now.* It's got to be nailed, one flubbed arpeggio, one flat half note, one misplaced pinky in the middle of a run of sixteenth notes, and *everyone* will hear. Everyone.

My parents' presence at a high school orchestra concert turned what should have been a routine event into something akin to the finals of the Olympic women's figure skating competition. Even from the blinding, floodlit stage I could practically see them in the audience, clucking at every error, grimacing at anything even slightly out of tune. Afterward, when the other parents—musically illiterate chumps—were patting their kids on the head and loading the tuba into the station wagon, I would receive my critique. "You were hesitating in the second part of the Haydn Variations." "You overanticipated in the Berceuse section of the Stravinsky." "Your tone was excellent in the first movement, but then your chops ran out." My brother, who was forced for a number of years to play the French horn, once was reduced to a screaming fight with our father in the school parking lot, the kind of fight possible only between fathers and sons. He'd bumbled too many notes, played out of tune, committed some treasonous infraction against the family reputation. My father gave him the business on the way to the car, eliciting the alto curses of a fourteen-year-old, pages of music everywhere, an instrument case slammed on the pavement.

This sort of rebellion was not my style. I cried instead. I cried in the seventh grade when the letter telling me I'd been accepted to the North Jersey Regional Band and Orchestra arrived three days late. I cried in the tenth grade when I ended up in the All-State Band instead of the orchestra. I cried when I thought I'd given a poor recital (never mind that the audience thought I was brilliant—all morons), cried before lessons (underprepared), cried after lessons (sentenced to a week of reviewing the loathsome F sharp étude). Mostly, though, I cried during practice drills supervised by my father. These were torture sessions wherein some innocent tooting would send my father racing downstairs from his attic study, screaming, "Count, count, you're not counting! Jesus Christ!" Out would come a pencil, if not an actual conductor's baton, and he would begin hitting the music stand, forcing me to repeat the tricky fingerings again and again, speeding up the tempo so that I'd be sure to hit each note when we took it back down to real time. These sessions would last for hours, my mouth muscles shaking, tears welling up from fatigue and exasperation. If we had a copy of the piano part, my mother would play the accompaniment, and together my parents would bark commands: "Articulate the eighth notes more. More staccato on the tonguing. Don't tap your foot, tap your toe inside your shoe." The postman heard a lot of this. The neighbors heard all of it. After practicing we'd eat dinner, but not before that song: "There's a smile on our face, and it seems to say all the wonderful things . . . " "Good practice session today," my mother would say, dishing out the casserole, WQXR's *Symphony Hall* playing over the kitchen speakers. "Yup, sounding pretty good," my father would say. "How about one more go at it before bed?"

My mother called my oboe a "horn." This infuriated me. "Do you have your horn?" she'd ask every single morning. "Do you need your horn for school today?" She maintained that this terminology was technically correct, that among musicians a "horn" was anything into which air was blown. My oboe was a $4,000 instrument, high-grade black granadilla with sterling silver keys. It was no horn. But such semantics are a staple of Music Is My Bag, the overfamiliar stance that reveals a desperate need for subcultural affiliation, the musical equivalent of people in the magazine business who refer to publications like *Glamour* and *Forbes* as "books." As is indicated by the use of "horn," there's a subtly macho quality to

Music Is My Bag. The persistent insecurity of musicians, especially classical musicians, fosters a kind of jargon that would be better confined to the military or major league baseball. Cellists talk about rock stops and rosin as though they were comparing canteen belts or brands of glove grease. They have their in-jokes and aphorisms: "The Rock Stops Here," "Eliminate Violins in Our Schools."

I grew up surrounded by phrases like "rattle off that solo," "nail that lick," and "build up your chops." "Chops" is a word that should be invoked only by rock-and-roll guitarists but is more often uttered with the flailing, badly timed anti-authority of the high school clarinet player. Like the violinist who plays "Eleanor Rigby" before rehearsal, the clarinet player's relationship to rock and roll maintains its distance. Rock music is about sex. It is something unloved by parents and therefore unloved by Music Is My Bag people, who make a vocation of pleasing their parents, of studying trig and volunteering at the hospital and making a run for the student government even though they're well aware they have no chance of winning. Rock and roll is careless and unstudied. It might possibly involve drinking. It most certainly involves dancing. It flies in the face of the central identity of Music Is My Baggers, who chose as their role models those painfully introverted characters from young adult novels: the klutz, the bookworm, the late bloomer. When given a classroom assignment to write about someone who inspires her, Music Is My Bag will write about her grandfather or perhaps Jean-Pierre Rampal. If the bad-attitude kid in the back row writes about AC/DC's Angus Young, Music Is My Bag will believe in her heart that he should receive a failing grade. Rock and roll, as her parents would say when the junior high drama club puts on a production of *Grease,* "is not appropriate for this age group." Even in the throws of adolescence, Music Is My Bag will deny adolescence. Even at age sixteen, she will hold her ears when the rock music gets loud, saying it ruins her sense of overtones, saying she has sensitive ears. Like a retiree, she will classify the whole genre as nothing but a bunch of noise, though it is likely that she is a fan of Yes.

During the years when I was a member of the New Jersey All-State Orchestra, I would carpool to rehearsals with the four or so other kids from my town who made All-State every year. This involved spending as much as two hours each way in station wagons driven by people's parents, and, inevitably, the issue of music would arise: what music would be played in the car? Among the most talented musicians in school was a girl named Elizabeth Ostling, who was eventually hired as the second flutist for the Boston Symphony Orchestra at age twenty-one, and at the age of fifteen was unaccountably possessed by an enthusiasm for the Christian singer Amy Grant. Next to Prokofiev and the Hindemith Flute Sonata, Amy Grant occupied the number-one spot in her studious, late-blooming heart. Since Elizabeth's mother, like many parents of Baggers, was devoted solely to her daughter's musical and academic career, she did most of the driving to such boony spots as Chatham High School, Monmouth Regional, and Long Branch Middle School. Mile after New Jersey Turnpike mile, we were serenaded by the wholesome synthesizers of songs like "Saved By Love" and "Wait for the Healing," only to spill out of the car and take no small relief in the sound of twenty-five of New Jersey's best student violinists playing "Eleanor Rigby" before the six-hour rehearsal.

To participate in a six-hour rehearsal of the New Jersey All-State Orchestra is to see the accessories of Bagdom tumble from purses, knapsacks, and totes; here more than any-place are the real McCoys, actual Music Is My Bag bags, canvas satchels filled with stereo Walkmans and A.P. math homework and Trapper Keeper notebooks featuring the piano-playing Schroeder from the *Peanuts* comic strip. When we paused for dinner I would embark on oboe maintenance, putting the reed in water, swabbing the instrument dry, removing the wads of wax that, during my orthodontic years, I placed over my front teeth to keep the inside of my mouth from bleeding. Just as I had hated the entropy of recess back in grade school, I loathed the dinner breaks at All-State rehearsals. To maximize rehearsal time, the wind section often ate separately from the strings, which left me alone with the band types, the horn players and percussionists who wore shirts with slogans like "Make Time for Halftime." They'd wolf down their sandwiches and commence with their jam session, a cacophonous white noise of scales, finger exercises, and memorized excerpts from their hometown marching numbers. During these dinner breaks, I'd generally hang with the other oboist. For some reason, this was almost always a tall girl who wore sneakers with corduroy pants and a turtleneck with nothing over it. This is fairly typical Music Is My Bag garb, though oboists have a particular spin on it, a spin characterized more than anything by lack of spin. Given the absence in most classical musicians of a style gene, this is probably a good thing. Oboists don't accessorize. They don't wear buttons on their jackets that say "Oboe Power" or "Who Are You Going to Tune To?"

There's high-end Bagdom and low-end Bagdom, with a lot of room in between. Despite my parents' paramilitary practice regimens, I have to give them credit for being fairly high-end Baggers. There were no piano-key scarves in our house, no "World's Greatest Trombonist" figurines, no plastic tumblers left over from my father's days as assistant director of the Stanford University Marching Band. Such accessories are the mandate of the lowest tier of Music Is My Bag, a stratum whose mascot is PDQ Bach, whose theme song is "Piano Man," and whose regional representative is the kid in high school who plays not only the trumpet but the piano, saxophone, flute, string bass, accordion, and wood block. This kid, considered a wunderkind by his parents and the rest of the band community, plays none of these instruments well, but the fact that he knows so many different sets of fingerings, the fact that he has the potential to earn some college money by performing as a one-man band at the annual state teachers' conference, makes him a hometown hero. He may not be a football player. He may not even gain access to the Ivy League. But in the realm of Music Is My Bag, the kid who plays every instrument, particularly when he can play Billy Joel songs on every instrument, is the alpha male.

The flip side of the one-man band are those Music Is My Baggers who are not musicians at all. These are the kids who twirl flags or rifles in the marching band, the ones who blast music in their rooms and play not air guitar but air keyboards, their hands fluttering out in front of them, the hand positions not nearly as important as the attendant head motions. This is the essence of Bagdom, which is to take greater pleasure in the reverb than the melody, to love the lunch break more than the rehearsal, the rehearsal more than the performance, the clarinet case more than the clarinet. It is to think nothing of sending away for the deluxe packet of limited-edition memorabilia that is being sold for the low, low price of one's entire personality. It is to let the trinkets do the talking.

I was twenty-one when I stopped playing the oboe. I wish I could come up with a big, dramatic reason why. I wish I could say that I sustained some kind of injury that prevented me from playing (it's hard to imagine what kind of injury could sideline an oboist—lip strain? carpal tunnel syndrome?), or that I was forced to sell my oboe in order to help a family member in crisis, or, better yet, that I suffered a violent attack in which my oboe was used as a weapon against me before being stolen and melted down for artillery. But the truth has more to do with what in college I considered to be an exceptionally long walk from my dormitory to the music building. Without the prodding of my parents or the structure of a state-run music education program, my oboe career had to run on self-motivation alone, and when my senior year started I neither registered for private lessons nor signed up for the orchestra, dodging countless calls from the director imploring me to reassume my chair.

Since then I haven't set foot in a rehearsal room, put together a folding music stand, fussed with a reed, marked up music, practiced scales, tuned an orchestra, or performed any of the countless activities that previously had dominated my existence. There are moments every now and then when I'll hear an oboe-dominated section of the Bach Mass in B Minor or the Berceuse section of Stravinsky's *Firebird Suite* and long to find a workable reed and pick the instrument up again. But then I imagine how terrible I'll sound after eight dormant years, and I just put the whole idea out of my mind before I start to feel sad about it. I can still smell the musty odor of my oboe case, the old-ladyish whiff of the velvet lining and the tubes of cork grease and the damp fabric of the key pads. Unlike the computer on which I now work, my oboe had the sense of being an ancient thing. Brittle and creaky, it was vulnerable when handled by strangers. It needed to be packed up tight, dried out in just the right places, kept away from the heat and the cold and from anyone too stupid to distinguish it from a clarinet.

What I really miss about the oboe is having my hands on it. I could come at that instrument from any angle and know every indentation on every key, every spot that leaked air, every nick on every square inch of wood. I knew precisely how its weight was distributed between my right thumb and left wrist, and I knew, above all, that the weight would feel the same way every time, every day, for every year that I played. But I put my oboe down, and I never picked it back up. I could have been a pretty good oboist if I had practiced, if I had ignored the set design and just played the instrument. But I didn't and I wasn't. When I look back I hardly recognize myself, that person who could play a Mozart sonata by memory, whose fingers could move three times faster than I now type—a person who was given a gift, but who walked away from it because of piano-key scarves and fedora hats and all those secondary melodies that eventually became the only thing I could hear.

Dagoberto Gilb

Steinbeck

Not being precocious in matters of literature, even to the end of my teenage years when I still thought of "book" more as a verb, long before I'd read a poetic sentence, even I knew of Steinbeck, *The Grapes of Wrath* and *East of Eden*. His name was bigger than these titles, than the movies that were made of the novels. His name was as up there as that of Marilyn Monroe, Sandy Koufax, John F. Kennedy.

Eventually, when books did become active nouns for me, John Steinbeck was in my first stack of them, and it was not a good experience. That's because I'd been drawn to read *Tortilla Flat.* If this were all there was, I would have left it at that, groaning about him as I did this novel. I mean, what's with these sweet, mystically dumb and lazy Mexican "paisanos"? What nonmedieval writer creates lines like: "I swear, what I have is thine. While I have a house, thou hast a house. Give me a drink." But this is how he had these "native" characters of the Monterey Peninsula speak to each other, even as, or especially when, they were drinking red wine by the gallon. Terrible as it was, I'm easier on the novel now: it is simply another of those "exoticized" novels by a writer whose home was near— though on the good side of the tracks—a historically earlier culture that fascinates for its "strangeness." It's what young writers often begin with once they are stricken by the sense of mystery that is around and in them, that isolating awe which drives them to write. It's what bad writers never know how to transcend.

Because what Steinbeck attributed to chromosomes in Mexican-Americans—lazy innocence and drunken happiness—he came to understand as social and political conditions when he matured to write about the people from the Dust Bowl and Central Valley of California. And that was when he became great, and that was when what he wrote about was what I wanted to read, what I admired and was inspired by. When what he wrote wasn't just about poor Okies rattling across the Southwest into California, or about lonely people living on a ranch, but about how people are, and how they should be and should be treated, and so about me, too, not to mention what I care about, and what I believe in: that the West is not the East, that the West is a land unique, ruggedly beautiful, as are the people from it.

The premier writer of the American West, Steinbeck didn't do Cowboys and Indians. You see hitchhikers and waitresses, truck drivers speeding by cotton and corn fields. You feel wind and it's dusty, and the sun is hot and too bright. There are trains pounding railroad tracks, rivers and creeks and bridges and long stretches of highway. There are lone oak trees in dry, grassy fields, vistas with rolling hills and mountains. Men hunt for wood to camp by a fire at night near gulleys with rocks and boulders. There are working ranches, and horseback riding and shooting rifles don't make the story.

Steinbeck tells us stories of work, the dream of what work can do for people. Lennie and George, in *Of Mice and Men,* are sent to the boss's ranch near Soledad for a job, expecting no more than to earn a living, hard as it comes. What they dream of is a house where they might listen to the rain outside, a couple of acres where they can raise rabbits in winter, have a chicken hutch, leave the thick cream on the milk, grow alfalfa, have a vegetable garden.

Remember when *cause* mattered? When it wasn't passé to care about the working poor? When being rich wasn't in itself the only state of achievement? In *The Grapes of Wrath,* Tom Joad, an ex-con guilty of beating a man, released from prison with four more years of probation, comes back to his Oklahoma home to find his parents, sharecroppers displaced by the cigar-chewing banker and anonymous corporations whose roaring tractors, rolling like tanks in a war, intend to pacify a land where families were born and buried.

The story of the Joads, traveling across the West to find work in the dreamland of California, is about disillusioned poor people who begin to organize against the meanest spirit of capitalism. Steinbeck takes on the dangerous and divisive issue of fair and decent labor; he is unafraid to talk about lousy wages and the abuse of workers, unafraid to extol the virtues of union and strikes. He allows Tom Joad, a man who can kill, to become inspired by a no-longer-religious preacher, to be the hero of his novel: "I been thinkin' a hell of a lot, thinkin' about our people livin' like pigs, an' the good lan' layin fallow, or maybe one fella with a million acres, while a hundred thousan' good farmers is starvin'. An' I been wonderin' if all our folks got together an' yelled. . . . "

The authorities say Steinbeck is sentimental, his work melodramatic. But if that's so, even if it's only that, I'm sentimental for him now. Because so many people, and so many writers, have left behind or never learned a respect for manual work, for people who carry and use tools for a living and get calluses and chapped hands and dirt under the nails, who bend and stoop, people who work by the hour or the basket, who build and fix things, who dig and plant and pick. The literary world is a powerful suit-and-tie business, and the well-dressed stories that editors look for are too much by writers whose game is played as professionally as Harvard MBAs, whose marketing goals are not meant to cause a reader to step outside the privileged cubicle to see who's sweeping the floors in the hours after they've gone home.

Wayne Koestenbaum

Celebrity Dreaming

1.

Over the last twenty years, I have dreamt frequently of celebrities, sometimes every night. In the mornings I write down my dreams in a blue notebook. Often I incorporate the material in a poem. Otherwise it lies fallow.

Many of my dream notes are in Manhattan Mini Storage. Recently I visited them.

After a star dream, I wake up thrilled: I've "scored," without effort, in my sleep! I've met Sophia Loren, Maria Callas, Joan Didion! The stars never pay much attention to me, but I don't mind. I'm content to be subordinate.

2.

Selected dreams of movie stars, 1978–1998:

Sophia Loren and I watched her latest movie at an Upper East Side theater.

Sophia Loren came over to my house for supper. I asked her what she was working on. She wouldn't say, although I begged.

Julie Andrews worked as a lounge singer.

Julie Andrews was exhausted.

I telephoned Peggy Wood (who played the Mother Abbess in *The Sound of Music*) to ask for advice on how to sing "Some Enchanted Evening." Peggy, jealous, offered no encouragement.

I packed Elizabeth Taylor's bag, including a nightgown with a cappuccino stain on it. Liz was incognito: her roommate didn't know that Liz was Liz.

I met Liz at Jackie Onassis's country house. I nearly told Liz that I'd just seen *The Only Game in Town,* but I didn't want to be gauche.

A midget rode on Liz Taylor's handlebars, while Sophia Loren sat atop a geometric sculpture that resembled her figure but was vastly inferior, and Lyle Lovett, in the background, posed as a supermodel.

Liza Minnelli tap-danced on a Flatiron District sidewalk.

Barbra Streisand played an athlete in a movie; later, I auditioned for a part in *One Flew over the Cuckoo's Nest,* its script covered in sauerkraut.

I led Bette Davis back from the dead. We sat on a beach. She wore asylum clothing: white tennies.

Ramon Novarro sang at a nightclub. He wore a Tarzan costume; his legs were flabby. I knew we were meant for each other, though I wondered how he could still be alive.

Keir Dullea, star of *Bunny Lake Is Missing,* gave a lecture on the poet Louise Bogan.

Charlie Chaplin sat near me in a fancy uptown Manhattan restaurant.

Alec Baldwin had plastic surgery so that the narcotics police wouldn't recognize him. A hot date told him she preferred the old face; she took a blowtorch to the fake layer and melted it.

Jean-Paul Belmondo spent the night at my house. He was distraught about Brigitte Bardot. I couldn't help him.

I played the part of Orestes in a photo-montage version of Oscar Wilde's *Salomé.**

3.

All of my celebrities resemble each other. The women are powerful, seductive, distant. The men are powerful, seductive, distant. Neither the men nor the women thoroughly endorse me, but they tolerate my proximity, and sometimes, they lead me on. Occasionally I manage to lure them into bed.

Usually they are too busy to be aggressive, though sometimes it is possible that they might turn rageful. I am a victim with a sneaky agenda, who wants to "make time" with them. I struggle to be nice, though niceness is an arduous masquerade. Sometimes, however, I behave aggressively; sometimes I retaliate against a celebrity who has gone too far.

4.

Selected dreams of writers, 1978–1998:

Joyce Carol Oates sent me a special-delivery thank-you note for a dinner I'd served her.

Joyce Carol Oates (wearing a negligee) hugged me and said she was hearing voices, which meant she was writing a story.

---

* Orestes does not appear in *Salomé.*

Joyce Carol Oates performed Salome's dance of the seven veils in a baseball stadium.

I spent all day writing Joyce Carol Oates a lengthy fan letter, endlessly revised.

Susan Sontag wore a pink miniskirt and sat like an odalisque on her couch. Three people were eavesdropping on our conversation; she shooed them away with a radical fist. I told her that I'd loved her ever since I'd read *On Photography* when I was twenty-one. She smiled at the praise.

Joan Didion, beside me on a couch, said, "We like people." She disapproved of writers who didn't like people. Wanting to be alone with me, Didion urged a dull intern with sharp literary tastes to leave the room.

I visited Elizabeth Hardwick, who was memorizing a Haydn sonata.

I applied for a job as Jean Rhys's secretary (she was a lawyer).

I saw Toni Morrison enter a bookstore.

I guarded Adrienne Rich's purse, containing health supplies. In an attempt to please her, I bought her a pair of shrunken nylons.

My psychiatrist lived with Marianne Moore.

John Ashbery's phone number was only one-digit different from mine, and consequently he often received my phone calls. At a Chelsea AIDS clinic, we conversed, and he found the phrase *blue velvet* in a poem of mine.

I slept with John Ashbery.

At a party, I began (in a trance) to flirt with James Merrill. I hoped to become his escort.

I suggested to W. H. Auden that we live together. He had dyed his hair and lost most of his wrinkles.

I visited James Schuyler, who was a young man living on a bayou.

I met Roland Barthes at a café in Cambridge, Massachusetts. His sexiness almost made me faint. I said, "Are you really Roland Barthes?" Indeed he was. He took me to his apartment on Brattle Street, and I fell into his arms. He massaged my fingers; I noted his beaky nose.

I was on a panel with Jacques Lacan. Rude, he chatted with another panelist while I was trying to deliver my paper.

A thin, strict woman—the sister of Thoreau or Hawthorne—owned a restaurant and wanted to sleep with me. We hugged. In lieu of sex, I recited an Emerson paragraph that mentioned her.

5.

If, in real life, I meet one of my celebrities, then dreams of that figure stop. I have dreamt about certain celebrities so obsessively over the past two decades that I imagine that the nocturnal narratives form a savings account, a supernatural bribe: if I dream enough about the star, eventually my brain waves will mingle with hers, and she'll get the message that I love her. My dreams about human magnitudes are a telepathic project—an attempt to influence a remote deity.

Sometimes the celebrity shows up only briefly in the dream—a cameo appearance. Other times, the star stays for the night. Her fame gives me a charge, but it is also an obstacle. It sits between us, an excuse for her indifference. If she manages to violate her renown to offer me an endearment, I will truly have accomplished something in my sleep.

Perversely, I believe my dreams to be aesthetic creations: their memory lingers for years. I feel toward them as toward a marvelous performance of a ballet, seen from a distance, yet perfectly recalled, and subject to restorative, retrospective idealization.

The dreams are acts of restitution: dead writers are reborn, retired singers perform again, dictators behave decently.

6.

Selected dreams of visual artists, 1978–1998:
I met Andy Warhol. I called him a "cunt."

7.

I have enough of a psychoanalytic bent to imagine that the celebrities in my dreams are screens for my parents as I remember them from childhood: omnipotent figures. And yet the dream stars are also grandiose self-portraits. I make no secret of the fact that I love fame; that I want to meet famous people; that I want to become famous. However, I am also afraid of fame. When, in waking life, I have the opportunity to meet a celebrity, I am bashful, diffident, uncharming. If I were to see a star walking toward me at a party, I would probably stoop to tie my shoes, and thus miss my chance.

The celebrities who fascinate me are usually old enough to be my parents. I am relatively uninterested in young stars. Nor am I preoccupied by stars my own age, with the exception of Alec Baldwin and a few, choice others.

8.

Selected dreams of opera singers, 1978–1998:
Maria Callas gave a concert at my yeshiva. I was sent to the basement for talking out loud during the program. Afterward I met Callas. I said "Bravo," and she said "Thank you." Her skin was very smooth. She said, "Wasn't it a wonderful performance?" I could see a bit of her breast. She showed me pictures she'd taken of her husband, Mr. Meneghini. Then she shut herself in the dressing room.

Maria Callas sang badly, and I looked into her mouth: an enormous, quixotic, original space. We were watching old movies, with which she had affinity.

I sat beside Leontyne Price in a car. We were talking about voice: hers. She said something noble about retirement.

I telephoned Leontyne Price and heard, on her answering machine, a tune from *Il Trovatore*. Then she picked up and apologized for having screened the call. I told her I was eager to hear her sing in New York, and she laughed, recognizing my insincerity. Then I said, "Well, bye, Leontyne," and tried to pronounce her name correctly.

Monserrat Caballé coached me in the role of Leonora in *Il Trovatore*.

Frederica von Stade gave a public interview, in the Met lobby, before a performance of *Der Rosenkavalier*. In order to preserve her voice, she sang her responses rather than spoke them.

I asked Renata Scotto out to dinner; after all, we'd belonged to the same theater troupe in Los Gatos, California.

Kathleen Battle put her foot down and burst into tears when she heard a student sing Gershwin songs unidiomatically.

Dawn Upshaw had a lousy apartment, no privacy.

I listened to a recording of *Madama Butterfly* sung by André Previn's first wife, Dory. ("Pre-Mia," I said to a fellow listener.)

An unidentified soprano was lowered into the center of the audience during an innovative staging of *Lucia di Lammermoor*. I was afraid she would land on me.

9.

I don't mind being a person who dreams about celebrities. I don't think the activity is pathetic or pathological. It clutters my nights with melodramas to which I must pay strict attention, behaving like a faithful scribe or historian.

I don't expect kindness from my celebrities; I expect only tolerance, a cold forbearance.

10.

Selected dreams of Anna Moffo, 1978–1998:

I stood in the wings watching Anna Moffo's Metropolitan Opera debut.

I attended a master class in Anna Moffo's white-carpeted living room.

I discovered that Anna Moffo had roles in the Jewish cinema long before her operatic debut.

I met Anna Moffo and her first husband, Mario Lanfranchi. She was singing *mélodies* by a nonexistent French composer named Janet.

I saw Anna Moffo in a combined production of *Rigoletto, Trovatore,* and *Butterfly;* her costume was a black-and-white bathrobe.

I discussed the last two notes of *La Traviata* with Anna Moffo.

A boy fell from the Met balcony while Anna Moffo sang *La Bohème*.

Anna Moffo left in my room a beautiful huge-buttoned coat, a purse, and a copy of her recent recording of an obscure Bellini opera.

As an innovative digression during *Butterfly*, Anna Moffo carried a tray of hair spray through the audience.

I ate ice cream with Anna Moffo while sitting on a rock.

I bought Anna Moffo a black umbrella and delivered it to her at the Met.

Anna Moffo lent me a copy of *Where the Wild Things Are:* a literary version, with more text, fewer pictures.

Anna Moffo and I shopped for antiques.

I went backstage to meet Anna Moffo at a 1968 Met gala. I told my boyfriend, "I know we're in a hurry to leave, but it's 1968 again, and this is my chance to meet Anna Moffo in 1968."

11.

Selected dreams of pop singers, 1978–1998:

In my mailbox I saw a postcard, addressed to my boyfriend, who had inquired whether a certain river was polluted: "Steve: River is OK. Tell Debbie Harry to stop peeing in it."

12.

In dreams, commodities function as celebrities. In 1996 I dreamt of a yellow patent leather Anna Sui purse that was really a shoe, and, a few months later, I dreamt of a blue Neutrogena face splash. The appearance of the word *Neutrogena,* in the dream, was as exciting as the arrival of a celebrity at a party: it lit up the surrounding bleakness.

13.

Selected dreams of composers and conductors, 1978–1998:

I agreed to be "kept" by Virgil Thomson, who promised to take me to Israel. All I'd need to spend of my own funds was one hundred dollars.

I went to the opera with Benjamin Britten. We sat in the front row. The sets were falling apart.

I flirted with Herbert von Karajan at a performance of *Tales of Hoffmann.*

Franz Schubert fought Rambo in a boxing ring. (Ronald Reagan watched.) Schubert needed to defend his honor. Before the fight began, I heard a beautiful Schubert composition. I wanted to tell him about its beauty, before he died.

14.

I am not the only person to dream of celebrities. A psychologist told me that he dreamt of shaking hands with Nixon. Another psychologist told me that he dreamt for years about Keanu Reeves, and that many of his patients started dreaming of Princess Diana after her death: "she functioned like Glinda, the Good Witch, stepping out of nowhere to let you know that you don't need to be afraid of your unconscious." A psychoanalyst said that his patients have recently been dreaming of characters from *Seinfeld.* A writer told me that he dreamt of seeing Pablo Picasso naked ("his penis was featureless, overly simplified, like an abstract painting"). The young man who cuts my hair confessed that he gave Leonardo DiCaprio a haircut on a beach in a dream; then they had sex. Another time he dreamt of

Christy Turlington, who said hello. He did not have sex with Christy. A fellow English professor confided that he dreamt of Hedy Lamarr, and that then, the next morning, he heard her name mentioned on the radio. He marveled at the coincidence. I, too, marvel at it, though I can't interpret it.

15.

Selected dreams of leaders, 1978–1998:

Princess Diana gave a book party at Area, the nightclub. The party seemed an illustration in a Sartre or Camus novel.

My mother dated Hitler. His first name was Franz. We called him Franz Hitlerino.

A woman friend of mine had phone sex with Dan Quayle. They stayed on the line all night.

16.

One of my earliest celebrity fantasies concerned Brigitte Bardot: in second grade, I fantasized that she was my mother, that she picked me up from school in a white limo, and that we traveled together to France. I decided that my name was Pierre, and, for a spell, I signed my papers "Pierre," and, sometimes, "Mary Poppins."

Eventually, my teacher put a stop to this nonsense.

David Sedaris

The Drama Bug

The man was sent to our class to inspire us, and personally speaking, I thought he did an excellent job. After introducing himself in a relaxed and genial manner, he started toward the back of the room, only to be stopped midway by what we came to know as "the invisible wall," that transparent barrier realized only by psychotics, drug fiends, and other members of the show business community.

I sat enthralled as he righted himself and investigated the imaginary wall with his open palms, running his hands over the seemingly hard surface in hopes of finding a way out. Moments later he was tugging at an invisible rope, then struggling in the face of a violent, fantastic wind.

You know you're living in a small town when you can reach the ninth grade without ever having seen a mime. As far as I was concerned, this man was a prophet, a genius, a pioneer in the field of entertainment—and here he was in Raleigh, North Carolina! It was a riot, the way he imitated the teacher, turning down the corners of his mouth and riffling through his imaginary purse in search of gum and aspirin. Was this guy funny or what!

I went home and demonstrated the invisible wall for my two-year-old brother, who pounded on the very real wall beside his playpen, shrieking and wailing in disgust. When my mother asked what I'd done to provoke him, I threw up my hands in mock innocence before lowering them to retrieve the imaginary baby that lay fussing at my feet. I patted the back of my little ghost to induce gas and was investigating its soiled diaper when I noticed my mother's face assume an expression she reserved for unspeakable horror. I had seen this look only twice before: once when she was caught in the path of a charging, rabid pig and then again when I told her I wanted a peach-colored velveteen blazer with matching slacks.

"I don't know who put you up to this," she said, "but I'll kill you myself before I watch you grow up to be a clown. If you want to paint your face and prance around on street corners, then you'll have to find some other place to live because I sure as hell won't have it in my house." She turned to leave. "*Or in my yard,*" she added.

Fearful of her retribution, I did as I was told, ending my career in mime with a whimper rather than the silent bang I had hoped for.

The visiting actor returned to our classroom a few months later, removing his topcoat to reveal a black body stocking worn with a putty-colored neck brace, the result of a recent automobile accident. This afternoon's task was to introduce us to the works of William Shakespeare, and once again I was completely captivated by his charm and skill. When the words became confusing, you needed only to pay attention to the actor's face and hands to understand that this particular character was not just angry, but vengeful. I loved the undercurrent of hostility that lay beneath the surface of this deceptively beautiful language. It seemed a shame that people no longer spoke this way, and I undertook a campaign to reintroduce Elizabethan English to the citizens of North Carolina.

"Perchance, fair lady, thou dost think me unduly vexed by the sorrowful state of thine quarters," I said to my mother as I ran the vacuum cleaner over the living-room carpet she was inherently too lazy to bother with. "These foul specks, the evidence of life itself, have sullied not only thine shag-tempered mat but also thine character. Be ye mad, woman? Were it a punishable crime to neglect thine dwellings, you, my feeble-spirited mistress, would hang from the tallest tree in penitence for your shameful ways. Be there not garments to launder and iron free of turbulence? See ye not the porcelain plates and hearty mugs waiting to be washed clean of evidence? Get thee to thine work, damnable lady, and quickly, before the products of thine very loins raise their collected fists in a spirit born both of rage and indignation, forcibly coaxing the last breath from the foul chamber of thine vain and upright throat. Go now, wastrel, and get to it!"

My mother reacted as if I had whipped her with a short length of yarn. The intent was there, but the weapon was strange and inadequate. I could tell by the state of my room that she spent the next day searching my dresser for drugs. The clothes I took pride in neatly folding were crammed tight into their drawers with no regard for color or category. I smelled the evidence of cigarettes and noticed the coffee rings on my desk. My mother had been granted forgiveness on several previous occasions, but mess with mine drawers and ye have just made thyself an enemy for life. Tying a feather to the shaft of my ballpoint pen, I quilled her a letter. "The thing that ye search for so desperately," I wrote, "resideth not in mine well-ordered chamber, but in the questionable content of thine own character." I slipped the note into her purse, folded twice and sealed with wax from the candles I now used to light my room. I took to brooding, refusing to let up until I received a copy of Shakespeare's collected plays. Once they were acquired, I discovered them dense and difficult to follow. Reading the words made me feel dull and stupid, but speaking them made me feel powerful. I found it best to simply carry the book from room to room, occasionally skimming for fun words I might toss into my ever fragrant vocabulary. The dinner hour became either unbearable or excruciating, depending on my mood.

"Methinks, kind sir, most gentle lady, fellow siblings all, that this barnyard fowl be most tasty and succulent, having simmered in its own sweet juices for such a time as it might take the sun to pass, rosy and full-fingered, across the plum-colored sky for the course of a twilight hour. 'Tis crisp yet juicy, this plump bird, satisfied in the company of such finely roasted neighbors. Hear me out, fine relations, and heed my words, for methinks it adventurous, and fanciful, too, to saddle mine fork with both fowl *and* carrot at the exact same time, the twin juices blending together in a delicate harmony which doth cajole and enliven mine tongue in a spirit of unbridled merriment! What say ye, fine father, sisters, and infant brother, too, that we raise our flagons high in celebration of this hearty feast, prepared lovingly and with utmost grace by this dutiful woman we have the good fortune to address as wife, wench, or mother!"

My enthusiasm knew no limits. Soon my mother was literally begging me to wait in the car while she stepped into the bank or grocery store.

I was at the orthodontist's office, placing a pox upon the practice of dentistry, when the visiting actor returned to our classroom.

"You missed it," my friend Lois said. "The man was so indescribably powerful that I was practically crying, that's how brilliant he was." She positioned her hands as if she were supporting a tray. "I don't know what more I can say. The words, they just don't exist. I could try to explain his realness, but you'd never be able to understand it. Never," she repeated. "Never, never, never."

Lois and I had been friends for six months when our relationship suddenly assumed a competitive edge. I'd never cared who made better grades or had more spending money. We each had our strengths; the important thing was to honor each other for the thing that person did best. Lois held her Chablis better than I, and I respected her for that. Her frightening excess of self-confidence allowed her to march into school wearing a rust-colored Afro wig, and I stood behind her one hundred percent. She owned more records than I did, and because she was nine months older, also knew how to drive a car and did so as if she were rushing to put out a fire. *Fine,* I thought, *good for her.* My superior wisdom and innate generosity allowed me to be truly happy for Lois up until the day she questioned my ability to understand the visiting actor. The first few times he visited, she'd been just like the rest of them, laughing at his neck brace and rolling her eyes at the tangerine-sized lump in his tights. *I* was the one who first identified his brilliance, and now she was saying I couldn't understand him? Methinks not.

"Honestly, woman," I said to my mother on our way to the dry cleaner, "to think that this low-lying worm might speak to me of greatness as though it were a thing invisible to mine eyes is more than I can bear. Her words doth strike mine heart with the force of a punishing blow, leaving me both stunned and highly vexed, too. Hear me, though, for I shall bide my time, quietly, and with cunning, striking back at the very hour she doth least expect it. Such an affront shall not go unchallenged, of that you may rest assured, gentle lady. My vengeance will hold the sweet taste of the ripest berry; and I shall savor it slowly."

"You'll get over it," my mother said. "Give it a week or two and I'm sure everything will be back to normal. I'm going in now to get your father's shirts and I want you to wait here, *in the car.* Trust me, this whole thing will be forgotten about in no time."

This had become her answer to everything. She'd done some asking around and concluded I'd been bitten by what her sister referred to as "the drama bug." My mother was convinced that this was a phase, just like all the others. A few weeks of fanfare and I'd drop show business, just like I had the guitar and my private detective agency. I hated having my life's ambition reduced to the level of a common cold. This wasn't a bug, but a full-fledged virus. It might lay low for a year or two, but this little germ would never go away. It had nothing to do with talent or initiative. Rejection couldn't weaken it, and no amount of success would ever satisfy it. Once diagnosed, the prognosis was terminal.

The drama bug seemed to strike hardest with Jews, homosexuals, and portly girls, whose faces were caked with acne medication. These were individuals who, for one reason or another, desperately craved attention. I would later discover it was a bad idea to gather more than two of these people in an enclosed area for any length of time. The stage was not only a physical place but also a state of mind, and the word *audience* was defined as anyone forced to suffer your company. We young actors were a string of lightbulbs left burning twenty-four hours a day, exhausting ourselves and others with our self-proclaimed brilliance.

I had the drama bug and Lois had a car. Weighing the depth of her momentary transgression against the rich rewards of her private chariot, I found it within my bosom to forgive my wayward friend. I called her the moment I learned the visiting actor had scheduled a production of *Hamlet* set to take place in the amphitheater of the Raleigh Rose Garden. He himself would direct and play the title role, but the other parts were up for grabs. We auditioned, and because we were the youngest and least experienced, Lois and I were assigned the roles of the traveling players Hamlet uses to bait his uncle Claudius. It wasn't the part I was hoping for, but I accepted my role with quiet dignity. I had a few decent speeches and planned to work them to the best of my ability.

Our fellow cast members were in their twenties and thirties and had wet their feet in such long-running outdoor dramas as *The Lost Colony* and *Tender Is the Lamb.* These were professionals, and I hoped to benefit from their experience, sitting literally at their feet as the director paced the lip of the stage addressing his clenched fist as "poor Yorick."

I worshiped these people. Lois slept with them. By the second week of rehearsal, she had abandoned Fortinbras in favor of Laertes, who, she claimed, had a "real way with the sword." Unlike me, she was embraced by the older crowd, attending late-night keg parties with Polonius and Ophelia and driving to the lake with the director while Gertrude and Rosencrantz made out in the backseat. The killer was that Lois was nowhere near as committed as I was. Her drama bug was the equivalent of a twenty-four-hour flu, yet there she was, playing bumper pool with Hamlet himself while I practiced lines alone in my room, dreaming up little ways to steal the show.

It was decided that as traveling players, Lois and I would make our entrance tumbling onto the outdoor stage. When she complained that the grass was irritating her skin, the director examined the wee pimples on her back and decided that, from this point on, the players would enter skipping. I had rehearsed my tumble until my brain lost its mooring and could be heard rattling inside my skull, and now, on the basis of one complaint, we were skipping? He'd already cut all my speeches, leaving me with the one line "Aye, my lord." That was it, three lousy syllables. A person could wrench more emotion out of a sneeze than all my dialogue put together. While the other actors strolled the Rose Garden memorizing their vengeful soliloquies, I skipped back and forth across the parking lot repeating, "Aye, my lord," in a voice that increasingly sounded like that of a trained parrot. Lois felt silly skipping and spoke to the director, who praised her instincts and announced that, henceforth, the players would enter walking.

The less I had to do, the more my fellow actors used me as a personal slave. I would have been happy to help them run lines, but instead, they wanted me to polish their crowns or trot over to a car, searching the backseat for a misplaced dagger.

"Looking for something to do? You can help Doogan glow-tape the props," the director said. "You can chase the spiders out of the dressing room, or better yet, why don't you run down to the store and get us some drinks."

For the most part, Lois sat in the shade doing nothing. Not only did she refuse to help out, but she was always the first one to hand me a large bill when placing an order for a thirty-cent diet soda. She'd search through her purse, bypassing the singles in favor of a ten or a twenty. "I need to break this anyway," she'd say. "If they charge you extra for a cup of ice, tell them to fuck themselves." During the rehearsal breaks she huddled in the stands, gossiping with the other actors while I was off anchoring ladders for the technicians.

When it came time for our big scene, Lois recited her lines as if she were reading the words from the surface of some distant billboard. She squinted and paused between syllables, punctuating each word with a question mark. "Who this? Has seen with tongue? In venom steeped?"

If the director had a problem with her performance, he kept it to himself. I, on the other hand, was instructed to remove the sweater from around my neck, walk slower, and drop the accent. It might have been easier to accept the criticism had he spread it around a little, but that seemed unlikely. She could enter the scene wearing sunglasses and eating pizza and that was "fine, Lois. Great work, babe."

By this time I was finding my own way home from rehearsal. Lois couldn't give me a ride, as she was always running off to some party or restaurant with what she referred to as "the gang from Elsinore."

"I can't go," I'd say, pretending I had been invited. "I really need to get home and concentrate on my line. You go ahead, though. I'll just call my mother. She'll pick me up."

"Are we vexed?" my mother would ask, pulling her station wagon into the parking lot.

"We are indeed," I answered. "And highly so."

"Let it go," she said. "Ten years from now I guarantee you won't remember any of these people. Time passes, you'll see." She frowned, studying her face in the rearview mirror. "Enough liquor, and people can forget anything. Don't let it get to you. If nothing else, this has taught you to skim money while buying their drinks."

I didn't appreciate her flippant attitude, but the business with the change was insightful.

"Round everything off to the nearest dollar," she said. "Hand them their change along with their drinks so they'll be less likely to count it—and never fold the bills, keep the money in a wad."

My mother had the vengeful part down. It was the craft of acting I thought she knew nothing about.

We were in dress rehearsal when the director approached Lois regarding a new production he hoped to stage that coming fall. It was to be a musical based on the lives of roving Gypsies. "And you," he said, "shall be my lusty bandit queen."

Lois couldn't sing; everyone knew that. Neither could she act or play the tambourine. "Yours is the heart of a Gypsy," he said, kneeling in the grass. "The vibrant soul of a nomad."

When I expressed an interest, he suggested I might enjoy working behind the scenes. He meant for me to hang lights or lug scenery, to become one of those guys with the low-riding pants, their tool belts burdened with heavy wrenches and thick rolls of gaffer tape. Anyone thinking I might be trusted with electrical wiring had to be a complete idiot, and that's what this man was. I looked at him clearly then, noticing the way his tights made a mockery of his slack calves and dumpy little basket. Vibrant soul of a nomad, indeed. If he were such a big stinking deal, what was he doing in Raleigh? His blow-dried hair, the cheap Cuban-heeled shoes, and rainbow-striped suspenders—it was all a sham. Why wear tights with suspenders when their only redeeming feature was that they stayed up on their own—that's how they got their name, tights. And acting? The man performed as if the audience were deaf. He shouted his lines, grinning like a jack-o'-lantern and flailing his arms as if his sleeves were on fire. His was a form of acting that never fails to embarrass me. Watching him was like opening the door to a singing telegram: you know it's supposed to be entertaining, but you can't get beyond the sad fact that this person actually thinks he's bringing some joy into your life. Somewhere he had a mother who sifted through a shoe box of mimeographed playbills, pouring herself another drink and wondering when her son would come to his senses and swallow some drain cleaner.

I finally saw Hamlet for who he really was and recognized myself as the witless Yorick who had blindly followed along behind him.

My mother attended the opening-night performance. Following my leaden "Aye, my lord," I lay upon the grassy stage as Lois poured a false vial of poison into my ear. As I lay dying, I opened my eyes just a crack, catching sight of my mother stretched out on her hard, stone pew, fighting off the moths that, along with a few dozen seniors, had been attracted by the light.

There was a cast party afterward, but I didn't go. I changed my clothes in the dressing room, where the actors stood congratulating one another, repeating the words "brilliant" and "intense" as if they were describing the footlights. Horatio asked me to run to the store for cigarettes, and I pocketed his money, promising to return "with lightning speed, my lord."

"You were the best in the whole show," my mother said, stopping for frozen pizza on our way home. "I mean it, you walked onto that stage and all eyes went right to you."

It occurred to me then that my mother was a better actor than I could ever hope to be. Acting is different than posing or pretending. When done with precision, it bears a striking resemblance to lying. Stripped of the costumes and grand gestures, it presents itself as an unquestionable truth. I didn't envy my mother's skill, neither did I contradict her.

That's how convincing she was. It seemed best, sitting beside her with a frozen pizza thawing on my lap, to simply sit back and learn.

Charles Simic

The Necessity of Poetry

Late night on MacDougal Street. An old fellow comes up to me and says: "Sir, I'm writing the book of my life and I need a dime to complete it." I give him a dollar.

Another night in Washington Square Park, a fat woman with a fright wig says to me: "I'm Esther, the Goddess of Love. If you don't give me a dollar, I'll put a curse on you." I give her a nickel.

One of those postwar memories: a baby carriage pushed by a humpbacked old woman, her son sitting in it, both legs amputated.

She was haggling with the greengrocer when the carriage got away from her. The street was steep so it rolled downhill with the cripple waving his crutch, his mother screaming for help, and everybody else laughing as if they were in the movies. Buster Keaton or somebody like that about to go over a cliff.

One laughed because one knew it would end well. One was surprised when it didn't.

I didn't tell you how I got lice wearing a German helmet. This used to be a famous story in our family. I remember those winter evenings just after the war with everybody huddled around the stove, talking and worrying late into the night. Sooner or later, somebody would bring up my German helmet full of lice. They thought it was the funniest thing they ever heard. Old people had tears of laughter in their eyes. A kid dumb enough to walk around with a German helmet full of lice. They were crawling all over it. Any fool could see them!

I sat there saying nothing, pretending to be equally amused, nodding my head while thinking to myself, what a bunch of idiots! All of them! They had no idea how I got the helmet, and I wasn't about to tell them.

It was in those first days just after the liberation of Belgrade, I was up in the old cemetery with a few friends, kind of snooping around. Then, all of a sudden, we saw them! A couple of German soldiers, obviously dead, stretched out on the ground. We drew closer to take a better look. They had no weapons. Their boots were gone, but there was a helmet that had fallen to the side of one of them. I don't remember what the others got, but I went for the helmet. I tiptoed so as not to wake the dead man. I also kept my eyes averted. I never saw his face, even if sometimes I think I did. Everything else about that moment is still intensely clear to me.

That's the story of the helmet full of lice.

Beneath the swarm of high-flying planes we were eating watermelon. While we ate the bombs fell on Belgrade. We watched the smoke rise in the distance. We were hot in the garden and asked to take our shirts off. The watermelon made a ripe, cracking noise as my mother cut it with a big knife. We also heard what we thought was thunder, but when we looked up, the sky was cloudless and blue.

My mother heard a man plead for his life once. She remembers the stars, the dark shapes of trees along the road on which they were fleeing the Austrian army in a slow-moving ox-cart. "That man sounded terribly frightened out there in the woods," she says. The cart went on. No one said anything. Soon they could hear the river they were supposed to cross.

In my childhood women mended stockings in the evening. To have a "run" in one's stock-ing was catastrophic. Stockings were expensive, and so was electricity. We would all sit around the table with a single lamp, my grandmother reading the papers, we children pre-tending to do our homework, while watching my mother spreading her red-painted fin-gernails inside the transparent stocking.

There was a maid in our house who let me put my hand under her skirt. I was five or six years old. I can still remember the dampness of her crotch and my surprise that there was all that hair there. I couldn't get enough of it. She would crawl under the table where I had my military fort and my toy soldiers. I don't remember what was said, if anything. Just her hand, firmly guiding mine to that spot.

They sit on the table, the tailors do. At least, they used to. A street of dim shops in Bel-grade where we went to have my father's coat narrowed and shortened so it would fit me. The tailor got off the table and stuck pins in my shoulder. "Don't squirm," my mother said. Outside it was getting dark. Large snowflakes fell.

   Years later in New York, on the same kind of afternoon, a dry-cleaning store window with an ugly, thick-legged woman on the chair in a white dress. She's having the hems raised by a gray-headed Jewish tailor, who kneels before her as if he is proposing marriage.

There was an expensive-looking suitcase on the railroad tracks, and they were afraid to come near it. Far from any station, it was on a stretch of track bordered by orchards where they had been stealing plums that afternoon. The suitcase, she remembers, had colorful labels, of what were probably world-famous hotels and ocean liners. During the war, of course, one heard of bombs, special ones, in the shape of toys, pens, soccer balls, exotic birds—so why not suitcases? For that reason they left it where it was.

   "I always wondered what was in it," my wife says. We were talking about the summer of 1944, of which we both had only a few clear recollections.

The world was going up in flames and I was studying violin. The baby Nero sawing away . . .

   My teacher's apartment was always cold. A large, almost empty room with a high ceil-ing already in shadow. I remember the first few screechy notes my violin would make and my teacher's stern words of reprimand. I was terrified of that old woman. I also loved her because after the scolding she would give me something to eat. Something rare and exotic, like chocolate filled with sweet liqueur. We'd sit in that big empty room, almost dark now. I'd be eating and she'd be watching me eat. "Poor child," she'd say, and I thought it had to do with my not practicing enough, my being dim-witted when she tried to explain something to me, but today I'm not sure that's what she meant. In fact, I suspect she had something else entirely in mind. That's why I'm writing this, to find out what it was.

When my grandfather was dying from diabetes, when he had already had one leg cut off at the knee and they were threatening to do the same to the other, his old buddy Savo Lozanic used to visit him every morning to keep him company. They would reminisce about this and that and even have a few laughs.

One morning my grandmother had to leave him alone in the house, as she had to attend the funeral of a distant relative. That's what gave him the idea. He hopped out of bed and into the kitchen, where he found candles and matches. He got back into his bed, somehow placed one candle above his head and the other at his feet, and lit them. Finally, he pulled the sheet over his face and began to wait.

When his friend knocked, there was no answer. The door being unlocked, Savo went in, calling from time to time. The kitchen was empty. A fat gray cat slept on the dining room table. When Savo entered the bedroom and saw the bed with the sheet and lit candles, he let out a wail and then broke into sobs as he groped for a chair to sit down.

"Shut up, Savo," my grandfather said sternly from under his sheet. "Can't you see I'm only practicing?"

Another story about time. This one about the time it took the people to quit their cells after beginning to suspect that the Germans were gone. In that huge prison in Milan all of a sudden you could hear a pin drop. Eventually they thought it best to remove their shoes before walking out.

My father was still tiptoeing hours later crossing a large empty piazza. There was a full moon above the dark palaces. His heart was in his mouth.

"It was just like an opera stage," he says. "All lit up, nobody in the audience, and nobody in the orchestra pit. Nevertheless, I felt like singing. Or perhaps screaming?"

He did neither. The year was 1944.

The streets are empty, it's raining, and we are sitting in the Hotel Sherman bar listening to the bluesy piano. I'm not yet old enough to order a drink, but my father's presence is so authoritative and intimidating that when he orders for me the waiters never dare to ask about my age.

We talk. My father remembers a fly that wouldn't let him sleep one summer afternoon fifty years ago. I tell him about an old gray overcoat twice my size, which my mother made me wear after the war. It was wintertime. People on the street would sometimes stop and watch me. The overcoat trailed the ground and made walking difficult. One day I was standing on the corner waiting to cross when a young woman gave me a small coin and walked away. I was so embarrassed.

"Was she pretty?" my father asks.

"Not at all," I tell him. She looked like a hick, maybe a nun.

"A Serbian Ophelia," my father thinks.

It's possible. Anything is possible.

The huge crowd cheering the dictator; the smiling faces of children offering flowers in welcome. How many times have I seen that? And always the same blond little girl curtsying!

Here she is surrounded by the high boots of the dignitaries and a couple of tightly leashed police dogs. The monster himself is patting her on the head and whispering in her ear.

I look in vain for someone with a troubled face.

The exiled general's grandson was playing war with his cheeks puffed to imitate bombs exploding. The grim daughter wrote down the old man's reminiscences. The whole apartment smelled of bad cooking.

The general was in a wheelchair. He wore a bib and smoked a cigar. The daughter smiled for me and my mother in a way that made her sharp little teeth show.

I liked the general better. He remembered some prime minister pretending to wipe his ass with a treaty he had just signed, the captured enemy officers drinking heavily and toasting some cabaret singer from their youth.

It's your birthday. The child you were appears on the street wearing a stupid grin. He wants to take you by the hand, but you won't let him.

"You've forgotten something," he whispers. And you, quiet as a mutt around an undertaker, since, of course, he (the child) doesn't exist.

There was an old fellow at the *Sun Times,* who was boss when I first came and worked as a mail clerk, who claimed to have read everything. His father was a janitor at the university library in Urbana, and Stanley, for that was his name, started as a kid. At first I didn't believe any of it; then I asked him about Gide, whom I was then reading. He recited for me the names of the major novels and their plots. What about Isaac Babel, Alain Fournier, Aldous Huxley, Ford Madox Ford? The same thing. It was amazing! Everything I had read or heard of he had already read. You should be on a quiz show, Stanley, people who overheard us said. Stanley had never been to college and had worked for the newspaper most of his life. He had a stutter, so I guess that explains why he never married or got ahead. So, all he did was read books. I had the impression that he loved every book he read. Only superlatives for Stanley, one book better than the other. If I started to criticize, he'd get pissed off. Who do I think I am? Smartass, he called me, and wouldn't talk to me about books for a few days. Stanley was pure enthusiasm. I was giddy myself at the thought of another book waiting for me to read at home.

The night of my farewell dinner in Chicago, I got very drunk. At some point, I went to the bathroom and could not find my way back. The restaurant was large and full of mirrors. I would see my friends seated in the distance, but when I hurried toward them, I would come face to face with myself in a mirror. With my new beard I did not recognize myself immediately and almost apologized. In the end, I gave up and sat at an old man's table. He ate in silence, and I lit a cigarette. Time passed. The place was emptying. The old man finally wiped his mouth and pushed his full, untouched wineglass toward me. I would have stayed with him indefinitely if one of the women from our party hadn't found me and led me outside.

Did I lie a little? Of course. I gave the impression that I had lived for years on the Left Bank and often sat at the tables of the famous cafés watching the existentialists in their passionate arguments. What justified these exaggerations in my eyes was the real possibility that I could have done something like that. Everything about my life already seemed a fluke, a series of improbable turns of events, so in my case fiction was no stranger than truth. Like when I told the woman on the train from Chicago that I was a Russian. I described our apartment in Leningrad, the terrors of the long siege during the war, the deaths of my parents before a German firing squad which we children had to witness, the DP camps in Europe. At some point during the long night I had to go to the bathroom and simply laugh.

How much of it did she believe? Who knows? In the morning she gave me a long kiss in parting, which could have meant anything.

My father and his best friend talking about how some people resemble animals. The bird-like wife of so and so, for example. The many breeds of dogs and their human look-alikes. The lady who is a cow. The widow next door who is a tigress, etc.

"And what about me?" says my father's friend.

"You look like a rat, Tony," he replies without a moment's hesitation, after which they just sit drinking without saying another word.

"You look like a young Franz Schubert," the intense-looking woman told me as we were introduced.

At that same party, I spoke to a lawyer who insisted we had met in London two years before. I explained my accent to a doctor by telling him that I was raised by a family of deaf-mutes.

There was a girl there, too, who kept smiling sweetly at me without saying anything. Her mother told me that I reminded her of her brother, who was executed by the Germans in Norway. She was going to give me more details, but I excused myself, telling everyone that I had a sudden and terrible toothache that required immediate attention.

I got the idea of sleeping on the roof in Manhattan on hot nights from my mother and father. That's what they did during the war, except it wasn't a roof but a large terrace on the top floor of a building in downtown Belgrade. There was a blackout, of course. I remember immense starry skies, and how silent the city was. I would begin to speak, but someone— I could not tell for a moment who it was—would put a hand over my mouth.

Like a ship at sea we were with stars and clouds up above. We were sailing full speed ahead. "That's where the infinite begins," I remember my father saying, pointing with his long, dark hand.

If my father has a ghost, he's standing outside some elegant men's store on Madison Avenue on a late summer evening. A tall man studying a pair of brown suede Italian shoes. He himself is impeccably dressed in a tan suit, a blue shirt of an almost purple hue with a silk tie the color of rusty rose. He seems in no hurry. At the age of fifty-three, with his hair thinning and slicked back, he could be an Italian or a South American. Belle Georgio, one waitress in Chicago used to call him. No one would guess by his appearance that he is almost always broke.

I'm packing parcels in the Lord & Taylor basement during the Christmas rush with a bunch of losers. One fellow is an inventor. He has a new kind of aquarium with piped music, which makes it look as if the fish are doing water ballet, but the world is not interested. Another man supports three ex-wives, so he has a night job in addition to this one. His eyes close all the time. He's so pale, he could pass for a stiff in an open coffin.

Then there's Felix, a mousy fellow a bit older than I who claims to be a distant relative of the English royal family. One time he brought the chart of his family tree to make us stop laughing and explained the connection. What does not make sense is his poverty. He said he was a writer but wouldn't tell us what kind. "Are you writing porno?" one Puerto Rican girl asked him.

Her name was Rosie. She liked boxing. One time she and I went on a date to watch the fights at the Garden. We sat in the Spanish section. "Kill him! Kill him!" she screamed all evening without interruption. At the end she was so tired she wouldn't even have a drink with me, and had to rush home.

At a poetry reading given by Allen Tate, I met a young poet who was attending a workshop given by Louise Bogan at NYU. I sat in a few times and accompanied my new friends for beers after class. One day I even showed two of my poems to Bogan. One was called "Red Armchair," and it had to do with an old chair thrown out on the sidewalk for the trashmen to pick up. The other poem I don't remember. Bogan was very kind. She fixed a few things but was generally encouraging, which surprised me, since I didn't think much of the poems myself.

The other critique of my poetry came later that fall and it was devastating. I had met a painter in a bar, an older fellow living in poverty with a wife and two small kids in a cold-water flat in the Village, where he painted huge, realistic canvases of derelicts in the manner of 1930s socialist realism. A skyscraper and underneath a poor man begging. The message was obvious, but the colors were nice.

Despite the difference in our ages, we saw each other quite a bit, talking art and literature, until one day I showed him my poems. We were sitting in his kitchen with a bottle of whiskey between us. He leaned back in the chair and read the poems slowly, slowly while I watched him closely. At some point I began to detect annoyance in him and then anger. Finally, he looked at me as if seeing me for the first time and said something like: "Simic, I thought you were a smart kid. This is pure shit you're writing!"

I was prepared for gentle criticism in the manner of Louise Bogan, even welcomed it, but his bluntness stunned me. I left in a daze. I was convinced he was right. If I'd had a pistol, I would have shot myself on the spot. Then, little by little, mulling over what he had said, I got pissed off. There were some good things in my poems, I thought. "Fuck him," I shouted to some guy who came my way in the street. Of course, he was right, too, and it hurt me that he was, but all the same.

I came out of my daze just as I was entering Central Park on Fifty-ninth Street. I had walked more than sixty blocks totally oblivious of my surroundings. I sat on a bench and reread my poems, crossing out most of the lines, attempting to rewrite them then and there, still angry, still miserable, and at the same time grimly determined.

There was this old guy in Washington Square Park who used to lecture me about Sacco and Vanzetti and the great injustice done to them. We'd share a bench from time to time, and I'd hear him say again and again how if shit was worth money the poor would be born without assholes. He wore gray gloves, walked with a cane, tipped his hat to ladies, and worried about me. "A kid just off the boat," he'd say to someone passing by. "Sure to get screwed if he doesn't watch out."

I went to see Ionesco's *Bald Soprano* with Boris. It was being presented at the small theater in the Village. There were only six people in the audience, and that included the two of us. They gave the performance anyway. When it came to the love scene with the woman who has three noses, the actors got carried away on the couch. Their voices went down to a whisper as they started undressing each other. Boris and I just looked at each other. The other four people had suddenly become invisible. I have no recollection of the rest of the play except that at the exit the streets were covered with newly fallen snow.

I was five minutes late from lunch at the insurance company where I was working and my boss chewed me out for being irresponsible in front of twenty or thirty other drudges. I sat at my desk for a while fuming, then I rose slowly, wrapped my scarf around my neck and put my gloves on in plain view of everybody, and walked out without looking back. I didn't have an overcoat and on the street it was snowing, but I felt giddy, deliriously happy at being free.

We were on our third bottle of wine when he showed me the pictures of his girlfriend. To my surprise, the photographs spread out on the table were of a naked woman shamelessly displaying herself. Leaning over my shoulder, he wanted me to note each detail, her crotch, her ass, her breasts, until I felt aroused. It was an odd situation. My host's pregnant wife was asleep in the next room. The photographs were spread all over the dining room table. There must've been close to a hundred of them. I looked and listened. From time to time, I could hear the wife snore.

Approaching Manhattan on the train at night, I remember the old Polish and Ukrainian women wielding their mops in the brightly lit towers. I'd be working on some ledger that wouldn't balance, and they'd be scrubbing floors on their knees. They were fat and they all wore flowered dresses. The youngest would stand on a chair and dust off the portrait of the grim founder of the company. The old black man who ran the elevator would bow to them like a headwaiter in a fancy restaurant as he took them from one floor to the next. That would make them laugh. You'd see they had teeth missing. More than a few teeth missing.

It was a window with a view of a large office with many identical desks at which men and women sat working. A woman got up with papers in hand and walked the length of the floor to where a man rose to meet her at the other end. He waved his arms as he talked, while she stood before him with her head lowered, and I went on tying my necktie in the hotel room across the street. I was about to turn away from the window when I realized that the man was yelling at the woman, and that she was sobbing.

Here's a scene for you. My father and I are walking down Madison, when I spot a blue overcoat in a store called the British American House. We study it, comment on the cut, and my father suggests I try it on. I know he has no money, but he insists since it's beginning to snow a little and I'm only wearing a tweed jacket. We go in, I put it on, and it fits perfectly. Immediately, I'm in love with it. We ask the price and it's $200—which was a lot of money in 1959. Too bad, I think, but then my father asks me if I want it. I think maybe he's showing off in front of the salesman or he's come into some money he hasn't told me about. Do you want it? he asks again while the salesman goes to attend to another customer. You've no money, George, I remind him, expecting him to contradict me or come to his senses. "Don't worry" is his reply.

I've seen him do this before and it embarrasses me. He asks for the boss and the two of them sequester themselves for a while. I stand around waiting for us to be kicked out. Instead, he emerges triumphant and I wear the overcoat into the street. A born con man. His manner and appearance inspired such confidence that with a small down payment and promise to pay the rest in a week or two, he'd get what he wanted. This was in the days before credit cards and credit bureaus, when store owners had to make such decisions on the spot. They trusted him, and he eventually did pay whatever he owed. The crazy thing was that he pulled this stunt only in the best stores. It would never occur to him to ask for credit from a grocer, and yet he often went hungry despite his huge salary.

My father had phenomenal debts. He borrowed money any chance he had and paid his bills only when absolutely necessary. It was nothing for him to spend the rent money the night before it was due. I lived in terror of my landlords and landladies while he seemingly never worried. We'd meet after work and he'd suggest dinner in a French restaurant and I'd resist, knowing it was his rent money he was proposing to spend. He'd describe the dishes and wines we could have in tantalizing detail, and I'd keep reminding him of the rent. He'd explain to me slowly, painstakingly, as if I were feeble-minded, that one should never worry about the future. We'll never be so young as we are tonight, he'd say. If we are smart, and we are, tomorrow we'll figure out how to pay the rent. In the end, who could say no? I never did.

On the street corner the card trickster was shuffling his three cards, using a large cardboard box as a table. The cards, the quick hands fluttered. It looked like a cockfight. Five of us watching without expression, our heads, in the meantime, buzzing with calculations and visions of riches. The day was cold so we all had to squint.

Tough guys, he said, time to place your bets.

I became more and more lucid the later it got. This was always my curse. Everybody was already asleep. I tried to wake my dearest, but she drew me down on her breasts sleepily. We loved, slowly, languidly, and then I talked to her for hours about the necessity of poetry while she slept soundly.

Susan Allen Toth

Cinematypes: Going to the Movies

I

Aaron takes me only to art films. That's what I call them, anyway: strange movies with vague poetic images I don't understand, long dreamy movies about a distant Technicolor past, even longer black-and-white movies about the general meaninglessness of life. We do not go unless at least one reputable critic has found the cinematography superb. We went to *The Devil's Eye,* and Aaron turned to me in the middle and said, "My God, this is *funny.*" I do not think he was pleased.

When Aaron and I go to the movies, we drive our cars separately and meet by the box office. Inside the theater he sits tentatively in his seat, ready to move if he can't see well, poised to leave if the film is disappointing. He leans away from me, careful not to touch the bare flesh of his arm against the bare flesh of mine. Sometimes he leans so far I am afraid he may be touching the woman on his other side instead. If the movie is very good, he leans forward too, peering between the heads of the couple in front of us. The light from the screen bounces off his glasses; he gleams with intensity, sitting there on the edge of his seat, watching the screen. Once I tapped him on the arm so I could whisper a comment in his ear. He jumped.

After *Belle de Jour,* Aaron said he wanted to ask me if he could stay overnight. "But I can't," he shook his head mournfully before I had a chance to answer, "because I know I never sleep well in strange beds." Then he apologized for asking. "It's just that after a film like that," he said, "I feel the need to assert myself."

II

Bob takes me only to movies that he thinks have a redeeming social conscience. He doesn't call them films. They tend to be about poverty, war, injustice, political corruption, struggling unions in the 1930s, and the military-industrial complex. Bob doesn't like propaganda movies, though, and he doesn't like to be too depressed either. We stayed away from *The Sorrow and the Pity;* it would be, he said, too much. Besides, he assured me, things are never that hopeless. So most of the movies we see are made in Hollywood. Because they are always very topical, these movies offer what Bob calls "food for thought." When we saw *Coming Home,* Bob's jaw set so firmly with the first half that I knew we would end up at Poppin' Fresh Pies afterward.

When Bob and I go to the movies, we take turns driving so no one owes anyone else anything. We park far away from the theater so we don't have to pay for a space. If it's raining or snowing, Bob offers to let me off at the door, but I can tell he'll feel better if I go with him while he parks, so we share the walk too. Inside the theater Bob will hold my hand when I get scared if I ask him. He puts my hand firmly on his knee and covers it completely with his own hand. His knee never twitches. After a while, when the scary part is past, he loosens his hand slightly and I know that is a signal to take mine away. He sits companionably close, letting his jacket just touch my sweater, but he does not infringe. He thinks I ought to know he is there if I need him.

One night after *The China Syndrome* I asked Bob if he wouldn't like to stay for a second drink, even though it was past midnight. He thought awhile about that, considering my offer from all possible angles, but finally he said no. Relationships today, he said, have a tendency to move too quickly.

III

Sam likes movies that are entertaining. By that he means movies that Will Jones of the *Minneapolis Tribune* loved and either *Time* or *Newsweek* rather liked; also movies that do not have sappy love stories, are not musicals, do not have subtitles, and will not force him to think. He does not go to movies to think. He liked *California Suite* and *The Seduction of Joe Tynan,* though the plots, he said, could have been zippier. He saw it all coming too far in advance, and that took the fun out. He doesn't like to know what is going to happen. "I just want my brain to be tickled," he says. It is very hard for me to pick out movies for Sam.

When Sam takes me to the movies, he pays for everything. He thinks that's what a man ought to do. But I buy my own popcorn, because he doesn't approve of it; the grease might smear his flannel slacks. Inside the theater, Sam makes himself comfortable. He takes off his jacket, puts one arm around me, and all during the movie he plays with my hand, stroking my palm, beating a small tattoo on my wrist. Although he watches the movie intently, his body operates on instinct. Once I inclined my head and kissed him lightly just behind his ear. He beat a faster tattoo on my wrist, quick and musical, but he didn't look away from the screen.

When Sam takes me home from the movies, he stands outside my door and kisses me long and hard. He would like to come in, he says regretfully, but his steady girlfriend in Duluth wouldn't like it. When the *Tribune* gives a movie four stars, he has to save it to see with her. Otherwise her feelings might be hurt.

IV

I go to some movies by myself. On rainy Sunday afternoons I often sneak into a revival house or a college auditorium for old Technicolor musicals, *Kiss Me Kate, Seven Brides for Seven Brothers, Calamity Jane,* even, once, *The Sound of Music.* Wearing saggy jeans so I can prop my feet on the seat in front, I sit toward the rear where no one will see me. I eat large handfuls of popcorn with double butter. Once the movie starts, I feel completely at home. Howard Keel and I are old friends; I grin back at him on the screen, admiring all his teeth. I know the sound tracks by heart. Sometimes when I get really carried away I hum along with Kathryn Grayson, remembering how I once thought I would fill out a formal like that. Skirts whirl, feet tap, acrobatic young men perform impossible feats, and then the camera dissolves into a dream sequence I know I can comfortably follow. It is not, thank God, Bergman.

If I can't find an old musical, I settle for Hepburn and Tracy, vintage Grant or Gable, on adventurous days Claudette Colbert or James Stewart. Before I buy my ticket I make sure it will all end happily. If necessary, I ask the girl at the box office. I have never seen *Stella Dallas* or *Intermezzo.* Over the years I have developed other peccadilloes: I will, for example, see anything that is redeemed by Thelma Ritter. At the end of *Daddy Long Legs* I wait happily for the scene where Fred Clark, no longer angry, at last pours Thelma a convivial drink. They smile at each other, I smile at them, I feel they are smiling at me. In the movies I go to by myself, the men and women always like each other.

The "Eye"

Saul Bellow

Graven Images

Harry S. Truman liked to say that as president of this country he was its most powerful citizen—but sometimes he added, smiling, the photographers were even more powerful. They could tell the commander in chief where to go, make him move his chair, cross his legs, hold up a letter, order him to smile or to look stern. He acknowledged their power and, as a political matter, deferred to their judgment. What the people thought of their chief executive would to some extent be decided by the photographers and the picture editors. Photographers may claim to be a priesthood interpreting the laws of light, and light is a universal mystery that the picture takers measure with their light meters. "In nature's book of infinite mystery, a little I can read," says the Egyptian soothsayer in *Antony and Cleopatra.* Pictures taken in the light must be developed in the shallow mystery of darkrooms. But photographers have nothing in common with soothsayers. Their interests, apart from the technical one, are social and political. To some extent, it is they who decide how you are to be publicly seen. Your "visual record" is in their hands.

Broadly speaking, your *amour propre* is the territory invaded by the picture takers. You may wish or not wish to be in public life. Some people have not the slightest desire to be in the papers or on TV. Others feel that papers and TV screens confer immortality. TV crews on a city street immediately attract big crowds. The arrival of television cameras offers people the opportunity each and every one of them has dreamt of—a shot at eternity. Not by deeds, not by prayers, but solely by their faces, grinning and mugging.

But this aspect of modern image-making or idolatry is not, for me, the most interesting one. What I discover when I search my soul is that I have formed a picture of myself as I wish to be seen, and that while photographers are setting up their lights and cameras I am summoning up and fortifying that picture. My intent is to triumph over the photographers' vision of me—their judgment as to what my place in photographic reality is to be. They have *technics*—Science—on their side. On my side there is vanity and deceit—there is, as I have already said, *amour propre;* there is, moreover, a nagging sense that my powers of candor are weakening and sagging, and that my face betrays how heavily it is mortgaged to death. *Amour propre,* with all its hypocritical tricks, is the product of your bourgeois outlook. Your aim is to gain general acceptance for your false self, to make propaganda, concealing your real motives—motives of personal advantage. You persuade people to view you as you need to be viewed if you are to put it over on them. We all are, insofar as we live for our *amour propre,* loyal to nothing except our secret, crippled objectives—the objectives of every "civilized" man.

Et cetera.

Yes, we're all too familiar with *amour propre,* thanks to the great romantic writers of the nineteenth century. But give clever people something to understand and you can count on them to understand it. So in facing the photographers it's not the exposure of my *amour propre* that concerns me. What I feel in making innumerable last-minute ego arrangements is that the real me will decide to withhold itself. I know that the best picture instruments of Germany or "state-of-the-art" Japan are constructed for ends very different from mine. What need is there to bring these powerful lenses up to the very tip of my nose? They will meaninglessly enlarge the pores of my skin. You will supply them with shots that remind viewers of the leg of a mosquito photographed through a microscope. The truth about you is that you have lost more hair than you thought and that your scalp is shining through— the truth is that you have huge paisley-shaped bruises under your eyes and that your bridgework when you smile is far from "photogenic." You are not simply shown—you are exposed. This exposure cannot be prevented. One can only submit to the merciless cruelty of "pure objectivity," which is so hard on your illusions.

Then, too, from a contemporary point of view, the daily and weekly papers—to say nothing of television—do not feel that they are honoring the truth if they do not tear away the tatters of vanity that cover our imperfections. No one is safe from exposure except the owners, the main stockholders, and the leading advertisers of the great national papers. Things weren't always like this. The "gentlemen" described by Aristotle are immune to shame—they are made that way; nothing shameful can touch these aristocrats. But Adam and Eve, when they had eaten the apple of self-consciousness, sewed fig leaves together to cover their nakedness.

It is the (not always conscious) premise of the photographer that his is the art of penetrating your private defenses. We, his subjects, can learn not to care. But we are not by any means an Aristotelian class, trained in the virtues. We are democrats and lead our petty lives in the shadow of shame. And for this as for all our weaknesses and vices there arise, in all civilized countries, entire classes of people, categories of specialists who specialize in *discovery* and exposure.

Their slogan is: Let the Record Show. And what the record shows is, of course, change and decay, instability, weakness and infirmity, darkness as endless and winding as the Malabar Caves as E. M. Forster years ago described them in *A Passage to India.*

A photograph that made me look worse than the Ruins of Athens was published by *Time* together with a line from William Blake: "The lineaments of gratified desire." Nowhere in the novel *Time* was reviewing had I so much as hinted that my face, with its lineaments, was anything like the faces Blake had in mind (faces of prostitutes, as his text explicitly tells us). But there was my dreary, sullen, tired, and aging mug. I was brought low by Blake's blazing words. But it is the prerogative of the mass media to bring you down when they think that you have gotten ahead of yourself—when they suspect you of flying too high. It doesn't damage us to be exposed, to appear in distorted shapes on film or slick paper or newsprint. I often remember how at the age of ninety-nine Freud's grandmother complained that in the paper "they made me look a hundred years old."

But picture editors and journalists often seem to feel that they are the public representatives of truth, and even that they are conferring some sort of immortality on you by singling you out. But you had better be prepared for rough treatment. Often your "privacy" is to them a cover for the lies and manipulations of *amour propre.*

Who would have thought that minor vanities might lead to such vexations? Your secrets will die in the glare of publicity. When the police strip Dimitri Karamazov to his foul underpants, he says to them, "Gentlemen, you have sullied my soul."

But the world has undergone a revolutionary transformation. Such simple, romantic standards of personal dignity and of the respect due to privacy are to be found today only in remote corners of backward countries. Maybe in the Pyrenees or in the forgotten backlands of Corsica—places where I shouldn't care to live. Everywhere else, the forces of insight are on the lookout. The function of their insights is to make your secrets public, for the public has a right to know, and it is the duty of journalists to deliver the secrets of people "in the news" to their readers. For every story has a story behind it—which is to say that your face, in its own way a story, the story that you present, has another, sometimes very different story underlying it, and it is through the skill of the photographer that these layers of story are revealed.

Painters and sculptors, whose publics are smaller, also approach our heads and faces with insight. They class themselves as artists and are more intellectually sophisticated—better educated than photographers. They have generally absorbed a certain amount of twentieth-century psychology, and their portraits may be filled or formed by their ideas and they may have a diagnostic intent. Do you want to know whether X, our subject, is a violent narcissist? Or whether his is a real, a human face, not a false ideological mask or disguise.

The photograph—to narrow it down—reduces us to two dimensions and it makes us small enough to be represented on a piece of paper or a frame of film. We have been trained by the camera to see the external world. We look *at* and not *into,* as one philosopher has put it. We do not allow ourselves to be *drawn* into what we see. We have been trained to go by the externals. The camera shows us only those, and it is we who do the rest. What we do this *with* is the imagination. What photographs have to show us is the external appearance of objects or beings in the real world, and this is only a portion of their reality. It is after all a convention.

I have known—and still know—many excellent photographers whose work I respect. There are demonic, sadistic camera technicians, too. All trades are like that. But neither the kindly nor the wicked ones can show us the realities we so hope—or long—to see.

Finally, there is the ancient Jewish rule forbidding graven images. My maternal grandfather refused to have his picture taken. But when he was dying my mother brought in a photographer and hid him behind the bushes.

This faded picture is one of my Old World legacies. I also inherited the brass family samovar and my mother's silver change purse. In this purse I now carry Betapace, Hytrin, and Coumadin tablets.

My grandfather's picture was taken in the late 1890s. He is sitting, dying in an apple orchard, his beard is spread over his upper body. His elbow rests on the top of his walking stick and his hand supports his head. His big eyes tell you that he is absorbed in *olam ha-bo*—the world to come, the next life. My mother used to say, "He would have been very angry with me. To make pictures was sinful [an *averah*], but I took the *averah* on myself."

When we were very young, my parents told us that until we came of age they would be responsible for our transgressions. But that is an altogether different matter. What I am saying here is that nowadays not even the nobs have their portraits painted, and the masses preserve the faces of ancestors in daguerreotypes and Kodaks. The critical mind sees an insignificant photographer hidden in the bushes, inserting a plate and pulling the cloth over his head. Perhaps the old man knew perfectly well that his picture was being taken. My mother was then old enough to bear the burden of this sin. She committed it because she loved him and was afraid of forgetting what he had looked like.

In any case, I have been not only photographed but cast in bronze and also painted. Since I am too impatient to sit still, painters and sculptors have worked from photographs. The Chicago Public Library exhibits the busts of bookish local boys. The artist who did my head was obliged to measure it while I was watching the Chicago Bulls on television. It was an important game and I didn't intend to miss it.

Considering the bronze head on display in the Harold Washington Library, I think that Pablo Picasso would have done it better. He might perhaps have given me a third eye and two noses. I'd have loved two noses.

But for a one-nose job, the bust in the Chicago library isn't at all bad.

Leslie Marmon Silko

Language and Literature from a Pueblo Indian Perspective

Where I come from, the words most highly valued are those spoken from the heart, unpremeditated and unrehearsed. Among the Pueblo people, a written speech or statement is highly suspect because the true feelings of the speaker remain hidden as she reads words that are detached from the occasion and the audience. I have intentionally not written a formal paper because I want you to *hear* and to experience English in a structure that follows patterns from the oral tradition. For those of you accustomed to being taken from point A to point B to point C, this presentation may be somewhat difficult to follow. Pueblo expression resembles something like a spider's web—with many little threads radiating from the center, crisscrossing one another. As with the web, the structure emerges as it is made, and you must simply listen and trust, as the Pueblo people do, that meaning will be made.

My task is a formidable one: I ask you to set aside a number of basic approaches that you have been using and probably will continue to use, and, instead, to approach language from the Pueblo perspective, one that embraces the whole of creation and the whole of history and time.

What changes would Pueblo writers make to English as a language for literature? I have some examples of stories in English that I will use to address this question. At the same time, I would like to explain the importance of storytelling and how it relates to a Pueblo theory of language.

So I will begin, appropriately enough, with the Pueblo Creation story, an all-inclusive story of how life began. In this story, Tse'itsi'nako, Thought Woman, by thinking of her sisters, and together with her sisters, thought of everything that is. In this way, the world was created. Everything in this world was a part of the original Creation; the people at home understood that far away there were other human beings, also a part of this world. The

Creation story even includes a prophecy that describes the origin of European and African peoples and also refers to Asians.

This story, I think, suggests something about why the Pueblo people are more concerned with story and communication and less concerned with a particular language. There are at least six, possibly seven, distinct languages among the twenty pueblos of the southwestern United States, for example, Zuñi and Hopi. And from mesa to mesa there are subtle differences in language. But the particular language being spoken isn't as important as what a speaker is trying to say, and this emphasis on the story itself stems, I believe, from a view of narrative particular to the Pueblo and other Native American peoples—that is, that language *is* story.

I will try to clarify this statement. At Laguna Pueblo, for example, many individual words have their own stories. So when one is telling a story and one is using words to tell the story, each word that one is speaking has a story of its own, too. Often the speakers, or tellers, will go into these word stories, creating an elaborate structure of stories within stories. This structure, which becomes very apparent in the actual telling of a story, informs contemporary Pueblo writing and storytelling as well as the traditional narratives. This perspective on narrative—of story within story, the idea that one story is only the beginning of many stories and the sense that stories never truly end—represents an important contribution of Native American cultures to the English language.

Many people think of storytelling as something that is done at bedtime, that it is something done for small children. But when I use the term *storytelling,* I'm talking about something much bigger than that. I'm talking about something that comes out of an experience and an understanding of that original view of Creation—that we are all part of a whole; we do not differentiate or fragment stories and experiences. In the beginning, Tse'itsi'nako, Thought Woman, thought of all things, and all of these things are held together as one holds many things together in a single thought.

So in the telling (and you will hear a few of the dimensions of this telling), first of all, as mentioned earlier, the storytelling always includes the audience, the listeners. In fact, a great deal of the story is believed to be inside the listener; the storyteller's role is to draw the story out of the listeners. The storytelling continues from generation to generation.

Basically, the origin story constructs our identity—with this story, we know who we are. We are the Lagunas. This is where we come from. We came this way. We came by this place. And so from the time we are very young, we hear these stories, so that when we go out into the world, when one asks who we are or where we are from, we immediately know: we are the people who came from the north. We are the people of these stories.

In the Creation story, Antelope says that he will help knock a hole in the Earth so that the people can come up, out into the next world. Antelope tries and tries; he uses his hooves but is unable to break through. It is then that Badger says, "Let me help you." And Badger very patiently uses his claws and digs a way through, bringing the people into the world. When the Badger clan people think of themselves, or when the Antelope people think of themselves, it is as people who are of *this* story, and this is *our* place, and we fit into the very beginning when the people first came, before we began our journey south.

Within the clans there are stories that identify the clan. One moves, then, from the idea of one's identity as a tribal person into clan identity, then to one's identity as a member of an extended family. And it is the notion of extended family that has produced a kind of story that some distinguish from other Pueblo stories, though Pueblo people do not. Anthropologists and ethnologists have, for a long time, differentiated the types of stories the Pueblos tell. They tended to elevate the old, sacred, and traditional stories and to brush aside family stories, the family's account of itself. But in Pueblo culture, these family stories are given equal recognition. There is no definite, preset pattern for the way one will hear the stories of one's own family, but it is a very critical part of one's childhood, and the storytelling continues throughout one's life. One will hear stories of importance to the family—sometimes wonderful stories—stories about the time a maternal uncle got the biggest deer that was ever seen and brought it back from the mountains. And so an individual's identity will extend from the identity constructed around the family—"I am from the family of my uncle who brought in this wonderful deer, and it was a wonderful hunt."

Family accounts include negative stories, too; perhaps an uncle did something unacceptable. It is very important that one keep track of all these stories—both positive and not so positive—about one's own family and other families. Because even when there is no way around it—old Uncle Pete *did* do a terrible thing—by knowing the stories that originate in other families, one is able to deal with terrible sorts of things that might happen within one's own family. If a member of the family does something that cannot be excused, one always knows stories about similarly inexcusable things done by a member of another family. But this knowledge is not communicated for malicious reasons. It is very important to understand this. Keeping track of all the stories within the community gives us all a certain distance, a useful perspective, that brings incidents down to a level we can deal with. If others have done it before, it cannot be so terrible. If others have endured, so can we.

The stories are always bringing us together, keeping this whole together, keeping this family together, keeping this clan together. "Don't go away, don't isolate yourself, but come here, because we have all had these kinds of experiences." And so there is this constant pulling together to resist the tendency to run or hide or separate oneself during a traumatic emotional experience. This separation not only endangers the group but the individual as well—one does not recover by oneself.

Because storytelling lies at the heart of Pueblo culture, it is absurd to attempt to fix the stories in time. "When did they tell the stories?" or "What time of day does the storytelling take place?"—these questions are nonsensical from a Pueblo perspective, because our storytelling goes on constantly: as some old grandmother puts on the shoes of a child and tells her the story of a little girl who didn't wear her shoes, for instance, or someone comes into the house for coffee to talk with a teenage boy who has just been in a lot of trouble, to reassure him that someone else's son has been in that kind of trouble, too. Storytelling is an ongoing process, working on many different levels.

Here's one story that is often told at a time of individual crisis (and I want to remind you that we make no distinctions between types of story—historical, sacred, plain gossip—because these distinctions are not useful when discussing the Pueblo *experience* of language). There was a young man who, when he came back from the war in Vietnam, had saved up his army pay and bought a beautiful red Volkswagen. He was very proud of it. One night he drove up to a place called the King's Bar, right across the reservation line. The bar is notorious for many reasons, particularly for the deep arroyo located behind it. The young man ran in to pick up a cold six-pack, but he forgot to put on his emergency brake. And his little red Volkswagen rolled back into the arroyo and was all smashed up. He felt very bad about it, but within a few days everybody had come to him with stories about other people who had lost cars and family members to that arroyo, for instance, George Day's station wagon, with his mother-in-law and kids inside. So everybody was saying, "Well, at least your mother-in-law and kids weren't in the car when it rolled in," and one can't argue with that kind of story. The story of the young man and his smashed-up Volkswagen was now joined with all the other stories of cars that fell into that arroyo.

Now I want to tell you a very beautiful little story. It is a very old story that is sometimes told to people who suffer great family or personal loss. This story was told by my Aunt Susie. She is one of the first generation of people at Laguna who began experimenting with English—who began working to make English speak for us, that is, to speak from the heart. (I come from a family intent on getting the stories told.) As you read the story, I think you will hear that. And here and there, I think, you will also hear the influence of the Indian school at Carlisle, Pennsylvania, where my Aunt Susie was sent (like being sent to prison) for six years.

This scene is set partly in Acoma, partly in Laguna. Waithea was a little girl living in Acoma and one day she said, "Mother, I would like to have some *yashtoah* to eat." *Yashtoah* is the hardened crust of corn mush that curls up. *Yashtoah* literally means "curled up." She said, "I would like to have some *yashtoah*," and her mother said, "My dear little girl, I can't make you any *yashtoah* because we haven't any wood, but if you will go down off the mesa, down below, and pick up some pieces of wood and bring them home, I will make you some *yashtoah*." So Waithea was glad and ran down the precipitous cliff of Acoma mesa. Down below, just as her mother had told her, there were pieces of wood, some curled, some crooked in shape, that she was to pick up and take home. She found just such wood as these.

She brought them home in a little wicker basket. First she called to her mother as she got home, "*Nayah, deeni!* Mother, upstairs!" The Pueblo people always called "upstairs" because long ago their homes were two, three stories, and they entered from the top. She said, "*Deeni! Upstairs!*" and her mother came. The little girl said, "I have brought the wood you wanted me to bring." And she opened her little wicker basket to lay out the pieces of wood, but here they were snakes. They were snakes instead of the crooked sticks of wood. And her mother said, "Oh my dear child, you have brought snakes instead!" She said, "Go take them back and put them back just where you got them." And the little girl ran down the mesa again, down below to the flats. And she put those snakes back just where she got them. They were snakes instead, and she was very hurt about this, and so she said, "I'm not going home. I'm going to Kawaik, the beautiful lake place Kawaik, and drown myself in that lake, *byn'yah'nah* [the 'west lake']. I will go there and drown myself."

So she started off, and as she passed by the Enchanted Mesa near Acoma, she met an old man, very aged, and he saw her running, and he said, "My dear child, where are you going?" "I'm going to Kawaik and jump into the lake there."

"Why?" "Well, because," she said, "my mother didn't want to make any *yashtoah* for me." The old man said, "Oh, no! You must not go, my child. Come with me and I will take you home." He tried to catch her, but she was very light and skipped along. And every time he would try to grab her she would skip faster away from him.

The old man was coming home with some wood strapped to his back and tied with yucca. He just let that strap go and let the wood drop. He went as fast as he could up the cliff to the little girl's home. When he got to the place where she lived, he called to her mother. "*Deeni!*" "Come on up!" And he said, "I can't. I just came to bring you a message. Your little daughter is running away. She is going to Kawaik to drown herself in the lake there." "Oh my dear little girl!" the mother said. So she busied herself with making the *yashtoah* her little girl liked so much. Corn mush curled at the top. (She must have found enough wood to boil the corn meal and make the *yashtoah*.)

While the mush was cooling off, she got the little girl's clothing, her *manta* dress and buckskin moccasins and all her other garments, and put them in a bundle—probably a yucca bag. And she started down as fast as she could on the east side of Acoma. (There used to be a trail there, you know. It's gone now, but it was accessible in those days.) She saw her daughter way at a distance and she kept calling: "Stsamaku! My daughter! Come back! I've got your *yashtoah* for you." But the little girl would not turn. She kept on ahead and she cried: "My mother, my mother, she didn't want me to have any *yashtoah*. So now I'm going to Kawaik and drown myself." Her mother heard her cry and said, "My little daughter, come back here!" "No," and she kept a distance away from her. And they came nearer and nearer to the lake. And she could see her daughter now, very plain. "Come back, my daughter! I have your *yashtoah*." But no, she kept on, and finally she reached the lake and she stood on the edge.

She had tied a little feather in her hair, which is traditional (in death they tie this feather on the head). She carried a feather, the little girl did, and she tied it in her hair with a piece of string; right on top of her head she put the feather. Just as her mother was about to reach her, she jumped into the lake. The little feather was whirling around and around in the depths below. Of course the mother was very sad. She went, grieved, back to Acoma and climbed her mesa home. She stood on the edge of the mesa and scattered her daughter's clothing, the little moccasins, the *yashtoah*. She scattered them to the east, to the west, to the north, to the south. And the pieces of clothing and the moccasins and *yashtoah* all turned into butterflies. And today they say that Acoma has more beautiful butterflies: red ones, white ones, blue ones, yellow ones. They came from this little girl's clothing.

Now this is a story anthropologists would consider very old. The version I have given you is just as Aunt Susie tells it. You can occasionally hear some English she picked up at Carlisle—words like *precipitous*. You will also notice that there is a great deal of repetition, and a little reminder about *yashtoah* and how it is made. There is a remark about the cliff trail at Acoma—that it was once there but is there no longer. This story may be told at a time of sadness or loss, but within this story many other elements are brought together. Things are not separated out and categorized; all things are brought together, so that the reminder about the *yashtoah* is valuable information that is repeated—a recipe, if you will. The information about the old trail at Acoma reveals that stories are, in a sense, maps, since even to this day there is little information or material about trails that is passed around with writing. In the structure of this story the repetitions are, of course, designed to help you remember. It is repeated again and again, and then it moves on.

There are a great many parallels between Pueblo experiences and those of African and Caribbean peoples—one is that we have all had the conqueror's language imposed on us.

But our experience with English has been somewhat different in that the Bureau of Indian Affairs schools were not interested in teaching us the canon of Western classics. For instance, we never heard of Shakespeare. We were given Dick and Jane, and I can remember reading that the robins were heading south for the winter. It took me a long time to figure out what was going on. I worried for quite a while about our robins in Laguna because they didn't leave in the winter, until I finally realized that all the big textbook companies are up in Boston and *their* robins do go south in the winter. But in a way, this dreadful formal education freed us by encouraging us to maintain our narratives. Whatever literature we were exposed to at school (which was damn little), at home the storytelling, the special regard for telling and bringing together through the telling, was going on constantly.

And as the old people say, "If you can remember the stories, you will be all right. Just remember the stories." When I returned to Laguna Pueblo after attending college, I wondered how the storytelling was continuing (anthropologists say that Laguna Pueblo is one of the more acculturated pueblos), so I visited an English class at Laguna-Acoma High School. I knew the students had cassette tape recorders in their lockers and stereos at home, and that they listened to Kiss and Led Zeppelin and were well informed about culture in general. I had with me an anthology of short stories by Native American writers, *The Man to Send Rain Clouds*. One story in the book is about the killing of a state policeman in New Mexico by three Acoma Pueblo men in the early 1950s. I asked the students how many had heard this story and steeled myself for the possibility that the anthropologists were right, that the old traditions were indeed dying out and the students would be ignorant of the story. But instead, all but one or two raised their hands—they had heard the story, just as I had heard it when I was young, some in English, some in Laguna.

One of the other advantages that we Pueblos have enjoyed is that we have always been able to stay with the land. Our stories cannot be separated from their geographical locations, from actual physical places on the land. We were not relocated like so many Native American groups who were torn away from their ancestral land. And our stories are so much a part of these places that it is almost impossible for future generations to lose them—there is a story connected with every place, every object in the landscape.

Dennis Brutus has talked about the "yet unborn" as well as "those from the past," and how we are still *all* in *this* place, and language—the storytelling—is our way of passing through or being with them, of being together again. When Aunt Susie told her stories, she would tell a younger child to go open the door so that our esteemed predecessors might bring their gifts to us. "They are out there," Aunt Susie would say. "Let them come in. They're here, they're here with us *within* the stories."

A few years ago, when Aunt Susie was 106, I paid her a visit, and while I was there she said, "Well, I'll be leaving here soon. I think I'll be leaving here next week, and I will be going over to the Cliff House." She said, "It's going to be real good to get back over there." I was listening, and I was thinking that she must be talking about her house at Paguate village, just north of Laguna. And she went on, "Well, my mother's sister [and she gave her Indian name] will be there. She has been living there. She will be there and we will be over there, and I will get a chance to write down these stories I've been telling you." Now you must understand, of course, that Aunt Susie's mother's sister, a great story-teller herself, has long since passed over into the land of the dead. But then I realized, too, that Aunt Susie wasn't talking about death the way most of us do. She was talking about "going over" as a journey, a journey that perhaps we can only begin to understand through an appreciation for the boundless capacity of language that, through storytelling, brings us together, despite great distances between cultures, despite great distances in time.

John Updike

Fast Art

The Andy Warhol Retrospective at New York's Museum of Modern Art is the perfect show for time-pressed Manhattanites; they can breeze through it at the clip of a fast walk, take it in through the corners of their eyes without ever breaking stride, and be able to talk about it afterwards entirely in terms of what they got out of it. Indeed, you can honorably discuss the show without attending it at all, if you've ever seen a Brillo box, a Campbell's soup can, a photograph of Marilyn Monroe, and a silver balloon. Here they are again, the dear old Warhol icons, full of empty content, or contented emptiness. Their vacuity gains through muchness, since if you miss one wall of silk-screened cans or Marilyns or dollar bills, another wall will deliver the same massage, and we can take in this art as we take in reality—while trying to ignore it. Not only does, say, a duplicated and garishly paint-smeared image of Liza Minnelli or Truman Capote not invite close attention, it sends it skidding the other way. Busy power-people should love this show; it repels lingering, and can be cruised for its high spots, which are all but indistinguishable from its low spots.

This is not denigration but an attempt at description. Warhol's art has the powerful effect of making nothing seem important. He was a considerable philosopher, and in his testament, *The Philosophy of Andy Warhol,* as extracted by Pat Hackett, we read: "Some critic called me the Nothingness Himself and that didn't help my sense of existence any. Then I realized that existence itself is nothing and I felt better." His great unfulfilled ambition (he couldn't have had too many) was a regular TV show; he was going to call it *Nothing Special.* He came to maturity in the postwar, early–Cold War era of existentialism and angst, and found himself greatly soothed by the spread of television and the tape recorder. In his *Philosophy,* he speaks this parable: "A whole day of life is like a whole day of television. TV never goes off the air once it starts for the day, and I don't either. At the end of the day the whole day will be a movie. A movie made for TV." The tape recorder completed his deliverance from direct, emotional involvement in his own life: "The acquisition of my tape recorder really finished whatever emotional life I might have had, but I was glad to see it go. Nothing was ever a problem again, because a problem just meant a good tape, and when a problem transforms itself into a good tape it's not a problem any more." Like the pidgin pronouncements of Gertrude Stein, Warhol's harbor amid their deadpan tumble of egocentric prattle an intermittent clairvoyance, a shameless gift for seeing what is there and saying it. The political turbulence and colorful noise of the Sixties did not hide from him the decade's essential revolution: "During the 60s, I think, people forgot what emotions were supposed to be. And I don't think they've ever remembered. I think that once you see emotions from a certain angle you can never think of them as real again."

What remains real, it would seem, is the semiotic shell, the mass of images with which a society economically bent on keeping us stirred up appeals to our oversolicited, overanalyzed, overdramatized, overliberated, and over-the-hill emotions. Warhol on sex, our great social lubricant and sales incentive, is especially withering: "After being alive, the next hardest work is having sex." Sex is not only work: "Sex is nostalgia for when you used to want it, sometimes. Sex is nostalgia for sex." Or: "Frigid people really make out." His obsessive silk-screening of Marilyn Monroe (of one particular face that she presented to the camera, her eyelids half lowered and her lips parted in a smile somewhat like a growl, a Fifties drive-in waitress's tired sizing-up of one more coarse but not totally uninteresting come-on) turns her into a Day-Glo–tinted, tarted-up mask, the gaudy sad skull left when she is viewed without desire. The repetition that was one of Warhol's key devices—two Liza Minnellis, ten Elizabeth Taylors, thirty-six Elvises, one hundred two Troy Donahues—has a mocking effect. In one of the many essays that introduce the tribute-laden, 478-page catalogue, John Cage is quoted as saying, "Andy has fought by repetition to show us that there is no repetition really, that everything we look at is worthy of our attention." To me the message seems the exact opposite: that everything is repeated, that everything is emptied and rendered meaningless by repetition. Warhol himself stated: "When you see a gruesome picture over and over again, it doesn't really have any effect."

Born Andrew Warhola in 1928, the son of an immigrant Carpatho-Russian coal miner, he came from Pittsburgh to New York in 1949, freshly graduated from Carnegie Tech. In *Pre-Pop Warbol,* an album of his commercial art published in 1988 by Panache Press at Random House, Tina S. Fredericks, who gave Warhol his professional start at *Glamour* magazine, writes, "I greeted a pale, blotchy boy, diffident almost to the point of disappearance but somehow immediately and immensely appealing. He seemed all one color: pale chinos, pale wispy hair, pale eyes, a strange beige birthmark over the side of his face (almost like a Helen Frankenthaler wash)." He was not only appealing and blotchy but persistent and resourceful; by the mid-Fifties he had become a very successful commercial artist. His drawings of shoes for I. Miller, done in the Ben Shahn–like blotted-line look that he had developed, were especially celebrated in the advertising world. He was industrious and quick, and never overdid his assignments, providing a light, artist-effacing touch. In *Pre-Pop Warbol* can be found a number of devices directly transferred to the "serious" art he began to produce in 1960—repetition, gold-leaf, a wallpaper flatness, monochrome washes across the outlines, and appropriation of ready-made elements such as embossed paper decorations. These early years also saw, in the hiring of his first assistant, Nathan Gluck, in 1955, the beginning of his famous "Factory" and (to quote Rupert Jasen Smith) "his art-by-committee philosophy." Warhol's first art sales were of shoe drawings rejected by I. Miller, displayed on the walls of the Serendipity restaurant in 1954. His first exhibit, containing paintings of Superman and a Pepsi-Cola advertisement and a before-and-after nose job all present in this 1989 retrospective, appeared behind mannequins in a window of Bonwit Teller in 1961. As late as 1963 he was still accepting more commercial commissions than he rejected. He saw, however, that the gallery and the museum were the path to true wealth and fame; he went, in his words, from the art business to business art. "I started as a commercial artist, and I want to finish as a business artist. . . . I wanted to be an Art Businessman or a Business Artist. Being good in business is the most fascinating kind of art."

"American money is very well-designed, really," Warhol said in one of the few aesthetic judgments offered in his *Philosophy.* "I like it better than any other kind of money." He drew dollar bills freehand, he silk-screened sheets of them, he became rich. He had an untroubled tabloid mentality; his eye naturally went to what interests most of us: money, advertisements, packages, lurid headlines, pictures of movie stars, photographs of electric chairs and gory automobile accidents. His early-Sixties pencilled and painted copies of screaming front pages from the *News,* the *Post,* and the *Mirror,* with Sinatra and Princess Margaret, Liz and Eddie carefully but not mechanically reproduced, make us smile, because these are familiar images we thought too lowly to be passed through the eye and hand and mind of an artist. They, and the soup cans and Coke bottles, are Pop comedy, our world brought home to us with that kiss of surprise which realism bestows. The multiple silk-screens possess, in the inevitable irregularities of the process and the overlay of colors, qualities that we can call painterly, and that reassure us.

But when we arrive, on the lower floor of this exhibition, at the blown-up and mono-chromed photos of car wrecks and electric chairs and race riots, a whiff of Sixties sulphur offends our nostrils in these odorless Eighties. Something too extreme and bleak is afoot. We wonder how much of our interest can be credited to Warhol, and how much to the inherent fascination of the original photographs. Where is the artist in all this? Is he working hard enough, or just peddling gruesome photos? We find ourselves getting indignant and hostile. Warhol in his lifetime inspired a great deal of hostile criticism, even in times when almost anything went, and the hostility relates, I think, to the truly radical notion his works embody: the erasure of the artist from art, his total surrender to mechanism and accident. Such a notion makes art critics uneasy, for if artists self-erase, art critics must be next in line, and it distresses the art viewer with the suspicion that he is being swindled—being sold, as it were, a silk-screen of the Brooklyn Bridge.

No sweat, the saying goes, and Warhol perfected sweatless art: movies without cutting, books without editing, painting without brushing. Up from blue-collar origins, he became the manager of the Factory. His lightest touch on the prayer wheel there produced a new billowing of replicated images, of Maos and cows and Mick Jaggers, of dollar signs and shoes, of mock-ads and packages, of helium-filled silver pillows. When each idea had had its scandalous and impudent little run, he came up with another, and although some, like the oxidization paintings produced by urinating on canvases covered with copper metallic paint,* will never replace Pollock in the hearts of museum curators, it must be said that for all the Sixties and much of the Seventies Warhol maintained quality controls. Almost everything produced was perfect in its way, with a commercial artist's clean precision and automatic tact. In the anarchic realm of the disappearing artist, the artist's ghost—wispy and powdery, Warhol came to look more and more ghostlike—exercised

---

* "Mixed mediums," in polite cataloguese.

taste. Not until the last rooms of this show do any of the canvases seem too much, like the visually noisy camouflage series, or too little, like the epochal religious paintings of Raphael and Leonardo reduced to coloring-book outlines and disfigured with manufacturers' logos.

In the realm of social behavior, too, a certain control kept Warhol productive and inventive. Though lesser members of his Factory descended into stoned orgies and ruinous addictions, he remained wrapped in a prophylactic innocence, going home every night (until 1971) to his mother—that same mother who, he remembered in his brief memoir of his childhood, used to read *Dick Tracy* to him in "her thick Czechoslovakian accent" and who would reward him with a Hershey bar "every time I finished a page in my coloring book." How much, really, of his mature work can be described as "coloring"! In one of his first self-abnegations he induced her to sign his works, and write his captions, in her own clumsy but clear handwriting. Julia Warhola presents a perspective on her son opposite from that of the critic who called him Nothingness Himself: Tina Fredericks quotes her as saying, "He represents at the same time the American and the European fused together and he's very keen and sensitive to everything that goes on every day and he registered it like . . . you know . . . a photographic plate. . . . He has this terrific energy and he goes out and he registers everything and he does that everything and he becomes everything. The everything man."

Everything and nothing, Warhol might have pointed out, are close to identical. He evidently did not quite discard the Roman Catholicism in which he was raised, paying daily visits to the Church of St. Vincent Ferrer on 66th Street and anonymously performing good works for the homeless. The closing paragraphs of the catalogue essay by Robert Rosenblum persuasively link Warhol's Catholicism with his sense of the iconic, his altarpiecelike diptychs, his fondness for gilt and memento mori. But surely, also, the profound hollowness we feel behind the canvases is a Catholic negativity, the abyss of lost faith. Protestantism, when it fades, leaves behind a fuzzy idealism; Catholicism, a crystalline cynicism. In the *Philosophy,* some of his remarks have the penetrating desolation we associate with maximists like La Rochefoucauld and Chamfort. "I think that just being alive is so much work at something you don't always want to do. Being born is like being kidnapped. And then sold into slavery." The equation of being born with being kidnapped takes one's breath away, and the Warhol "works" on display in New York assume a new light when seen as the fruits of a kind of cosmic slavery. Work he did, while pretending to do nothing. If the show in its early rooms has the gaiety of a department store, it takes on downstairs the sombre, claustral mood of a catacomb. Negatived skulls and *Mona Lisas* suggest the inversions of a black mass. The glamorized women, we notice, are almost all of them dead or grazed by death—Marilyn, Jackie, Natalie, Liz. And Warhol himself, unexpectedly dead in a hospital when not yet sixty, a victim perhaps of the distracted medical attention that celebrities risk receiving from the awed staff, has joined the Pop martyrs, the mummified media saints.

There was an efficient churchly atmosphere to his show, of duty discharged and superstition placated. Visitors, I noticed, kept glancing slyly at one another, as if to ask, "How foolish do *you* feel?" One woman, with a seemly irreverence, combed her hair in front of a Warhol self-portrait whose framing glass reflected back from that dead opaque face. It might have been an act of oblation. Andy has become—what he must have wanted all along—an icon.

Craft Essays

Patricia Hampl

Reviewing Anne Frank

Book reviewing is the bread-and-butter labor of the writing life. In fact, it's considered hack work—though not by me. I have always been idealistic, even romantic, about reviewing. My affection may be rooted in the fact that writing book reviews was the first way I got published. Reviews provided the first sweet literary money I earned.

Fundamentally, literature is a conversation, strangely intimate, conducted between writer and reader—countless writers, unknown readers. Reviewing has never struck me as having much to do with assigning scores or handing out demerits. The reviewer's job— and pleasure—is akin to any reader's. It is the pleasure of talk. If nobody *talks* about books, if they are not discussed or somehow contended with, literature ceases to be a conversation, ceases to be dynamic. Most of all, it ceases to be intimate. It degenerates into a monologue or a mutter. An unreviewed book is a struck bell that gives no resonance. Without reviews, literature would be oddly mute in spite of all those words on all those pages of all those books. Reviewing makes of reading a participant sport, not a spectator sport.

But no assignment has been as daunting as the one given me to review the new "Definitive Edition" of Anne Frank's *Diary*. The *Diary* is a book like no other. For one thing, virtually all books assigned for review are just off the press. A reviewer is a kind of first reader, an explorer describing a new book, like a new country, to the people who have yet to travel there. But who does not know about Anne Frank and her heartbreaking diary? It was first published over fifty years ago, and has been translated into virtually every language in the world that sustains a book culture. Most readers know this book, like very few others, from childhood, and they carry it into adulthood.

Even if they haven't read it, people know the story and the essential personality of its extraordinary author. Besides the familiarity of the book, who on earth would claim to "review" Anne Frank? The book seemed to defy the very enterprise of book reviewing. I suppose the emotion ruling me as I approached my task was a paralyzing diffidence. Who was I to write about this icon of the Holocaust?

I procrastinated as long as I could. I did everything to keep from writing the review. I was very good at this. I read the book slowly, I underlined passages, I took notes, jotting down lines from the *Diary*, some of them passages I remembered with surprising sharpness from girlhood when I had first read the book, some of them new to me. The more I felt the power of the book, the more hopeless I felt. I missed the first deadline and called my editor, begging for an extension. Granted! A reprieve.

Then I procrastinated some more. I developed a sudden urgency about cleaning my oven and sorting out my sock drawer. I called friends, made lunch dates (I never go out to lunch when I'm working). I asked my friends what *they* thought about Anne Frank. I had a ferocious resistance to writing the review. I found yet another way to avoid writing which

I could at least call "research": I dug up "The Development of Anne Frank," an essay about Anne Frank by John Berryman which I remembered having read or having heard about years before. I took notes on *that*.

I saw from a note in the text that the essay had been written in 1967. I had been Berryman's student at the University of Minnesota that year, taking two courses in "Humanities of the Western World" from him in a packed, overheated room with fifty or sixty other undergraduates. The room smelled of wet wool (our damp winter coats) and cigarette smoke (his unfiltered cigarettes which pitched perilously from his wildly gesticulating hand).

We understood Berryman was "a great poet." *Life* magazine had done a big picture story about him in Ireland, catching his Old Testament beard in the salt wind, the hand and the cigarette in motion against an abysmal sea. He talked about literature in a fierce, angry way, full of astonishment; he had an ability to bring a roomful of undergraduates to tears by reading aloud the farewell scene between Hector and Andromache in the *Iliad*. Mechanical engineering students, taking the class as a distribution requirement, looked down with red, embarrassed faces, twisting their paperback Homers.

Berryman killed himself only a few years after I graduated. He jumped from a bridge on campus, a bridge I had walked across every day. I couldn't remember his ever saying anything about Anne Frank, but reading his essay about her all these years later brought him powerfully back, the force of his inquiring mind, his determination to understand what was at stake in her book, his assumption of the greatness of this little girl who kept a diary.

I still hadn't written a word.

But I had finally wandered into the task at hand. Though I ended up referring only briefly to a remark in Berryman's essay when I wrote my own review (a kind of private homage to him), it wasn't so much what his essay said that began to unlock my own timidity. Rather, it was the tone I felt in his essay, a voice that was so poised on *trying to understand* that it had no room for the kind of hand wringing I was indulging in myself.

Berryman began by telling how he had first come across Anne Frank's *Diary* in 1952 when the first installment of the translated text appeared in *Commentary* magazine. "I read it with amazement," he says in his essay. He was so galvanized by her writing that "the next day, when I went to town to see my analyst, I stopped in the magazine's offices . . . to see if proofs of the *Diary's* continuation were available, and they were." Then, "like millions of people later," he wrote, "I was bowled over with pity and horror and admiration for the astounding doomed little girl."

But he didn't stop with this emotional anchor. He demanded, right from the start, that he think as well as feel. "But what I *thought* was: a sane person. A sane person, in the twentieth century." Berryman had found the tip of his subject: How had such extraordinary sanity come to be developed in the crushing circumstances of Anne Frank's life which were the worst circumstances of the century? It wasn't necessary to remember the details of his own tragic end for me to feel his urgency in searching for "a sane person in the twentieth century."

I liked the naturalness of this beginning, the casualness of his saying he was "bowled over." I liked how, having established his feeling, he refused to dwell on it but pushed on to a thought. I could feel a mind at work, and more than that: I felt a story unfolding. He was writing a *story,* I suddenly thought, the story of his relation to this book. The ideas were like characters in the story that he kept looking at from one angle and then another in order to make sense of them, in order to come to a conclusion, much the way a story must bring its characters to some resolving, if mysterious, finale.

Strangely enough, it was at this point (if I remember correctly) that I made my first mark on paper, my first stab at my own response to Anne Frank. I wrote the first three paragraphs of my review, quite easily, as if there had been no procrastination, no moaning and groaning at all for several weeks of fretful false starts. After reading Berryman's essay, I knew what to do—at least for three paragraphs.

> On Tuesday, March 28, 1944, Gerrit Bolkestein, Education Minister of the Dutch Government in exile, delivered a radio message from London urging his war-weary countrymen to collect "vast quantities of simple, everyday material" as part of the historical record of the Nazi occupation.
>
> "History cannot be written on the basis of official decisions and documents alone," he said. "If our descendants are to understand fully what we as a nation have had to endure and overcome during these years, then what we really need are ordinary documents—a diary, letters."
>
> In her diary the next day, Anne Frank mentions this broadcast, which she and her family heard on a clandestine radio in their Amsterdam hiding place. "Ten years after the war," she writes on March 29, "people would find it very amusing to read how we lived, what we ate and what we talked about as Jews in hiding."

No one, reading the opening paragraphs of John Berryman's essay about being bowled over and astonished to find in this little girl's diary "a sane person in the twentieth century" and then reading the opening of my review, which is a straightforward piece of historical information, would imagine that I had finally been nudged off the dime by his essay. Berryman's tone is personal and immediate. Mine is distanced (I never make use of the first person pronoun in my entire review) and rests its authority on certain historical facts I present to the reader dispassionately.

I got the hint about the Dutch Education Minister's clandestine radio message from the foreword to the "Definitive Edition," but I tracked down the exact quotation from the speech at the library. If I wasn't going to allow myself the kind of authority and presence that Berryman had with the use of the personal pronoun, I needed to achieve that sense of immediacy another way. Direct quotation from the minister's speech mimicked the clandestine wartime radio transmission.

I tried to make Anne Frank's knowledge of the minister's radio message part of this story—as indeed it actually was. I wanted the reader to see history happening as it happened for Anne Frank herself. That is why I began the review in a storylike way: "On Tuesday, March 28, 1944, Gerrit Bolkestein, Education Minister of the Dutch Government in exile, delivered a radio message from London urging . . . " In order to bolster the authority of this information in every way possible—and thereby to bolster the authority of my own narrative—I called the public library to find out what day of the week March 28 fell on in the year 1944 so that, casually, I could note that it was a Tuesday. I had to seduce the reader not with my emotional authority but with the authority of simple facts. A small thing, but words *are* small, and each one can count for a lot.

It is odd—even to me—that reading Berryman's very personal (though closely ana-lytical) essay should have shown me the way into my own piece about Anne Frank. I had a number of constraints that hadn't hampered him. For one thing, I had much less space: My editor allotted me a certain number of words and no more. The reviewer's humble pie. Berryman had written an essay, a more open, luxurious form.

Still, many reviewers use the first person voice, and Berryman certainly had won me over partly because of his very immediate presence in his own essay. So why did I steer away from that voice? I think I understood, after reading Berryman's beautiful essay, the different task I had before me. What Berryman had done in 1967 didn't need to be done again. But I benefited from the freedom of his prose, the genuineness of his inquiry. It was a model for me—not a model of style, but of intention. I wasn't coming upon Anne Frank's *Diary* as it came out in proofs for the first time. I was responding to a definitive edition of a book that has long been a classic. I did not need to present myself as having been moved by the *Diary*. History had provided several generations of such readers. I needed to get out of the way.

Also, while I had been procrastinating by having lunch with my friends, one of my luncheon companions mentioned that there had been (and continues to be) an ugly, demented attempt to deny the authenticity of the *Diary*. Like many such anti-Holocaust theories, this one tries to prove that while there might have been a little girl named Anne Frank who had died during the war of "natural causes" (or in some versions had not died but been "lost" or who was herself a fabrication), this child had never written a diary. "The Diary of Anne Frank," these conspiracy theorists claim, was written by adults—by Anne Frank's father (whose presence as the sole survivor of his murdered family the theory does not account for) or by some others engaged in a "Jewish plot."

It was all quite mad.

The reason these allegations about the *Diary* had won any attention at all hinged on the fact that there are indeed several versions of Anne Frank's diaries. In preparing the first edition of the book, her father was compelled, partly by his own sense of discretion and partly by space limitations imposed on him by the original Dutch publisher, to make dele-tions. In 1986 a "Critical Edition" was published that meticulously presents Anne's origi-nal diary, plus the version she was working on for her proposed fictionalized version, "The Secret Annex," and the edition her father published—which is the edition all the world has come to know. The book I was reviewing was the restored, original diary, published for the first time in a reader's edition.

I studied the distinctions among the various texts carefully in the Critical Edition and attempted to present these distinctions briefly but clearly in a reference to the Critical Edi-tion. This Critical Edition had been published in 1986 partly to refute the crazy allegations of the conspiracy theorists. I wanted to use my review, in part, to alert readers to any false claims made in this regard.

Berryman's essay made me powerfully aware of the time which had passed between his first response to the book in 1952, hardly seven years after Anne Frank's death in Bergen-Belsen, and my reading of the 1995 Definitive Edition when she would have been sixty-six. His task was to give the psychological project of the *Diary* its due. It was not yet clear, in 1967, that the *Diary* was a classic work of human development. Its very popular-ity had obscured, Berryman felt, its most important subject which was, he said, "even more mysterious and fundamental than St. Augustine's" in his *Confessions:* namely, "the conversion of a child into a person." My task was more modest. Beyond the basic biographical information which, for most readers, I knew would be unnecessary, I had to place the book in its public history.

With this in mind, I made reference at the end of the review to the book's age—fifty years old, and to Philip Roth's use of Anne Frank as a fictional character in his novel *The Ghost Writer.* I wanted to show how Anne Frank has entered our lives as a permanent presence, that to invoke her name is to invoke a person we know and who shall always be missing because her presence in her book has made her so alive it is "unthinkable and disorienting," as I say in my review, "to know that this life was crushed."

I remember feeling a kind of relief (not satisfaction, but the more unburdened feeling that the word "relief" suggests) when I stumbled upon the word "disorienting." For I felt this had something to do with the enduring grief and regret that mention of Anne Frank brings forward within us. My sense of being "disoriented" by her death was somehow related to Berryman's relief in finding a "sane person in the twentieth century." We *should* be disoriented by such hellish hatred. I was writing my review, after all, as children were dying from similar sectarian hatred in Bosnia. I too needed to find a sane person in the twentieth century. A child especially.

Finally, I wanted to remind people of the extraordinary person Anne Frank was, the splendid writer, the utterly natural girl/woman, and the gifted thinker. All my notes paid off, just as my luncheon with my friend had: I had many passages which I was able to use to present Anne Frank to readers not only as the icon of a murdered child but as the strong and vital writer she was. I came away from my reading of the *Diary* convinced absolutely that, had she lived, Anne Frank would have written many books and that we would know her not only as the author of her diary. And I came away with a clear answer to those sentimentalists who ask their appalling question: Would anyone really care about the diary if she hadn't died? Oh yes.

But maybe I always knew the answer to that question. When I was a girl, first reading the *Diary,* I treasured it because Anne fought and contended with her mother just as I did; she battled to become a person—the very thing Berryman honored most in her. I *needed* Anne Frank then—not because she was the child who died and put a face on the six million murdered (I was not yet capable of taking that in) but because, like me, she was determined to live, to grow up to be herself and no one else. She was, simply, my friend. I don't think I was able to keep in mind that she was dead. I went to her *Diary,* quite simply as she went to Kitty, for a friendship not to be found anywhere else but in books. As Anne Frank wrote to Kitty in a letter in her red plaid notebook, "Paper is more patient than people." It is the secret motto not only of a sensitive teenager but of any writer.

About two weeks after my review was published, I received a small white envelope, addressed in a careful hand in blue ink, forwarded to me from the *New York Times Book Review* which had received it. There was no return address, but the envelope was postmarked New York. A fan letter, I thought, with a brief flutter of vanity.

Inside was a single sheet, my name written again with the careful blue ink, and below that a crazy quilt of black headlines apparently photocopied from various articles in newspapers and periodicals. All of them claimed in their smudged, exclamatory way to have evidence of the "Anne Frank Zionist Plot" or the "Frank Lies." The headlines were all broken off and crammed into one another; bits and pieces of the articles to which they belonged overlapped. There wasn't a complete sentence on the entire mashed and deranged page.

But there it was: The small insane mind responding spasmodically to the sane person John Berryman had been so relieved to discover as a middle-aged man, sick in his own mind and heart, the same sane person so many girls recognize as their truest friend as they move into the rough and beautiful terrain of womanhood.

I stood in my bright kitchen, holding that piece of paper, disoriented all over again. The paper literally felt *dirty,* perhaps because of the smudged typefaces. It was the sooty look of old-fashioned pornography.

I did with it the only thing possible: I burned it. Somehow it required burning, not just tossing out. I burned it in the kitchen sink, and watched the clotted ashes swirl down the garbage disposal.

My fury was mixed with something else—with disbelief, I think. I don't know what it will take to convince me of the world's capacity to hate life, its dark instinct to smash what blooms. Anne Frank knew this hard truth as a child. She refused to cave in to it even as she acknowledged it: "I hear the approaching thunder that, one day, will destroy us too, I feel the suffering of millions." The conversation she began with Kitty, her imaginary correspondent, was founded on a discipline of compassion. Even in acknowledging her own likely death, she felt not only for herself but felt as well "the suffering of millions." It made her into that extra thing—not a child, not a woman, but an artist.

This was the sane person who, John Berryman says at the end of his essay, "remained able to weep with pity, in Auschwitz, for naked gypsy girls driven past to the crematory. . . . " We seek her still, this sane person we long for at the end of our terrible century that tried so desperately to erase her.

Bret Lott

Toward a Definition of Creative Nonfiction

The Reverend Francis Kilvert, an English curate in the Welsh Border region, kept a journal of his life—where he went, what he did, what he dreamt, who he knew, and what he thought—from 1870 to 1879. In the journal he wrote, "Why do I keep this voluminous journal! I can hardly tell. Partly because life appears to me such a curious and wonderful thing that it almost seems a pity that even such a humble and uneventful life as mine should pass altogether away without some record such as this." *Kilvert's Diary,* published in 1941 and reprinted in 1960, serves as a beautiful, moving, and genuine glimpse into country life of that time nonetheless. All well and good, but how does it help define what creative nonfiction is?

That passage serves, I hold, to illuminate as best as any passage from any piece of literature I can find the longing each of us carries, or ought to carry, in our hearts as human beings first, and as writers second. Creative nonfiction is, in one form or another, for better and worse, in triumph and failure, the attempt to keep from passing altogether away the lives we have lived.

And though that may sound like a definitive pronouncement on what creative nonfiction is, I mean what I say in giving this essay the title it has: *Toward* a Definition of Creative Nonfiction. We aren't going to arrive anywhere here. We can no more understand what creative nonfiction is by trying to define it than we can learn how to ride a bike by looking at a bicycle tire, a set of handlebars, the bicycle chain itself. Sure, we'll have something of an idea, maybe a glimpse into the importance of finding your balance when we look at how narrow those tires are. But until we get on that thing and try to steer it with this weirdly twisted metal tube and actually try to synchronize pushing down on the pedals and pushing forward at the same time, we won't have a clue.

Any definition of true worth to you as a writer will and must come to you experientially. What creative nonfiction is will reveal itself to you only at the back end of things, once you have written it. Kilvert wrote his journal in the midst of his life, looking back at what had happened that day, trying to piece together the meaning of his life from the shards of it, however exquisitely beautiful or sharply painful they were. It was the piecing together of it that mattered, and that matters to us here, today.

And because we are human beings, as such we are pattern makers, a species desirous of order, no matter how much we as "artists" may masquerade otherwise. Yet looking back at our lives to find that order—and here is the sticky part—must *not* be an effort to reorder our lives as we want them to be seen; rather, we are after, in creative nonfiction, an understanding of what it is that has happened, and in that way to see order, however chaotic it may be.

Frank O'Connor, arguably the most important and influential short story writer of this century, wrote in a letter to a friend, " . . . there are occasions when we all feel guilt and remorse; we all want to turn back time. But even if we were able, things would go in precisely the same way, because the mistakes we make are not in our judgments but in our natures. It is only when we do violence to our natures that we are justified in our regrets . . . We are what we are, and within our limitations we have made our own efforts. They seem puny in the light of eternity, but they didn't at the time, and they weren't."

It is in creative nonfiction we try to divine from what we have done, who we have known, what we have dreamt and how we have failed, an order to our lives. "The test of a first-rate intelligence," F. Scott Fitzgerald wrote in his landmark essay "The Crack-Up," "is the ability to hold two opposed ideas in the mind at the same time, and still retain the ability to function." The two opposed ideas of creative nonfiction are finding order in chaos without reforming chaos into order; retaning the ability to function is the act of writing all this down for someone else to understand.

So let's begin with just that much: a desire not to let slip altogether away our lives as we have known them, and to put an order—again, for better and worse—to our days.

Creative nonfiction can take any form, from the letter to the list, from the biography to the memoir, from the journal to the obituary. When I say we are trying to find order in what has happened, I do *not* mean creative nonfiction is simply writing about what happened to me. Rather, it is writing about oneself *in relation to* the subject at hand. A book review is creative nonfiction in that it is a written record of the reviewer *in relation to* the book in question; John Krakauer's fantastic book *Into the Wild* is a biography of an idealistic young man, Chris McCandless, who upon graduation from college disappeared into the wild, his decomposed body found four months later in an abandoned bus in the Alaskan wilderness. The biography becomes creative nonfiction as the author increasingly identifies himself with the young man, increasingly recognizing in the stupidity of the boy's folly his own reckless self—Krakauer sees himself *in relation to* the subject at hand: the death of Chris McCandless. This essay itself is a form of creative nonfiction in that it is my attempt at defining an abstract through the smallest of apertures: my own experience *in relation to* creative nonfiction. So creative nonfiction is not solely, What happened to me today, and why is it important?

Creative nonfiction can be and often is a euphemism for the personal essay, and my earlier assertion that creative nonfiction's being understood only through its being written is borne out rather handily in the meaning of the word *essay* itself.

The French word *essai* means to attempt something, to give something a trial run, to test. Michel de Montaigne, considered the writer who identified if not invented the form, was the first to use the word *essai* to describe his writings, the first collection of which was entitled strangely enough *Essais,* and which was written between 1572 and 1574. This notion of the attempt, of testing one's words lined up in an order one deems close enough to reveal a personal understanding so that all may have that same understanding is, and will always be, only an attempt. The essay as trial run is inherent to any definition of creative nonfiction; you will only come to know this form by running your own tests.

Montaigne, a landowner and lawyer from a nominally wealthy family in the Perigord region of France, wrote out of his own interests, but wrote convinced that it was his own interest as a human being in a matter or topic at hand that made his attempts universal: "Each man bears the entire form of man's estate," he wrote, and therefore, he reasoned, what he was attempting to render in words might make his attempts of interest to all. Philip Lopate, in his indispensable anthology *The Art of the Personal Essay,* writes, "What Montaigne tells us about himself is peculiarly, charmingly specific and daily: he is on the short side, has a loud, abrasive voice, suffers from painful kidney stones, scratches his ears a lot (the insides itch), loves sauces, is not sure radishes agree with him, does his best thinking on horseback, prefers glass to metal cups, moves his bowels regularly in the morning, and so on. It is as if the self were a new continent, and Montaigne its first explorer."

The self as continent, and you its first explorer: another definition of creative nonfiction. For self, however at the center of what you are writing or however tangential, must inform the heart of the tale you are telling. It is indeed *self* that is the *creative* element of creative nonfiction. Without you and who you are, a piece of writing that tells what happened is simply nonfiction: a police report. But when I begin to incorporate the sad and glorious fact that the way I see it shapes and forms what it is to be seen, I end up with creative nonfiction.

As a kind of sidebar, I'd like to interject here the fact that one doesn't have to have had a bizarre life before that life becomes worthy of writing about. Contrary to popular belief, that belief borne out by even the most cursory look at the lineup of victim-authors on afternoon and morning TV talk shows and evening newsmagazines, one's life needn't have been wracked by incest or murder or poorly executed plastic surgery to be worthy of examination. Which is, of course, not to say that those lives are not worth writing about. They most certainly are. But E. B. White's words from the introduction to his *Letters of E. B. White* speak as eloquently as I have seen to this matter of whether or not one's life has been miserable enough to record: "If an unhappy childhood is indispensable for a writer, I am ill-equipped: I missed out on all that and was neither deprived nor unloved.

It would be inaccurate, however, to say that my childhood was untroubled. The normal fears and worries of every child were in me developed to a high degree; every day was an awesome prospect. I was uneasy about practically everything: the uncertainty of the future, the dark of the attic, the panoply and discipline of school, the transitoriness of life, the mystery of the church and of God, the frailty of the body, the sadness of afternoon, the shadow of sex, the distant challenge of love and marriage, the far-off problem of a livelihood."

These normal fears, if we have been paying the least bit of attention to our lives, inform us all; and if E. B. White, who is the greatest American essayist of this century, found in that uneasiness the material for a lifetime, we too have all we need.

But *how* do we look at ourselves in order best to inform our readers that who we are matters, and is worthy of their attention? In the Tyndale commentary on the Book of Proverbs, Derek Kidner writes that the sayings and aphorisms of King Solomon, and to a lesser degree Lemuel and Agur, constitute "not a portrait album of a book of manners: [the Book of Proverbs] offers a key to life. The samples of behavior which it holds up to view are all assessed by one criterion, which could be summed up in the question, 'Is this wisdom, or is this folly?'" I believe that this same criterion is one that helps define creative nonfiction as well. In examining the self as continent, in seeing the way self shades and informs the meaning of what has happened, the writer must be inquiring of himself, Is this wisdom, or is this folly? The self as inquisitor of self is integral to an examination of one's life; it calls for a kind of ruthlessness about seeing oneself in relation to others: Why did I do that? What was I thinking? Who was I trying to kid? What did I hope to achieve? These questions must be asked, and asked with all the candor and courage and objectivity one can muster, though objectivity is an abstract to be hoped for, and not to be achieved; it is, after all, *you* who is writing about you.

Which brings me to another major point on our way toward a definition: creative nonfiction cannot at any time be self-serving. There is no room here for grandstanding of oneself. To my way of thinking—and this is me speaking as a follower of Christ, and therefore one well aware of my transgressions, my iniquities, my falling short of the glory of God—ninety-nine times out of a hundred the answer to the question, Is this wisdom, or is this folly? is, Folly. Hands down.

Phillip Lopate writes, "The enemy of the personal essay is self-righteousness, not just because it is tiresome and ugly in itself, but because it slows down the dialectic of self-questioning. . . . The essayist is someone who lives with the guilty knowledge that he is 'prejudiced' (Mencken called his essay collections *Prejudices*) and has a strong predisposition for or against certain everyday phenomena. It then becomes his business to attend to these inner signals, these stomach growls, these seemingly indefensible intuitions, and try to analyze what lies underneath them, the better to judge them."

So, our definition thus far: a desire not to let slip altogether away our lives as we have known them; to put an order, for better and worse, to our days; this is only a test; the self as continent, you its first explorer; is his wisdom, or is this folly?; no self-righteousness.

This last point, however, seems at odds with the entire notion of the personal essay, all this business about me: isn't talk about myself in relation to others by definition egotistical? Wasn't I taught in seventh grade never to include 'I' in an essay? Who cares about what I think in the first place?

Thoreau, in answer to this assertion we have had pounded into our heads most of our lives, wrote in the opening of *Walden,* "In most books the I, or first person, is omitted; in this it will be retained; that, in respect to egotism, is the main difference. We commonly do not remember that it is, after all, always the first person that is speaking." And if one is honestly seeking to understand, circling with a cold eye one's relation to events, places, people—whatever the subject of the essay—then that search's chances of being construed as egotistical will be dismissed. Seventeenth-century English writer Alexander Smith wrote, "The speaking about one self is not necessarily offensive. A modest, truthful man speaks better about himself than about anything else, and on that subject his speech is likely to be most profitable to his hearers . . . If he be without taint of boastfulness, of self-sufficiency, of hungry vanity, the world will not press the charge home."

Another element of any definition of creative nonfiction must include the form's circling bent, its way of looking again and again at itself from all angles in order to see itself most fully. The result is literary triangulation, a finding of the subject in a three-dimensional grid through digression, full-frontal assault, guerrilla tactics and humble servitude, all in an effort, simply, to see. The creative nonfiction form attempts in whatever way it can to grab hold hard and sure its subject in any manner possible. Eudora Welty writes in *One Writer's Beginnings,* "In writing, as in life, the connections of all sorts of relationships and kinds lie in wait of discovery, and give out their signals to the Geiger counter of the charged imagination, once it is drawn into the right field . . . What I do make my stories out of is the whole fund of my feelings, my responses to the real experiences of my own life, to the relationships that formed and changed it, that I have given most of myself to, and so learned my way toward a dramatic counterpart." The dramatic counterpart of which she here writes is, of course, her stories—fiction—but I maintain that this "whole fund" of feelings, the complete range of our responses to our own real experiences, must inform creative nonfiction as well. Only when we use our "whole fund" can we circle our subjects in the most complete way, wringing from our stores of knowledge and wisdom and the attendant recognition of how little we have of both—*the essence of who we are*—then coupling those recognitions with what in fact we do not know altogether, will we find what we have come looking for: ourselves and, by grace and by luck, the larger world perhaps we hadn't seen before.

Lopate writes, "The personal essay is the reverse of that set of Chinese boxes that you keep opening, only to find a smaller one within. Here you start with the small—the package of flaws and limits—and suddenly find a slightly larger container, insulated by the essay's successful articulation and the writer's self-knowledge."

I agree with Lopate in how the essay reveals larger and larger selves in itself, but rather than the Chinese box, the image that comes to my mind is that of the Russian nesting dolls, one person inside another inside another. But instead of finding smaller selves inside the self, the opposite occurs, as with Lopate's boxes: we find nested inside that smallest of selves a larger self, and a larger inside that, until we come to the whole of humanity within our own hearts.

Now back to our definition: a desire not to let slip altogether away our life as we have known it; to put an order, for better and worse, to our days; this is only a test; the self as continent, you its first explorer; is this wisdom, or is this folly?; no self-righteousness, though it is always the first person talking; circle the subject to see it most whole.

I'm saving perhaps the most conundrum-like element for nearly last. What role, we have to ask once all these prior elements are taken into account, does *truth* have here? If you look at the pieces of our definition thus far, each one contains within it the angle of perception: the fact that it is only me who is seeing. That is, I don't want to let slip away my life as I have seen it, but who is to say I am telling the truth? In my attempt to put order to my days, am I deluding myself, inflicting an order that was and is now nowhere to be seen? If this is only a test, who is to say I pass? If I am the explorer of my self as continent, what does my discovery matter—didn't Leif Erikson set up shop in North America 500 years before Columbus discovered the place? Isn't one man's wisdom another man's folly? How do I know if I'm not being self-righteous unless there's somebody outside myself to cut me down to size? In circling my subject, isn't it me who determines my course, my longitude and latitude, and therefore am I, by definition, being the most subjective of anyone on planet earth when it comes to my subject?

The answer to each and every one of these questions is: continue to question. Only through rigorous and ruthless questioning of the self can we hope to arrive at any kind of truth.

If you wish to understand creative nonfiction, hope to find a definition, then it is up to you to embrace the fact that, as Montaigne saw, "Each man bears the entire form of man's estate." Inherent to that form are the eccentricities, egotism, foolishness, and fraud of all mankind; inherent as well are the wisdom and self-recognition, the worth and value and merit available to mankind, once enough scouring of what we know and do not know has taken place. V. S. Pritchett, in his memoir *Midnight Oil,* wrote, "The true autobiography of this egotist is exposed in all its intimate foliage in his work. But there is a period when a writer has not yet become one, or, just having become one, is struggling to form his talent, and it is from this period that I have selected most of the scenes and people in this book. It *is* a selection, and it is neither a confession nor a volume of literary reminiscences, but as far as I am able I have put in my 'truth.'"

Pritchett puts the word *truth* in quotation marks; he predicates it with the possessive pronoun *my.* We must recognize that this is the deepest truth we can hope to attain on our own: quotation marks, calling it our own. Only when we have scoured as clean as possible by self-inquiry, even interrogation, what we *perceive,* can we approach calling it *truth;* and even then that crutch of the quotation marks and the assignation of who it belongs to—me—must be acknowledged.

Finally, we have to try and further illuminate *why* we write creative nonfiction. Certainly that first element—a desire not to let slip altogether away our lives as we have known them—is a beginning point, but simply trying to capture our lives before they slip away seems more *reactive* than *proactive.* Writing is, I believe, both, and so any definition must encompass both the reactive and the proactive.

Karen Blixen, AKA Isak Dinesen, in a dinner meeting speech she gave in 1959 at the National Institute of Arts and Letters in New York, addressed the subject, "On Mottoes of My Life." In it she said, "The family of Finch Hatton, of England, have on their crest the device *Je responderay,* 'I will answer.' . . . I liked it so much I asked Denys . . . if I might have it for my own. He generously made me a present of it and even had a seal cut for me, with the words carved on it. The device was meaningful and dear to me for many reasons, two in particular. The first . . . was its high evaluation of the idea of the answer in itself.

For an answer is a rarer thing than is generally imagined. There are many highly intelligent people who have no answer at all in them. . . . Secondly, I liked the Finch Hatton device for its ethical content. I will answer *for* what I say or do; I will answer *to* the impression I make. I will be responsible."

This is the proactive element of creative nonfiction, and the final element of my *essai* to define creative writing: *our responsibility as human beings to answer for and to our lives.* It is a responsibility that must encompass all the elements laid out in all this talk about definitions; it is a responsibility that must be woven through the recognition of the fleeting nature of this span of days we have been given, woven through our attempt to see order in chaos, through our understanding that we are only attempting this test and through our being the first explorers of the continent of ourselves. This responsibility to answer for and to ourselves must be woven through the interrogation of self as to whether this is folly or wisdom, through the pledge to humility and to avoiding the abyss of self-righteousness, through the recognition that it is always and only me—the first person—talking, and through the relentless circling of the subject to see it most completely. And this responsibility to answer for and to ourselves must be woven through our recognition that the only truth I can hope to approach will finally and always and only be *my truth.*

But if we are rigorous enough, fearless enough, and humble enough to attempt this responsibility, this way of seeing—for creative nonfiction, like fiction, like poetry, is simply and complexly a way of seeing—the rewards we will reap will be great: we will *understand.* To understand, and nothing more, and that is everything.

Cynthia Ozick

She: Portrait of the Essay as a Warm Body

> The essay does not allow us to forget our usual sensations and opinions. It does something even more potent: it makes us deny them.

An essay is a thing of the imagination. If there is information in an essay, it is by-the-by, and if there is an opinion, one need not trust it for the long run. A genuine essay rarely has an educational, polemical, or sociopolitical use; it is the movement of a free mind at play. Though it is written in prose, it is closer in kind to poetry than to any other form. Like a poem, a genuine essay is made of language and character and mood and temperament and pluck and chance.

I speak of a "genuine" essay because fakes abound. Here the old-fashioned term *poetaster* may apply, if only obliquely. As the poetaster is to the poet—a lesser aspirant—so the average article is to the essay: a look-alike knockoff guaranteed not to wear well. An article is often gossip. An essay is reflection and insight. An article often has the temporary advantage of social heat—what's hot out there right now. An essay's heat is interior. An article can be timely, topical, engaged in the issues and personalities of the moment; it is likely to be stale within the month. In five years it may have acquired the quaint aura of a rotary phone. An article is usually Siamese-twinned to its date of birth. An essay defies its date of birth—and ours, too. (A necessary caveat: some genuine essays are popularly called "articles"—but this is no more than an idle, though persistent, habit of speech. What's in a name? The ephemeral is the ephemeral. The enduring is the enduring.)

A small historical experiment. Who are the classic essayists who come at once to mind? Montaigne, obviously. Among the nineteenth-century English masters, the long row of Hazlitt, Lamb, De Quincey, Stevenson, Carlyle, Ruskin, Newman, Martineau, Arnold. Of the Americans, Emerson. Nowadays, admittedly, these are read only by specialists and literature majors, and by the latter only under compulsion. However accurate this observation, it is irrelevant to the experiment, which has to do with beginnings and their disclosures. Here, then, are some introductory passages:

> One of the pleasantest things in the world is going a journey; but I like to go by myself. I can enjoy society in a room; but out of doors, nature is company enough for me. I am then never less alone than when alone.
>
> —*William Hazlitt, "On Going a Journey"*

> To go into solitude, a man needs to retire as much from his chamber as from society. I am not solitary whilst I read and write, though nobody is with me. But if a man would be alone, let him look at the stars.
>
> —*Ralph Waldo Emerson, "Nature"*

> I have often been asked, how I first came to be a regular opium-eater; and have suffered, very unjustly, in the opinion of my acquaintance, from being reputed to have brought upon myself all the sufferings which I shall have to record, by a long course of indulgence in this practice purely for the sake of creating an artificial state of pleasurable excitement. This, however, is a misrepresentation of my case.
>
> —*Thomas De Quincey, "Confessions of an English Opium-Eater"*

> The human species, according to the best theory I can form of it, is composed of two distinct races, *the men who borrow, and the men who lend.*
>
> —*Charles Lamb, "The Two Races of Men"*

> I saw two hareems in the East; and it would be wrong to pass them over in an account of my travels; though the subject is as little agreeable as any I can have to treat. I cannot now think of the two mornings thus employed without a heaviness of heart greater than I have ever brought away from Deaf and Dumb Schools, Lunatic Asylums, or even Prisons.
>
> —*Harriet Martineau, "The Hareem"*

> The future of poetry is immense, because in poetry, where it is worthy of its high destinies, our race, as time goes on, will find an ever surer and surer stay. There is not a creed which is not shaken, not an accredited dogma which is not shown to be questionable, not a received tradition which does not threaten to dissolve. . . . But for poetry the idea is everything; the rest is a world of illusion, of divine illusion.
>
> —*Matthew Arnold, "The Study of Poetry"*

The changes wrought by death are in themselves so sharp and final, and so terrible and melancholy in their consequences, that the thing stands alone in man's experience, and has no parallel upon earth. It outdoes all other accidents because it is the last of them. Sometimes it leaps suddenly upon its victims, like a Thug; sometimes it lays a regular siege and creeps upon their citadel during a score of years. And when the business is done, there is sore havoc made in other people's lives, and a pin knocked out by which many subsidiary friendships hung together.

—*Robert Louis Stevenson, "Aes Triplex"*

It is recorded of some people, as of Alexander the Great, that their sweat, in consequence of some rare and extraordinary constitution, emitted a sweet odour, the cause of which Plutarch and others investigated. But the nature of most bodies is the opposite, and at their best they are free from smell. Even the purest breath has nothing more excellent than to be without offensive odour, like that of very healthy children.

—*Michel de Montaigne, "Of Smells"*

What might such a little anthology of beginnings reveal? First, that language differs from one era to the next: archaism intrudes, if only in punctuation and cadence. Second, that splendid minds may contradict each other (outdoors, Hazlitt never feels alone; Emerson urges others to go outdoors in order to feel alone). Third, that the theme of an essay can be anything under the sun, however trivial (the smell of sweat) or crushing (the thought that we must die). Fourth, that the essay is a consistently recognizable and venerable—or call it ancient—form. In English, Addison and Steele in the eighteenth century, Bacon and Browne in the seventeenth, Lyly in the sixteenth, Bede in the eighth. And what of the biblical Koheleth (Ecclesiastes), who may be the oldest essayist reflecting on one of the oldest subjects—world-weariness?

So the essay is ancient and various; but this is a commonplace. Something else, more striking yet, catches our attention—the essay's power. By "power" I mean precisely the capacity to do what force always does: coerce assent. Never mind that the shape and inclination of any essay is against coercion or suasion, or that the essay neither proposes nor purposes to get us to think like its author—at least not overtly. If an essay has a "motive," it is linked more to happenstance and opportunity than to the driven will. A genuine essay is not a doctrinaire tract or a propaganda effort or a broadside. Thomas Paine's "Common Sense" and Emile Zola's "J'Accuse . . . !" are heroic landmark writings; but to call them essays, though they may resemble the form, is to misunderstand. The essay is not meant for the barricades; it is a stroll through someone's mazy mind. This is not to say that no essayist has ever been intent on making a moral argument, however obliquely—George Orwell is a case in point. At the end of the day the essay turns out to be a force for agreement. It co-opts agreement; it courts agreement; it seduces agreement. For the brief hour we give to it, we are sure to fall into surrender and conviction. And this will occur even if we are intrinsically roused to resistance.

To illustrate: I may not be persuaded by Emersonianism as an ideology, but Emerson—his voice, his language, his music—persuades me. When we look for words of praise, not for nothing do we speak of "commanding" or "compelling" prose. If I am a skeptical rationalist or an advanced biochemist, I may regard (or discard) the idea of the soul as no better than a puff of warm vapor. But here is Emerson on the soul: "When it breathes through [man's] intellect, it is genius; when it breathes through his will, it is virtue; when it flows through his affection, it is love." And then—well, I am in thrall; I am possessed; I believe.

The novel has its own claims on surrender. It suspends our participation in the society we ordinarily live in, so that for the time we are reading, we forget it utterly. But the essay does not allow us to forget our usual sensations and opinions. It does something even more potent: it makes us deny them. The authority of a masterly essayist—the authority of sublime language and intimate observation—is absolute. When I am with Hazlitt, I know no greater companion than nature. When I am with Emerson, I know no greater solitude than nature.

And what is oddest about the essay's power to lure us into its lair is how it goes about this work. We feel it when a political journalist comes after us with a point of view—we feel it the way the cat is wary of the dog. A polemic is a herald, complete with feathered hat and trumpet. A tract can be a trap. Certain magazine articles have the scent of so much per word. What is indisputable is that all of these are more or less in the position of a lepidopterist with his net: they mean to catch and skewer. They are focused on prey—us. The genuine essay, in contrast, never thinks of us; the genuine essay may be the most self-centered (the politer word would be subjective) arena for human thought ever devised.

Or else, though still not having us in mind (unless as an embodiment of common folly), it is not self-centered at all. When I was a child, I discovered in the public library a book that enchanted me then, and the idea of which has enchanted me for life. I have no recollection of either the title or the writer—and anyhow, very young readers rarely take note of authors; stories are simply and magically *there*. The characters include, as I remember them, three or four children and a delightful relation who is a storyteller, and the scheme is this: each child calls out a story element, most often an object, and the storyteller gathers up whatever is supplied (blue boots, a river, a fairy, a pencil box) and makes out of these random, unlikely, and disparate offerings a tale both logical and surprising. An essay, it seems to me, may be similarly constructed—if so deliberate a term applies. The essayist, let us say, unexpectedly stumbles over a pair of old blue boots in a corner of the garage, and this reminds her of when she last wore them—twenty years ago, on a trip to Paris, where on the bank of the Seine she stopped to watch an old fellow sketching, with a box of colored pencils at his side. The pencil wiggling over his sheet is a grayish pink, which reflects the threads of sunset pulling westward in the sky, like the reins of a fairy cart . . . and so on. The mind meanders, slipping from one impression to another, from reality to memory to dreamscape and back again.

In the same way Montaigne, when contemplating the unpleasantness of sweat, ends with the pure breath of children. Stevenson, starting out with mortality, speaks first of ambush, then of war, and finally of a displaced pin. No one is freer than the essayist—free to leap out in any direction, to hop from thought to thought, to begin with the finish and finish with the middle, or to eschew beginning and end and keep only a middle. The marvel is that out of this apparent causelessness, out of this scattering of idiosyncratic seeing and telling, a coherent world is made. It is coherent because, after all, an essayist must be an artist, and every artist, whatever the means, arrives at a sound and singular imaginative frame—call it, on a minor scale, a cosmogony.

Into this frame, this work of art, we tumble like tar babies, and are held fast. What holds us there? The authority of a voice, yes; the pleasure—sometimes the anxiety—of a new idea, an untried angle, a snatch of reminiscence, bliss displayed or shock conveyed. An essay can be the product of intellect or memory, lightheartedness or gloom, well-being or disgruntlement. But always we sense a certain quietude, on occasion a kind of detachment. Rage and revenge, I think; belong to fiction. The essay is cooler than that. Because it so often engages in acts of memory, and despite its gladder or more antic incarnations, the essay is by and large a serene or melancholic form. It mimics that low electric hum, which sometimes rises to resemble actual speech, that all human beings carry inside their heads—a vibration, garrulous if somewhat indistinct, that never leaves us while we are awake. It is the hum of perpetual noticing: the configuration of someone's eyelid or tooth, the veins on a hand, a wisp of string caught on a twig; some words your fourth-grade teacher said, so long ago, about the rain; the look of an awning, a sidewalk, a bit of cheese left on a plate. All day long this inescapable hum drums on, recalling one thing and another, and pointing out this and this and this. Legend has it that Titus, emperor of Rome, went mad because of the buzzing of a gnat that made her home in his ear; and presumably the gnat, flying out into the great world and then returning to her nest, whispered what she had seen and felt and learned there. But an essayist is more resourceful than an emperor, and can be relieved of this interior noise, if only for the time required to record its murmurings. To seize the hum and set it down for others to hear is the essayist's genius.

It is a genius bound to leisure, and even to luxury, if luxury is measured in hours. The essay's limits can be found in its own reflective nature. Poems have been wrested from the inferno of catastrophe or war, and battlefield letters, too; these are the spontaneous bursts and burnings that danger excites. But the meditative temperateness of an essay requires a desk and a chair, a musing and a mooning, a connection to a civilized surround; even when the subject itself is a wilderness of lions and tigers, mulling is the way of it. An essay is a fireside thing, not a conflagration or a safari.

This may be why, when we ask who the essayists are, we discover that though novelists may now and then write essays, true essayists rarely write novels. Essayists are a species of metaphysician: they are inquisitive, and analytic, about the least grain of being. Novelists go about the strenuous business of marrying and burying their people, or else they send them to sea, or to Africa, or at the least out of town. Essayists in their stillness ponder love and death. It is probably an illusion that men are essayists more often than women, especially since women's essays have in the past frequently assumed the form of unpublished correspondence. (Here I should, I suppose, add a note about maleness and femaleness as a literary issue—what is popularly termed "gender," as if men and women were French or German tables and sofas. I *should* add such a note—it is the fashion, or, rather, the current expectation or obligation—but nothing useful can be said about any of it.) Essays are written by men. Essays are written by women. That is the long and the short of it. John Updike, in a genially confident discourse on maleness ("The Disposable Rocket"), takes the view—though he admits to admixture—that the "male sense of space must differ from that of the female, who has such interesting, active, and significant inner space. The space that interests men is outer." Except, let it be observed, when men write essays, since it is only inner space—interesting, active, significant—that can conceive and nourish the contemplative essay. The "ideal female body," Updike adds, "curves around centers of repose," and no phrase could better describe the shape of the ideal essay—yet women are no fitter as essayists than men. In promoting the felt salience of sex, Updike nevertheless drives home an essayist's point. Essays, unlike novels, emerge from the sensations of the self. Fiction creeps into foreign bodies: the novelist can inhabit not only a sex not his own but also beetles and noses and hunger artists and nomads and beasts. The essay is, as we say, personal.

And here is an irony. Though I have been intent on distinguishing the marrow of the essay from the marrow of fiction, I confess that I have been trying all along, in a subliminal way, to speak of the essay as if it—or she—were a character in a novel or a play: moody, fickle, given to changing her clothes, or the subject, on a whim; sometimes obstinate, with a mind of her own, or hazy and light; never predictable. I mean for her to be dressed—and addressed—as we would Becky Sharp, or Ophelia, or Elizabeth Bennet, or Mrs. Ramsay, or Mrs. Wilcox, or even Hester Prynne. Put it that it is pointless to say (as I have done repeatedly, disliking it every time) "the essay," or "an essay." The essay—an essay—is not an abstraction; she may have recognizable contours, but she is highly colored and individuated; she is not a type. She is too fluid, too elusive, to be a category. She may be bold, she may be diffident, she may rely on beauty or cleverness, on eros or exotica. Whatever her story, she is the protagonist, the secret self's personification. When we knock on her door, she opens to us; she is a presence in the doorway; she leads us from room to room. Then why should we not call her "she"? She may be privately indifferent to us, but she is anything but unwelcoming. Above all, she is not a hidden principle or a thesis or a construct: she is *there,* a living voice. She takes us in.

PART

IV

— Nature and Science —

Nature, landscape, and the physical world have long been sources of discovery for essay writers in America. Ralph Waldo Emerson and Henry David Thoreau, perhaps our best-known essayists on this subject, helped usher in the modern era of nature writing with their use of vivid description and their ardor for the landscapes around them. Their influence can be seen in writers such as John Muir, John Burroughs, and Rachel Carson, whose works are at the foundation of the environmental movement.

The writers in this section continue and reshape the tradition of observing phenomena and the natural world. Whether seeking to understand animal behavior, a region or terrain, or a scientific process, the essays reflect perspectives and ideas as varied as the geography of a nation. Some of the works here, such as Edward Hoagland's "The Courage of Turtles" and Linda Hogan's "The Bats," examine interactions between human and other animal environments. Gretel Ehrlich's "The Solace of Open Spaces" and Barry Lopez's craft essay "Landscape and Narrative" ponder physical landscapes as metaphors for interior landscapes. In the field of science, Richard McCann's "The Resurrectionist" gives us a candid story about organ transplantation; Floyd Skloot's "Wild in the Woods: Confessions of a Demented Man" details his experience of being "demented" due to a brain virus; and Terry Tempest Williams's "The Clan of One-Breasted Women" focuses on nuclear testing in the 1950s and the menacing effect it has had on her family. The voices in this section are as diverse as the subject matter. We encounter meditation (Ehrlich), elegy and anger (Williams), raw emotion (McCann), restraint (Hoagland), and observation (Hogan).

Journalistic creative nonfiction combines the seemingly detached realm of scientific inquiry with the art of writing. Some of these works explain subjects or processes through humanistic viewpoints, as in Atul Gawande's "Final Cut," which weighs the clinical and personal aspects of diagnosis and autopsy. Diane Ackerman's "The Psychopharmacology of Chocolate," on the other hand, combines anecdotes with scientific explanations to analyze the craving for chocolate.

Stephen Jay Gould takes a different approach in "A Biological Homage to Mickey Mouse" by applying evolutionary principles to an iconic cartoon character.

It may be said that research rather than pure observation marks a key difference between personal and journalistic nature and science writing. In his essay on craft, "Life Is a Narrative," Edward O. Wilson notes that "science writers are in the difficult position of locating themselves somewhere between the two stylistic poles of literature and science." While nature writing is situated closer to the "literary pole"—perhaps explaining why creative nonfiction on nature tends to be more personal and identity-centered—"the pole nearest science is occupied primarily by scientists who choose to deliver their dispatches from the front to a broader public." As we can see, much creative nonfiction on Nature and Science deals, in some way, with the tension between physical nature and human nature.

This tension can be explored through many different styles. An essay might be marked by a sense of wit and play (Gould), might be serious and contemplative (Gawande), or might be somewhere in between (Ackerman). As with the personal essays, these works all seem to acknowledge in their own way the fact of mystery: at the heart of natural and scientific inquiry is the search for answers.

As Wilson writes, "Science, like the rest of culture, is based on the manufacture of narrative." This bond between nature and literature is further examined in Barry Lopez's "Landscape and Narrative" and Annie Dillard's "Seeing." These works are invaluable not only as craft pieces on storytelling and observation but also as paragons of essay writing. In exploring the art of perception and verbalization, they bring us back to the necessity and pleasure of pure wonder.

The "I"

Gretel Ehrlich

The Solace of Open Spaces

It's May and I've just awakened from a nap, curled against sagebrush the way my dog taught me to sleep—sheltered from wind. A front is pulling the huge sky over me, and from the dark a hailstone has hit me on the head. I'm trailing a band of two thousand sheep across a stretch of Wyoming badlands, a fifty-mile trip that takes five days because sheep shade up in hot sun and won't budge until it's cool. Bunched together now, and excited into a run by the storm, they drift across dry land, tumbling into draws like water and surge out again onto the rugged, choppy plateaus that are the building blocks of this state.

The name Wyoming comes from an Indian word meaning "at the great plains," but the plains are really valleys, great arid valleys, sixteen hundred square miles, with the horizon bending up on all sides into mountain ranges. This gives the vastness a sheltering look.

Winter lasts six months here. Prevailing winds spill snowdrifts to the east, and new storms from the northwest replenish them. This white bulk is sometimes dizzying, even nauseating, to look at. At twenty, thirty, and forty degrees below zero, not only does your car not work, but neither do your mind and body. The landscape hardens into a dungeon of space. During the winter, while I was riding to find a new calf, my jeans froze to the saddle, and in the silence that such cold creates I felt like the first person on earth, or the last.

Today the sun is out—only a few clouds billowing. In the east, where the sheep have started off without me, the benchland tilts up in a series of eroded red-earthed mesas, planed flat on top by a million years of water; behind them, a bold line of muscular scarps rears up ten thousand feet to become the Big Horn Mountains. A tidal pattern is engraved into the ground, as if left by the sea that once covered this state. Canyons curve down like galaxies to meet the oncoming rush of flat land.

To live and work in this kind of open country, with its hundred-mile views, is to lose the distinction between background and foreground. When I asked an older ranch hand to describe Wyoming's openness, he said, "It's all a bunch of nothing—wind and rattlesnakes—and so much of it you can't tell where you're going or where you've been and it don't make much difference." John, a sheepman I know, is tall and handsome and has an explosive temperament. He has a perfect intuition about people and sheep. They call him "Highpockets," because he's so long-legged; his graceful stride matches the distances he has to cover. He says, "Open space hasn't affected me at all. It's all the people moving in on it." The huge ranch he was born on takes up much of one county and spreads into another state; to put 100,000 miles on his pickup in three years and never leave home is not unusual. A friend of mine has an aunt who ranched on Powder River and didn't go off her place for eleven years. When her husband died, she quickly moved to town, bought a car, and drove around the States to see what she'd been missing.

Most people tell me they've simply driven through Wyoming, as if there were nothing to stop for. Or else they've skied in Jackson Hole, a place Wyomingites acknowledge uncomfortably because its green beauty and chic affluence are mismatched with the rest of the state. Most of Wyoming has a "lean-to" look. Instead of big, roomy barns and Victorian houses, there are dugouts, low sheds, log cabins, sheep camps, and fence lines that look like driftwood blown haphazardly into place. People here still feel pride because they live in such a harsh place, part of the glamorous cowboy past, and they are determined not to be the victims of a mining-dominated future.

Most characteristic of the state's landscape is what a developer euphemistically describes as "indigenous growth right up to your front door"—a reference to waterless stands of salt sage, snakes, jack rabbits, deerflies, red dust, a brief respite of wildflowers, dry washes, and no trees. In the Great Plains the vistas look like music, like Kyries of grass, but Wyoming seems to be the doing of a mad architect—tumbled and twisted, ribboned with faded, deathbed colors, thrust up and pulled down as if the place had been startled out of a deep sleep and thrown into a pure light.

I came here four years ago. I had not planned to stay, but I couldn't make myself leave. John, the sheepman, put me to work immediately. It was spring, and shearing time. For fourteen days of fourteen hours each, we moved thousands of sheep through sorting corrals to be sheared, branded, and deloused. I suspect that my original motive for coming here was to "lose myself" in new and unpopulated territory. Instead of producing the numbness I thought I wanted, life on the sheep ranch woke me up. The vitality of the people I was working with flushed out what had become a hallucinatory rawness inside me. I threw away my clothes and bought new ones; I cut my hair. The arid country was a clean slate. Its absolute indifference steadied me.

Sagebrush covers 58,000 square miles of Wyoming. The biggest city has a population of fifty thousand, and there are only five settlements that could be called cities in the whole state. The rest are towns, scattered across the expanse with as much as sixty miles between them, their populations two thousand, fifty, or ten. They are fugitive-looking, perched on a barren, windblown bench, or tagged onto a river or a railroad, or laid out straight in a farming valley with implement stores and a block-long Mormon church. In the eastern part of the state, which slides down into the Great Plains, the new mining settlements are boomtowns, trailer cities, metal knots on flat land.

Despite the desolate look, there's a coziness to living in this state. There are so few people (only 470,000) that ranchers who buy and sell cattle know one another statewide; the kids who choose to go to college usually go to the state's one university, in Laramie; hired hands work their way around Wyoming in a lifetime of hirings and firings. And despite the physical separation, people stay in touch, often driving two or three hours to another ranch for dinner.

Seventy-five years ago, when travel was by buckboard or horseback, cowboys who were temporarily out of work rode the grub line—drifting from ranch to ranch, mending fences or milking cows, and receiving in exchange a bed and meals. Gossip and messages traveled this slow circuit with them, creating an intimacy between ranchers who were three and four weeks' ride apart. One old-time couple I know, whose turn-of-the-century homestead was used by an outlaw gang as a relay station for stolen horses, recall that if you were traveling, desperado or not, any lighted ranch house was a welcome sign. Even now, for someone who lives in a remote spot, arriving at a ranch or coming to town for supplies is cause for celebration. To emerge from isolation can be disorienting. Everything looks bright, new, vivid. After I had been herding sheep for only three days, the sound of the camp tender's pickup flustered me. Longing for human company, I felt a foolish grin take over my face; yet I had to resist an urgent temptation to run and hide.

Things happen suddenly in Wyoming, the change of seasons and weather; for people, the violent swings in and out of isolation. But good-naturedness is concomitant with severity. Friendliness is a tradition. Strangers passing on the road wave hello. A common sight is two pickups stopped side by side far out on a range, on a dirt track winding through the sage. The drivers will share a cigarette, uncap their thermos bottles, and pass a battered cup, steaming with coffee, between windows. These meetings summon up the details of several generations, because, in Wyoming, private histories are largely public knowledge.

Because ranch work is a physical and, these days, economic strain, being "at home on the range" is a matter of vigor, self-reliance, and common sense. A person's life is not a series of dramatic events for which he or she is applauded or exiled but a slow accumulation of days, seasons, years, fleshed out by the generational weight of one's family and anchored by a land-bound sense of place.

In most parts of Wyoming, the human population is visibly outnumbered by the animal. Not far from my town of fifty, I rode into a narrow valley and startled a herd of two hundred elk. Eagles look like small people as they eat car-killed deer by the road. Antelope, moving in small, graceful bands, travel at sixty miles an hour, their mouths open as if drinking in the space.

The solitude in which westerners live makes them quiet. They telegraph thoughts and feelings by the way they tilt their heads and listen; pulling their Stetsons into a steep dive over their eyes, or pigeon-toeing one boot over the other, they lean against a fence with a fat wedge of Copenhagen beneath their lower lips and take in the whole scene. These detached looks of quiet amusement are sometimes cynical, but they can also come from a dry-eyed humility as lucid as the air is clear.

Conversation goes on in what sounds like a private code; a few phrases imply a complex of meanings. Asking directions, you get a curious list of details. While trailing sheep I was told to "ride up to that kinda upturned rock, follow the pink wash, turn left at the dump, and then you'll see the water hole." One friend told his wife on roundup to "turn at the salt lick and the dead cow," which turned out to be a scattering of bones and no salt lick at all.

Sentence structure is shortened to the skin and bones of a thought. Descriptive words are dropped, even verbs; a cowboy looking over a corral full of horses will say to a wrangler, "Which one needs rode?" People hold back their thoughts in what seems to be a dumbfounded silence, then erupt with an excoriating perceptive remark. Language, so compressed, becomes metaphorical. A rancher ended a relationship with one remark: "You're a bad check," meaning bouncing in and out was intolerable, and even coming back would be no good.

What's behind this laconic style is shyness. There is no vocabulary for the subject of feelings. It's not a hangdog shyness, or anything coy—always there's a robust spirit in evidence behind the restraint, as if the earth-dredging wind that pulls across Wyoming had carried its people's voices away but everything else in them had shouldered confidently into the breeze.

I've spent hours riding to sheep camp at dawn in a pickup when nothing was said; eaten meals in the cookhouse when the only words spoken were a mumbled "Thank you, ma'am" at the end of dinner. The silence is profound. Instead of talking, we seem to share one eye. Keenly observed, the world is transformed. The landscape is engorged with detail, every movement on it chillingly sharp. The air between people is charged. Days unfold, bathed in their own music. Nights become hallucinatory; dreams, prescient.

Spring weather is capricious and mean. It snows, then blisters with heat. There have been tornadoes. They lay their elephant trunks out in the sage until they find houses, then slurp everything up and leave. I've noticed that melting snowbanks hiss and rot, viperous, then drip into calm pools where ducklings hatch and livestock, being trailed to summer range, drink. With the ice cover gone, rivers churn a milkshake brown, taking culverts and small bridges with them. Water in such an arid place (the average annual rainfall where I live is less than eight inches) is like blood. It festoons drab land with green veins; a line of cottonwoods following a stream; a strip of alfalfa; and, on ditch banks, wild asparagus growing.

I've moved to a small cattle ranch owned by friends. It's at the foot of the Big Horn Mountains. A few weeks ago, I helped them deliver a calf who was stuck halfway out of his mother's body. By the time he was freed, we could see a heartbeat, but he was straining against a swollen tongue for air. Mary and I held him upside down by his back feet, while Stan, on his hands and knees in the blood, gave the calf mouth-to-mouth resuscitation. I have a vague memory of being pneumonia-choked as a child, my mother giving me her air, which may account for my romance with this windswept state.

If anything is endemic to Wyoming, it is wind. This big room of space is swept out daily, leaving a bone yard of fossils, agates, and carcasses in every stage of decay. Though it was water that initially shaped the state, wind is the meticulous gardener, raising dust and pruning the sage.

I try to imagine a world in which I could ride my horse across uncharted land. There is no wilderness left; wildness, yes, but true wilderness has been gone on this continent since the time of Lewis and Clark's overland journey.

Two hundred years ago, the Crow, Shoshone, Arapaho, Cheyenne, and Sioux roamed the intermountain West, orchestrating their movements according to hunger, season, and warfare. Once they acquired horses, they traversed the spines of all the big Wyoming ranges—the Absarokas, the Wind Rivers, the Tetons, the Big Horns—and wintered on the unprotected plains that fan out from them. Space was life. The world was their home.

What was life-giving to Native Americans was often nightmarish to sodbusters who had arrived encumbered with families and ethnic pasts to be transplanted in nearly uninhabitable land. The great distances, the shortage of water and trees, and the loneliness created unexpected hardships for them. In her book *O Pioneers!*, Willa Cather gives a settler's version of the bleak landscape:

> The little town behind them had vanished as if it had never been, had fallen
> behind the swell of the prairie, and the stern frozen country received them into
> its bosom. The homesteads were few and far apart; here and there a windmill
> gaunt against the sky, a sod house crouching in a hollow.

The emptiness of the West was for others a geography of possibility. Men and women who amassed great chunks of land and struggled to preserve unfenced empires were, despite their self-serving motives, unwitting geographers. They understood the lay of the land. But by the 1850s the Oregon and Mormon trails sported bumper-to-bumper traffic. Wealthy landowners, many of them aristocratic absentee landlords, known as remittance men because they were paid to come West and get out of their families' hair, overstocked the range with more than a million head of cattle. By 1885 the feed and water were desperately short, and the winter of 1886 laid out the gaunt bodies of dead animals so closely together that when the thaw came, one rancher from Kaycee claimed to have walked on cowhide all the way to Crazy Woman Creek, twenty miles away.

Territorial Wyoming was a boy's world. The land was generous with everything but water. At first there was room enough, food enough, for everyone. And, as with all beginnings, an expansive mood set in. The young cowboys, drifters, shopkeepers, schoolteachers, were heroic, lawless, generous, rowdy, and tenacious. The individualism and optimism generated during those times have endured.

John Tisdale rode north with the trail herds from Texas. He was a college-educated man with enough money to buy a small outfit near the Powder River. While driving home from the town of Buffalo with a buckboard full of Christmas toys for his family and a winter's supply of food, he was shot in the back by an agent of the cattle barons who resented the encroachment of small-time stockmen like him. The wealthy cattlemen tried to control all the public grazing land by restricting membership in the Wyoming Stock Growers Association, as if it were a country club. They ostracized from roundups and brandings cowboys and ranchers who were not members, then denounced them as rustlers. Tisdale's death, the second such cold-blooded murder, kicked off the Johnson County cattle war, which was no simple good-guy-bad-guy shoot-out but a complicated class struggle between landed gentry and less affluent settlers—a shocking reminder that the West was not an egalitarian sanctuary after all.

Fencing ultimately enforced boundaries, but barbed wire abrogated space. It was stretched across the beautiful valleys, into the mountains, over desert badlands, through buffalo grass. The "anything is possible" fever—the lure of any new place—was constricted. The integrity of the land as a geographical body, and the freedom to ride anywhere on it, were lost.

I punched cows with a young man named Martin, who is the great-grandson of John Tisdale. His inheritance is not the open land that Tisdale knew and prematurely lost but a rage against restraint.

Wyoming tips down as you head northeast; the highest ground—the Laramie Plains—is on the Colorado border. Up where I live, the Big Horn River leaks into difficult, arid terrain. In the basin where it's dammed, sandhill cranes gather and, with delicate legwork, slice through the stilled water. I was driving by with a rancher one morning when he commented that cranes are "old-fashioned." When I asked why, he said, "Because they mate for life." Then he looked at me with a twinkle in his eyes, as if to say he really did believe in such things but also understood why we break our own rules.

In all this open space, values crystalize quickly. People are strong on scruples but tenderhearted about quirky behavior. A friend and I found one ranch hand, who's "not quite right in the head," sitting in front of the badly decayed carcass of a cow, shaking his finger and saying, "Now, I don't want you to do this ever again!" When I asked what was wrong with him, I was told, "He's goofier than hell, just like the rest of us." Perhaps because the West is historically new, conventional morality is still felt to be less important than rock-bottom truths. Though there's always a lot of teasing and sparring, people are blunt with one another, sometimes even cruel, believing honesty is stronger medicine than sympathy, which may console but often conceals.

The formality that goes hand in hand with the rowdiness is known as the Western Code. It's a list of practical do's and don'ts, faithfully observed. A friend, Cliff, who runs a trapline in the winter, cut off half his foot while chopping a hole in the ice. Alone, he dragged himself to his pickup and headed for town, stopping to open the ranch gate as he left, and getting out to close it again, thus losing, in his observance of rules, precious time and blood. Later, he commented, "How would it look, them having to come to the hospital to tell me their cows had gotten out?"

Accustomed to emergencies, my friends doctor each other from the vet's bag with relish. When one old-timer suffered a heart attack in hunting camp, his partner quickly stirred up a brew of red horse liniment and hot water and made the half-conscious victim drink it, then tied him onto a horse and led him twenty miles to town. He regained consciousness and lived.

The roominess of the state has affected political attitudes as well. Ranchers keep up with world politics and the convulsions of the economy but are basically isolationists. Being used to running their own small empires of land and livestock, they're suspicious of big government. It's a "don't fence me in" holdover from a century ago. They still want the elbow room their grandfathers had, so they're strongly conservative, but with a populist twist.

Summer is the season when we get our "cowboy tans"—on the lower parts of our faces and on three fourths of our arms. Excessive heat, in the nineties and higher, sends us outside with the mosquitoes. In winter we're tucked inside our houses, and the white wasteland outside appears to be expanding, but in summer all the greenery abridges space. Summer is a go-ahead season. Every living thing is off the block and in the race: battalions of bugs in flight and biting; bats swinging around my log cabin as if the bases were loaded and someone had hit a home run. Some of summer's high-speed growth is ominous: larkspur, death camas, and green greasewood can kill sheep—an ironic idea, dying in this desert from eating what is too verdant. With sixteen hours of daylight, farmers and ranchers irrigate feverishly. There are first, second, and third cuttings of hay, some crews averaging only four hours of sleep a night for weeks. And, like the cowboys who in summer ride the night rodeo circuit, nighthawks make daredevil dives at dusk with an eerie whirring sound like a plane going down on the shimmering horizon.

In the town where I live, they've had to board up the dance-hall windows because there have been so many fights. There's so little to do except work that people wind up in a state of idle agitation that becomes fatalistic, as if there were nothing to be done about all this untapped energy. So the dark side to the grandeur of these spaces is the small-mindedness that seals people in. Men become hermits; women go mad. Cabin fever explodes into suicides, or into grudges and lifelong family feuds. Two sisters in my area inherited a ranch but found they couldn't get along. They fenced the place in half. When one's cows got out and mixed with the other's, the women went at each other with shovels. They ended up in the same hospital room but never spoke a word to each other for the rest of their lives.

After the brief lushness of summer, the sun moves south. The range grass is brown. Livestock is trailed back down from the mountains. Water holes begin to frost over at night. Last fall Martin asked me to accompany him on a pack trip. With five horses, we followed a river into the mountains behind the tiny Wyoming town of Meeteetse. Groves of aspen, red and orange, gave off a light that made us look toasted. Our hunting camp was so high that clouds skidded across our foreheads, then slowed to sail out across the warm valleys. Except for a bull moose who wandered into our camp and mistook our black gelding for a rival, we shot at nothing.

One of our evening entertainments was to watch the night sky. My dog, a dingo bred to herd sheep, also came on the trip. He is so used to the silence and empty skies that when an airplane flies over he always looks up and eyes the distant intruder quizzically. The sky, lately, seems to be much more crowded than it used to be. Satellites make their silent passes in the dark with great regularity. We counted eighteen in one hour's viewing. How odd to think that while they circumnavigated the planet, Martin and I had moved only six miles into our local wilderness and had seen no other human for the two weeks we stayed there.

At night, by moonlight, the land is whittled to slivers—a ridge, a river, a strip of grassland stretching to the mountains, then the huge sky. One morning a full moon was setting in the west just as the sun was rising. I felt precariously balanced between the two as I loped across a meadow. For a moment, I could believe that the stars, which were still visible, work like cooper's bands, holding together everything above Wyoming.

Space has a spiritual equivalent and can heal what is divided and burdensome in us. My grandchildren will probably use space shuttles for a honeymoon trip or to recover from heart attacks, but closer to home we might also learn how to carry space inside ourselves in the effortless way we carry our skins. Space represents sanity, not a life purified, dull, or "spaced out" but one that might accommodate intelligently any idea or situation.

From the clayey soil of northern Wyoming is mined bentonite, which is used as a filler in candy, gum, and lipstick. We Americans are great on fillers, as if what we have, what we are, is not enough. We have a cultural tendency toward denial, but, being affluent, we strangle ourselves with what we can buy. We have only to look at the houses we build to see how we build *against* space, the way we drink against pain and loneliness. We fill up space as if it were a pie shell, with things whose opacity further obstructs our ability to see what is already there.

Edward Hoagland

The Courage of Turtles

Turtles are a kind of bird with the governor turned low. With the same attitude of removal, they cock a glance at what is going on, as if they need only to fly away. Until recently they were also a case of virtue rewarded, at least in the town where I grew up, because, being humble creatures, there were plenty of them. Even when we still had a few bobcats in the woods the local snapping turtles, growing up to forty pounds, were the largest carnivores. You would see them through the amber water, as big as greeny wash basins at the bottom of the pond, until they faded into the inscrutable mud as if they hadn't existed at all.

When I was ten I went to Dr. Green's Pond, a two-acre pond across the road. When I was twelve I walked a mile or so to Taggart's Pond, which was lusher, had big water snakes and a waterfall; and shortly after that I was bicycling way up to the adverturesome vastness of Mud Pond, a lake-sized body of water in the reservoir system of a Connecticut city, possessed of cat-backed little islands and empty shacks and a forest of pines and hardwoods along the shore. Otters, foxes and mink left their prints on the bank; there were pike and perch. As I got older, the estates and forgotten back lots in town were parceled out and sold for nice prices, yet, though the woods had shrunk, it seemed that fewer people walked in the woods. The new residents didn't know how to find them. Eventually, exploring, they did find them, and it required some ingenuity and doubling around on my part to go for eight miles without meeting someone. I was grown by now, I lived in New York, and that's what I wanted on the occasional weekends when I came out.

Since Mud Pond contained drinking water I had felt confident nothing untoward would happen there. For a long while the developers stayed away, until the drought of the mid–1960s. This event, squeezing the edges in, convinced the local water company that the pond really wasn't a necessity as a catch basin, however; so they bulldozed a hole in the earthen dam, bulldozed the banks to fill in the bottom, and landscaped the flow of water that remained to wind like an English brook and provide a domestic view for the houses which were planned. Most of the painted turtles of Mud Pond, who had been inaccessible as they sunned on their rocks, wound up in boxes in boys' closets within a matter of days. Their footsteps in the dry leaves gave them away as they wandered forlornly. The snappers and the little musk turtles, neither of whom leave the water except once a year to lay their eggs, dug into the drying mud for another siege of hot weather, which they were accustomed to doing whenever the pond got low. But this time it was low for good; the mud baked over them and slowly entombed them. As for the ducks, I couldn't stroll in the woods and not feel guilty, because they were crouched beside every stagnant pothole, or were slinking between the bushes with their heads tucked into their shoulders so that I wouldn't see them. If they decided I had, they beat their way up through the screen of trees, striking their wings dangerously, and wheeled about with that headlong, magnificent velocity to locate another poor puddle.

I used to catch possums and black snakes as well as turtles, and I kept dogs and goats. Some summers I worked in a menagerie with the big personalities of the animal kingdom, like elephants and rhinoceroses. I was twenty before these enthusiasms began to wane, and it was then that I picked turtles as the particular animal I wanted to keep in touch with. I was allergic to fur, for one thing, and turtles need minimal care and not much in the way of quarters. They're personable beasts. They see the same colors we do and they seem to see just as well, as one discovers in trying to sneak up on them. In the laboratory they unravel the twists of a maze with the hot-blooded rapidity of a mammal. Though they can't run as fast as a rat, they improve on their errors just as quickly, pausing at each crossroads to look left and right. And they rock rhythmically in place, as we often do, although they are hatched from eggs, not the womb. (A common explanation psychologists give for our pleasure in rocking quietly is that it recapitulates our mother's heartbeat *in utero*.)

Snakes, by contrast, are dryly silent and priapic. They are smooth movers, legalistic, unblinking, and they afford the humor which the humorless do. But they make challenging captives; sometimes they don't eat for months on a point of order—if the light isn't right, for instance. Alligators are sticklers too. They're like war-horses, or German shepherds, and with their bar-shaped, vertical pupils adding emphasis, they have the *idée fixe* of eating, eating, even when they choose to refuse all food and stubbornly die. They delight in tossing a salamander up towards the sky and grabbing him in their long mouths as he comes down. They're so eager that they get the jitters, and they're too much of a proposition for a casual aquarium like mine. Frogs are depressingly defenseless: that moist, extensive back, with the bones almost sticking through. Hold a frog and you're holding its skeleton. Frogs' tasty legs are the staff of life to many animals—herons, raccoons, ribbon snakes—though they themselves are hard to feed. It's not an enviable role to be the staff of life, and after frogs you descend down the evolutionary ladder a big step to fish.

Turtles cough, burp, whistle, grunt and hiss, and produce social judgments. They put their heads together amicably enough, but then one drives the other back with the suddenness of two dogs who have been conversing in tones too low for an onlooker to hear. They pee in fear when they're first caught, but exercise both pluck and optimism in trying to escape, walking for hundreds of yards within the confines of their pen, carrying the weight of that cumbersome box on legs which are cruelly positioned for walking. They don't feel that the contest is unfair; they keep plugging, rolling like sailorly souls—a bobbing, infirm gait, a brave, sea-legged momentum—stopping occasionally to study the lay of the land. For me, anyway, they manage to contain the rest of the animal world. They can stretch out their necks like a giraffe, or loom underwater like an apocryphal hippo. They browse on lettuce thrown on the water like a cow moose which is partly submerged. They have a penguin's alertness, combined with a build like a Brontosaurus when they rise up on tiptoe. Then they hunch and ponderously lunge like a grizzly going forward.

Baby turtles in a turtle bowl are a puzzle in geometrics. They're as decorative as pansy petals, but they are also self-directed building blocks, propping themselves on one another in different arrangements, before upending the tower. The timid individuals turn fearless, or vice versa. If one gets a bit arrogant he will push the others off the rock and afterwards climb down into the water and cling to the back of one of those he has bullied, tickling him with his hind feet until he bucks like a bronco. On the other hand, when this same milder-mannered fellow isn't exerting himself, he will stare right into the face of the sun for hours. What could be more lionlike? And he's at home in or out of the water and does lots of metaphysical tilting. He sinks and rises, with an infinity of levels to choose from; or, elongating himself, he climbs out on the land again to perambulate, sits boxed in his box, and finally slides back in the water, submerging into dreams.

I have five of these babies in a kidney-shaped bowl. The hatchling, who is a painted turtle, is not as large as the top joint of my thumb. He eats chicken gladly. Other foods he will attempt to eat but not with sufficient perseverance to succeed because he's so little. The yellow-bellied terrapin is probably a yearling, and he eats salad voraciously, but no meat, fish or fowl. The Cumberland terrapin won't touch salad or chicken but eats fish and all of the meats except for bacon. The little snapper, with a black crenelated shell, feasts on any kind of meat, but rejects greens and fish. The fifth of the turtles is African. I acquired him only recently and don't know him well. A mottled brown, he unnerves the green turtles, dragging their food off to his lairs. He doesn't seem to want to be green—he bites the algae off his shell, hanging meanwhile at daring, steep, head-first angles.

The snapper was a Ferdinand until I provided him with deeper water. Now he snaps at my pencil with his downturned and fearsome mouth, his swollen face like a napalm victim's. The Cumberland has an elliptical red mark on the side of his green-and-yellow head. He is benign by nature and ought to be as elegant as his scientific name (*Pseudemys scripta elegans*), except he has contracted a disease of the air bladder which has permanently inflated it; he floats high in the water at an undignified slant and can't go under. There may have been internal bleeding, too, because his carapace is stained along its ridge. Unfortunately, like flowers, baby turtles often die. Their mouths fill up with a white fungus and their lungs with pneumonia. Their organs clog up from the rust in the water, or diet troubles, and, like a dying man's, their eyes and heads become too prominent. Toward the end, the edge of the shell becomes flabby as felt and folds around them like a shroud.

While they live they're like puppies. Although they're vivacious, they would be a bore to be with all the time, so I also have an adult wood turtle about six inches long. Her shell is the equal of any seashell for sculpturing, even a Cellini shell; it's like an old, dusty, richly engraved medallion dug out of a hillside. Her legs are salmon-orange bordered with black and protected by canted, heroic scales. Her plastron—the bottom shell—is splotched like a margay cat's coat, with black ocelli on a yellow background. It is convex to make room for the female organs inside, whereas a male's would be concave to help him fit tightly on top of her. Altogether, she exhibits every camouflage color on her limbs and shells. She has a turtleneck neck, a tail like an elephant's, wise old pachydermous hind legs, and the face of a turkey—except that when I carry her she gazes at the passing ground with a hawk's eyes and mouth. Her feet fit to the fingers of my hand, one to each one, and she rides looking down. She can walk on the floor in perfect silence, but usually she lets her shell knock portentously, like a footstep, so that she resembles some grand, concise, slow-moving id. But if an earthworm is presented, she jerks swiftly ahead, poises above it, and strikes like a mongoose, consuming it with wild vigor. Yet she will climb on my lap to eat bread or boiled eggs.

If put into a creek, she swims like a cutter, nosing forward to intercept a strange turtle and smell him. She drifts with the current to go downstream, maneuvering behind a rock when she wants to take stock, or sinking to the nether levels, while bubbles float up. Getting out, choosing her path, she will proceed a distance and dig into a pile of humus, thrusting herself to the coolest layer at the bottom. The hole closes over her until it's as small as a mouse's hole. She's not as aquatic as a musk turtle, not quite as terrestrial as the box turtles in the same woods, but because of her versatility she's marvelous, she's everywhere. And though she breathes the way we breathe, with scarcely perceptible movements of her chest, sometimes instead she pumps her throat ruminatively, like a pipe smoker sucking and puffing. She waits and blinks, pumping her throat, turning her head, then sets off like a loping tiger in slow motion, hurdling the jungly lumber, the pea vine and twigs. She estimates angles so well that when she rides over the rocks, sliding down a drop-off with her rugged front legs extended, she has the grace of a rodeo mare.

But she's well off to be with me rather than at Mud Pond. The other turtles have fled—those that aren't baked into the bottom. Creeping up the brooks to sad, constricted marshes, burdened as they are with that box on their backs, they're walking into a setup where all their enemies move thirty times faster than they. It's like the nightmare most of us have whimpered through, where we are weighted down disastrously while trying to flee; fleeing our home ground, we try to run.

I've seen turtles in still worse straits. On Broadway, in New York, there is a penny arcade which used to sell baby terrapins that were scrawled with bon mots in enamel paint, such as KISS ME BABY. The manager turned out to be a wholesaler as well, and once I asked him whether he had any larger turtles to sell. He took me upstairs to a loft room devoted to the turtle business. There were desks for the paper work and a series of racks that held shallow tin bins atop one another, each with several hundred babies crawling around in it. He was a smudgy-complexioned, serious fellow and he did have a few adult terrapins, but I was going to school and wasn't actually planning to buy; I'd only wanted to see them. They were aquatic turtles, but here they went without water, presumably for weeks, lurching about in those dry bins like handicapped citizens, living on gumption. An easel where the artist worked stood in the middle of the floor. She had a palette and a clip attachment for fastening the babies in place. She wore a smock and a beret, and was homely, short, and eccentric-looking, with funny black hair, like some of the ladies who show their paintings in Washington Square in May. She had a cold, she was smoking, and her hand wasn't very steady, although she worked quickly enough. The smile that she produced for me would have looked giddy if she had been happier, or drunk. Of course the turtles' doom was sealed when she painted them, because their bodies inside would continue to grow but their shells would not. Gradually, invisibly, they would be crushed. Around us their bellies— two thousand belly shells—rubbed on the bins with a mournful, momentous hiss.

Somehow there were so many of them I didn't rescue one. Years later, however, I was walking on First Avenue when I noticed a basket of living turtles in front of a fish store. They were as dry as a heap of old bones in the sun; nevertheless, they were creeping over one another gimpily, doing their best to escape. I looked and was touched to discover that they appeared to be wood turtles, my favorites, so I bought one. In my apartment I looked closer and realized that in fact this was a diamondback terrapin, which was bad news. Diamondbacks are tidewater turtles from brackish estuaries, and I had no sea water to keep him in. He spent his days thumping interminably against the baseboards, pushing for an opening through the wall. He drank thirstily but would not eat and had none of the hearty, accepting qualities of wood turtles. He was morose, paler in color, sleeker and more Oriental in the carved ridges and rings that formed his shell. Though I felt sorry for him, finally I found his unrelenting presence exasperating. I carried him, struggling in a paper bag, across town to the Morton Street Pier on the Hudson. It was August but gray and windy. He was very surprised when I tossed him in; for the first time in our association, I think, he was afraid. He looked afraid as he bobbed about on top of the water, looking up at me from ten feet below. Though we were both accustomed to his resistance and rigidity, seeing him still pitiful, I recognized that I must have done the wrong thing. At least the river was salty, but it was also bottomless; the waves were too rough for him, and the tide was coming in, bumping him against the pilings underneath the pier. Too late, I realized that he wouldn't be able to swim to a peaceful inlet in New Jersey, even if he could figure out which way to swim. But since, short of diving in after him, there was nothing I could do, I walked away.

Linda Hogan

The Bats

The first time I was fortunate enough to catch a glimpse of mating bats was in the darkest corner of a zoo. I was held spellbound, seeing the fluid movement of the bats as they climbed each other softly and closed their wings together. They were an ink black world hanging from a rafter. The graceful angles of their dark wings opened and jutted out like an elbow or knee poking through a thin, dark sheet. A moment later it was a black, silky shawl pulled tight around them. Their turning was beautiful, a soundless motion of wind blowing great dark dunes into new configurations.

A few years later, in May, I was walking in a Minneapolis city park. The weather had been warm and humid. For days it had smelled of spring, but the morning grew into a sudden cold snap, the way Minnesota springs are struck to misery by a line of cold that travels in across the long, gray plains. The grass was crisp. It cracked beneath my feet. Chilled to the bone, and starting home, I noticed what looked like a brown piece of fur lying among the frosted blades of new grass. I walked toward it and saw the twiglike legs of a bat, wings folded like a black umbrella whose inner wires had been broken by a windstorm.

The bat was small and brown. It had the soft, furred body of a mouse with two lines of tiny black nipples exposed on the stomach. At first I thought it was dead, but as I reached toward it, it turned its dark, furrowed face to me and bared its sharp teeth. A fierce little mammal, it looked surprisingly like an angry human being. I jumped back. I would have pulled back even without the lightning fast memory of tales about rabid bats that tangle in a woman's hair.

In this park, I'd seen young boys shoot birds and turtles. Despite the bat's menacing face, my first thought was to protect it. Its fangs were still bared, warning me off. When I touched it lightly with a stick, it clamped down like it would never let go. I changed my mind; I decided it was the children who needed protection. Still, I didn't want to leave it lying alone and vulnerable in the wide spiny forest of grass blades that had turned sharp and brittle in the cold.

Rummaging through the trash can I found a lidded box and headed back toward the bat when I came across another bat. This bat, too, was lying brown and inert on the grass. That's when it occurred to me that the recent warm spell had been broken open by the cold and the bats, shocked back into hibernation, had stopped dead in flight, rendered inactive by the quick drop in temperature.

I placed both bats inside the box and carried them home. Now and then the weight would shift and there was the sound of scratching and clawing. I wondered if the warmth from my hands was enough heat to touch them back to life.

At home, I opened the box. The two bats were mating. They were joined together, their broken umbrella wings partly open, then moving, slumping, and opening again. These are the most beautiful turnings, the way these bodies curve and glide together, fold and open. It's elegant beyond compare, more beautiful than eels circling each other in the dark waters.

I put them in a warm corner outside, nestled safe in dry leaves and straw. I looked at them several times a day. Their fur, in the springtime, was misted with dewy rain. They mated for three days in the moldering leaves and fertile earth, moving together in that liquid way, then apart, like reflections on a mirror, a four-chambered black heart beating inside the closed tissue of wings. Between their long, starry finger bones were dark webbings of flesh, wings for sailing jagged across the evening sky. The black wing membranes were etched like the open palm of a human hand, stretched open, offering up a fortune for the reading. As I watched, the male stretched out, opened his small handlike claws to scratch his stomach, closed them again, and hid the future from my eyes.

By the fourth day, the male had become thin and exhausted. On that day he died and the female flew away with the new life inside her body.

For months after that, the local boys who terrorized the backyards of neighbors would not come near where I lived. I'd shown one the skeleton of the male and told them there were others. I could hear them talking in the alley late at night, saying, "Don't go in there. She has bats in her yard." So they'd smoke their cigarettes in a neighbor's yard while the neighbor watched them like a hawk from her kitchen window. My house escaped being vandalized.

My family lived in Germany once when I was a child. One day, exploring a forest with a friend, we came across a cave that went back into the earth. The dark air coming from inside the cave was cool, musty, and smelled damp as spring, but the entryway itself was dark and forboding, the entrance to a world we didn't know. Gathering our courage, we returned the next day with flashlights and stolen matches. It was late afternoon, almost dusk, when we arrived back at the cave. We had no more than just sneaked inside and held up the light when suddenly there was a roaring tumult of sound. Bats began to fly. We ran outside to twilight just as the sky above us turned gray with a fast-moving cloud of their ragged wings, flying up, down, whipping air, the whole sky seething. Afraid, we ran off toward the safety of our homes, half-screaming, half-laughing through the path in the forest. Not even our skirts catching on the brambles slowed us down.

Later, when we mentioned the cave of bats, we were told that the cave itself had been an ammunition depot during World War II, and that bat guano was once used in place of gunpowder. During the war, in fact, the American military had experimented with bats carrying bombs. It was thought that they could be used to fly over enemy lines carrying explosives that would destroy the enemy. Unfortunately, one of them flew into the attic of the general's house and the bomb exploded. Another blew up a colonel's car. They realized that they could not control the direction a bat would fly and gave up on their strategy of using life to destroy life.

Recently I visited a cave outside of San Antonio with writer and friend Naomi Nye. It was only a small mouth of earth, but once inside it, the sanctuaries stretched out for long distances, a labyrinth of passageways. No bats have inhabited that cave since people began to intrude, but it was still full of guano. Some of it had been taken out in the 1940s to be used as gunpowder. Aside from that, all this time later, the perfect climate inside the cave preserved the guano in its original form, with thick gray layers, as fresh and moist as when the bats had lived there.

Bats hear their way through the world. They hear the sounds that exist at the edges of our lives. Leaping through blue twilight they cry out a thin language, then listen for its echo to return. It is a dusky world of songs a pitch above our own. For them, the world throws back a language, the empty space rising between hills speaks an open secret then lets the bats pass through, here or there, in the dark air. Everything answers, the corner of a house, the shaking leaves on a wind-blown tree, the solid voice of bricks. A fence post talks back. An insect is located. A wall sings out its presence. There are currents of air loud as ocean waves, a music of trees, stones, charred stovepipes. Even our noisy silences speak out in a dark dimension of sound that is undetected by our limited hearing in the loud, vibrant land in which we live.

Once, Tennessee writer Jo Carson stuck her hearing aid in my ear and said, "Listen to this." I could hear her speak, listening through the device. I could hear the sound of air, even the noise of cloth moving against our skin, and a place in the sky. All of it drowned out the voices of conversation. It was how a bat must hear the world, I thought, a world alive in its whispering songs, the currents of air loud as waves of an ocean, a place rich with the music of trees and stones.

It is no wonder that bats have been a key element in the medicine bundles of some southern tribes. Bats are people from the land of souls, land where moon dwells. They are listeners to our woes, hearers of changes in earth, predictors of earthquake and storm. They live with the goddess of night in the lusty mouth of earth.

Some of the older bundles, mistakenly opened by non-Indians, were found to contain the bones of a bat, wrapped carefully in brain-tanned rawhide. The skeletons were intact and had been found naturally rather than killed or trapped by people, which would have rendered them neutral; they would have withdrawn their assistance from people. Many Indian people must have waited years, searching caves and floors and the ground beneath trees where insects cluster, in order to find a small bony skull, spine, and the long finger bones of the folded wings. If a bat skeleton were found with meat still on it, it was placed beside an anthill, and the ants would pick the bones clean.

I believe it is the world-place bats occupy that allows them to be of help to people, not just because they live inside the passageways between earth and sunlight, but because they live in double worlds of many kinds. They are two animals merged into one, a milk-producing rodent that bears live young, and a flying bird. They are creatures of the dusk, which is the time between times, people of the threshold, dwelling at the open mouth of inner earth like guardians at the womb of creation.

The bat people are said to live in the first circle of holiness. Thus, they are intermediaries between our world and the next. Hearing the chants of life all around them, they are listeners who pass on the language and songs of many things to human beings who need wisdom, healing, and guidance through our lives, we who forget where we stand in the world. Bats know the world is constantly singing, know the world inside the turning and twisting of caves, places behind and beneath our own. As they scuttle across cave ceilings, they leave behind their scratch marks on the ceiling like an ancient alphabet written by diviners who traveled through and then were gone from the thirteen-month world of light and dark.

And what curing dwells at the center of this world of sounds above our own? Maybe it's as if earth's pole to the sky lives in a weightless cave, poking through a skin of dark and night and sleep.

At night, I see them out of the corner of my eye, like motes of dust, as secret as the way a neighbor hits a wife, a ghost cat slinks into a basement, or the world is eaten through by rust down to the very heart of nothing. What an enormous world. No wonder it holds our fears and desires. It is all so much larger than we are.

I see them through human eyes that turn around a vision, eyes that see the world upside down before memory rights it. I don't hear the high-pitched language of their living, don't know if they have sorrow or if they tell stories longer than a rainstorm's journey, but I see them. How can we get there from here, I wonder, to the center of the world, to the place where the universe carries down the song of night to our human lives. How can we listen or see to find our way by feel to the heart of every yes or no? How do we learn to trust ourselves enough to hear the chanting of earth? To know what's alive or absent around us, and penetrate the void behind our eyes, the old, slow pulse of things, until a wild flying wakes up in us, a new mercy climbs out and takes wing in the sky?

Richard McCann

The Resurrectionist

Here is what happened:

I was cut apart.

The liver of a dead person was placed inside me so I might live again. This took twelve hours and thirty-three units of blood.

But who was I afterward?

I could still recall the body I'd had when I was ten, the body in which I carried what I called "myself," walking along the C&O Railroad tracks or crossing the divided highway that separated our house from the woods a heavy, modest body, dressed in husky-size jeans from Monkey Ward and a brown corduroy car coat that my mother chose, identical to those my uncles wore back in the mining towns they lived in. I could recall the body I'd had, nervous and tentative, when I first made love at seventeen. But these bodies were gone, as was the body into which I'd been born, these bodies I'd called "mine" without hesitation, intact and separate and entire.

Three months after my liver transplant I flew to Nashville to visit my mother in the nursing home. She sat in a blue housecoat at a folding card table, slowly spooning a Dixie cup of ice cream to her mouth. "Marie, your son's here," the nurse kept telling her. But my mother wouldn't look up except to look through me. She'd begun her own metamorphosis since the last time I'd seen her, withdrawing into the form of a bony old woman who only sometimes recognized my brother or me.

"Is this your son Richard?" the nurse asked, a grade-school teacher prompting a forgetful pupil. My mother shook her head: no, no.

At night I sat at her bedside. "I'm here," I whispered as she slept. "I made it through. I'm here."

I didn't know if she could hear me. For a while I tried to work on the letter of gratitude I was planning to send to the strangers the transplant coordinator referred to as my "donor family," though I knew nothing about them or their loved one whose liver I'd received. I couldn't figure what to write to them that would seem neither too rehearsed nor too intimate, though I planned to repeat some remarks I'd heard in a support group meeting, thanking them for "the gift of life" and assuring them that the highest form of giving occurred, as theirs had, when neither the donor nor the recipient was known to one another.

For a moment my mother shifted beneath her blanket, murmuring in her sleep. I put down the pencil and closed my eyes. *In just a second,* I thought, *she'll say my name.*

"Mother," I said, though she said nothing further. I wanted us back as we had been, restored to what I felt were our real and original bodies, my mother smoking a cigarette on the stoop of our old house in Silver Spring and me beside her with a bottle of Pepsi in my hand, though I knew if my mother were able to ask what had happened to the liver I was born with—the one she'd given me, I sometimes imagined, for it had once been a part of her as well as of me—I could have told her only what the surgeon had told me: "It was sent to pathology and burned."

I flew home the next morning. On the plane I noticed the man beside me staring as one by one I swallowed the half-dozen immunosuppressants that kept my body from rejecting the organ it would forever perceive as foreign, and for a moment I felt my own sudden strangeness, even to myself, as if I were a distinct biological phenomenon, constructed in a manner different from that of my fellow passengers hurtling though space in a pressurized cabin, drinking coffee and reading their magazines.

"I'm a liver transplant recipient," I told my seatmate.

He wanted to know if my new liver was male or female or white or black.

I said I didn't know; he said that if it were him he'd sure want to find out.

But I didn't, or at least I didn't think so, and I was relieved when the plane began its descent. Somewhere over the Alleghenies my seatmate had asked if I'd heard about a man with AIDS who'd gotten a liver from a baboon.

No, I hadn't.

But in my transplant support group I had heard of recipients who'd waived their rights to anonymity to arrange what they sometimes called "reunions," inviting their donor families over for *yahrzeit* rituals and barbecues, and I'd heard of donor families who'd secured the names of recipients, showing up unannounced on their doorsteps, bearing bouquets of mixed flowers and brightly colored mylar balloons.

"Maybe it's kind of like discovering you're adopted or finding your birth mother," one woman said, confiding to our support group her anxious plans for meeting the mother of the teenage boy whose lungs she'd received.

No one dared the obvious: the mother was the mother of a child who was dead, even if his lungs were still drawing breath on earth.

Sometimes I too fantasized that I had an alternate family that was eager to receive me as flesh and blood, especially as my mother retreated farther and farther into a world from which I was excluded, as when she imagined that I was her dead brother and called me by his name. But my fantasies of a happy meeting with a donor family were vague and unspecific, even less concrete than the fantasies I'd concocted as a child, waiting for George Maharis from Route 66 to pull up to the house in his Corvette, ready to speed me away to what I felt sure was my real future.

My fantasies of a painful meeting, however, were explicit and detailed with dread. What would I say if my donor family were to ask to place their hands on my belly so they could feel the liver softly pulsing within?

How could I refuse them? I owed these people everything. I was alive because of a decision they'd made while standing in the bright fluorescence of a hospital corridor. Wasn't the liver more theirs than mine?

I imagined myself hesitating when they reached to touch me, and I imagined them demanding of me, with what I would have agreed was a rightful anger, "Who do you think you are?"

We are made of the dust of old stars, our grade-school teacher told us; we are made of leaves and sediment and the mulch of life. But I was made also of something rescued from the graveyard, I realized after the transplant, and if I was now among the resurrected, I was also the resurrectionist—the name given in the nineteenth century to the grave robbers who sold corpses for dissection to physicians and anatomists, trafficking in bodies and parts.

I don't recall when I began to think of what is medically called "the non-heart-beating cadaver donor" as neither a noble but faceless benefactor nor as a nonhuman organ source, but rather as someone particular and separate who'd lived his own life before he died. I don't recall when I began to think of a donor organ as a bearer of its own set of cellular memories and not just as some sort of bloodied and perishable apparatus that one could airlift a great distance in an Igloo cooler marked HUMAN HEART or HUMAN EYES. In the eleven months I spent waiting for a transplant, I could barely acknowledge what was happening to my own body as my liver rapidly failed: abdomen grossly distended from accumulated fluids; muscle wasting as my body cannibalized itself for nutrients and proteins; pale stools streaked with bile; profound and constant exhaustion; brief spells of aphasia; cramps and sudden hemorrhages, blood puddling in my mouth from ruptured esophageal varices; skin the color of copper and eyes the color of urine.

I do recall a spring afternoon a month before my transplant, when I was lying on the grass in Rock Creek Park, back from the transplant clinic where I'd overheard a nurse telling someone in the next room—I couldn't see who—that a high number of teenage donors die not from car wrecks but from suicide.

I didn't want to know this, not as I myself was growing so desperate for a donor. As soon as I left the clinic, I asked a taxi driver to take me to Rock Creek Park—"Are you all right?" he kept asking, afraid of my appearance—where I'd often gone when I was well to sunbathe with my friends, though now I was alone. I paid the fare; then I was lying on the unmowed grass, attempting to lose myself in the song I could hear playing on a far-off radio, pretending that my whole life consisted of just one word: *sunny, sunny. . . .*

But it didn't work. My donor had begun to claim me, or so it seemed; I felt as if he'd somehow been constructing himself inside me without my knowledge as I was dying, though he was still alive and waiting for nothing unforeseen. Perhaps he's here right now in this park, I thought, or perhaps he's in another part of the city, crossing a street against traffic or standing at a pay phone or waiting for the bus that will bear him home from work. For a moment it seemed as if there were but the two of us left in the world, me and my blood brother, though one of us would soon be dying.

Don't die, I wanted to whisper, though I didn't know if I was speaking to him or myself.

I suppose I found out four weeks later: the hospital paged me past midnight to say they'd located a suitable donor.

My friend Sarah drove me to the E.R. The whole way I kept checking and rechecking the contents of the small suitcase I'd packed six months before—silk dressing gown, twenty-dollar bill, packet of Dentyne, razor and toothbrush and comb; I couldn't stop touching these things, as if they were all that was left holding me to earth.

I knew what would happen when we got to the hospital—X ray, EKG, and enema; introduction of IV lines, one in the left hand and another beneath the collarbone, for sedatives and cyclosporine and antibiotics. For months, I'd been trying to prepare myself for the transplant surgery, studying the booklets the doctor had given me, one with drawings of abdomens marked with dotted lines to represent incision sites, and another with a diagram showing how a pump-driven external system of plastic tubing would route my blood outside my body during the time when I would have no liver.

I was prepared to wake in the ICU, as in fact I did, unable to speak or move, brain buzzing like high voltage from prednisone.

But I was not prepared for what came the week after that: the impact of the realization that I had participated in the pain and violence and grief of a human death. *You have to face what you've done,* I kept telling myself as, each day, I watched myself in the mirror, growing healthier, until even my jaundiced eyes were white again: I had taken a liver from a brain-dead corpse that had been maintained on a ventilator during the removal of its organs, so that it looked like a regular surgical patient, prepped and draped, with an anesthesiologist standing by its head to monitor blood pressure and maintain homeostasis, its chest visibly rising and falling with regulated breath.

"It's not like you killed him," my friends kept telling me.

"I know, I know," I said to quiet them, though I didn't know, not really. But I did know, as perhaps my friends did not, that it isn't just children who believe they can kill with the power of a thought or a word. After all, I had sat in the clinic waiting room with other transplant candidates, joking that we should take a rifle up to the roof to shoot some people whose organs we might like. "I wish we'd been at the Texas Book Depository with Oswald," one man had said.

At night in bed I often thought of the person who'd died; when I was quiet, I could feel myself quietly grieving him, just as I was grieving my own body, so deeply wounded and cut apart, though still alive.

"I'm sorry," I wanted to tell him.

Sometimes I woke in the middle of the night, troubled to realize that I had taken a piece of him inside me, as if I had eaten him to stay alive. When this happened I often forced myself to think of it longer, though I didn't want to, as if I were a member of a tribe I'd read about a long time before in an old ethnographic text that described how the bereaved dripped the bodily fluids of the dead into their rice, which they then made themselves eat as an act of reverence and love.

In this state, I could not console myself. I got up and sat on the sofa. *So here I am,* I thought, *right on the edge of the unspeakable. . . .*

Other nights I thought of the donor with a great tenderness, sometimes perceiving him as male and sometimes as female. These nights, I placed my hand over what seemed to be still her liver, not mine, and slowly massaged the right side of my body—a broken reliquary with a piece of flesh inside—all the way from my hip to the bottom of my rib cage. "It's okay, it's okay," I whispered over and over, as if I were attempting to quiet a troubled spirit not my own.

If I could, I would undo what I have done, I thought, though I knew that if I had to, I would do it again.

I wasn't new to survivor guilt. After all, I'd been living for a long time in the midst of the AIDS epidemic while so many of my close friends died: Larry, Ed, Darnell, Allen, Ricardo, Paul, George, Arcadio, Jaime, Wally, Billy, Victor, and David.

In this sense, it had been a relief to be diagnosed, to have a progressive disease that threatened my life, to be bivouacked with the others. "It's like you're one of us now," my friend Kenny had told me. "It's like you've got AIDS."

But I couldn't tell him it wasn't true, at least not after the transplant; it wasn't the same at all. I'd outlived everyone, even myself.

What did Lazarus want after he stumbled from the cave, tied hand and foot with graveclothes, his face bound about with a napkin? *Loose him,* Jesus said, and *Let him go.*

I survived. It's two years since the transplant. Here I am, in my new life.

I want to unfurl.

I want to become my gratitude.

I want to fly around the world.

I want to be a man with a suntan. The man in the Arrow shirt.

And above all, this: I want to complete what I've written here—these fragments, these sticky residues of trauma—by adding just one more line before the words THE END: "It's a miracle."

It is a miracle, of course. I know that. Just the other day, for instance, stopping at a sidewalk fruit stand and buying a blood orange: *Oh,* I thought, *this will replace the blood I lost.* I carried the orange to the park, where I sat in the sun, lazily devouring its juicy flesh, its piercing wine-red tartness. *There's nothing more than this I need,* I thought. *I'm alive. I'm alive.*

But what happens after the miracle? What happens after the blinding light of change withdraws and the things of the earth resume their shadows?

What happened to Lazarus after his resurrection? On this, the Gospel According to St. John is silent. Did Lazarus speak after he was commanded from the grave and his shroud was loosed? Did he thank the One who was his Savior and then walk back into the house with his sisters Mary and Martha so they could wash him clean? Or did he turn in anger toward his Savior, demanding to know why He had tarried so long with His Apostles before coming? *If thou hadst been here, I had not died.*

Where did he go afterward? Did he live a long life? Did he forget his time in the grave?

Here is where I went after my resurrection: Miami Beach, Sarasota, Raleigh, Nashville, Peterborough, Madrid, Barcelona, New York City, and Provincetown.

And I went back as an inpatient to the hospital—five more times, at least to date. The hepatitis goes on, the doctor tells me. The transplant doesn't cure it. It gives the virus a new liver to infect and feast upon. (*Dear donor, forgive me, I can't save your life. . . .*)

A year after the transplant, just after the anniversary the social worker called my "first birthday," these things happened: low-grade fever; weight gain; edema; jaundice; sudden and unwanted elevations in alkaline phosphatase, bilirubin, and liver enzymes. *This can't be happening,* I thought, *not again.*

"We need to biopsy the liver," the doctor said. He said we needed to measure the progression of the disease by assessing the extent of new cirrhotic scarring. I knew what that meant: it meant the story wasn't over, as I so badly wanted it to be. It meant that things were uncertain.

"Don't worry," the doctor said as he sorted through my file. "We can always discuss retransplantation."

No, I thought, I can't hear that word, not ever again, especially if it's applied to me. Where was the miracle now? I was supposed to have been restored. I was supposed to have been made whole. I wanted to loose the graveclothes; I wanted to unbind the napkin from my face; I wanted to be through with death forever.

Instead I was sitting in a windowless medical office, waiting for the phlebotomist to come and draw more blood. I wasn't sure I had the heart for more miracles.

Did Lazarus believe he was done with death after his resurrection? There's no record of whether Christ cured him of the sickness that had killed him in the first place, before he rose again; there's no record of the pain his body must have felt after having lain four days in its grave—long enough to have begun to decompose and (as the Gospel says) *to stinketh.*

As for me: For three weeks I got worse, then I slowly got better. A few months later the doctor said there'd be no need to discuss retransplantation, at least not yet, at least not in the immediate future.

It wasn't a miracle that pulled me back, at least not then: I was saved not by a sudden and divine intervention but by the persistent and real efforts of physicians, some with Cartier watches and others wearing scuffed shoes. The story didn't end with a tongue of flame or a blinding light. Each morning and evening I monitor myself for organ rejection, as I'll do for the rest of my life: blood pressure, temperature, weight. I go to the clinic for blood draws; I await faxes detailing test results.

Here is what happens after the resurrection:

Your body hurts, because it's hard to come to life again after lying so long in a grave, but you set goals and you labor to meet them, holding yourself up with your IV pole as you shuffle down the hospital corridor, slowly building back your strength. You learn your medications; you learn to pack your wounds with sterile gauze; you learn to piss into a bottle and shit into a pan. It's work, preparing yourself for sunlight.

Then the day comes when you are allowed to wash your hair and shower. A little while later you're walking down a street.

People you've not seen in ages stop to ask how you're doing; you say you're doing fine, you're doing great. It's life again, dear ordinary life! Life as you hungered for it, with its pleasures and its requirements.

Yes, it's life again, your life, but it's not the same, not quite. Or so it seems, because you can't forget how it felt to lie in the close darkness of that grave; you can't forget the acrid smell of the earth or the stink of the moldering graveclothes, especially now that you know, as you never did before, that you're headed back to the grave again, as is everyone, and you know this with a clarity you cherish and despise.

The gift of life is saturated with the gift of death.

Sometimes, sleepless at night, I imagine I'm back in the hospital the night of my transplant, lying naked in a cubicle behind a thin curtain, waiting for a nurse to prep me for surgery. *This is how it feels to lie in a cold room,* I tell myself, because this might be my last night on earth and I want to feel everything, to feel once more how life feels, each breath in and each breath out.

The nurse comes in and instructs me to lie on my side. She administers an enema. *This is how it feels to be filled with warm water.* I go to the toilet and afterwards I look at myself for a moment in the bathroom mirror. When I return to the cubicle and lie down, the nurse says she must shave the hair from my abdomen, all the way from my groin to my chest. "I hope my hands are warm enough," she says, spreading the shaving soap across my stomach. She touches the cold razor to my belly, and I think, *This is how it feels to be alive.*

Floyd Skloot

Wild in the Woods: Confessions of a Demented Man

> My twin, the nameless one, wild in the woods.
> —*John Berryman, "Dream Song 255"*

I am demented. I have been clinically demented for a decade, ever since contracting a virus that attacked my brain in December of 1988. I display dementia's classic "multiple cognitive deficits that include memory impairment but not impairment of consciousness" and am totally disabled. You might never know, just looking at me.

There are, however, a few tips to the naked eye. My brain damage manifests itself in specific motor malfunctions. So I walk like Phillip Dean in James Salter's classic 1967 novel, *A Sport and a Pastime,* who in a bad moment "feels awkward, as if the process of movement had suddenly asserted all its complexity and everything had to be commanded." This is an accurate description of how I feel when I walk. I have to think about every step or else the whole process of walking breaks down. Like Dean, I walk "as if made of wood," only I do it that way all the time. If I bend to pick up a dropped coin, I will probably fall over. I can be tripped by a gust of wind. Few of my shirts are free of permanent stains from spills or splashes, and there are squiggles of ink on everything I wear. Watch me accidentally ladle the oat bran I've just cooked into the sink instead of a cereal bowl or struggle to affix the plastic blade attachment guide to my beard trimmer. See me open the pantry and stare into it with no recollection of what I was after an instant before, or start a bath by rubbing soap over my still-dry body. Play cards with me and wonder why I discard an ace just after you've picked up an ace off the pile or suddenly follow the rules of poker while we're playing casino. Try to teach me how to operate a new microwave oven or program an unfamiliar calculator. If the cat moves across my field of vision, hear my conversation stop as I forget what I am telling you. If I ask you to pass the "steam wheels" just wait a moment till I correct myself and request the "cream cheese." If we drive together and I tell you to turn left, be sure to turn right.

Dementia is a loaded word. To health professionals, it refers to "a precipitous decline in mental function from a previous state" and has clear diagnostic criteria. But to almost everyone else, it refers to doddering senility. Either that or craziness; the dictionary offers "madness" and "insanity" as synonyms. Dementia is the Halloween of illnesses, a horror mask, a nightmare affliction, its victims akin to Freddy Krueger or Michael "The Shape" Myers. It is so fearsome because it is so transformative. The demented are seen as out of control or out of touch, as zombies, given over to primal impulses. Plug "demented" into a search engine on the World Wide Web and you get referred to sites like "The Demented Pinhead Figurine," "Lunatic Lounge, the Home of Stupid Human Noises," or "The Doctor Demento Halloween Show."

We decry what we fear. We shroud it in myth, heap abuse upon it, use language and gesture to banish it from sight or render it comic. By shrinking its monstrousness, we tame it. So a new disease such as AIDS is known first as the gay cancer, or chronic fatigue syndrome is known first as the yuppie flu, officially trivialized, shunted aside. And there is little we fear so much as losing our minds. Synonyms for "demented" are "daft," "deranged," "maniacal," "psycho," "unbalanced." Or, more colloquially, "bananas," "flipped out," "nutty as a fruitcake," "out of one's tree." The demented are like monkeys, it would seem.

I became demented overnight. Sudden onset is one factor that distinguishes my form of dementia from the more common form associated with Alzheimer's disease. For the Alzheimer's patient, who is usually over sixty, dementia develops slowly, inexorably. Mine developed on the night of December 7, 1988, without prelude and without time to prepare, momentously, the way it does in people suffering strokes or tumors, a bullet to the brain or exposure to toxic substances like carbon monoxide. For me, it was how I imagine the day some sixty-five million years ago when a huge meteorite struck the earth, turning summer to winter in an instant. Not that I noticed right away.

When I woke up in a hotel room in Washington, D.C., after a long flight east, a taxi ride from the airport, a quick run around the mall, and a light dinner, I simply felt sick. Though I noticed that it was almost impossible for me to tie my shoes, that I could not quite get the hang of shaving myself and that operating the elevator was a bafflement, I could not make sense of these observations. My notebook from the seminar I had come to attend remained empty of notes; I spent most of the time upstairs in bed. For six weeks afterward, I thought I had a terrible flu, and that the confusion and mistakes, the inability to find my way back to the office from a coffee break or to sustain an idea during a meeting, saying "adequate" when I meant "accurate" or calling my "cubicle" a "crucifix," were connected to this bad bug I had caught. What it felt like was a gradual lowering of the blinds or one of those slow-motion descents of a shaken sheet as it softly rides the air down to cover your body. One day, driving on a familiar stretch of I–205, headed for the doctor's office, I had to pull over onto the shoulder and stop driving. I did not risk driving again for six years. I could not fill out the forms needed by doctors or insurers. Armed with a plastic cup, I walked to the bathroom to give a urine sample, used the cup for a quick drink from the faucet and returned to the examination room having forgotten to pee at all. I could not remember the doctors or what they were telling me, could not describe the history of my illness without notes, could not find my way back from the examining room to the waiting room.

Have you ever been delirious? Gripped by high fever or certain brain infections, diseases or injuries; after too much to drink, sniff or snort; after too many pharmaceuticals or too long a run, people can lapse into delirium. It is a short-term mental state characterized by confusion and disorientation. Most people have been there. Dementia resembles delirium in the same way an ultra-marathon resembles a dash across the street. Same basic components, vastly different scale. If you've run delirium's course once or twice in your life, try to imagine a version that never ends.

In May of 1989, six months after becoming ill, I was examined by Muriel Lezak, associate professor of neurology and psychiatry at Oregon Health Sciences University. Dr. Lezak, acclaimed author of the 1983 Oxford University Press textbook, *Neuropsychological Assessment,* conducted exhaustive tests with an empathy and tenderness that moved me to tears. She found extensive problems in my ability to learn and remember, a tendency toward slowed processing, fragmented visual recall and an overall "difficulty in keeping track of ongoing mental activity." To her, I appeared lost within the thickets of my own thought processes. My responses struck her as "very fragmented into bits" and these bits "were scattered rather helter-skelter as [if I] had seemingly lost sight of the original overall plan," all suggestive of a "significant visual learning deficit." I could not put things together, could not make sense of what I saw. She found that I had "great difficulty in organizing and synthesizing visual material when the burden of making structure" was upon me. She summed up our session up by saying, "Mr. Skloot no longer is automatically accurate in handling basic arithmetic or writing tasks, as one might suspect he normally would be."

You never dream of hearing such things said about you. But dementia is a biological catastrophe whose essence is intellectual diminishment, and I had diminished all right. Big-time. My IQ was down about 15%. Unable to exercise, metabolism gone haywire, my body weight was up almost as much. I was, in many ways, so unrecognizable to myself that I dreaded looking in the mirror, confusing what was happening inside my head with what might show itself outside. People kept saying I looked good. The hard edge from rigorous training for marathon running and long-distance racing was gone; I looked softer, which apparently was not a bad thing. I *was* softer. I was also slower. I felt denser, tamped down, compacted. I lived with greater stillness; I had time, had an emptiness where there had always been fullness—of mind, of purpose, of agenda. I had so few defenses against the world—not only because my immune system was scrambled, but because I found myself more emotionally open—that I felt utterly exposed.

A process had begun that required me to redefine myself, to construct a new sense of who I was and how I dealt with the world as an intellectual shadow of my former self. It would be years before I could make much headway. Fortunately, my dementia does not appear to be progressive; at least it has not gotten worse over the last decade and is classified as static. I got where I was going fast, and have stayed there, as though beamed down.

Now I had an opportunity to reconfigure myself. At least that was one way to look at this. Becoming ill afforded me the chance to discover and align my emotional state with my new biological state.

The word *dementia* has its root in the Latin *dementare,* meaning "senseless." Yet I have found my senses heightened following the loss of intellectual force. My responsiveness to odor is so strong that sometimes I think I've become a beagle. Intensely spiced foods—Indian, Thai, Mexican—taste exaggerated in their richness; I can become exhausted and confused by eating these cuisines. My skin often tingles, sometimes for no discernible reason, sometimes in response to the slightest stimulus. The same process that stripped me of significant intellectual capacity and numbed my mind seems to have triggered a corresponding heightening of sensory and emotional awareness. Sometimes this can be a maelstrom, sometimes a baptismal immersion. Forced out of the mind, away from my customary cerebral mode of encounter, I have found myself dwelling more in the wilder realms of sense and emotion. Out of mind and into body, into heart. An altered state.

This is actually biology at work. Dementia is, after all, a symptom of organic brain damage. It is a condition, a disorder of the central nervous system, brought about in my case by a viral assault on brain tissue. When the assault wiped out certain intellectual processes it also affected emotional processes. I am not talking about compensatory or reactive emotional conditions; I mean the same virus zapped certain emotion-controlling neural tissue, transforming the way I felt and responded, loosening my controls.

It has not been customary to recognize the neurology of emotion. For centuries, at least since Descartes famously wrote, "I think, therefore I am," in his 1637 *Discourse on Method,* scientists have tended to focus their attention on the seemingly measurable mental processes of memory, thinking or language production. Emotions, on the other hand, were thought of primarily as distractions to mental activity, difficult to assess objectively, either from within or without.

But in the last two decades, neuroscientists have made it clear that, as John E. Dowling says, in *Creating Mind: How the Brain Works,* "feelings and emotions—fear, sadness, anger, anxiety, pleasure, hostility, and calmness—localize to certain brain regions." Dowling notes that "lesions in these areas can lead to profound changes in a person's emotional behavior and personality, as well as in the ability to manage one's life." This is what has happened to me.

Intelligence is only part of the story of human consciousness. The longer I dwell in this new, demented state, the more I think intelligence may not even be the most critical part. I have become aware of the way changes in my emotional experience intersect with changes in my intellectual experience to demand and create a fresh experience of being in the world, an encounter that feels spiritual in nature. I have been rewoven.

This concept of emotion turns Descartes upside down. It also gives a clue about where to turn within the wilderness of dementia. After all, when one way through the wilderness is blocked, survival dictates finding an alternative way. For me, since the softening of intellectual powers coincided with an intensification of emotional response, the way through this wilderness seemed obvious.

I noticed almost immediately after my illness began that my emotional condition was as altered as my intellectual condition. It was apparent in small, everyday experiences that had never touched me deeply before, such as being moved to tears by seeing an outfielder make a diving catch, hearing the opening chords of a favorite nocturne, feeling the first spring breezes on my skin as I stood on the porch, observing my dog's yawn or finding a grapefruit in the refrigerator, neatly sectioned by my wife and wrapped in plastic for my breakfast. I could also erupt in tears over the least frustration—trying without success to decipher a menu, to replenish the lead in a pencil, to operate a new boom box. It was apparent as well in the emotional upheaval that accompanies chronic illness, with its attendant loss of companionship and livelihood, freedom and diversion. I would look out my window, see joggers clomp by and, unable to run myself as I used to every day, be filled with a despair I once would have suppressed. Although I had nothing but time on my hands, the least delay in a bank or doctor's office would irritate me beyond all rationality. The gift of a portable phone from my former colleagues, with a note saying they hoped it would let them talk with me more often, shattered me with joy. Sometimes the emotional upwelling was embarrassing, as when the opening chords of the overture to *The King and I* sent me into a torrent of ecstatic tears. The arrival of two acceptances of my poems from literary magazines also broke me up. I was turning into a sentimental slob.

This was not merely a matter of being victimized by emotional storms. There was also disinhibition, a new freedom to express the sentiments I was feeling. At first I was swamped with ungovernable emotions, but soon learned to swim within them, even to surf upon them. My relationship with my daughter deepened. Love and passion entered my life for the first time in decades. My brother's advancing terminal illness, which took his life in the summer of 1997, was something I could face openly with him after years of estrangement, spending time in his presence, crying with him, finding for the first time in decades the possibility of sharing the warmth we felt for each other.

Losses in my intellectual capacities are clear and measurable, the kind of losses that can be evaluated and scored. Changes in my emotional life seem every bit as great. But, perhaps in part because my form of dementia is not as grave as that of Alzheimer's sufferers, these changes offer a counterbalance to my mental losses. I feel differently, but in many ways I feel more fully, more richly. It is as though I have been given an area of psychological life in which to compensate for what is missing.

In the spring of 1993, I married Beverly and moved to the woods. This is something I could never have imagined myself doing. In fact, it is the opposite of what I thought was needed after getting sick. Logic dictated that I stay in the center of things, close to friends, doctors, services and entertainment. I should live where anything I might need was within walking distance. To do otherwise, I reasoned, would be to further isolate myself, and illness had isolated me enough already. It never occurred to me that city life could have a deleterious effect on chronic illness, or that it represented a clinging to old ways, or that the time had come to consider a new way of living, since brain damage had changed so much about me.

I believed in the importance of staying connected to the city, even though my intuition was urging me elsewhere. For instance, the first act of independence I had performed, about eight months after getting sick, was to spend a week alone at the Oregon coast in a small room overlooking the sea. The motel was called The Ocean Locomotion, though stillness was its primary attraction. I could walk the hundred yards from my room to a colossal piece of driftwood shaped like a davenport, plunked just beyond the tide line, and watch the breakers, the zany behavior of gulls, or the sunset. Occasionally a ship would drift across the horizon. At the time, I could not have rationally explained why it felt vital for me to leave the city and be alone in nature. But I was drawn there and knew that being away from the city was good for me. Back in Portland, I lived for a year in an urban townhouse close to the Willamette River and spent several hours every day sitting or walking on its bank, pulled there, trying always to find more and more deserted sites. Still, I remained in the city till 1993.

By then Beverly had entered my life. I knew that in 1989 she had purchased twenty acres of hilly forest land in rural western Oregon, built a small, round house in the middle of the site, and had been living there by herself ever since. In time, she took me to see it.

The place, located two miles outside a small town of 1,100 and fifty miles from the nearest urban center, is so isolated that the closest neighbor is over a quarter of a mile away, and that neighbor is a vintner who does not even live on the winery property. The land is officially a tree farm, its rocky and irregular acreage filled with Douglas fir, oak, maple, the occasional wild cherry. Beverly left it rough and harvests nothing. The landscape is laced with blackberry vines, wild rose, hazel and poison oak, and what has been cleared for gardens is under continual assault from what remains wild. A winter creek cuts through the middle and during its months of loud life there is also a lovely view south into the Eola Valley through naked trees. Some mornings mist rises from the valley floor, climbs the hillside, blankets the house for a while and then leaves a blazing sky behind, the whole show like a short drama entitled Hope. Some mornings cattle and horses call from the small farms at the base of the hill; once a llama that had gotten loose found its way up to the house, trailed by a massive billy goat with one broken, off-center horn.

I learned that nothing here obeys the rules imposed on it. The ground is hard, basaltic, unforgiving. Beverly dug out a small pond, working her pick and shovel like a convict, lined the hole with plastic and filled it with water plants that the deer ate almost before she could get back inside the house and clean off. They stepped through the plastic liner in their zeal, so she replaced it with a smaller, pre-formed pond liner and the deer now use it as their personal drinking fountain. She allowed a friend from work to keep bees in a small grove for a season or two, but the hive failed and now there are only wild bees on the premises. This is a place that does not tame, that fights back at efforts to diminish it.

When we discussed the possibility of my joining her, the idea of living in the country was appealing to me for several wrong reasons. A lifelong urbanite, I was born in Brooklyn, New York, raised there and on Long Island and have spent much of my life in cities. Not just in cities, but in apartments. At the time Beverly and I began to be together, I was living in a new apartment building downtown, right in the middle of Portland's hubbub, walking distance from the bookstores, theater, concert hall, artsy cinema, restaurants, the Safeway. For nature, I had the Willamette, two blocks to the east, so polluted that the Environmental Protection Agency keeps threatening to add it to the Superfund cleanup list.

I still equated the city with self-sufficiency. But after spending a few weekends at Beverly's place in the woods, I began to consider escaping the frenzy, fleeing the noise and congestion. It would always be difficult for me to think clearly, but being surrounded by urban commotion made it worse. I felt scattered. I had come to see that it was impossible to truly slow down in the city. It was impossible to find harmony between my surroundings and my newly diminished self, reined-in, slowed down, isolated from the worlds of work, running and community that I had always lived in. There was too much stimulation, too much outer life for a person in my situation. I had nothing but time on my hands, yet was living where time seemed accelerated. I needed an emptier place, pared down, humbler: a home that fit my circumstances.

But of course, rural life is hardly empty. My isolated, quiet, dull, out-of-the-way home of the last half-decade is actually teeming with life. It offers life in its immediacy, to be experienced without the mediation of thought or explanation, and gives time to contemplate. You don't need to be quick, just open and responsive, to get what this hill is about. Dwindling well water, the delicate system by which electricity is delivered to us, the boundaries established for herbs or flowers or vegetables—the human imprint is fragile and contingent. Yesterday as I was writing this very paragraph, the power went out in a gust of wind and took along my thoughts. It takes rigor and flexibility to hold on, a dedication of soul, but the rewards are worth it. I had seen *myself* as dulled and emptied too, so it has been instructive to be reminded of how much life goes on beneath surfaces that appear quiet.

One spring night shortly before we got married, Beverly and I dragged her mattress outside and hauled it onto a platform made from a couple of chaise lounges. We protected ourselves with an altar of citronella candles and a down comforter, and prepared to spend a night under the stars. This was a first for me. Nice and peaceful, arm around my sweetheart, gazing up at the constellations, impressed by how much I could see. Then the action began. Bats swooped to catch the bugs. Owls started calling. I could hear deer moving through the woods just to the east of us, frogs in the pond. A skunk sashayed underneath our chaises and headed toward the compost pile. My first response was the fear of a city boy stalked, then laughter and soon a joy so vast that I felt caressed by it.

There are some days, when Beverly is at work and I am here alone, that I do not speak aloud at all during the daylight hours. Yet I am not restless or bored, don't yearn for the city, and this is not an exile. Till I got here, gave up my city home and began learning how to be in these woods, I did not really understand how much I needed to live like this. Functioning now at a more appropriate tempo, looking closely at the world I live in because there is not much else to do, I understand more about what has happened to me.

When the coastal wind blows hard through the trees and I see them swaying, I lose my balance, even in bed, because the damage to my brain has affected the system by which I hold myself in place. To retain balance is work for me. It requires a focus on what holds still. I need to stop thinking altogether to do it right. Seeing those trees every morning also reminds me that this is a land of second growth. The timber on much of our hill was harvested many years ago, and I live within the density of what grew back. It is a good place for me to live, a workshop in survival, in coming back from damage.

A person doesn't escape to a place like this. It's not exile; it's home.

I am not getting any better. But I am also not getting any worse. At fifty-two, after eleven years of living with static dementia, I have discovered just where that leaves me. Since I cannot presume that I will remember anything, I must live fully in the present. Since I cannot presume that I will understand anything, I must feel and experience my life in the moment and not always press to formulate ideas about it. Since I cannot escape my body and the limits it has imposed on me, I must learn to be at home in it. Since I can do so little, it is good to live in a place where there is so little to do. And since I cannot presume that I will master anything I do, I must relinquish mastery as a goal and seek harmony instead.

The short, grizzled guy living atop the Amity Hills looks like me and for the most part seems like me. He goes out in a storm to bring in a few logs for the wood stove; he uses the homemade privy balanced between a pair of oak when the power is out, which means the well cannot pump, which means the toilet cannot be used; he has learned to catch live mice in his gloved hands in his bedroom in the middle of the night and release them unharmed in the woods; he sits in an Adirondack chair reading while bees work the rosemary and hyssop nearby. He is my twin, all right, my demented self, wild in the woods, someone I did not know I had inside me.

Terry Tempest Williams

The Clan of One-Breasted Women

I belong to a Clan of One-Breasted Women. My mother, my grandmothers, and six aunts have all had mastectomies. Seven are dead. The two who survive have just completed rounds of chemotherapy and radiation.

I've had my own problems: two biopsies for breast cancer and a small tumor between my ribs diagnosed as a "borderline malignancy."

This is my family history.

Most statistics tell us breast cancer is genetic, hereditary, with rising percentages attached to fatty diets, childlessness, or becoming pregnant after thirty. What they don't say is living in Utah may be the greatest hazard of all.

We are a Mormon family with roots in Utah since 1847. The "word of wisdom" in my family aligned us with good foods—no coffee, no tea, tobacco, or alcohol. For the most part, our women were finished having their babies by the time they were thirty. And only one faced breast cancer prior to 1960. Traditionally, as a group of people, Mormons have a low rate of cancer.

Is our family a cultural anomaly? The truth is, we didn't think about it. Those who did, usually the men, simply said, "bad genes." The women's attitude was stoic. Cancer was part of life. On February 16, 1971, the eve of my mother's surgery, I accidentally picked up the telephone and overheard her ask my grandmother what she could expect.

"Diane, it is one of the most spiritual experiences you will ever encounter."

I quietly put down the receiver.

Two days later, my father took my brothers and me to the hospital to visit her. She met us in the lobby in a wheelchair. No bandages were visible. I'll never forget her radiance, the way she held herself in a purple velvet robe, and how she gathered us around her.

"Children, I am fine. I want you to know I felt the arms of God around me."

We believed her. My father cried. Our mother, his wife, was thirty-eight years old.

A little over a year after Mother's death, Dad and I were having dinner together. He had just returned from St. George, where the Tempest Company was completing the gas lines that would service southern Utah. He spoke of his love for the country, the sandstoned landscape, bare-boned and beautiful. He had just finished hiking the Kolob trail in Zion National Park. We got caught up in reminiscing, recalling with fondness our walk up Angel's Landing on his fiftieth birthday and the years our family had vacationed there.

Over dessert, I shared a recurring dream of mine. I told my father that for years, as long as I could remember, I saw this flash of light in the night in the desert—that this image had so permeated my being that I could not venture south without seeing it again, on the horizon, illuminating buttes and mesas.

"You did see it," he said.

"Saw what?"

"The bomb. The cloud. We were driving home from Riverside, California. You were sitting on Diane's lap. She was pregnant. In fact, I remember the day, September 7, 1957. We had just gotten out of the Service. We were driving north, past Las Vegas. It was an hour or so before dawn, when this explosion went off. We not only heard it, but felt it. I thought the oil tanker in front of us had blown up. We pulled over and suddenly, rising from the desert floor, we saw it, clearly, this golden-stemmed cloud, the mushroom. The sky seemed to vibrate with an eerie pink glow. Within a few minutes, a light ash was raining on the car."

I stared at my father.

"I thought you knew that," he said. "It was a common occurrence in the fifties."

It was at this moment that I realized the deceit I had been living under. Children growing up in the American Southwest, drinking contaminated milk from contaminated cows, even from the contaminated breasts of their mothers, my mother—members, years later, of the Clan of One-Breasted Women.

It is a well-known story in the Desert West, "The Day We Bombed Utah," or more accurately, the years we bombed Utah: above ground atomic testing in Nevada took place from January 27, 1951 through July 11, 1962. Not only were the winds blowing north covering "low-use segments of the population" with fallout and leaving sheep dead in their tracks, but the climate was right. The United States of the 1950s was red, white, and blue. The Korean War was raging. McCarthyism was rampant. Ike was it, and the cold war was hot. If you were against nuclear testing, you were for a communist regime.

Much has been written about this "American nuclear tragedy." Public health was secondary to national security. The Atomic Energy Commissioner, Thomas Murray, said, "Gentlemen, we must not let anything interfere with this series of tests, nothing."

Again and again, the American public was told by its government, in spite of burns, blisters, and nausea, "It has been found that the tests may be conducted with adequate assurance of safety under conditions prevailing at the bombing reservations." Assuaging public fears was simply a matter of public relations. "Your best action," an Atomic Energy Commission booklet read, "is not to be worried about fallout." A news release typical of the times stated, "We find no basis for concluding that harm to any individual has resulted from radioactive fallout."

On August 30, 1979, during Jimmy Carter's presidency, a suit was filed, *Irene Allen v. The United States of America*. Mrs. Allen's case was the first on an alphabetical list of twenty-four test cases, representative of nearly twelve hundred plaintiffs seeking compensation from the United States government for cancers caused by nuclear testing in Nevada.

Irene Allen lived in Hurricane, Utah. She was the mother of five children and had been widowed twice. Her first husband, with their two oldest boys, had watched the tests from the roof of the local high school. He died of leukemia in 1956. Her second husband died of pancreatic cancer in 1978.

In a town meeting conducted by Utah Senator Orrin Hatch, shortly before the suit was filed, Mrs. Allen said, "I am not blaming the government, I want you to know that, Senator Hatch. But I thought if my testimony could help in any way so this wouldn't happen again to any of the generations coming up after us . . . I am happy to be here this day to bear testimony of this."

God-fearing people. This is just one story in an anthology of thousands.

On May 10, 1984, Judge Bruce S. Jenkins handed down his opinion. Ten of the plaintiffs were awarded damages. It was the first time a federal court had determined that nuclear tests had been the cause of cancers. For the remaining fourteen test cases, the proof of causation was not sufficient. In spite of the split decision, it was considered a landmark ruling. It was not to remain so for long.

In April 1987, the Tenth Circuit Court of Appeals overturned Judge Jenkins's ruling on the ground that the United States was protected from suit by the legal doctrine of sovereign immunity, a centuries-old idea from England in the days of absolute monarchs.

In January 1988, the Supreme Court refused to review the Appeals Court decision. To our court system it does not matter whether the United States government was irresponsible, whether it lied to its citizens, or even that citizens died from the fallout of nuclear testing. What matters is that our government is immune: "The King can do no wrong."

In Mormon culture, authority is respected, obedience is revered, and independent thinking is not. I was taught as a young girl not to "make waves" or "rock the boat."

"Just let it go," Mother would say. "You know how you feel, that's what counts."

For many years, I have done just that—listened, observed, and quietly formed my own opinions, in a culture that rarely asks questions because it has all the answers. But one by one, I have watched the women in my family die common, heroic deaths. We sat in waiting rooms hoping for good news, but always receiving the bad. I cared for them, bathed their scarred bodies, and kept their secrets. I watched beautiful women become bald as Cytoxan, cisplatin, and Adriamycin were injected into their veins. I held their foreheads as they vomited green-black bile, and I shot them with morphine when the pain became inhuman. In the end, I witnessed their last peaceful breaths, becoming a midwife to the rebirth of their souls.

The price of obedience has become too high.

The fear and inability to question authority that ultimately killed rural communities in Utah during atmospheric testing of atomic weapons is the same fear I saw in my mother's body. Sheep. Dead sheep. The evidence is buried.

I cannot prove that my mother, Diane Dixon Tempest, or my grandmothers, Lettie Romney Dixon and Kathryn Blackett Tempest, along with my aunts developed cancer from nuclear fallout in Utah. But I can't prove they didn't.

My father's memory was correct. The September blast we drove through in 1957 was part of Operation Plumbbob, one of the most intensive series of bomb tests to be initiated. The flash of light in the night in the desert, which I had always thought was a dream, developed into a family nightmare. It took fourteen years, from 1957 to 1971, for cancer to manifest in my mother—the same time, Howard L. Andrews, an authority in radioactive fallout at the National Institutes of Health, says radiation cancer requires to become evident. The more I learn about what it means to be a "downwinder," the more questions I drown in.

What I do know, however, is that as a Mormon woman of the fifth generation of Latter-day Saints, I must question everything, even if it means losing my faith, even if it means becoming a member of a border tribe among my own people. Tolerating blind obedience in the name of patriotism or religion ultimately takes our lives.

When the Atomic Energy Commission described the country north of the Nevada Test Site as "virtually uninhabited desert terrain," my family and the birds at Great Salt Lake were some of the "virtual uninhabitants."

One night, I dreamed women from all over the world circled a blazing fire in the desert. They spoke of change, how they hold the moon in their bellies and wax and wane with its phases. They mocked the presumption of even-tempered beings and made promises that they would never fear the witch inside themselves. The women danced wildly as sparks broke away from the flames and entered the night sky as stars.

And they sang a song given to them by Shoshone grandmothers:

Ah ne nah, nah	Consider the rabbits
nin nah nah—	How gently they walk on the earth—
ah ne nah, nah	Consider the rabbits
nin nah nah—	How gently they walk on the earth—
Nyaga mutzi	We remember them
oh ne nay—	We can walk gently also—
Nyaga mutzi	We remember them
oh ne nay—	We can walk gently also—

The women danced and drummed and sang for weeks, preparing themselves for what was to come. They would reclaim the desert for the sake of their children, for the sake of the land.

A few miles downwind from the fire circle, bombs were being tested. Rabbits felt the tremors. Their soft leather pads on paws and feet recognized the shaking sands, while the roots of mesquite and sage were smoldering. Rocks were hot from the inside out and dust devils hummed unnaturally. And each time there was another nuclear test, ravens watched the desert heave. Stretch marks appeared. The land was losing its muscle.

The women couldn't bear it any longer. They were mothers. They had suffered labor pains but always under the promise of birth. The red hot pains beneath the desert promised death only, as each bomb became a stillborn. A contract had been made and broken between human beings and the land. A new contract was being drawn by the women, who understood the fate of the earth as their own.

Under the cover of darkness, ten women slipped under a barbed-wire fence and entered the contaminated country. They were trespassing. They walked toward the town of Mercury, in moonlight, taking their cues from coyote, kit fox, antelope squirrel, and quail. They moved quietly and deliberately through the maze of Joshua trees. When a hint of daylight appeared they rested, drinking tea and sharing their rations of food. The women closed their eyes. The time had come to protest with the heart, that to deny one's genealogy with the earth was to commit treason against one's soul.

At dawn, the women draped themselves in mylar, wrapping long streamers of silver plastic around their arms to blow in the breeze. They wore clear masks, that became the faces of humanity. And when they arrived at the edge of Mercury, they carried all the butterflies of a summer day in their wombs. They paused to allow their courage to settle.

The town that forbids pregnant women and children to enter because of radiation risks was asleep. The women moved through the streets as winged messengers, twirling around each other in slow motion, peeking inside homes and watching the easy sleep of men and women. They were astonished by each stillness and periodically would utter a shrill note or low cry just to verify life.

The residents finally awoke to these strange apparitions. Some simply stared. Others called authorities, and in time the women were apprehended by wary soldiers dressed in desert fatigues. They were taken to a white, square building on the other edge of Mercury. When asked who they were and why they were there, the women replied, "We are mothers and we have come to reclaim the desert for our children."

The soldiers arrested them. As the ten women were blindfolded and handcuffed, they began singing:

> You can't forbid us everything
> You can't forbid us to think—
> You can't forbid our tears to flow
> And you can't stop the songs that we sing.

The women continued to sing louder and louder, until they heard the voices of their sisters moving across the mess:

> *Ah ne nah, nah*
> *nin nah nah—*
> *Ah ne nah, nah*
> *nin nah nah—*
> *Nyaga mutzi*
> *oh ne nay—*
> *Nyaga mutzi*
> *oh ne nay—*

"Call for reinforcements," one soldier said.

"We have," interrupted one woman, "we have—and you have no idea of our numbers."

I crossed the line at the Nevada Test Site and was arrested with nine other Utahns for trespassing on military lands. They are still conducting nuclear tests in the desert. Ours was an act of civil disobedience. But as I walked toward the town of Mercury, it was more than a gesture of peace. It was a gesture on behalf of the Clan of One-Breasted Women.

As one officer cinched the handcuffs around my wrists, another frisked my body. She found a pen and a pad of paper tucked inside my left boot.

"And these?" she asked sternly.

"Weapons," I replied.

Our eyes met. I smiled. She pulled the leg of my trousers back over my boot.

"Step forward, please," she said as she took my arm.

We were booked under an afternoon sun and bused to Tonopah, Nevada. It was a two-hour ride. This was familiar country. The Joshua trees standing their ground had been named by my ancestors, who believed they looked like prophets pointing west to the Promised Land. These were the same trees that bloomed each spring, flowers appearing like white flames in the Mojave. And I recalled a full moon in May, when Mother and I had walked among them, flushing out mourning doves and owls.

The bus stopped short of town. We were released.

The officials thought it was a cruel joke to leave us stranded in the desert with no way to get home. What they didn't realize was that we were home, soul-centered and strong, women who recognized the sweet smell of sage as fuel for our spirits.

The "Eye"

Diane Ackerman

The Psychopharmacology of Chocolate

What food do you crave? Ask the question with enough smoldering emphasis on the last word, and the answer is bound to be chocolate. It was first used by the Indians of Central and South America. The Aztecs called it *xocoatl* ("chocolate"), declared it a gift from their white-bearded god of wisdom and knowledge, Quetzalcoatl, and served it as a drink to members of the court—only rulers and soldiers could be trusted with the power it conveyed. The Toltecs honored the divine drink by staging rituals in which they sacrificed chocolate-colored dogs. Itzá human-sacrifice victims were sometimes given a mug of chocolate to sanctify their journey. What Hernán Cortés found surrounding Montezuma was a society of chocolate worshipers who liked to perk up their drink with chili peppers, pimiento, vanilla beans, or spices, and serve it frothing and honey-thick in gold cups. To cure dysentery, they added the ground-up bones of their ancestors. Montezuma's court drank two thousand pitchers of chocolate each day, and he himself enjoyed a chocolate ice made by pouring the drink over snow brought to him by runners from the mountains. Impressed by the opulence and restorative powers of chocolate, Cortés introduced it to Spain in the sixteenth century. It hit the consciousness of Europe like a drug cult. Charles V decided to mix it with sugar, and those who could afford it drank it thick and cold; they, too, occasionally added orange, vanilla, or various spices. Brillat-Savarin reports that "The Spanish ladies of the New World are madly addicted to chocolate, to such a point that, not content to drink it several times each day, they even have it served to them in church." Today, chocolate-zombies haunt the streets of every city, dreaming all day of that small plunge of chocolate waiting for them on the way home from work. In Vienna, the richest chocolate cakes are decorated with edible gold leaf. More than once, I've been seriously tempted to fly to Paris for the afternoon, just to go to Angelina, a restaurant on the rue de Rivoli where they melt a whole chocolate bar into each cup of hot chocolate. How many candy bars *don't* contain chocolate? Chocolate, which began as an upper-class drink, has become déclassé, trendy, cloaked in a tackiness it doesn't deserve. For example, an ad in *Chocolatier Magazine* offers a one-quarter-pound chocolate "replica of a 5-1/4 inch floppy disk." In fact, the company can provide an entire "computer work-station comprised of a chocolate terminal, chocolate computer keyboard, chocolate chip and chocolate byte." Their slogan is "Boots up into your mouth, not in your disk drive." One September weekend in 1984, the Fontainbleau Hotel in Miami offered a Chocolate Festival Weekend, with special rates, menus, and events. People could fingerpaint in chocolate syrup, attend lectures on chocolate, sample chocolates from an array of companies, learn cooking techniques, or watch a TV actor be dunked in six hundred gallons of chocolate syrup. Five thousand people attended. Chocolate festivals rage in cities all across America, and there are highly popular chocolate tours in Europe. In Manhattan last month I heard one woman, borrowing the jargon of junkies, say to another, "Want to do some chocolate?"

Because chocolate is such an emotional food, one we eat when we're blue, jilted, premenstrual, or generally in need of TLC, scientists have been studying its chemistry. In 1982, two psychopharmacologists, Dr. Michael Liebowitz and Dr. Donald Klein, proposed an explanation for why lovesick people pig out on chocolate. In the course of their work with intense, thrill-seeking women who go into post-thrill depressions, they discovered that they all had something in common—in their depressed phase, virtually all of them ate large amounts of chocolate. They speculated that the phenomenon might well be related to the brain chemical phenylethylamine (PEA), which makes us feel the roller coaster of passion we associate with falling in love, an amphetaminelike rush. But when the rush of love ends, and the brain stops producing PEA, we continue to crave its natural high, its emotional speed. Where can one find lots of this luscious, love-arousing PEA? In chocolate. So it's possible that some people eat chocolate because it reproduces the sense of well-being we enjoy when we're in love. A sly beau once arrived at my apartment with three Droste chocolate apples, and every wedge I ate over the next two weeks, melting lusciously in my mouth, filled me with amorous thoughts of him.

Not everyone agrees with the PEA hypothesis. The Chocolate Manufacturer's Association argues that:

> the PEA content of chocolate is extremely small, especially in comparison with that of some other commonly consumed foods. The standard serving size of three and a half ounces of smoked salami contains 6.7 mg of phenylethylamine; the same size serving of cheddar cheese contains 5.8 mg of phenylethylamine. The standard 1.5-ounce serving of chocolate (the size of the average chocolate bar) contains much less than 1 mg (.21 mg). Obviously, if Dr. Liebowitz's theory were true, people would be eating salami and cheese in far greater amounts than they are today.

And Dr. Liebowitz himself, in *The Chemistry of Love,* later asked of chocolate craving:

> Could this be an attempt to raise their PEA levels? The problem is that PEA present in food is normally quickly broken down by our bodies, so that it doesn't even reach the blood, let alone the brain. To test the effect of ingesting PEA, researchers at the National Institute of Mental Health ate pounds of chocolate, and then measured the PEA levels in their urine for the next few days; the PEA levels didn't budge.

As a thoroughgoing chocoholic, I should say that I do indeed eat a lot of cheese. Smoked salami is too unhealthy for me even to consider; the Cancer Society has suggested that people should not eat foods that are smoked or contain nitrites. So, it's entirely possible that cheese fills some of my PEA need. What else do chocoholics eat? In other words, what is the total consumption of PEA from all sources? Chocolate may be a more appealing, even if smaller, source of PEA because of its other associations with luxury and reward. The NIMH study tested average people, but suppose people who crave chocolate aren't average? Isn't that the idea? Liebowitz now says that PEA may break down too fast to affect the brain. We still know very little about the arcane ways in which some drugs do this, not enough to completely dismiss chocolate's link with PEA.

Wurtman and others argue that we crave chocolate because it's a carbohydrate, which, like other carbohydrates, prompts the pancreas to make insulin, which ultimately leads to an increase in that neurotransmitter of calm, serotonin. If this were true, a plate of pasta, or potatoes, or bread would be equally satisfying. Chocolate also contains theobromine ("food of the gods"), a mild, caffeinelike substance, so, for the sake of argument, let's say it's just the serotonin and the relative of caffeine we crave, a calm stimulation, a culinary oxymoron few foods provide.* It might even explain why some women crave chocolate when they're due to menstruate, since women who suffer PMS have been found to have lower levels of serotonin, and premenstrual women in general eat 30 percent more carbohydrates than they do at other times of the month. But if it were as simple as that, a doughnut and a cup of coffee would do the trick. Furthermore, there's a world of difference between people who enjoy chocolate, women who crave chocolate only at certain times of the month, and serious chocoholics. Chocoholics don't crave potato chips and pasta; they crave chocolate. Substitutes in any combination won't do. Only the chocoholic in a household fresh out of chocolate, on a snowy night when the roads are impassable, knows how specific that craving can be. I'm not sure why some people crave chocolate, but I am convinced that it's a specific need, and therefore the key to solving a specific chemical mystery to which we'll one day find the solution.

The Four Seasons restaurant in Manhattan serves a chocolate bombe that's the explosive epitome of chocolate desserts, two slices of which (the standard serving) few people are able to finish because it's so piquantly rich. On the waterfront in St. Louis I once had a mousse called "Chocolate Suicide," which was drug-level chocolate. I felt as if my brain had been hung up in a smokehouse. I can still remember the first time I had Godiva chocolates at a friend's house; they were Godivas from the original factory in Brussels, with a perfect sheen, a twirling aroma, heady but not jarring, and a way of delicately melting on the tongue. One of the reasons why chocolates are superb in Belgium, Vienna, Paris, and some of our American cities is that chocolate candy is in considerable part a dairy product. The chocolate flavor may come from the plant, but the silken, melting delight comes from the milk, cream, and butter, which must be fresh. The people who create designer chocolates have learned that their confections must provide just the right melting sensation, and feel quintessentially creamy and luscious, with no grittiness or aftertaste, for people to be thoroughly wowed by them. In George Orwell's *1984,* sex is forbidden and chocolate is "dull-brown crumbly stuff that tasted . . . like the smoke of a rubbish fire." Just before Julia and Winston risk making love, they eat real, full-bodied "dark and shiny" chocolate. Their amorous feast had its precedents. Montezuma drank an extra cup of chocolate before he went to visit his women's quarters. Glamorous movie stars like Jean Harlow used to be shown eating boxes of chocolates. M. F. K. Fisher, the diva of gastronomy, once con-

---

* In a one-and-a-half-ounce milk-chocolate bar, there are about nine milligrams of caffeine (which the plant may use as an insecticide); a five-ounce cup of brewed coffee has about 115 milligrams; a twelve-ounce cola drink has between thirty-two and sixty-five.

fided that her mother's doctor prescribed chocolate as a cure for debilitating lovesickness. On the other hand, Aztec women were forbidden chocolate; what secret terror was it thought to unleash in them?

Atul Gawande

Final Cut

Your patient is dead; the family is gathered. And there is one last thing that you have to ask about: the autopsy. How should you go about it? You could do it offhandedly, as if it were the most ordinary thing in the world: "Shall we do an autopsy, then?" Or you could be firm, use your Sergeant Joe Friday voice: "Unless you have strong objections, we will need to do an autopsy, ma'am." Or you could take yourself out of it: "I am sorry, but they require me to ask, Do you want an autopsy done?"

What you can't be nowadays is mealymouthed about it. I once took care of a woman in her eighties who had given up her driver's license only to get hit by a car—driven by someone even older—while she was walking to a bus stop. She sustained a depressed skull fracture and cerebral bleeding, and, despite surgery, she died a few days later. So, on the spring afternoon after the patient took her last breath, I stood beside her and bowed my head with the tearful family. Then, as delicately as I could—not even using the awful word—I said, "If it's all right, we'd like to do an examination to confirm the cause of death."

"An *autopsy?*" a nephew said, horrified. He looked at me as if I were a buzzard circling his aunt's body. "Hasn't she been through enough?"

The autopsy is in a precarious state these days. A generation ago, it was routine; now it has become a rarity. Human beings have never quite become comfortable with the idea of having their bodies cut open after they die. Even for a surgeon, the sense of violation is inescapable.

Not long ago, I went to observe the dissection of a thirty-eight-year-old woman I had taken care of who had died after a long struggle with heart disease. The dissecting room was in the sub-basement, past the laundry and a loading dock, behind an unmarked metal door. It had high ceilings, peeling paint, and a brown tiled floor that sloped down to a central drain. There was a Bunsen burner on a countertop, and an old-style grocer's hanging scale, with a big clock-face red-arrow gauge and a pan underneath, for weighing organs. On shelves all around the room there were gray portions of brain, bowel, and other organs soaking in formalin in Tupperware-like containers. The facility seemed run-down, chintzy, low-tech. On a rickety gurney in the corner was my patient, sprawled out, completely naked. The autopsy team was just beginning its work.

Surgical procedures can be grisly, but dissections are somehow worse. In even the most gruesome operations—skin grafting, amputations—surgeons maintain some tenderness and aestheticism toward their work. We know that the bodies we cut still pulse with life, and that these are people who will wake again. But in the dissecting room, where the person is gone and only the shell remains, you naturally find little delicacy, and the difference is visible in the smallest details. There is, for example, the simple matter of how a body is moved from gurney to table. In the operating room, we follow a careful, elaborate procedure for the unconscious patient, involving a canvas-sleeved rolling board and several gentle movements. We don't want so much as a bruise. Down here, by contrast, someone grabbed my patient's arm, another person a leg, and they just yanked. When her skin stuck to the stainless-steel dissecting table, they had to wet her and the table down with a hose before they could pull her the rest of the way.

The young pathologist for the case stood on the sidelines and let a pathology assistant take the knife. Like many of her colleagues, the pathologist had not been drawn to her field by autopsies but by the high-tech detective work that she got to do on tissue from living patients. She was happy to leave the dissection to the assistant, who had more experience at it anyway.

The assistant was a tall, slender woman of around thirty with straight sandy-brown hair. She was wearing the full protective garb of mask, face shield, gloves, and blue plastic gown. Once the body was on the table, she placed a six-inch metal block under the back, between the shoulder blades, so that the head fell back and the chest arched up. Then she took a scalpel in her hand, a big No. 6 blade, and made a huge Y-shaped incision that came down diagonally from each shoulder, curving slightly around each breast before reaching the midline, and then continued down the abdomen to the pubis.

Surgeons get used to the opening of bodies. It is easy to detach yourself from the person on the table and become absorbed by the details of method and anatomy. Nevertheless, I couldn't help wincing as she did her work: she was holding the scalpel like a pen, which forced her to cut slowly and jaggedly with the tip of the blade. Surgeons are taught to stand straight and parallel to their incision, hold the knife between the thumb and four fingers, like a violin bow, and draw the belly of the blade through the skin in a single, smooth slice to the exact depth desired. The assistant was practically sawing her way through my patient.

From there, the evisceration was swift. The assistant flayed back the skin flaps. With an electric saw, she cut through the exposed ribs along both sides. Then she lifted the rib cage as if it were the hood of a car, opened the abdomen, and removed all the major organs—including the heart, the lungs, the liver, the bowels, and the kidneys. Then the skull was sawed open, and the brain, too, was removed. Meanwhile, the pathologist was at a back table, weighing and examining everything, and preparing samples for microscopy and thorough testing.

For all this, however, I had to admit: the patient came out looking remarkably undisturbed. The assistant had followed the usual procedure and kept the skull incision behind the woman's ears, where it was completely hidden by her hair. She had also taken care to close the chest and abdomen neatly, sewing the incision tight with weaved seven-cord thread. My patient seemed much the same as before, except now a little collapsed in the middle. (The standard consent allows the hospital to keep the organs for testing and research. This common and long-established practice has caused huge controversy in Britain—the media have branded it "organ stripping"—but in America it remains generally accepted.) Most families, in fact, still have open-casket funerals after autopsies. Morticians employ fillers to restore a corpse's shape, and when they're done you cannot tell that an autopsy has been performed.

Still, when it is time to ask for a family's permission to do such a thing, the images weigh on everyone's mind—not least the doctor's. You strive to achieve a cool, dispassionate attitude toward these matters. But doubts nevertheless creep in.

One of the first patients for whom I was expected to request an autopsy was a seventy-five-year-old retired New England doctor who died one winter night while I was with him. Herodotus Sykes (not his real name, but not unlike it, either) had been rushed to the hospital with an infected, rupturing abdominal aortic aneurysm and taken to emergency surgery. He survived it, and recovered steadily until, eighteen days later, his blood pressure dropped alarmingly and blood began to pour from a drainage tube in his abdomen. "The aortic stump must have blown out," his surgeon said. Residual infection must have weakened the suture line where the infected aorta had been removed. We could have operated again, but the patient's chances were poor, and his surgeon didn't think he would be willing to take any more.

He was right. No more surgery, Sykes told me. He'd been through enough. We called Mrs. Sykes, who was staying with a friend about two hours away, and she set out for the hospital.

It was about midnight. I sat with him as he lay silent and bleeding, his arms slack at his sides, his eyes without fear. I imagined his wife out on the Mass Pike, frantic, helpless, with six lanes, virtually empty at that hour, stretching far ahead.

Sykes held on, and at 2:15 A.M. his wife arrived. She turned ashen at the sight of him, but she steadied herself. She gently took his hand in hers. She squeezed, and he squeezed back. I left them to themselves.

At 2:45, the nurse called me in. I listened with my stethoscope, then turned to Mrs. Sykes and told her that he was gone. She had her husband's Yankee reserve, but she broke into quiet tears, weeping into her hands, and seemed suddenly frail and small. A friend who had come with her soon appeared, took her by the arm, and led her out of the room.

We are instructed to request an autopsy on everyone as a means of confirming the cause of death and catching our mistakes. And this was the moment I was supposed to ask—with the wife despondent and reeling with shock. But surely, I began to think, here was a case in which an autopsy would be pointless. We knew what had happened—a persistent infection, a rupture. We were sure of it. What would cutting the man apart accomplish?

And so I let Mrs. Sykes go. I could have caught her as she walked through the ICU's double doors. Or even called her on the phone later. But I never did.

Such reasoning, it appears, has become commonplace in medicine. Doctors are seeking so few autopsies that in recent years the *Journal of the American Medical Association* has twice felt the need to declare "war on the nonautopsy." According to the most recent statistics available, autopsies have been done in fewer than 10 percent of deaths; many hospitals do none. This is a dramatic turnabout. Through much of the twentieth century, doctors diligently obtained autopsies in the majority of all deaths—and it had taken centuries to reach this point. As Kenneth Iserson recounts in his fascinating almanac, *Death to Dust,* physicians have performed autopsies for more than two thousand years. But for most of history they were rarely performed. If religions permitted them at all—Islam, Shinto, orthodox Judaism, and the Greek Orthodox Church still frown on them—it was generally only for legal purposes. The Roman physician Antistius performed one of the earliest forensic examinations on record, in 44 B.C., on Julius Caesar, documenting twenty-three wounds, including a final, fatal stab to the chest. In 1410, the Catholic Church itself ordered an autopsy—on Pope Alexander V, to determine whether his successor had poisoned him. No evidence of this was apparently found.

The first documented postmortem examination in the New World was actually done for religious reasons, though. It was performed on July 19, 1533, on the island of Española (now the Dominican Republic), upon conjoined female twins connected at the lower chest, to determine if they had one soul or two. The twins had been born alive, and a priest had baptized them as two separate souls. A disagreement subsequently ensued about whether he was right to have done so, and when the "double monster" died at eight days of age an autopsy was ordered to settle the issue. A surgeon, one Johan Camacho, found two virtually complete sets of internal organs, and it was decided that two souls had lived and died.

Even in the nineteenth century, however, long after church strictures had loosened, people in the West seldom allowed doctors to autopsy their family members for medical purposes. As a result, the practice was largely clandestine. Some doctors went ahead and autopsied hospital patients immediately after death, before relatives could turn up to object. Others waited until burial and then robbed the graves, either personally or through accomplices, an activity that continued into the twentieth century. To deter such autopsies, some families would post nighttime guards at the grave site—hence the term "graveyard shift." Others placed heavy stones on the coffins. In 1878, one company in Columbus, Ohio, even sold "torpedo coffins," equipped with pipe bombs rigged to blow up if they were tampered with. Yet doctors remained undeterred. Ambrose Bierce's *The Devil's Dictionary,* published in 1906, defined "grave" as "a place in which the dead are laid to await the coming of the medical student."

By the turn of the twentieth century, however, prominent physicians such as Rudolf Virchow in Berlin, Karl Rokitansky in Vienna, and William Osler in Baltimore began to win popular support for the practice of autopsy. They defended it as a tool of discovery, one that had already been used to identify the cause of tuberculosis, reveal how to treat appendicitis, and establish the existence of Alzheimer's disease. They also showed that autopsies prevented errors—that without them doctors could not know when their diagnoses were incorrect. Moreover, most deaths were a mystery then, and perhaps what clinched the argument was the notion that autopsies could provide families with answers—give the story of a loved one's life a comprehensible ending. Once doctors had insured a dignified and respectful dissection at the hospital, public opinion turned. With time, doctors who did *not* obtain autopsies were viewed with suspicion. By the end of the Second World War, the autopsy was firmly established as a routine part of death in Europe and North America.

So what accounts for its decline? In truth, it's not because families refuse—to judge from recent studies, they still grant that permission up to 80 percent of the time. Instead, doctors, once so eager to perform autopsies that they stole bodies, have simply stopped asking. Some people ascribe this to shady motives. It has been said that hospitals are trying to save money by avoiding autopsies, since insurers don't pay for them, or that doctors avoid them in order to cover up evidence of malpractice. And yet autopsies lost money and uncovered malpractice when they were popular, too.

Instead, I suspect, what discourages autopsies is medicine's twenty-first-century, tall-in-the-saddle confidence. When I failed to ask Mrs. Sykes whether we could autopsy her husband, it was not because of the expense, or because I feared that the autopsy would uncover an error. It was the opposite: I didn't see much likelihood that an error would be found. Today, we have MRI scans, ultrasound, nuclear medicine, molecular testing, and much more. When somebody dies, we already know why. We don't need an autopsy to find out.

Or so I thought. Then I had a patient who changed my mind.

He was in his sixties, whiskered and cheerful, a former engineer who had found success in retirement as an artist. I will call him Mr. Jolly, because that's what he was. He was also what we call a vasculopath—he did not seem to have an undiseased artery in him. Whether because of his diet or his genes or the fact that he used to smoke, he had had, in the previous decade, one heart attack, two abdominal aortic aneurysm repairs, four bypass operations to keep blood flowing past blockages in his leg arteries, and several balloon procedures to keep hardened arteries open. Still, I never knew him to take a dark view of his lot. "Well, you can't get miserable about it," he'd say. He had wonderful children. He had beautiful grandchildren. "But, aargh, the wife," he'd go on. She would be sitting right there at the bedside and would roll her eyes, and he'd break into a grin.

Mr. Jolly had come into the hospital for treatment of a wound infection in his legs. But he soon developed congestive heart failure, causing fluid to back up into his lungs. Breathing became steadily harder for him, until we had to put him in the ICU, intubate him, and place him on a ventilator. A two-day admission turned into two weeks. With a regimen of diuretics and a change in heart medications, however, his heart failure reversed, and his lungs recovered. And one bright Sunday morning he was reclining in bed, breathing on his own, watching the morning shows on the TV set that hung from the ceiling. "You're doing marvelously," I said. I told him we would transfer him out of intensive care by the afternoon. He would probably be home in a couple of days.

Two hours later, a code-blue emergency call went out on the overhead speakers. When I got to the ICU and saw the nurse hunched over Mr. Jolly, doing chest compressions, I blurted out an angry curse. He'd been fine, the nurse explained, just watching TV, when suddenly he sat upright with a look of shock and then fell back, unresponsive. At first, he was asystolic—no heart rhythm on the monitor—and then the rhythm came back, but he had no pulse. A crowd of staffers set to work. I had him intubated, gave him fluids and epinephrine, had someone call the attending surgeon at home, someone else check the morning lab test results. An X-ray technician shot a portable chest film.

I mentally ran through possible causes. There were not many. A collapsed lung, but I heard good breath sounds with my stethoscope, and when his X-ray came back the lungs looked fine. A massive blood loss, but his abdomen wasn't swelling, and his decline happened so quickly that bleeding just didn't make sense. Extreme acidity of the blood could do it, but his lab tests were fine. Then there was cardiac tamponade—bleeding into the sac that contains the heart. I took a six-inch spinal needle on a syringe, pushed it through the skin below the breastbone, and advanced it to the heart sac. I found no bleeding. That left only one possibility: a pulmonary embolism—a blood clot that flips into the lung and instantly wedges off all blood flow. And nothing could be done about that.

I went out and spoke to the attending surgeon by phone and then to the chief resident, who had just arrived. An embolism was the only logical explanation, they agreed. I went back into the room and stopped the code. "Time of death: 10:23 A.M.," I announced. I phoned his wife at home, told her that things had taken a turn for the worse, and asked her to come in.

This shouldn't have happened; I was sure of it. I scanned the records for clues. Then I found one. In a lab test done the day before, the patient's clotting had seemed slow, which wasn't serious, but an ICU physician had decided to correct it with vitamin K. A frequent side effect of vitamin K is blood clots. I was furious. Giving the vitamin was completely unnecessary—just fixing a number on a lab test. Both the chief resident and I lit into the physician. We all but accused him of killing the patient.

When Mrs. Jolly arrived, we took her to a family room where it was quiet and calm. I could see from her face that she'd already surmised the worst. His heart had stopped suddenly, we told her, because of a pulmonary embolism. We said the medicines we gave him may have contributed to it. I took her in to see him and left her with him. After a while, she came out, her hands trembling and her face stained with tears. Then, remarkably, she thanked us. We had kept him for her all these years, she said. Maybe so, but neither of us felt any pride about what had just happened.

I asked her the required question. I told her that we wanted to perform an autopsy and needed her permission. We thought we already knew what had happened, but an autopsy would confirm it, I said. She considered my request for a moment. If an autopsy would help us, she finally said, then we could do it. I said, as I was supposed to, that it would. I wasn't sure I believed it.

I wasn't assigned to the operating room the following morning, so I went down to observe the autopsy. When I arrived, Mr. Jolly was already laid out on the dissecting table, his arms splayed, skin flayed back, chest exposed, abdomen open. I put on a gown, gloves, and a mask, and went up close. The assistant began buzzing through the ribs on the left side with the electric saw, and immediately blood started seeping out, as dark and viscous as crankcase oil. Puzzled, I helped him lift open the rib cage. The left side of the chest was full of blood. I felt along the pulmonary arteries for a hardened, embolized clot, but there was none. He hadn't had an embolism after all. We suctioned out three liters of blood, lifted the left lung, and the answer appeared before our eyes. The thoracic aorta was almost three times larger than it should have been, and there was an half-inch hole in it. The man had ruptured an aortic aneurysm and had bled to death almost instantly.

In the days afterward, I apologized to the physician I'd reamed out over the vitamin, and pondered how we had managed to miss the diagnosis. I looked through the patient's old X-rays and now saw a shadowy outline of what must have been his aneurysm. But none of us, not even the radiologists, had caught it. Even if we had caught it, we wouldn't have dared to do anything about it until weeks after treating his infection and heart failure, and that would have been too late. It disturbed me, however, to have felt so confident about what had happened that day and to have been so wrong.

The most perplexing thing was his final chest X-ray, the one we had taken during the code blue. With all that blood filling the chest, I should have seen at least a haze over the left side. But when I pulled the film out to look again, there was nothing.

How often do autopsies turn up a major misdiagnosis in the cause of death? I would have guessed this happened rarely, in 1 or 2 percent of cases at most. According to three studies done in 1998 and 1999, however, the figure is about 40 percent. A large review of autopsy studies concluded that in about a third of the misdiagnoses the patients would have been expected to live if proper treatment had been administered. George Lundberg, a pathologist and former editor of the *Journal of the American Medical Association,* has done more than anyone to call attention to these figures. He points out the most surprising fact of all: the rates at which misdiagnosis is detected in autopsy studies have not improved since at least 1938.

With all the recent advances in imaging and diagnostics, it's hard to accept that we not only get the diagnosis wrong in two out of five of our patients who die but that we have also failed to improve over time. To see if this could really be true, doctors at Harvard put together a simple study. They went back into their hospital records to see how often autopsies picked up missed diagnoses in 1960 and 1970, before the advent of CT, ultrasound, nuclear scanning, and other technologies, and then in 1980, after those technologies became widely used. The researchers found no improvement. Regardless of the decade, physicians missed a quarter of fatal infections, a third of heart attacks, and almost two-thirds of pulmonary emboli in their patients who died.

In most cases, it wasn't technology that failed. Rather, the physicians did not consider the correct diagnosis in the first place. The perfect test or scan may have been available, but the physicians never ordered it.

In a 1976 essay, the philosophers Samuel Gorovitz and Alasdair MacIntyre explored the nature of fallibility. Why would a meteorologist, say, fail to correctly predict where a hurricane was going to make landfall? They saw three possible reasons. One was ignorance: perhaps science affords only a limited understanding of how hurricanes behave. A second reason was ineptitude: the knowledge is available, but the weatherman fails to apply it correctly. Both of these are surmountable sources of error. We believe that science will overcome ignorance, and that training and technology will overcome ineptitude. The third possible cause of error the philosophers posited, however, was an insurmountable kind, one they termed "necessary fallibility."

There may be some kinds of knowledge that science and technology will never deliver, Gorovitz and MacIntyre argued. When we ask science to move beyond explaining how things (say, hurricanes) generally behave to predicting exactly how a particular thing (say, Thursday's storm off the South Carolina coast) will behave, we may be asking it to do more than it can. No hurricane is quite like any other hurricane. Although all hurricanes follow predictable laws of behavior, each one is continuously shaped by myriad uncontrollable, accidental factors in the environment. To say precisely how one specific hurricane will behave would require a complete understanding of the world in all its particulars—in other words, omniscience.

It's not that it's impossible to predict anything; plenty of things are completely predictable. Gorovitz and MacIntyre give the example of a random ice cube in a fire. Ice cubes are so simple and so alike that you can predict with complete assurance that an ice cube will melt. But when it comes to inferring exactly what is going on in a particular person, are people more like ice cubes or like hurricanes?

Right now, at about midnight, I am seeing a patient in the emergency room, and I want to say that she is an ice cube. That is, I believe I can understand what's going on with her, that I can discern all her relevant properties. I believe I can help her.

Charlotte Duveen, as we will call her, is forty-nine years old, and for two days she has had abdominal pain. I begin observing her from the moment I walk through the curtains into her room. She is sitting cross-legged in the chair next to her stretcher and greets me with a cheerful, tobacco-beaten voice. She does not look sick. No clutching the belly. No gasping for words. Her color is good—neither flushed nor pale. Her shoulder-length brown hair has been brushed, her red lipstick neatly applied.

She tells me the pain started out crampy, like a gas pain. But then, during the course of the day, it became sharp and focused, and as she says this she points to a spot in the lower right part of her abdomen. She has developed diarrhea. She constantly feels as if she has to urinate. She doesn't have a fever. She is not nauseated. Actually, she is hungry. She tells me that she ate a hot dog at Fenway Park two days ago and visited the exotic birds at the zoo a few days before that, and she asks if either might have anything to do with this. She has two grown children. Her last period was three months ago. She smokes half a pack a day. She used to use heroin but says she's clean now. She once had hepatitis. She has never had surgery.

I feel her abdomen. It could be anything, I think: food poisoning, a virus, appendicitis, a urinary-tract infection, an ovarian cyst, a pregnancy. Her abdomen is soft, without disten-sion, and there is an area of particular tenderness in the lower right quadrant. When I press there, I feel her muscles harden reflexively beneath my fingers. On the pelvic exam, her ovaries feel normal. I order some lab tests. Her white blood cell count comes back elevated. Her urinalysis is normal. A pregnancy test is negative. I order an abdominal CT scan.

I am sure I can figure out what's wrong with her, but, if you think about it, that's a curious faith. I have never seen this woman before in my life, and yet I presume that she is like the others I've examined. Is it true? None of my other patients, admittedly, were forty-nine-year-old women who had had hepatitis and a drug habit, had recently been to the zoo and eaten a Fenway frank, and had come in with two days of mild lower-right-quadrant pain. Yet I still believe. Every day, we take people to surgery and open their abdomens, and, broadly speaking, we know what we will find: not eels or tiny chattering machines or a pool of blue liquid but coils of bowel, a liver to one side, a stomach to the other, a blad-der down below. There are, of course, differences—an adhesion in one patient, an infec-tion in another—but we have catalogued and sorted them by the thousands, making a statistical profile of mankind.

I am leaning toward appendicitis. The pain is in the right place. The timing of her symptoms, her exam, and her white blood cell count all fit with what I've seen before. She's hungry, however; she's walking around, not looking sick, and this seems unusual. I go to the radiology reading room and stand in the dark, looking over the radiologist's shoulder at the images of Duveen's abdomen flashing up on the monitor. He points to the appendix, wormlike, thick, surrounded by gray, streaky fat. It's appendicitis, he says confi-dently. I call the attending surgeon on duty and tell him what we've found. "Book the OR," he says. We're going to do an appendectomy.

 This one is as sure as we get. Yet I've worked on similar cases in which we opened the patient up and found a normal appendix. Surgery itself is a kind of autopsy. "Autopsy" lit-erally means "to see for oneself," and, despite our knowledge and technology, when we look we're often unprepared for what we find. Sometimes it turns out that we had missed a clue along the way, made a genuine mistake. Sometimes we turn out wrong despite doing everything right.

Whether with living patients or dead, however, we cannot know until we look. Even in the case of Mr. Sykes, I now wonder whether we put our stitches in correctly, or whether the bleeding had come from somewhere else entirely. Doctors are no longer asking such questions. Equally troubling, people seem happy to let us off the hook. In 1995, the United States National Center for Health Statistics stopped collecting autopsy statistics altogether. We can no longer even say how rare autopsies have become.

From what I've learned looking inside people, I've decided human beings are somewhere between a hurricane and an ice cube: in some respects, permanently mysterious, but in others—with enough science and careful probing—entirely scrutable. It would be as foolish to think we have reached the limits of human knowledge as it is to think we could ever know everything. There is still room enough to get better, to ask questions of even the dead, to learn from knowing when our simple certainties are wrong.

Stephen Jay Gould

A Biological Homage to Mickey Mouse

Age often turns fire to placidity. Lytton Strachey, in his incisive portrait of Florence Nightingale, writes of her declining years:

> Destiny, having waited very patiently, played a queer trick on Miss Nightingale. The benevolence and public spirit of that long life had only been equaled by its acerbity. Her virtue had dwelt in hardness. . . . And now the sarcastic years brought the proud woman her punishment. She was not to die as she had lived. The sting was to be taken out of her; she was to be made soft; she was to be reduced to compliance and complacency.

I was therefore not surprised—although the analogy may strike some people as sacrilegious—to discover that the creature who gave his name as a synonym for insipidity had a gutsier youth. Mickey Mouse turned a respectable fifty last year. To mark the occasion, many theaters replayed his debut performance in *Steamboat Willie* (1928). The original Mickey was a rambunctious, even slightly sadistic fellow. In a remarkable sequence, exploiting the exciting new development of sound, Mickey and Minnie pummel, squeeze, and twist the animals on board to produce a rousing chorus of "Turkey in the Straw." They honk a duck with a tight embrace, crank a goat's tail, tweak a pig's nipples, bang a cow's teeth as a stand-in xylophone, and play bagpipe on her udder.

Christopher Finch, in his semiofficial pictorial history of Disney's work, comments: "The Mickey Mouse who hit the movie houses in the late twenties was not quite the well-behaved character most of us are familiar with today. He was mischievous, to say the least, and even displayed a streak of cruelty." But Mickey soon cleaned up his act, leaving to gossip and speculation only his unresolved relationship with Minnie and the status of Morty and Ferdie. Finch continues: "Mickey . . . had become virtually a national symbol, and as such he was expected to behave properly at all times. If he occasionally stepped out of line, any number of letters would arrive at the Studio from citizens and organizations who

Mickey's evolution during 50 years (left to right). As Mickey became increasingly well behaved over the years, his appearance became more youthful. Measurements of three stages in his development revealed a larger relative head size, larger eyes, and an enlarged cranium—all traits of juvenility. *Source:* © Disney Enterprises, Inc.

felt that the nation's moral well-being was in their hands. . . . Eventually he would be pressured into the role of straight man."

As Mickey's personality softened, his appearance changed. Many Disney fans are aware of this transformation through time, but few (I suspect) have recognized the coordinating theme behind all the alterations—in fact, I am not sure that the Disney artists themselves explicitly realized what they were doing, since the changes appeared in such a halting and piecemeal fashion. In short, the blander and inoffensive Mickey became progressively more juvenile in appearance. (Since Mickey's chronological age never altered—like most cartoon characters he stands impervious to the ravages of time—this change in appearance at a constant age is a true evolutionary transformation. Progressive juvenilization as an evolutionary phenomenon is called neoteny. More on this later.)

The characteristic changes of form during human growth have inspired a substantial biological literature. Since the head-end of an embryo differentiates first and grows more rapidly in utero than the foot-end (an antero-posterior gradient, in technical language), a newborn child possesses a relatively large head attached to a medium-sized body with diminutive legs and feet. This gradient is reversed through growth as legs and feet overtake the front end. Heads continue to grow but so much more slowly than the rest of the body that relative head size decreases.

In addition, a suite of changes pervades the head itself during human growth. The brain grows very slowly after age three, and the bulbous cranium of a young child gives way to the more slanted, lower-browed configuration of adulthood. The eyes scarcely grow at all and relative eye size declines precipitously. But the jaw gets bigger and bigger. Children, compared with adults, have larger heads and eyes, smaller jaws, a more prominent, bulging cranium, and smaller, pudgier legs and feet. Adult heads are altogether more apish, I'm sorry to say.

Mickey, however, has traveled this ontogenetic pathway in reverse during his fifty years among us. He has assumed an ever more childlike appearance as the ratty character of *Steamboat Willie* became the cute and inoffensive host to a magic kingdom. By 1940, the former tweaker of pig's nipples gets a kick in the ass for insubordination (as the Sorcerer's Apprentice in *Fantasia*). By 1953, his last cartoon, he has gone fishing and cannot even subdue a squirming clam.

The Disney artists transformed Mickey in clever silence, often using suggestive devices that mimic nature's own changes by different routes. To give him the shorter and pudgier legs of youth, they lowered his pants line and covered his spindly legs with a baggy outfit. (His arms and legs also thickened substantially—and acquired joints for a floppier appearance.) His head grew relatively larger and its features more youthful. The length of Mickey's snout has not altered, but decreasing protrusion is more subtly suggested by a pronounced thickening. Mickey's eye has grown in two modes: first, by a major, discontinuous evolutionary shift as the entire eye of ancestral Mickey became the pupil of his descendants, and second, by gradual increase thereafter.

Mickey's improvement in cranial bulging followed an interesting path since his evolution has always been constrained by the unaltered convention of representing his head as a circle with appended ears and an oblong snout. The circle's form could not be altered to provide a bulging cranium directly. Instead, Mickey's ears moved back, increasing the distance between nose and ears, and giving him a rounded, rather than a sloping, forehead.

To give these observations the cachet of quantitative science, I applied my best pair of dial calipers to three stages of the official phylogeny—the thin-nosed, ears-forward figure of the early 1930s (stage 1), the later-day Jack of Mickey and the Beanstalk (1947, stage 2), and the modern mouse (stage 3). I measured three signs of Mickey's creeping juvenility: increasing eye size (maximum height) as a percentage of head length (base of the nose to top of rear ear); increasing head length as a percentage of body length; and increasing cranial vault size measured by rearward displacement of the front ear (base of the nose to top of front ear as a percentage of base of the nose to top of rear ear).

All three percentages increased steadily—eye size from 27 to 42 percent of head length; head length from 42.7 to 48.1 percent of body length; and nose to front ear from 71.7 to a whopping 95.6 percent of nose to rear ear. For comparison, I measured Mickey's young "nephew" Morty Mouse. In each case, Mickey has clearly been evolving toward youthful stages of his stock, although he still has a way to go for head length.

You may, indeed, now ask what an at least marginally respectable scientist has been doing with a mouse like that. In part, fiddling around and having fun, of course. (I still prefer *Pinocchio* to *Citizen Kane*.) But I do have a serious point—two, in fact—to make. We must first ask why Disney chose to change his most famous character so gradually and persistently in the same direction. National symbols are not altered capriciously and market researchers (for the doll industry in particular) have spent a good deal of time and practical effort learning what features appeal to people as cute and friendly. Biologists also have spent a great deal of time studying a similar subject in a wide range of animals.

In one of his most famous articles, Konrad Lorenz argues that humans use the characteristic differences in form between babies and adults as important behavioral cues. He believes that features of juvenility trigger "innate releasing mechanisms" for affection and nurturing in adult humans. When we see a living creature with babyish features, we feel an automatic surge of disarming tenderness. The adaptive value of this response can scarcely be questioned, for we must nurture our babies. Lorenz, by the way, lists among his releasers the very features of babyhood that Disney affixed progressively to Mickey: "a relatively large head, predominance of the brain capsule, large and low-lying eyes, bulging cheek region, short and thick extremities, a springy elastic consistency, and clumsy movements." (I propose to leave aside for this article the contentious issue of whether or not our affectionate response to babyish features is truly innate and inherited directly from ancestral

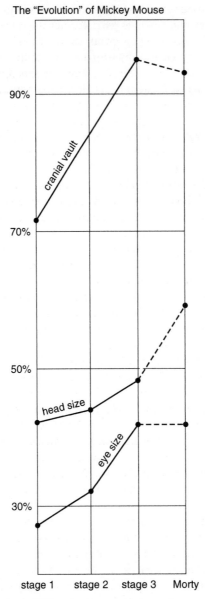

The "Evolution" of Mickey Mouse

At an early stage in his evolution, Mickey had a smaller head, cranial vault, and eyes. He evolved toward the characteristics of his young nephew Morty.

primates—as Lorenz argues—or whether it is simply learned from our immediate experience with babies and grafted upon an evolutionary predisposition for attaching ties of affection to certain learned signals. My argument works equally well in either case for I only claim that babyish features tend to elicit strong feelings of affection in adult humans, whether the biological basis be direct programming or the capacity to learn and fix upon signals. I also treat as collateral to my point the major thesis of Lorenz's article—that we respond not to the totality or *Gestalt,* but to a set of specific features acting as releasers. This argument is important to Lorenz because he wants to argue for evolutionary identity in modes of behavior between other vertebrates and humans, and we know that many birds, for example, often respond to abstract features rather than *Gestalten.* Lorenz's article, published in 1950, bears the title *Ganzheit und Teil in der tierischen und menschlichen Gemeinschaft*—"Entirety and part in animal and human society." Disney's piecemeal change of Mickey's appearance does make sense in this context—he operated in sequential fashion upon Lorenz's primary releasers.)

Lorenz emphasizes the power that juvenile features hold over us, and the abstract quality of their influence, by pointing out that we judge other animals by the same criteria— although the judgment may be utterly inappropriate in an evolutionary context. We are, in short, fooled by an evolved response to our own babies, and we transfer our reaction to the same set of features in other animals.

Many animals, for reasons having nothing to do with the inspiration of affection in humans, possess some features also shared by human babies but not by human adults— large eyes and a bulging forehead with retreating chin, in particular. We are drawn to them, we cultivate them as pets, we stop and admire them in the wild—while we reject their small-eyed, long-snouted relatives who might make more affectionate companions or objects of admiration. Lorenz points out that the German names of many animals with features mimicking human babies end in the diminutive suffix *chen,* even though the animals are often larger than close relatives without such features—*Rotkehlchen* (robin), *Eichhörnchen* (squirrel), and *Kaninchen* (rabbit), for example.

In a fascinating section, Lorenz then enlarges upon our capacity for biologically inappropriate response to other animals, or even to inanimate objects that mimic human features. "The most amazing objects can acquire remarkable, highly specific emotional values by 'experiential attachment' of human properties. . . . Steeply rising, somewhat overhanging cliff faces or dark storm-clouds piling up have the same, immediate display value as a human being who is standing at full height and leaning slightly forwards"—that is, threatening.

We cannot help regarding a camel as aloof and unfriendly because it mimics, quite unwittingly and for other reasons, the "gesture of haughty rejection" common to so many human cultures. In this gesture, we raise our heads, placing our nose above our eyes. We then half-close our eyes and blow out through our nose—the "harumph" of the stereotyped upperclass Englishman or his well-trained servant. "All this," Lorenz argues quite cogently, "symbolizes resistance against all sensory modalities emanating from the disdained counterpart." But the poor camel cannot help carrying its nose above its elongate eyes, with mouth drawn down. As Lorenz reminds us, if you wish to know whether a camel will eat out of your hand or spit, look at its ears, not the rest of its face.

In his important book *Expression of the Emotions in Man and Animals,* published in 1872, Charles Darwin traced the evolutionary basis of many common gestures to originally adaptive actions in animals later internalized as symbols in humans. Thus, he argued for evolutionary continuity of emotion, not only of form. We snarl and raise our upper lip in fierce

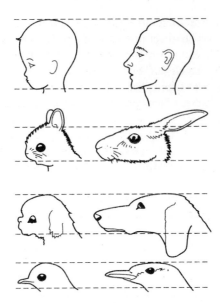

Humans feel affection for animals with juvenile features: large eyes, bulging craniums, retreating chins (left column). Small-eyed, long-snouted animals (right column) do not elicit the same response. From *Studies in Animal and Human Behavior*, vol. II, by Konrad Lorenz, 1971. Methuen & Co. Ltd.

anger—to expose our nonexistent fighting canine tooth. Our gesture of disgust repeats the facial actions associated with the highly adaptive act of vomiting in necessary circumstances. Darwin concluded, much to the distress of many Victorian contemporaries: "With mankind some expressions, such as the bristling of the hair under the influence of extreme terror, or the uncovering of the teeth under that of furious rage, can hardly be understood, except on the belief that man once existed in a much lower and animal-like condition."

In any case, the abstract features of human childhood elicit powerful emotional responses in us, even when they occur in other animals. I submit that Mickey Mouse's evolutionary road down the course of his own growth in reverse reflects the unconscious discovery of this biological principle by Disney and his artists. In fact, the emotional status of most Disney characters rests on the same set of distinctions. To this extent, the magic kingdom trades on a biological illusion—our ability to abstract and our propensity to transfer inappropriately to other animals the fitting responses we make to changing form in the growth of our own bodies.

Donald Duck also adopts more juvenile features through time. His elongated beak recedes and his eyes enlarge; he converges on Huey, Louie, and Dewey as surely as Mickey approaches Morty. But Donald, having inherited the mantle of Mickey's original misbehavior, remains more adult in form with his projecting beak and more sloping forehead.

Mouse villains or sharpies, contrasted with Mickey, are always more adult in appearance, although they often share Mickey's chronological age. In 1936, for example, Disney made a short entitled *Mickey's Rival*. Mortimer, a dandy in a yellow sports car, intrudes upon Mickey and Minnie's quiet country picnic. The thoroughly disreputable Mortimer has a head only 29 percent of body length, to Mickey's 45, and a snout 80 percent of head length, compared with Mickey's 49. (Nonetheless, and was it ever different, Minnie transfers her affection until an obliging bull from a neighboring field dispatches Mickey's rival.) Consider also the exaggerated adult features of other Disney characters—the swaggering bully Peg-leg Pete or the simple, if lovable, dolt Goofy.

As a second, serious biological comment on Mickey's odyssey in form, I note that his path to eternal youth repeats, in epitome, our own evolutionary story. For humans are neotenic. We have evolved by retaining to adulthood the originally juvenile features of our ancestors. Our australopithecine forebears, like Mickey in *Steamboat Willie,* had projecting jaws and low vaulted craniums.

Our embryonic skulls scarcely differ from those of chimpanzees. And we follow the same path of changing form through growth: relative decrease of the cranial vault since brains grow so much more slowly that the bodies after birth, and continuous relative increase of the jaw. But while chimps accentuate these changes, producing an adult strikingly different in form from a baby, we proceed more slowly down the same path and never get nearly so far. Thus, as adults, we retain juvenile features. To be sure, we change enough to produce a notable difference between baby and adult, but our alteration is far smaller than that experienced by chimps and other primates.

A marked slowdown of developmental rates has triggered our neoteny. Primates are slow developers among mammals, but we have accentuated the trend to a degree matched by no other mammal. We have very long periods of gestation, markedly extended childhoods, and the longest life span of any mammal. The morophological features of external youth have served us well. Our enlarged brain is, at least in part, a result of extending rapid prenatal growth rates to later ages. (In all mammals, the brain grows rapidly in utero but often very little after birth. We have extended this fetal phase in postnatal life.)

But the changes in timing themselves have been just as important. We are preeminently learning animals, and our extended childhood permits the transference of culture

Dandified, disreputable Mortimer (here stealing Minnie's affections) has strikingly more adult features than Mickey. His head is smaller in proportion to body length; his nose is a full 80 percent of head length. *Source:* © Disney Enterprises, Inc.

Cartoon villains are not the only Disney characters with exaggerated adult features. Goofy, like Mortimer, has a small head relative to body length and a prominent snout. *Source:* © Disney Enterprises, Inc.

by education. Many animals display flexibility and play in childhood but follow rigidly programmed patterns as adults. Lorenz writes, in the same article cited above: "The characteristic which is so vital for the human peculiarity of the true man—that of always remaining in a state of development—is quite certainly a gift which we owe to the neotenous nature of mankind."

In short, we, like Mickey, never grow up although we, alas, do grow old. Best wishes to you, Mickey, for your next half-century. May we stay as young as you, but grow a bit wiser.

Craft Essays

Annie Dillard

Seeing

When I was six or seven years old, growing up in Pittsburgh, I used to take a precious penny of my own and hide it for someone else to find. It was a curious compulsion; sadly, I've never been seized by it since. For some reason I always "hid" the penny along the same stretch of sidewalk up the street. I would cradle it at the roots of a sycamore, say, or in a hole left by a chipped-off piece of sidewalk. Then I would take a piece of chalk, and, starting at either end of the block, draw huge arrows leading up to the penny from both directions. After I learned to write I labeled the arrows: SURPRISE AHEAD or MONEY THIS WAY. I was greatly excited, during all this arrow-drawing, at the thought of the first lucky passer-by who would receive in this way, regardless of merit, a free gift from the universe. But I never lurked about. I would go straight home and not give the matter another thought, until, some months later, I would be gripped again by the impulse to hide another penny.

It is still the first week in January, and I've got great plans. I've been thinking about seeing. There are lots of things to see, unwrapped gifts and free surprises. The world is fairly studded and strewn with pennies cast broadside from a generous hand. But—and this is the point—who gets excited by a mere penny? If you follow one arrow, if you crouch motionless on a bank to watch a tremulous ripple thrill on the water and are rewarded by the sight of a muskrat kit paddling from its den, will you count that sight a chip of copper only, and go your rueful way? It is dire poverty indeed when a man is so malnourished and fatigued that he won't stoop to pick up a penny. But if you cultivate a healthy poverty and simplicity, so that finding a penny will literally make your day, then, since the world is in fact planted in pennies, you have with your poverty bought a lifetime of days. It is that simple. What you see is what you get.

I used to be able to see flying insects in the air. I'd look ahead and see, not the row of hemlocks across the road, but the air in front of it. My eyes would focus along that column of air, picking out flying insects. But I lost interest, I guess, for I dropped the habit. Now I can see birds. Probably some people can look at the grass at their feet and discover all the crawling creatures. I would like to know grasses and sedges—and care. Then my least journey into the world would be a field trip, a series of happy recognitions. Thoreau, in an expansive mood, exulted, "What a rich book might be made about buds, including, perhaps, sprouts!" It would be nice to think so. I cherish mental images I have of three perfectly happy people. One collects stones. Another—an Englishman, say—watches clouds. The third lives on a coast and collects drops of seawater which he examines microscopically and mounts. But I don't see what the specialist sees, and so I cut myself off, not only from the total picture, but from the various forms of happiness.

Unfortunately, nature is very much a now-you-see-it, now-you-don't affair. A fish flashes, then dissolves in the water before my eyes like so much salt. Deer apparently ascend bodily into heaven; the brightest oriole fades into leaves. These disappearances stun me into stillness and concentration; they say of nature that it conceals with a grand nonchalance, and they say of vision that it is a deliberate gift, the revelation of a dancer who for my eyes only flings away her seven veils. For nature does reveal as well as conceal: now-you-don't-see-it, now-you-do. For a week last September migrating red-winged blackbirds were feeding heavily down by the creek at the back of the house. One day I went out to investigate the racket; I walked up to a tree, an Osage orange, and a hundred birds flew away. They simply materialized out of the tree. I saw a tree, then a whisk of color, then a tree again. I walked closer and another hundred blackbirds took flight. Not a branch, not a twig budged: the birds were apparently weightless as well as invisible. Or, it was as if the leaves of the Osage orange had been freed from a spell in the form of red-winged blackbirds; they flew from the tree, caught my eye in the sky, and vanished. When I looked again at the tree the leaves had reassembled as if nothing had happened. Finally I walked directly to the trunk of the tree and a final hundred, the real diehards, appeared, spread, and vanished. How could so many hide in the tree without my seeing them? The Osage orange, unruffled, looked just as it had looked from the house, when three hundred redwinged blackbirds cried from its crown. I looked downstream where they flew, and they were gone. Searching, I couldn't spot one. I wandered downstream to force them to play their hand, but they'd crossed the creek and scattered. One show to a customer. These appearances catch at my throat; they are the free gifts, the bright coppers at the roots of trees.

It's all a matter of keeping my eyes open. Nature is like one of those line drawings of a tree that are puzzles for children: Can you find hidden in the leaves a duck, a house, a boy, a bucket, a zebra, and a boot? Specialists can find the most incredibly well-hidden things. A book I read when I was young recommended an easy way to find caterpillars to rear: you simply find some fresh caterpillar droppings, look up, and there's your caterpillar. More recently an author advised me to set my mind at ease about those piles of cut stems on the ground in grassy fields. Field mice make them; they cut the grass down by degrees to reach the seeds at the head. It seems that when the grass is tightly packed, as in a field of ripe grain, the blade won't topple at a single cut through the stem; instead, the cut stem simply drops vertically, held in the crush of grain. The mouse severs the bottom again and again, the stem keeps dropping an inch at a time, and finally the head is low enough for the mouse to reach the seeds. Meanwhile, the mouse is positively littering the field with its little piles of cut stems into which, presumably, the author of the book is constantly stumbling.

If I can't see these minutiae, I still try to keep my eyes open. I'm always on the lookout for antlion traps in sandy soil, monarch pupae near milkweed, skipper larvae in locust leaves. These things are utterly common, and I've not seen one. I bang on hollow trees near water, but so far no flying squirrels have appeared. In flat country I watch every sunset in hopes of seeing the green ray. The green ray is a seldom-seen streak of light that rises from the sun like a spurting fountain at the moment of sunset; it throbs into the sky for two seconds and disappears. One more reason to keep my eyes open. A photography professor at the University of Florida just happened to see a bird die in midflight; it jerked, died, dropped, and smashed on the ground. I squint at the wind because I read Steward Edward White: "I have always maintained that if you looked closely enough you could *see* the wind—the dim, hardly-made-out, fine debris fleeing high in the air." White was an excellent observer, and devoted an entire chapter of *The Mountains* to the subject of seeing deer: "As soon as you can forget the naturally obvious and construct an artificial obvious, then you too will see deer."

But the artificial obvious is hard to see. My eyes account for less than one percent of the weight of my head; I'm bony and dense; I see what I expect. I once spent a full three minutes looking at a bullfrog that was so unexpectedly large I couldn't see it even though a dozen enthusiastic campers were shouting directions. Finally I asked, "What color am I looking for?" and a fellow said, "Green." When at last I picked out the frog, I saw what painters are up against: the thing wasn't green at all, but the color of wet hickory bark.

The lover can see, and the knowledgeable. I visited an aunt and uncle at a quarter-horse ranch in Cody, Wyoming. I couldn't do much of anything useful, but I could, I thought, draw. So, as we all sat around the kitchen table after supper, I produced a sheet of paper and drew a horse. "That's one lame horse," my aunt volunteered. The rest of the family joined in: "Only place to saddle that one is his neck"; "Looks like we better shoot the poor thing, on account of those terrible growths." Meekly, I slid the pencil and paper down the table. Everyone in that family, including my three young cousins, could draw a horse. Beautifully. When the paper came back it looked as though five shining, real quarter horses had been corralled by mistake with a papier-mâché moose; the real horses seemed to gaze at the monster with a steady, puzzled air. I stay away from horses now, but I can do a creditable goldfish. The point is that I just don't know what the lover knows; I just can't see the artificial obvious that those in the know construct. The herpetologist asks the native, "Are there snakes in that ravine?" "Nosir." And the herpetologist comes home with, yessir, three bags full. Are there butterflies on that mountain? Are the bluets in bloom, are there arrowheads here, or fossil shells in the shale?

Peeping through my keyhole I see within the range of only about thirty percent of the light that comes from the sun; the rest is infrared and some little ultraviolet, perfectly apparent to many animals, but invisible to me. A nightmare network of ganglia, charged and firing without my knowledge, cuts and splices what I do see, editing it for my brain. Donald E. Carr points out that the sense impressions of one-celled animals are *not* edited for the brain: "This is philosophically interesting in a rather mournful way, since it means that only the simplest animals perceive the universe as it is."

A fog that won't burn away drifts and flows across my field of vision. When you see fog move against a backdrop of deep pines, you don't see the fog itself, but streaks of clearness floating across the air in dark shreds. So I see only tatters of clearness through a pervading obscurity. I can't distinguish the fog from the overcast sky; I can't be sure if the light is direct or reflected. Everywhere darkness and the presence of the unseen appalls. We estimate now that only one atom dances alone in every cubic meter of intergalactic space. I blink and squint. What planet or power yanks Halley's Comet out of orbit? We haven't seen that force yet; it's a question of distance, density, and the pallor of reflected light. We rock, cradled in the swaddling band of darkness. Even the simple darkness of night whispers suggestions to the mind. Last summer, in August, I stayed at the creek too late.

Where Tinker Creek flows under the sycamore log bridge to the tear-shaped island, it is slow and shallow, fringed thinly in cattail marsh. At this spot an astonishing bloom of life supports vast breeding populations of insects, fish, reptiles, birds, and mammals. On windless summer evenings I stalk along the creek bank or straddle the sycamore log in absolute stillness, watching for muskrats. The night I stayed too late I was hunched on the log staring spellbound at spreading, reflected stains of lilac on the water. A cloud in the sky suddenly lighted as if turned on by a switch; its reflection just as suddenly materialized on the water upstream, flat and floating, so that I couldn't see the creek bottom, or life in the water under the cloud. Downstream, away from the cloud on the water, water turtles smooth as beans were gliding down with the current in a series of easy, weightless push-offs, as men bound on the moon. I didn't know whether to trace the progress of one turtle I was sure of, risking sticking my face in one of the bridge's spider webs made invisible by the gathering dark, or take a chance on seeing the carp, or scan the mudbank in hope of seeing a muskrat, or follow the last of the swallows who caught at my heart and trailed it after them like streamers as they appeared from directly below, under the log, flying upstream with their tails forked, so fast.

But shadows spread, and deepened, and stayed. After thousands of years we're still strangers to darkness, fearful aliens in an enemy camp with our arms crossed over our chests. I stirred. A land turtle on the bank, startled, hissed the air from its lungs and withdrew into its shell. An uneasy pink here, an unfathomable blue there, gave great suggestion of lurking beings. Things were going on. I couldn't see whether that sere rustle I heard was a distant rattlesnake, slit-eyed, or a nearby sparrow kicking in the dry flood debris slung at the foot of a willow. Tremendous action roiled the water everywhere I looked, big action, inexplicable. A tremor welled up beside a gaping muskrat burrow in the bank and I caught my breath, but no muskrat appeared. The ripples continued to fan upstream with a steady, powerful thrust. Night was knitting over my face an eyeless mask, and I still sat transfixed. A distant airplane, a delta wing out of nightmare, made a gliding shadow on the creek's bottom that looked like a stingray cruising upstream. At once a black fin slit the pink cloud on the water, shearing it in two. The two halves merged together and seemed to dissolve before my eyes. Darkness pooled in the cleft of the creek and rose, as water collects in a well. Untamed, dreaming lights flickered over the sky. I saw hints of hulking underwater shadows, two pale splashes out of the water, and round ripples rolling close together from a blackened center.

At last I stared upstream where only the deepest violet remained of the cloud, a cloud so high its underbelly still glowed feeble color reflected from a hidden sky lighted in turn by a sun halfway to China. And out of that violet, a sudden enormous black body arced over the water. I saw only a cylindrical sleekness. Head and tail, if there was a head and tail, were both submerged in cloud. I saw only one ebony fling, a headlong dive to darkness; then the waters closed, and the lights went out.

I walked home in a shivering daze, up hill and down. Later I lay open-mouthed in bed, my arms flung wide at my sides to steady the whirling darkness. At this latitude I'm spinning 836 miles an hour round the earth's axis; I often fancy I feel my sweeping fall as a breakneck arc like the dive of dolphins, and the hollow rushing of wind raises hair on my neck and the side of my face. In orbit around the sun I'm moving 64,800 miles an hour. The solar system as a whole, like a merry-go-round unhinged, spins, bobs, and blinks at the speed of 43,200 miles an hour along a course set east of Hercules. Someone has piped, and we are dancing a tarantella until the sweat pours. I open my eyes and I see dark, muscled forms curl out of water, with flapping gills and flattened eyes. I close my eyes and I see stars, deep stars giving way to deeper stars, deeper stars bowing to deepest stars at the crown of an infinite cone.

"Still," wrote van Gogh in a letter, "a great deal of light falls on everything." If we are blinded by darkness, we are also blinded by light. When too much light falls on everything, a special terror results. Peter Freuchen describes the notorious kayak sickness to which Greenland Eskimos are prone. "The Greenland fjords are peculiar for the spells of completely quiet weather, when there is not enough wind to blow out a match and the water is like a sheet of glass. The kayak hunter must sit in his boat without stirring a finger so as not to scare the shy seals away. . . . The sun, low in the sky, sends a glare into his eyes, and the landscape around moves into the realm of the unreal. The reflex from the mirror-like water hypnotizes him, he seems to be unable to move, and all of a sudden it is as if he were floating in a bottomless void, sinking, sinking, and sinking. . . . Horror-stricken, he tries to stir, to cry out, but he cannot, he is completely paralyzed, he just falls and falls." Some hunters are especially cursed with this panic, and bring ruin and sometimes starvation to their families.

Sometimes here in Virginia at sunset low clouds on the southern or northern horizon are completely invisible in the lighted sky. I only know one is there because I can see its reflection in still water. The first time I discovered this mystery I looked from cloud to no-cloud in bewilderment, checking my bearings over and over, thinking maybe the ark of the covenant was just passing by south of Dead Man Mountain. Only much later did I read the explanation: polarized light from the sky is very much weakened by reflection, but the light in clouds isn't polarized. So invisible clouds pass among visible clouds, till all slide over the mountains; so a greater light extinguishes a lesser as though it didn't exist.

In the great meteor shower of August, the Perseid, I wail all day for the shooting stars I miss. They're out there showering down, committing harakiri in a flame of fatal attraction, and hissing perhaps at last into the ocean. But at dawn what looks like a blue dome clamps down over me like a lid on a pot. The stars and planets could smash and I'd never know. Only a piece of ashen moon occasionally climbs up or down the inside of the dome, and our local star without surcease explodes on our heads. We have really only that one light, one source for all power, and yet we must turn away from it by universal decree. Nobody here on the planet seems aware of this strange, powerful taboo, that we all walk about carefully averting our faces, this way and that, lest our eyes be blasted forever.

Darkness appalls and light dazzles; the scrap of visible light that doesn't hurt my eyes hurts my brain. What I see sets me swaying. Size and distance and the sudden swelling of meanings confuse me, bowl me over. I straddle the sycamore log bridge over Tinker Creek in the summer. I look at the lighted creek bottom: snail tracks tunnel the mud in quavering curves. A crayfish jerks, but by the time I absorb what has happened, he's gone in a billowing smokescreen of silt. I look at the water: minnows and shiners. If I'm thinking minnows, a carp will fill my brain till I scream. I look at the water's surface: skaters, bubbles, and leaves sliding down. Suddenly, my own face, reflected, startles me witless. Those snails have been tracking my face! Finally, with a shuddering wrench of the will, I see clouds, cirrus clouds. I'm dizzy, I fall in. This looking business is risky.

Once I stood on a humped rock on nearby Purgatory Mountain, watching through binoculars the great autumn hawk migration below, until I discovered that I was in danger of joining the hawks on a vertical migration of my own. I was used to binoculars, but not, apparently, to balancing on humped rocks while looking through them. I staggered. Everything advanced and receded by turns; the world was full of unexplained foreshortenings and depths. A distant huge tan object, a hawk the size of an elephant, turned out to be the browned bough of a nearby loblolly pine. I followed a sharp-shinned hawk against a featureless sky, rotating my head unawares as it flew, and when I lowered the glass a glimpse of my own looming shoulder sent me staggering. What prevents the men on Palomar from falling, voiceless and blinded, from their tiny, vaulted chairs?

I reel in confusion; I don't understand what I see. With the naked eye I can see two million light-years to the Andromeda galaxy. Often I slop some creek water in a jar and when I get home I dump it in a white china bowl. After the silt settles I return and see tracings of minute snails on the bottom, a planarian or two winding round the rim of water, roundworms shimmying frantically, and finally, when my eyes have adjusted to these dimensions, amoebae. At first the amoebae look like muscae volitantes, those curled moving spots you seem to see in your eyes when you stare at a distant wall. Then I see the amoebae as drops of water congealed, bluish, translucent, like chips of sky in the bowl. At length I choose one individual and give myself over to its idea of an evening. I see it dribble a grainy foot before it on its wet, unfathomable way. Do its unedited sense impressions include the fierce focus of my eyes? Shall I take it outside and show it Andromeda, and blow its little endoplasm? I stir the water with a finger, in case it's running out of oxygen. Maybe I should get a tropical aquarium with motorized bubblers and lights, and keep this one for a pet. Yes, it would tell its fissioned descendants, the universe is two feet by five, and if you listen closely you can hear the buzzing music of the spheres.

Oh, it's mysterious lamplit evenings, here in the galaxy, one after the other. It's one of those nights when I wander from window to window, looking for a sign. But I can't see. Terror and a beauty insoluble are a ribband of blue woven into the fringes of garments of things both great and small. No culture explains, no bivouac offers real haven or rest. But it could be that we are not seeing something. Galileo thought comets were an optical illusion. This is fertile ground: since we are certain that they're not, we can look at what our scientists have been saying with fresh hope. What if there are *really* gleaming, castellated cities hung upside-down over the desert sand? What limpid lakes and cool date palms have our caravans always passed untried? Until, one by one, by the blindest of leaps, we light on the road to these places, we must stumble in darkness and hunger. I turn from the window. I'm blind as a bat, sensing only from every direction the echo of my own thin cries.

I chanced on a wonderful book by Marius von Senden, called *Space and Sight*. When Western surgeons discovered how to perform safe cataract operations, they ranged across Europe and America operating on dozens of men and women of all ages who had been blinded by cataracts since birth. Von Senden collected accounts of such cases; the histories are fascinating. Many doctors had tested their patients' sense perceptions and ideas of space both before and after the operations. The vast majority of patients, of both sexes and all ages, had, in von Senden's opinion, no idea of space whatsoever. Form, distance, and size were so many meaningless syllables. A patient "had no idea of depth, confusing it with roundness." Before the operation a doctor would give a blind patient a cube and a sphere; the patient would tongue it or feel it with his hands, and name it correctly. After the operation the doctor would show the same objects to the patient without letting him touch them; now he had no clue whatsoever what he was seeing. One patient called lemonade "square" because it pricked on his tongue as a square shape pricked on the touch of his hands. Of another postoperative patient, the doctor writes, "I have found in her no notion of size, for example, not even within the narrow limits which she might have encompassed with the aid of touch. Thus when I asked her to show me how big her mother was, she did not stretch out her hands, but set her two index-fingers a few inches apart." Other doctors reported their patients' own statements to similar effect. "The room he was in . . . he knew to be but part of the house, yet he could not conceive that the whole house could look bigger"; "Those who are blind from birth . . . have no real conception of height or distance. A house that is a mile away is thought of as nearby, but requiring the taking of a lot of steps. . . . The elevator that whizzes him up and down gives no more sense of vertical distance than does the train of horizontal."

For the newly sighted, vision is pure sensation unencumbered by meaning: "The girl went through the experience that we all go through and forget, the moment we are born. She saw, but it did not mean anything but a lot of different kinds of brightness." Again, "I asked the patient what he could see; he answered that he saw an extensive field of light, in which everything appeared dull, confused, and in motion. He could not distinguish objects." Another patient saw "nothing but a confusion of forms and colours." When a newly sighted girl saw photographs and paintings, she asked, "'Why do they put those dark marks all over them?' 'Those aren't dark marks,' her mother explained, 'those are shadows. That is one of the ways the eye knows that things have shape. If it were not for shadows many things would look flat.' 'Well, that's how things do look,' Joan answered. 'Everything looks flat with dark patches.'"

But it is the patients' concepts of space that are most revealing. One patient, according to his doctor, "practiced his vision in a strange fashion; thus he takes off one of his boots, throws it some way off in front of him, and then attempts to gauge the distance at which it lies; he takes a few steps towards the boot and tries to grasp it; on failing to reach it, he moves on a step or two and gropes for the boot until he finally gets hold of it." "But even at this stage, after three weeks' experience of seeing," von Senden goes on, "'space,' as he conceives it, ends with visual space, i.e., with colour-patches that happen to bound his view. He does not yet have the notion that a larger object (a chair) can mask a smaller one (a dog), or that the latter can still be present even though it is not directly seen."

In general the newly sighted see the world as a dazzle of color-patches. They are pleased by the sensation of color, and learn quickly to name the colors, but the rest of seeing is tormentingly difficult. Soon after his operation a patient "generally bumps into one of these colour-patches and observes them to be substantial, since they resist him as tactual objects do. In walking about it also strikes him—or can if he pays attention—that he is continually passing in between the colours he sees, that he can go past a visual object, that a part of it then steadily disappears from view; and that in spite of this, however he twists and turns—whether entering the room from the door, for example, or returning back to it—he always has a visual space in front of him. Thus he gradually comes to realize that there is also a space behind him, which he does not see."

The mental effort involved in these reasonings proves overwhelming for many patients. It oppresses them to realize, if they ever do at all, the tremendous size of the world, which they had previously conceived of as something touchingly manageable. It oppresses them to realize that they have been visible to people all along, perhaps unattractively so, without their knowledge or consent. A disheartening number of them refuse to use their new vision, continuing to go over objects with their tongues, and lapsing into apathy and despair. "The child can see, but will not make use of his sight. Only when pressed can he with difficulty be brought to look at objects in his neighbourhood; but more than a foot away it is impossible to bestir him to the necessary effort." Of a twenty-one-year-old girl, the doctor relates, "Her unfortunate father, who had hoped for so much from this operation, wrote that his daughter carefully shuts her eyes whenever she wishes to go about the house, especially when she comes to a staircase, and that she is never happier or more at ease than when, by closing her eyelids, she relapses into her former state of total blindness." A fifteen-year-old boy, who was also in love with a girl at the asylum for the blind, finally blurted out, "No, really, I can't stand it any more; I want to be sent back to the asylum again. If things aren't altered, I'll tear my eyes out."

Some do learn to see, especially the young ones. But it changes their lives. One doctor comments on "the rapid and complete loss of that striking and wonderful serenity which is characteristic only of those who have never yet seen." A blind man who learns to see is ashamed of his old habits. He dresses up, grooms himself, and tries to make a good impression. While he was blind he was indifferent to objects unless they were edible; now, "a sifting of values sets in . . . his thoughts and wishes are mightily stirred and some few of the patients are thereby led into dissimulation, envy, theft and fraud."

On the other hand, many newly sighted people speak well of the world, and teach us how dull is our own vision. To one patient, a human hand, unrecognized, is "something bright and then holes." Shown a bunch of grapes, a boy calls out, "It is dark, blue and shiny. . . . It isn't smooth, it has bumps and hollows." A little girl visits a garden. "She is greatly astonished, and can scarcely be persuaded to answer, stands speechless in front of the tree, which she only names on taking hold of it, and then as 'the tree with the lights in it.'" Some delight in their sight and give themselves over to the visual world. Of a patient just after her bandages were removed, her doctor writes, "The first things to attract her attention were her own hands; she looked at them very closely, moved them repeatedly to and fro, bent and stretched the fingers, and seemed greatly astonished at the sight." One girl was eager to tell her blind friend that "men do not really look like trees at all," and astounded to discover that her every visitor had an utterly different face. Finally, a twenty-two-year-old girl was dazzled by the world's brightness and kept her eyes shut for two weeks. When at the end of that time she opened her eyes again, she did not recognize any objects, but, "the more she now directed her gaze upon everything about her, the more it could be seen how an expression of gratification and astonishment overspread her features; she repeatedly exclaimed: 'Oh God! How beautiful!'"

I saw color-patches for weeks after I read this wonderful book. It was summer; the peaches were ripe in the valley orchards. When I woke in the morning, color-patches wrapped round my eyes, intricately, leaving not one unfilled spot. All day long I walked among shifting color-patches that parted before me like the Red Sea and closed again in silence, transfigured, whenever I looked back. Some patches swelled and loomed, while others vanished utterly, and dark marks flitted at random over the whole dazzling sweep. But I couldn't sustain the illusion of flatness. I've been around for too long. Form is condemned to an eternal danse macabre with meaning: I couldn't unpeach the peaches. Nor can I remember ever having seen without understanding; the color-patches of infancy are lost. My brain then must have been smooth as any balloon. I'm told I reached for the moon; many babies do. But the color-patches of infancy swelled as meaning filled them; they arrayed themselves in solemn ranks down distances which unrolled and stretched before me like a plain. The moon rocketed away. I live now in a world of shadows that shape and distance color, a world where space makes a kind of terrible sense. What gnosticism is this, and what physics? The fluttering patch I saw in my nursery window—silver and green and shape-shifting blue—is gone; a row of Lombardy poplars takes its place, mute, across the distant lawn. That humming oblong creature pale as light that stole along the walls of my room at night, stretching exhilaratingly around the corners, is gone, too, gone the night I ate of the bittersweet fruit, put two and two together and puckered forever my brain. Martin Buber tells this tale: "Rabbi Mendel once boasted to his teacher Rabbi Elimelekh that evenings he saw the angel who rolls away the light before the darkness, and mornings the angel who rolls away the darkness before the light. 'Yes,' said Rabbi Elimelekh, 'in my youth I saw that too. Later on you don't see these things any more.'"

Why didn't someone hand those newly sighted people paints and brushes from the start, when they still didn't know what anything was? Then maybe we all could see color-patches too, the world unraveled from reason, Eden before Adam gave names. The scales would drop from my eyes; I'd see trees like men walking; I'd run down the road against all orders, hallooing and leaping.

Seeing is of course very much a matter of verbalization. Unless I call my attention to what passes before my eyes, I simply won't see it. It is, as Ruskin says, "not merely unnoticed, but in the full, clear sense of the word, unseen." My eyes alone can't solve analogy tests using figures, the ones which show, with increasing elaborations, a big square, then a small square in a big square, then a big triangle, and expect me to find a small triangle in a big triangle. I have to say the words, describe what I'm seeing. If Tinker Mountain erupted, I'd be likely to notice. But if I want to notice the lesser cataclysms of valley life, I have to maintain in my head a running description of the present. It's not that I'm observant; it's just that I talk too much. Otherwise, especially in a strange place, I'll never know what's happening. Like a blind man at the ball game, I need a radio.

When I see this way I analyze and pry. I hurl over logs and roll away stones; I study the bank a square foot at a time, probing and tilting my head. Some days when a mist covers the mountains, when the muskrats won't show and the microscope's mirror shatters, I want to climb up the blank blue dome as a man would storm the inside of a circus tent, wildly, dangling, and with a steel knife claw a rent in the top, peep, and, if I must, fall.

But there is another kind of seeing that involves a letting go. When I see this way I sway transfixed and emptied. The difference between the two ways of seeing is the difference between walking with and without a camera. When I walk with a camera, I walk from shot to shot, reading the light on a calibrated meter. When I walk without a camera, my own shutter opens, and the moment's light prints on my own silver gut. When I see this second way I am above all an unscrupulous observer.

It was sunny one evening last summer at Tinker Creek; the sun was low in the sky, upstream. I was sitting on the sycamore log bridge with the sunset at my back, watching the shiners the size of minnows who were feeding over the muddy sand in skittery schools. Again and again, one fish, then another turned for a split second across the current and flash! the sun shot out from its silver side. I couldn't watch for it. It was always just happening somewhere else, and it drew my vision just as it disappeared: flash, like a sudden dazzle of the thinnest blade, a sparking over a dun and olive ground at chance intervals from every direction. Then I noticed white specks, some sort of pale petals, small, floating from under my feet on the creek's surface, very slow and steady. So I blurred my eyes and gazed towards the brim of my hat and saw a new world. I saw the pale white circles roll up, roll up, like the world's turning, mute and perfect, and I saw the linear flashes, gleaming silver, like stars being born at random down a rolling scroll of time. Something broke and something opened. I filled up like a new wineskin. I breathed an air like light; I saw a light like water. I was the lip of a fountain the creek filled forever; I was ether, the leaf in the zephyr; I was flesh-flake, feather, bone.

When I see this way I see truly. As Thoreau says, I return to my senses. I am the man who watches the baseball game in silence in an empty stadium. I see the game purely; I'm abstracted and dazed. When it's all over and the white-suited players lope off the green field to their shadowed dugouts, I leap to my feet; I cheer and cheer.

But I can't go out and try to see this way. I'll fail, I'll go mad. All I can do is try to gag the commentator, to hush the noise of useless interior babble that keeps me from seeing just as surely as a newspaper dangled before my eyes. The effort is really a discipline requiring a lifetime of dedicated struggle; it marks the literature of saints and monks of every order East and West, under every rule and no rule, discalced and shod. The world's spiritual geniuses seem to discover universally that the mind's muddy river, this ceaseless flow of trivia and trash, cannot be dammed, and that trying to dam it is a waste of effort that might lead to madness. Instead you must allow the muddy river to flow unheeded in the dim channels of consciousness; you raise your sights; you look along it, mildly, acknowledging its presence without interest and gazing beyond it into the realm of the real where subjects and objects act and rest purely, without utterance. "Launch into the deep," says Jacques Ellul, "and you shall see."

The secret of seeing is, then, the pearl of great price. If I thought he could teach me to find it and keep it forever I would stagger barefoot across a hundred deserts after any lunatic at all. But although the pearl may be found, it may not be sought. The literature of illumination reveals this above all: although it comes to those who wait for it, it is always, even to the most practiced and adept, a gift and a total surprise. I return from one walk knowing where the killdeer nests in the field by the creek and the hour the laurel blooms. I return from the same walk a day later scarcely knowing my own name. Litanies hum in my ears; my tongue flaps in my mouth Ailinon, alleluia! I cannot cause light; the most I can do is try to put myself in the path of its beam. It is possible, in deep space, to sail on solar wind. Light, be it particle or wave, has force: you rig a giant sail and go. The secret of seeing is to sail on solar wind. Hone and spread your spirit till you yourself are a sail, whetted, translucent, broadside to the merest puff.

When her doctor took her bandages off and led her into the garden, the girl who was no longer blind saw "the tree with the lights in it." It was for this tree I searched through the peach orchards of summer, in the forests of fall and down winter and spring for years. Then one day I was walking along Tinker Creek thinking of nothing at all and I saw the tree with the lights in it. I saw the backyard cedar where the mourning doves roost charged and transfigured, each cell buzzing with flame. I stood on the grass with the lights in it, grass that was wholly fire, utterly focused and utterly dreamed. It was less like seeing than like being for the first time seen, knocked breathless by a powerful glance. The flood of fire abated, but I'm still spending the power. Gradually the lights went out in the cedar, the colors died, the cells unflamed and disappeared. I was still ringing. I had been my whole life a bell, and never knew it until at that moment I was lifted and struck. I have since only very rarely seen the tree with the lights in it. The vision comes and goes, mostly goes, but I live for it, for the moment when the mountains open and a new light roars in spate through the crack, and the mountains slam.

Barry Lopez

Landscape and Narrative

One summer evening in a remote village in the Brooks Range of Alaska, I sat among a group of men listening to hunting stories about the trapping and pursuit of animals. I was particularly interested in several incidents involving wolverine, in part because a friend of mine was studying wolverine in Canada, among the Cree, but, too, because I find this animal such an intense creature. To hear about its life is to learn more about fierceness.

Wolverines are not intentionally secretive, hiding their lives from view, but they are seldom observed. The range of their known behavior is less than that of, say, bears or wolves. Still, that evening no gratuitous details were set out. This was somewhat odd, for wolverine easily excite the imagination; they can loom suddenly in the landscape with authority, with an aura larger than their compact physical dimensions, drawing one's immediate and complete attention. Wolverine also have a deserved reputation for resoluteness in the worst winters, for ferocious strength. But neither did these attributes induce the men to embellish.

I listened carefully to these stories, taking pleasure in the sharply observed detail surrounding the dramatic thread of events. The story I remember most vividly was about a man hunting a wolverine from a snow machine in the spring. He followed the animal's tracks for several miles over rolling tundra in a certain valley. Soon he caught sight ahead of a dark spot on the crest of a hill—the wolverine pausing to look back. The hunter was catching up, but each time he came over a rise the wolverine was looking back from the next rise, just out of range. The hunter topped one more rise and met the wolverine bounding toward him. Before he could pull his rifle from its scabbard the wolverine flew across the engine cowl and the windshield, hitting him square in the chest. The hunter scrambled his arms wildly, trying to get the wolverine out of his lap, and fell over as he did so. The wolverine jumped clear as the snow machine rolled over, and fixed the man with a stare. He had not bitten, not even scratched the man. Then the wolverine walked away. The man thought of reaching for the gun, but no, he did not.

The other stories were like this, not so much making a point as evoking something about contact with wild animals that would never be completely understood.

When the stories were over, four or five of us walked out of the home of our host. The surrounding land, in the persistent light of a far northern summer, was still visible for miles—the striated, pitched massifs of the Brooks Range; the shy, willow-lined banks of the John River flowing south from Anaktuvuk Pass; and the flat tundra plain, opening with great affirmation to the north. The landscape seemed alive because of the stories. It was precisely these ocherous tones, this kind of willow, exactly this austerity that had informed the wolverine narratives. I felt exhilaration, and a deeper confirmation of the stories. The mundane tasks which awaited me I anticipated now with pleasure. The stories had renewed in me a sense of the purpose of my life.

This feeling, an inexplicable renewal of enthusiasm after storytelling, is familiar to many people. It does not seem to matter greatly what the subject is, as long as the context is intimate and the story is told for its own sake, not forced to serve merely as the vehicle for an idea. The tone of the story need not be solemn. The darker aspects of life need not be ignored. But I think intimacy is indispensable—a feeling that derives from the listener's trust and a story-teller's certain knowledge of his subject and regard for his audience. This intimacy deepens if the storyteller tempers his authority with humility, or when terms of idiomatic expression, or at least the physical setting for the story, are shared.

I think of two landscapes—one outside the self, the other within. The external land-scape is the one we see—not only the line and color of the land and its shading at different times of the day, but also its plants and animals in season, its weather, its geology, the record of its climate and evolution. If you walk up, say, a dry arroyo in the Sonoran Desert you will feel a mounding and rolling of sand and silt beneath your foot that is distinctive. You will anticipate the crumbling of the sedimentary earth in the arroyo bank as your hand reaches out, and in that tangible evidence you will sense a history of water in the region. Perhaps a black-throated sparrow lands in a paloverde bush—the resiliency of the twig under the bird, that precise shade of yellowish-green against the milk-blue sky, the fluttering whir of the arriving sparrow, are what I mean by "the landscape." Draw on the smell of creosote bush, or clack stones together in the dry air. Feel how light is the desiccated dropping of the kangaroo rat. Study an animal track obscured by the wind. These are all elements of the land, and what makes the landscape comprehensible are the relationships between them. One learns a landscape finally not by knowing the name or identity of everything in it, but by perceiving the relationships in it—like that between the sparrow and the twig. The dif-ference between the relationships and the elements is the same as that between written his-tory and a catalog of events.

The second landscape I think of is an interior one, a kind of projection within a per-son of a part of the exterior landscape. Relationships in the exterior landscape include those that are named and discernible, such as the nitrogen cycle, or a vertical sequence of Ordovician limestone, and others that are uncodified or ineffable, such as winter light falling on a particular kind of granite, or the effect of humidity on the frequency of a blackpoll warbler's burst of song. That these relationships have purpose and order, how-ever inscrutable they may seem to us, is a tenet of evolution. Similarly, the speculations, intuitions, and formal ideas we refer to as "mind" are a set of relationships in the interior landscape with purpose and order; some of these are obvious, many impenetrably subtle. The shape and character of these relationships in a person's thinking, I believe, are deeply influenced by where on this earth one goes, what one touches, the patterns one observes in nature—the intricate history of one's life in the land, even a life in the city, where wind, the chirp of birds, the line of a falling leaf, are known. These thoughts are arranged, fur-ther, according to the thread of one's moral, intellectual, and spiritual development. The interior landscape responds to the character and subtlety of an exterior landscape; the shape of the individual mind is affected by land as it is by genes.

In stories like those I heard at Anaktuvuk Pass about wolverine, the relationship between separate elements in the land is set forth clearly. It is put in a simple framework of sequential incidents and apposite detail. If the exterior landscape is limned well, the lis-tener often feels that he has heard something pleasing and authentic—trustworthy. We derive this sense of confidence I think not so much from verifiable truth as from an under-standing that lying has played no role in the narrative. The storyteller is obligated to engage the reader with a precise vocabulary, to set forth a coherent and dramatic rendering of incidents—and to be ingenuous.

When one hears a story one takes pleasure in it for different reasons—for the euphony of its phrases, an aspect of the plot, or because one identifies with one of the characters. With certain stories certain individuals may experience a deeper, more profound sense of well-being. This latter phenomenon, in my understanding, rests at the heart of storytelling as an elevated experience among aboriginal peoples. It results from bringing two landscapes together. The exterior landscape is organized according to principles or laws or tendencies beyond human control. It is understood to contain an integrity that is beyond human analysis and unimpeachable. Insofar as the storyteller depicts various subtle and obvious relationships in the exterior landscape accurately in his story, and insofar as he orders them along traditional lines of meaning to create the narrative, the narrative will "ring true." The listener who "takes the story to heart" will feel a pervasive sense of congruence within himself and also with the world.

Among the Navajo and, as far as I know, many other native peoples, the land is thought to exhibit a sacred order. That order is the basis of ritual. The rituals themselves reveal the power in that order. Art, architecture, vocabulary, and costume, as well as ritual, are derived from the perceived natural order of the universe—from observations and meditations on the exterior landscape. An indigenous philosophy—metaphysics, ethics, epistemology, aesthetics, and logic—may also be derived from a people's continuous attentiveness to both the obvious (scientific) and ineffable (artistic) orders of the local landscape. Each individual, further, undertakes to order his interior landscape according to the exterior landscape. To succeed in this means to achieve a balanced state of mental health.

I think of the Navajo for a specific reason. Among the various sung ceremonies of this people—Enemyway, Coyoteway, Red Antway, Uglyway—is one called Beautyway. In the Navajo view, the elements of one's interior life—one's psychological makeup and moral bearing—are subject to a persistent principle of disarray. Beautyway is, in part, a spiritual invocation of the order of the exterior universe, that irreducible, holy complexity that manifests itself as all things changing through time (a Navajo definition of beauty, hózhǫ́ǫ́). The purpose of this invocation is to recreate in the individual who is the subject of the Beautyway ceremony that same order, to make the individual again a reflection of the myriad enduring relationships of the landscape.

I believe story functions in a similar way. A story draws on relationships in the exterior landscape and projects them onto the interior landscape. The purpose of storytelling is to achieve harmony between the two landscapes, to use all the elements of story—syntax, mood, figures of speech—in a harmonious way to reproduce the harmony of the land in the individual's interior. Inherent in story is the power to reorder a state of psychological confusion through contact with the pervasive truth of those relationships we call "the land."

These thoughts, of course, are susceptible to interpretation. I am convinced, however, that these observations can be applied to the kind of prose we call nonfiction as well as to traditional narrative forms such as the novel and the short story, and to some poems. Distinctions between fiction and nonfiction are sometimes obscured by arguments over what constitutes "the truth." In the aboriginal literature I am familiar with, the first distinction made among narratives is to separate the authentic from the inauthentic. Myth, which we tend to regard as fictitious or "merely metaphorical," is as authentic, as real, as the story of a wolverine in a man's lap. (A distinction is made, of course, about the elevated nature of myth—and frequently the circumstances of myth-telling are more rigorously prescribed than those for the telling of legends or vernacular stories—but all of these narratives are rooted in the local landscape. To violate *that* connection is to call the narrative itself into question.)

The power of narrative to nurture and heal, to repair a spirit in disarray, rests on two things: the skillful invocation of unimpeachable sources and a listener's knowledge that no hypocrisy or subterfuge is involved. This last simple fact is to me one of the most imposing aspects of the Holocene history of man.

We are more accustomed now to thinking of "the truth" as something that can be explicitly stated, rather than as something that can be evoked in a metaphorical way outside science and Occidental culture. Neither can truth be reduced to aphorism or formulas. It is something alive and unpronounceable. Story creates an atmosphere in which it becomes discernible as a pattern. For a storyteller to insist on relationships that do not exist is to lie. Lying is the opposite of story. (I do not mean to confuse ignorance with deception, or to imply that a storyteller can perceive all that is inherent in the land. Every storyteller falls short of a perfect limning of the landscape—perception and language both fail. But to make up something that is not there, something which can never be corroborated in the land, to knowingly set forth a false relationship, is to be lying, no longer telling a story.)

Because of the intricate, complex nature of the land, it is not always possible for a storyteller to grasp what is contained in a story. The intent of the storyteller, then, must be to evoke, honestly, some single aspect of all that the land contains. The storyteller knows that because different individuals grasp the story at different levels, the focus of his regard for truth must be at the primary one—with who was there, what happened, when, where, and why things occurred. The story will then possess similar truth at other levels—the integrity inherent at the primary level of meaning will be conveyed everywhere else. As long as the storyteller carefully describes the order before him, and uses his storytelling skill to heighten and emphasize certain relationships, it is even possible for the story to be more successful than the storyteller himself is able to imagine.

I would like to make a final point about the wolverine stories I heard at Anaktuvuk Pass. I wrote down the details afterward, concentrating especially on aspects of the biology and ecology of the animals. I sent the information on to my friend living with the Cree. When, many months later, I saw him, I asked whether the Cree had enjoyed these insights of the Nunamiut into the nature of the wolverine. What had they said?

"You know," he told me, "how they are. They said, 'That could happen.'"

In these uncomplicated words the Cree declared their own knowledge of the wolverine. They acknowledged that although they themselves had never seen the things the Nunamiut spoke of, they accepted them as accurate observations, because they did not consider story a context for misrepresentation. They also preserved their own dignity by not overstating their confidence in the Nunamiut, a distant and unknown people.

Whenever I think of this courtesy on the part of the Cree I think of the dignity that is ours when we cease to demand the truth and realize that the best we can have of those substantial truths that guide our lives is metaphorical—a story. And the most of it we are likely to discern comes only when we accord one another the respect the Cree showed the Nunamiut. Beyond this—that the interior landscape is a metaphorical representation of the exterior landscape, that the truth reveals itself most fully not in dogma but in the paradox, irony, and contradictions that distinguish compelling narratives—beyond this there are only failures of imagination: reductionism in science; fundamentalism in religion; fascism in politics.

Our national literatures should be important to us insofar as they sustain us with illumination and heal us. They can always do that so long as they are written with respect for both the source and the reader, and with an understanding of why the human heart and the land have been brought together so regularly in human history.

Edward O. Wilson

Life Is a Narrative

Let me tell you a story. It is about two ants. In the early 1960s, when I was a young professor of zoology at Harvard University, one of the vexing mysteries of evolution was the origin of ants. That was far from a trivial problem in science. Ants are the most abundant of insects, the most effective predators of other insects, and the busiest scavengers of small dead animals. They transport the seeds of thousands of plant species, and they turn and enrich more soil than earthworms. In totality (they number roughly in the million billions and weigh about as much as all of humanity), they are among the key players of Earth's terrestrial environment. Of equal general interest, they have attained their dominion by means of the most advanced social organization known among animals.

I had chosen these insects for the focus of my research. It was the culmination of a fascination that dated back to childhood. Now, I spent a lot of time thinking about how they came to be. At first the problem seemed insoluble, because the oldest known ants, found in fossil deposits up to 57 million years old, were already advanced anatomically. In fact, they were quite similar to the modern forms all about us. And just as today, these ancient ants were among the most diverse and abundant of insects. It was as though an opaque curtain had been lowered to block our view of everything that occurred before. All we had to work with was the tail end of evolution.

Somewhere in the world the Ur-ants awaited discovery. I had many conversations with William L. Brown, a friend and fellow myrmecologist, about where the missing links might turn up and what traits they possess that could reveal their ancestry among the nonsocial wasps. We guessed that they first appeared in the late Mesozoic era, 65 million or more years ago, far back enough to have stung and otherwise annoyed the last of the dinosaurs. We were not willing to accept the alternative hypothesis favored by some biblical creationists, that ants did not evolve at all but appeared on Earth full-blown.

Because well-preserved fossils had already been collected by the tens of thousands from all around the northern hemisphere over a period of two centuries without any trace of the Ur-species, I was afraid I would never see one in my lifetime. Then, as so often happens in science, a chance event changed everything. One Sunday morning in 1967, a middle-aged couple, Mr. and Mrs. Edmund Frey, were strolling along the base of the seaside bluffs at Cliffwood Beach, New Jersey, collecting bits of fossilized wood and amber from a thin layer of clay freshly exposed by a storm the day before. They were especially interested in the amber, which are jewel-like fragments of fossil tree sap. In one lump they rescued, clear as yellow glass, were two beautifully preserved ants. At first, that might have seemed nothing unusual: museums, including the one at Harvard, are awash in amber ants. What made these specimens important, however, was their age: about 90 million years, from the middle of the Cretaceous period, Mesozoic era, in the Age of Dinosaurs.

The Freys were willing to share their find, and soon the two specimens found their way to me for examination. There they came close to disaster. As I nervously fumbled the amber piece out of its mailing box I dropped it to the floor, where it broke into two halves. Luck stayed with me, however. The break was as clean as though made by a jeweler, and each piece contained an undamaged specimen. Within minutes I determined that the ants were the long-sought Holy Grail of ant paleontology, or at least very close to it. Brown and I later formally placed them in a new genus, Sphecomyrma freyi (literally, "Frey's wasp ant"). They were more primitive than all other known ants, living and fossil. Moreover, in a dramatic confirmation of evolution as a predictive theory, they possessed most of the intermediate traits that according to our earlier deductions should connect modern ants to the nonsocial wasps.

As a result of the discovery, other entomologists intensified their search, and many more ant fossils of Mesozoic age were soon found. Originating from deposits in New Jersey, Canada, Siberia, and Brazil, they compose a mix of primitive and more advanced species. Bit by bit, they have illuminated the history of ants from near the point of origin over 100 million years ago to the start of the great radiative spread that created the modern fauna.

Science consists of millions of stories like the finding of New Jersey's dawn ants. These accounts, some electrifying, most pedestrian, become science when they can be tested and woven into cause-and-effect explanations to become part of humanity's material worldview. Science, like the rest of culture, is based on the manufacture of narrative. That is entirely natural, and in a profound sense it is a Darwinian necessity. We all live by narrative, every day and every minute of our lives. Narrative is the human way of working through a chaotic and unforgiving world bent on reducing our bodies to malodorous catabolic molecules. It delays the surrender of our personal atoms and compounds back to the environment for the assembly of more humans, and ants.

By narrative we take the best stock we can of the world and our predicament in it. What we see and recreate is seldom the blinding literal truth. Instead, we perceive and respond to our surroundings in narrow ways that most benefit our organismic selves. The narrative genius of Homo sapiens is an accommodation to the inherent inability of the three pounds of our sensory system and brain to process more than a minute fraction of the information the environment pours into them. In order to keep the organism alive, that fraction must be intensely and accurately selective. The stories we tell ourselves and others are our survival manuals.

With new tools and models, neuroscientists are drawing close to an understanding of the conscious mind as narrative generator. They view it as an adaptive flood of scenarios created continuously by the working brain. Whether set in the past, present, or future, whether fictive or reality based, the free-running constructions are our only simulacrum of the world outside the brain. They are everything we will ever possess as individuals. And, minute by minute, they determine whether we live or die.

The present in particular is constructed from sensations very far in excess of what can be put into the simulacrum. Working at a frantic pace, the brain summons memories—past scenarios—to help screen and organize the incoming chaos. It simultaneously creates imaginary scenarios to create fields of competing options, the process we call decision-making. Only a tiny fraction of the narrative fragments—the focus—is selected for higher-order processing in the prefrontal cortex. That segment constitutes the theater of running symbolic imagery we call the conscious mind. During the story-building process, the past is reworked and returned to memory storage. Through repeated cycles of recall and supplementation the brain holds on to shrinking segments of the former conscious states. Across generations the most important among these fragments are communicated widely and converted into history, literature, and oral tradition. If altered enough, they become legend and myth. The rest disappear. The story I have just told you about Mesozoic ants is all true as best I can reconstruct it from my memory and notes. But it is only a little bit of the whole truth, most of which is beyond my retrieval no matter how hard I might try.

This brings me to the relation between science and literature. Science is not a subculture separate from that of literature. Its knowledge is the totality of what humanity can verify about the real world, testable by repeated experiment or factual observation, bound to related information by general principles, and—this is the part most often missed—ultimately subject to cause-and-effect explanations consilient across the full range of disciplines. The most democratic of human mental activity, it comprises the nonfiction stories you can take to the bank.

Everyone can understand the process of science, and, once familiar with a modest amount of factual information and the elementary terminology of particular disciplines, he or she can grasp the intuitive essence of at least some scientific knowledge. But the scientific method is not natural to the human mind. The phenomena it explicates are by and large unfamiliar to ordinary experience. New scientific facts and workable theories, the silver and gold of the scientific enterprise, come slow and hard, less like nuggets lying on a streambed than ore dug from mines. To enjoy them while maintaining an effective critical attitude requires mental discipline. The reason, again, is the innate constraints of the human brain. Gossip and music flow easily through the human mind, because the brain is genetically predisposed to receive them. Theirs is a Paleolithic cogency. Calculus and reagent chemistry, in contrast, come hard, like ballet on pointe. They have become relevant only in modern, postevolutionary times. Of the hundreds of fellow scientists I have known for more than fifty years, from graduate students to Nobelists, all generally prefer at random moments of their lives to listen to gossip and music rather than to scientific lectures. Trust me: physics is hard even for physicists. Somewhere on a distant planet, there may exist a species that hereditarily despises gossip and thrives on calculus. But I doubt it.

The central task of science writing for a broad audience is, in consequence, how to make science human and enjoyable without betraying nature. The best writers achieve that end by two means. They present the phenomena as a narrative, whether historical, evolutionary, or phenomenological, and they treat the scientists as protagonists in a story that contains, at least in muted form, the mythic elements of challenge and triumph.

To wring honest journalism and literature from honest science, the writer must overcome formidable difficulties. First is the immensity and exponential growth of the primary material itself, which has experienced a phenomenally short doubling time of fifteen years for over three hundred years, all the while coupled with a similarly advancing technology. It has spread its reach into every conceivable aspect of material existence, from the origin of the universe to the creative process of the mind itself. Its relentless pursuit of detail and theory long ago outstripped the minds of individual scientists themselves to hold it. So fragmented are the disciplines and specialized the language resulting from the growth that experts in one subject often cannot grasp the technical reports of experts in closely similar specialties. Insect neuroendocrinologists, for example, have a hard time understanding mammalian neuroendocrinologists, and the reverse. To see this change in science graphically you need only place opened issues of a premier journal such as Nature or Science from fifty years ago side by side with issues of the same journal today. The science writer must somehow thread his way into this polyglot activity, move to a promising sector of the front, and, then, accepting a responsibility the research scientists themselves typically avoid, turn the truth of it into a story interesting to a broad public.

A second obstacle to converting science into literature is the standard format of research reportage in the technical journals. Scientific results are by necessity couched in specialized language, trimmed for brevity, and delivered raw. Metaphor is unwelcome except in small homeopathic doses. Hyperbole, no matter how brilliant, spells death to a scientific reputation. Understatement and modesty, even false modesty, are preferred, because in science discovery counts for everything and personal style next to nothing. In pure literature, metaphor and personal style are, in polar contrast, everything. The creative writer, unlike the scientist, seeks channels of cognitional and emotional expression already deeply carved by instinct and culture. The most successful innovator in literature is an honest illusionist. His product, as Picasso said of visual art, is the lie that helps us to see the truth. Imagery, phrasing, and analogy in pure literature are not crafted to report empirical facts. They are instead the vehicles by which the writer transfers his own feelings directly into the minds of his readers in order to evoke the same emotional response.

The central role of pure literature is the transmission of the details of human experience by artifice that directs aesthetic reaction. Originality and power of metaphor, not new facts and theory, are coin of the realm in creative writing. Their source is an intuitive understanding of human nature as opposed to an accurate knowledge of the material world, at least in the literal, quantifiable form required for science. Metaphor in the best writing strikes the mind in an idiosyncratic manner. Its effect ripples out in a hypertext of culture-bound meaning, yet it triggers emotions that transcend culture. Technical scientific reporting tries to achieve exactly the reverse: it narrows meaning and avoids metaphor in order to preserve literalness and repeatability. It saves emotional resonance for another day and venue.

To illustrate the difference, I've contrived the following imaginary examples of the two forms of writing applied to the same subject, the search for life in a deep cave:

> SCIENCE. The central shaft of the cavern descends from the vegetated rim to the oblique slope of fallen rock at the bottom, reaching a maximum depth of 86 meters before giving way to a lateral channel. On the floor of this latter passageway we found a small assemblage of troglobitic invertebrates, including two previously undescribed eyeless species of the carabid subfamily Bembidini (see also Harrison, in press).

> LETTERS. After an hour's rappel through the Hadean darkness we at last reached the floor of the shaft almost 300 feet below the fern-lined rim. From there we worked our way downward across a screelike rubble to the very bottom. Our headlamps picked out the lateral cavern exactly where Romero's 1926 map claimed it to be. Rick pushed ahead and within minutes shouted back that he had found blind, white cave inhabitants. When we caught up, he pointed to scurrying insects he said were springtails and, to round out the day, at least two species of ground beetles new to science.

In drawing these distinctions in the rules of play, I do not mean to depict scientists as stony Pecksniffs. Quite the contrary. They vary enormously in temperament, probably to the same degree as a random sample from the nonscientific population. Their conferences and seminars are indistinguishable in hubbub from business conventions. Nothing so resembles an ecstatic prospector as a scientist with an important discovery to report to colleagues, to family, to grant officers, to anyone who will listen.

A scientist who has made an important discovery is as much inclined to show off and celebrate as anyone else. Actually, this can be accomplished in a technical article, if done cautiously. The heart of such a report is always the Methods and Materials, followed by Results, all of which must read like your annual tax report. But up front there is also the Introduction, where the author briefly explains the significance of the topic, what was known about it previously, who made the previous principal advances, and what aspect of the whole the author's own findings are meant to address. A smidgen of excitement, maybe even a chaste metaphor or two, is allowed in the Introduction. Still more latitude is permitted for the Discussion, which follows the Results. Here the writer is expected to expatiate on the data and hypotheses as inclination demands. He or she may also push the envelope and make cautious guesses about what lies ahead for future researchers. However, there must be no outbursts such as, "I was excited to find . . ." or "This is certain to be a major advance."

Science writers are in the difficult position of locating themselves somewhere between the two stylistic poles of literature and science. They risk appearing both as journalists to the literati and as amateurs to the scientists. But these judgments, if made, are ignorant and unfair. Enormous room for original thought and expression exists in science writing. Its potential is nothing less than the establishment of what Sir Charles Snow called the third culture, a concept also recently promoted by the author and literary agent John Brockman.

The position nearest the literary pole is that broadly classified as nature writing. With roots going back to nineteenth-century romanticism, it cultivates the facts and theories of science but relies heavily on personal narrative and aesthetic expression. Thanks to writers of the first rank such as Annie Dillard, Barry Lopez, Peter Matthiessen, Bill McKibben, David Quammen, and Jonathan Weimer (a representative but far from exclusive list!), nature writing has become a distinctive American art form.

The pole nearest science is occupied primarily by scientists who choose to deliver their dispatches from the front to a broader public. Ranging from memoirs to philosophical accounts of entire disciplines, their writing resonates with a certain firsthand authority but is constrained to modesty in emotional expression by the conventions of their principal trade. Writing scientists also frequently struggle with the handicap imposed by the lack of connection of their subject to ordinary human experience: few tingles of the spine come from bacterial genetics, and generally the only tears over physical chemistry come as a result of trying to learn it. Despite the inherent difficulties, science writing is bound to grow in influence, because it is the best way to bridge the two cultures into which civilization is still split. Most educated people who are not professionals in the field do not understand science and technology, despite the profound effect of these juggernauts of modernity on every aspect of their lives. Symmetrically, most scientists are semiliterate journeymen with respect to the humanities. They are thus correspondingly removed from the heart and spirit of our species. How to solve this problem is more than just a puzzle for creative writers. It is, if you will permit a scientist a strong narrative-laden metaphor, the central challenge of education in the twenty-first century.

PART

V

— Culture and Society —

So much of creative nonfiction centers on the act of interpretation, for as we write, we interpret our lives: our pasts, our families, our histories. We extend that interpretation to the world around us as well, and recognize, as the writers in this section do, that we are surely social creatures, influenced by political, cultural, and economic currents. "Culture and Society" is a broad topic, but the writers here hone the field for us: from the idea of the American dream to issues of sexual and ethnic identity, war, AIDS, racism, consumer culture, and what it means to contend with the personal as political and the political as personal. Perhaps more than any other subject in this text, Culture and Society insists on blurred boundaries between the inward "I" and the critical "Eye."

As the writers in the "I" section come to understand aspects of themselves, they also discover something about the world around them. Often the pieces hinge on matters of identity and awareness, from Dorothy Allison's excerpt from *Two or Three Things I Know for Sure,* which focuses on sexual identity, to Margaret Atwood's "The Female Body" and Alice Walker's "Becoming What We're Called," which examine ideas about language and gender. Gerald Early's "Life with Daughters: Watching the Miss America Pageant" takes on subjects of race and beauty, while Maxine Hong Kingston's "No Name Woman" and Bharati Mukherjee's "Two Ways to Belong in America" deal with ethnic identity and immigration.

The range of voices and styles here are equally varied. Allison's memoir is narrative, confessional, and intensely personal; Atwood's piece is experimental, drawing on poetic and postmodern elements of fragmentation. Kingston's contemporary classic has a story-within-a-story framework, while Early's essay is analytical, using the Miss America pageant as a point of departure. What all of these voices have in common is a sense of immediacy and honesty, a desire to interpret personal perspective and experience. As with the works of journalistic creative nonfiction, these essays return to considerations of class, culture, and economics, locating the individual within broader contexts beyond the self.

Perhaps because of its origins in reportage, much of the journalistic creative nonfiction in this section looks at ideas of equality and justice. Here again the difference between the personal and the journalistic can become difficult to discern. Lawrence Otis Graham's "Invisible Man," for instance, is a personal essay in that it is based on his experiences as a busboy in an all-white country club. Yet this method is also a journalistic technique of research and investigation, which Graham uses to explore the nature and reality of racism. Graham's point of view is personal but the subject of investigation is the behavior of others. Susan Sontag's excerpt from *AIDS and Its Metaphors* is a discussion piece that seeks insight and discovery in the manner of a more traditional essay, while Michael Herr's "Illumination Rounds" gives us narrative glimpses into the Vietnam War. As with the essays in all of the preceding sections, structure and subject are closely connected. The fragmentation in Herr's work, for instance, reflects the chaos and randomness of wartime, while the diary form in Graham's essay emphasizes the role of observation and participation.

The art of researching and writing about cultural, social, and personal progress is addressed in three craft essays. In her contemporary classic "On Keeping a Notebook," Joan Didion, one of the first practitioners of New Journalism, discusses the ever-present role of the "I." Part of the point of keeping track of our perceptions is, as Didion says, "keeping in touch" with ourselves and who we once were. By keeping a record of our perceptions, we can track our development as thinkers and writers engaged in the business of observing the world. Barbara Ehrenreich's "Getting Ready" is the introduction to her best-selling *Nickel and Dimed: On (Not) Getting By in America,* an exposé of the jobs available to working-class America. Like Graham, she uses an experiential, investigative approach in this book, and "Getting Ready" is a view into what this method requires. Finally, Lee Gutkind, founder and editor of the influential journal *Creative Nonfiction,* provides a comprehensive look at the field—its definitions, controversies, and "rules"—in "The Creative Nonfiction Police." As Gutkind writes:

> More than any other literary genre, the creative nonfiction writer must rely on his or her own conscience and sensitivity to others and display a higher morality and a healthy respect for fairness and justice . . . . This sounds so simple—yet it is so difficult . . . . As writers we intend to make a difference, to affect someone's life over and above our own. To say something that matters—this is why we write. To impact upon society, to put a personal stamp on history.

The "I"

Dorothy Allison

from Two or Three Things I Know for Sure

I had this girlfriend once scared all my other girlfriends off. Big, blond, shy, and butch, just out of the army, drove a two-door Chevy with a reinforced trunk and wouldn't say why.

"What you carry in that thing, girl? You moving contraband state to state?" I was joking, teasing, putting my hand on her butt, grinning at her scowl, touching her in places she couldn't quite admit she liked.

"I an't moving nothing," she told me.

"Uh-huh. Right. So how come I feel so moved?"

She blushed. I love it when women blush, especially those big butch girls who know you want them. And I wanted her. I did. I wanted her. But she was a difficult woman, wouldn't let me give her a backrub, read her palm, or sew up the tear in her jeans—all those ritual techniques Southern femmes have employed in the seduction of innocent butch girls. A basic error, this one was not from the South. Born in Chicago, she was a Yankee runaway raised in Barbados by a daddy who worked as a Mafia bagman and was never really sure if he was bringing up a boy or a girl. He'd bought her her first three-piece suit, then cursed at how good it looked on her and signed the permission form that let her join the army at seventeen.

"My daddy loves me, he just don't understand me. Don't know how to talk to me when I go back." She told me that after I'd helped her move furniture for two hours and we were relaxing over a shared can of beer and stories of how she'd gotten to Tallahassee. I just nodded, pretty sure her daddy understood her as much as he could stand.

I seduced her in the shower. It was all that furniture-moving, I told her, and insisted I couldn't go out in the condition I was in. Simple courtesy. I sent her in the shower first, came in after, and then soaped her back in businesslike fashion so she'd relax a little more. I kept chatting—about the women's center, books I'd read, music, and oh! how long and thick her toenails were. I got down on my knees to examine her toenails.

"Woman," I said, "you have the most beautiful feet."

I let the water pour down over both of us. It was a silly thing, to talk that way in that situation, but sex is like that. There I was, kneeling for her, naked, my hands on her legs, my mouth just where I wanted it to be. I smiled before I leaned forward. She clenched her fists in my hair, moaned when my tongue touched her. The muscles in her thighs began to jump. We nearly drowned in that shower.

"Don't laugh at me," she said later when we were lying limp on wet sheets, and I promised. No.

"Whiskey and cigarettes," she mumbled. "I move whiskey and cigarettes without tax stamps, for the money, that's what I move."

I smiled and raked my teeth across her throat. "Uh-huh."

"And . . . " She paused. I put one leg between her thighs and slid myself up and down until we fit tight, the bone of my hip resting against the arch of her pubic mound, the tangle of her blond curls wiry on my belly. I pushed up off her throat and waited. She looked up at me. Her cheeks were bright red, her eyes almost closed, pearly tears showing at the corners.

"Shaklee! Shaklee products. Oh God! I sell cleaning supplies door to door."

I bit her shoulder, didn't laugh. I rocked her on my leg until she relaxed and laughed herself. I rocked her until she could forgive me for asking. Then she took hold of me and rolled me over and showed me that she wanted me as much as I had wanted her.

"You're quite a story," I whispered to her after.

"Don't tell," she begged.

"Who would I tell?"

Who needs to know?

Not until I was thirty-four did my sister Anne and I sit down together to talk about our lives. She came out on the porch, put a six-pack on my lap, and gave me a wary careful grin.

"All right," Anne said. "You drink half the six-pack and then we'll talk."

"I can't drink," I said.

"I know." She grinned at me.

I frowned. Then, very deliberately, I pulled one of the cans free from the plastic loop, popped it open, and drank deeply. The beer wasn't as cold as it should have been, but the taste was sweet and familiar.

"Not bad," I complimented Anne.

"Yeah, I gave up on those fifty-nine-cent bargains. These days I spend three dollars or I don't buy."

"I'm impressed."

"Oh, don't start. You've never been impressed with anything I've done or said or thought of doing. You were so stuck up you never noticed me at all."

"I noticed." I looked at her, remembering her at thirteen—the first time she had accused me of being weird, making fun of me for not wearing makeup or even knowing what kind of clothes I should have been begging Mama to buy me. "You don't do nothing but read, do you?" Her words put her in the hated camp of my stepfather, who was always snatching books out of my hands and running me out of the house.

"We didn't like each other much," Anne said.

"We didn't know each other."

"Yeah? Well, Mama always thought you peed rose water."

"But you were beautiful. Hell, you didn't even have to pee, you were so pretty. People probably offered to pee for you."

"Oh, they offered to do something, right enough." She gave me a bitter smile.

"You made me feel so ugly."

"You made me feel so stupid."

I couldn't make a joke out of that. Instead, I tried to get her to look at me. I reached over and put my hand on her arm.

When we were girls, my little sister Anne had light shiny hair, fine skin, and guileless eyes. She was a girl whose walk at twelve made men stop to watch her pass, a woman at thirteen who made grown men murderous and teenage boys sweaty with hunger. My mother watched her with the fear of a woman who had been a beautiful girl. I watched her with painful jealousy. Why was she so pretty when I was so plain? When strangers in the grocery store smiled at her and complimented Mama on "that lovely child," I glared and turned away. I wanted to be what my little sister was. I wanted all the things that appeared to be possible for her.

It took me years to learn the truth behind that lie. It took my sister two decades to tell me what it was really like being beautiful, about the hatred that trailed over her skin like honey melting on warm bread.

My beautiful sister had been dogged by contempt just like her less beautiful sisters—more, for she dared to be different yet again, to hope when she was supposed to have given up hope, to dream when she was not the one they saved dreams for. Her days were full of boys sneaking over to pinch her breasts and whisper threats into her ears, of girls who warned her away from their brothers, of thin-lipped adults who lost no opportunity to tell her she really didn't know how to dress.

"You think you pretty, girl? Ha! You an't nothing but another piece of dirt masquerading as better."

"You think you something? What you thinking, you silly bitch?"

I think she was beautiful. I think she still is.

My little sister learned the worth of beauty. She dropped out of high school and fell in love with a boy who got a bunch of his friends to swear that the baby she was carrying could just as easily have been theirs as his. By eighteen she was no longer beautiful, she was ashamed: staying up nights with her bastard son, living in my stepfather's house, a dispatcher for a rug company, unable to afford her own place, desperate to give her life to the first man who would treat her gently.

"Sex ruined that girl," I heard a neighbor tell my mama. "Shoulda kept her legs closed, shoulda known what would happen to her."

"You weren't stupid," I said, my hand on Anne's arm, my words just slightly slurred.

"Uh-huh. Well, you weren't ugly."

We popped open more cans and sat back in our chairs. She talked about her babies. I told her about my lovers. She cursed the men who had hurt her. I told her terrible stories about all the mean women who had lured me into their beds when it wasn't me they really wanted. She told me she had always hated the sight of her husband's cock. I told her that sometimes, all these years later, I still wake up crying, not sure what I have dreamed about, but remembering something bad and crying like a child in great pain. She got a funny look on her face.

"I made sure you were the one," she said. "The one who had to take him his glasses of tea, anything at all he wanted. And I hated myself for it. I knew every time, when you didn't come right back—I knew he was keeping you in there, next to him, where you didn't want to be any more than I did."

She looked at me, then away. "But I never really knew what he was doing," she whispered. "I thought you were so strong. Not like me. I knew I wasn't strong at all. I thought you were like Mama, that you could handle him. I thought you could handle anything. Every time he'd grab hold of me and hang on too long, he'd make me feel so bad and frightened and unable to imagine what he wanted, but afraid, so afraid. I didn't think you felt like that. I didn't think it was the same for you."

We were quiet for a while, and then my sister leaned over and pressed her forehead to my cheek.

"It wasn't fair, was it?" she whispered.

"None of it was," I whispered back, and put my arms around her.

"Goddamn!" she cursed. "Goddamn!" And started to cry. Just that fast, I was crying with her.

"But Mama really loved you, you know," Anne said.

"But you were beautiful."

She put her hands up to her cheeks, to the fine webs of wrinkles under her eyes, the bruised shadows beneath the lines. The skin of her upper arms hung loose and pale. Her makeup ended in a ragged line at her neck, and below it, the skin was puckered, freckled, and sallow.

I put my hand on her head, on the full blond mane that had been her glory when she was twelve. Now she was thirty-two, and the black roots showing at her scalp were sprinkled with gray. I pulled her to me, hugged her, and kissed her neck. Slowly we quieted our crying, holding on to each other. Past my sister's shoulder, I saw her girl coming toward us, a chubby dark child with nervous eyes.

"Mama. Mama, y'all all right?"

My sister turned to her daughter. For a moment I thought she was going to start crying again, but instead she sighed. "Baby," she called, and she put her hands out to touch those little-girl porcelain cheeks. "Oh baby, you know how your mama gets."

"You know how your mama gets." The words echoed in me. If I closed my eyes, I could see again the yellow kitchens of our childhood, where Mama hung her flowered curtains every time we moved, as if they were not cotton but spirit. It was as if every move were another chance to begin again, to claim some safe and clean space for herself and her girls. Every time, we watched her, thinking this time maybe it would be different. And when different did not come, when, every time, the same nightmarish scenes unfolded—shouting and crying and Mama sitting hopelessly at her kitchen table—she spoke those words.

"Oh, girls, you know how your mama gets."

I clenched my hands on my thighs, seeing my niece's mouth go hard. She clamped her teeth as I remembered clamping mine, looked away as I would have done, not wanting to see two tired, half-drunk women looking back at her with her own features. I shook my head once and caught her glance, the wise and sullen look of a not quite adolescent girl who knew too much.

"Pretty girl," I said. "Don't look so hard."

Her mouth softened slightly. She liked being told she was pretty. At eleven so had I. I waved her to my hip, and when she came, I pushed her hair back off her face, using the gestures my mama had used on me. "Oh, you're going to be something special," I told her. Something special.

"My baby's so pretty," Anne said. "Look at her. My baby's just the most beautiful thing in the whole wide world." She grinned, and shook her head. "Just like her mama, huh?" Her voice was only a little bitter, only a little cruel. Just like her mama.

I looked into my niece's sunburned frightened face. Like her mama, like her grandmama, like her aunts—she had that hungry desperate look that trusts nothing and wants everything. She didn't think she was pretty. She didn't think she was worth any-thing at all.

"Let me tell you a story," I whispered. "Let me tell you a story you haven't heard yet." Oh, I wanted to take her, steal her, run with her a thousand miles away from the daddy who barely noticed her, the men who had tried to do to her what my stepfather had done to me. I wanted to pick her up and cradle her. I wanted to save her.

My niece turned her face to me, open and trusting, waiting to be taken away, to be persuaded, or healed, or simply distracted.

All right, I thought. That will do. For one moment, this moment leading to the next, the act of storytelling connecting to the life that might be possible, I held her attention and began.

"Let me tell you about your mama."

My niece looked from me to my sister, and my sister stared at me uncertainly, won-dering if I was going to hurt her, her and her girl.

"Sit down, baby. I got a story to tell you. Look at your mama. You know how she is? Well, let me tell you about the day death was calling your mama's name, death was singing her song and luring her away. She was alone, as alone as only a woman waiting to birth a baby can be. All she saw was darkness. All she heard was her blood singing death. But in the deepest part of that night she heard something else. She heard the baby in her belly crying soft, too weak to make a big noise, too small to know it was alive at all. That's when your mama saved her own life—by choosing it, by claiming it, alone and scared as she was. By pulling you into the world and loving you with her whole heart."

I watched my sister's eyes go wide, watched her mouth work. "Now you telling stories about me?"

I just smiled. "Oh, I got one or two."

That night I sat with my niece and watched my sister going in and out her back door, picking up and sweeping, scolding her dogs for jumping up on her clean work clothes. My niece was sleepy, my sister exhausted. Their features were puffy, pale, and too much alike. I surprised myself then, turning my niece's face to mine and starting another story.

"When your mama was a girl," I told her, "she was so beautiful people said the sun shone brighter when she walked out in the day. They said the moon took on glitter when she went out in the night. But, strangest of all, people said the June bugs catching sight of her would begin to light and try to sing an almost human song. It got to the point she had to stay home and hide to keep the sun from getting too hot, the moon from burning up, the June bugs from going hoarse and dying out."

"Ahhh." The two of them looked at me, almost smiling, almost laughing, waiting. I put my hand out, not quite touching my sister's face, and drew my fingers along the line of her neck from just below her ear to the softness of her chin. With my other hand I made the same gesture along my niece's face.

"See here?" I whispered. "This is where you can see it. That's the mark of the beautiful Gibson women, both of you have it."

My niece touched her cheek, mouth open.

"Here?" she asked.

Yes.

Two or three things I know, two or three things I know for sure, and one of them is that if we are not beautiful to each other, we cannot know beauty in any form.

Margaret Atwood

The Female Body

> . . . entirely devoted to the subject of "The Female Body." Knowing how well
> you have written on this topic . . . this capacious topic . . .
> —letter from *Michigan Quarterly Review*

1.

I agree, it's a hot topic. But only one? Look around, there's a wide range. Take my own, for instance.

I get up in the morning. My topic feels like hell. I sprinkle it with water, brush parts of it, rub it with towels, powder it, add lubricant. I dump in the fuel and away goes my topic, my topical topic, my controversial topic, my capacious topic, my limping topic, my nearsighted topic, my topic with back problems, my badly behaved topic, my vulgar topic, my outrageous topic, my aging topic, my topic that is out of the question and anyway still can't spell, in its oversized coat and worn winter boots, scuttling along the sidewalk as if it were flesh and blood, hunting for what's out there, an avocado, an alderman, an adjective, hungry as ever.

2.

The basic Female Body comes with the following accessories: garter belt, panti-girdle, crinoline, camisole, bustle, brassiere, stomacher, chemise, virgin zone, spike heels, nose ring, veil, kid gloves, fishnet stockings, fichu, bandeau, Merry Widow, weepers, chokers, barrettes, bangles, beads, lorgnette, feather boa, basic black, compact, Lycra stretch one-piece with modesty panel, designer peignoir, flannel nightie, lace teddy, bed, head.

3.

The Female Body is made of transparent plastic and lights up when you plug it in. You press a button to illuminate the different systems. The circulatory system is red, for the heart and arteries, purple for the veins; the respiratory system is blue; the lymphatic system is yellow; the digestive system is green, with liver and kidneys in aqua. The nerves are done in orange and the brain is pink. The skeleton, as you might expect, is white.

The reproductive system is optional, and can be removed. It comes with or without a miniature embryo. Parental judgment can thereby be exercised. We do not wish to frighten or offend.

4.

He said, I won't have one of those things in the house. It gives a young girl a false notion of beauty, not to mention anatomy. If a real woman was built like that she'd fall on her face.

She said, If we don't let her have one like all the other girls she'll feel singled out. It'll become an issue. She'll long for one and she'll long to turn into one. Repression breeds sublimation. You know that.

He said, It's not just the pointy plastic tits, it's the wardrobes. The wardrobes and that stupid male doll, what's his name, the one with the underwear glued on.

She said, Better to get it over with when she's young. He said, All right, but don't let me see it.

She came whizzing down the stairs, thrown like a dart. She was stark naked. Her hair had been chopped off, her head was turned back to front, she was missing some toes and she'd been tattooed all over her body with purple ink in a scrollwork design. She hit the potted azalea, trembled there for a moment like a botched angel, and fell.

He said, I guess we're safe.

5.

The Female Body has many uses. It's been used as a door knocker, a bottle opener, as a clock with a ticking belly, as something to hold up lampshades, as a nutcracker, just squeeze the brass legs together and out comes your nut. It bears torches, lifts victorious wreaths, grows copper wings and raises aloft a ring of neon stars; whole buildings rest on its marble heads.

It sells cars, beer, shaving lotion, cigarettes, hard liquor; it sells diet plans and diamonds, and desire in tiny crystal bottles. Is this the face that launched a thousand products? You bet it is, but don't get any funny big ideas, honey, that smile is a dime a dozen.

It does not merely sell, it is sold. Money flows into this country or that country, flies in, practically crawls in, suitful after suitful, lured by all those hairless pre-teen legs. Listen, you want to reduce the national debt, don't you? Aren't you patriotic? That's the spirit. That's my girl.

She's a natural resource, a renewable one luckily, because those things wear out so quickly. They don't make 'em like they used to. Shoddy goods.

6.

One and one equals another one. Pleasure in the female is not a requirement. Pair-bonding is stronger in geese. We're not talking about love, we're talking about biology. That's how we all got here, daughter.

Snails do it differently. They're hermaphrodites, and work in threes.

7.

Each Female Body contains a female brain. Handy. Makes things work. Stick pins in it and you get amazing results. Old popular songs. Short circuits. Bad dreams.

Anyway: each of these brains has two halves. They're joined together by a thick cord; neural pathways flow from one to the other, sparkles of electric information washing to and fro. Like light on waves. Like a conversation. How does a woman know? She listens. She listens in.

The male brain, now, that's a different matter. Only a thin connection. Space over here, time over there, music and arithmetic in their own sealed compartments. The right brain doesn't know what the left brain is doing. Good for aiming though, for hitting the target when you pull the trigger. What's the target? Who's the target? Who cares? What matters is hitting it. That's the male brain for you. Objective.

This is why men are so sad, why they feel so cut off, why they think of themselves as orphans cast adrift, footloose and stringless in the deep void. What void? she asks. What are you talking about? The void of the universe, he says, and she says Oh and looks out the window and tries to get a handle on it, but it's no use, there's too much going on, too many rustlings in the leaves, too many voices, so she says, Would you like a cheese sandwich, a piece of cake, a cup of tea? And he grinds his teeth because she doesn't understand, and wanders off, not just alone but Alone, lost in the dark, lost in the skull, searching for the other half, the twin who could complete him.

Then it comes to him: he's lost the Female Body! Look, it shines in the gloom, far ahead, a vision of wholeness, ripeness, like a giant melon, like an apple, like a metaphor for "breast" in a bad sex novel; it shines like a balloon, like a foggy noon, a watery moon, shimmering in its egg of light.

Catch it. Put it in a pumpkin, in a high tower, in a compound, in a chamber, in a house, in a room. Quick, stick a leash on it, a lock, a chain, some pain, settle it down, so it can never get away from you again.

Gerald Early

Life with Daughters:
Watching the Miss America Pageant

The theater is an expression of our dream life—of our unconscious aspirations.
—David Mamet, "A Tradition of the Theater as Art," *Writing in Restaurants*

Aunt Hester went out one night,—where or for what I do not know,—and happened to be absent when my master desired her presence.
—Frederick Douglass, *Narrative of the Life of Frederick Douglass*

Adults, older girls, shops, magazines, newspapers, window signs—all the world had agreed that a blue-eyed, yellow-haired, pink-skinned doll was what every girl child treasured.
—Toni Morrison, *The Bluest Eye*

It is now fast become a tradition—if one can use that word to describe a habit about which I still feel a certain amount of shamefacedness—for our household to watch the Miss America contest on television every year. The source of my embarrassment is that this program remains, despite its attempts in recent years to modernize its frightfully antique quality of "women on parade," a kind of maddeningly barbarous example of the persistent, hard, crass urge to sell: from the plugs for the sponsor that are made a part of the script (that being an antique of fifties and sixties television; the show does not remember its history so much as it seems bent on repeating it) to the constant references to the success of some of the previous contestants and the reminders that this is some sort of scholarship competition, the program has all the cheap earnestness of a social uplift project being played as a musical revue in Las Vegas. Paradoxically, it wishes to convince the public that it is a common entertainment while simultaneously wishing to convey that it is more than mere entertainment. The Miss America pageant is the worst sort of "Americanism," the soft smile of sex and the hard sell of toothpaste and hair dye ads wrapped in the dreamy ideological gauze of "making it through one's own effort." In a perverse way, I like the show; it is the only live television left other than sports, news broadcasts, performing arts awards programs, and speeches by the president. I miss live TV. It was the closest thing to theater for the masses. And the Miss America contest is, as it has been for some time, the most perfectly rendered theater in our culture, for it so perfectly captures what we yearn for: a low-class ritual, a polished restatement of vulgarity, that wants to open the door to high-class respectability by way of plain middle-class anxiety and ambition. Am I doing all right? the contestants seem to ask in a kind of reassuring, if numbed, way. The contest brings together all the American classes in a show-biz spectacle of classlessness and tastelessness.

My wife has been interested in the Miss America contest since childhood, and so I ascribe her uninterrupted engagement with America's cultural passage into fall (Miss America, like college and pro football, signifies for us as a nation the end of summer; the contest was invented, back in 1921, by Atlantic City merchants to prolong the summer season past Labor Day) as something mystically and uniquely female. She, as a black woman, had a long-standing quarrel with the contest until Vanessa Williams was chosen the first black Miss America in September 1983. Somehow she felt vindicated by Williams for all those years as a black girl in Dallas, watching white women win the crown and thumb their noses at her, at her blackness, at her straightened hair, her thick lips, her wide nose. She played with white Barbie dolls as a little girl and had, I suppose, a "natural," or at least an understandable and predictable, interest in seeing the National White Barbie Doll chosen every year because for such a long time, of course, the Miss America contest, with few exceptions, was a totemic preoccupation with and representation of a particularly stilted form of patriarchal white supremacy. In short, it was a national white doll contest. And well we know that every black girl growing up in the fifties and early sixties had her peculiar love-hate affair with white dolls, with mythicized white femininity. I am reminded of this historical instance: everyone knows that in the Brown versus Topeka Board of Education case (the case that resulted in the Supreme Court decision to integrate public schools) part of the sociological evidence used by the plaintiffs to show the psychological damage suffered by blacks because of Jim Crow was an account by Kenneth Clarke of how, when offered a choice between a black doll and a white doll, little black girls invariably chose the white doll because they thought it "prettier."

On the front page of the January 6, 1962, *Pittsburgh Courier*, a black weekly, is a picture of a hospitalized black girl named Connie Smith holding a white doll sent to her by Attorney General Robert Kennedy. Something had occurred between 1954, when the Supreme Court made its decision, and 1962 which made it impossible for Kennedy to send the girl a black doll, and this impossibility was to signal, ironically, that the terms of segregation and the terms of racial integration, the very icon of them, were to be exactly the same. Kennedy could not send the girl a black doll, as it would have implied, in the age of integration, that he was, in effect, sending her a Jim Crow toy, a toy that would emphasize the girl's race. In the early sixties such a gesture would have been considered condescending. To give the black girl a white doll in the early sixties was to mainstream the black girl into the culture, to say that she was worthy of the same kind of doll that a white girl would have. But how can it be that conservatism and liberalism, segregation and integration, could produce, fantastically, the same results, the identical iconography: a black girl hugging a white doll because everyone thinks it is best for her to have it? How can it be that at one time the white doll is the sign of the black girl's rejection and inferiority and fewer than ten years later it is the sign of her acceptance and redemption? Those who are knowledgeable about certain aspects of the black mind or the collective black consciousness realize, of course, that the issues of segregation and integration, of conservatism and liberalism, of acceptance and rejection, of redemption and inferiority, are all restatements of the same immovable and relentless reality of the meaning of American blackness; that this is all a matter of the harrowing and compelling intensity that is called, quaintly, race pride. And in this context, the issue of white dolls, this fetishization of young white feminine beauty, and the complexity of black girlhood becomes an unresolved theme stated in a strident key. Blacks have preached for a long time about how to heal their daughters of whiteness: in the November 1908 issue of *The Colored American Magazine*, E. A. Johnson wrote an article entitled, "Negro Dolls for Negro Babies," in which he said, "I am convinced that one of the best ways to teach Negro children to respect their own color would be to see to it that the children be given colored dolls to play with. . . . To give a Negro child a white doll means to create in it a prejudice against its own color, which will cling to it through life." Lots of black people believed this and, for all I know, probably still do, as race pride, or the lack thereof, burns and crackles like a current through most African-American public and private discourse. Besides, it is no easy matter to wish white dolls away.

A few years ago I was thumbing through an album of old family photographs and saw one of me and my oldest sister taken when I was four and she was nine. It struck me, transfixed me really, as it was a color photo and most of the old family pictures taken when I was a boy were black-and-white because my mother could not afford to have color pictures developed. We, my sister and I, are sitting on an old stuffed blue chair and she is holding a white doll in her hand, displaying it for the picture. I remember the occasion very well, as my sister was to be confirmed in our small, all-black Episcopal church that day, and she was, naturally, proud of the moment and wanted to share it with her favorite toy. That, I remembered, was why these were color pictures. It was a special day for the family, a day my mother wanted to celebrate by taking special pictures. My mother is a very dark woman who has a great deal of race pride and often speaks about my sisters' having black dolls. I was surprised, in looking at the picture recently, that they ever owned a white one, that indeed a white one had been a favorite.

My wife grew up—enjoyed the primary years of black girlhood, so to speak—during the years 1954 through 1962; she was about five or six years younger than my oldest sister. She lived in a southern state, or a state that was a reasonable facsimile of a southern state. She remembers that signs for colored and white bathrooms and water fountains persisted well into the mid-sixties in Texas. She remembers also Phyllis George, the Miss America from Denton, Texas, who went on to become a television personality for several years. She has always been very interested in George's career, and she has always disliked her. "She sounds just like a white girl from Texas," my wife likes to say, always reminding me that while both blacks and whites in Texas have accents, they do not sound alike. George won the contest in 1971, my wife's freshman year at the University of Pennsylvania and around the time she began to wear an Afro, a popular hairstyle for young black women in the days of "our terrible blackness" or "our black terribleness." It was a year fraught with complex passages into black womanhood for her. To think that a white woman from Texas should win the Miss America title that year! For my wife, the years of watching the Miss America contest were nothing more, in some sense continue to be nothing more, than an expression of anger made all the worse by the very unconscious or semiconscious nature of it. But if the anger has been persistent, so has her enormous capacity to "take it"; for in all these years it has never occurred to her to refuse to watch because, like the black girl being offered the white doll, like all black folk being offered white gifts, she has absolutely no idea how that is done, and she is not naïve enough to think that a simple refusal would be an act of empowerment. Empowerment comes only through making demands of our bogeymen, not by trying to convince ourselves we are not tormented. Yet, paradoxically, among blacks there is the bitter hope that a simplistic race pride will save us, a creed that masks its complex contradictions beneath lapping waves of bourgeois optimism and bourgeois anguish; for race pride clings to the opposing notions that the great hope (but secret fear) of an African-American future is, first, that blacks will always remain black and, second, that the great fear (but secret hope) of an African-American future is that blacks will not always remain black but evolve into something else. Race pride, which at its most insistent argues that blackness is everything, becomes, in its attempt to be the psychological quest for sanity, a form of dementia that exists as a response to that form of white dementia that says blackness is nothing. Existing as it does as a reactive force battling against a white preemptive presumption, race pride begins to take on the vices of an unthinking dogma and the virtues of a disciplined religious faith, all in the same instance. With so much at stake, race pride becomes both the act of making a virtue of a necessity and making a necessity of a virtue and, finally, making a profound and touching absurdity of both virtue and necessity. In some ways my wife learned her lessons well in her youth: she never buys our daughters white dolls.

My daughters, Linnet, age ten, and Rosalind, age seven, have become staunch fans of beauty contests in the last three years. In that time they have watched, in their entirety, several Miss America pageants, one Miss Black America contest, and one Miss USA. At first, I ascribed this to the same impulse that made my wife interested in such events when she was little: something secretly female, just as an interest in professional sports might be ascribed to something peculiarly male. Probably it is a sort of resentment that black girls harbor toward these contests. But that could not really be the case with my daughters.

After all, they have seen several black entrants in these contests and have even seen black winners. They also have black dolls.

Back in the fall of 1983 when Vanessa Williams became Miss America, we, as a family, had our picture taken with her when she visited St. Louis. We went, my wife and I, to celebrate the grand moment when white American popular culture decided to embrace black women as something other than sexual subversives or fat, kindly maids cleaning up and caring for white families. We had our own, well, royalty, and royal origins mean a great deal to people who have been denied their myths and their right to human blood. White women reformers may be ready to scrap the Miss America contest. (And the contest has certainly responded to the criticism it has been subjected to in recent years by muting some of the fleshier aspects of the program while, in its attempts to be even more the anxiety-ridden middle-class dream-wish, emphasizing more and more the magic of education and scholarly attainments.) It is now the contest that signifies the quest for professionalism among bourgeois women, and the first achievement of the professional career is to win something in a competition. But if there is a movement afoot to bring down the curtain finally on Miss America, my wife wants no part of it: "Whites always want to reform and end things when black people start getting on the gravy train they've been enjoying for years. What harm does the Miss America contest do?" None, I suppose, especially since black women have been winning lately.

Linnet and Rosalind were too young when we met Vanessa Williams to recall anything about the pictures, but they are amazed to see themselves in a bright, color Polaroid picture with a famous person, being part of an event which does not strike a chord in their consciousness because they cannot remember being alive when it happened. I often wonder if they attach any significance to the pictures at all. They think Vanessa is very pretty, prettier than their mother, but they attach no significance to being pretty—that is to say, no real value; they would not admire someone simply because he or she was good-looking. They think Williams is beautiful, but they do not wish that she was their mother. And this issue of being beautiful is not to be taken lightly in the life of a black girl. About two years ago Linnet started coming home from school wishing aloud that her hair was long and blond so that she could fling it about, the way she saw many of her white classmates doing. As she attends a school that is more than 90 percent white, it seemed inevitable to my wife that one of our daughters would become sensitive about her appearance. At this time Linnet's hair was not straightened and she wore it in braids. Oddly, despite the fact that she wanted a different hairstyle that would permit her hair to "blow in the wind," so to speak, she vehemently opposed having it straightened, although my wife has straightened hair, after having worn an Afro for several years. I am not sure why Linnet did not want her hair straightened; perhaps, after seeing her teenage cousin have her hair straightened on several occasions, the process of hair straightening seemed distasteful or disheartening or frightening. Actually, I do not think Linnet wanted to change her hair to be beautiful; she wanted to be like everyone else. But perhaps this is simply wishful thinking here or playing with words because Linnet must have felt her difference as being a kind of ugliness. Yet she is not a girl who is subject to illusion. Once, about a year earlier, when she had had a particularly rough day in school, I told her, in a father's patronizing way with a daughter, that I thought she was the most beautiful girl in the world. She looked at me strangely when I said that and then replied matter-of-factly: "I don't think I'm beautiful at all. I think I'm just ordinary. There is nothing wrong with that, is there,

Daddy? Just to be ordinary?" "Are you unhappy to be ordinary?" I asked. She thought for a moment, then said quietly and finally, "No. Are you?"

Hair straightening, therefore, was not an option and would not have been even if Linnet had wanted it, because my wife was opposed to having Linnet's hair straightened at her age. At first, Linnet began going to school with her hair unbraided. Unfortunately, this turned out to be a disastrous hairdo, as her hair shrank during the course of a day to a tangled mess. Finally, my wife decided to have both Linnet and Rosalind get short Afro haircuts. Ostensibly, this was to ease the problem of taking swim lessons during the summer. In reality, it was to end Linnet's wishes for a white hairstyle by, in effect, foreclosing any possibility that she could remotely capture such a look. Rosalind's hair was cut so that Linnet would not feel that she was being singled out. (Alas, the trials of being both the second and the younger child!) At first, the haircuts caused many problems in school. Some of the children—both black and white—made fun of them. Brillo heads, they were called, and fungus and Afro heads. One group of black girls at school refused to play with Linnet. "You look so ugly with that short hair," they would say. "Why don't you wear your hair straight like your mom? Your mom's hair is so pretty." Then, for the first time, the girls were called niggers by a white child on their school bus, although I think neither the child nor my daughters completely understood the gravity of that obscenity. People in supermarkets would refer to them as boys unless they were wearing dresses. Both girls went through a period when they suffered most acutely from that particular American disease, that particularly African-American disease, the conjunction of oppression and exhibitionistic desire: self-consciousness. They thought about their hair all the time. My wife called the parents of the children who teased them. The teasing stopped for the most part, although a few of the black girls remained so persistent that the white school counselor suggested that Linnet's and Rosalind's hair be straightened. "I'm white," he said, "and maybe I shouldn't get into this, but they might feel more comfortable if they wore a different hairstyle." My wife angrily rejected that bit of advice. She had them wear dresses more often to make them look unmistakably like girls, although she refused out of hand my suggestion of having their ears pierced. She is convinced that pierced ears are just a form of mutilation, primitive tattooing or scarring passing itself off as something fashionable. Eventually, the girls became used to their hair. Now, after more than a year, they hardly think about it, and even if Linnet wears a sweat suit or jeans, no one thinks she is a boy because she is budding breasts. Poor Rosalind still suffers on occasion in supermarkets because she shows no outward signs of sexual maturity. Once, while watching Linnet look at her mother's very long and silken straight hair, the hair that the other black girls at school admire, always calling it pretty, I asked her if she would like to have hers straightened.

"Not now," she said. "Maybe when I'm older. It'll be something different."

"Do you think you will like it?" I asked.

"Maybe," she said.

And in that "maybe," so calmly and evenly uttered, rests the complex contradictions, the uneasy tentative negotiations of that which cannot be compromised yet can never be realized in this flawed world as an ideal; there is, in that "maybe," the epistemology of race pride for black American women so paradoxically symbolized by their straightened hair. In the February 1939 issue of *The Atlantic Monthly*, a black woman named Kimbal Goffman (possibly a pseudonym) wrote an essay entitled "Black Pride" in which she accused blacks of being ashamed of their heritage and, even more damningly in some of her barbs obviously aimed at black women, of their looks:

> . . . why are so many manufacturers becoming rich through the manufacture of bleaching preparations? Why are hair-straightening combs found in nearly every Negro home? Why is the following remark made so often to a newborn baby, when grandma or auntie visits it for the first time? "Tell Mother she must pinch your nose every morning. If she doesn't, you're gonna have a sure 'nough darky nose."

According to Goffman, blacks do not exploit what society has given them; they are simply ashamed to have what they have, tainted as it is with being associated with a degraded people, and long to be white or to have possessions that would accrue a kind of white status. In the essay, blacks in general receive their share of criticism but only black women are criticized in a gender-specific way that their neurotic sense of inferiority concerning physical appearance is a particularly dangerous form of reactionism as it stigmatizes each new generation. According to Goffman, it is black women, because they are mothers, who perpetuate their sense of inferiority by passing it on to their children. In this largely Du Boisian argument, Goffman advises, "Originality is the backbone of all progress." And, in this sense, originality means understanding blackness as something uncontrolled or uninfluenced by what whites say it is. This is the idealism of race pride that demands both purity and parity. Exactly one year later, in the February 1940 issue of *The Brown American*, a black magazine published in Philadelphia, Lillian Franklin McCall wrote an article about the history of black women beauty shop owners and entrepreneurs entitled "Appointment at Seven." The opening paragraph is filled with dollar signs:

> The business of straightening milady's insistent curls tinkles cash registers in the country to the tune of two million and a half dollars a year. And that covers merely the semi-monthly session with the hairdresser for the estimated four million of Eve's sepia adult daughters by national census. Today there is a growing trend to top off the regular, "Shampoo and wave," with a facial; and, perhaps, a manicure. New oil treatments and rinses prove a lure, too, so milady finds her beauty budget stepped up from approximately $39 yearly for an average $1.25 or $1.50 "hair-do," to $52.00 per year if she adds a facial to the beauty rite, and $10 more, for the manicure.

In a Booker T. Washington tone, McCall goes on to describe how the establishment of a black beauty culture serves as a source of empowerment for black women:

> Brown business it is, in all its magnitude for Miss Brown America receives her treatments from the hands of Negro beauticians and her hair preparations and skin dreams come, usually from Negro laboratories.

She then tells the reader that leading companies in this field were founded by black women: Madam C. J. Walker, Mrs. Annie Turbo Malone, Madame Sara Spencer Washington. And one is struck by the absences that this essay evokes, not only in comparison to Goffman's piece but also to Elsie Johnson McDougald's major manifesto on black women, "The Task of Negro Womanhood," that appeared in Alain Locke's seminal 1925 anthology of African-American thought, *The New Negro*. In McDougald's piece, which outlines all the economic status and achievements of black women at the time, there is absolutely no mention of black beauty culture, no mention of Madame C. J. Walker, although her newspaper ads were among the biggest in black newspapers nationwide during the twenties. (And why did McDougald not mention black women's beauty workers and businesspeople culture along with the nurses, domestics, clerks, and teachers she discusses at length? It can scarcely be because she, as a trained and experienced writer on black sociological matters, did not think of it.)[1] It is not simply money or black woman's industry or endeavor that makes the black woman present or a presence; it is beauty culture generally which finally brings her into being, and specifically, her presence is generated by her hair. What for one black woman writer, Goffman, is an absence and thus a sign of degradation, is for another a presence and a sign of economic possibilities inherent in feminine aesthetics.

What did I see as a boy when I passed the large black beauty shop on Broad and South streets in Philadelphia where the name of its owner, Adele Reese, commanded such respect or provoked such jealousy? What did I see there but a long row of black women dressed immaculately in white tunics, washing and styling the hair of other black women? That was a sign of what culture, of what set of politics? The sheen of those straightened heads, the entire enterprise of the making of black feminine beauty: was it an enactment of a degradation inspirited by a bitter inferiority or was it a womanly laying on of hands where black women were, in their way, helping themselves to live through and transcend their degradation? As a boy, I used to watch and wonder as my mother straightened my sisters' hair every Saturday night for church on Sunday morning. Under a low flame on the stove, the hot comb would glow dully; from an open jar of Apex bergamot hair oil or Dixie Peach, my mother would extract blobs and place them on the back of one hand, deftly applying the oil to strands of my sisters' hair with the other. And the strange talk about a "light press" or a "heavy press" or a "close press" to get the edges and the ends; the concern about the hair "going back" if caught in the rain. Going back where, I wondered. To Africa? To the bush? And the constant worry and vigil about burning, getting too close to the scalp. I can remember hearing my sisters' hair sizzle and crackle as the comb passed through with a kind of pungent smell of actually burning hair. And I, like an intentional moth, with lonely narrow arcs, hovered near this flame of femininity with a fascinated impertinence. Had I witnessed the debilitating nullity of absence or was it the affirmation of an inescapable presence? Had I witnessed a mutilation or a rite of devotion? Black women's hair is, I decided even as a boy, unintelligible. And now I wonder, is the acceptance of the reigns of black women as Miss America a sign that black beauty has become part of the mainstream culture? Is the black woman now truly a presence?

We, I and my wife and our daughters, sat together and watched the latest Miss America contest. We did what we usually do. We ate popcorn. We laughed at all the talent numbers, particularly the ones when the contestants were opera singers or dancers. We laughed when the girls tried to answer grand social questions—such as "How can we inspire children to achieve and stay in school?" or "How can we address the problem of mainstreaming physically disadvantaged people?"—in thirty seconds. In fact, as Rosalind told me after the show, the main reason my daughters watch the Miss America pageant is that "it's funny." My daughters laugh because they cannot understand why the women are doing what they are doing, why they are trying so hard to please, to be pleasing. This must certainly be a refreshing bit of sanity, as the only proper response for such a contest is simply to dismiss it as hilarious; this grandiose version of an elocution, charm school, dance and music recital, which is not a revelation of talent but a reaffirmation of bourgeois cultural conditioning. And this bit of sanity on my daughters' part may prove hopeful for our future, for our American future, for our African-American future, if black girls are, unlike my wife when she was young, no longer angry. When it was announced that Miss Missouri, Debbye Turner, the third black to be Miss America, was the winner, my children were indifferent. It hardly mattered to them who won, and a black woman's victory meant no more than if any other contestant had prevailed. "She's pretty," Linnet said. She won two dollars in a bet with my wife, who did not think it possible that another black Miss America would be chosen. "Vanessa screwed up for the whole race," she told me once. "It's the race burden, the sins of the one become the original sins of us all." Linnet said simply, "She'll win because she is the best." Meritocracy is still a valid concept with the young.

For me, it was almost to be expected that Miss Turner would win. First, she received more precontest publicity than any other contestant in recent years, with the possible exception of the black woman who was chosen Miss Mississippi a few years ago. Second, after the reign of Vanessa Williams, one would think that the Miss America powers that be very much wanted to have another black win and have a successful reign so that the contest itself could both prove its good faith (to blacks) and forestall criticism from white feminists and liberals (who are always put in a difficult position when the object of their disapproval is a black woman). As with the selection of Williams, the contest gained a veneer of post-modernist social and political relevance not only by selecting a black again but by having an Asian, a kidney donor, and a hearing-impaired woman among the top ten finalists. This all smacks of affirmative action or the let's-play-fair-with-the-underrepresented doctrine, which, as Miss Virginia pointed out after the contest, smacks of politics. But the point she missed, of course, is the point that all people who oppose affirmative action miss. The selection process for the Miss America contest has always been political. Back in the days when only white college women, whose main interest in most instances was a degree in MRS, could win, the contest was indeed just as political as it is now, a clear ideological bow to both patriarchal ideals and racism. It is simply a matter of which politics you prefer, and while no politics are perfect, some are clearly better than others. But in America, it must be added, the doctrine of fair play should not even be graced with such a sophisticated term as "political." It is more our small-town, bourgeois Christian, muscular myth of ethical rectitude, the tremendous need Americans feel to be decent. So Miss Turner is intended to be both the supersession of Vanessa Williams—a religious vet student whose ambitions are properly, well, post-modernist Victorianism, preach do-goodism, evoke the name of God whenever you speak of your ambitions, and live with smug humility—and the redemption of the image of black women in American popular culture, since the Miss America contest is one of the few vehicles of display and competition for women in popular culture.

And if my daughters have come to one profound penetration of this cultural rite, it is that the contest ought to be laughed at in some ways, as most of the manifestations of popular culture ought to be for being the shoddy illusions that they are. For one always ought to laugh at someone or a group of someones who are trying to convince you that nothing is something—and that is not really the same as someone trying to convince you that you can have something for nothing, because in the popular culture business, the price for nothing is the same as the price for something; this "nothing is something" is, in fact, in most cases what the merchandising of popular culture is all about. (But as Mother reminded me as a boy: nothing is nothing and something is something. Accept no substitutes!) For my children, the contest can be laughed at because it is so completely meaningless to them; they know it is an illusion despite its veneer as a competition. And it is that magical word, competition, which is used over and over again all night long by the host and hostesses of the Miss America show (a contest, like most others these days, from the SATs to professional sports, that is made up of a series of competitions within the framework of larger competitions in such a pyramid that the entire structure of the outside world, for the bourgeois mind, is a frightful maze, a strangulating skein of competitions), that is the touchstone of reality, the momentous signifier that the sponsors of the pageant hope will give this extravaganza new significance and new life. For everything that we feel is important now is a matter of competition, beating out someone else for a prize, for some cheap prestige, a moment of notice before descending to cipherhood again; competition ranging from high culture (literary prizes, which seem to be awarded every day in the week, and classical music competitions for every instrument in a symphony orchestra, because of course for high culture one can never have enough art) to mid-culture (the entire phenomenon of American education, from academic honors to entrance require-ments for prestigious schools, because of course for the middle class one can never have enough education or enough professionalism) to low culture (playing the lottery and vari-ous forms of gambling, because of course for the lower class one can never hope enough for money). And the more stringent and compulsively expressed the competition is (and the Miss America contest has reached a new height of hysteria in both the stridency and compulsion of the competition), the more legitimate and noteworthy it is.

Everyone in our culture wants to win a prize. Perhaps that is the grand lesson we have taken with us from kindergarten in the age of the perversions of Dewey-style education: everyone gets a ribbon, and praise becomes a meaningless narcotic to soothe egoistic dis-temper. And in our bourgeois coming-of-age, we simply crave more and more ribbons and praise, the attainment of which becomes all the more delightful and satisfying if they are gotten at someone else's expense. Competition, therefore, becomes in the end a kind of laissez-faire psychotherapy that structures and orders our impossible rages of ambition, our rages to be noticed. But competition does not produce better people (a myth we have swal-lowed whole); it does not even produce better candidates; it simply produces more desper-ately grasping competitors. The "quality" of the average Miss America contestant is not significantly better now than it was twenty-five years ago, although the desires of today's contestants may meet with our approval (who could possibly disapprove of a black woman who wishes to be a vet in this day of careerism as the expression of independence and polit-ical empowerment), but then the women of twenty-five years ago wanted what their audi-ences approved of as well. That is not necessarily an advance or progress; that is simply a recognition that we are all bound by the mood and temper of our time. So, in this vast com-petition, this fierce theatrical warfare where all the women are supposed to love their neigh-bor while they wish to beat her brains out, this warfare so pointedly exposed before the nation, what we have chosen is not the Royal American Daughter (although the contest's preoccupation with the terminology of aristocracy mirrors the public's need for such a per-son as the American princess) but rather the Cosmopolitan Girl. As the magazine ad states:[2]

> Can a girl be too Busy? I'm taking seventeen units at Princeton, pushing on with
> my career during vacations and school breaks, study singing and dancing when
> I can, try never to lose track of my five closest chums, steal the time for Michael
> Jackson and Thomas Hardy, work for an anti-drug program for kids and, oh yes,
> I hang out with three horses, three cats, two birds and my dog Jack. My favorite

magazine says "too busy" just means you don't want to miss anything . . . I love that magazine. I guess you can say I'm That Cosmopolitan Girl.

When one reads about these women in the Miss America contest, that is precisely what they sound like: the Cosmopolitan Girl who knows how to have serious fun, and she has virtually nothing with which to claim our attention except a moralistic bourgeois diligence. To use a twenties term: she sounds "swell." She is an amalgam of both lead characters portrayed by Patty Duke on her old TV show: the studious, serious kid and the "typical" wacky but good-hearted suburban teenager, or, to borrow Ann Douglas's concept, she is the Teen Angel: the bourgeois girl who can do everything, is completely self-absorbed with her leisure, and has a heart of gold. Once again, with the Miss America contest we have America's vehement preoccupation with innocence, with its inability to deal with the darkness of youth, the darkness of its own uselessly expressed ambition, the dark complexity of its own simplistic morality of sunshine and success, the darkness, righteous rage, and bitter depth of its own daughters. Once again, when the new Miss America, victorious and smiling, walks down the runway, we know that runway, that victory march, to be the American catwalk of supreme bourgeois self-consciousness and supreme illusion. We are still being told that nothing is something.

Nonetheless, the fact that Miss Turner won struck both my wife and me as important, as something important for the race. We laughed during the contest, but we did not laugh when she was chosen. We wanted her to win very much; it is impossible to escape that need to see the race uplifted, to thumb your nose at whites in a competition. It is impossible for blacks not to want to see their black daughters elevated to the platforms where white women are. Perhaps this tainted desire, an echoing "Ballad of the Brown Girl" that resounds in the unconscious psyche of all black people, is the unity of feeling which is the only race pride blacks have ever had since they became Americans; for race pride for the African American, finally, is something that can only be understood as existing on the edge of tragedy and history and is, finally, that which binds both together to make the African American the darkly and richly complicated person he or she is. In the end, both black women magazine writers quoted earlier were right: race pride is transcending your degradation while learning to live in it and with it. To paraphrase an idea of Dorothy Sayers, race pride must teach blacks that they are not to be saved *from* degradation but saved *in* it.

A few days after the contest I watched both my daughters playing Barbies, as they call it. They squat on the floor on their knees, moving their dolls around through an imaginary town and in imaginary houses. I decided to join them and squatted down too, asking them the rules of their game, which they patiently explained as though they did not mind having me, the strange adult, invade their children's world. I told them it was hard for me to squat and asked if I could simply sit down, but they said that one always plays Barbies while squatting. It was a rule that had to be obeyed. As they went along, explaining relationships among their myriad dolls and the several landscapes, as complicated a genealogy as anything Faulkner ever dreamed up, a theater as vast as the entire girlhood of the world, they told me that one particular black Ken doll and one particular black Barbie doll were married and that the dolls had a child. Then Rosalind held up a white doll that someone, probably a grandparent, had given them (my wife is fairly strict on the point of our daughters' not having white dolls, but I guess a few have slipped through), explaining that this doll was the daughter of the black Ken and Barbie.

"But," I said, "how could two black dolls have a white daughter?"

"Oh," said Rosalind, looking at me as if I were an object deserving of only her indulgent pity, "we're not racial. That's old-fashioned. Don't you think so, Daddy? Aren't you tired of all that racial stuff?"

Bowing to that wisdom which, it is said, is the only kind that will lead us to Christ and to ourselves, I decided to get up and leave them to their play. My knees had begun to hurt and I realized, painfully, that I was much too old, much too at peace with stiffness and inflexibility, for children's games.

Notes

[1] Richard Wright tells a story in his 1956 account of the Bandung conference, entitled *The Color Curtain*, that emphasizes the absence of the black woman. He relates how a white woman journalist knocks on his hotel room door during the course of the conference and confides the strange behavior of her roommate—a black woman journalist from Boston. Her roommate walks around in the middle of the night and the white woman often covertly spies her in "a dark corner of the room . . . bent over a tiny blue light, a very low and a very blue flame. . . . It seemed like she was combing her hair, but I wasn't sure. Her right arm was moving and now and then she would look over her shoulder toward my bed." The white woman thinks that the black woman is practicing voodoo. But Wright soon explains that the black woman is simply straightening her hair.

> "But why would she straighten her hair? Her hair seems all right" [the white woman journalist asks].
>
> "Her hair is all right. But it's not straight. It's kinky. But she does not want you, a white woman, to see her when she straightens her hair. She would feel embarrassed—"
>
> "Why?"
>
> "Because you were born with straight hair, and she wants to look as much like you as possible. . . . "
>
> The woman stared at me, then clapped her hands to her eyes and exclaimed:
>
> "Oh!"
>
> I leaned back and thought: here in Asia, where everybody was dark, the poor American Negro woman was worried about the hair she was born with. Here, where practically nobody was white, her hair would have been acceptable; no one would have found her "inferior" because her hair was kinky; on the contrary, the Indonesians would perhaps have found her different and charming.

The conversation continues with an account of the black woman's secretive skin lightening treatments. What is revealing in this dialogue which takes on both political and psychoanalytic proportions is the utter absence of the black woman's voice, her presence. She is simply the dark, neurotic ghost that flits in the other room while the black male and the white female, both in the same room, one with dispassionate curtness and the other with sentimentalized guilt, consider the illness that is enacted before them as a kind of bad theater. Once again, the psychopathology of the black American is symbolized by the black woman's straightened hair, by her beauty culture.

[2] Jacques Barzun, "Culture High and Dry," *The Culture We Deserve* (Middletown, Conn.: Wesleyan University Press, 1989).

Maxine Hong Kingston

No Name Woman

"You must not tell anyone," my mother said, "what I am about to tell you. In China your father had a sister who killed herself. She jumped into the family well. We say that your father has all brothers because it is as if she had never been born.

"In 1924 just a few days after our village celebrated seventeen hurry-up weddings— to make sure that every young man who went 'out on the road' would responsibly come home—your father and his brothers and your grandfather and his brothers and your aunt's new husband sailed for America, the Gold Mountain. It was your grandfather's last trip. Those lucky enough to get contracts waved good-bye from the decks. They fed and guarded the stowaways and helped them off in Cuba, New York, Bali, Hawaii. 'We'll meet in California next year,' they said. All of them sent money home.

"I remember looking at your aunt one day when she and I were dressing; I had not noticed before that she had such a protruding melon of a stomach. But I did not think, 'She's pregnant,' until she began to look like other pregnant women, her shirt pulling and the white tops of her black pants showing. She could not have been pregnant, you see, because her husband had been gone for years. No one said anything. We did not discuss it. In early summer she was ready to have the child, long after the time when it could have been possible.

"The village had also been counting. On the night the baby was to be born the villagers raided our house. Some were crying. Like a great saw, teeth strung with lights, files of people walked zigzag across our land, tearing the rice. Their lanterns doubled in the disturbed black water, which drained away through the broken bunds. As the villagers closed in, we could see that some of them, probably men and women we knew well, wore white masks. The people with long hair hung it over their faces. Women with short hair made it stand up on end. Some had tied white bands around their foreheads, arms, and legs.

"At first they threw mud and rocks at the house. Then they threw eggs and began slaughtering our stock. We could hear the animals scream their death—the roosters, the pigs, a last great roar from the ox. Familiar wild heads flared in our night windows; the villagers encircled us. Some of the faces stopped to peer at us, their eyes rushing like searchlights. The hands flattened against the panes, framed heads, and left red prints.

"The villagers broke in the front and the back doors at the same time, even though we had not locked the doors against them. Their knives dripped with the blood of our animals. They smeared blood on the doors and walls. One woman swung a chicken, whose throat she had slit, splattering blood in red arcs about her. We stood together in the middle of our house, in the family hall with the pictures and tables of the ancestors around us, and looked straight ahead.

"At that time the house had only two wings. When the men came back we would build two more to enclose our courtyard and a third one to begin a second courtyard. The villagers pushed through both wings, even your grandparents' rooms, to find your aunt's, which was also mine until the men returned. From this room a new wing for one of the younger families would grow. They ripped up her clothes and shoes and broke her combs, grinding them underfoot. They tore her work from the loom. They scattered the cooking fire and rolled the new weaving in it. We could hear them in the kitchen breaking our bowls and banging the pots. They overturned the great waist-high earthenware jugs; duck eggs, pickled fruits, vegetables burst out and mixed in acrid torrents. The old woman from the next field swept a broom through the air and loosed the spirits-of-the-broom over our heads. 'Pig.' 'Ghost.' 'Pig,' they sobbed and scolded while they ruined our house.

"When they left, they took sugar and oranges to bless themselves. They cut pieces from the dead animals. Some of them took bowls that were not broken and clothes that were not torn. Afterward we swept up the rice and sewed it back up into sacks. But the smells from the spilled preserves lasted. Your aunt gave birth in the pigsty that night. The next morning when I went up for the water, I found her and the baby plugging up the family well.

"Don't let your father know that I told you. He denies her. Now that you have started to menstruate, what happened to her could happen to you. Don't humiliate us. You wouldn't like to be forgotten as if you had never been born. The villagers are watchful."

Whenever she had to warn us about life, my mother told stories that ran like this one, a story to grow up on. She tested our strength to establish realities. Those in the emigrant generations who could not reassert brute survival died young and far from home. Those of us in the first American generations have had to figure out how the invisible world the emigrants built around our childhoods fit in solid America.

The emigrants confused the gods by diverting their curses, misleading them with crooked streets and false names. They must try to confuse their offspring as well, who, I suppose, threaten them in similar ways—always trying to get things straight, always trying to name the unspeakable. The Chinese I know hide their names; sojourners take new names when their lives change and guard their real names with silence.

Chinese-Americans, when you try to understand what things in you are Chinese, how do you separate what is peculiar to childhood, to poverty, insanities, one family, your mother who marked your growing with stories, from what is Chinese? What is Chinese tradition and what is the movies?

If I want to learn what clothes my aunt wore, whether flashy or ordinary, I would have to begin, "Remember Father's drowned-in-the-well sister?" I cannot ask that. My mother has told me once and for all the useful parts. She will add nothing unless powered by Necessity, a river-bank that guides her life. She plants vegetable gardens rather than lawns; she carries the odd-shaped tomatoes home from the fields and eats food left for the gods.

Whenever we did frivolous things, we used up energy; we flew high kites. We children came up off the ground over the melting cones our parents brought home from work and the American movie on New Year's Day—*Oh, You Beautiful Doll* with Betty Grable one year, and *She Wore a Yellow Ribbon* with John Wayne another year. After the one carnival ride each, we paid in guilt; our tired father counted his change on the dark walk home.

Adultery is extravagance. Could people who hatch their own chicks and eat the embryos and the heads for delicacies and boil the feet in vinegar for party food, leaving only the gravel, eating even the gizzard lining—could such people engender a prodigal aunt? To be a woman, to have a daughter in starvation time was a waste enough. My aunt could not have been the lone romantic who gave up everything for sex. Women in the old China did not choose. Some man had commanded her to lie with him and be his secret evil. I wonder whether he masked himself when he joined the raid on her family.

Perhaps she encountered him in the fields or on the mountain where the daughters-in-law collected fuel. Or perhaps he first noticed her in the marketplace. He was not a stranger because the village housed no strangers. She had to have dealings with him other than sex. Perhaps he worked an adjoining field, or he sold her the cloth for the dress she sewed and wore. His demand must have surprised, then terrified her. She obeyed him; she always did as she was told.

When the family found a young man in the next village to be her husband, she stood tractably beside the best rooster, his proxy, and promised before they met that she would be his forever. She was lucky that he was her age and she would be the first wife, an advantage secure now. The night she first saw him, he had sex with her. Then he left for America. She had almost forgotten what he looked like. When she tried to envision him, she only saw the black and white face in the group photograph the men had had taken before leaving.

The other man was not, after all, much different from her husband. They both gave orders: she followed. "If you tell your family, I'll beat you. I'll kill you. Be here again next week." No one talked sex, ever. And she might have separated the rapes from the rest of living if only she did not have to buy her oil from him or gather wood in the same forest. I want her fear to have lasted just as long as rape lasted so that the fear could have been contained. No drawn-out fear. But women at sex hazarded birth and hence lifetimes. The fear did not stop but permeated everywhere. She told the man, "I think I'm pregnant." He organized the raid against her.

On nights when my mother and father talked about their life back home, sometimes they mentioned an "outcast table" whose business they still seemed to be settling, their voices tight. In a commensal tradition, where food is precious, the powerful older people made wrongdoers eat alone. Instead of letting them start separate new lives like the Japanese, who could become samurais and geishas, the Chinese family, faces averted but eyes glowering sideways, hung on to the offenders and fed them leftovers. My aunt must have lived in the same house as my parents and eaten at an outcast table. My mother spoke about the raid as if she had seen it, when she and my aunt, a daughter-in-law to a different household, should not have been living together at all. Daughters-in-law lived with their husbands' parents, not their own; a synonym for marriage in Chinese is "taking a daughter-in-law." Her husband's parents could have sold her, mortgaged her, stoned her. But they had sent her back to her own mother and father, a mysterious act hinting at disgraces not told me. Perhaps they had thrown her out to deflect the avengers.

She was the only daughter; her four brothers went with her father, husband, and uncles "out on the road" and for some years became western men. When the goods were divided among the family, three of the brothers took land, and the youngest, my father, chose an education. After my grandparents gave their daughter away to her husband's family, they had dispensed all the adventure and all the property. They expected her alone to keep the traditional ways, which her brothers, now among the barbarians, could fumble without detection. The heavy, deep-rooted women were to maintain the past against the flood, safe for returning. But the rare urge west had fixed upon our family, and so my aunt crossed boundaries not delineated in space.

The work of preservation demands that the feelings playing about in one's guts not be turned into action. Just watch their passing like cherry blossoms. But perhaps my aunt, my forerunner, caught in a slow life, let dreams grow and fade and after some months or years went toward what persisted. Fear at the enormities of the forbidden kept her desires delicate, wire and bone. She looked at a man because she liked the way the hair was tucked behind his ears, or she liked the question-mark line of a long torso curving at the shoulder and straight at the hip. For warm eyes or a soft voice or a slow walk—that's all—

a few hairs, a line, a brightness, a sound, a pace, she gave up family. She offered us up for a charm that vanished with tiredness, a pigtail that didn't toss when the wind died. Why, the wrong lighting could erase the dearest thing about him.

It could very well have been, however, that my aunt did not take subtle enjoyment of her friend, but, a wild woman, kept rollicking company. Imagining her free with sex doesn't fit, though. I don't know any women like that, or men either. Unless I see her life branching into mine, she gives me no ancestral help.

To sustain her being in love, she often worked at herself in the mirror, guessing at the colors and shapes that would interest him, changing them frequently in order to hit on the right combination. She wanted to look back.

On a farm near the sea, a woman who tended her appearance reaped a reputation for eccentricity. All the married women blunt-cut their hair in flaps about their ears or pulled it back in tight buns. No nonsense. Neither style blew easily into heart-catching tangles. And at their weddings they displayed themselves in their long hair for the last time. "It brushed the back of my knees," my mother tells me. "It was braided, and even so, it brushed the backs of my knees."

At the mirror my aunt combed individuality into her bob. A bun could have been contrived to escape into black streamers blowing in the wind or in quiet wisps about her face, but only the older women in our picture album wear buns. She brushed her hair back from her forehead, tucking the flaps behind her ears. She looped a piece of thread, knotted into a circle between her index fingers and thumbs, and ran the double strand across her forehead. When she closed her fingers as if she were making a pair of shadow geese bite, the string twisted together catching the little hairs. Then she pulled the thread away from her skin, ripping the hairs out neatly, her eyes watering from the needles of pain. Opening her fingers, she cleaned the thread, then rolled it along her hairline and the tops of the eyebrows. My mother did the same to me and my sisters and herself. I used to believe that the expression "caught by the short hairs" meant a captive held with a depilatory string. It especially hurt at the temples, but my mother said we were lucky we didn't have to have our feet bound when we were seven. Sisters used to sit on their beds and cry together, she said, as their mothers or their slave removed the bandages for a few minutes each night and let the blood gush back into their veins. I hope that the man my aunt loved appreciated a smooth brow, that he wasn't just a tits-and-ass man.

Once my aunt found a freckle on her chin, at a spot that the almanac said predestined her for unhappiness. She dug it out with a hot needle and washed the wound with peroxide.

More attention to her looks than these pullings of hairs and pickings at spots would have caused gossip among the villagers. They owned work clothes and good clothes, and they wore good clothes for feasting the new seasons. But since a woman combing her hair hexes beginnings, my aunt rarely found an occasion to look her best. Women looked like great sea snails—the corded wood, babies, and laundry they carried were the whorls on their backs. The Chinese did not admire a bent back; goddesses and warriors stood straight. Still there must have been a marvelous freeing of beauty when a worker laid down her burden and stretched and arched.

Such commonplace loveliness, however, was not enough for my aunt. She dreamed of a lover for the fifteen days of New Year's, the time for families to exchange visits, money, and food. She plied her secret comb. And sure enough she cursed the year, the family, the village, and herself.

Even as her hair lured her imminent lover, many other men looked at her. Uncles, cousins, nephews, brothers would have looked, too, had they been home between journeys. Perhaps they had already been restraining their curiosity, and they left, fearful that their glances, like a field of nesting birds, might be startled and caught. Poverty hurt, and that was their first reason for leaving. But another, final reason for leaving the crowded house was the never-said.

She may have been unusually beloved, the precious only daughter, spoiled and mirror-gazing because of the affection the family lavished on her. When her husband left, they welcomed the chance to take her back from the in-laws; she could live like the little daughter for just a while longer. There are stories that my grandfather was different from other people, "crazy ever since the little Jap bayoneted him in the head." He used to put his naked penis on the dinner table, laughing. And one day he brought home a baby girl, wrapped up inside his brown western-style greatcoat. He had traded one of his sons, probably my father, the youngest, for her. My grandmother made him trade back. When he finally got a daughter of his own, he doted on her. They must have all loved her, except perhaps my father, the only brother who never went back to China, having once been traded for a girl.

Brothers and sisters, newly men and women, had to efface their sexual color and present plain miens. Disturbing hair and eyes, a smile like no other, threatened the ideal of five generations living under one roof. To focus blurs, people shouted face to face and yelled from room to room. The immigrants I know have loud voices, unmodulated to American tones even after years away from the village where they called their friendships out across the fields. I have not been able to stop my mother's screams in public libraries or over telephones. Walking erect (knees straight, toes pointed forward, not pigeon-toed, which is Chinese-feminine) and speaking in an inaudible voice, I have tried to turn myself American-feminine. Chinese communication was loud, public. Only sick people had to whisper. But at the dinner table, where the family members came nearest one another, no one could talk, not the outcasts nor any eaters. Every word that falls from the mouth is a coin lost. Silently they gave and accepted food with both hands. A preoccupied child who took his bowl with one hand got a sideways glare. A complete moment of total attention is due everyone alike. Children and lovers have no singularity here, but my aunt used a secret voice, a separate attentiveness.

She kept the man's name to herself throughout her labor and dying; she did not accuse him that he be punished with her. To save her inseminator's name she gave silent birth.

He may have been somebody in her own household, but intercourse with a man outside the family would have been no less abhorrent. All the village were kinsmen, and the titles shouted in loud country voices never let kinship be forgotten. Any man within visiting distance would have been neutralized as a lover—"brother," "younger brother," "older brother"—115 relationship titles. Parents researched birth charts probably not so much to assure good fortune as to circumvent incest in a population that has but one hundred surnames. Everybody has eight million relatives. How useless then sexual mannerisms, how dangerous.

As if it came from an atavism deeper than fear, I used to add "brother" silently to boys' names. It hexed the boys, who would or would not ask me to dance, and made them less scary and as familiar and deserving of benevolence as girls.

But, of course, I hexed myself also—no dates. I should have stood up, both arms waving, and shouted out across libraries, "Hey, you! Love me back." I had no idea, though, how to make attraction selective, how to control its direction and magnitude. If I made myself American-pretty so that the five or six Chinese boys in the class fell in love with me, everyone else—the Caucasian, Negro, and Japanese boys—would too. Sisterliness, dignified and honorable, made much more sense.

Attraction eludes control so stubbornly that whole societies designed to organize relationships among people cannot keep order, not even when they bind people to one another from childhood and raise them together. Among the very poor and the wealthy, brothers married their adopted sisters, like doves. Our family allowed some romance, paying adult brides' prices and providing dowries so that their sons and daughters could marry strangers. Marriage promises to turn strangers into friendly relatives—a nation of siblings.

In the village structure, spirits shimmered among the live creatures, balanced and held in equilibrium by time and land. But one human being flaring up into violence could open up a black hole, a maelstrom that pulled in the sky. The frightened villagers, who depended on one another to maintain the real, went to my aunt to show her a personal, physical representation of the break she made in the "roundness." Misallying couples snapped off the future, which was to be embodied in true offspring. The villagers punished her for acting as if she could have a private life, secret and apart from them.

If my aunt had betrayed the family at a time of large grain yields and peace, when many boys were born, and wings were being built on many houses, perhaps she might have escaped such severe punishment. But the men—hungry, greedy, tired of planting in dry soil, cuckolded—had been forced to leave the village in order to send food-money home. There were ghost plagues, bandit plagues, wars with the Japanese, floods. My Chinese brother and sister had died of an unknown sickness. Adultery, perhaps only a mistake during good times, became a crime when the village needed food.

The round moon cakes and round doorways, the round tables of graduated size that fit one roundness inside another, round windows and rice bowls—these talismans had lost their power to warn this family of the law: A family must be whole, faithfully keeping the descent line by having sons to feed the old and the dead who in turn look after the family. The villagers came to show my aunt and lover-in-hiding a broken house. The villagers were speeding up the circling of events because she was too shortsighted to see that her infidelity had already harmed the village, that waves of consequences would return unpredictably, sometimes in disguise, as now, to hurt her. This roundness had to be made coin-sized so that she would see its circumference: Punish her at the birth of her baby. Awaken her to the inexorable. People who refused fatalism because they could invent small resources insisted on culpability. Deny accidents and wrest fault from the stars.

After the villagers left, their lanterns now scattering in various directions toward home, the family broke their silence and cursed her. "Aiaa, we're going to die. Death is coming. Death is coming. Look what you've done. You've killed us. Ghost! Dead Ghost! Ghost! You've never been born." She ran out into the fields, far enough from the house so that she could no longer hear their voices, and pressed herself against the earth, her own land no more. When she felt the birth coming, she thought that she had been hurt. Her body seized together. "They've hurt me too much," she thought. "This is gall, and it will kill me." With forehead and knees against the earth, her body convulsed and then relaxed. She turned on her back; lay on the ground. The black well of sky and stars went out and out forever; her body and her complexity seemed to disappear. She was one of the stars, a bright dot in blackness, without home, without a companion, in eternal cold and silence.

An agoraphobia rose in her, speeding higher and higher, bigger and bigger; she would not be able to contain it; there would be no end to fear.

Flayed, unprotected against space, she felt pain return, focusing her body. This pain chilled her—a cold, steady kind of surface pain. Inside, spasmodically, the other pain, the pain of the child, heated her. For hours she lay on the ground, alternately body and space. Sometimes a vision of normal comfort obliterated reality: She saw the family in the evening gambling at the dinner table, the young people massaging their elders' backs. She saw them congratulating one another, high joy on the mornings the rice shoots came up. When these pictures burst, the stars drew yet further apart. Black space opened.

She got to her feet to fight better and remembered that old-fashioned women gave birth in their pigsties to fool the jealous, pain-dealing gods, who do not snatch piglets. Before the next spasms could stop her, she ran to the pigsty, each step a rushing out into emptiness. She climbed over the fence and knelt in the dirt. It was good to have a fence enclosing her, a tribal person alone.

Laboring, this woman who had carried her child as a foreign growth that sickened her every day, expelled it at last. She reached down to touch the hot, wet, moving mass, surely smaller than anything human, and could feel that it was human after all—fingers, toes, nails, nose. She pulled it up on to her belly, and it lay curled there, butt in the air, feet precisely tucked one under the other. She opened her loose shirt and buttoned the child inside. After resting, it squirmed and thrashed and she pushed it up to her breast. It turned its head this way and that until it found her nipple. There, it made little snuffling noises. She clenched her teeth at its preciousness, lovely as a young calf, a piglet, a little dog.

She may have gone to the pigsty as a last act of responsibility: She would protect this child as she had protected its father. It would look after her soul, leaving supplies on her grave. But how would this tiny child without family find her grave when there would be no marker for her anywhere, neither in the earth nor the family hall? No one would give her a family hall name. She had taken the child with her into the wastes. At its birth the two of them had felt the same raw pain of separation, a wound that only the family pressing tight could close. A child with no descent line would not soften her life but only trail after her, ghostlike, begging her to give it purpose. At dawn the villagers on their way to the fields would stand around the fence and look.

Full of milk, the little ghost slept. When it awoke, she hardened her breasts against the milk that crying loosens. Toward morning she picked up the baby and walked to the well.

Carrying the baby to the well shows loving. Otherwise abandon it. Turn its face into the mud. Mothers who love their children take them along. It was probably a girl; there is some hope of forgiveness for boys.

"Don't tell anyone you had an aunt. Your father does not want to hear her name. She has never been born." I have believed that sex was unspeakable and words so strong and fathers so frail that "aunt" would do my father mysterious harm. I have thought that my family, having settled among immigrants who had also been their neighbors in the ancestral land, needed to clean their name, and a wrong word would incite the kinspeople even here. But there is more to this silence: They want me to participate in her punishment. And I have.

In the twenty years since I heard this story I have not asked for details nor said my aunt's name; I do not know it. People who comfort the dead can also chase after them to hurt them further—a reverse ancestor worship. The real punishment was not the raid swiftly inflicted by the villagers, but the family's deliberately forgetting her. Her betrayal so maddened them, they saw to it that she would suffer forever, even after death. Always hungry, always needing, she would have to beg food from other ghosts, snatch and steal it from those whose living descendants give them gifts. She would have to fight the ghosts massed at crossroads for the buns a few thoughtful citizens leave to decoy her away from village and home so that the ancestral spirits could feast unharassed. At peace, they could act like gods, not ghosts, their descent lines providing them with paper suits and dresses, spirit money, paper houses, paper automobiles, chicken, meat, and rice into eternity— essences delivered up in smoke and flames, steam and incense rising from each rice bowl. In an attempt to make the Chinese care for people outside the family, Chairman Mao encourages us now to give our paper replicas to the spirits of outstanding soldiers and workers, no matter whose ancestors they may be. My aunt remains forever hungry. Goods are not distributed evenly among the dead.

My aunt haunts me—her ghost drawn to me because now, after fifty years of neglect, I alone devote pages of paper to her, though not origamied into houses and clothes. I do not think she always means me well. I am telling on her, and she was a spite suicide, drowning herself in the drinking water. The Chinese are always very frightened of the drowned one, whose weeping ghost, wet hair hanging and skin bloated, waits silently by the water to pull down a substitute.

Bharati Mukherjee

Two Ways to Belong in America

This is a tale of two sisters from Calcutta, Mira and Bharati, who have lived in the United States for some thirty-five years, but who find themselves on different sides in the current debate over the status of immigrants. I am an American citizen and she is not. I am moved that thousands of long-term residents are finally taking the oath of citizenship. She is not.

Mira arrived in Detroit in 1960 to study child psychology and pre-school education. I followed her a year later to study creative writing at the University of Iowa. When we left India, we were almost identical in appearance and attitude. We dressed alike, in saris; we expressed identical views on politics, social issues, love and marriage in the same Calcutta convent-school accent. We would endure our two years in America, secure our degrees, then return to India to marry the grooms of our father's choosing.

Instead, Mira married an Indian student in 1962 who was getting his business administration degree at Wayne State University. They soon acquired the labor certifications necessary for the green card of hassle-free residence and employment.

Mira still lives in Detroit, works in the Southfield, Michigan, school system, and has become nationally recognized for her contributions in the fields of pre-school education and parent-teacher relationships. After 36 years as a legal immigrant in this country, she clings passionately to her Indian citizenship and hopes to go home to India when she retires.

In Iowa City in 1963, I married a fellow student, an American of Canadian parentage. Because of the accident of his North Dakota birth, I bypassed labor-certification requirements and the race-related "quota" system that favored the applicant's country of origin over his or her merit. I was prepared for (and even welcomed) the emotional strain that came with marrying outside my ethnic community. In thirty-three years of marriage, we have lived in every part of North America. By choosing a husband who was not my father's selection, I was opting for fluidity, self-invention, blue jeans and T-shirts, and renouncing three thousand years (at least) of caste-observant, "pure culture" marriage in the Mukherjee family. My books have often been read as unapologetic (and in some quarters overenthusiastic) texts for cultural and psychological "mongrelization." It's a word I celebrate.

Mira and I have stayed sisterly close by phone. In our regular Sunday morning conversations, we are unguardedly affectionate. I am her only blood relative on this continent. We expect to see each other through the looming crises of aging and ill health without being asked. Long before Vice President Gore's "Citizenship U.S.A." drive, we'd had our polite arguments over the ethics of retaining an overseas citizenship while expecting the permanent protection and economic benefits that come with living and working in America.

Like well-raised sisters, we never said what was really on our minds, but we probably pitied one another. She, for the lack of structure in my life, the erasure of Indianness, the absence of an unvarying daily core. I, for the narrowness of her perspective, her uninvolvement with the mythic depths or the superficial pop culture of this society. But, now, with the scapegoating of "aliens" (documented or illegal) on the increase, and the targeting of long-term legal immigrants like Mira for new scrutiny and new self-consciousness, she and I find ourselves unable to maintain the same polite discretion. We were always unacknowledged adversaries, and we are now, more than ever, sisters.

"I feel used," Mira raged on the phone the other night. "I feel manipulated and discarded. This is such an unfair way to treat a person who was invited to stay and work here because of her talent. My employer went to the I.N.S. and petitioned for the labor certification. For over thirty years, I've invested my creativity and professional skills into the improvement of *this* country's pre-school system. I've obeyed all the rules, I've paid my taxes, I love my work, I love my students, I love the friends I've made. How dare America now change its rules in midstream? If America wants to make new rules curtailing benefits of legal immigrants, they should apply only to immigrants who arrive after those rules are already in place."

To my ears, it sounded like the description of a long-enduring, comfortable yet loveless marriage, without risk or recklessness. Have we the right to demand, and to expect, that we be loved? (That, to me is the subtext of the arguments by immigration advocates.) My sister is an expatriate, professionally generous and creative, socially courteous and gracious, and that's as far as her Americanization can go. She is here to maintain an identity, not to transform it.

I asked her if she would follow the example of others who have decided to become citizens because of the anti-immigration bills in Congress. And here, she surprised me. "If America wants to play the manipulative game, I'll play it too," she snapped. "I'll become a U.S. citizen for now, than change back to Indian when I'm ready to go home. I feel some kind of irrational attachment to India that I don't to America. Until all this hysteria against legal immigrants, I was totally happy. Having my green card meant I could visit any place in the world I wanted to and then come back to a job that's satisfying and that I do very well."

In one family, from two sisters alike as peas in a pod, there could not be a wider divergence of immigrant experience. America spoke to me—I married it—I embraced the demotion from expatriate aristocrat to immigrant nobody, surrendering those thousands of years of "pure culture," the saris, the delightfully accented English. She retained them all. Which of us is the freak?

Mira's voice, I realize, is the voice not just of the immigrant South Asian community but of an immigrant community of the millions who have stayed rooted in one job, one city, one house, one ancestral culture, one cuisine, for the entirety of their productive years. She speaks for greater numbers than I possibly can. Only the fluency of her English and the anger, rather than fear, born of confidence from her education, differentiate her from the seamstresses, the domestics, the technicians, the shop owners, the millions of hard-working but effectively silenced documented immigrants as well as their less fortunate "illegal" brothers and sisters.

Nearly twenty years ago, when I was living in my husband's ancestral homeland of Canada, I was always well-employed but never allowed to feel part of the local Quebec or larger Canadian society. Then, through a Green Paper that invited a national referendum on the unwanted side effects of "nontraditional" immigration, the Government officially turned against its immigrant communities, particularly those from South Asia.

I felt then the same sense of betrayal that Mira feels now. I will never forget the pain of that sudden turning, and the casual racist outbursts the Green Paper elicited. That sense of betrayal had its desired effect and drove me, and thousands like me, from the country.

Mira and I differ, however, in the ways in which we hope to interact with the country that we have chosen to live in. She is happier to live in America as expatriate Indian than as an immigrant American. I need to feel like a part of the community I have adopted (as I tried to feel in Canada as well). I need to put roots down, to vote and make the difference that I can. The price that the immigrant willingly pays, and that the exile avoids, is the trauma of self-transformation.

Alice Walker

Becoming What We're Called

"Boy, Man, Fellow, Chap"

Last night before I could stop myself I put my arms around a dear friend who'd just said she'd see us later, "you guys!" and told her I don't like being called "guy." In fact, I told her, noting her puzzled expression, I detest it.

I remember once, many years ago, attending a spring festival in the seaside village of this same friend. The air was scented with early flowers, the sun was shining brightly off the ocean. My friend found a table for us not far from the grill on which hot dogs and tofu burgers were being flipped. Within minutes, unbeckoned, three teenage maidens brought us overflowing platters of food, freshly prepared, lovingly arranged, a feast. One was brown-haired, one blond, and one as red-headed as the daughter of my next-hill-over neighbors, who was named after the Irish Goddess Bridget. I suppose it was partly this that caused me to think of the three young women, so solicitous, so gracefully nurturing, as Goddesses. Thanking them, I was just about to comment on the Goddess nature of their behavior when my friend said cheerfully, "Thank you, you guys!" I felt they had not been seen, that their essential nature had been devalued, but I said nothing, not wanting to offend my friend.

Sometimes I think these struggles about identity will never end; this one reminds me of nothing so much as of the battle black people seem to have lost a decade ago against the word "nigger." Seeking to redeem it, to render it harmless, many people deliberately kept it alive among themselves. Now, because of rap, it is commonplace to hear it bouncing through the air, no matter where you are, and if you are not fond of it, you feel all the assault such a negative description brings. (*Nigger:* a vulgar, offensive term of hostility and contempt, as used by Negrophobes.) Recently, for instance, two other friends and I were walking through the San Francisco Botanical Garden, the only black people there, the only black women. It is crucial, living in the city, to have access to nature: a place where you can relax, be yourself, and relate to the magnificence of the earth without thinking every moment of life in a racist, violent society. We stood by a pond on which there were hundreds of birds and marveled at the way the fluttering of their wings stirred the air. It was a beautiful day. The sun was warm, the sky blue, the Asian magnolias in full expression. Suddenly, out of nowhere, it seemed, we heard, very loud, "black nigger black . . . dah, dah, dah." We looked about for the racist white man who had dared shatter our peace. He was not there. Instead, the retreating back of a young black man, bopping in tune to music from his Walkman, told the story. He was singing along with someone whose refrain, "black nigger black," he echoed. We watched as he swung along, oblivious to the beauty all around him, his attention solely on this song. He went the length of the garden, seeing nothing; only thinking of how he was black and a nigger and this was all the identity he had. It was like watching him throw mud, or worse, all over himself.

I have asked people, both men and women, why they like "you guys." Some admit they picked it up from a television commercial that seemed cute to them. Others add, incredibly, that they felt it was an all-inclusive term for males and females; they considered it gender free. Some recalled the expression "guys and gals" and said, laughing, nobody wanted to be "gals." I tried to imagine everyone in American calling themselves and each other "you gals." How many men would accept it? Personally, for gender-free inclusivity, I prefer the Southern expression "you all."

After the completion of *Warrior Marks,* a film we made about female genital mutilation, Pratibha Parmar and I premiered it in ten European and American cities, an exhausting but at times exhilarating tour. But after about the third city, we realized that the most exhausting thing was neither the travel nor the stress we experienced as we anticipated each audience's response to the film; it was having, at every theater, to endure the following questions: How long did it take "you guys" to do this? What was it like for "you guys" to travel and film in Africa? The women asking us these questions seemed blind to us, and in their blindness we felt our uniqueness as female creators disappear. We had recently been in societies where some or all of a woman's genitalia were forcibly cut from her by other women who collaborated—wholeheartedly, by now—with men. To us, the refusal to acknowledge us as women seemed a verbal expression of this same idea. It made us quite ill. After all, it would have been impossible for "guys" to make the film we had made. No women would have talked to them, for one thing. Each night, over and over, we told the women greeting us: We are not "guys." We are women. Many failed to get it. Others were amused. One woman amused *us*, she had so much difficulty not saying "you guys," every two minutes, even after we'd complained!

It would seem from the dictionary that the verb "guy" is another word for "guide," or "control": bearing a very real resemblance to "husband." It means "to steady, stay, or direct by means of a guy, from the French *guying*." The noun means "a boy or man; fellow; chap." It means "a person whose appearance or dress is odd." Again, as a verb, "guy" can mean "to tease; to ridicule." And this last is how I feel it when the word is used by men referring to women, and by women referring to themselves. I see in its use some women's obsequious need to be accepted at any cost, even at the cost of erasing their own femaleness, and that of other women. Isn't it at least ironic that after so many years of struggle for women's liberation, women should end up calling themselves this?

I think my friend is probably exasperated with me because of what I said to her last night. After all, "you guys" is a habitual expression in conversation around the world; I am asking her not to call me something that comes easily, apparently, to her. I think perhaps I am a trying friend to have; one who wonders, as I can't help but do, why this should be so. The magic of naming is that people often become what they are called. What in me evokes this word from her? I will call her up in a day or two and suggest we go for a walk and discuss this issue in the open arena of nature, where the larkspur is not called delphinium and the hummingbird is not labeled dove. Grass is not called tree and rocks are not called bears. When I look at her I see a black woman daily overcoming incredible odds to live a decent, honest, even merry life. Someone who actively nurtures community wherever she goes. Someone who has raised a strong daughter and now showers affection and attention on a beautiful grandchild. I see someone who dances like a Nubian and cooks like a Creole. I don't respect "guys" enough to obliterate the woman that I see by calling her by their name.

The "Eye"

Lawrence Otis Graham

Invisible Man

I drive up the winding lane past a long stone wall and beneath an archway of sixty-foot maples. At one bend of the drive, a freshly clipped lawn and a trail of yellow daffodils slope gently up to the four-pillared portico of a white Georgian colonial. The building's six huge chimneys, the two wings with slate-gray shutters, and the white brick façade loom over a luxuriant golf course. Before me stands the hundred-year-old Greenwich Country Club—*the* country club—in the affluent, patrician, and very white town of Greenwich, Connecticut, where there are eight clubs for 59,000 people.

I'm a thirty-year-old corporate lawyer at a midtown Manhattan firm, and I make $105,000 a year. I'm a graduate of Princeton University (1983) and Harvard Law School (1988), and I've written eleven nonfiction books. Although these might seem like good credentials, they're not the ones that brought me here. Quite frankly, I got into this country club the only way that a black man like me could—as a $7-an-hour busboy.

After seeing dozens of news stories about Dan Quayle, Billy Graham, Ross Perot, and others who either belonged to or frequented white country clubs, I decided to find out what things were really like at a club where I saw no black members.

I remember stepping up to the pool at a country club when I was ten and setting off a chain reaction: Several irate parents dragged their children out of the water and fled. Back then, in 1972, I saw these clubs only as a place where families socialized. I grew up in an affluent white neighborhood in Westchester, and all my playmates and neighbors belonged somewhere. Across the street, my best friend introduced me to the Westchester Country Club before he left for Groton and Yale. My teenage tennis partner from Scarsdale introduced me to the Beach Point Club on weekends before he left for Harvard. The family next door belonged to the Scarsdale Golf Club. In my crowd, the question wasn't "Do you belong?" It was "Where?"

My grandparents owned a Memphis trucking firm, and as far back as I can remember, our family was well off and we had little trouble fitting in—even though I was the only black kid on the high school tennis team, the only one in the orchestra, the only one in my Roman Catholic confirmation class.

Today, I'm back where I started—on a street of five- and six-bedroom colonials with expensive cars, and neighbors who all belong somewhere. As a young lawyer, I realize that these clubs are where business people network, where lawyers and investment bankers meet potential clients and arrange deals. How many clients and deals am I going to line up on the asphalt parking lot of my local public tennis courts?

I am not ashamed to admit that I one day want to be a partner and a part of this network. When I talk to my black lawyer or investment-banker friends or my wife, a brilliant black woman who has degrees from Harvard College, law school, and business school, I learn that our white counterparts are being accepted by dozens of these elite institutions. So why shouldn't we—especially when we have the same ambitions, social graces, credentials, and salaries?

My black Ivy League friends and I talk about black company vice-presidents who have to beg white subordinates to invite them out for golf or tennis. We talk about the club in Westchester that rejected black Scarsdale resident and millionaire magazine publisher Earl Graves, who sits on *Fortune* 500 boards, owns a Pepsi distribution franchise, raised three bright Ivy League children, and holds prestigious honorary degrees. We talk about all the clubs that face a scandal and then run out to sign up one quiet, deferential black man who will remove the taint and deflect further scrutiny.

I wanted some answers. I knew I could never be treated as an equal at this Greenwich oasis—a place so insular that the word "Negro" is still used in conversation. But I figured I could get close enough to understand what these people were thinking and why country clubs were so set on excluding people like me.

March 28 to April 7, 1992

I invented a completely new résumé for myself. I erased Harvard, Princeton, and my upper-middle-class suburban childhood from my life. So that I'd have to account for fewer years, I made myself seven years younger—an innocent twenty-three. I used my real name and made myself a graduate of the same high school. Since it was ludicrous to pretend I was from "the streets," I decided to become a sophomore-year dropout from Tufts University, a midsize college in suburban Boston. My years at nearby Harvard had given me enough knowledge about the school to pull it off. I contacted some older friends who owned large companies and restaurants in the Boston and New York areas and asked them to serve as references. I was already on a leave of absence from my law firm to work on a book.

I pieced together a wardrobe with a polyester blazer, ironed blue slacks, black loafers, and a horrendous pink, black, and silver tie, and I set up interviews at clubs. Over the telephone, five of the eight said that I sounded as if I would make a great waiter. But when I met them, the club managers told me I "would probably make a much better busboy."

"Busboy? Over the phone, you said you needed a waiter," I argued. "Yes, I know I said that, but you seem very alert, and I think you'd make an excellent busboy instead."

The maître d' at one of the clubs refused to accept my application. Only an hour earlier, she had enthusiastically urged me to come right over for an interview. Now, as two white kitchen workers looked on, she would only hold her hands tightly behind her back and shake her head emphatically.

April 8 to 11

After interviewing at five clubs and getting only two offers, I made my final selection in much the way I had decided on a college and a law school: I went for prestige. Not only was the Greenwich Country Club celebrating its hundredth anniversary but its roster boasted former president Gerald Ford (an honorary member), baseball star Tom Seaver, former Securities and Exchange Commission chairman and U.S. ambassador to the Netherlands John Shad, as well as former Timex spokesman John Cameron Swayze. Add to that a few dozen *Fortune* 500 executives, bankers, Wall Street lawyers, European entrepreneurs, a Presbyterian minister, and cartoonist Mort Walker, who does "Beetle Bailey." [The Greenwich Country Club did not respond to any questions from *New York* magazine about the club and its members.]

For three days, I worked on my upper-arm muscles by walking around the house with a sterling silver tray stacked high with heavy dictionaries. I allowed a mustache to grow in, then added a pair of arrestingly ugly Coke-bottle reading glasses.

April 12 (Sunday)

Today was my first day at work. My shift didn't start until 10:30 A.M., so I laid out my clothes at home: a white button-down shirt, freshly ironed cotton khaki pants, white socks, and white leather sneakers. I'd get my official club uniform in two days. Looking in my wallet, I removed my American Express gold card, my Harvard Club membership ID, and all of my business cards.

When I arrived at the club, I entered under the large portico, stepping through the heavy doors and onto the black and white checkerboard tiles of the entry hall.

A distracted receptionist pointed me toward Mr. Ryan's[1] office. I walked past glistening silver trophies and a guest book on a pedestal to a windowless office with three desks. My new boss waved me in and abruptly hung up the phone.

"Good morning, Larry," he said with a sufficiently warm smile. The tight knot in his green tie made him look more fastidious than I had remembered from the interview.

"Hi, Mr. Ryan. How's it going?"

Glancing at his watch to check my punctuality, he shook my hand and handed me some papers. "Oh, and by the way, where'd you park?"

"In front, near the tennis courts."

Already shaking his head, he tossed his pencil onto the desk. "That's off limits to you. You should always park in the back, enter in the back, and leave from the back. No exceptions."

"I'll do the forms right now," I said. "And then I'll be an official busboy."

Mr. Ryan threw me an ominous nod. "And Larry, let me stop you now. We don't like that term 'busboy.' We find it demeaning. We prefer to call you busmen."

Leading me down the center stairwell to the basement, he added, "And in the future, you will always use the back stairway by the back entrance." He continued to talk as we trotted through a maze of hallways. "I think I'll have you trail with Carlos or Hector—no, Carlos. Unless you speak Spanish?"

"No." I ran to keep up with Mr. Ryan.

"That's the dishwasher room, where Juan works. And over here is where you'll be working." I looked at the brass sign. MEN'S GRILL.

It was a dark room with a mahogany finish, and it looked like a library in a large Victorian home. Dark walls, dark wood-beamed ceilings. Deep-green wool carpeting. Along

---

[1] All names of club members and personnel have been changed.

one side of the room stood a long, highly polished mahogany bar with liquor bottles, wineglasses, and a two-and-a-half-foot-high silver trophy. Fifteen heavy round wooden tables, each encircled with four to six broad wooden armchairs padded with green leather on the backs and seats, broke up the room. A big-screen TV was set into the wall along with two shelves of books.

"This is the Men's Grill," Mr. Ryan said. "Ladies are not allowed except on Friday evenings."

Next was the brightly lit connecting kitchen. "Our kitchen serves hot and cold foods. You'll work six days a week here. The club is closed on Mondays. The kitchen serves the Men's Grill and an adjoining room called the Mixed Grill. That's where the ladies and kids can eat."

"And what about men? Can they eat in there, too?"

This elicited a laugh. "Of course they can. Time and place restrictions apply only to women and kids."

He showed me the Mixed Grill, a well-lit, pastel-blue room with glass French doors and white wood trim.

"Guys, say hello to Larry. He's a new busman at the club."

I waved.

"And this is Rick, Stephen, Drew, Buddy, and Lee." Five white waiters dressed in white polo shirts with blue "1892" club insignias nodded while busily slicing lemons.

"And this is Hector and Carlos, the other busmen." Hector, Carlos, and I were the only nonwhites on the serving staff. They greeted me in a mix of English and Spanish.

"Nice to meet all of you," I responded.

"Thank God," one of the taller waiters cried out. "Finally—somebody who can speak English."

Mr. Ryan took me and Carlos through a hall lined with old black-and-white portraits of former presidents of the club. "This is our one hundredth year, so you're joining the club at an important time," Mr. Ryan added before walking off. "Carlos, I'm going to leave Larry to trail with you—and no funny stuff."

Standing outside the ice room, Carlos and I talked about our pasts. He was twenty-five, originally from Colombia, and hadn't finished school. I said I had dropped out, too.

As I stood there talking, Carlos suddenly gestured for me to move out of the hallway. I looked behind me and noticed something staring down at us. "A video camera?"

"They're around," Carlos remarked quietly while scooping ice into large white tubs. "Now watch me scoop ice."

After we carried the heavy tubs back to the grill, I saw another video camera pointed down at us. I dropped my head.

"You gonna live in the Monkey House?" Carlos asked.

"What's that?"

We climbed the stairs to take our ten-minute lunch break before work began. "Monkey House is where workers live here," Carlos said.

I followed him through a rather filthy utility room and into a huge white kitchen. We got on line behind about twenty Hispanic men and women—all dressed in varying uniforms. At the head of the line were the white waiters I'd met earlier.

I was soon handed a hot plate with two red lumps of rice and some kind of sausage-shaped meat. There were two string beans, several pieces of zucchini, and a thin, broken slice of dried meat loaf that looked as if it had been cooked, burned, frozen, and then reheated.

I followed Carlos, plate in hand, out of the kitchen. To my surprise, we walked back into the dank and dingy utility room, which turned out to be the workers' dining area.

The white waiters huddled together at one end of the tables, while the Hispanic workers ate quietly at the other end. Before I could decide which end to integrate, Carlos directed me to sit with him on the Hispanic end.

I was soon back downstairs working in the grill. At my first few tables, I tried to avoid making eye contact with members as I removed dirty plates and wiped down tables and chairs. I was sure I'd be recognized.

At around 1:15, four men who looked to be in their mid- to late fifties sat down at a six-chair table while pulling off their cotton windbreakers and golf sweaters.

"It's these damned newspeople that cause all the problems," said Golfer No. 1, shoving his hand deep into a popcorn bowl. "These Negroes wouldn't even be thinking about golf. They can't afford to join a club, anyway."

Golfer No. 2 squirmed out of his navy-blue sweater and nodded in agreement. "My big problem with this Clinton fellow is that he apologized." As I stood watching from the corner of the bar, I realized the men were talking about Governor Bill Clinton's recent apology for playing at an all-white golf club in Little Rock, Arkansas.

"Holt, I couldn't agree with you more," added Golfer No. 3, a hefty man who was biting off the end of a cigar.

"You got any iced tea?" Golfer No. 1 asked as I put the silverware and menus around the table. Popcorn flew out of his mouth as he attempted to speak and chew at the same time.

"Yes, we certainly do."

Golfer No. 3 removed a beat-up Rolex from his wrist. "It just sets a bad precedent. Instead of apologizing, he should try to discredit them—undercut them somehow. What's to apologize for?" I cleared my throat and backed away from the table.

Suddenly, Golfer No. 1 waved me back to his side. "Should we get four iced teas or just a pitcher and four glasses?"

"I'd be happy to bring whatever you'd like, sir."

Throughout the day, I carried "bus buckets" filled with dirty dishes from the grill to the dishwasher room. And each time I returned to the grill, I scanned the room for recognizable faces. After almost four hours of running back and forth, clearing dishes, wiping down tables, and thanking departing members who left spilled coffee, dirty napkins, and unwanted business cards in their wake, I helped out in the coed Mixed Grill.

"Oh, busboy," a voice called out as I made the rounds with two pots of coffee. "Here, busboy. Here, busboy," the woman called out. "Busboy, my coffee is cold. Give me a refill."

"Certainly, I would be happy to." I reached over for her cup.

The fiftyish woman pushed her hand through her straw-blonde hair and turned to look me in the face. "Decaf, thank you."

"You are quite welcome."

Before I turned toward the kitchen, the woman leaned over to her companion. "My goodness. Did you hear that? That busboy has diction like an educated white person."

A curly-haired waiter walked up to me in the kitchen. "Larry, are you living in the Monkey House?"

"No, but why do they call it that?"

"Well, no offense against you, but it got that name since it's the house where the workers have lived at the club. And since the workers used to be Negroes—blacks—it was nicknamed the Monkey House. And the name just stuck—even though Negroes have been replaced by Hispanics."

April 13 (Monday)

I woke up and felt a pain shooting up my calves. As I turned to the clock, I realized I'd slept for eleven hours. I was thankful the club is closed on Mondays.

April 14 (Tuesday)

Rosa, the club seamstress, measured me for a uniform in the basement laundry room while her barking gray poodle jumped up on my feet and pants. "Down, Margarita, down," Rosa cried with pins in her mouth and marking chalk in her hand. But Margarita ignored her and continued to bark and do tiny pirouettes until I left with all of my new country club polo shirts and pants.

Today, I worked exclusively with the "veterans," including sixty-five-year-old Sam, the Polish bartender in the Men's Grill. Hazel, an older waitress at the club, is quick, charming, and smart—the kind of waitress who makes any restaurant a success. She has worked for the club nearly twenty years and has become quite territorial with certain older male members.

Members in the Mixed Grill talked about hotel queen and Greenwich resident Leona Helmsley, who was on the clubhouse TV because of her upcoming prison term for tax evasion.

"I'd like to see them haul her off to jail," one irate woman said to the rest of her table. "She's nothing but a garish you-know-what."

"In every sense of the word," nodded her companion as she adjusted a pink headband in her blondish-white hair. "She makes the whole town look bad. The TV keeps showing those aerial shots of Greenwich and that dreadful house of hers."

A third woman shrugged her shoulders and looked into her bowl of salad. "Well, it is a beautiful piece of property."

"Yes, it is," said the first woman. "But why here? She should be in those other places like Beverly Hills or Scarsdale or Long Island, with the rest of them. What's she doing here?"

Woman No. 3 looked up. "Well, you know, he's not Jewish."

"Really?"

"So that explains it," said the first woman with an understanding expression on her tanned forehead. "Because, you know, the name didn't sound Jewish."

The second woman agreed: "I can usually tell."

April 15 (Wednesday)

Today, we introduced a new extended menu in the two grill rooms. We added shrimp quesadillas ($6) to the appetizer list—and neither the members nor Hazel could pronounce the name of the dish or fathom what it was. One man pounded on the table and demanded to know which country the dish had come from. He told Hazel how much he hated "changes like this. I like to know that some things are going to stay the same."

Another addition was the "New Dog in Town" ($3.50). It was billed as knackwurst, but one woman of German descent sent the dish back: "This is not knackwurst—this is just a big hot dog."

As I wiped down the length of the men's bar, I noticed a tall stack of postcards with color photos of nude busty women waving hello from sunny faraway beaches. I saw they had been sent from vacationing members with fond regards to Sam or Hazel. Several had come from married couples. One glossy photo boasted a detailed frontal shot of a red-haired beauty who was naked except for a shoestring around her waist. On the back, the message said, Dear Sam, Pull string in an emergency. Love always, The Atkinson Family.

April 16 (Thursday)

This afternoon, I realized I was doing okay. I was fairly comfortable with my few "serving" responsibilities and the rules that related to them:

- When a member is seated, bring out the silverware, cloth napkin, and a menu.
- Never take an order for food, but always bring water or iced tea if it is requested by a member or waiter.
- When a waiter takes a chili or salad order, bring out a basket of warm rolls and crackers, along with a scoop of butter.
- When getting iced tea, fill a tall glass with ice and serve it with a long spoon, a napkin on the bottom, and a lemon on the rim.
- When a member wants his alcoholic drink refilled, politely respond, "Certainly, I will have your waiter come right over."
- Remember that the member is always right.
- Never make offensive eye contact with a member or his guest.
- When serving a member fresh popcorn, serve to the left.
- When a member is finished with a dish or glass, clear it from the right.
- Never tell a member that the kitchen is out of something.

But there were also some "informal" rules that I discovered (but did not follow) while watching the more experienced waiters and kitchen staff in action:

- If you drop a hot roll on the floor in front of a member, apologize and throw it out. If you drop a hot roll on the floor in the kitchen, pick it up and put it back in the bread warmer.
- If you have cleared a table and are 75 percent sure that the member did not use the fork, put it back in the bin with the other clean forks.
- If, after pouring one glass of Coke and one of diet Coke, you get distracted and can't remember which is which, stick your finger in one of them to taste it.
- If a member asks for decaffeinated coffee and you have no time to make it, use regular and add water to cut the flavor.
- When members complain that the chili is too hot and spicy, instead of making a new batch, take the sting out by adding some chocolate syrup.

- If you're making a tuna on toasted wheat and you accidentally burn one side of the bread, don't throw it out. Instead, put the tuna on the burned side and lather on some extra mayo.

April 17 (Friday)

Today, I heard the word "nigger" four times. And it came from someone on the staff.

In the grill, several members were discussing Arthur Ashe, who had recently announced that he had contracted AIDS through a blood transfusion.

"It's a shame that poor man has to be humiliated like this," one woman golfer remarked to a friend over pasta and vegetable salad. "He's been such a good example for his people."

"Well, quite frankly," added a woman in a white sun visor, "I always knew he was gay. There was something about him that just seemed too perfect."

"No, Anne, he's not gay. It came from a blood transfusion."

"Umm," said the woman. "I suppose that's a good reason to stay out of all those big city hospitals. All that bad blood moving around."

Later that afternoon, one of the waiters, who had worked in the Mixed Grill for two years, told me that Tom Seaver and Gerald Ford were members. Of his brush with greatness, he added, "You know, Tom's real first name is George."

"That's something."

"And I've seen O. J. Simpson here, too."

"O. J. belongs here, too?" I asked.

"Oh, no, there aren't any black members here. No way. I actually don't even think there are any Jews here, either."

"Really? Why is that?" I asked.

"I don't know. I guess it's just that the members probably want to have a place where they can go and not have to think about Jews, blacks, and other minorities. It's not really hurting anyone. It's really a WASP club. . . . But now that I think of it, there is a guy here who some people think is Jewish, but I can't really tell. Upstairs, there's a Jewish secretary too."

"And what about O. J.?"

"Oh, yeah, it was so funny to see him out there playing golf on the eighteenth hole." The waiter paused and pointed outside the window. "It never occurred to me before, but it seemed so odd to see a black man with a golf club here on this course."

April 18 (Saturday)

When I arrived, Stephen, one of the waiters, was hanging a poster and sign-up sheet for a soccer league whose main purpose was to "bridge the ethnic and language gap" between white and Hispanic workers at the country clubs in the Greenwich area. I congratulated Stephen on his idea.

Later, while I was wiping down a table, I heard a member snap his fingers in my direction. I turned to see a group of young men smoking cigars. They seemed to be my age or a couple of years younger. "Hey, do I know you?" the voice asked.

As I turned slowly toward the voice, I could hear my own heartbeat. I was sure it was someone I knew.

"No," I said, approaching the blond cigar smoker. He had on light green khaki pants and a light yellow V-neck cotton sweater adorned with a tiny green alligator. As I looked at the other men seated around the table, I noticed that all but one had alligators on their sweaters or shirts.

"I didn't think so. You must be new—what's your name?"

"My name is Larry. I just started a few days ago."

The cigar-smoking host grabbed me by the wrist while looking at his guests. "Well, Larry, welcome to the club. I'm Mr. Billings. And this is Mr. Dennis, a friend and new member."

"Hello, Mr. Dennis," I heard myself saying to a freckle-faced young man who puffed uncomfortably on his fat roll of tobacco.

The first cigar smoker gestured for me to bend over as if he were about to share some important confidence. "Now, Larry, here's what I want you to do. Go get us some of those peanuts and then give my guests and me a fresh ashtray. Can you manage that?"

It was Easter Sunday, and the Easter-egg hunt began with dozens of small children scampering around the tulips and daffodils while well-dressed parents watched wistfully from the rear patio of the club. A giant Easter bunny gave out little baskets filled with jelly beans to parents and then hopped over to the bushes, where he hugged the children. As we peered out from the closed blinds in the grill, we saw women in mink, husbands in gray suits, children in Ralph Lauren and Laura Ashley. Hazel let out a sigh. "Aren't they beautiful?" she said. For just a moment, I found myself agreeing.

As I raced around taking out orders of coffee and baskets of hot rolls, I got a chance to see groups of families. Fathers seemed to be uniformly taller than six feet. Most of them were wearing blue blazers, white shirts, and incredibly out-of-style silk ties—the kind with little blue whales or little green ducks floating downward. They were bespectacled and conspicuously clean-shaven.

The "ladies," as the club prefers to call them, almost invariably had straight blonde hair. Whether or not they had brown roots and whether they were twenty-five or forty-eight, ladies wore their hair blonde, straight, and off the face. No dangling earrings, five-carat diamonds, or designer handbags. Black velvet or pastel headbands were de rigueur.

There were also groups of high school kids who wore torn jeans, sneakers or unlaced L. L. Bean shoes and sweatshirts that said things like HOTCHKISS LACROSSE or ANDOVER CREW. At one table, two boys sat talking to two girls.

"No way, J.C.," one of the girls cried in disbelief while playing with the straw in her diet Coke.

The strawberry-blonde girl next to her flashed her unpainted nails in the air. "Way. She said that if she didn't get her grades up by this spring, they were going to take her out altogether."

"And where would they send her?" one of the guys asked.

The strawberry blonde's grin disappeared as she leaned in close. "Public school."

The group, in hysterics, shook the table. The guys stomped their feet.

"Oh, my God, J.C., oh, J.C., J.C.," the diet Coke girl cried.

Sitting in a tableless corner of the room, beneath the TV, was a young, dark-skinned black woman dressed in a white uniform and a thick wool coat. On her lap was a baby with silky white-blond hair. The woman sat patiently, shifting the baby in her lap while glancing over to where the baby's family ate, two tables away.

I ran to the kitchen, brought back a glass of tea, and offered it to her. The woman looked up at me, shook her head, and then turned back to the gurgling infant.

April 21 (Tuesday)

While Hector and I stood inside a deep walk-in freezer, we scooped balls of butter into separate butter dishes and talked about our plans. "Will you go finish school sometime?" he asked as I dug deep into a vat of frozen butter.

"Maybe. In a couple years, when I save more money, but I'm not sure."

I felt lousy about having to lie.

Just as we were all leaving for the day, Mr. Ryan came down to hand out the new policies for those who were going to live in the Monkey House. Since it had recently been renovated, the club was requiring all new residents to sign the form. The policy included a rule that forbade employees to have overnight guests. Rule 14 stated that the club management had the right to enter an employee's locked bedroom at any time, without permission and without giving notice.

As I was making rounds with my coffeepots, I overheard a raspy-voiced woman talking to a mother and daughter who were thumbing through a catalogue of infants' clothing.

"The problem with au pairs is that they're usually only in the country for a year."

The mother and daughter nodded in agreement.

"But getting one that is a citizen has its own problems. For example, if you ever have to choose between a Negro and one of these Spanish people, always go for the Negro."

One of the women frowned, confused. "Really?"

"Yes," the raspy-voiced woman responded with cold logic. "Even though you can't trust either one, at least Negroes speak English and can follow your directions."

Before I could refill the final cup, the raspy-voiced woman looked up at me and smiled. "Oh, thanks for the refill, Larry."

April 22 (Wednesday)

"This is our country, and don't you forget it. They came here and have to live by our rules!" Hazel pounded her fist into the palm of her pale white hand.

I had made the mistake of telling her I had learned a few Spanish phrases to help me communicate better with some of my co-workers. She wasn't impressed.

"I'll be damned if I'm going to learn or speak one word of Spanish. And I'd suggest you do the same," she said. She took a long drag on her cigarette while I loaded the empty shelves with clean glasses.

Today, the TV was tuned to testimony and closing arguments from the Rodney King police-beating trial in California.

"I am so sick of seeing that awful videotape," one woman said to friends at her table. "It shouldn't be on TV."

At around two, Lois, the club's official secretary, asked me to help her send out a mailing to six hundred members after my shift.

She took me up to her office on the main floor and introduced me to the two women who sat with her.

"Larry, this is Marge, whom you'll talk with in three months, because she's in charge of employee benefits."

I smiled at the brunette.

"And Larry, this is Sandy, whom you'll talk with after you become a member at the club, because she's in charge of members' accounts."

Both Sandy and I looked up at Lois with shocked expressions.

Lois winked, and at the same moment, the three jovial women burst out laughing.

Lois sat me down at a table in the middle of the club's cavernous ballroom and had me stamp ANNUAL MEMBER GUEST on the bottom of small postcards and stuff them into envelopes.

As I sat in the empty ballroom, I looked around at the mirrors and the silver and crystal chandeliers that dripped from the high ceiling. I thought about all the beautiful weddings and debutante balls that must have taken place in that room. I could imagine members asking themselves, "Why would anybody who is not like us want to join a club where they're not wanted?"

I stuffed my last envelope, forgot to clock out, and drove back to the Merritt Parkway and into New York.

April 23 (Thursday)

"Wow, that's great," I said to Mr. Ryan as he posted a memo entitled "Employee Relations Policy Statement: Employee Golf Privileges."

After quickly reading the memo, I realized this "policy" was a crock. The memo opened optimistically: "The club provides golf privileges for staff. . . . Current employees will be allowed golf privileges as outlined below." Unfortunately, the only employees that the memo listed "below" were department heads, golf-management personnel, teaching assistants, the general manager, and "key staff that appear on the club's organizational chart."

At the end of the day, Mr. Ryan handed me my first paycheck. The backbreaking work finally seemed worthwhile. When I opened the envelope and saw what I'd earned— $174.04 for five days—I laughed out loud.

Back in the security of a bathroom stall, where I had periodically been taking notes since my arrival, I studied the check and thought about how many hours—and how hard—I'd worked for so little money. It was less than one tenth of what I'd make in the same time at my law firm. I went upstairs and asked Mr. Ryan about my paycheck.

"Well, we decided to give you $7 an hour," he said in a tone overflowing with generosity. I had never actually been told my hourly rate. "But if the check looks especially big, that's because you got some extra pay in there for all of your terrific work on Good Friday. And by the way, Larry, don't tell the others what you're getting, because we're giving you a special deal and it's really nobody else's business."

I nodded and thanked him for his largess. I stuffed some more envelopes, emptied out my locker, and left.

The next morning, I was scheduled to work a double shift. Instead, I called and explained that I had a family emergency and would have to quit immediately. Mr. Ryan was very sympathetic and said I could return when things settled down. I told him, "No, thanks," but asked that he send my last paycheck to my home. I put my uniform and the key to my locker in a brown padded envelope, and I mailed it all to Mr. Ryan.

Somehow it took two months of phone calls for me to get my final paycheck ($123.74, after taxes and a $30 deduction).

I'm back at my law firm now, dressed in one of my dark gray Paul Stuart suits, sitting in a handsome office thirty floors above midtown. It's a long way from the Monkey House, but we have a long way to go.

Michael Herr

Illumination Rounds

We were all strapped into the seats of the Chinook, fifty of us, and something, someone was hitting it from the outside with an enormous hammer. How do they do that? I thought, we're a thousand feet in the air! But it had to be that, over and over, shaking the helicopter, making it dip and turn in a horrible out-of-control motion that took me in the stomach. I had to laugh, it was so exciting, it was the thing I had wanted, almost what I had wanted except for that wrenching, resonant metal-echo; I could hear it even above the noise of the rotor blades. And they were going to fix that, I knew they would make it stop. They had to, it was going to make me sick.

They were all replacements going in to mop up after the big battles on Hills 875 and 876, the battles that had already taken on the name of one great battle, the battle of Dak To. And I was new, brand new, three days in-country, embarrassed about my boots because they were so new. And across from me, ten feet away, a boy tried to jump out of the straps and then jerked forward and hung there, his rifle barrel caught in the red plastic webbing of the seat back. As the chopper rose again and turned, his weight went back hard against the webbing and a dark spot the size of a baby's hand showed in the center of his fatigue jacket. And it grew—I knew what it was, but not really—it got up to his armpits and then started down his sleeves and up over his shoulders at the same time. It went all across his waist and down his legs, covering the canvas on his boots until they were dark like everything else he wore, and it was running in slow, heavy drops off his fingertips. I thought I could hear the drops hitting the metal strip on the chopper floor. Hey! . . . Oh, but this isn't anything at all, it's not real, it's just some *thing* they're going through that isn't real. One of the door gunners was heaped up on the floor like a cloth dummy. His hand had the bloody raw look of a pound of liver fresh from the butcher paper. We touched down on the same lz we had just left a few minutes before, but I didn't know it until one of the guys shook my shoulder, and then I couldn't stand up. All I could feel of my legs was their shaking, and the guy thought I'd been hit and helped me up. The chopper had taken eight hits, there was shattered plastic all over the floor, a dying pilot up front, and the boy was hanging forward in the straps again, he was dead, but not (I knew) really dead.

It took me a month to lose that feeling of being a spectator to something that was part game, part show. That first afternoon, before I'd boarded the Chinook, a black sergeant had tried to keep me from going. He told me I was too new to go near the kind of shit they were throwing around up in those hills. ("You a reporter?" he'd asked, and I'd said, "No, a writer," dumbass and pompous, and he'd laughed and said, "Careful. You can't use no eraser up where you wanna go.") He'd pointed to the bodies of all the dead Americans lined in two long rows near the chopper pad, so many that they could not even cover all of them decently. But they were not real then, and taught me nothing. The Chinook had come in, blowing my helmet off, and I grabbed it up and joined the replacements waiting to board. "Okay, man," the sergeant said. "You gotta go, you gotta go. All's I can say is, I hope you get a clean wound."

The battle for Hill 875 was over, and some survivors were being brought in by Chinook to the landing strip at Dak To. The 173rd Airborne had taken over 400 casualties, nearly 200 killed, all on the previous afternoon and in the fighting that had gone on all through the night. It was very cold and wet up there, and some girls from the Red Cross had been sent up from Pleiku to comfort the survivors. As the troops filed out of the helicopters, the girls waved and smiled at them from behind their serving tables. "Hi, soldier! What's your name?" "Where you from, soldier?" "I'll bet some hot coffee would hit the spot about now."

And the men from the 173rd just kept walking without answering, staring straight ahead, their eyes rimmed with red from fatigue, their faces pinched and aged with all that had happened during the night. One of them dropped out of line and said something to a loud, fat girl who wore a Peanuts sweatshirt under her fatigue blouse and she started to cry. The rest just walked past the girls and the large, olive-drab coffee urns. They had no idea of where they were.

A senior NCO in the Special Forces was telling the story: "We was back at Bragg, in the NCO Club, and this schoolteacher comes in an' she's real good-lookin'. Dusty here grabs her by the shoulders and starts runnin' his tongue all over her face like she's a fuckin ice-cream cone. An' you know what she says? She says, 'I like you. You're different.'"

At one time they would have lighted your cigarette for you on the terrace of the Continental Hotel. But those days are almost twenty years gone, and anyway, who really misses them? Now there is a crazy American who looks like George Orwell, and he is always sleeping off his drinks in one of the wicker chairs there, slumped against a table, starting up with violence, shouting and then going back to sleep. He makes everyone nervous, especially the waiters; the old ones who had served the French and the Japanese and the first American journalists and OSS types ("those noisy bastards at the Continental," Graham Greene called them) and the really young ones who bussed the tables and pimped in a modest way. The little elevator boy still greets the guests each morning with a quiet "*Ca va?*" but he is seldom answered, and the old baggage man (he also brings us grass) will sit in the lobby and say, "How are you tomorrow?"

"Ode to Billy Joe" plays from speakers mounted on the terrace's corner columns, but the air seems too heavy to carry the sound right, and it hangs in the corners. There is an exhausted, drunk master sergeant from the 1st Infantry Division who has bought a flute from the old man in khaki shorts and pith helmet who sells instruments along Tu Do Street. The old man will lean over the butt-strewn flower boxes that line the terrace and play "Frère Jacques" on a wooden stringed instrument. The sergeant has brought the flute, and he is playing it quietly, pensively, badly.

The tables are crowded with American civilian construction engineers, men getting $30,000 a year from their jobs on government contracts and matching that easily on the black market. Their faces have the look of aerial photos of silicone pits, all hung with loose flesh and visible veins. Their mistresses were among the prettiest, saddest girls in Vietnam. I always wondered what they had looked like before they'd made their arrangements with the engineers. You'd see them at the tables there, smiling their hard, empty smiles into those rangy, brutal, scared faces. No wonder those men all looked alike to the Vietnamese. After a while they all looked alike to me. Out on the Bien Hoa Highway, north of Saigon, there is a monument to the Vietnamese war dead, and it is one of the few graceful things left in the country. It is a modest pagoda set above the road and approached by long flights of gently rising steps. One Sunday, I saw a bunch of these engineers gunning their Harleys up those steps, laughing and shouting in the afternoon sun. The Vietnamese had a special name for them to distinguish them from all other Americans: it translated out to something like "The Terrible Ones," although I'm told that this doesn't even approximate the odium carried in the original.

There was a young sergeant in the Special Forces, stationed at the C Detachment in Can Tho, which served as the SF headquarters for IV Corps. In all, he had spent thirty-six months in Vietnam. This was his third extended tour, and he planned to come back again as soon as he possibly could after this current hitch was finished. During his last tour he had lost a finger and part of a thumb in a fire-fight, and he had been generally shot up enough times for the three Purple Hearts which mean that you don't have to fight in Vietnam anymore. After all that, I guess they thought of him as a combat liability, but he was such a hard charger that they gave him the EM Club to manage. He ran it well and seemed happy, except that he had gained a lot of weight in the duty, and it set him apart from the rest of the men. He loved to horse around with the Vietnamese in the compound, leaping on them from behind, leaning heavily on them, shoving them around and pulling their ears, sometimes punching them a little hard in the stomach, smiling a stiff small smile that was meant to tell them all that he was just being playful. The Vietnamese would smile too, until he turned to walk away. He loved the Vietnamese, he said, he really *knew* them after three years. As far as he was concerned, there was no place in the world as fine as Vietnam. And back home in North Carolina he had a large, glass-covered display case in which he kept his medals and decorations and citations, the photographs taken during three tours and countless battles, letters from past commanders, a few souvenirs. The case stood in the center of the living room, he said, and every night his wife and three kids would move the kitchen table out in front of it and eat their dinner there.

At 800 feet we knew we were being shot at. Something hit the underside of the chopper but did not penetrate it. They weren't firing tracers, but we saw the brilliant flickering blips of light below, and the pilot circled and came down very fast, working the button that released fire from the flex guns mounted on either side of the Huey. Every fifth round was a tracer, and they sailed out and down, incomparably graceful, closer and closer, until they met the tiny point of light coming from the jungle. The ground fire stopped, and we went on to land at Vinh Long, where the pilot yawned and said, "I think I'll go to bed early tonight and see if I can wake up with any enthusiasm for this war."

A twenty-four-year-old Special Forces captain was telling me about it. "I went out and killed one VC and liberated a prisoner. Next day the major called me in and told me that I'd killed fourteen VC and liberated six prisoners. You want to see the medal?"

There was a little air-conditioned restaurant on the corner of Le Loi and Tu Do, across from the Continental Hotel and the old opera house which now served as the Vietnamese Lower House. Some of us called it the Graham Greene Milk Bar (a scene in *The Quiet American* had taken place there), but its name was Givral. Every morning they baked their own baguettes and croissants, and the coffee wasn't too bad. Sometimes, I'd meet there with a friend of mine for breakfast.

He was a Belgian, a tall, slow-moving man of thirty who'd been born in the Congo. He professed to know and love war, and he affected the mercenary sensibility. He'd been photographing the Vietnam thing for seven or eight years now, and once in a while he'd go over to Laos and run around the jungles there with the government, searching for the dreaded Pathet Lao, which he pronounced "Paddy Lao." Other people's stories of Laos always made it sound like a lotus land where no one wanted to hurt anyone, but he said that whenever he went on ops there he always kept a grenade taped to his belly because he was a Catholic and knew what the Paddy Lao would do to him if he were captured. But he was a little crazy that way, and tended to dramatize his war stories.

He always wore dark glasses, probably even during operations. His pictures sold to the wire services, and I saw a few of them in the American news magazines. He was very kind in a gruff, offhanded sort of way, kindness embarrassed him, and he was so graceless among people, so eager to shock, that he couldn't understand why so many of us liked him. Irony was the effect he worked for in conversation, that and a sense of how exquisite the war could be when all of its machinery was running right. He was explaining the finish of an operation he'd just been on in War Zone C, above Cu Chi.

"There were a lot of dead VC," he said. "Dozens and dozens of them! A lot of them were from the same village that has been giving you so much trouble lately. VC from top to bottom—Michael, in that village the fucking *ducks* are VC. So the American commander had twenty or thirty of the dead flown up in a sling load and dropped into the village. I should say it was a drop of at least two hundred feet, all those dead Viet Congs, right in the middle of the village."

He smiled (I couldn't see his eyes).

"Ah, Psywar!" he said, kissing off the tips of his fingers.

Bob Stokes of *Newsweek* told me this: In the big Marine hospital in Danang they have what is called the "White Lie Ward," where they bring some of the worst cases, the ones who can be saved but who will never be the same again. A young marine was carried in, still unconscious and full of morphine, and his legs were gone. As he was being carried into the ward, he came out of it briefly and saw a Catholic chaplain standing over him.

"Father," he said, "am I all right?"

The chaplain didn't know what to say. "You'll have to talk about that with the doctors, son."

"Father, are my legs okay?"

"Yes," the chaplain said. "Sure."

By the next afternoon the shock had worn off and the boy knew all about it. He was lying on his cot when the chaplain came by.

"Father," the Marine said, "I'd like to ask you for something."

"What, son?"

"I'd like to have that cross." And he pointed to the tiny silver insignia on the chaplain's lapel.

"Of course," the chaplain said. "But why?"

"Well, it was the first thing I saw when I came to yesterday, and I'd like to have it."

The chaplain removed the cross and handed it to him. The Marine held it tightly in his fist and looked at the chaplain.

"You lied to me, Father," he said. "You cocksucker. You lied to me."

His name was Davies, and he was a gunner with a helicopter group based at Tan Son Nhut airport. On paper, by the regulations, he was billeted in one of the big "hotel" BEQ's in Cholon, but he only kept his things there. He actually lived in a small two-story Vietnamese house deeper inside of Cholon, as far from the papers and the regulations as he could get. Every morning he took an Army bus with wire-grille windows out to the base and flew missions, mostly around War Zone C, along the Cambodian border, and most nights he returned to the house in Cholon where he lived with his "wife" (whom he'd found in one of the bars) and some other Vietnamese who were said to be the girl's family. Her mamma-san and her brother were always there, living on the first floor, and there were others who came and went. He seldom saw the brother, but every few days he would find a pile of labels and brand names torn from cardboard cartons, American products that the brother wanted from the PX.

The first time I saw him he was sitting alone at a table on the Continental terrace, drinking a beer. He had a full, drooping mustache and sharp, sad eyes, and he was wearing a denim workshirt and wheat jeans. He also carried a Leica and a copy of *Ramparts*, and I just assumed at first that he was a correspondent. I didn't know then that you could buy *Ramparts* at the PX, and after I'd borrowed and returned it we began to talk. It was the issue that featured left-wing Catholics like Jesus Christ and Fulton Sheen on the cover. "*Catholique?*" one of the bar girls said later that night. "*Moi aussi*," and she kept the magazine. That was when we were walking around Cholon in the rain trying to find Hoa, his wife. Mamma-san had told us that she'd gone to the movies with some girlfriends, but Davies knew what she was doing.

"I hate that shit," he said. "It's so uncool."

"Well, don't put up with it."

"Yeah."

Davies' house was down a long, narrow alley that became nothing more than a warren at the end, smelling of camphor smoke and fish, crowded but clean. He would not speak to Mamma-san, and we walked straight up to the second floor. It was one long room that had a sleeping area screened off in an arrangement of filmy curtains. At the top of the stairs there was a large poster of Lenny Bruce, and beneath it, in a shrine effect, was a low table with a Buddha and lighted incense on it.

"Lenny," Davies said.

Most of one wall was covered with a collage that Davies had done with the help of some friends. It included glimpses of burning monks, stacked Viet Cong dead, wounded Marines screaming and weeping, Cardinal Spellman waving from a chopper, Ronald Reagan, his face halved and separated by a stalk of cannabis; pictures of John Lennon peering through wire-rimmed glasses, Mick Jagger, Jimi Hendrix, Dylan, Eldridge Cleaver, Rap Brown; coffins draped with American flags whose stars were replaced by swastikas and dollar signs; odd parts clipped from *Playboy* pictures, newspaper headlines (FARMERS BUTCHER HOGS TO PROTEST PORK PRICE DIP), photo captions (*President Jokes with Newsmen*), beautiful girls holding flowers, showers of peace symbols; Ky standing at attention and saluting, a small mushroom cloud forming where his genitalia should have been; a map of the western United States with the shape of Vietnam reversed and fitted over California and one large, long figure that began at the bottom with shiny leather boots and rouged knees and ascended in a microskirt, bare breasts, graceful shoulders and a long neck, topped by the burned, blackened face of a dead Vietnamese woman.

By the time Davies' friends showed up, we were already stoned. We could hear them below, laughing and rapping with Mama, and then they came up the stairs, three spades and two white guys.

"It sure do smell *peculiar* up here," one of them said.

"Hi, you freaky li'l fuckers."

"This grass is Number Ten," Davies said. "Every time I smoke this grass over here it gives me a bad trip."

"Ain' nuthin' th' matter with that grass," someone said. "It ain't the grass."

"Where's Hoa?"

"Yeah, Davies, where's your ole lady at?"

"She's out hustling Saigon tea, and I'm fucking sick of it." He tried to look really angry, but he only looked unhappy.

One of them handed off a joint and stretched out. "Hairy day today," he said.

"Where'd you fly?"

"Bu Dop."

"Bu Dop!" one of the spades said, and he started to move toward the joint, jiving and working his shoulders, bopping his head. "Bu Dop, budop, bu dop dop *dop!*"

"Funky funky Bu Dop."

"Hey, man, can you OD on grass?"

"I dunno, baby. Maybe we could get jobs at the Aberdeen Proving Grounds smokin' dope for Uncle Sugar."

"Wow, I'm stoned. Hey, Davies, you stoned?"

"Yeah," Davies said.

It started to rain again, so hard that you couldn't hear drops, only the full force of the water pouring down on the metal roof. We smoked a little more, and then the others started to leave. Davies looked like he was sleeping with his eyes open.

"That goddamn pig," he said. "Fuckin' whore. Man, I'm paying out all this bread for the house and those people downstairs. I don't even know who they are, for Christ's sake. I'm really . . . I'm getting sick of it."

"You're pretty short now," someone said. "Why don't you cut out?"

"You mean just split?"

"Why not?"

Davies was quiet for a long time.

"Yeah," he finally said. "This is bad. This is really bad. I think I'm going to get out of here."

A bird colonel, commanding a brigade of the 4th Infantry Division: "I'll bet you always wondered why we call 'em Dinks up in this part of the country. I thought of it myself. I'll tell you, I never *did* like hearing them called Charlie. See, I had an uncle named Charlie, and I liked him too. No, Charlie was just too damn good for the little bastards. So I just thought, What are they *really* like? and I came up with rinky-dink. Suits 'em just perfect, Rinky-Dink. 'Cept that was too long, so we cut it down some. And that's why we call 'em Dinks."

One morning before dawn, Ed Fouhy, a former Saigon bureau chief for CBS, went out to 8th Aerial Port at Tan Son Nhut to catch the early military flight to Danang. They boarded as the sun came up, and Fouhy strapped in next to a kid in rumpled fatigues, one of those soldiers you see whose weariness has gone far beyond physical exhaustion, into that state where no amount of sleep will ever give him the kind of rest he needs. Every torpid movement they make tells you that they are tired, that they'll stay tired until their tours are up and the big bird flies them back to the World. Their eyes are dim with it, their faces almost puffy, and when they smile you have to accept it as a token.

There was a standard question you could use to open a conversation with troops, and Fouhy tried it. "How long you been in-country?" he asked.

The kid half lifted his head; that question could *not* be serious. The weight was really on him, and the words came slowly.

"All fuckin' day," he said.

"You guys out to do a story on me suntahm," the kid said. He was a helicopter gunner, six-three with an enormous head that sat in bad proportion to the rest of his body and a line of picket teeth that were always on show in a wet, uneven smile. Every few seconds he would have to wipe his mouth with the back of his hand, and when he talked to you his face was always an inch from yours, so that I had to take my glasses off to keep them dry. He was from Kilgore, Texas, and he was on his seventeenth consecutive month in-country.

"Why should we do a story about you?"

"'Cause I'm so fuckin' good," he said, "'n' that ain' no shit, neither. Got me one hunnert 'n' fifty-se'en gooks kilt. 'N' fifty caribou." He grinned and stanched the saliva for a second. "Them're all certified," he added.

The chopper touched down at Ba Xoi and we got off, not unhappy about leaving him. "Lis'n," he said laughing, "you git up onna ridgeline, see y' keep yer head down. Y'heah?"

"Say, how'd you get to be a co-respondent an' come ovah to this raggedly-ass motherfucker?"

He was a really big spade, rough-looking even when he smiled, and he wore a gold nose-bead fastened through his left nostril. I told him that the nose-bead blew my mind, and he said that was all right, it blew everybody's mind. We were sitting by the chopper pad of an lz above Kontum. He was trying to get to Dak To, I was heading for Pleiku, and we both wanted to get out of there before nightfall. We took turns running out to the pad to check the choppers that kept coming in and taking off, neither of us having any luck, and after we'd talked for an hour he laid a joint on me and we smoked.

"I been here mor'n eight months now," he said. "I bet I been in mor'n twenny fire-fights. An' I ain' hardly fired back once."

"How come?"

"Shee-it, I go firin' back, I might kill one a th' Brothers you dig it?"

I nodded, no Viet Cong ever called *me* honky, and he told me that in his company alone there were more than a dozen Black Panthers and that he was one of them. I didn't say anything, and then he said that he wasn't just a Panther; he was an agent for the Panthers, sent over here to recruit. I asked him what kind of luck he'd been having, and he said fine, real fine. There was a fierce wind blowing across the lz, and the joint didn't last very long.

"Hey, baby," he said, "that was just some shit I tol' you. Shit, I ain't no Panther. I was just fuckin' with you, see what you'd say."

"But the Panthers have guys over here. I've met some."

"Tha' could be," he said, and he laughed.

A Huey came in, and he jogged out to see where it was headed. It was going to Dak To, and he came back to get his gear. "Later, baby," he said. "An' luck." He jumped into the chopper, and as it rose from the strip he leaned out and laughed, bringing his arm up and bending it back toward him, palm out and the fist clenched tightly in the Sign.

One day I went out with the ARVN on an operation in the rice paddies above Vinh Long, forty terrified Vietnamese troops and five Americans, all packed into three Hueys that dropped us up to our hips in paddy muck. I had never been in a rice paddy before. We spread out and moved toward the marshy swale that led to the jungle. We were still twenty feet from the first cover, a low paddy wall, when we took fire from the treeline. It was probably the working half of a crossfire that had somehow gone wrong. It caught one of the ARVN in the head, and he dropped back into the water and disappeared. We made it to the wall with two casualties. There was no way of stopping their fire, no room to send a flanking party, so gunships were called and we crouched behind the wall and waited. There was a lot of fire coming from the trees, but we were all right as long as we kept down. And I was thinking, Oh man, so this is a rice paddy, yes, wow! when I suddenly heard an electric guitar shooting right up in my ear and a mean, rapturous black voice singing, coaxing, "Now c'mon baby, stop actin' so crazy," and when I got it all together I turned to see a grinning black corporal hunched over a cassette recorder. "Might's well," he said. "We ain' goin' *no*where till them gunships come."

That's the story of the first time I ever heard Jimi Hendrix, but in a war where a lot of people talked about Aretha's "Satisfaction" the way other people speak of Brahms' Fourth, it was more than a story; it was Credentials. "Say, that Jimi Hendrix is my main man," someone would say. "He has *definitely* got his shit together!" Hendrix had once been in the 101st Airborne, and the Airborne in Vietnam was full of wiggy-brilliant spades like him, really mean and really good, guys who always took care of you when things got bad. That music meant a lot to them. I never once heard it played over the Armed Forces Radio Network.

I met this kid from Miles City, Montana, who read the *Stars and Stripes* every day, checking the casualty lists to see if by some chance anybody from his town had been killed. He didn't even know if there was anyone else from Miles City in Vietnam, but he checked anyway because he knew for sure that if there *was* someone else and they got killed, he would be all right. "I mean, can you just see *two* guys from a raggedy-ass town like Miles City getting killed in Vietnam?" he said.

The sergeant had lain out near the clearing for almost two hours with a wounded medic. He had called over and over for a medevac, but none had come. Finally, a chopper from another outfit, a LOH, appeared, and he was able to reach it by radio. The pilot told him that he'd have to wait for one of his own ships, they weren't coming down, and the sergeant told the pilot that if he did not land for them he was going to open fire from the ground and fucking well *bring* him down. So they were picked up that way, but there were repercussions.

The commander's code name was Mal Hombre, and he reached the sergeant later that afternoon from a place with the call signal Violent Meals.

"God *damn* it, Sergeant," he said through the static, "I thought you were a professional soldier."

"I waited as long as I could, Sir. Any longer, I was gonna lose my man."

"This outfit is perfectly capable of taking care of its own dirty laundry. Is that clear, Sergeant?"

"Colonel, since when is a wounded trooper 'dirty laundry'?"

"At ease, Sergeant," Mal Hombre said, and radio contact was broken.

There was a spec 4 in the Special Forces at Can Tho, a shy Indian boy from Chinle, Arizona, with large, wet eyes the color of ripe olives and a quiet way of speaking, a really nice way of putting things, kind to everyone without ever being stupid or soft about it. On the night that the compound and the airstrip were hit, he came and asked me if there was a chaplain anywhere around. He wasn't very religious, he said, but he was worried about tonight. He'd just volunteered for a "suicide squad," two jeeps that were going to drive across the air-strip with mortars and a recoilless rifle. It looked bad, I had to admit; there were so few of us in the compound that they'd had to put me on the reaction force. It might be bad. He just had a feeling about it, he'd seen what always happened to guys whenever they got that feeling, at least he *thought* it was that feeling, a bad one, the worst he'd ever had.

I told him that the only chaplains I could think of would be in the town, and we both knew that the town was cut off.

"Oh," he said. "Look, then. If I get it tonight . . . "

"It'll be okay."

"Listen, though. If it happens . . . I think it's going to . . . will you make sure the colonel tells my folks I was looking for a chaplain anyway?"

I promised, and the jeeps loaded and drove off. I heard later that there had been a brief firefight, but that no one had been hurt. They didn't have to use the recoilless. They all drove back into the compound two hours later. The next morning at breakfast he sat at another table, saying a lot of loud, brutal things about the gooks, and he wouldn't look at me. But at noon he came over and squeezed my arm and smiled, his eyes fixed somewhere just to the right of my own.

For two days now, ever since the Tet Offensive had begun, they had been coming by the hundreds to the province hospital at Can Tho. They were usually either very young or very old or women, and their wounds were often horrible. The more lightly wounded were being treated quickly in the hospital yard, and the more serious cases were simply placed in one of the corridors to die. There were just too many of them to treat, the doctors had worked without a break, and now, on the second afternoon, the Viet Cong began shelling the hospital.

One of the Vietnamese nurses handed me a cold can of beer and asked me to take it down the hall where one of the Army surgeons was operating. The door of the room was ajar, and I walked right in. I probably should have looked first. A little girl was lying on the table, looking with wide dry eyes at the wall. Her left leg was gone, and a sharp piece of bone about six inches long extended from the exposed stump. The leg itself was on the floor, half wrapped in a piece of paper. The doctor was a major, and he'd been working alone. He could not have looked worse if he'd lain all night in a trough of blood. His hands were so slippery that I had to hold the can to his mouth for him and tip it up as his head went back. I couldn't look at the girl.

"Is it all right?" he said quietly.

"It's okay now. I expect I'll be sick as hell later on."

He placed his hand on the girl's forehead and said, "Hello, little darling." He thanked me for bringing the beer. He probably thought that he was smiling, but nothing changed anywhere in his face. He'd been working this way for nearly twenty hours.

The Intel report lay closed on the green field table, and someone had scrawled "What does it all mean?" across the cover sheet. There wasn't much doubt about who had done that; the S-2 was a known ironist. There were so many like him, really young captains and majors who had the wit to cut back their despair, a wedge to set against the bitterness. What got to them sooner or later was an inability to reconcile their love of service with their contempt for the war, and a lot of them finally had to resign their commissions, leave the profession.

We were sitting in the tent waiting for the rain to stop, the major, five grunts and myself. The rains were constant now, ending what had been a dry monsoon season, and you could look through the tent flap and think about the Marines up there patrolling the hills. Someone came in to report that one of the patrols had discovered a small arms cache.

"An arms cache!" the major said. "What happened was, one of the grunts was out there running around, and he tripped and fell down. That's about the only way we ever find any of this shit."

He was twenty-nine, young in rank, and this was his second tour. The time before, he had been a captain commanding a regular Marine company. He knew all about grunts and patrols, arms caches and the value of most Intelligence.

It was cold, even in the tent, and the enlisted Marines seemed uncomfortable about lying around with a stranger, a correspondent there. The major was a cool head, they knew that; there wasn't going to be any kind of hassle until the rain stopped. They talked quietly among themselves at the far end of the tent, away from the light of the lantern. Reports kept coming in: reports from the Vietnamese, from recon, from Division, situation reports, casualty reports, three casualty reports in twenty minutes. The major looked them all over.

"Did you know that a dead Marine costs eighteen thousand dollars?" he said. The grunts all turned around and looked at us. They knew how the major had meant that because they knew the major. They were just seeing about me.

The rain stopped, and they left. Outside, the air was still cool, but heavy, too, as though a terrible heat was coming on. The major and I stood by the tent and watched while an F-4 flew nose-down, released its load against the base of a hill, leveled and flew upward again.

"I've been having this dream," the major said. "I've had it two times now. I'm in a big examination room back at Quantico. They're handing out questionnaires for an aptitude test. I take one and look at it, and the first question says, 'How many kinds of animals can you kill with your hands?'"

We could see rain falling in a sheet about a kilometer away. Judging by the wind, the major gave it three minutes before it reached us.

"After the first tour, I'd have the goddamndest nightmares. You know, the works. Bloody stuff, bad fights, guys dying, *me* dying . . . I thought they were the worst," he said. "But I sort of miss them now."

Susan Sontag

AIDS and Its Metaphors

By metaphor I meant nothing more or less than the earliest and most succinct definition I know, which is Aristotle's, in his *Poetics* (1457b). "Metaphor," Aristotle wrote, "consists in giving the thing a name that belongs to something else." Saying a thing is or is like something-it-is-not is a mental operation as old as philosophy and poetry, and the spawning ground of most kinds of understanding, including scientific understanding, and expressiveness. (To acknowledge which I prefaced the polemic against metaphors of illness I wrote ten years ago with a brief, hectic flourish of metaphor, in mock exorcism of the seductiveness of metaphorical thinking.) Of course, one cannot think without metaphors. But that does not mean there aren't some metaphors we might well abstain from or try to retire. As, of course, all thinking is interpretation. But that does not mean it isn't sometimes correct to be "against" interpretation. . . .

AIDS quickly became a global event—discussed not only in New York, Paris, Rio, Kinshasa but also in Helsinki, Buenos Aires, Beijing, and Singapore—when it was far from the leading cause of death in Africa, much less in the world. There are famous diseases, as there are famous countries, and these are not necessarily the ones with the biggest populations. AIDS did not become so famous just because it afflicts whites too, as some Africans bitterly assert. But it is certainly true that were AIDS only an African disease, however many millions were dying, few outside of Africa would be concerned with it. It would be one of those "natural" events, like famines, which periodically ravage poor, overpopulated countries and about which people in rich countries feel quite helpless. Because it is a

world event—that is, because it affects the West—it is regarded as not just a natural disaster. It is filled with historical meaning. (Part of the self-definition of Europe and the neo-
European countries is that it, the First World, is where major calamities are
history-making, transformative, while in poor, African or Asian countries they are part of a
cycle, and therefore something like an aspect of nature.) Nor has AIDS become so publi-
cized because, as some have suggested, in rich countries the illness first afflicted a group of
people who were all men, almost all white, many of them educated, articulate, and knowledgeable about how to lobby and organize for public attention and resources devoted to
the disease. AIDS occupies such a large part in our awareness because of what it has been
taken to represent. It seems the very model of all the catastrophes privileged populations
feel await them.

What biologists and public health officials predict is something far worse than can be
imagined or than society (and the economy) can tolerate. No responsible official holds out
the slightest hope that the African economies and health services can cope with the spread
of the disease predicted for the near future, while every day one can read the direst estimates of the cost of AIDS to the country that has reported the largest number of cases, the
United States. Astonishingly large sums of money are cited as the cost of providing minimum care to people who will be ill in the next few years. (This is assuming that the reas-
surances to "the general population" are justified, an assumption much disputed within
the medical community.) Talk in the United States, and not only in the United States, is of
a national emergency, "possibly our nation's survival." An editorialist at *The New York Times*
intoned last year: "We all know the truth, every one of us. We live in a time of plague such
as has never been visited on our nation. We can pretend it does not exist, or exists for
those others, and carry on as if we do not know. . . . " And one French poster shows a
giant UFO-like black mass hovering over and darkening with spidery rays most of the
familiar hexagon shape of the country lying below. Above the image is written: "It depends
on each of us to erase that shadow" (*Il depend de chacun de nous d'effacer cette ombre.*) And
underneath: "France doesn't want to die of AIDS" (*La France ne veut pas mourir du sida*).
Such token appeals for mass mobilization to confront an unprecedented menace appear, at
frequent intervals, in every mass society. It is also typical of a modern society that the
demand for mobilization be kept very general and the reality of the response fall well short
of what seems to be demanded to meet the challenge of the nation-endangering menace.
This sort of rhetoric has a life of its own: it serves some purpose if it simply keeps in circu-
lation an ideal of unifying communal practice that is precisely contradicted by the pursuit
of accumulation and isolating entertainments enjoined on the citizens of a modern mass
society.

The survival of the nation, of civilized society, of the world itself is said to be at
stake—claims that are a familiar part of building a case for repression. (An emergency
requires "drastic measures," et cetera.) The end-of-the-world rhetoric that AIDS has
evoked does inevitably build such a case. But it also does something else. It offers a stoic,
finally numbing contemplation of catastrophe. The eminent Harvard historian of science
Stephen Jay Gould has declared that the AIDS pandemic may rank with nuclear weaponry
"as the greatest danger of our era." But even if it kills as much as a quarter of the human
race—a prospect Gould considers possible—"there will still be plenty of us left and we
can start again." Scornful of the jeremiads of the moralists, a rational and humane scientist
proposes the minimum consolation: an apocalypse that doesn't have any meaning. AIDS is

a "natural phenomenon," not an event "with a moral meaning," Gould points out; "there is no message in its spread." Of course, it is monstrous to attribute meaning, in the sense of moral judgment, to the spread of an infectious disease. But perhaps it is only a little less monstrous to be invited to contemplate death on this horrendous scale with equanimity.

Much of the well-intentioned public discourse in our time expresses a desire to be candid about one or another of the various dangers which might be leading to all-out catastrophe. And now there is one more. To the death of oceans and lakes and forests, the unchecked growth of populations in the poor parts of the world, nuclear accidents like Chernobyl, the puncturing and depletion of the ozone layer, the perennial threat of nuclear confrontation between the superpowers or nuclear attack by one of the rogue states not under superpower control—to all these, now add AIDS. In the countdown to a millennium, a rise in apocalyptic thinking may be inevitable. Still, the amplitude of the fantasies of doom that AIDS has inspired can't be explained by the calendar alone, or even by the very real danger the illness represents. There is also the need for an apocalyptic scenario that is specific to "Western" society, and perhaps even more so to the United States. (America, as someone has said, is a nation with the soul of a church—an evangelical church prone to announcing radical endings and brand-new beginnings.) The taste for worst-case scenarios reflects the need to master fear of what is felt to be uncontrollable. It also expresses an imaginative complicity with disaster. The sense of cultural distress or failure gives rise to the desire for a clean sweep, a tabula rasa. No one wants a plague, of course. But, yes, it would be a chance to begin again. And beginning again—that is very modern, very American, too.

AIDS may be extending the propensity for becoming inured to vistas of global annihilation which the stocking and brandishing of nuclear arms has already promoted. With the inflation of apocalyptic rhetoric has come the increasing unreality of the apocalypse. A permanent modern scenario: apocalypse looms . . . and it doesn't occur. And it still looms. We seem to be in the throes of one of the modern kinds of apocalypse. There is the one that's not happening, whose outcome remains in suspense: the missiles circling the earth above our heads, with a nuclear payload that could destroy all life many times over, that haven't (so far) gone off. And there are ones that are happening, and yet seem not to have (so far) the most feared consequences—like the astronomical Third World debt, like overpopulation, like ecological blight; or that happen and then (we are told) didn't happen— like the October 1987 stock market collapse, which was a "crash," like the one in October 1929, and was not. Apocalypse is now a long-running serial: not "Apocalypse Now" but "Apocalypse From Now On." Apocalypse has become an event that is happening and not happening. It may be that some of the most feared events, like those involving the irreparable ruin of the environment, have already happened. But we don't know it yet, because the standards have changed. Or because we do not have the right indices for measuring the catastrophe. Or simply because this is a catastrophe in slow motion. (Or *feels* as if it is in slow motion, because we know about it, can anticipate it; and now have to wait for it to happen, to catch up with what we think we know.)

Modern life accustoms us to live with the intermittent awareness of monstrous, unthinkable—but, we are told, quite probable—disasters. Every major event is haunted, and not only by its representation as an image (an old doubling of reality now, which began in 1839, with the invention of the camera). Besides the photographic or electronic simulation of events, there is also the calculation of their eventual outcome. Reality has bifurcated, into the real thing and an alternative version of it, twice over. There is the event and its image. And there is the event and its projection. But as real events often seem to have no more reality for people than images, and to need the confirmation of their images, so our reaction to events in the present seeks confirmation in a mental outline, with appropriate computations, of the event in its projected, ultimate form.

Future-mindedness is as much the distinctive mental habit, and intellectual corruption, of this century as the history-mindedness that, as Nietzsche pointed out, transformed thinking in the nineteenth century. Being able to estimate how matters will evolve into the future is an inevitable byproduct of a more sophisticated (quantifiable, testable) understanding of process, social as well as scientific. The ability to project events with some accuracy into the future enlarged what power consisted of, because it was a vast new source of instructions about how to deal with the present. But in fact the look into the future, which was once tied to a vision of linear progress, has, with more knowledge at our disposal than anyone could have dreamed, turned into a vision of disaster. Every process is a prospect, and invites a prediction bolstered by statistics. Say: the number now . . . in three years, in five years, in ten years; and, of course, at the end of the century. Anything in history or nature that can be described as changing steadily can be seen as heading toward catastrophe. (Either the too little and becoming less: waning, decline, entropy. Or the too much, ever more than we can handle or absorb: uncontrollable growth.) Most of what experts pronounce about the future contributes to this new double sense of reality—beyond the doubleness to which we are already accustomed by the comprehensive duplication of everything in images. There is what is happening now. And there is what it portends: the imminent, but not yet actual, and not really graspable, disaster.

Two kinds of disaster, actually. And a gap between them, in which the imagination flounders. The difference between the epidemic we have and the pandemic that we are promised (by current statistical extrapolations) feels like the difference between the war we have, so-called limited wars, and the unimaginably more terrible ones we could have the latter (with all the appurtenances of science fiction) being the sort of activity people are addicted to staging for fun, as electronic games. For beyond the real epidemic with its inexorably mounting death toll (statistics are issued by national and international health organizations every week, every month) is a qualitatively different, much greater disaster which we think both will and will not take place. Nothing is changed when the most appalling estimates are revised downward, temporarily, which is an occasional feature of the display of speculative statistics disseminated by health bureaucrats and journalists. Like the demographic predictions, which are probably just as accurate, the big news is usually bad.

A proliferation of reports or projections of unreal (that is, ungraspable) doomsday eventualities tends to produce a variety of reality-denying responses. Thus, in most discussions of nuclear warfare, being rational (the self-description of experts) means not acknowledging the human reality, while taking in emotionally even a small part of what is at stake for human beings (the province of those who regard themselves as the menaced) means insisting on unrealistic demands for the rapid dismantling of the peril. This split of public attitude, into the inhuman and the all-too-human, is much less stark with AIDS. Experts denounce the stereotypes attached to people with AIDS and to the continent where it is presumed to have originated, emphasizing that the disease belongs to much wider populations than the groups initially at risk, and to the whole world, not just to Africa.* For while AIDS has turned out, not surprisingly, to be one of the most meaning-laden of diseases, along with leprosy and syphilis, clearly there are checks on the impulse to stigmatize people with the disease. The way in which the illness is such a perfect repository for people's most general fears about the future to some extent renders irrelevant the predictable efforts to pin the disease on a deviant group or a dark continent.

Like the effects of industrial pollution and the new system of global financial markets, the AIDS crisis is evidence of a world in which nothing important is regional, local, limited; in which everything that can circulate does, and every problem is, or is destined to become, worldwide. Goods circulate (including images and sounds and documents, which circulate fastest of all, electronically). Garbage circulates: the poisonous industrial wastes of St. Etienne, Hannover, Mestre, and Bristol are being dumped in the coastal towns of West Africa. People circulate, in greater numbers than ever. And diseases. From the untrammeled intercontinental air travel for pleasure and business of the privileged to the unprecedented migrations of the underprivileged from villages to cities and, legally and illegally, from country to country—all this physical mobility and interconnectedness (with its consequent dissolving of old taboos, social and sexual) is as vital to the maximum functioning of the advanced, or world, capitalist economy as is the easy transmissibility of goods and images and financial instruments. But now that heightened, modern interconnectedness in space, which is not only personal but social, structural, is the bearer of a health menace sometimes described as a threat to the species itself; and the fear of AIDS is of a piece with attention to other unfolding disasters that are the byproduct of advanced society, particularly those illustrating the degradation of the environment on a world scale. AIDS is one of the dystopian harbingers of the global village, that future which is already here and always before us, which no one knows how to refuse.

That even an apocalypse can be made to seem part of the ordinary horizon of expectation constitutes an unparalleled violence that is being done to our sense of reality, to our humanity. But it is highly desirable for a specific dreaded illness to come to seem ordinary. Even the disease most fraught with meaning can become just an illness. It has happened with leprosy, though some ten million people in the world, easy to ignore since almost all live in Africa and the Indian subcontinent, have what is now called, as part of its wholesome dedramatization, Hansen's disease (after the Norwegian physician who, over a century ago, discovered the bacillus). It is bound to happen with AIDS, when the illness is

---

* "AIDS cannot be stopped in any country unless it is stopped in all countries," declared the retiring head of the World Health Organization in Geneva, Dr. Halfdan Mahler, at the Fourth International Conference on AIDS (Stockholm, June 1988), where the global character of the AIDS crisis was a leading theme. "This epidemic is worldwide and is sparing no continent," said Dr. Willy Rozenbaum, a French AIDS specialist. "It cannot be mastered in the West unless it is overcome everywhere." In contrast to the rhetoric of global responsibility, a specialty of the international conferences, is the view, increasingly heard, in which AIDS is regarded as a kind of Darwinian test of a society's aptitude for survival, which may require writing off those countries that can't defend themselves. A German AIDS specialist, Dr. Eike Brigitte Helm, has declared that it "can already be seen that in a number of parts of the world AIDS will drastically change the population structure. Particularly in Africa and Latin America. A society that is not able, somehow or other, to prevent the spread of AIDS has very poor prospects for the future." [Sontag's note]

much better understood and, above all, treatable. For the time being, much in the way of individual experience and social policy depends on the struggle for rhetorical ownership of the illness: how it is possessed, assimilated in argument and in cliché. The age-old, seemingly inexorable process whereby diseases acquire meanings (by coming to stand for the deepest fears) and inflict stigma is always worth challenging, and it does seem to have more limited credibility in the modern world, among people willing to be modern—the process is under surveillance now. With this illness, one that elicits so much guilt and shame, the effort to detach it from these meanings, these metaphors, seems particularly liberating, even consoling. But the metaphors cannot be distanced just by abstaining from them. They have to be exposed, criticized, belabored, used up.

Not all metaphors applied to illnesses and their treatment are equally unsavory and distorting. The one I am most eager to see retired—more than ever since the emergence of AIDS—is the military metaphor. Its converse, the medical model of the public weal, is probably more dangerous and far-reaching in its consequences, since it not only provides a persuasive justification for authoritarian rule but implicitly suggests the necessity of state-sponsored repression and violence (the equivalent of surgical removal or chemical control of the offending or "unhealthy" parts of the body politic). But the effect of the military imagery on thinking about sickness and health is far from inconsequential. It overmobilizes, it overdescribes, and it powerfully contributes to the excommunicating and stigmatizing of the ill.

No, it is not desirable for medicine, any more than for war, to be "total." Neither is the crisis created by AIDS a "total" anything. We are not being invaded. The body is not a battlefield. The ill are neither unavoidable casualties nor the enemy. We—medicine, society—are not authorized to fight back by any means whatever. . . . About that metaphor, the military one, I would say, if I may paraphrase Lucretius:[1] Give it back to the war-makers.

Craft Essays

Joan Didion

On Keeping a Notebook

"'That woman Estelle,'" the note reads, "'is partly the reason why George Sharp and I are separated today.' *Dirty crepe-de-Chine wrapper, hotel bar, Wilmington RR, 9:45 a.m. August Monday morning.*"

Since the note is in my notebook, it presumably has some meaning to me. I study it for a long while. At first I have only the most general notion of what I was doing on an

---

[1] Lucretius: Titus Lucretius Carus (c. 50 B.C. [exact birth and death unknown]); a Roman poet and philosopher best known for a six-volume hexameter poem, *De rerum natura* (On the Nature of Things), in which he denounces religious belief as the source of human wickedness and misery.

August Monday morning in the bar of the hotel across from the Pennsylvania Railroad station in Wilmington, Delaware (waiting for a train? missing one? 1960? 1961? why Wilmington?), but I do remember being there. The woman in the dirty crepe-de-Chine wrapper had come down from her room for a beer, and the bartender had heard before the reason why George Sharp and she were separated today. "Sure," he said, and went on mopping the floor. "You told me." At the other end of the bar is a girl. She is talking, pointedly, not to the man beside her but to a cat lying in the triangle of sunlight cast through the open door. She is wearing a plaid silk dress from Peck & Peck, and the hem is coming down.

Here is what it is: The girl has been on the Eastern Shore, and now she is going back to the city, leaving the man beside her, and all she can see ahead are the viscous summer sidewalks and the 3 A.M. long-distance calls that will make her lie awake and then sleep drugged through all the steaming mornings left in August (1960? 1961?). Because she must go directly from the train to lunch in New York, she wishes that she had a safety pin for the hem of the plaid silk dress, and she also wishes that she could forget about the hem and the lunch and stay in the cool bar that smells of disinfectant and malt and make friends with the woman in the crepe-de-Chine wrapper. She is afflicted by a little self-pity, and she wants to compare Estelles. That is what that was all about.

Why did I write it down? In order to remember, of course, but exactly what was it I wanted to remember? How much of it actually happened? Did any of it? Why do I keep a notebook at all? It is easy to deceive oneself on all those scores. The impulse to write things down is a peculiarly compulsive one, inexplicable to those who do not share it, useful only accidentally, only secondarily, in the way that any compulsion tries to justify itself. I suppose that it begins or does not begin in the cradle. Although I have felt compelled to write things down since I was five years old, I doubt that my daughter ever will, for she is a singularly blessed and accepting child, delighted with life exactly as life presents itself to her, unafraid to go to sleep and unafraid to wake up. Keepers of private notebooks are a different breed altogether, lonely and resistant rearrangers of things, anxious malcontents, children afflicted apparently at birth with some presentiment of loss.

My first notebook was a Big Five tablet, given to me by my mother with the sensible suggestion that I stop whining and learn to amuse myself by writing down my thoughts. She returned the tablet to me a few years ago; the first entry is an account of a woman who believed herself to be freezing to death in the Arctic night, only to find, when day broke, that she had stumbled onto the Sahara Desert, where she would die of the heat before lunch. I have no idea what turn of a five-year-old's mind could have prompted so insistently "ironic" and exotic a story, but it does reveal a certain predilection for the extreme which has dogged me into adult life; perhaps if I were analytically inclined I would find it a truer story than any I might have told about Donald Johnson's birthday party or the day my cousin Brenda put Kitty Litter in the aquarium.

So the point of my keeping a notebook has never been, nor is it now, to have an accurate factual record of what I have been doing or thinking. That would be a different impulse entirely, an instinct for reality which I sometimes envy but do not possess. At no point have I ever been able successfully to keep a diary; my approach to daily life ranges from the grossly negligent to the merely absent, and on those few occasions when I have tried dutifully to record a day's events, boredom has so overcome me that the results are mysterious at best. What is this business about "shopping, typing piece, dinner with E, depressed"? Shopping for what? Typing what piece? Who is E? Was this "E" depressed, or was I depressed? Who cares?

In fact I have abandoned altogether that kind of pointless entry; instead I tell what some would call lies. "That's simply not true," the members of my family frequently tell me when they come up against my memory of a shared event. "The party was *not* for you, the spider was *not* a black widow, *it wasn't that way at all.*" Very likely they are right, for not only have I always had trouble distinguishing between what happened and what merely might have happened, but I remain unconvinced that the distinction, for my purposes, matters. The cracked crab that I recall having for lunch the day my father came home from Detroit in 1945 must certainly be embroidery, worked into the day's pattern to lend verisimilitude; I was ten years old and would not now remember the cracked crab. The day's events did not turn on cracked crab. And yet it is precisely that fictitious crab that makes me see the afternoon all over again, a home movie run all too often, the father bearing gifts, the child weeping, an exercise in family love and guilt. Or that is what it was to me. Similarly, perhaps it never did snow that August in Vermont; perhaps there never were flurries in the night wind, and maybe no one else felt the ground hardening and summer already dead even as we pretended to bask in it, but that was how it felt to me, and it might as well have snowed, could have snowed, did snow.

How it felt to me: that is getting closer to the truth about a notebook. I sometimes delude myself about why I keep a notebook, imagine that some thrifty virtue derives from preserving everything observed. See enough and write it down, I tell myself, and then some morning when the world seems drained of wonder, some day when I am only going through the motions of doing what I am supposed to do, which is write—on that bankrupt morning I will simply open my notebook and there it will all be, a forgotten account with accumulated interest, paid passage back to the world out there: dialogue overheard in hotels and elevators and at the hatcheck counter in Pavillon (one middle-aged man shows his hat check to another and says, "That's my old football number"); impressions of Bettina Aptheker and Benjamin Sonnenberg and Teddy ("Mr. Acapulco") Stauffer; careful *aperçus* about tennis bums and failed fashion models and Greek shipping heiresses, one of whom taught me a significant lesson (a lesson I could have learned from F. Scott Fitzgerald, but perhaps we all must meet the very rich for ourselves) by asking, when I arrived to interview her in her orchid-filled sitting room on the second day of a paralyzing New York blizzard, whether it was snowing outside.

I imagine, in other words, that the notebook is about other people. But of course it is not. I have no real business with what one stranger said to another at the hatcheck counter in Pavillon; in fact I suspect that the line "That's my old football number" touched not my own imagination at all, but merely some memory of something once read, probably "The Eighty-Yard Run." Nor is my concern with a woman in a dirty crepe-de-Chine wrapper in a Wilmington bar. My stake is always, of course, in the unmentioned girl in the plaid silk dress. *Remember what it was to be me:* that is always the point.

It is a difficult point to admit. We are brought up in the ethic that others, any others, all others, are by definition more interesting than ourselves; taught to be diffident, just this side of self-effacing. ("You're the least important person in the room and don't forget it," Jessica Mitford's governess would hiss in her ear on the advent of any social occasion; I copied that into my notebook because it is only recently that I have been able to enter a room without hearing some such phrase in my inner ear.) Only the very young and the very old may recount their dreams at breakfast, dwell upon self, interrupt with memories of beach picnics and favorite Liberty lawn dresses and the rainbow trout in a creek near Colorado Springs. The rest of us are expected, rightly, to affect absorption in other people's favorite dresses, other people's trout.

And so we do. But our notebooks give us away, for however dutifully we record what we see around us, the common denominator of all we see is always, transparently, shamelessly, the implacable "I." We are not talking here about the kind of notebook that is patently for public consumption, a structural conceit for binding together a series of graceful *pensées;* we are talking about something private, about bits of the mind's string too short to use, an indiscriminate and erratic assemblage with meaning only for its maker.

And sometimes even the maker has difficulty with the meaning. There does not seem to be, for example, any point in my knowing for the rest of my life that, during 1964, 720 tons of soot fell on every square mile of New York City, yet there it is in my notebook, labeled "FACT." Nor do I really need to remember that Ambrose Bierce liked to spell Leland Stanford's name "£eland $tanford" or that "smart women almost always wear black in Cuba," a fashion hint without much potential for practical application. And does not the relevance of these notes seem marginal at best?:

> In the basement museum of the Inyo County Courthouse in Independence, California, sign pinned to a mandarin coat: "This MANDARIN COAT was often worn by Mrs. Minnie S. Brooks when giving lectures on her TEAPOT COLLECTION."

> Redhead getting out of car in front of Beverly Wilshire Hotel, chinchilla stole, Vuitton bags with tags reading:
> > MRS. LOU FOX
> > HOTEL SAHARA
> > VEGAS

Well, perhaps not entirely marginal. As a matter of fact, Mrs. Minnie S. Brooks and her MANDARIN COAT pull me back into my own childhood, for although I never knew Mrs. Brooks and did not visit Inyo County until I was thirty, I grew up in just such a world, in houses cluttered with Indian relics and bits of gold ore and ambergris and the souvenirs my Aunt Mercy Farnsworth brought back from the Orient. It is a long way from that world to Mrs. Lou Fox's world, where we all live now, and is it not just as well to remember that? Might not Mrs. Minnie S. Brooks help me to remember what I am? Might not Mrs. Lou Fox help me to remember what I am not?

But sometimes the point is harder to discern. What exactly did I have in mind when I noted down that it cost the father of someone I know $650 a month to light the place on the Hudson in which he lived before the Crash? What use was I planning to make of this line by Jimmy Hoffa: "I may have my faults, but being wrong ain't one of them"? And although I think it interesting to know where the girls who travel with the Syndicate have their hair done when they find themselves on the West Coast, will I ever make suitable use of it? Might I not be better off just passing it on to John O'Hara? What is a recipe for sauerkraut doing in my notebook? What kind of magpie keeps this notebook? "*He was born the night the* Titanic *went down.*" That seems a nice enough line, and I even recall who said it, but is it not really a better line in life than it could ever be in fiction?

But of course that is exactly it: not that I should ever use the line, but that I should remember the woman who said it and the afternoon I heard it. We were on her terrace by the sea, and we were finishing the wine left from lunch, trying to get what sun there was, a California winter sun. The woman whose husband was born the night the *Titanic* went down wanted to rent her house, wanted to go back to her children in Paris. I remember wishing that I could afford the house, which cost $1,000 a month. "Someday you will," she said lazily. "Someday it all comes." There in the sun on her terrace it seemed easy to believe in someday, but later I had a low-grade afternoon hangover and ran over a black snake on the way to the supermarket and was flooded with inexplicable fear when I heard the checkout clerk explaining to the man ahead of me why she was finally divorcing her husband. "He left me no choice," she said over and over as she punched the register. "He has a little seven-month-old baby by her, he left me no choice." I would like to believe that my dread then was for the human condition, but of course it was for me, because I wanted a baby and did not then have one and because I wanted to own the house that cost $1,000 a month to rent and because I had a hangover.

It all comes back. Perhaps it is difficult to see the value in having one's self back in that kind of mood, but I do see it; I think we are well advised to keep on nodding terms with the people we used to be whether we find them attractive company or not. Otherwise they turn up unannounced and surprise us, come hammering on the mind's door at 4 A.M. of a bad night and demand to know who deserted them, who betrayed them, who is going to make amends. We forget all too soon the things we thought we could never forget. We forget the loves and the betrayals alike; forget what we whispered and what we screamed, forget who we were. I have already lost touch with a couple of people I used to be; one of them, a seventeen-year-old, presents little threat, although it would be of some interest to me to know again what it feels like to sit on a river levee drinking vodka-and-orange-juice and listening to Les Paul and Mary Ford and their echoes sing "How High the Moon" on the car radio. (You see I still have the scenes, but I no longer perceive myself among those present, no longer could even improvise the dialogue.) The other one, a twenty-three-year-old, bothers me more. She was always a good deal of trouble, and I suspect she will reappear when I least want to see her, skirts too long, shy to the point of aggravation, always the injured party, full of recriminations and little hurts and stories I do not want to hear again, at once saddening me and angering me with her vulnerability and ignorance, an apparition all the more insistent for being so long banished.

It is a good idea, then, to keep in touch, and I suppose that keeping in touch is what notebooks are all about. And we are all on our own when it comes to keeping those lines open to ourselves: your notebook will never help me, nor mine you. "*So what's new in the whiskey business?*" What could that possibly mean to you? To me it means a blonde in a Pucci bathing suit sitting with a couple of fat men by the pool at the Beverly Hills Hotel. Another man approaches, and they all regard one another in silence for a while. "So what's new in the whiskey business?" one of the fat men finally says by way of welcome, and the blonde stands up, arches one foot and dips it in the pool, looking all the while at the cabaña where Baby Pignatari is talking on the telephone. That is all there is to that, except that several years later I saw the blonde coming out of Saks Fifth Avenue in New York with her California complexion and a voluminous mink coat. In the harsh wind that day she looked old and irrevocably tired to me, and even the skins in the mink coat were not worked the way they were doing them that year, not the way she would have wanted them done, and there is the point of the story. For a while after that I did not like to look in the mirror, and my eyes would skim the newspapers and pick out only the deaths, the cancer victims, the premature coronaries, the suicides, and I stopped riding the Lexington Avenue IRT because I noticed for the first time that all the strangers I had seen for years— the man with the seeing-eye dog, the spinster who read the classified pages every day, the fat girl who always got off with me at Grand Central—looked older than they once had.

It all comes back. Even that recipe for sauerkraut: even that brings it back. I was on Fire Island when I first made that sauerkraut, and it was raining, and we drank a lot of bourbon and ate the sauerkraut and went to bed at ten, and I listened to the rain and the Atlantic and felt safe. I made the sauerkraut again last night and it did not make me feel any safer, but that is, as they say, another story.

Barbara Ehrenreich

Getting Ready *from* **Nickel and Dimed**

The idea that led to this book arose in comparatively sumptuous circumstances. Lewis Lapham, the editor of *Harper's,* had taken me out for a $30 lunch at some understated French country-style place to discuss future articles I might write for his magazine. I had the salmon and field greens, I think, and was pitching him some ideas having to do with pop culture when the conversation drifted to one of my more familiar themes—poverty. How does anyone live on the wages available to the unskilled? How, in particular, we wondered, were the roughly four million women about to be booted into the labor market by welfare reform going to make it on $6 or $7 an hour? Then I said something that I have since had many opportunities to regret: "Someone ought to do the old-fashioned kind of journalism—you know, go out there and try it for themselves." I meant someone much younger than myself, some hungry neophyte journalist with time on her hands. But Lapham got this crazy-looking half smile on his face and ended life as I knew it, for long stretches at least, with the single word *"You."*

The last time anyone had urged me to forsake my normal life for a run-of-the-mill low-paid job had been in the seventies, when dozens, perhaps hundreds, of sixties radicals started going into the factories to "proletarianize" themselves and organize the working class in the process. Not this girl. I felt sorry for the parents who had paid college tuition for these blue-collar wannabes and sorry, too, for the people they intended to uplift. In my own family, the low-wage way of life had never been many degrees of separation away; it was close enough, in any case, to make me treasure the gloriously autonomous, if not always well-paid, writing life. My sister has been through one low-paid job after another—phone company business rep, factory worker, receptionist—constantly struggling against what she calls "the hopelessness of being a wage slave." My husband and companion of seventeen years was a $4.50-an-hour warehouse worker when I fell in with him, escaping eventually and with huge relief to become an organizer for the Teamsters. My father had been a copper miner; uncles and grandfathers worked in the mines or for the Union Pacific. So to me, sitting at a desk all day was not only a privilege but a duty: something I owed to all those people in my life, living and dead, who'd had so much more to say than anyone ever got to hear.

Adding to my misgivings, certain family members kept reminding me unhelpfully that I could do this project, after a fashion, without ever leaving my study. I could just pay myself a typical entry-level wage for eight hours a day, charge myself for room and board plus some plausible expenses like gas, and total up the numbers after a month. With the prevailing wages running at $6–$7 an hour in my town and rents at $400 a month or more, the numbers might, it seemed to me, just barely work out all right. But if the question was whether a single mother leaving welfare could survive without government assistance in the form of food stamps, Medicaid, and housing and child care subsidies, the answer was well known before I ever left the comforts of home. According to the National Coalition for the Homeless, in 1998—the year I started this project—it took, on average nationwide, an hourly wage of $8.89 to afford a one-bedroom apartment, and the Preamble Center for Public Policy was estimating that the odds against a typical welfare recipient's landing a job at such a "living wage" were about 97 to 1. Why should I bother to confirm these unpleasant facts? As the time when I could no longer avoid the assignment approached, I began to feel a little like the elderly man I once knew who used a calculator to balance his checkbook and then went back and checked the results by redoing each sum by hand.

In the end, the only way to overcome my hesitation was by thinking of myself as a scientist, which is, in fact, what I was educated to be. I have a Ph.D. in biology, and I didn't get it by sitting at a desk and fiddling with numbers. In that line of business, you can think all you want, but sooner or later you have to get to the bench and plunge into the everyday chaos of nature, where surprises lurk in the most mundane measurements. Maybe when I got into the project, I would discover some hidden economies in the world of the low-wage worker. After all, if almost 30 percent of the workforce toils for $8 an hour or less, as the Washington-based Economic Policy Institute reported in 1998, they may have found some tricks as yet unknown to me. Maybe I would even be able to detect in myself the bracing psychological effects of getting out of the house, as promised by the wonks who brought us welfare reform. Or, on the other hand, maybe there would be unexpected costs—physical, financial, emotional—to throw off all my calculations. The only way to find out was to get out there and get my hands dirty.

In the spirit of science, I first decided on certain rules and parameters. Rule one, obviously enough, was that I could not, in my search for jobs, fall back on any skills derived from my education or usual work—not that there were a lot of want ads for essayists anyway. Two, I had to take the highest-paying job that was offered me and do my best to hold it; no Marxist rants or sneaking off to read novels in the ladies' room. Three, I had to take the cheapest accommodations I could find, at least the cheapest that offered an acceptable level of safety and privacy, though my standards in this regard were hazy and, as it turned out, prone to deterioration over time.

I tried to stick to these rules, but in the course of the project, all of them were bent or broken at some time. In Key West, for example, where I began this project in the late spring of 1998, I once promoted myself to an interviewer for a waitressing job by telling her I could greet European tourists with the appropriate *Bonjour* or *Guten Tag,* but this was the only case in which I drew on any remnant of my actual education. In Minneapolis, my final destination, where I lived in the early summer of 2000, I broke another rule by failing to take the best-paying job that was offered, and you will have to judge my reasons for doing so yourself. And finally, toward the very end, I did break down and rant—stealthily, though, and never within hearing of management.

There was also the problem of how to present myself to potential employers and, in particular, how to explain my dismal lack of relevant job experience. The truth, or at least a drastically stripped-down version thereof, seemed easiest: I described myself to interviewers as a divorced homemaker reentering the workforce after many years, which is true as far as it goes. Sometimes, though not always, I would throw in a few housecleaning jobs, citing as references former housemates and a friend in Key West whom I have at least helped with after-dinner cleanups now and then. Job application forms also want to know about education, and here I figured the Ph.D. would be no help at all, might even lead employers to suspect that I was an alcoholic washout or worse. So I confined myself to three years of college, listing my real-life alma mater. No one ever questioned my background, as it turned out, and only one employer out of several dozen bothered to check my references. When, on one occasion, an exceptionally chatty interviewer asked about hobbies, I said "writing" and she seemed to find nothing strange about this, although the job she was offering could have been performed perfectly well by an illiterate.

Finally, I set some reassuring limits to whatever tribulations I might have to endure. First, I would always have a car. In Key West I drove my own; in other cities I used Rent-A-Wrecks, which I paid for with a credit card rather than my earnings. Yes, I could have walked more or limited myself to jobs accessible by public transportation. I just figured that a story about waiting for buses would not be very interesting to read. Second, I ruled out homelessness as an option. The idea was to spend a month in each setting and see whether I could find a job and earn, in that time, the money to pay a second month's rent. If I was paying rent by the week and ran out of money I would simply declare the project at an end; no shelters or sleeping in cars for me. Furthermore, I had no intention of going hungry. If things ever got to the point where the next meal was in question, I promised myself as the time to begin the "experiment" approached, I would dig out my ATM card and cheat.

So this is not a story of some death-defying "undercover" adventure. Almost anyone could do what I did—look for jobs, work those jobs, try to make ends meet. In fact, millions of Americans do it every day, and with a lot less fanfare and dithering.

I am, of course, very different from the people who normally fill America's least attractive jobs, and in ways that both helped and limited me. Most obviously, I was only visiting a world that others inhabit full-time, often for most of their lives. With all the real-life assets I've built up in middle age—bank account, IRA, health insurance, multiroom home— waiting indulgently in the background, there was no way I was going to "experience poverty" or find out how it "really feels" to be a long-term low-wage worker. My aim here was much more straightforward and objective—just to see whether I could match income to expenses, as the truly poor attempt to do every day. Besides, I've had enough unchosen encounters with poverty in my lifetime to know it's not a place you would want to visit for touristic purposes; it just smells too much like fear.

Unlike many low-wage workers, I have the further advantages of being white and a native English speaker. I don't think this affected my chances of getting a job, given the willingness of employers to hire almost anyone in the tight labor market of 1998 to 2000, but it almost certainly affected the *kinds* of jobs I was offered. In Key West, I originally sought what I assumed would be a relatively easy job in hotel housekeeping and found myself steered instead into waitressing, no doubt because of my ethnicity and my English skills. As it happened, waitressing didn't provide much of a financial advantage over housekeeping, at least not in the low-tip off-season when I worked in Key West. But the experience did help determine my choice of other localities in which to live and work. I ruled out places like New York and L.A., for example, where the working class consists mainly of people of color and a white woman with unaccented English seeking entry-level jobs might only look desperate or weird.

I had other advantages—the car, for example—that set me off from many, though hardly all, of my coworkers. Ideally, at least if I were seeking to replicate the experience of a woman entering the workforce from welfare, I would have had a couple of children in tow, but mine are grown and no one was willing to lend me theirs for a monthlong vacation in penury. In addition to being mobile and unencumbered, I am probably in a lot better health than most members of the long-term low-wage workforce. I had everything going for me.

If there were other, subtler things different about me, no one ever pointed them out. Certainly I made no effort to play a role or fit into some imaginative stereotype of low-wage working women. I wore my usual clothes, wherever ordinary clothes were permitted, and my usual hairstyle and makeup. In conversations with coworkers, I talked about my real children, marital status, and relationships; there was no reason to invent a whole new life. I did modify my vocabulary, however, in one respect: at least when I was new at a job and worried about seeming brash or disrespectful, I censored the profanities that are—thanks largely to the Teamster influence—part of my normal speech. Other than that, I joked and teased, offered opinions, speculations, and, incidentally, a great deal of health-related advice, exactly as I would do in any other setting.

Several times since completing this project I have been asked by acquaintances whether the people I worked with couldn't, uh, *tell*—the supposition being that an educated person is ineradicably different, and in a superior direction, from your workaday drones. I wish I could say that some supervisor or coworker told me even once that I was special in some enviable way—more intelligent, for example, or clearly better educated than most. But this never happened, I suspect because the only thing that really made me "special" was my inexperience. To state the proposition in reverse, low-wage workers are no more homogeneous in personality or ability than people who write for a living, and no less likely to be funny or bright. Anyone in the educated classes who thinks otherwise ought to broaden their circle of friends.

There was always, of course, the difference that only I knew—that I wasn't working for the money, I was doing research for an article and later a book. I went home every day not to anything resembling a normal domestic life but to a laptop on which I spent an hour or two recording the day's events—very diligently, I should add, since note taking was seldom an option during the day. This deception, symbolized by the laptop that provided a link to my past and future, bothered me, at least in the case of people I cared about and wanted to know better. (I should mention here that names and identifying details have been altered to preserve the privacy of the people I worked with and encountered in other settings during the course of my research. In most cases, I have also changed the names of the places I worked and their exact locations to further ensure the anonymity of people I met.)

In each setting, toward the end of my stay and after much anxious forethought, I "came out" to a few chosen coworkers. The result was always stunningly anticlimactic, my favorite response being, "Does this mean you're not going to be back on the evening shift next week?" I've wondered a lot about why there wasn't more astonishment or even indignation, and part of the answer probably lies in people's notion of "writing." Years ago, when I married my second husband, he proudly told his uncle, who was a valet parker at the time, that I was a writer. The uncle's response: "Who isn't?" Everyone literate "writes," and some of the low-wage workers I have known or met through this project write journals and poems—even, in one case, a lengthy science fiction novel.

But as I realized very late in this project, it may also be that I was exaggerating the extent of the "deception" to myself. There's no way, for example, to pretend to be a waitress: the food either gets to the table or not. People knew me as a waitress, a cleaning person, a nursing home aide, or a retail clerk not because I acted like one but because that's what I *was,* at least for the time I was with them. In every job, in every place I lived, the work absorbed all my energy and much of my intellect. I wasn't kidding around. Even though I suspected from the start that the mathematics of wages and rents were working against me, I made a mighty effort to succeed.

I make no claims for the relevance of my experiences to anyone else's, because there is nothing typical about my story. Just bear in mind, when I stumble, that this is in fact the *best*-case scenario: a person with every advantage that ethnicity and education, health and motivation can confer attempting, in a time of exuberant prosperity, to survive in the economy's lower depths.

Lee Gutkind

The Creative Nonfiction Police

I am giving a reading at St. Edwards University in Austin, Texas. It is a Thursday evening after a day of meeting classes and answering questions about essay writing, but now, in the auditorium, the audience is sparse, perhaps 60 or so in a space that seats nearly 250. My host is embarrassed; she informs me that a popular Latino poet is reading on campus at the same time, so the potential audience is divided. I have a feeling that I am the lesser of the two. This is a city with a high percentage of Mexican-American residents. And poetry is written to be read aloud, unlike nonfiction, which is factual and informative and which, students might assume, can be tedious and boring.

Of course, I am a *creative* nonfiction writer, "creative" being indicative of the style in which the nonfiction is written so as to make it more dramatic and compelling. We embrace many of the techniques of the fiction writer, including dialogue, description, plot, intimacy of detail, characterization, point of view; except, because it is nonfiction—and this is the difference—it is true.

Writing nonfiction so that it reads like fiction is challenging and, some critics say, virtually impossible unless the author takes liberties in style and content, which may corrupt the nonfiction—making it untrue, or partially true, or shading the meaning and misleading readers. A comment from John Berendt, author of *Midnight in the Garden of Good and Evil*, is frequently cited as indicative of the danger inherent in the form. Berendt made up transitions in order to move from scene to scene in his book. Creative nonfiction writers aren't supposed to make up anything in the scenes or between the scenes, including transitions, but Berendt said he was making the experience easier for himself and more enjoyable for his readers, a process he called "rounding the corners."

This then is the subject we are discussing in the auditorium after my reading—what writers can do or can't do in walking that thin blurred line between fiction and nonfiction. After all, if you are encouraged to use "literary techniques," straying from the literal truth for the sake of the narrative can be easy. The questions pile up, one after another; the audience is engaged. "How can you be certain that the dialogue you are recreating from an incident that occurred months ago is accurate?" asks one audience member. Another demands, "How can you look through the eyes of your characters if you are not inside their heads?"

I am answering as best I can, but as I try repeatedly to explain, such questions have a lot to do with the believability of your narrative and a writer's ethical and moral boundaries. After a while, I throw up my hands and say, "Listen! I am not the creative nonfiction police."

There is a woman in the audience—someone I had noticed earlier during my reading. She is in the front row—hard to miss—older than most of the undergraduates, blonde, attractive, in her late 30s maybe. She has the alert yet composed look of a nurse, a person only semi-relaxed, always ready to act or react. She has taken her shoes off and propped her feet on the stage; I remember how her toes wiggled as she laughed at the essay I had been reading. But when I say, "I am not the creative nonfiction police," although many people chuckle, this woman suddenly jumps to her feet, whips out a badge, and points in my direction. "Well I am," she announces. "Someone has to be. And you are under arrest." Then she scoops up her shoes and storms barefooted from the room. The Q and A ends and I rush into the hallway, but she is gone. My host says the woman is a stranger. No one knows her. She is a mystery to everyone, especially me.

The bigger mystery, however, then and now, is the set of parameters that govern or define creative nonfiction—the concepts writers must consider while laboring in or struggling with what we call the literature of reality, beginning with the difference between fiction and nonfiction, which is truth, or at least a measure of truth, because most fiction, on some level, is true. But how is the truth in nonfiction determined? Who is the final arbiter of truth? The line between fiction and nonfiction is often debated, but is there a single dividing point or an all-encompassing truth to tell?

Historians and journalists rely on sources—documents and interviews—but how do they know if the documents are accurate or the witnesses' perceptions valid? Witnesses in court will usually tell what they see as the truth—but how many innocent people have been convicted based on testimony of a sincere and objective bystander? In *All the President's Men*, Woodward and Bernstein insisted on the corroboration of two sources, but who is to say two sources are enough? A good historian exhausts the available sources, but sooner or later has to make decisions about which to accept and reject.

And why, I wonder, are we always questioning the ethics of nonfiction writers? Are there no ethical boundaries in poetry and fiction? Are we more deceived by Truman Capote, who did not take notes and relied on memory to retell the horrible story of the murder of the Clutter family in *In Cold Blood,* or Michael Chabon who disguised real characters and situations in his novel, *Wonder Boys*? Many writers in Pittsburgh knew the story as intimately as Chabon, but considered it improper and potentially hurtful to the characters and their families to write about it. David Leavitt's career was significantly damaged when, in his novel, *While England Sleeps*, he described the esteemed poet Sir Stephen Spender, masked by another name and body, in a way that endangered his reputation. Spender triggered litigation to halt the distribution of Leavitt's book. The ethical boundaries of the narrative are not, however, a new dilemma or debate. Henry David Thoreau lived for two years on Walden Pond while documenting only one year. Which part of the two years did he choose and how often, in his painstaking process of revision, did he combine two or three days—or even four weeks—into one?

This technique that Thoreau evidently employed, by the way, is called "compression" —meaning that multiple incidents or situations combined or compressed in order to flesh out the narrative, allowing a writer to build a more compelling, fully executed three-dimensional story.

In her book about Geoffrey Masson, *In the Freud Archives*, Janet Malcolm combined a series of conversations about the same subject or incident into one. Malcolm did not admit to altering facts of the conversations—only when and how the conversations occurred. Does this violate some sort of ethical or moral bond with the reader or the subject? Probably not, as long as the information is not manufactured—which is the reason that Masson's suit against *The New Yorker* and Malcolm went all the way to the U.S. Supreme Court. Masson was initially contending that Malcolm manufactured quotes; he may not have been aware of the use of compression or would not have been disturbed by it had his attorneys not questioned the technique while investigating information subpoenaed from Malcolm.

Another Janet—Janet Cooke, formerly a reporter for *The Washington Post*—was awarded the Pulitzer Prize for her depiction of an eight-year-old boy dealing drugs on the streets of the nation's capital. But curious reporters searching for the subject of the story eventually forced Cooke to admit that he didn't exist. He was a composite of a number of kids she had met. Cooke lost her job—her reputation was ruined. Unfortunately, others have not learned from her mistakes.

In the past couple of years, a number of journalists have been discovered and disgraced for fudging the truth. In 1997, Stephen Glass admitted to fabricating parts of 27 articles for *The New Republic, The New York Times, George,* and *Harper's*. He even provided fake supporting material, including self-created Web sites, to outfox his fact-checkers. And a columnist for *The Boston Globe*, Patricia Smith, admitted to fabricating the people and the quotations in four of her columns in 1999. In one case she made up an entire story about a woman dying of cancer.

Ironically, the journalistic community has been unceasingly critical of creative nonfiction while virtually ignoring its own misdeeds. In a 1997 feature in *Vanity Fair Magazine*, "Me, Myself and I," James Wolcott boiled all creative nonfiction down into what he called "confessional writing" and took to task as "navel gazers" nearly any writer who had been the least bit self-revelatory in their work. Wolcott zeroed in on the memoir and made it seem as if that was the creative nonfiction genre in its totality, while ignoring the significant information-oriented work done by John McPhee, Annie Dillard, Tracy Kidder, Gay Talese, and many others.

Wolcott reserved an especially interesting title and role for me as "the godfather behind creative nonfiction." He abhorred the fact that I traveled and talked about creative nonfiction all over the world, wrote books about creative nonfiction, published a journal (*Creative Nonfiction*), directed a creative nonfiction writers' conference, and taught creative nonfiction. He called me a "human octopus."

Wolcott's observation that memoirists are overly self-obsessed was not new or particularly enlightening. This criticism has been pouring forth from dozens of directions since publication of *The Kiss,* in which Kathryn Harrison relates the details of her affair with the Presbyterian minister who is her father. Many people objected to this book because they found the subject morally indefensible—a separate or moot point. Or because they simply didn't want to know all the sordid details of the relationship; this was something personal and private—something that ought to have been fictionalized. Which it was in two of Harrison's novels, neither of which readers paid any attention to. So Harrison tried the same story in nonfiction—and achieved fame and, perhaps, fortune.

I don't find *The Kiss* particularly skillful or memorable, but I don't object to the story. My major problems concern the innocent victims of Harrison's quest to unload her anxieties. While I don't justify her father's actions, I wonder about the toll this will take on her children when they are old enough to read the book or when the parents of their classmates discuss Harrison in front of their children—an incident that could lead to embarrassment and continued distress. And what of her father's new family, his wife and children—and his congregation? Is he to be punished without being permitted to defend or explain himself?

The Perfect Storm, although not a memoir, is another popular book whose author Sebastian Junger has been accused of victimizing characters. Ray Leonard, a retired forest service ecologist, is depicted as curled on his bunk, "sullen and silent, sneaking gulps off a whiskey bottle" while his sailboat, *The Satori,* is sinking. The incident was never verified and, in fact, *The Satori* was found on a beach, intact, a few days later. It never went down. It is hard to know whether Leonard was a coward—but he is presented as one. Junger never contacted Leonard because the rest of his story and the fate of *The Satori* was irrelevant to the narrative, he said.

The Kiss and *The Perfect Storm* are troubling examples of how an author's need to write the perfect narrative or to share the pain and anxiety of a traumatic life can create innocent victims who may or may not be guilty of corruption, brutality, indecency, cowardice, or responsibility, but who will hardly ever have the opportunity to have their day in court. I understand that writing from memory is often unverifiable, but I believe that memoirists don't go far enough to confront and try to satisfy their own moral and ethical landscape.

I said at the beginning that I wasn't the creative nonfiction police or the literary judiciary. But I am "the godfather behind creative nonfiction," after all, according to *Vanity Fair*. The real point is that I have been doing this for a long time—more than a dozen published books and 25 years of teaching; I may be the first person to teach creative non-fiction on a full-time basis—anywhere. So I would like to recommend a code for creative nonfiction writers—kind of a checklist. The word "checklist" is carefully chosen. There are no rules, laws, specific prescriptions relating to what to do and not to do as a creative nonfiction writer. The gospel according to Lee Gutkind or anyone else doesn't and should-n't exist. It's more a question of doing the right thing, being fair, following the golden rule. Treating others with courtesy and respect and using common sense.

First, strive for the truth. Be certain that everything you write is as accurate and hon-est as you can make it. I don't mean that everyone who has shared the experience you are writing about should agree that your account is true. As I said, everyone has his or her own very precious, private, and shifting truth. But be certain your narrative is as true to your memory as possible.

Second, recognize the important distinction between recollected conversation and fabricated dialogue. Don't make anything up and don't tell your readers what you think your characters are thinking during the time about which you are writing. If you want to know how or what people are or were thinking, then ask them. Don't assume or guess.

Third, don't round corners—or compress situations or characters—unnecessarily. Not that rounding corners or compressing characters or incidents are absolutely wrong, but if you do experiment with these techniques, make certain you have a good reason. Making literary decisions based on good narrative principles is often legitimate—you are, after all, writers. But stop to consider the people about whom you are writing. Unleash your venom on the guilty parties; punish them as they deserve. But also ask yourself: who are the innocent victims? How have I protected them? Adults can file suits against you, but are you violating the privacy or endangering the emotional stability of children? Are you being fair to the aged or infirm?

Fourth, one way to protect the characters in your book, article, or essay is to allow them to defend themselves—or at least to read what you have written about them. Few writers do this because they are afraid of litigation or ashamed or embarrassed about the intimacies they have revealed. But sharing your narrative with the people about whom you are writing doesn't mean that you have to change what you say about them; rather, it only means that you are being responsible to your characters and the stories that you are reveal-ing. I understand why you would not want to share your narrative; it could be dangerous. It could ruin your friendship, your marriage, your future. But by the same token so too could the publication of your book. And this is the kind of responsible action you might appreciate if the shoe were on the other foot.

I have on occasion shared parts of books with characters I have written about—with positive results. First, my characters corrected my mistakes. But, more importantly, when you come face to face with a character, you are able to communicate on a different and deeper level. When you show them what you think, they think and feel—when they read what you have written—they may get angry—an action in itself which is interesting to observe and write about.

Or they may feel obliged to provide their side of their situation—a side that you have been hesitant to listen to or interpret. With the text in the middle, as a filter, it is possible to discuss personal history as a story somewhat disconnected from the reality you are experiencing. It provides a way to communicate as an exercise in writing—it filters and distances the debate. Moreover, it defines and cements your own character. The people about whom you have written may not like what you have said—and may in fact despise you for saying it—but they can only respect and admire the forthright way in which you have approached them. No laws govern the scope of good taste and personal integrity.

More than in any other literary genre, the creative nonfiction writer must rely on his or her own conscience and sensitivity to others and display a higher morality and a healthy respect for fairness and justice. We all harbor resentments, hatreds, and prejudices, but that doesn't necessarily mean, because we are writers, that we are being given special dispensation to behave in a way that is unbecoming to ourselves and hurtful to others. This sounds so simple—yet it is so difficult. The moral and ethical responsibility of the creative nonfiction writer is to practice the golden rule and to be as fair and truthful as possible— to write both for art's sake and for humanity's sake. In other words, we police ourselves.

By saying this, I do not feel that I am being overly simplistic. As writers we intend to make a difference, to affect someone's life over and above our own. To say something that matters—this is why we write. To impact upon society, to put a personal stamp on history. Remember that art and literature are our legacies to other generations. We will be forgotten, but our books and essays, our stories and poems will always, somewhere, have a life.

Wherever you draw the line between fiction and nonfiction remember the basic rules of good citizenship: Do not recreate incidents and characters who never existed; do not write to do harm to innocent victims; do not forget your own story, but while considering your struggle and the heights of your achievements, think repeatedly about how your story will impact on and relate to your reader. Over and above the creation of a seamless narrative, you are seeking to touch and affect someone else's life—which is the goal creative nonfiction writers share with novelists and poets. We all want to connect with another human being—as many people as possible—in such a way that they will remember us and share our legacy with others.

Someday, I hope to connect with the woman with the badge and the bare feet face-to-face. The truth is, I have never forgotten her. She has, in some strange way, become an accouterment to my conscience, standing over me as I write, forcing me to ask the questions about my work that I have recommended to you. Perhaps she is here today, as I am proofreading this essay—somewhere. But from this point on I am hoping you too will feel her shadow over your shoulders each time you sit down, address your keyboard, and begin to write.

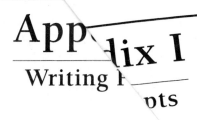

Appendix I
Writing Prompts

Part I: Portraits

Every Picture Tells a Story: *The "I."* Jamaica Kincaid's "Biography of a Dress" begins with a photograph, and the progress of her essay is an exercise in memory. She meditates on the story behind the picture, imbuing a two-dimensional object with full and textured meaning. This prompt requires that you find an old picture of yourself and proceed to reconstruct the time in which the picture was taken. Choosing the right photograph is critical here. Perhaps it was taken at a turning point—perhaps on your parents' last vacation before their divorce or just before you moved from one place to another. The moment should be meaningful and evocative of a specific time. Keeping in mind the necessity of writing with the senses, travel back to that room or environment by recalling the objects, sights, and associations there. Who else is in the picture? Who took it? What was the occasion? What memories or ideas does the photograph trigger?

Separate Paths. Write a memoir piece about a person you know (from your family or perhaps among your childhood friends) who took a divergent path from your own. Look at the way John Edgar Wideman explores the differences and similarities between himself and his brother in his excerpt from *Brothers and Keepers* and the way Bernard Cooper handles his tensions with his father in "Picking Plums." Use the advantages of the personal essay form to weave assertion with illustration, anecdote with commentary. Remember that this is as much an essay about you as it is about your subject. Don't shirk on self-analysis. Use your memory and, where appropriate, your imagination.

Investigating the Family. Beverly Lowry's nonfiction book *Crossed Over,* from which "Secret Ceremonies of Love and Death" is sprung, is a bridge text, combining memoir with literary journalism. This prompt encourages you to be both interviewer and, possibly, subject. Think of a fascinating story in your family that you've

heard many times but not always same way. Perhaps different members
of your family have different ver e event. Maybe you were at the center of
the event, or perhaps it took pl you were born and you're investigating its
veracity. Pinpoint the story, f and make sure it's one that has always interested you. Then go about irng others in your family to come up with a version that you believe to begMake sure to ask specific questions. The story can
be humorous or serious ith into consideration ideas on truth and perception,
your goal here is to emith a true or composite "true" story about your family.

More than Just a J he "Eye." Using Tom Wolfe's "Yeager" as a model, write a
profile of an indipaying particular attention to his or her job and what that
job represents. Wolfe, Yeager is an emblematic figure of bravery and derring-
do. In your p, you might write a portrait about someone you know who is a
magnetic chter, has a particularly interesting job, or both. The subject obviously doest have to be famous; the only requirement is that he or she be interesting toou. Study Susan Orlean's "Meet the Shaggs" and, for further reading,
look ater essay "The American Man, Age Ten," from her collection *The Bullfighter
Checks Her Makeup*. Here Orlean profiles a seemingly ordinary boy made extraordinary by the author's deep interest in him and her recognition that "[ten] is around
the age when guys get screwed up about girls."

Part II: Place

More than Just a Job: The "I." Using Thomas Lynch's "The Undertaking" and
Lawrence Otis Graham's "Invisible Man" as models, write an essay describing a job
you currently have or once had. What is the name of the company where you
work or worked? What is the company's mission, its role in the community? What
is your role in the company? Like Lynch, you'll want to describe both what the job
stands for and how it relates to you. Every workplace has its own jargon and hier-
archies, and part of your task in this essay will be to capture the particulars of
speech, setting, and culture. As well as focusing on the unique aspects of the job
itself, you could also analyze power relationships—between you and your boss,
for instance, or you and a coworker. This essay lends itself well to segmentation.

Tales out of School. This prompt encourages you to frame your own educational
story. Reread Stuart Dybek's "Field Trips" and look for the ways in which the
author combines voice, personal reflection, and narrative. Write your own "tale
out of school," using the essay or memoir form to dramatize or portray your experiences in education. You could write about one particular class, year, or school.
You could follow Dybek's lead and write about a field trip. Or you could cover
moments from all or most of your educational history, taking a retrospective view.

Along the way, make clear to your reader not only the details of your experience but also, by inference and/or assertion, what you believe education should and should not be.

Meditation on Place. In "Saturday Night, and Sunday Morning," James Alan McPherson meditates on the city of Chicago and blues music. John McPhee takes a similar, though more experimental, approach in his segmented portrait of Atlantic City, "In Search of Marvin Gardens." Perhaps you live in a city or town that has a rich history or holds particular cultural significance. Do research about your chosen place. Consider certain aspects about it that fascinate you. Then write a segmented essay in which you meditate on a particular place, combining any or all of the following: history, culture, politics, geography, topography, weather, the arts, and personal reflection.

Museum Immersion. Perhaps, like Sarah Vowell in "What He Said There," you are interested in the intersection of past and present. Go to the Web site of your local bureau of tourism and look up nearby museums. You may find strange and obscure collections, like the Ships in Bottles Museum, the Pretzel Museum, or the Gallery of Obscure Patents. Go to a museum or an exhibit that for whatever reason captures your interest, and absorb yourself in it. Perhaps, like Vowell, your approach will be critical, introspective, even humorous. You may need to supplement your observations with research.

Part III: Creativity and the Arts

Arts Pilgrimage. Think of a figure, ideally someone in the arts, whom you've long admired or whom you wish you knew more about. Perhaps you live near the Andy Warhol museum or near the route John Steinbeck's Joads took to get to California. Perhaps a writer, artist, musician, or actor grew up not far from where you live, or perhaps he or she lived nearby during an important personal or creative period. Take a pilgrimage to the town, city, or neighborhood where he or she lived and/or worked. Walk around and research how this place informed your subject. Note how things have changed in the time since your subject lived here. Write an essay or meditation in the form of a pilgrimage. What does this figure or artist mean—both to you and, more expansively, to culture and the arts?

What's Your Bag? Keeping in mind Meghan Daum's essay "Music Is My Bag," recall your own experience as part of a subculture. Perhaps, like Daum, you were a member of a band or orchestra and your whole existence revolved around that experience. Maybe, like David Sedaris, you, too, had "The Drama Bug." Maybe you were the member of a team, club, or group that had its own culture and set of rules. What was your bag? What was your bug? If Daum's household was filled with music, what was your household filled with? If Sedaris's sole pursuit was drama, what was your obsession and why? This is an opportunity to combine a variety of forms within a single essay: self-portrait, process analysis, and criticism. Like *Meditation on Place,* this piece lends itself well to segmentation.

Critical Immersion. We know that in immersion journalism, the writer can become so fully absorbed in a subject that by the time he or she sits down to write the piece, it is almost as if the writer is channeling the subject's voice. The same can apply to in-depth criticism. The reviewer or critic reads, watches, or listens to everything related to his or her subject. Choose one area of the arts—music, dance, theater, film, literature, or popular culture—and one artist. Study as much as you can of that artist's work, then write a critical piece around an organizing subject. What is it about this artist or icon that moves you? How can you make sense of the artist and his or her relationship to his or her work? What ideas are at the center of it? Note, for example, how Wayne Koestenbaum uses "dreams," John Updike uses "repetition," Saul Bellow uses "image," and Leslie Marmon Silko uses "story" as the linchpins of their essays, and look for similar words or controlling ideas around which to focus your piece.

Every Picture Tells a Story: *The "Eye."* One liberating exercise an essayist can undertake is to step outside of him or herself and try to imagine other people's lives. So here's a prompt where you can leave yourself behind for a while. Step 1: Go to http://www.foundmagazine.com or pick up the *found* book, by Davy Rothbart. Step 2: Locate the found object that, for whatever reason, most interests you. Take your time browsing. Linger over the individual objects until one inspires you above all the rest. Step 3: Once you've decided on a found object, use it as inspiration for an essay. Alternatively, you could find your own item that inspires you or sparks your curiosity. Extrapolate from your find and describe the object thoroughly, reflecting on its use, meaning, or history; help us understand what drew you to it and what it means both personally and as a cultural artifact.

Part IV: Nature and Science

I Am the Walrus. With Edward Hoagland's "The Courage of Turtles" and Linda Hogan's "The Bats" as guides, do a close study of one particular animal or living creature. Look at its habits, habitat, patterns, and evolutionary role. Paying careful attention to specific detail, describe the creature as thoroughly as you can. And, where appropriate, look for ways to connect your own experience or interests with the observed creature. Why are you drawn to this animal? What does your interest say about you, your life, and the environment in which you live?

A Walk in the Woods. Annie Dillard's "Seeing," from her Pulitzer Prize–winning book *A Pilgrim at Tinker Creek,* is a series of linked observations about keeping one's eyes open to the wonders of the natural world. On its surface, the piece seems a collection of Dillard's own walks, in which she observes all the minutiae of nature. But Dillard doesn't just observe and identify; she filters her seeing through her own unique perspective in richly cadenced language, connecting her observations with fragments of thought and reflection. This prompt invites you to take a cue from Dillard, Gretel Ehrlich, Barry Lopez, and Terry Tempest Williams, and open your eyes to a natural environment. Go to your favorite public park or natural landscape and take a walk in the woods (or mountains, tundra, beach-front, hill, field, swamp, glade). Allow yourself to absorb the landscape and really *see.* The course of your essay may be a quest toward one particularly interesting object or view. Or, like Dillard and Ehrlich, your piece might be structured around an idea—"seeing" or "solace," for example—made up of a series of obser-vations and ruminations. The piece might be discursive, traveling from one moment of sharp observation to another. What do you see? What are you really seeing?

Anatomies: In the first century A.D., Seneca wrote a famous piece about his asthma and here, in contemporary literature Richard McCann, Floyd Skloot, Lucy Grealy, Margaret Atwood, Thomas Lynch, Terry Tempest Williams, Gerald Early, and others have written pieces with the body as a point of departure. Perhaps you have suffered a physical ailment that resulted in a change in the way you were perceived. Perhaps this change had to do with your private sense of self, as it did for Richard McCann and Floyd Skloot. Perhaps the body became inextricably tied to public perception, as it did with Lucy Grealy, whose feelings of isolation, shame, and alienation are so candidly portrayed in "Mirrorings." This prompt encourages you to remember a physical condition from childhood or from the present that has left you or someone you know scarred, healed, or never quite the same.

Why Is the Sky Blue? You don't have to be a scientist to have a scientist's curiosity. Take a problem in science and explain it. With Diane Ackerman's book *A Natural History of the Senses* in mind, unravel a scientific "fact," as she does in "The Psychopharmacology of Chocolate." Begin this prompt with a question, some-thing you've always wondered, along the lines of "Why do we crave chocolate?" Then, over the course of your essay, set about answering the question, drawing on scientific research. Research has never been more accessible (though, with the

Internet, confirming scientific "fact" requires particular diligence). Look at the way Stephen Jay Gould, in "A Biological Homage to Mickey Mouse," makes science writing accessible for a general audience. The more curious you are about the question that begins your essay, the more lively and searching your prose will be. In exploring your topic, seek not only to explain but also to discover an idea that you could, for instance, connect back to yourself.

Part V: Culture and Society

On the Many Meanings of a Word. The history of the personal essay is full of writers anchoring their ruminations to a single word—sometimes an abstract noun, sometimes a concrete noun. Historical examples include Seneca's "On Noise," Montaigne's "On Liars," William Hazlitt's "On the Pleasure of Hating," Langston Hughes's "Bop," and Jorge Luis Borges's "Blindness." This prompt asks you to create an essay out of a single word. Take your time picking a word that, for whatever reason, resonates with you. Research the history of the word and its various meanings. The more layered the word, the richer your essay will be. The word could be abstract, like Annie Dillard's "Seeing." It could be concrete like Joan Didion's "On Keeping a Notebook." Think about structuring your essay in sections that alternate between personal memories generated by the word and rumination, analysis, and philosophical consideration. Look for ways to tie your own personal history to the meaning(s) of the word. Ultimately, your essay should show the relationship between the concrete and the abstract, your life and a broader idea.

Where You're from and Who You Are. Some of the finest contemporary essays and memoirs are ultimately about identity: how one perceives oneself within and outside of a community and culture. Drawing on such pieces as Maxine Hong Kingston's "No Name Woman" and Dorothy Allison's excerpt from *Two or Three Things I Know for Sure,* write a memoir or essay about a central aspect of your identity. Perhaps you'll want to construct the piece around a visit, as Allison does, or a series of recollections as Kingston does. Keep in mind as you sit down to write that there are preconceived notions about nearly every place and every ethnicity. Perhaps you grew up in the South and now live in the North. How have you dealt with assumptions about each culture? Perhaps you have been subject to broad and damaging stereotypes. As you begin the piece, keep in mind questions such as: What assumptions do people have about you? How have you handled these situations? And to what extent have you embraced or resisted the stereotypes?

Point/Counterpoint. A tried and true strategy in traditional argumentation is to understand, in full measure, the opposing side's opinion. This prompt encourages you to go one further by immersing yourself in something that in your normal life you would disagree with or ignore. In "Life with Daughters: Watching the Miss America Pageant," Gerald Early makes an effort to understand the appeal of a cultural phenomenon. By taking the pageant seriously and analyzing it from all angles, he creates a thought-provoking analysis that examines the pageant from metaphorical, cultural, and historical viewpoints. Similarly, you might, for example, explore a pop cultural trend or phenomenon that you would ordinarily ignore. What emotions is your subject tapping into? What is the appeal? Did you find yourself falling under your subject's sway? How has the immersion changed or solidified your point of view? How might you critically examine and interpret your subject?

Writing Undercover. Think of a social system or occurrence that disturbs you or that you believe is wrong. Perhaps, like Barbara Ehrenreich, you're concerned about economic injustice and have always wondered how a person can actually get by in America on minimum wage. As she notes in "Getting Started," her introduction to *Nickel and Dimed,* Ehrenreich began with a hypothesis, then like a scientist she tested her hypothesis by taking a series of minimum-wage jobs, trying (and failing) to make a living. Think of a similar experiment in experiential journalism that you might undertake or plan to undertake. You don't need to try to spend a year living on six dollars an hour, but you might spend a week living in a way that's completely outside your own experience. Note how Lawrence Otis Graham uses experiential technique to examine invisibility, race, class, and perception. Ultimately your work should involve both research and experience. It should begin with an idea or question, then put that idea or question to the test.

Appendix II

Suggestions for Further Reading: A Selection of Creative Nonfiction Books by North American Authors Since 1960

Part I: Portraits

The "I"

Hilton Als, *The Women*

Russell Baker, *Growing Up*

Jo Ann Beard, *The Boys of My Youth*

Augusten Burroughs, *Running with Scissors*

Frank Conroy, *Stop-Time*

Harry Crews, *A Childhood*

Mark Doty, *Heaven's Coast*

Dave Eggers, *A Heartbreaking Work of Staggering Genius*

Paula Fox, *Borrowed Finery*

Marita Golden, *Migrations of the Heart*

Kathryn Harrison, *The Kiss*

Maureen Howard, *Facts of Life*

Mary Karr, *The Liar's Club*

Leonard Kriegel, *Flying Solo*

Li-Young Lee, *The Winged Seed*

Thylias Moss, *Tale of a Sky-Blue Dress*

Nasdijj, *The Blood Runs like a River Through My Dreams*

Michael Ondaatje, *Running in the Family*

Ntozake Shange, *If I Can Cook/You Know God Can*

Sue William Silverman, *Because I Remember Terror, Father, I Remember You*

Geoffrey Wolff, *The Duke of Deception*

Tobias Wolff, *This Boy's Life*

The "Eye"

Truman Capote, *In Cold Blood*

Darcy Frey, *The Last Shot*

Elizabeth Gilbert, *The Last American Man*

David Halberstam, *Firehouse*

Jane Kramer, *The Last Cowboy*

Adrian Nicole LeBlanc, *Random Family*

J. Anthony Lukas, *Common Ground: A Turbulent Decade in the Lives of Three American Families*

Norman MacLean, *Young Men and Fire*

Sylvia Nasar, *A Beautiful Mind*

George Plimpton, *Paper Lion*

Eileen Pollack, *Woman Walking Ahead*

Gary Smith, *Beyond the Game*

Gay Talese, *Fame and Obscurity*

Studs Terkel, *Working*

Calvin Trillin, *Killings*

Part II: Place

The "I"

Rick Bragg, *All Over but the Shoutin'*

Alan Cheuse, *Fall out of Heaven*

David James Duncan, *Riverteeth*

Diana Hume George, *The Lonely Other: A Woman Watching America*

Wendy Gimbel, *Havana Dreams*

Mary Gordon, *Seeing Through Places*

Garrett Hongo, *Volcano*

Teresa Jordan, *Riding the White Horse Home*

Michael Martone, *The Flatness and Other Landscapes*

Frank McCourt, *Angela's Ashes*

Colleen J. McElroy, *A Long Way from St. Louie*

Willie Morris, *North Toward Home*

Kathleen Norris, *Dakota: A Spiritual Geography*

Chris Offutt, *The Same River Twice*

Michael Perry, *Population: 485*

Ishmael Reed, *Shrovetide in Old New Orleans*

Mark Salzman, *Lost in Place: Growing up Absurd in Suburbia*

Kate Simon, *Bronx Primitive*

Annick Smith, *Homestead*

Gary Soto, *Living up the Street*

D. J. Waldie, *Holy Land: A Suburban Memoir*

Sara Wheeler, *Terra Incognita*

The "Eye"

John Berendt, *Midnight in the Garden of Good and Evil*

H. G. "Buzz" Bissinger, *Friday Night Lights*

Tim Cahill, *Pass the Butterworms*

James Conaway, *Napa: The Story of an American Eden*

Ian Frazier, *Great Plains*

Eddy Harris, *Mississippi Solo*

Tony Horwitz, *Confederates in the Attic*

Pico Iyer, *Global Soul*

Sebastian Junger, *The Perfect Storm*

Jon Krakauer, *Into the Wild*

William Least-Heat Moon, *Blue Highways*

Mary Morris, *Nothing to Declare*

Eleanor Munro, *On Glory Roads*

Sheila Nickerson, *Disappearance: A Map*

Andrew X. Pham, *Catfish and Mandala*

Paul Theroux, *The Old Patagonian Express: By Train Through the Americas*

Part III: Creativity and The Arts

The "I"

Don Asher, *Notes from a Battered Grand*

Joseph Brodsky, *Less than One*

Anatole Broyard, *Kafka Was the Rage*

Jay Cantor, *On Becoming One's Own Mother*

John D'Agata, *Halls of Fame*

Andre Dubus, *Broken Vessels*

Stanley Elkin, *Pieces of Soap*

Joseph Epstein, *Snobbery: The American Version*

Anne Fadiman, *Ex Libris: Confessions of a Common Reader*

Jonathan Franzen, *How to Be Alone*

William Gass, *Tests of Time*

Albert Goldbarth, *Many Circles*

Jim Harrison, *The Raw and the Cooked*

Pauline Kael, *Deeper into Movies*

Ursula K. Le Guin, *Dancing at the Edge of the World*

Hilary Masters, *In Montaigne's Tower*

Carole Maso, *Break Every Rule*

Azar Nafisi, *Reading Lolita in Tehran*

Philip Roth, *Reading Myself and Others*

Marjorie Sandor, *The Night Gardener*

Lynne Sharon Schwartz, *Ruined by Reading: A Life in Books*

David Shields, *Remote*

The "Eye"

Nicholson Baker, *The Size of Thoughts*

Lester Bangs, *Psychotic Reactions and Carburetor Dung*

Charles Baxter, *Burning Down the House*

Arthur C. Danto, *The Transfiguration of the Commonplace*

Guy Davenport, *The Geography of the Imagination*

Nicholas Delbanco, *The Beaux Arts Trio: A Portrait*

W. S. Di Piero, *Out of Eden: Essays on Modern Art*

Don Foster, *Author Unknown*

Gary Giddins, *Visions of Jazz*

Elizabeth Hardwick, *Bartleby in Manhattan*

Lewis Hyde, *The Gift*

Janet Malcolm, *The Silent Woman*

Joyce Carol Oates, *The Profane Art*

Luc Sante, *The Factory of Facts*

Lawrence Weschler, *Boggs: A Comedy of Values*

Part IV: Nature and Science

The "I"

Edward Abbey, *Desert Solitaire*

Kim Barnes, *In the Wilderness*

Wendell Berry, *The Recollected Essays, 1965–1980*

Jane Brox, *Here and Nowhere Else*

Franklin Burroughs, *Billy Watson's Croker Sack*

David Carroll, *Swampwalker's Journal: A Wetlands Year*

James Galvin, *The Meadow*

Vicki Hearne, *Adam's Task*

Sue Hubbell, *A Country Year*

Susanna Kaysen, *Girl, Interrupted*

William Kittredge, *Owning It All*

Verlyn Klinkenborg, *The Rural Life*

Peter Matthiessen, *The Snow Leopard*

Ellen Meloy, *Raven's Exile: A Season on the Green River*

N. Scott Momaday, *The Way to Rainy Mountain*

Doug Peacock, *Grizzly Years*

Noel Perrin, *First Person Rural*

Janice Ray, *Ecology of a Cracker Childhood*

Chet Raymo, *The Soul of the Night*

Gary Snyder, *A Place in Space*

Wallace Stegner, *Wolf Willow*

William Warner, *Beautiful Swimmers*

The "Eye"

David Abram, *The Spell of the Sensuous*

Natalie Angier, *Woman: An Intimate Geography*

Richard Dawkins, *The Selfish Gene*

Helen Fisher, *Anatomy of Love: A Natural History of Mating, Marriage and Why We Stray*

Jerome Groopman, *The Measure of Our Days*

Steve Jones, *Darwin's Ghost*

Bill McKibben, *The End of Nature*

John Hanson Mitchell, *Living at the End of Time*

Michael Paterniti, *Driving Mr. Albert*

Steven Pinker, *How the Mind Works*

Michael Pollan, *The Botany of Desire*

David Quammen, *Wild Thoughts from Wild Places*

Richard Selzer, *The Exact Location of the Soul*

Oliver Sacks, *The Man Who Mistook His Wife for a Hat*

Lewis Thomas, *The Lives of a Cell*

Part V: Culture and Society

The "I"

Paula Gunn Allen, *Off the Reservation*

Maya Angelou, *I Know Why the Caged Bird Sings*

Edward Ball, *Slaves in the Family*

James Carroll, *God, My Father and the War that Came Between Us*

Stanley Crouch, *Notes of a Hanging Judge*

Toi Derricotte, *The Black Notebooks*

Michael Dorris, *The Broken Cord*

Henry Louis Gates, Jr., *Thirteen Ways of Looking at a Black Man*

Ray Gonzalez, *Memory Fever: A Journey Beyond El Paso Del Norte*

John Hockenberry, *Moving Violations*

bell hooks, *Talking Back*

Eric Liu, *The Accidental Asian: Notes of a Native Speaker*

Nancy Mairs, *Waist-High in the World*

Alex Haley and Malcolm X, *The Autobiography of Malcolm X*

Nathan McCall, *Makes Me Wanna Holler*

Paul Monette, *Becoming a Man*

Tim O'Brien, *If I Die in a Combat Zone, Box Me up and Ship Me Home*

Paisley Rekdal, *The Night My Mother Met Bruce Lee*

Adrienne Rich, *Blood, Bread and Poetry: Selected Prose*

Richard Rodriguez, *The Hunger of Memory*

Randy Shilts, *And the Band Played On*

Brent Staples, *Parallel Time*

The "Eye"

Ted Conover, *Newjack: Guarding Sing Sing*

Paul Fussell, *Class*

Malcolm Gladwell, *The Tipping Point*

Francine du Plessix Gray, *Adam and Eve in the City*

Jonathan Harr, *A Civil Action*

Alex Kotlowitz, *There Are No Children Here*

Norman Mailer, *Executioner's Song*

Katha Pollitt, *Reasonable Creatures: Essays on Women and Feminism*

Eric Schlosser, *Fast Food Nation: The Dark Side of the All-American Meal*

Neil Sheehan, *A Bright Shining Lie: John Paul Vann and America in Vietnam*

Mark Slouka, *Cyberspace and the Hi-tech War on Reality*

David Foster Wallace, *A Supposedly Fun Thing I'll Never Do Again*

Cornel West, *Race Matters*

Patricia J. Williams, *The Alchemy of Race and Rights*

Alec Wilkinson, *Big Sugar: Seasons in the Cane Fields of Florida*

Author Biographies

I. Portraits

Bernard Cooper was born in 1951 in Oklahoma City and grew up in Los Angeles. He has published a short story collection, *Guess Again* (2000); a novel, *A Year of Rhymes* (1993); and many essays in such periodicals as *Harper's, Ploughshares, Paris Review,* and *Georgia Review.* His essays and memoirs are collected in *Truth Serum* (1997) and *Maps to Anywhere* (1992), a mélange of poetry and prose covering a wide range of topics from AIDS to his father's aging to the extinction of the dinosaur to the loss of his brother to leukemia. Cooper is currently the art critic for *Los Angeles Magazine.*

Tony Earley was born in 1961 in Texas and grew up in North Carolina. He is the author of a short story collection, *Here We Are in Paradise* (1994); a novel, *Jim the Boy* (2000); and a collection of essays/autobiographical reflections called *Somehow Form a Family: Stories That Are Mostly True* (2001). His work has appeared in *Harper's,* the *New Yorker, Oxford American,* and *Best American Short Stories.* Earley was named one of the best young writers in America by *Granta* in 1996 and the *New Yorker* in 1999.

Lucy Grealy was born in 1963 in Dublin and died in 2002 in New York City. Throughout her life, she struggled with a facial disfigurement caused by cancer, a subject she wrote about in her memoir, *Autobiography of a Face* (1994). She received an M.F.A. from the University of Iowa and taught at Amherst College, Bennington College, and The New School University. In addition to her memoir, she published *Everyday Alibis* (1985), which contains poems and a novel, and the essay collection *As Seen on TV: Provocations* (2000).

Tracy Kidder was born in 1945 in New York City. In his Pulitzer Prize–and National Book Award–winning books, he has found compelling drama in the lives of ordinary people. *The Soul of a New Machine* (1981) details the human face behind the rush to create a new computer. *House* (1985) documents the process of building a new home. *Among Schoolchildren* (1989) covers a year in the life of a classroom, and *Old Friends* (1993) takes on two years at a nursing home. His latest books are *Home Town* (1999), a book about intersecting lives in the town of Northampton, Massachusetts; and *Mountains Beyond Mountains* (2003), a portrait of a heroic public heath doctor.

Jamaica Kincaid was born Elaine Potter Richardson in 1949 in Antigua. At the age of 17 she immigrated to the United States and later became a staff writer for the *New Yorker.* The impact of British colonialism in Antigua is a subject she frequently returns to in her work. She is the author of six books of fiction, including *Annie John* (1985), *Lucy* (1990), and *At the Bottom of the River* (1983), and the novels *Autobiography of My Mother* (1996) and *Mr. Potter* (2003). Her nonfiction includes *My Brother* (1997), an account of her brother's death from AIDS; *A Small Place* (2000), a narrative history of Antigua; and *My Garden Book* (2001).

Phillip Lopate was born in 1943 in Jamaica, New York. Best known for his personal essays, he is also editor of the widely regarded *The Art of the Personal Essay: An Anthology from the Classical Era to the Present* (1994), which helped revitalize interest in personal nonfiction narrative. A versatile writer of novels, poems, essays, nonfiction, and film criticism, his nonfiction books include *Being with Children*

(1975); *Bachelorhood: Tales of the Metropolis* (1989); *Against Joie de Vivre* (1989); *Portrait of My Body* (1996); and *Totally, Tenderly, Tragically: Essays and Criticism from a Lifelong Love Affair with the Movies* (1998).

Beverly Lowry was born in 1938 in Memphis, Tennessee and grew up in Mississippi. She has published six novels, including *Daddy's Girl* (1981) and *The Track of Real Desires* (1994). A journalist and essayist, she published her first book of nonfiction in 1992: *Crossed Over: A Murder, a Memoir.* The book chronicled the death of her son in a hit-and-run and her unlikely friendship with Texas death row inmate Karla Fay Tucker. The state of Texas executed Tucker on February 3, 1998, less than a year after "Secret Ceremonies of Love and Death" was published. Lowry's most recent book of nonfiction is *Her Dream of Dreams: The Rise and Triumph of Madam C. J. Walker* (2003).

Susan Orlean was born in 1955 in Cleveland, Ohio. Currently a staff writer for the *New Yorker,* she has worked as a reporter in Oregon and Boston and has written for magazines such as *Rolling Stone, Vogue,* and *Esquire.* Orlean is known for her literary journalistic profiles of extraordinary people and her observations of social and cultural behavior. Her collected essays include *Saturday Night* (1990) and *The Bullfighter Checks Her Makeup* (2000). She is also the author of a book-length profile, *The Orchid Thief* (1998), upon which the film *Adaptation* is loosely based.

Scott Russell Sanders was born in 1945 in Memphis, Tennessee. His novels, stories, memoirs, and essays are particularly well known for their focus on the place of human beings in nature. Several of his personal essays, including "The Inheritance of Tools," are considered contemporary classics in the genre. His books include *Stone Country* (1985), *In Limestone Country* (1991), *The Paradise of Bombs* (1993), *Staying Put:*

Making a Home in a Restless World (1993), *Writing from the Center* (1995), *A Place Called Freedom* (1997), *Hunting for Hope: A Father's Journey* (1998), and *The Force of Spirit* (2000).

Lê Thi Diem Thúy was born in 1972 in Saigon. She and her father left Vietnam in 1979 by boat and spent time at a Singapore refugee camp before settling in Southern California. Her account of these childhood events appears in *The Gangster We Are All Looking For* (2001). Though the title story was included in *Best American Essays 1997,* Lê's publisher, Knopf, brought the book out as a novel. Lê is also known for her work as a performance artist.

John Edgar Wideman was born in 1941 in Washington, D.C., and grew up in the Homewood section of Pittsburgh, where much of his work is set. In college he was an All Ivy League basketball player and received a Rhodes Scholarship in 1963. In 1967 Wideman published his first novel, *A Glance Away.* He has published 10 novels, including *Sent for You Yesterday* (1983) and *Philadelphia Fire* (1990); three short story collections; the memoir *Brothers and Keepers* (1984); and two additional books of nonfiction: *Fatheralong: A Meditation on Fathers and Sons, Race and Society* (1994) and *Hoop Roots: Basketball, Race, and Love* (2001).

Tom Wolfe was born in 1930 in Richmond, Virginia. He is widely credited with popularizing the term "New Journalism" and has been one of its most celebrated pioneers and practitioners. His highly influential books include his portrait of Ken Kesey and the Merry Pranksters, *The Electric Kool-Aid Acid Test* (1968); his critique of art criticism and the art world, *The Painted Word* (1975); and his group portrait of the early years of the U.S. space program, *The Right Stuff* (1979), from which "Yeager" is excerpted. Wolfe has also written the novels *Bonfire of the Vanities* (1987) and *A Man in Full* (1998). His most recent book is the essay collection *Hooking Up* (2000).

II. Place

André Aciman was born in 1951 to Jewish parents living in Alexandria, Egypt. His family's move from Turkey to Egypt in the early 1900s, and the subjects of home, family, and exile, are touchstones in much of his work, including the memoir *Out of Egypt* (1994) and the essay collection *False Papers* (2000). Aciman has also lived in Italy and France and now resides in the United States, where he teaches French literature. A frequent contributor to publications such as the *New Yorker,* the *New York Times Magazine,* and the *New Republic,* he also edited and contributed to *Letters of Transit: Five Authors Reflect on Exile, Identity, Language, and Loss* (1999).

Judith Ortiz Cofer was born in 1952 in Puerto Rico and moved to New Jersey in 1960. A poet and novelist as well as an essayist, Cofer is known for her experiments in language and form and her interest in breaking the boundaries of genre. Her first novel, *The Line of the Sun* (1989), was nominated for a Pulitzer Prize. She is also the author of the award-winning *Silent Dancing: A Partial Remembrance of a Puerto Rican Childhood* (1990); *The Latin Deli: Prose and Poetry* (1993); *An Island like You: Stories of the Barrio* (1995); and *The Year of the Revolution* (1998).

Edwidge Danticat was born in 1969 in Port-au-Prince, Haiti, and raised in Brooklyn, New York. Her M.F.A. thesis at Brown University was *Breath, Eyes, Memory* (1994), a novel about four generations of Haitian women struggling against poverty and powerlessness. She is also the author of the novels *The Farming of Bones* (1998) and

The Dew Breaker (2004); a novel for young readers, *Behind the Mountains* (2002); and the short story collection *Krik? Krak!* (1995). Her nonfiction has appeared in publications such as *Best American Essays* and the *New York Times.* In her nonfiction book *After the Dance: A Walk Through Carnival in Jacmel* (2002), Danticat travels to a coastal village in Haiti to take part in her first Carnival.

Vivian Gornick was born in 1935 in New York City. Her essays span the spectrum of memoir, personal essay, criticism, and literary journalism. Her books include *In Search of Ali Mahmoud* (1973); *Essays in Feminism* (1978); *Fierce Attachments: A Memoir* (1987); *Approaching Eye Level: Personal Essays* (1996); *The End of the Novel of Love: Critical Essays* (1997), which was nominated for the National Book Critics' Circle Award; and *The Situation and the Story: The Art of Personal Narrative* (2001), a book on writing and craft.

Chang-rae Lee was born in 1965 in Seoul, South Korea, and immigrated to the United States with his family when he was three years old. The lives of first- and second-generation immigrants and themes of assimilation and Asian American identity figure prominently in his work, including his first novel, *Native Speaker* (1995), which won the PEN/Hemingway Award; and his second novel, *A Gesture Life* (1999). Lee's most recent novel is *Aloft* (2004).

Thomas Lynch was born in 1948 in Detroit and lives in Milford, Michigan, where he is the town's funeral director. His work in "the dismal trade," as he calls it, infuses his writing, which is acclaimed for its lyricism and meditations on the business of life and death. His volumes of poetry include *Skating with Heather Grace* (1986) and *Still Life in Milford* (1998). He has published the essay collections *The*

Undertaking: Life Studies from the Dismal Trade (1997), a finalist for the National Book Award; and *Bodies in Motion and at Rest* (2000).

John McPhee was born in 1931 in Princeton, New Jersey. An acclaimed nonfiction writer, he is probably best known for his essays on the natural world and on humans' effect upon the environment. His books include *The Pine Barrens* (1968); *Coming into the Country* (1977), a collection of essays on Alaska considered a classic of American nature writing; *Table of Contents* (1985); *The Control of Nature* (1989); the Pulitzer Prize–winning *Annals of the Former World* (1998); and *The Founding Fish* (2002). McPhee has also published profiles such as *A Sense of Where You Are: A Profile of William Warren Bradley* (1965); *Encounters with the Archdruid* (1971); and *The Curve of Binding Energy* (1974), which explores the subject of nuclear energy.

James Alan McPherson was born in 1943 in Savannah, Georgia, and educated at Morris Brown College, Harvard Law School, and the University of Iowa Writers' Workshop. His fiction includes the short story collections *Hue and Cry* (1969) and *Elbow Room* (1978), which won the Pulitzer Prize. He has published a memoir, *Crabcakes* (1998); and an essay collection, *A Region Not Home: Reflections from Exile* (2000). He has also edited two essay collections: *Railroad: Trains and Train People in American Culture* (1976) and *Fathering Daughters: Reflections by Men* (1998). Much of McPherson's work deals with the formation of American ideals and culture within frameworks such as race and class.

Naomi Shihab Nye was born in 1954 in St. Louis, Missouri, to a Palestinian father and a mother of German and Swiss decent. Her poetry collections include *Different Ways to Pray* (1980); *The Yellow Glove* (1986); *Red Suitcase* (1994); and *Words Under the Words* (1995). As in many of her poems, Nye's essay collection *Never in a Hurry* (1996) travels across time and cultures, traversing landscapes such as the American Southwest as well as her grandparents' home in Palestine.

Jonathan Raban was born in 1942 in England and now lives in Seattle. Known for his insightful travel essays and explorations, he has written about a wide range of geographies, from a sailing trip around the British Isles to a variety of excursions into the American landscape, from Alaska to the Mississippi River to the Florida Keys. His books include *Old Glory: An American Voyage* (1981); *Coasting* (1986); *For Love and Money: Writing, Reading, Travelling* (1987); *Hunting Mister Heartbreak: A Discovery of America* (1991); *Bad Land: An American Romance* (1996), which won a National Book Critics' Circle Award; and *Passage to Juneau: A Sea and Its Meanings* (1999).

Sarah Vowell was born in 1969 in Oklahoma and raised in Montana. Her work takes on a range of issues from American history to popular culture. Her lively and humorous observations are broadcast on public radio's *This American Life*. Her essay collections include *Radio On: A Listener's Diary* (1997); *Take the Cannoli: Stories from the New World* (2000); and *The Partly Cloudy Patriot* (2002). She has also published articles and essays in places such as the *Los Angeles Times, Salon,* and *Time.*

III. Creativity and the Arts

Saul Bellow was born in 1915 in Quebec, the son of Jewish immigrants from St. Petersburg, Russia. He lived and taught in Chicago for many years and is the recipient of numerous honors and awards, including National Book Awards for his novels *Augie March* (1954); *Herzog* (1965); and *Mr. Sammler's Planet* (1971); and a Pulitzer Prize for his novel *Humboldt's Gift* (1976). He has published a range of essays, lectures, and criticism, as well as the memoir *To Jerusalem and Back* (1976) and the essay collection *It All Adds Up: From the Dim Past to the Uncertain Future* (1994). In 1976 Bellow received the Nobel Prize for Literature.

Meghan Daum was born in 1970 in Palo Alto, California, and raised primarily in New Jersey. A contributor to public radio's *This American Life* as well as publications such as *Harper's* and the *New Yorker,* Daum's observations of cultural trends and habits are characterized by her witty, fresh, honest, and often ironic voice. She is the author of the essay collection *My Misspent Youth* (2001). In 1999 she moved from New York City to rural Nebraska, which provided the inspiration for her most recent book, the novel *The Quality of Life Report* (2003).

Dagoberto Gilb was born in 1950 in Los Angeles. After graduating from the University of California, he moved to El Paso and for 16 years made his living as a construction worker. In 1994 he published the PEN/Hemingway Award–winning short story collection, *The Magic of Blood,* which the writer Annie Proulx described as a "world of bills and debts and being laid off, of old trucks, paychecks that bounce, greedy landladies, fights, cheap girls, drugs, unemployment compensation, difficult bosses, color of skin, language games, a hunger for work." Gilb is also the author of two other works of fiction: *The Last Known Residence of Mickey Acuña* (1995) and *Woodcuts of Women* (2001). "Steinbeck" was first commissioned by the *New York Times* for the John Steinbeck Centennial

and appears in Gilb's collection of essays, *Gritos* (2003).

Patricia Hampl was born in 1946 in St. Paul, Minnesota. She is perhaps best known for her two memoirs, *A Romantic Education* (1981) and *Virgin Time: In Search of the Contemplative Life* (1992). In these books she explores her Roman Catholic upbringing and her Czech heritage while traveling to places such as Assisi and Eastern Europe. The author of numerous critical essays, stories, and poems, Hampl has also published *Spillville* (1987), a meditation on a summer Antonín Dvořák spent in Iowa; and *I Could Tell You Stories* (1999), a book of critical and craft essays on the subject of essay writing, with particular focus on the memoir form.

Wayne Koestenbaum was born in 1958 in San Jose, California, and lives in New York City. An accomplished poet and critic, much of his work explores the aesthetics and ideas of the creative arts, popular culture, and celebrity. His volumes of poetry include *Rhapsodies of a Repeat Offender* (1994) and *The Milk of Inquiry* (1999). His nonfiction essays and critical inquiries appear in numerous magazines and journals, including the *New York Times* and *Vogue*. His books are *Double Talk: The Erotics of Male Literary Collaboration* (1989); *The Queen's Throat: Homosexuality, and the Mystery of Desire* (1993); *Jackie Under My Skin: Interpreting An Icon* (1995); *Cleavage: Essays on Sex, Stars, and Aesthetics* (2000); and *Andy Warhol* (2001).

Bret Lott was born in 1958 in Los Angeles, California, and currently lives in South Carolina. His family's Southern heritage is the subject of his novel *Jewel* (1991), and much of his work deals with the intersections of past and present within generations of families. His other novels include *The Man Who Owned Vermont* (1987), *A Stranger's House* (1988), and *The Hunt Club* (1998). Lott has also published two short story collections and a memoir, *Fathers, Sons, and Brothers* (1997).

Cynthia Ozick was born in 1928 in New York City. Her subject matter spans poetry and criticism, Judaism and mysticism, politics and history, and her essays range from meditations on art, aesthetics, and fame to critical studies of writers and their work. Her essay collections include *Art & Ardor* (1983); *Metaphor & Memory* (1989); *Fame & Folly* (1996); and *Quarrel & Quandary* (2000). The recipient of numerous awards and honors, Ozick's books of fiction include *The Pagan Rabbi and Other Stories* (1971); *The Messiah of Stockholm* (1987); *The Shawl* (1989); and *The Puttermesser Papers* (1997).

David Sedaris was born in 1957 in Raleigh, North Carolina. He lived in Chicago and New York before moving to Paris, where he currently resides. He is widely acclaimed for his hilarious and moving essays and memoir pieces on subjects ranging from his family to the jobs he has held to cultural and personal identity. In 2001 *Time* magazine named him "Humorist of the Year." In addition to being a commentator for NPR, Sedaris is a contributor to magazines such as *Harper's* and the *New Yorker*. He is the author of collected essays, stories, and observations, including *Holidays on Ice* (1997), *Barrel Fever* (1994), *Naked* (1997), *Me Talk Pretty One Day* (2000), *Dress Your Family in Corduroy and Demin* (2004).

Leslie Marmon Silko, a Laguna Pueblo Indian, was born in 1948 in Albuquerque, New Mexico. As with her first novel, *Ceremony* (1977), her fiction, poetry, and nonfiction have received great critical praise.

Silko often draws on oral tradition as she examines the relationships between native culture and white society. Some of her other books are the novel *Almanac of the Dead* (1991) and the story and poetry collection *Storyteller* (1981). Her nonfiction essays, memoir pieces, and criticisms include *Sacred Water: Narratives and Pictures* (1993) and *Yellow Woman and a Beauty of the Spirit* (1996).

Charles Simic was born in 1938 in Belgrade, Yugoslavia, and immigrated to the United States at the age of 16. Author of over 60 books, he won a Pulitzer Prize for his volume of poetry *The World Doesn't End* in 1989. Some of his other books of poetry are *Hotel Insomnia* (1992); *Walking the Black Cat* (1996); *Jackstraws* (1999); and *The Voice at 3:00 a.m.* (2003). In much of his work Simic returns to childhood experiences and images of war, often depicted through taut, surrealistic language. He has also published numerous books of essays and memoir pieces, including *The Uncertain Certainty: Interviews, Essays, and Notes on Poetry* (1985); *Wonderful Words, Silent Truth* (1990); *The Unemployed Fortune-Teller* (1994); *Orphan Factory* (1997); and *A Fly in the Soup* (2000).

Susan Allen Toth was born in 1940 in Ames, Iowa, and attended Smith College, the University of California, Berkeley, and the University of Minnesota. Her memoir-driven work is known for its wit and introspection, and many of her essays focus on travel explorations. Her books include the memoirs *Blooming: A Small Town Girlhood* (1981) and *Ivy Days: Making My Way out East* (1984); the essay collections *How to Prepare for Your High School Reunion, and Other Midlife Musings* (1988); *Leaning into the Wind: A Memoir of Midwest Weather* (2003); and a trilogy of travelogues about

Britain, including *England for All Seasons* (1997).

John Updike was born in 1932 in Shillington, Pennsylvania, and has lived for many years in Massachusetts. Known for his chronicles of postwar American life, his work is distinguished for its intelligence, wit, and richly detailed language. He has published more than 50 books, including novels, short stories, poetry, essays, and criticism. His novels include *The Centaur* (1963); *Rabbit Is Rich* (1981) and *Rabbit at Rest* (1990), both of which won Pulitzer Prizes; and *Gertrude and Claudius* (2000). Some of his short story collections are *Problems and Other Stories* (1979) and *Licks of Love* (2000). His essay collections include *Assorted Prose* (1965); *Picked-Up Pieces* (1975); *Hugging the Shore* (1983); *Just Looking: Essays on Art* (1989); *Odd Jobs* (1991); and *More Matter* (1991).

IV. Nature and Science

Diane Ackerman was born in 1948 in Waukegan, Illinois. A poet, journalist, and essayist, Ackerman has been widely praised for her skill at observing and describing the details of the natural world. Her books of memoir and essay include *Twilight of the Tenderfoot: A Western Memoir* (1980); *On Extended Wings: An Adventure in Flight* (1987); *The Moon by Whale Light, and Other Adventures Among Bats, Penguins, Crocodilians, and Whales* (1991); *The Rarest of the Rare: Vanishing Animals, Timeless Worlds* (1995); and *A Slender Thread: Crisis, Healing, and Nature* (1997). "The Psychopharmacology of Chocolate" appeared in her book *A Natural History of the Senses* (1990). She has also written *A Natural History of Love* (1994) and *A Natural History of My Garden* (2001).

Annie Dillard was born in 1945 in Pittsburgh, Pennsylvania. She received a B.A. and M.A. from Hollins College and in 1974 published a collection of poetry, *Tickets for a Prayer Wheel*. In 1975, her collection of essays, *Pilgrim at Tinker Creek,* a series of meditations drawing on theology, philosophy, natural science, and physics, received the Pulitzer Prize in nonfiction. Dillard's fascination with the natural world and her lyricism in describing its wonders have led critics to compare her to Henry David Thoreau. A novelist, poet, and essayist, her nonfiction books include *Teaching a Stone to Talk: Expeditions and Encounters* (1982); *Encounters with Chinese Writers* (1984); *An American Childhood* (1987); *The Writing Life* (1989); and *For the Time Being* (1999).

Gretel Ehrlich was born in 1946 in Santa Barbara, California. The landscapes of the American West, particularly Wyoming, are the focus of much of her work, including her award-winning collection of essays, *The Solace of Open Spaces* (1985). She has also published poetry; the short story collections *Wyoming Stories* (1986) and *Drinking Dry Clouds* (1991); and the novel *Heart Mountain* (1988). Ehrlich's nonfiction books include *A Match to the Heart* (1994), which recounts her recovery experience after being struck by lightning; and works involving travel, such as *Islands, the Universe, Home* (1991) and *This Cold Heaven: Seven Seasons in Greenland* (2001).

Atul Gawande was born in 1965 in Brooklyn, and was educated at Stanford and Oxford, where he was a Rhodes Scholar. He received his M.D. from Harvard Medical School and an M.P.H. from the Harvard School of Public Health. He is currently a surgical resident at a hospital in Boston and a staff writer on medicine and science for the *New Yorker.* In his book of essays, *Complications: A Surgeon's Notes on an Imperfect Science* (2002), in which "Final Cut" appears, Gawande describes his profession as an "enterprise of constantly changing knowledge, uncertain information, fallible individuals, and at the same time lives on the line." Among his concerns are medical ethics and how the human psyche contributes to the way doctors treat their patients.

Stephen Jay Gould was born in 1941 in New York City and died in 2002. Primarily a paleontologist and an evolutionary biologist, Gould was a leading popular scientist throughout his lifetime. He published over 25 books including *The Panda's Thumb: More Reflections in Natural History,* which won the 1981 American Book Award for Science; *The Mismeasure of Man,* winner of the National Book Critics' Circle Award in 1982; *Wonderful Life* (1991), winner of The Science Book Prize in 1990; *Questioning the Millennium: A Rationalist's Guide to a Precisely Arbitrary Countdown* (1997); *The Structure of Evolutionary Theory* (2002); and *Triumph and Tragedy in Mudville: A Lifelong Passion for Baseball* (2003).

Edward Hoagland was born in 1932 in New York City and grew up in Connecticut and New York. He has said about his upbringing: "As a child, since I couldn't talk to people, I became close to animals. I became an observer, and in all my books, even the novels, witnessing things is what counts." His essays are perhaps best known for their focus on animals and the natural world, with narrative observations that return to the subject of human relationships. His books include *Notes from the Century Before: A Journal from British Columbia* (1969); *The Courage of Turtles* (1971); *Walking the Dead Diamond River* (1973); *Red*

Wolves and Black Bears (1976); *African Calliope* (1979); *Balancing Acts* (1992); *Tigers and Ice* (1999); and the memoir *Compass Points: How I Lived* (2001). He is also the author of five books of fiction.

Linda Hogan was born in 1947 in Denver, Colorado. A member of the Chickasaw tribe, she often writes about her Native American heritage and the intertwined themes of nature, community, and myth. Her books include critically acclaimed novels such as *Mean Spirit* (1990) and *Solar Storms* (1995); volumes of poetry such as *Seeing Through the Sun* (1985) and *The Book of Medicines* (1993), which won a National Book Critics' Circle Award; and numerous essays, including the collection *Dwellings: A Spiritual History of the Living World* (1995) and the memoir *The Woman Who Watches over the World* (2001).

Barry Lopez was born in 1945 in Port Chester, New York, and has lived for much of his life on the West Coast. He is a widely acclaimed writer on nature, landscape, and the environment. His nonfiction books and essay collections include *Of Wolves and Men* (1978); *Winter Dreams* (1981); *Arctic Dreams: Imagination and Desire in a Northern Landscape* (1986), which won the National Book Award; *Crossing Open Ground* (1988); *The Rediscovery of North America* (1991); and *About This Life: Journeys on the Threshold of Memory* (1998). His most recent book is the short story collection *Light Action in the Caribbean* (2000).

Richard McCann was born in 1940 in Cleveland, Ohio. A poet and essayist whose work appears in publications such as the *Atlantic Monthly, Ploughshares,* and *The Nation,* his work includes the poetry collection *Ghost Letters* (1994), which deals with the devastation of AIDS. McCann has said:

"For the past fifteen years my work—whether in fiction, poetry, or creative non-fiction—has derived from autobiographical explorations of the meaning and experience of the body, particularly the sexual body and the body in illness." His essay "The Resurrectionist," selected for *Best American Essays 2000,* is about his experience receiving a liver transplant. McCann is also coeditor of *Things Shaped in Passing: More "Poets for Life" Writing from the AIDS Pandemic* (1997).

Floyd Skloot was born in 1947 in Brooklyn. An essayist, poet, and novelist, Skloot's life and work were changed forever, as he has written, "since contracting a virus that attacked [his] brain in December of 1988." His experiences with illness are chronicled in his collection of award-winning essays, *In the Shadow of Memory* (2003), as well as in *The Night-Side: Seven Years in the Kingdom of the Sick* (1996). His books of poetry include *Poppies* (1994); *The Fiddler's Trance* (2001); and *The Evening Light* (2001).

Terry Tempest Williams was born in 1955 in Utah, where she currently lives. An environmentalist, her connection to her Mormon family and the landscape of Utah are major forces in her work. "The Clan of One-Breasted Women," taken from her book *Refuge: An Unnatural History of Family and Place* (1991), is about the deaths of many women in Williams's family, including her mother, due to radiation from aboveground atomic testing in Nevada from the 1950s until the early 1960s. Her other nonfiction books and essay collections include *Pieces of White Shell: A Journey to Navajo Land* (1984); *Coyote's Canyon* (1988); *An Unspoken Hunger* (1994); *Leap* (2000); and *Red: Passion and Patience in the Desert* (2001).

Edward O. Wilson was born in 1929 in Birmingham, Alabama. In 1955, he received his Ph.D. in biology from Harvard, where he has taught ever since. Wilson began his career as an entomologist, and his early research, demonstrating that ants communicate through the discharge of pheromones, opened a new area of biochemical study. *Sociobiology: The New Synthesis,* which Wilson published in 1975, is considered a groundbreaking book. The first detailed study of the emerging science of sociobiology, it brought its author both fame and controversy, since its most debated tenet is that human behavior is genetically based. Wilson is the author of two Pulitzer Prize–winning books, *On Human Nature* (1978) and *The Ants* (1990, with Bert Hölldobler). Among his other works are the memoir *Naturalist* (1995); *The Diversity of Life* (1992); and *Consilience* (1998).

V. Culture and Society

Dorothy Allison was born in 1949. Raised in Greenville, South Carolina, she grew up in poverty and suffered physical and sexual abuse by her stepfather. Her childhood is the subject of much of her work, including the novel *Bastard out of Carolina* (1992), which was a National Book Award finalist and winner of the Lambda Literary Award. Known for her feminism, which she has called "a substitute religion that made sense," Allison's other publications include the short story collection *Trash* (1988); the poetry collection *The Women Who Hate Me* (1991); the memoir *Two or Three Things I Know for Sure* (1994); the essay collection *Skin: Talking About Sex, Class, and Literature* (1994); and the novel *Cavedweller* (1998).

Margaret Atwood, born in 1939 and raised in Ontario and Quebec, has published over 30 acclaimed novels and collections of poems, essays, and stories. An important critic, she has helped define contemporary Canadian literature and has a distinguished reputation among feminist writers in North America and abroad. Among her best-known works are the novels *Surfacing* (1972); *The Handmaid's Tale* (1986), which received Canada's Governor General's Award; *Cat's Eye* (1989); *Alias Grace* (1996); the Booker Prize–winning *The Blind Assassin* (2000); and *Oryx and Crake* (2003). Atwood's story collections include *Wilderness Tips and Other Stories* (1991) and *Good Bones and Simple Murders* (1994). A recent book, *Negotiating with the Dead* (2002), is a collection of essays on the art and craft of writing.

Joan Didion was born in 1934 in Sacramento, California, where she was raised. A fifth-generation Californian who frequently writes about her home state, Didion has lived primarily in Los Angeles and New York. She is regarded as one of the most insightful journalists and observers of American culture and politics, and her essay collections *Slouching Towards Bethlehem* (1968) and *The White Album* (1979) are considered American classics. These were followed by nonfiction books such as *Salvador* (1983); *Miami* (1987); *After Henry* (also published as *Sentimental Journeys*) (1992); and *Where I Was From* (2003). She is also a novelist whose books include *Play It as It Lays* (1970); *A Book of Common Prayer* (1977); and *The Last Thing He Wanted* (1996).

Stuart Dybek was born in 1942 in Chicago. His upbringing in a Catholic household in working-class Slavic and Mexican neighborhoods has influenced much of his writing. He is the author of a collection of poems, *Brass Knuckles* (1979), and three short story collections: *Childhood and Other Neighborhoods* (1980); *The Coast of Chicago* (1990); and *I Sailed with Magellan* (2003). Widely published in such magazines as the *New Yorker,* the *Atlantic, Harper's,* and the *Paris Review,* Dybek has received numerous awards and honors, including a lifetime achievement award from the American Academy of Arts and Letters and a PEN/Malamud Award for Excellence in Short Story. "Field Trips" is part of an in-progress collection of personal essays about his youth in Chicago.

Gerald Early was born in 1952 in Philadelphia and graduated from the University of Pennsylvania in 1974. He received his Ph.D. from Cornell and is currently director of Afro-American Studies at Washington University in St. Louis. An essayist, poet, critic, and anthologist, Early has written about music, sports, politics, the arts, and many aspects of culture. His books include *Tuxedo Junction: Essays on American Culture* (1990); *The Culture of Bruising: Essays on Literature, Prizefighting, and Modern American Culture* (1991); *Speech and Power: The African-American Essay and Its Cultural Content from Polemics to Pulpit* (1993); *Lure and Loathing: Essays on Race, Identity, and Ambivalence of Assimilation* (1993); *Daughters: On Family and Fatherhood* (1994); and *One Nation Under Groove: Motown and American Culture* (1996).

Barbara Ehrenreich was born in 1941 in Butte, Montana. She received a Ph.D. in biology, which has influenced her work on issues such as health care. A widely regarded essayist, journalist, and social commentator, her subjects also include family, gender politics, class, and economics. Her best-selling book *Nickel and Dimed: On (Not) Getting by in America* (2001) sheds light on the lives of the American working class. A work of experiential literary journalism, it chronicles Ehrenreich's two years of working minimum-wage jobs. Her other nonfiction books and essay collections include *The Hearts of Men* (1983); *Fear of Falling: The Inner Life of the Middle Class* (1989); *The Worst Years of Our Lives* (1990); *The Snarling Citizen* (1995); *Blood Rites* (1997); and *Global Woman: Nannies, Maids, and Sex Workers in the New Economy* (2003).

Lawrence Otis Graham was born in 1962 in New York City. He attended Princeton and Harvard Law School and has worked as an attorney, business consultant, and adjunct professor. He became well known upon publishing two experiential essays on race in *New York* magazine. For one of these essays, "Invisible Man," Graham worked as a busboy at an all-white country club in Greenwich, Connecticut, and he exposes the subtle and overt racism directed at him and other non-white staff members. Graham has published over 12 books of nonfiction, including *Member of the Club: Reflections on Life in a Racially Polarized World* (1995) and *Our Kind of People: Inside America's Black Upper Class* (1999).

Lee Gutkind was born in 1943 in Pittsburgh, Pennsylvania. Founder and editor of the literary journal *Creative Nonfiction,* he is considered a pioneer in the field of creative nonfiction. His nonfiction books include *Bike Fever* (1973); *The Best Seat in Baseball, But You Have To Stand: The Game as Umpires See It* (1975); *Our Roots Grow Deeper Than We Know* (1985); *Many Sleepless Nights* (1988); *Stuck in Time: The Tragedy of Childhood Mental Illness* (1993); *Creative Nonfiction: How to Live It and Write It* (1996); *The Art of Creative Nonfiction* (1997); *An Unspoken Art: Profiles of Veterinary Life* (1997); and *Forever Fat* (2003). A frequent contributor to journals and publications, Gutkind is also the editor of numerous anthologies, including *The Essayist at Work: Profiles of Creative Nonfiction Writers* (1998).

Michael Herr was born in 1940 in Syracuse, New York, and attended Syracuse University before beginning his career as a journalist. In 1967, *Esquire* sent him to Vietnam, where he began writing dispatches that captured the war in all of its graphic and vivid horror. He did not publish a collection of these pieces until *Dispatches* in 1977. Herr served as a writer and consultant for the films *Apocalypse Now,* directed by Francis Ford Coppola; and *Full Metal Jacket,* directed by Stanley Kubrick. He has also written *The Big Room* (1987), a collection of biographical sketches of celebrities who had some connection to Las Vegas; *Walter Winchell* (1990), a novel based on one of these sketches; and *Kubrick* (2000), an elegy and loose biography about his filmmaking friend.

Maxine Hong Kingston was born in 1940 in Stockton, California, the eldest of six children, to Chinese immigrants who ran a laundry. Her writing relies heavily on memory and imagination, combining autobiography, history, and myth. In a 1987 interview she said, "The artist's memory winnows out; it edits for what is important and significant. Memory, my own memory, shows me what is unforgettable, and helps me get to an essence that will not die, and that haunts me until I can out it into a form, which is writing." Her books include *The Woman Warrior: Memoirs of a Girlhood Among Ghosts* (1976), which won the National Book Critics' Circle Award for nonfiction; *China Men* (1980); *Hawai'i One Summer* (1987); the novel *Tripmaster Monkey: His Fake Book* (1988); and *The Fifth Book of Peace* (2003).

Bharati Mukherjee was born in 1940 in Calcutta, India, and grew up in a Bengali Brahmin family. She came to the United States in 1961 to study creative writing at the University of Iowa Writers' Workshop.

After spending several years in Canada, Mukherjee returned to the United States to teach and write. Her short story collections are *The Middleman and Other Stories* (1988); which won the National Book Critics' Circle Award; and *Darkness* (1985). Her novels include *Wife* (1975); *Jasmine* (1989); *The Holder of the World* (1993); and *Desirable Daughters* (2002). She has also written two academic books and with her husband, the writer Clark Blaise, collaborated on the nonfiction books *Days and Nights in Calcutta* (1977) and *The Sorrow and the Terror: The Haunting Legacy of the Air India Tragedy* (1987).

Susan Sontag was born in 1933 in New York City, raised in Los Angeles and Tucson Arizona, and after graduating from high school at 15 earned multiple degrees from the University of Chicago and Harvard. She is best known for her works of criticism and analyses of contemporary culture, including *Against Interpretation* (1966); *On Photography* (1977), which won the National Book Critics' Circle Award for Criticism; *Illness as Metaphor* (1978); *AIDS and Its Metaphors* (1989); *Where the Stress Falls* (2001); and *Regarding the Pain of Others* (2002). Her novels include *In America*, which won a National Book Award in 2000. Her short story collections are *I, Etcetera* (1978) and *The Way We Live Now* (1991). Sontag has said her desire is to be an *écrivain*, what the French call someone whose profession is a writer without specialization.

Alice Walker was born in 1944 in Eatonton, Georgia, the eighth and youngest child of sharecroppers. She published her first book of poetry, *Once*, in 1968. After working in the civil rights movement and as a caseworker for the New York City Welfare Department, she taught at various colleges around the country. Widely acclaimed for her portrayals of African American women, particularly in the South, Walker's novels include *Meridian* (1976); *The Color Purple* (1982), which won a Pulitzer Prize; *The Temple of My Familiar* (1989); and *The Way Forward Is with a Broken Heart* (2000). Walker's books of essays range from the political to the personal and include *In Search of Our Mothers' Gardens* (1983); *Living by the Word* (1988); *Warrior Marks* (1993, with Pratibha Parmar); *Anything We Love Can Be Saved* (1997); and *Sent by Earth* (2001).

Credits

"A Literary Pilgrim Progresses to the Past" by André Aciman. Originally appeared in *The New York Times*, August 28, 2000. Copyright © 2000 by The New York Times. Reprinted with permission.

From *A Natural History of the Senses* by Diane Ackerman, copyright © 1990 by Diane Ackerman. Used by permission of Random House, Inc.

From "Two or Three Things I know for Sure" by Dorothy Allison, copyright © 1995 by Dorothy Allison. Used by permission of Dutton, a division of Penguin Group (USA) Inc.

"The Female Body" from *Good Bones and Simple Murders* by Margaret Atwood, copyright © 1983, 1992, 1994, by O.W. Toad Ltd. A Nan A. Talese Book. Used by permission of Doubleday, a division of Random House, Inc. and McClelland & Stewart Ltd., *The Canadian Publishers*.

"Graven Images" by Saul Bellow. Copyright © 1997 by Saul Bellow, reprinted with the permission of The Wylie Agency, Inc.

"Silent Dancing" by Judith Ortiz Cofer is reprinted with permission from the publisher of *Silent Dancing: A Partial Remembrance of a Puerto Rican Childhood* (Houston: Arte Público Press: University of Houston, 1990)

"Picking Plums" by Bernard Cooper. Copyright ©1992 by Bernard Cooper. Reprinted by permission of the author.

"Westbury Court" by Edwidge Danticat. First published in *New Letters*, Volume 65, Issue 4. Copyright © 1999 by Edwidge Danticat. Reprinted by permission of the author and Aragi, Inc.

"Music is My Bag: Confessions of a Lapsed Oboist" by Meghan Daum. Originally appeared in *Harper's Magazine,* March 2000. Copyright © 2000 by Meghan Daum. Reprinted by permission of the author.

"On Keeping a Notebook" from "Slouching Towards Bethlehem" by Joan Didion. Copyright © 1966, 1968, renewed 1996 by Joan Didion. Reprinted by permission of Farrar, Straus and Giroux, LLC.

"Seeing" from "Pilgrim at Tinker Creek" by Annie Dillard. Copyright © 1974 by Annie Dillard. Reprinted by permission of Harper Collins Publishers, Inc.

"I'm Going To Live The Life I Sing About in My Song" by Thomas A. Dorsey. Copyright © 1941 (Renewed) Unichappell Music Inc. Rights for Extended Renewal Term in U.S. assigned to Warner-Tamerlane Publishing Corp. All Rights Reserved. Used by Permission, Warner Bros. Publications U.S. Inc., Miami, FL 33014.

"Precious Lord Take My Hand," a.k.a. "Take My Hand Precious Lord," by Thomas A. Dorsey. Copyright © 1938 (Renewed) Unichappell Music Inc. Rights for Extended Renewal Term in U.S. assigned to Warner-Tamerlane Publishing Corp. All Rights Reserved. Used by Permission, Warner Bros. Publications U.S. Inc., Miami, FL 33014.

"Field Trips" by Stuart Dybek. Copyright © 1999 by Stuart Dybek. Reprinted by permission of the author.

From *Somehow Form A Family: Stories That Are Mostly True* by Tony Earley. Copyright © 2001 by Tony Earley. Reprinted by permission of Algonquin Books of Chapel Hill.

"Life with Daughters: Watching the Miss America Pageant," from *Daughters on Family and Fatherhood* by Gerald Early (1994). Essay was originally published in *The Kenyon Review,* 1990. Copyright © 1990 by Gerald Early. Reprinted by permission of the author.

Introduction from *Nickel and Dimed: On (Not) Getting by in America* by Barbara Ehrenreich, copyright © 2001 by Barbara Ehrenreich. Reprinted by permission of Henry Holt and Company, LLC.

"The Solace of Open Spaces," from *The Solace of Open Spaces* by Gretel Ehrlich, copyright © 1985 by Gretel Ehrlich. Used by permission of Viking Penguin, a division of Penguin Group (USA) Inc.

"Final Cut" from *Complications: A Young Surgeon's Notes on an Imperfect Science* by Atul Gawande, copyright © 2002 by Atul Gawande. Reprinted by permission of Henry Holt and Company, LLC.

"Steinbeck" from *Gritos: Essays* by Dagoberto Gilb. Copyright © 2003 by Dagoberto Gilb. Used by permission.

Excerpt from "The Situation and the Story" by Vivian Gornick. Copyright © 2001 by Vivian Gornick. Reprinted by permission of Farrar, Straus and Giroux, LLC.

"A Biological Homage to Mickey Mouse," from *The Panda's Thumb: More Reflections in Natural History* by Stephen Jay Gould. Copyright © 1980 by Stephen Jay Gould. Used by permission of W. W. Norton & Company, Inc.

"Invisible Man" by Lawrence Otis Graham. First published in *New York.* Copyright © 1992 by Lawrence Otis Graham. Reprinted by permission of International Creative Management, Inc.

"Mirrorings" by Lucy Grealy. Copyright © 1993 by *Harper's Magazine.* All rights reserved. Reproduced from the February issue by special permission.

"The Creative Nonfiction Police" by Lee Gutkind. Copyright © 2001 by Lee Gutkind. Originally appeared in *AWP,* December 2001. Reprinted by permission of the author.

"Reviewing Anne Frank," from *I Could Tell You Stories: Sojourns in the Land of Memory* by Patricia Hampl. Copyright © 1999 by Patricia Hampl. Used by permission of W. W. Norton & Company, Inc.

From "Dispatches" by Michael Herr, copyright © 1977 by Michael Herr. Used by permission of Alfred A. Knopf, a division of Random House, Inc.

"The Courage of Turtles" from *The Courage of Turtles* by Edward Hoagland. Published by Lyons & Burford. Copyright © 1968, 1970, 1993 by Edward Hoagland. Reprinted by permission of Lescher & Lescher, Ltd. All rights reserved.

"The Bats," from *Dwellings: A Spiritual History of the Living World* by Linda Hogan. Copyright © 1995 by Linda Hogan. Used by permission of W. W. Norton & Company, Inc.

"Making the Truth Believable" by Tracy Kidder. Copyright © 1993 by Tracy Kidder. Reprinted by permission of Georges Borchardt, Inc., for the author.